THE NAVAL CHRONICLE

VOLUME I

THE NAVAL CHRONICLE

The Contemporary Record of the Royal Navy at War

Volume I 1793 - 1798

Consolidated Edition
containing a

GENERAL AND BIOGRAPHICAL HISTORY

of

THE ROYAL NAVY

of the

UNITED KINGDOM

From the Occupation of Toulon to the Battle of the Nile

*War Reports, Commanding Officers' Gazette Letters of Naval Actions, Narratives
taken from Foreign Sources, Intelligence Reports on the Fleets of Europe and of the
American Republic, Letters from Serving Officers on Naval Strategy, Tactics, Gunnery,
Ship Design, and Professional Concerns, and With a Variety of Original Papers on
Nautical Subjects.*

*

*Under the Guidance of Several Literary and Professional Men,
and Prepared for General Use by:*

NICHOLAS TRACY

STACKPOLE BOOKS

CHATHAM PUBLISHING

LONDON

Copyright © Nicholas Tracy 1998

First published in Great Britain in 1998 by
Chatham Publishing,
61 Frith Street,
London W1V 5TA
Chatham Publishing is an imprint of Gerald Duckworth & Co Ltd

First published in North America in 1999 by
Stackpole Books,
5067 Ritter Road, Mechanicsburg,
PA 17055-6921

UK hardback edition
ISBN 0 86176 070 1
US hardback edition
ISBN 0-8117-1107-2

British Library Cataloguing in Publication Data
A catalogue record for this book is available from the British Library

A Library of Congress Catalog Card No. is available on request

Printed and bound in Great Britain

Contents

Editor's Preface

The pages of *The Naval Chronicle*, which began publication two hundred years ago in 1799 and continued for twenty years, are filled with the most important original published documentation of the Royal Navy, the navies of France, Spain, Portugal, the Netherlands, Denmark, Sweden, Russia, the Ottoman Empire, and of the American Republic. Joyce Gold, the publisher and printer of *The Naval Chronicle*, set out, 'under the guidance of several literary and professional men' to preserve for history the achievements of naval men and women of his age, especially of the twenty-two years of naval war which had begun in 1793 following the execution of King Louis XVI. Amongst the literary men were the Reverend James Stanier Clarke who, with John M'Arthur, was to be Lord Nelson's first biographer. Clarke acted as editor of *The Naval Chronicle* for at least the first two years. S and J Jones served editorial functions at different times. Well over a thousand pages were published each year until 1819, when, the navy having been reduced to a peace establishment, publication stopped.

The content of these volumes, besides editorial comment on naval affairs, included action reports forwarded to the Admiralty and published in the *London Gazette*, intelligence of foreign naval preparations, 'philosophical papers' discussing technical naval and maritime matters, letters to the editor apparently from naval officers, some of whom were professional writers but who nonetheless usually employed pseudonyms, biographies of naval officers, historical essays, anecdotes, stories, and poetry, with plates to illustrate the text. In 'Retrospective' sections, and in 'Biographical Memoirs', a conscientious effort was made to provide an accurate account of the war from its commencement in 1793, and content also included historical material from earlier times.

In the preface to the first volume Gold's, and Clarke's, intentions were laid out:

'The leading objects in this publication are, to do good, and to give pain to no one; to render justice unto those who deserve praise, and have experienced neglect; to cheer the uniformity of which the mariner so constantly complains, and to render him sensible of the sources from whence much amusement and instruction may be derived; and also to enable the public to form a more correct and enlarged idea of that profession, by whose exertions Great Britain stands pre-eminent in the scale of political importance...' I ii-iii

Although predominantly a journal for and about naval officers, *The Naval Chronicle* was also alive to the merits of the common sailor and marine, provided they knew their place. Mutineers, cowards and corrupt pursers were deemed worthy of the cat, noose, and gaol, although a grudging nod was given to those who showed repentance before they died. The sailors' place was in a practical world where the need was for good victuals, and paternalistic rule which mitigated the evils of their 'simplicity' by protecting them and their families from waterside 'sharks'. Considerable space in the pages of *The Naval Chronicle* was devoted to sailors' benevolent funds, and to efforts to improve the chance of surviving shipwreck. Towards the end of the war, a sympathetic hearing began to be given to those who argued for a reform of the methods of discipline. Experience had led to a growing understanding that fear could not command the fighting spirit which won battles.

Gold quickly realised his goal. *The Naval Chronicle* was immediately recognised as the most reliable and comprehensive record of naval events. In the preface to the thirteenth volume, Gold wrote with some pride that 'The thirteen columns we have raised, will hereafter be often pilfered, to set off the works of those, who would otherwise search in vain for such materials.' In the following volume, writing immediately after the death of Vice-Admiral Lord Nelson in the battle of Trafalgar, he was able to repeat those words, and add:

'Very fully has the truth of them been confirmed, by what has since taken place; for never was any poor devil so plucked, and pulled, and gutted, as our *Chronicle* has been, since the lamented death of our illustrious Hero, Lord Nelson.'

Readers of the novels of Patrick O'Brian and C S Forester will find that they too have quarried many of their stories from the pages of *The Naval Chronicle*. Gold's list of entries in *The Naval Chronicle* on Lord Nelson, many of which have been reproduced in the Consolidated Edition, ran to four pages in length.

Apparently it was not only Britons who found *The Naval Chronicle* an invaluable reference. 'S.S.', in a letter to the Editor dated 19 November 1810, wrote that during the recent negotiations concerning a settlement between France and Britain Emperor Napoleon had got his minister of marine, M Rivière, to request that he be sent copies of *The Naval Chronicle*, 'as it was read with much interest.'

'What pleasure the Emperor can derive from reading a work, every line of which records some of those enterprises which have immortalised our naval heroes, and have so completely thwarted his ambitious views of universal empire, I cannot devise, unless it be his intention to profit by the many great examples which are portrayed therein, or to have them translated, in the hope that the navy of the "Great Nation" may vainly endeavour to imitate the glorious deeds of the British Tars.' XXIV 393-394

In the thirty-first volume, 'Arion', one of the anonymous correspondents, wrote of the role of the Royal Navy in the defeat by Britain and her allies of Buonapartism:

'It was this arm of her power, which, amidst the wreck of nations, and the overthrow of mighty empires and states, brought into the ports of Great Britain the treasures of the whole world. It was the Royal Navy of Great Britain that prepared the way for the glorious fields fought in the peninsula - and the laurels that adorn the brows of the great Wellington. It was the Royal Navy of Great Britain that carried the terrors of her power to every shore; displayed the ensigns of her strength to cheer desponding nations; and, amidst preponderating gloom, shed a never-failing stream of hope.

'If it were to be asked, what would at this time have been the situation of Great Britain, had not her victorious fleets, under the favour of Divine Providence, protected her shores - been a shield to her commerce and her numerous colonies - *what answer could be given?*' XXXI 367-379

Truly, it is a rewarding thing to read right through the twenty or more thousand pages. For those who do not have the time to read the whole, or do not have access to the original, however, it is possible to abstract the contents. Perhaps a quarter of Gold's pages were devoted to events before the outbreak of war in 1793. The material which was included to entertain the serving officers who subscribed, the stories and the poetry, can largely be set aside, not because they are always without merit, but because they add little to the modern reader's knowledge of the naval war. It is also possible, and a necessity, to eliminate most of the reports of ship movements, most of the reports of courts martial, and also some of the gazette letters describing minor actions in the trade war which continued with little break for so many years. This material is invaluable to professional historians, but for the rest of us is of secondary importance.

Abstraction proves to be of positive value when the material is reorganised by sequence and content. In the first place, this structure has enabled the present editor to realise to some extent the avowed intention of the original publisher, Gold, by bringing together the material he inserted to cover the period 1793-1798 prior to the publication of the first volume of *The Naval Chronicle*. Of no less value has been the creation of thematic sections which gather and organise the technical papers, and letters to the editor on technical subjects, which originally were scattered at random throughout the volumes. In order to make the Consolidated Edition of *The Naval Chronicle* a work of the greatest value to the modern student of the naval campaigns of 1793 to 1815, editorial notes have been added whenever it appears that reference to modern research will be of value to readers, and to explain to modern readers references which must have seemed self-evident to those of the early nineteenth century.

Inevitably, over the twenty years of publication the format employed changed to some extent. In preparing the Consolidated Edition a compromise path has been followed to retain much of the original format, but at the same time to provide a consistency throughout. To do so, volumes have been divided into 'chapters' which bring together material, often widely spaced in the original eclectic organisation, which bear on a particular episode or naval command during a one- or two-year period, with additional thematic chapters as appendices. These chapter headings, and the editorial notes, either in the larger type or in square brackets, which introduce the following entries, are entirely modern. Within the individual chapters, headings introducing entries are also modern, but refer directly to the original headings used in the first edition, and conform as nearly as possible to them. Volume and page references attached to those headings are those of the first edition. Some of the longer entries, those which conveyed a summary of current naval news, have internal headings. Some of these are from the first edition, but most have been added to eliminate the difficulty readers might find in locating material. Simple, fourth level, headings giving a date or place are directly transferred from the first edition, but where it has been useful, the month or year has been added next to the simple statement of date. The captions to the original *Naval Chronicle* engravings reproduced in the Consolidated Edition are adapted from those of the first edition, some of which ran to four or five pages of text.

A compromise has also been made in the reproduction of the texts themselves. Some spelling has been modernised and made consistent, but generally the nineteenth-century forms have been retained as they are attractive when they do not obscure the sense. The editors of the first edition sometimes had difficulty with foreign words, and, while an effort has been made to track these down and correct them, the editor of the Consolidated Edition may have missed a few himself. He has also made so bold as to introduce paragraph divisions into some of the court martial reports, and parliamentary records, which in the first edition often ran for pages without any at all. Some punctuation has been added where the sense requires it. Footnotes are mostly original to the first edition, but to conform with modern usage they have been moved whenever possible to the end of a phrase or sentence. A few have been deleted where they serve no purpose in the modern edition, or are too long to be accommodated. The spelling of Napoleon Buonaparté's name gradually changed in *The Naval Chronicle*, first eliminating the acute accent, then the 'u' and final 'e'. Towards the end of the war, Napoleon's given name came into some use, but generally *The Naval Chronicle* made a point of treating his pretensions to imperial status with contempt, and preferred to refer to him as Buonaparte or Bonapart. The present editor has attempted to mirror this shifting form in his own notes.

All these changes are designed to facilitate access to the invaluable and exciting material collected in *The Naval Chronicle*. The index to the modern edition located at the end of Volume V corrects a major limitation of the first edition, and the references at the heads of entries to the volume and page number of the original enables students who need to refer to the first edition to find their way with relative ease.

NICHOLAS TRACY

Introduction to Volume I

Although the Marine Française went to war in 1793 in disarray due to the effects of the Revolution, it was by no means clear that it would not prove to be capable of using revolutionary ruthlessness as effectively as did the French army to transform the military map of Europe. This was not to prove to be the case, but the struggle was to be long between the mobilisation of the Channel Fleet, under the command of Admiral 'Black Dick' Howe, in 1793, and Rear-Admiral Nelson's annihilating victory at the battle of the Nile in the summer of 1798. This period was reported on retrospectively by *The Naval Chronicle*, publication of which was not to commence until 1799. Its conscientious efforts to preserve the historical record have left us with a vast amount of material, collated here into a chronological narrative. For convenience, this has been divided into chapters, each of which focuses on action in a particular theatre during a span of at most two years.

The most complete reportage for 1793 is of the Mediterranean theatre, where the French fleet base of Toulon was surrendered by its population to the protection of the British fleet, and its Spanish allies. Extensive reportage, however, was also given to operations in the West Indies, where British forces directed their efforts to seizing control of the valuable island commerce. In the early summer of 1794 occurred the first of the great naval battles of the war, the battle of the Glorious First of June, when the Channel Fleet engaged the Brest fleet which had sailed to escort home a much needed grain convoy. Reports by officers who took part in the battle, and biographical memoirs of their exploits, continued to appear in *The Naval Chronicle* for twenty years.

The focus of attention in 1795 continued to be on naval action in Home Waters, primarily associated with support of royalist forces in western France. In the Mediterranean, following the forced withdrawal from Toulon, action was dominated by French military operations in Italy. The British Mediterranean Fleet, having participated in the liberation of Corsica, sought to control the coastal communications between France and Italy. This led to two minor skirmishes with the Toulon fleet. French occupation of the Netherlands added the Dutch to Britain's enemies in 1795, which led to combined operations in South Africa and Ceylon. Spain was also forced to make peace with France.

Now controlling both the Dutch and Spanish fleets, the French government was able to pursue a plan developed with Irish nationalists to invade Ireland, as a step towards the invasion of England. This strategy was defeated by the weakness of France's naval supply organisation, and by the weather in January 1797 when the attempt was made. Stunning defeats of the Spanish fleet, on St Valentine's Day 1797 off Cape St Vincent, and of the Dutch fleet at Camperdown in October 1797, greatly reduced the danger of invasion, but anti-invasion planning and action continued, and late in 1798 a final French effort to support a nationalist rising in Ireland had to be met, ashore in Northern Ireland, and in the Irish Sea.

These victories were all the more remarkable, and important in British naval and social history, because they occurred in close conjunction to the great mutinies that were staged in the Channel Fleet at Spithead in April 1797, and at the Nore in May. The Spithead mutiny was a model of controlled industrial action, and led to greater government respect for seamen's interests. The Nore mutiny was less well managed, came close to being treasonable, and ended violently with the execution of the leaders.

Cape St Vincent and Camperdown had diverted the focus of French efforts back to the Mediterranean, where Napoleon Buonaparté was placed in command of an expedition to seize Malta, and Egypt, as stepping stones to the conquest of India. Nelson's destruction of the Toulon fleet in Aboukir Bay near Alexandria put an end to that danger, and also ensured the continued independence of the Kingdom of Naples. The battle of the Nile, which virtually eliminated the Toulon fleet, also established a new standard for victory. The year ended with the occupation of Minorca, which provided the British fleet with the ideal base for control of the French Mediterranean coast.

Volume I concludes with two Appendices consisting of papers from *The Naval Chronicle* on naval tactics and strategy, and on ship design, respectively.

1793 – Home Waters

IN JANUARY 1793, following the execution of Louis XIV, the French National Convention declared war against Britain, the Netherlands and Spain. They, with Sardinia, allied with Prussia and Austria in what became known as 'The First Coalition'. The French had already commenced hostilities against Britain on 2 January when the harbour batteries at Brest had opened fire on the 16-gun brig *Childers*. With only a short and unsettled break in 1802-03, Britain and France were to be at war for the next twenty-two years.

The Marine de la République Française entered the war with a strong fleet constructed during the last years of the *ancien régime*, but its cost had helped precipitate revolution, not only by its pressure on the central treasury, but also because it became impossible to pay the wages owed to seamen and dockyard mates. The effect of the revolution on naval discipline and leadership was devastating. Less predictably, revolution did not lead to any creative developments in ship design, signalling, or tactics as had taken place in the middle of the century, and had led to unparalleled success during the American Revolutionary War.

In contrast, the Royal Navy was in good shape, and in material terms mobilisation was able to take place faster than in any previous war. Manning was always a problem, but Britain still had the mercantile resources to support the largest population of seamen in Europe, and the ability to recruit them for the navy, albeit by the rough methods of the press. The sympathy which existed between officers and seamen, however, was under stress due to the revolution, and was to worsen as the fleet expanded to an unprecedented size. The crew of the *Culloden* mutinied in December 1793 and that of the *Windsor Castle* in November 1794, forerunners of the great mutinies of 1797.

When war was declared, Lord Chatham was at the Admiralty as First Lord. The first strategic requirements attended to were the convoy of trade, the reinforcement of the small squadron in the West Indies, and the maintenance in the Channel of a fleet able to prevent the enemy at Brest from acting offensively, and ready to send detachments to match any French

1

deployment. A substantial British squadron was also found to watch the Toulon fleet. Command of the Channel Fleet was given to Admiral Lord Howe, Britain's most experienced sailor, and an innovator in tactics and signalling, who established a distant blockade of Brest, operating out of Spithead.

Although *The Naval Chronicle* did not commence publication until 1798, a diary of the first month of the war appeared in the early numbers, items from which are reproduced here. Some of the more extensive items in this section, which might not have been placed there when later *The Naval Chronicle* took on its final form, have been relocated in one or other of the relevant chapters. More extensive coverage of the early years of the war were inserted in later numbers. The biographical memoir of Earl Howe, which was published after his great victory in May and June of 1794, remarked on the controversy over his operational method. Distant blockade had been standard during the American War, and reduced the wear on equipment and men, but did not provide quick response to French naval movements west towards Ireland, or southwest to the Indies. When later Admiral the Earl St Vincent established a close blockade of Brest, however, that was to be no less controversial. (See Appendix I, 'Strategy and Tactics'.) The biographical memoir of Rear-Admiral Kingsmill, which was published in Volume 5 of the first editions, provides the opening entry for this volume. In it is a description of the outbreak of war. It also provides an extensive account of the cruiser operations in the western approaches in defence of trade, which Kingsmill directed from Cork. Other reports of cruiser actions were printed as 'Gazette Letters', which later came to be one of the most important parts of *The Naval Chronicle*, and provided a continuous account of naval engagements. It has not been possible to reproduce many of those relating to single-ship engagements in this edition, but a few examples have been inserted. This section closes with an anecdote of naval life, many of which *The Naval Chronicle* included in its pages from time to time. The one inserted here will be recognised by readers of Patrick O'Brian's novels.

Outbreak of War
From the 'Biographical Memoirs of Sir Robert Kingsmill, Bart.' V 202-03

England, after a state of tranquillity, which, though it continued more than two years, was not unattended with much anxiety, owing to the civil disturbances then subsisting in France, and the very turbulent conduct of those people towards every country, whither their intrigue, their murderous principles, or their ravages were capable of extending their effects, found itself suddenly, though perhaps not unexpectedly, involved with the other countries which had preceded them in misfortune, in the general convulsion which appeared to threaten the total subversion of every social principle, and every wise regulation of what is called government, throughout the greater part of Europe. To enter into any disquisition or discussion of the causes which produced this dangerous and destructive political system, were, in this place, totally irrelevant; suffice it to say, that Britain considering it absolutely incompatible with her internal safety, and the welfare of her subjects, to continue any longer a silent spectator of those horrors which she beheld gradually approaching towards her, without, at least, attempting to divert the dreadful current, resolved no longer to brook those indignities which were hourly attempted to be forced upon her, and at the commencement of the year 1793, came to the resolution of equipping a sufficient force to withstand those attacks with which she was so vauntingly, and insolently threatened.

Historical Memoir of Naval Transactions During the Present War from its Commencement in 1793 (January-June) [I 212-13, 423-30; II 486-489]

Many are the heroes of the dark rolling sea! Thy sails are like the clouds of the morning, and thy ships like the light of Heaven; and thou thyself like a pillar of fire that giveth light in the night. *Ossian*

[This retrospective survey, modelled on the journalistic method employed for contemporary news from 1799 to 1818, was not continued after June 1793.]

We have made some slight alteration in the title to this department of our *Chronicle*, as also in its arrangement, in order to take in a more extensive scope of Naval History, and to be enabled to record every circumstance, however minute, that relates to it. Our first design was to have noticed only the principal actions that had taken place during the War; but on further consideration we have adopted the following plan as more interesting to our readers, especially professional men, and also as being more valuable to the future historian.

Enlistment bounty
On the 10th of January 1793, at a Common Council of the City of London, it was resolved - "That the sum of forty shillings for every able seaman, and twenty shillings for every ordinary seaman, over and above the Bounty granted by his Majesty, be given, during the pleasure of the Court, and not exceeding one month from the above date, to every such seaman as shall enter into the service of his Majesty's Navy." - The Corporation of King's Lynn also offered a bounty of two pounds to able-bodied seamen, in addition to his Majesty's Proclamation.

West Indies expedition
Early in this month (January 1793) the Navy Board contracted for 2,400 weight of tonnage, to carry three regiments to the West Indies.

January 19 1793 The *Queen*, of 98 guns, Commodore Alan Gardner, Captain Hutt, went out of Portsmouth Harbour. - she sailed for the West Indies in March.

French commence hostilities
January 11. Captain Barlow, of the *Childers* Sloop of War, 14 guns, arrived at the Admiralty with following intelligence:

The *Childers* cruised off Brest Harbour, and stood within three quarters of a mile of three batteries: her colours were not then hoisted; the battery on her starboard side fired a shot, which went over her. The *Childers* then hoisted the British colours, and the Fort hoisted the National colours, with a red pendant over the ensign; which was answered by the other two Forts. The *Childers* was then driven by the tide of flood within half a mile of the Forts; and Captain Barlow was obliged, it being calm, to have her oars out, to keep her from drifting too far in. Immediately a cross heavy fire began by signal from the three batteries. Providentially a breeze of wind sprung up, and the *Childers* made sail. Being a small object, only one shot hit, which struck one of her guns, and split into three pieces, without injuring any one: the pieces were collected, and slung - the shot weighed forty-eight pounds. The Flag Ship at Brest, which at this early period was nearly ready for sea, was the *Terrible*, of 110 guns; one of the new Ships launched at the beginning of the American war.

Lieutenants invited to seek employment
23 January. A note was pasted up in the drawing-room of the Admiralty, notifying to all Lieutenants of the Navy resident in the metropolis, that such, as were desirous of immediate employment should enter their names in a book ready for that purpose.

French embargo Calais
2 February. Captain Thomas Hammond, of the *Carteret* packet, arrived at Dover, with the intelligence, that an embargo had taken place the preceding day at Calais, and the other ports of France, on all French, English, Prussian, Dutch, and Russian vessels; except the packets, and bye-boats, employed between Dover and Calais. Information arrived on the 6th that the packets also were detained. Orders were immediately dispatched by Government for the detention of all French Ships. - It was reported at the time, that about eighty English vessels were in the different ports of France, with from 800 to 1000 seamen. - In the ports of Great Britain, the number of French ships were very few, not more than six, or eight.

Dutch fitting fleet for sea
The Dutch, at the beginning of this month, were fitting out their navy as expeditiously as possible. - The Court of Madrid had already ordered the fitting out of twenty sail of the line, and six frigates.

French ships in British ports embargoed
On the 4th of February 1793, a general embargo was laid on all French ships and vessels whatever; and on the 11th Mr. Dundas [Henry Dundas, Home Secretary] presented to the House of Commons the message from his Majesty [George III], that the French had declared war against Great Britain, and the United Provinces. General reprisals were immediately granted against the ships, goods, and subjects of France. Our frigates and brigs were soon very successful in taking or curbing the trade, both fair and piratical, of our enemies. The English government had just concluded a treaty of commerce with Russia, had taken a large body of German troops into its service; and had engaged the King of Sardinia, for a yearly subsidy of £200,000, to join the Austrians in Italy with a very considerable military force. Alliances were also formed with Austria, Prussia, Spain, Holland, Portugal, and Russia, all of whom agreed, with more or less reservation, to shut their ports against the vessels of France. The King of the Two Sicilies agreed to furnish 6000 men, and four ships of the line to the common cause.

Squadron sails to guard Channel Islands
The following squadron sailed on the 7th of February, by express from the Admiralty, with every frigate, and sloop, ready for sea, to prevent a descent on the islands of Jersey,

and Guernsey, which was mediated by the French: - *Hannibal*, 74, Captain Colpoys, as Commodore; *Hector*, 74, Captain Montagu; *Orion*, 74, Captain Duckworth; and *June*, 32 guns, Captain Hood.

War!

On the 9th of February, the following letter was received by Government, dated Dover, the 8th instant, 1793:

"I have the honour to inform your Lordships, that the *Carteret* and *Express* packet-boats are this morning arrived from Calais, the respective masters whereof bring an account that WAR was declared at Paris on Friday last, (Feb. 1) against the English and Dutch."

Letters of marque

February 11. Letters of marque against the French were issued from the Admiralty. - The Court of Spain engaged to assist the confederacy against France with sixty sail of different rates. - The Portuguese were to send six sail of the line to sea, and four frigates, besides four large ships, in the course of the summer.

Macbride hoists his flag

In the evening of the 10th, Admiral Macbride hoisted his flag on board his Majesty's Ship *Iphigenia*, then in the Downs.

French fleet attacks Cagliari

On the 16th of February, intelligence was received at Turin, that on the 27th of January 1793, the French Squadron in the Gulph of Cagliari, consisting of twenty or twenty-one ships, of which four were bomb-vessels, and seven Ships of the Line, having approached the city of Cagliari, began to bombard it, and were answered by a brisk firing of red-hot balls. This attack was continued for three days, when the Ships retired out of the reach of the cannon, but without quitting the Gulph. Several of the Ships were damaged in their Masts and Rigging, and one was set on fire by a red-hot ball, but by the timely assistance of the others the fire was extinguished. The Bombs produced no effect but upon the suburbs below the city, and only five men were killed. During the cannonading, the French attempted to land in several places to procure provisions, but they were every where repulsed by the militia, and lost upwards of 500 men.

London fitting for Duke of Clarence

20 February. An order was received in his Majesty's Dock-Yard at Plymouth, to fit the *London*, of 98 guns, with all possible dispatch, for the flag of his Royal Highness the Duke of Clarence.

Seamen recalled

18 February. A proclamation was issued, recalling all Mariners from the service of foreign states.

To counteract whatever insidious attempts might be made to sap the wooden walls of Great Britain, the following proclamation was issued:

"George R.

Whereas attempts may be made to seduce some of our subjects, contrary to their allegiance and duty to us, to enter on board French ships or vessels of war, or other ships or vessels of France, with intent to commit hostilities against us or our subjects; or otherwise to adhere, or give aid or comfort to our enemies upon the sea: Now we, in order that none of our subjects may ignorantly incur the guilt and penalties of such breaches of their allegiance and duty, have thought it necessary, by and with the advice of our Privy Council, to publish this our royal Proclamation; hereby notifying, and declaring, that all persons, being our subjects, who shall enter or serve on board any French ships or vessels of war, or other ships or vessels of France, with intent to commit hostilities against Us or our subjects, or who shall otherwise adhere, or give aid or comfort to our enemies upon the sea, will thereby become liable to suffer the pains of death, and all other pains and penalties of high treason and piracy. And we do hereby declare our royal intention and firm resolution to proceed against all such offenders according to law."

Gardner sails for West Indies

On the 22d February, Admiral Gardner kissed hands; being appointed to the command of the following Squadron, then under sailing orders for the West Indies. His flag was hoisted on the 6th of March:

Queen	98 guns	Rear Admiral Gardner
		Captain Hutt
Orion	74	Captain Duckworth
Hector	74	Captain G. Montague
Culloden	74	Captain Sir T. Rich, Bart.
Heroine	32	Captain A.H. Gardner
Andromeda	32	Captain J. Salisbury
Rattlesnake	16	Captain A. Monat

The above Squadron sailed from St. Helen's on the 26th of March.

Hull merchants request convoy

27 February. At a meeting of the merchants and ship-owners of Hull, in the preceding week, it was resolved that a requisition should be made to the Minister for two frigates, two sloops, and two cutters, or such other force as Government shall please to grant, to rendezvous in the Humber; and to act as convoy, or otherwise, for the protection of the coasting trade, and safety of the Port: as also for convoys for the trade to Italy, Spain, and Portugal; for the Baltic fleets; and for the Greenland ships: for a battalion, or such body of militia as may be had, to be quartered in the town; and for an able engineer to take a survey of the citadel, and to report what is proper to be done to put it in a state of defence.

List of French squadron at sea

March. The following list was circulated during the month, as an authentic one of the French force then at sea:

Le Republicain	110 guns	*La Tourville*	74 guns
L'Achille	74	*L'Experiment*	40
Frigates:	*La Thetis*	*La Surveillante* *La Concorde*	*La Réunion*

with two other vessels of less force: in all ten sail.

Spanish declaration

23 March. Spain declared war against France.

Female patriotic subscription
3 April. The female patriotic subscription, for the relief of the widows and children of those, who may fall during the war, amounted to £500. Her Royal Highness the duchess of York contributed yearly £50 - The Duchess of Buccleugh, Countess Pembroke, and Lady Mary Cooke, subscribed each £100.

East Indiamen sail
5 April. In the morning, about seven o'clock, Rear-Admiral Gell sailed from St. Helen's, with the East Indiamen under convoy, and the following Squadron:

St. George	98 guns	Rear-Admiral Gell
		Captain T. Foley
Boyne	98	Captain W.A. Otway
Ganges	74	Captain A.J.P. Molloy
Edgar	74	Captain A. Bertie
Powerful[1]	74	Captain T. Hicks
Egmont	74	Captain A. Dickson
Phaeton	38	Captain Sir A.S. Douglass

2 May. Admiral Gell, in the St. George, 98 guns, with the Egmont, 74, Captain A. Dickson, and Ganges, 74, Captain. J.A.P. Molloy, cruised off Cape Finisterre until the 15th.

Parker C-in-C Portsmouth
10 April. Admiral Sir Peter Parker, Bart. kissed hands, on being appointed Commander in chief at Portsmouth.

Ships in commission
6 May. Number of Ships of the line in commission, sixty-five.

Hood hoists flag
Lord Hood's flag, red at the fore-top, was hoisted in the evening of the 6th of May, on board the Victory, 110 guns.

Jamaica rewards Bligh for bread fruit expedition
The Assembly and Council of Jamaica voted the sum of £10,000 as a gratuity for the Bread Fruit Tree expedition: five thousand pounds of the above sum were voted to Captain W. Bligh, as commander on that service.

The Porte declares neutrality
9 May. The Grand Seignior issued an official notification of his intention to remain neutral during the present war. He, at the same time, forbade the vessels of the hostile powers to engage each other within three miles of his coast; and directed, that when they were engaged in open sea, none of his vessels should interfere to assist either party.

Anecdote of French recruitment methods
A young French gentleman, who was taken prisoner in the Dumourier privateer, and who acted in the capacity of interpreter, informed a midshipman on board the Phaeton,

---

1 The Powerful continued the Convoy to the East Indies.

that he had served for three years at Lubeck, as an apprentice to a merchant; and having returned to Bourdeaux, in order to enter into partnership with his father, on his arrival there, he was summoned before the municipality, who gave him his choice to depart instantly for the frontier to join the national troops, or to go to sea in a privateer: - he chose in consequence to go on board the *Dumourier*.

Naval vote

Naval Supplies granted by Parliament for the Year 1793:

December 20, 1792

For 25,000 men, including 5,000 marines	£ 1,300,000

February 11, 1793

For an addition of 20,000 men	£ 1,040,000

March 5

Ordinary, including half-pay	£ 669,205/5/10
Extraordinaries	£ 387,710

March 12

Towards paying off the Navy Debt	£ 575,000
	£ 3,971,915/5/10

Ordnance

Sea Service, not provided for in 1791	£ 32,068/15/4

March 20

To reimburse losses, sustained by persons concerned in the Nova Scotia Whale Fishery	£ 1,420/3/0

Hood sails for Mediterranean, promotions

A few hours after the fleet under the command of Vice Admiral Lord Hood, which sailed for the Mediterranean at the end of May, quitted the Offing at Portsmouth, a signal was made to bring to, when a promotion took place in favour of several young officers, who had distinguished themselves by their continual exertions in fitting out the fleet; after which it proceeded with a fair wind down Channel. On the 29th of May, they were seen from Maker Heights cruising to the westward. The men of war, Indiamen, and merchantmen, amounted to 150 sail. They seemed to cover the Channel.

Howe hoists flag as C-in-C Channel Fleet

On the 29th of May, Lord Howe hoisted the union flag at the main top, as commander in chief, on board his Majesty's ship *Queen Charlotte*, at Portsmouth.

Dutch news

A Dutch squadron, during this month, was cruising in the North Seas, consisting of one ship of 68 guns, five frigates, and one schooner, under the command of Commodore Byland.

Channel Fleet Operations
From the 'Biographical Memoir of Earl Howe.' [I 18-19]

On the commencement of the war with France, in 1793, his Lordship [Earl Howe], at the particular request of his sovereign, accepted the painful and arduous command of the Western Squadron. Powers, such as have been seldom delegated to any commander in chief, were wisely entrusted to his prudence. By the short cruises which he made, the fleet was never obliged to remain long in harbour to refit: but was constantly ready to engage the enemy. He entirely altered the signals, then in use, for others more simple and perfect; and, by the system he adopted throughout, prepared the way for the glorious successes which have followed. Yet still, such is the irritated state of the public mind, such a tendency does it possess to murmur; and so perfectly ignorant were the public in general of every thing relating to the natural and real objects of the Western Squadron, that the very means which Lord Howe employed to insure, as far as man could insure, a certain victory, should the French fleet put to sea, were ridiculed at home in terms painful to recollect, and highly indelicate to repeat.

Anecdote of Lord Howe [XXX 112]

Lord Howe, whilst Admiral of the Channel-Fleet, was at one time so unpopular in the navy, from his supposed *shyness*, that the officers of his own ship declined to drink his health at their mess. This was a source of mortification to the Chaplain, a *protegé* of his Lordship's, who took the ingenious mode of doing it in the following way. When called upon for a toast, he said, - "If you please, Gentlemen, I'll give you the *two first words of the third Psalm*," which was immediately drank. On referring to the book, it was discovered that the words were, "Lord! How." After the glorious first of June, the above was the favourite toast throughout the navy.

Trade Defence
From the 'Biographical Memoirs of Sir Robert Kingsmill, Bart.' [V 203-206]

A promotion of Flag-Officers followed almost as a natural consequence, this resolution [to bring a fleet forward for service]. On the 1st of February 1793, Mr. Kingsmill was promoted to the rank of Rear-Admiral of the White Squadron, and had scarcely experienced this advancement, ere his merits were still farther rewarded by his being appointed to command in chief on the Irish station. Taking all the concomitant circumstances into consideration, no appointment whatever, perhaps, was more judiciously made on any occasion; as an Officer his judgment, his zeal, and his prudence, appeared to point him out as peculiarly fitted to a command which certainly required all those different traits of conduct. His gallantry and activity in any case of sudden emergency were indubitable, and the private, the personal (if it may be so termed) qualification of his being a native of the country, marked him out, independent of every other circumstance, as a man that must be peculiarly grateful to those among whom in some cases it might be necessary for him to display his authority. The event fully established the truth of that theoretical reasoning on which it may be supposed the appointment itself was founded, while his private demeanour most deservedly acquired him the love, the esteem, and the affection of those who were unconnected with the service, his public conduct not only raised the highest esteem in all those persons who served under his orders, but in those who had most judiciously confided to him so important a trust.

The passage between Ushant and Cape Clear intersects, as it is well known, the track of all ships bound to England from the East or West Indies, the Levant, and in short every other quarter of the world, the Baltic, and Ports of Sweden or Denmark excepted, together with a very inconsiderable portion of ships, who, warned of any peculiarly imminent danger, have sometimes gone north about. The advantage which has rewarded on many occasions, particularly in former wars, the cruisers, as well those belonging to the King as to private persons, who devote their time and attention to this marauding service; encouraged an unremitting perseverance, that required the strictest attention to prevent from becoming most extremely injurious to the British commerce. To adopt the term commonly used to express the peculiar situation of naval affairs in that quarter; the entrance of the Irish and English Channels became, from the instant hostilities commenced, most grievously infested by cruisers belonging to the enemy, of all descriptions. The injury effected against the British trade in consequence of this measure, might have been of the most serious kind, if the utmost diligence, surmounted by activity, had not been used in counteraction of it. The mere list of vessels, many of them considerable in point of force, which fell into the hands of different cruisers acting under the orders of Sir Robert, would form of themselves a proof sufficiently indelible of that right to public applause, which his conduct justly procured him. Scarce a month passed for a considerable period without the capture of some vessel of consequence; but these successes were trivial in comparison with that which he had the fortune to effect in the month of June 1796. A squadron of frigates consisting of four sail, had been fitted out at Brest for the express purpose of committing depredations against the British trade in that particular quarter. The vessels composing it were selected with the utmost care, and considered of the first character as sailers in the whole French navy. They were manned with chosen crews, and commanded by officers held in the highest estimation for gallantry and nautical knowledge. Notwithstanding these precautions, the enemy had scarcely made their appearance on the station ere they were met, engaged, defeated, and captured. The first dawning of this progressive success was announced in the following plain narrative, officially communicated by the Vice-Admiral to the Secretary of the Admiralty:

"Sir, By my last of the 10th instant, you were acquainted, for the information of my Lords Commissioners of the Admiralty, that his Majesty's ships *Unicorn* and *Santa Margarita*, part of the squadron under my orders, had sent in a large ship, under Swedish colours, laden with Dutch property from Surinam; and that Lieutenant Carpenter, of the *Unicorn*, who brought her here, told me he had left our ships in chase of three sails, supposed to be enemies.

Their Lordships will now have the satisfaction of being informed that those three sail were French frigates, *viz. La Tribune*, of 40 guns, *La Tamise*, of 36 guns (formerly the *Thames*), and *La Legere*, of 24 guns, under the command of Commodore Moulston. Notwithstanding that superiority, his Majesty's two frigates, immediately on ascertaining what they were, crowded sail after them; upon which the enemy formed in a line of battle, but shortly after declining to come to an action, they separated and endeavoured to escape. Captain Williams, in the *Unicorn*, pursued the largest, *La Tribune*, and I have no doubt will give a good account of her, while Captain Martin chased and came up with *La Tamise*, which struck to him after a smart action, wherein thirty-three of the enemy were killed, and nineteen wounded; and only two men were killed and three wounded, on board the *Santa Margarita*. Unluckily, as the *Legere* could not be attended to during this chase and engagement, she got off.

Their Lordships will find more particulars on this subject in the inclosed letter to me from Captain Martin, who is safely arrived here with his prize; which capture is the most active and successful of all the enemy's cruisers against our trade.

The credit of the British name has been so eminently well supported on this occasion, by the zeal, spirit, and judgment with which his Majesty's ships were conducted, that it becomes wholly unnecessary for me farther to express my sense of the merits of their Captains, Officers, and crews. I am, Sir, &c.

R. KINGSMILL."

To render this success complete in every respect, the *Legere* was captured in a few days afterward. "I have the satisfaction", says the Admiral, in his official dispatch, "of acquainting you, for the information of my Lords Commissioners of the Admiralty, that the whole of the squadron which had sailed from Brest, under the orders of Commodore Moulston, is in our possession; *La Legere*, a fine coppered corvette, of 22 guns, being now brought in here by his Majesty's ships *Apollo* and *Doris*. Separated as those ships were, the capturing of them is a rare instance of success, and a proof of the activity of his Majesty's cruisers on that station."

"Separated as they were," was a term peculiarly apposite and modest, in respect to the situation of this luckless squadron, and the circumstances, under which it passed into the hands of the British. The *Proserpine*, of 44 guns, which, according to the létter of Captain Williams, who at that time commanded the *Unicorn*, and captured the *Tribune*, had parted from her companions on the evening preceding the first action, in a fog, was captured four days afterward off Cape Clear, by Lord Amelius Beauclerk, who commanded the *Dryad*.

Brutal Events on the Brig Glory, from 'Gazette Letters'[2]
Extract of a Letter from Portsmouth, February 18, 1793 [1 213-14]

Arrived the *Juno* man of war, Captain Samuel Hood, with a small French privateer called *L'Entreprenant*, which had taken the *Glory*, Benson, from London, and was retaken by the *Juno*, and with the privateer brought into harbour.

The privateer, Michael François Vaniere commander, had fired a dozen shot at the brig, and finding she would not bring to, boarded her with fifteen men, who bound Mr. Benson, the master, hands and feet, and lashed him down to the chest; putting all his crew in irons, stripping them of every article, and otherwise mal-treating them: but the instant the *Juno* brought the privateer and brig to, the privateer's crew released Mr. Benson and his men; who, feeling a strong resentment at their inhuman usage, were actuated by the impulse of the moment to retaliate in their turn. The following particulars, of this early instance of French barbarity, were afterwards sent by Captain Benson, from Portsmouth, to the owners of the *Juno* [sic, *Glory?*] at Chepstow.

The valuation of the *Glory* and cargo will be taken to-morrow: the salvage, consisting of one-eighth of the total value, goes to the officers and crew of the *Juno*, as a recompence for their vigilance. We were chased for two hours by the privateer, before she could

2 This is intended to supply whatever may be omitted in our Biography, and Memoirs of Navigation; the whole together will in time, we trust, form an extensive naval history.

come up with us; and after being boarded, they put the whole of my people in irons on the deck, and led me down to the cabin, where they placed me upon my back, and lashed me to my chest by the neck, arms, and legs, with my head hanging over. I was in the most excruciating pain for four hours and an half. In this helpless condition, one of the cowardly miscreants (they disgrace even the name of Frenchmen) snapped a pistol at my breast, and another made a thrust at me with a cutlass, which fortunately went in an oblique direction through my coat and jacket. They cut off my dog's head, for the purpose, they said, of representing the fate of the whole crew upon our arrival in France. In the interim, the *Juno* frigate most providentially hove into sight and gave chase, when we were all immediately liberated. It is difficult at all times to keep the passions within a due state of subordination: it was at that moment totally impossible for me to subdue my rage; and, snatching a cutlass from the hands of the man who untied me, I almost at one stroke severed his left arm from his body; when, fearing the further effects of my frenzy, he jumped out of the cabin window and was drowned. Another followed his example, and jumped off the taffrel; and the Captain, dreading the just vengeance which was awaiting him, took a pistol and shot himself through the head. I was not yet reduced to reason, and, before the *Juno*'s crew could overpower me, had cut and lacerated three other of the Frenchmen so dreadfully, that they were entirely covered with blood, and now lie in the hospital without hopes of recovery. Those only who suffer can feel, and though the moderate part of mankind may blame me for rashness, my own heart acquits me of any deliberate or unprovoked act of cruelty.

Action between
H.M.S. Nymph and the French National Frigate Cleopatra
From the 'Historical Memoir of Naval Transactions.' [1 426-428]

The capture of the *Cleopatra* frigate, 40 guns, 320 men, by Captain Edward Pellew, in the *Nymphe*, 32 guns, 250 ment, on the 18th of June, was accomplished with a gallantry not to be paralleled in any country but our own, and vindicated the superiority of the Brtish navy. At day break he descried the enemy, who had sailed three days from St. Maloes, without taking any thing. Captain Pellew bore down immediately; all was silent until they came within hale: he then ordered the crew of the *Nymphe* from their quarters to the shrouds, when *Long live King George the Third!* was given with three cheers. The French Captain, M. Jean Mullon, ordered his ship, in the same manner, to be manned; and, coming forward on the gangway, waved his hat, exclaiming, *Vive la Nation!* which his crew accompanied with three cheers. Captain Pellew's putting on his hat was the signal to the *Nymphe* to begin action. One more desperate was never fought; they were engaged, throughout, yard arm and yard arm. The first shot was fired about half past six in the morning. The sails and rigging were so much intermixed during the engagement, that the crew of the *Nymphe* actually went from their own yards to those of the *Cleopatra*, and cut the men from their quarters. At length a shot from the *Nymphe* carried away the mizzen mast of *La Cleopatra*, and another disabled the wheel of her tiller; so that she became ungovernable, and fell aboard the *Nymphe*.

Captain Pellew, fromt he cloud of smoke in which both ships were involved, not knowing the real cause, concluded his adversary intended to board him, and prepared to receive it: when finding they did not advance, he immediately gave orders to board *La Cleopatra*. The first party was led by Mr. Amherst Morris, and the next by the

This view represents the engagement between the *Nymphe*, 32 guns, 250 men, and the *Cleopatra* French frigate, 40 guns and 320 men, at the time when the *Cleopatra*, being disabled and unmanageable by the loss of her tiller and mizen mast, fell on board *La Nymphe*. [Plate 18]

second Lieutenant, Mr. George Luke, who himself struck the French colours, and hoisted the British flag.

One instance of cool intrepidity in our countrymen, during the action, deserves to be recorded amid the many that occurred. In the heat of this most desperate engagement, the rigging of the two ships was entangled; and, as the mast of the *Nymphe* was much wounded, Captain Pellew was fearful, that any strain might bring it down. He therefore offered ten guineas to any man who would go up and cut the rigging; upon which two seamen, in defiance of all danger, ran up the shrouds and performed it. - the engagement lasted 55 minutes.

On the twenty-second, Captain Pellew's letter to the Admiralty appeared in the Gazette:

To Mr. Stephens, dated off Portland, June 19, 1793.

"I have the honour to inform you that at day light yesterday morning, I was so fortunate as to fall in with the national French frigate *La Cleopatra*, mounting 40 guns, and manned with 320 men, commanded by Monsieur Jean Mullon, three days from St. Maloes, and had taken nothing.

We brought her to close action at half past six, and in fifty-five minutes took possession of her; the two ships having fallen on board each other, we boarded from the quarter-deck, and struck her colours; and finding it impossible to clear the ships, then hanging head and stern, we came to anchor, which divided us, after we had received on board 150 prisoners. The enemy fought us like brave men, neither ship firing a shot until we had hailed. Her captain was killed; three lieutenants wounded; the number of men not yet ascertained, but from the best accounts, about sixty; her mizzen mast overboard, and her tiller shot off.

I am extremely concerned she was not purchased at a less expense of valuable officers and men, on our part, whose loss I cannot sufficiently regret, and to whose gallantry I cannot possibly do justice. We had 23 men killed, and 27 wounded, of which a list is inclosed.

I am very particularly indebted to my first lieutenant, Mr. Amherst Morris, and no less so to Lieutenants George Luke, and Richard Pellowe, and I was ably seconded on the quarter deck by Lieutenant John Whitaker, of the marines, and Mr. Thomson, the master; and I hope I do not presume in recommending those officers to their Lordships protection and favour: And I should do injustice to my brother Captain Israel Pellew, who was accidentally on board, if I could possibly omit saying how much I owe him for his very distinguished firmness, and the encouraging example he held forth to a young ship's company, by taking upon him to directions of some guns on the main deck."

A list of the Killed and Wounded on board his Majesty's Ship La Nymphe, Edward Pellew, Esq. Captain, in an Engagement with La Cleopatra, a French Frigate, off the Start, on the 18th of June, 1793

Killed

Mr. Tobias James, Boatswain	Mr. Richard Pearse, Master's Mate
Mr. George Boyd, Midshipman	Mr. John Davie, Midshipman
Mr. Samuel Edsall, Ditto	Together with 14 seaman, and 4 private marines

Wounded

Lieut. George Luke, 2nd Lieutenant	Mr. John A. Norway, Midshipman
Mr. John Whitaker, Lieut. of Marines	Mr. John Plaine, Midshipman
Together with 17 seamen, and 6 private marines	

The *Nymphe*, with her prize, arrived in Portsmouth Harbour on Friday the 21st. She was cheered by all the ships as she passed, and her crew returned the compliment. On Sunday evening, the 23d, the French Captain, who fell soon after the action began, was buried, by Captain Pellew, in Portsmouth Church-yard. The body was followed only by his own officers. The inscription on the coffin was dictated by them:

Citoyen Mullon, Slain in battle with *La Nymphe*, June18th,1793, Aged 42 Years.

The *Cleopatra* was the frigate which hove in sight when Captain Faulknor, in the *Venus*, was engaging the *Prosperpine*.

On Saturday the 29th of June, Captain Edward Pellew, and his brother Lieutenant Israel Pellew, were introduced to the King by the Earl of Chatham [the First Lord]; when the former received his Majesty's thanks, with the honour of knighthood, and the latter kissed hands on being promoted to the rank of post captain.

[An account of this action was also published in the biographical memoir of Sir Edward Pellew, Bart. Vol. 18 pp. 443-447.]

View of Captain Ellison's action, off Guernsey, with an enemy's squadron. 8th June
1794. Engraved by Rickards, from a drawing by J.T. Lee, Esq. [Plate 253]

Anecdote of Life in the Navy
*From 'An account of a Curious Fish Observed by M. Vaillant, in His
voyage from the Cape of Good Hope.'* [167]

I embarked in the *Ganges*, commanded by Captain Paarde-hooper. We sailed from
False Bay the 14th of July, 1784, accompanied by four other of the company's ships. We
had scarcely cleared the bay, when contrary winds drove us to the southward, where an
horrible tempest assailed us, and we were driven by a violent gale to the latitude of 37°
south. I felt by experience how much reason the Portuguese had to call the southernmost
part of Africa the Cape of Tempests.

The four vessels sailed in company, without losing sight of each other; and we even
visited one another, when the weather was calm, and we could hoist out our boats.

When this kind of intercourse was rendered impracticable by high winds and too
stormy sea, we had recourse to another, that of mutually writing letters, of which the
gulls and terns were the carriers.

These birds, beaten by the winds, and tired with their flight, would pitch upon our
yards to rest themselves, where the sailors easily caught them. Having fastened our
little epistles to their legs, we then let them fly, and, making a noise to prevent their
alighting again on the vessel, obliged them to wing their course to the next. There they
were caught again by the crew, and sent back to us in the same manner with answers to
our letters.

This correct view of the action by the squadron under the command of Commodore Sir John Borlase Warren, and the French frigates under Monsieur Desgarceaux, on the twenty-ninth of April, 1794, is taken from the southward, to windward of the ships; at the moment when Sir John Warren in the *Flora*, after having fired into and passed *La Babet*, is engaging *La Pomone*, and *L'Engageante* - which ships kept in a close line: *La Resolue*, being the headmost ship of the enemy, luffing up occasionally, and raking the *Flora*. The *Arethusa* is coming up next; who engaged, and captured *La Babet*.

The *Concorde*, *Melampus*, and *Nymphe*, are advancing, under a press of sail; the latter on the starboard tack, and to leeward. Plate 33

1793-1794 – Mediterranean

TO WATCH THE TOULON FLEET, a substantial British squadron commanded by Vice-Admiral Samuel Lord Hood was sailed in four groups in the spring of 1793 to co-operate with the Spanish Admiral Don Juan de Langara based at Minorca. The prospect of an Hispano-British fleet engaging the French Toulon fleet, however, was shortlived. To reassert their authority in Toulon after the local overthrow of the Jacobins, the government in Paris sent an army south, and the Toulonese, out of desperation, invited Hood to occupy the port. Hood landed two regiments of British infantry and 200 marines, and a Spanish army was rushed across the frontier, to provide its landward defence. Small contingents were also sent by Naples, Piedmont and Sardinia. Command of the troops was given to the Spanish Rear-Admiral Don Federico Gravina. The French fleet moved into the inner harbour and landed its gunpowder. About 5000 of their crews were put onboard four disarmed and unserviceable 74s, and sailed under passport to the Atlantic ports.

Professional and national jealousies impeded the defence. Gravina was promoted within the Spanish service, and instructed to take command of the allied forces. To support him, Langara moved his three-deck flagship into a position broadside on to *Victory* with two other three-deckers on her bow and quarter. Hood, however, resisted this attempted intimidation.

After winning a desperate fight to control the high ground overlooking Toulon harbour, the French army used its artillery, under the command of the young General Napoleon Buonaparté, to overcome the fire from *Princess Royal*, 98, a Spanish 74, and two floating batteries. On 14 December the defences on the landward side were driven in. Toulon was taken, thousands of the leading citizens being guillotined.

Before Toulon was evacuated, British and Spanish incendiary parties, commanded by Sir Sydney Smith who had made his own way to Toulon from the Levant, were sent to destroy the arsenal and the ships in the harbour, but they were unable to burn more than ten of the Toulon fleet.

17

Hood was able to get fifteen French ships out of Toulon before the fall. Soon after the evacuation, Captain Samuel Hood, the Admiral's cousin, returned from a cruise in the *Juno* frigate late at night and brought her right into the inner harbour, where she took the ground, but was so fortunate as to bring her out again under a heavy fire from the batteries.

While still in occupation of Toulon, Lord Hood had sent a small squadron made up of three ships and two frigates under Commodore Robert Lindzee to attempt to persuade the French garrisons on Corsica to declare for the royalists. Corsica had only been incorporated into France in 1768 in the teeth of strong local opposition led by General Paoli, who again sought British assistance to establish an independent government. When the fleet was forced to leave Toulon, Hood moved to Hyères Bay on the Riviera, but on 24 January 1794 officers sent to communicate with Paoli returned with encouraging reports. Hood decided to return to San Fiorenzo Bay, and, with the anchorage secure, he moved on to lay siege to Bastia, using only sailors and marines, and with Paoli's irregulars in support. Bastia capitulated 21 May, and a Corsican Corte voted to separate from France and accept a British viceroy, Sir Gilbert Elliott. On 10 August Calvi was taken after another difficult siege during which Captain Horatio Nelson received the wound which destroyed his right eye.

The Naval Chronicle led its account of the occupation and siege of Toulon with an extended biographical memoir of Vice-Admiral Lord Hood, and supported it with an extensive file of 'Toulon Papers' of which it has only been possible here to reproduce a letter from Sir Sidney Smith describing his efforts to destroy the French fleet during the final assault of the French army. Apart from those files, a letter from Captain Edward Cooke was published, describing his daring work in making the initial contact with the Toulonese who wished to place their city under the protection of British forces, and his later experience in fighting to hold the perimeter around Toulon. In the memoir of the public services of Sir Charles Brisbane, published ten years later, was recorded another man's part in the defence and final demolition of perimeter forts. The question of whether Hood had been well advised to use Smith, who was present at Toulon at his own initiative, rather than employ one of his own officers, became a matter of discussion by *Naval Chronicle* correspondents in the months after Cochrane's participation in the 1809 fireship attack on the Brest fleet in Basque Roads. This correspondence has been reproduced here.

Juno's adventure following the withdrawal from Toulon was dramatically described in *The Naval Chronicle*'s biographical memoir of Sir Samuel Hood. Operations in Corsica were not extensively recorded in *The Naval Chronicle* but a brief description formed part of the biographical memoir of Lord Nelson. This section of the Mediterranean theatre in 1793 concludes with a list of the French ships found in Toulon, annotated to show which had been captured, which destroyed, and which had survived under French command.

British Occupation of Toulon
'From the Biographical Memoirs of Lord Hood.' II 37-45

On the commencement of the present War in (1793) Lord Hood was immediately called forth to command a powerful fleet, destined for the Mediterranean; where on his arrival such unprecedented events ensued, that we may venture to say, any more difficult, or more perplexing, never fell to the lot of a British Admiral. From respect unto those who are now living, and whose names would be introduced, were we to enter into a minute detail of the proceedings at Toulon, and Corsica, we shall at present only touch upon some of the principal leading features, and, having drawn the outline with truth and accuracy, shall leave it to a more distant period, to fill up the shades, and to insert the bold touches of history.

It had never formed a part of the responsibility of any officer, except the subject of the present memoir, to combine the momentous duties of a naval commander in chief, with the important ones of civil commissioner of the interests of one of the largest and most valuable ports in Europe; and this at a moment that was rendered particularly critical, from his being coalesced with the Spaniards, who were jealous of his authority, and who secretly endeavoured, as we shall now prove, to overthrow the good cause they openly professed to support.

Such was the task of difficulty, and danger, which Lord Hood had to perform, with the eyes of all Europe watching the manner in which it was executed: nothing but firmness, and a zealous diligence, could have surmounted such a trial.[1]

Although the task which Lord Hood had to fulfill was thus unexampled and difficult, the distinguished thanks which he received are public testimonies of its able accomplishment. His Lordship's services were acknowledged by the Kings of Sardinia, and Naples, under their own hands; his Holiness the Pope also manifested, in the same manner, his deep sense of the important benefits he had derived from the zeal, and care of Admiral Lord Hood: a present of a very elegant set of the Pia Clementia, which had hitherto been never given to any but crowned heads, was sent him by his Holiness.[2]

We shall now briefly state those interesting circumstances which led to the taking possession of Toulon, with some of the principal transactions of that short period, during which it remained under a British Admiral's government, and protection. This

---

1 The *details of a fleet* consisting of upwards of thirty British ships, and vessels, with seven French ships armed, and manned, under the direction of the French Rear Admiral Trogoffe: - the Correspondence with the Secretary of the Admiralty, and Secretary of State; with the several British Ambassadors, Ministers, and Consuls, in Spain, Italy, Constantinople, the States of Barbary, and the islands in the Mediterranean; the *Foreign Correspondence* with the sections of Toulon, and Marseilles; the negotiations, and correspondence, with the Austrian minister, and generals; with the Tuscan minister, and governors; with the Kings of Sardinia, and Naples, and their secretaries of state, generals, and naval commanding officers; with the Pope, and his secretary of state, Cardinal Zeladi; with the senates of Genoa, and Venice; with the grand master of Malta, and the Corsican General Paoli, and his adherents. - Scarce a day passed but the admiral received letters from one, or other, of the above great personages, written in French, Spanish, and Italian, which he answered in the most punctual manner.

2 In six large folio volumes, containing engravings of the statues, busts, and other antiques, at Rome.

Portrait of the Right Honourable
Samuel Lord Viscount Hood,
Admiral of the White, and
Governor of Greenwich
Hospital. Engraved by Ridley,
from an original painting by
Hickel. Plate 151

subject has never been correctly laid before the public; and we are happy in being able to state Facts, of the utmost importance to the history of the present war, which have hitherto been only confined to the knowledge of a few persons. In a future number will be published further documents, under the title of Toulon Papers, to which we can at present only refer.

On the 23d of August (1793), Commissioners came on board the *Victory*, Lord Hood's flag-ship, from Marseilles, with full powers from the Sections of the departments of The Mouths of the Rhone, to treat for peace; and they declared that a Monarchial Government in France was the leading object of their negotiation. They expected to be met by commissioners from Toulon, deputed by the Sections of the Department of the Var, for the same purpose. Lord Hood sent on shore to Toulon, and Marseilles, a proclamation and also a preliminary declaration, which produced the desired effect, and made a favourable impression.

On the 25th of August, the deputies of all the sections at Toulon agreed to Lord Hood's proposal, and signed a declaration, consisting of eight articles, which was addressed to his Lordship, and invested him provisionally with the harbour, and forts of Toulon. On the 26th, Captain Imbert, commander of *L'Apollon*, 74 guns, and also a member of the general committee of the sections, came on board the *Victory*, as a special commissioner from the said committee to Lord Hood, ratifying what they had done. He gave in a general state of the French line of battle ships in commission, in the outer road, with remarks on the character of the officers, and men. When Captain Imbert had given the strongest assurances that Louis XVII had been proclaimed by the sections, that they had sworn to acknowledge him, and were resolved no longer to endure the despotism of their tyrants, but would use their utmost endeavours to restore Peace to their distracted country, Lord Hood resolved to land 1500 men, and to take possession of the forts which commanded the ships in The Road.

Rear-Admiral St. Julien, a turbulent spirit, to whom the Seamen had given the command of the French fleet, in the room of the former commander in chief, Trogoffe, had manned the forts on the left of the harbour, and threatened resistance; but Lord Hood, animated by the same bold enterprise for which he has always been distinguished, and impressed with the great importance of gaining possession of Toulon, and its dependencies, determined to make every effort that could be performed by the fleet which he commanded. Accordingly, at midnight, on the 27th, he made the necessary arrangements for disembarking the troops, as near as possible to the great fort, called La Malgue, without their being annoyed by those batteries in the possession of St. Julien, on the opposite shore; and the following day (August 28), at noon, the Honourable Captain Elphinstone (now Lord Keith), entered the fort of La Malgue, at the head of the troops. In pursuance of Lord Hood's directions, he immediately took the command as governor, and sent a flag of truce, with peremptory notice to St. Julien, that such ships as did not proceed without delay into the inner harbour, and put their powder on shore, would be treated as enemies. St. Julien, however, was found to have escaped during the night, with the greater part of the crews of seven line of battle ships, which were principally attached to him: all but these seven ships removed into the inner harbour, in the course of the evening. The Spanish Fleet, under the command of Don Juan de Langara, appeared in sight, as the British troops were in the act of landing, to take possession of Fort La Malgue.

Having thus taken possession of Toulon, and the adjacent forts, Lord Hood issued on the same evening another proclamation, which greatly soothed the minds of the inhabitants.[3] The English troops in Fort La Malgue received on the twenty-ninth of August a reinforcement of 1000 men, who were disembarked from the Spanish Fleet. On the same day the British fleet turned into the outer road of Toulon, followed by the Spanish, and anchored at noon without the smallest obstruction. The junction of two such powerful fleets that had often met in fierce contention, but now rode peaceably at anchor in one of the finest harbours in the world, amid the glad acclamations of thousands, formed a most noble sight: as the flags of Great Britain, and Spain, waved promiscuously together in all their grandeur, they cheered the hearts of the gazing multitude, and seemed to promise a speedy termination to the Calamities of France. The British fleet had anchored but a short time in the outer road, when a numerous deputation, from the civil and military departments, came on board the *Victory* with an address to his Lordship.[4]

On the 30th of August Lord Hood judged it expedient, for the more effectual preservation of good order and discipline in the town, to appoint Rear Admiral Goodall governor of Toulon, and its dependencies. A part of Carteaux's army, consisting of 750 men, some cavalry, and ten pieces of cannon, approached the village of Ollioulle, near Toulon, on the same day; but Captain Elphinstone, governor of Fort La Malgue, immediately marched out at the head of six hundred troops, English and Spanish: he attacked the enemy with great spirit, and, soon making them abandon their posts on all sides, took four pieces of cannon, with horses, ammunition, two stand of colours, &c. as particularly stated in his letter to Lord Hood.[5] Our loss amounted to one captain killed, and nine men wounded. The Spaniards had three men killed, and as many wounded. In this attack Captain Elphinstone displayed a knowledge of military tactics, which was not expected from an officer in the British Navy. The particular objects which the French general had in view are developed in an intercepted letter sent by him to Colonel Mouriel, who commanded the advanced part of his army, which Governor Elphinstone defeated.[6]

Lord Mulgrave arrived at Toulon on the 6th of September, and, at the request of

3 Letters and proclamations relative to the British occupation of Toulon were published in the *Naval Chronicle* vol. 2 pp. 102-119, 192-201 & 288-303; *Toulon Papers* No. V.

4 *Ibid.* No. VI.

5 *Ibid.* No. VII.

6 *Ibid.* No. VIII.

Lord Hood, accepted the command of the British troops, with the rank of brigadier general, until his Majesty's pleasure was known. In consequence of the report, which his Lordship made, respecting the forces necessary to defend the several posts in the vicinity of Toulon, Lord Hood dispatched a pressing letter to Sir Robert Boyd, governor of Gibraltar, requesting 1500 soldiers, with artillery-men, and an able engineer. During the short time Lord Mulgrave commanded the forces at Toulon, he gave on all occasions distinguished proofs of his intrepidity, and professional abilities.

By the middle of September, our posts began to be kept in a constant alarm, from the increasing numbers of Carteaux's army on the west, and that of Italy on the east; each of them consisting nearly of 6000 men. At the same time, Lord Hood had apprehensions of some desperate attempt being made within, by upwards of 5000 disaffected seamen; the committee general of the sections, and the French Rear Admiral Trogroffe, represented the getting rid of them, as absolutely necessary for our own safety. This more especially was evident as previous to Lord Hood's taking possession of Toulon, they had agreed that these men should be sent home; provided they did not take any active part in obstructing the British fleet: they now in consequence began to be extremely clamorous and unruly; it was therefore, judged expedient to embark them in four of the most unserviceable ships, *Le Patriot*, *L'Apollon*, *L'Orion*, and *L'Entreprenant*, to each of which a passport was given.[7] These ships were totally dismantled of their guns, except two on the forecastle for signals, in case of distress; they had no small arms, and only twenty cartridges on board of each, and sailed as flags of truce; two for Brest, one for Rochefort, and one for L'Orient.

In addition to the motives just related, which induced Lord Hood to act thus, and to adhere strictly to the Convention, previously formed with the Civil and Military Government of Toulon, there were also others that had a powerful influence on his mind, but which were only known to a few. Amid the mass of the 5000 seamen, who were reputed turbulent, and disaffected, many were devoted to the cause of the inhabitants of Toulon, and were ready to make every sacrifice in favour of Monarchy; therefore, as it was confidently rumoured that Brest, Rochefort, and the other sea ports of France would take an active part in the same cause, there was good reason to hope that the arrival of these seamen would accelerate, at the several ports, similar exertions in behalf of the French monarch. The Convention however suspected their designs, and, having tried many in a summary manner, caused them to be put to death.

His Majesty's ships *Bedford*, and *Leviathan*, arrived at Toulon, September 28, with 800 Sardinian troops; and also Marshall Forteguerri, Commodore of the Sicilian ships, with 2000 troops from Naples, in two ships of the line, two frigates, and two sloops. This served considerably to cheer the spirits of the garrison, and of the inhabitants of Toulon, as for the last fortnight scarcely a day had passed, without their being attacked from one quarter or the other. Carteaux's army at this time amounted to 8000 men on the west, and that to the east, under Le Poype, to 7000; with reinforcements continually pouring into both.

The enemy had also opened a battery of twenty-four 24 pounders, upon our gun-boats, and the ships that covered them; and though they were soon dismounted by the ships under the direction of Rear Admiral Gell, and the works totally destroyed, with very great slaughter, yet the enemy, two or three successive times, renewed their works,

7 *Ibid.* No. IX.   Chart of Toulon

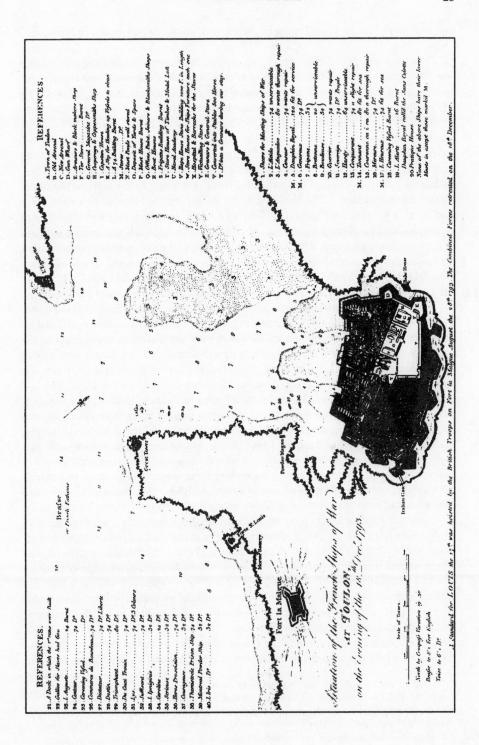

REFERENCES.

A. *Town of Toulon*
B. *Old Arsenal*
C. *New Arsenal*
D. *Gun Wharf*
E. *Armourer & Black maker's Shop*
F. *Tar Store .... Burnt*
G. *General & Ordnance Magazine*
H. *General & Oppoveable Ship*
I. *Careening House*
J. *Ditto for Boating up Vessels to clean*
K. *A 74 Building Barns*
L. *D°*
M. *Stores ..... D°*
N. *Mast Ponds will used*
O. *Deposits of Cords & Spars*
P. *Mast House Burnt*
Q. *Office, Paint, Joiners & Blacksmiths Shops*
R. *Boat House*
S. *Frigates Building Burnt*
T. *Store House of Timber & Model Loft*
U. *Naval Academy*
V. *Rope House -Rone Building none F. in Length*
W. *Store House for Ships Furnace each one*
X. *Hospital & Barracks for the Slaves*
Y. *Victualling Stores*
Z. *General & General's Store*
2. *Covered into Stables 300 Horse*
3. *D°into a Granary during our stay*

Stores for Mooring Ships of War
1. *L'Sobile .... 74 unserviceable*
2. *L'Orgueilleux .... So wants thorough repair*
3. *L'Heureux .... 74 wants repair*
M. 4. *Dauphin Royal ... 110 fit for service*
M. 6. *Commerce .... 74 D°*
7. *Pepone .... 32* ┐
8. *Brutonne .... 20* ├ *unserviceable*
9. *Bonhleure .... 32* ┘
10. *Guerrier .... 74 wants repair*
11. *Souverge .... 74 D° People*
12. *Hardy .... 64 unserviceable*
13. *Conquerant ...... 74 a slight repair*
M. 14. *Tonnant .... So fit for sea*
15. *Guerrière on i. on. So a thorough repair*
M. 16. *Moreau .... 74 D°*
M. 17. *L'Heureux .... 74 fit for sea*
18. *Careening Vessel Burnt*
19. *L. Merte .... 16 Burnt*
Dauphin Royal entild the Sans Culotte
20. *Pretager House*
None of the above Ships have their lower
Masts in except those marked M.

REFERENCES.

21. *A Dock in which the Frame were Built*
22. *Gallies for Slaves had Gun*
23. *L'Auguste .... 74 Burnt*
24. *Centaur .... 74 D°*
25. *Careening Vessel .... D°*
26. *Commerce de Bourdeaux. 74 D°*
27. *Destateur .... 74 D° Liberté*
28. *Destin .... 74 D°*
29. *Triomphant .... 80 D°*
30. *De Caux Trraun ...... 74 D°*
31. *Lys .... 74 D° 3 Colours*
32. *Suffisant .... 74 D°*
33. *L'Apoigique .... 34 D°*
34. *Caroline .... 32 D°*
35. *Serieux .... 32 D°*
36. *Barn Provision ...... 74 D°*
37. *Courageux .... 32 D°*
38. *Thermisdeek Prison Ship 74 D°*
39. *Montreal Powder Ship . 32 D°*
40. *L'Iris ...... D° ...... 32 D°*

Brassac
or French Fishermen

Situation of the French Ships of War
AT TOULON
on the Evening of the 18.th Dec.r 1793.

Scale of Toises

North by Compass Variation 19.30
Brafic to 31.° Fort English
Toise to 6.° D°

A Standard for LOUIS the 17.th was hoisted by the British Troops on Fort la Malgue August the 28.th 1793. The Combined Forces retreated on the 18.th December.

and persevered to the last moment in their attack upon our gun-boats, and advanced ships.

During the night of the 30th of September, the French availing themselves of a fog, very unexpectedly surprised a post occupied by the Spaniards, and thereby got possession of the Height of Pharon, immediately over Toulon; but at noon, on the 1st of October, when in the very act of establishing themselves with about 2000 men, they were attacked by the troops under the command of Lord Mulgrave, and after a short, but spirited action, were driven from the Height with great slaughter. Many of the flying parties were forced at the point of the bayonet headlong over the rocks. The loss of the English, Spaniards, Sardinians, and Neapolitans, amounted only to seven killed, and seventy-two wounded. The loss of the French was nearly 1450 killed and wounded, and 48 taken prisoners. The batteries of the enemy on the Hauteur de Ranier were destroyed in the night of the 8th October, with a considerable quantity of artillery and ammunition. The ensuing night a very successful sortie was made under the command of Captain Brereton, assisted by Lieutenant Sericold of the navy, and the seamen under his command: the enemy's batteries, which had recently been erected, were destroyed. The French, notwithstanding these defeats, obtained possession of Cape Le Brun, on the 15th, but were again overcome, and driven from thence with considerable loss.

Our readers must already have perceived with what labour; even at this period, Toulon was preserved by the valour and perseverance of a British admiral, assisted by his brave followers. These obstacles, however, were as nothing, in comparison to the treachery, and peculiar difficulties, by which he was surrounded. On the 18th of October Don Langara informed Lord Hood of the arrival of Don Valdes, to take upon him the command of the Spanish troops at Toulon, in the room of Admiral Gravina, who had been wounded on the 1st of October at the Heights of Pharon: on the 23d of the same month, Lord Hood was much surprised to receive another letter from Don Langara, acquainting him, that on account of the valour and good conduct of Admiral Gravina, his Catholic Majesty had promoted him to the rank of lieutenant general, and had appointed him *commander in chief of the combined forces at Toulon.* This Lord Hood very properly resisted; the town, and its dependent forts, were yielded up to the British troops alone, and were taken possession of by his Lordship; their Sardinian, and Sicilian Majesties, had been graciously pleased to confide their respective troops entirely to his Lordship's disposal, or to act under whatever British officer he might judge fit to appoint; he therefore felt it to be his duty to put the Sardinian and Sicilian troops together with the British under the command of Major General O'Hara, the moment he arrived, and who even then was off the port eventually subject to such orders as might afterwards be received from his Lordship. This unexpected measure of the court of Spain, together with the daily encroachments which the Spanish officers, supported by their commander in chief, made to obtain power, laid the foundation of that distrust which afterwards subsisted between the English, and Spaniards.[8]

Major General O'Hara, and Major General Dundas, arrived on the 22d of October; the former with a commission to be Governor of Toulon and its dependencies. Lord

8 The British Admiral had at this time only ten sail of the line in the harbour of Toulon; the menacing position in which Don Langara placed his ships at anchor, consisting of twenty one ships of the line, excited much animadversion. Under pretence of moving his fleet into more convenient births, he brought his own ship alongside to bear on the *Victory*, and anchored two three-deckers on her bow and quarter.

9 This squadron was commanded by Commodore Linzee, brother-in-law to Lord Hood, now Vice Admiral of the Red.

View of Toulon

View of Toulon, with the portrait of a polacre in the fore-ground. These vessels,
with three masts, are usually navigated in the Levant, and other parts of the
Mediterranean, with square sails upon the main mast, and lateen sails upon the fore
and mizen masts. Some of them, however, carry square sails upon all the three
masts, particularly those of Provence in France. Each of their masts is commonly
formed of one piece, so that they have neither topmasts, nor top gallant masts;
neither have they any horses to their yards, because the men stand upon the topsail
yard, to loose, or furl the top gallant sail, and on the lower yard to reef, loose, or furl
the top sail; whose yard is lowered sufficiently down for that purpose. Plate 21

Hood had the mortification to find at this critical juncture, that Sir Robert Boyd was so
sparing of succours for the defence of Toulon, that only half the number were sent
which he had so earnestly requested by letter early in September.

Lord Hood, finding his fleet much weakened by such a number of seamen who
were sent on shore to defend the various posts, judged it expedient to dispatch a ship to
the Grand Master of Malta, requesting that 1500 Maltese seamen might be sent to
serve in the British fleet, during its continuance in the Mediterranean, who should have
the same wages per month as his own seamen. The Grand Master in the most handsome
manner furnished the desired reinforcement.

The Spanish Admiral about this period proposed a joint expedition against Corsica;
but Lord Hood, aware of the different interests and views which the Spaniards might
have, wisely declined the undertaking unless he had instructions from home to that
purpose: adding in reply, that feeling much for General Paoli, he had a month before, as
a voluntary act of his own, sent a squadron to Corsica[9] to try what could be effected to

assist this veteran general; but owing to wrong information, and General Paoli not commencing the attack by land, at the same moment the squadron did by sea, the ships, after making a complete breach in the fort of St. Florence, were obliged to retreat with the loss of 50 men killed and wounded, and two line of battle ships much damaged.

The Spanish admiral began at this time more openly to disclose the treachery, which had been long concealed under a base hypocrisy, more worthy of an Inquisitor General, than of a Naval Officer. On the 12th of November, Don Langara, as if anxious to contrive some ground for an open rupture, renewed his desire of co-operating with a squadron of the British ships in attacking Corsica, and at the same instant proposed a joint expedition against some French ships that were at Tunis; but this was also declined by Lord Hood, as the Bey of Tunis had given no just cause of offence to his Britannic Majesty. Don Langara, however, still pursuing the object in his own mind, and finding he had not hitherto succeeded, as he could wish, wrote another letter to Lord Hood, claiming his right to an equal partition of power, in the naval, military, and civil departments of Toulon; and complaining that Corsican vessels, wearing the Corsican flag, had been received in the Port. Lord Hood still baffled the Spaniard by a reply that was moderate, but firm: *Do not, I entreat your Excellency, let us be discussing points our courts only can settle. The inhabitants of Corsica, who have never acknowledged themselves subjects of France, and navigate from ports in the island, not possessed by the French, have, I humbly conceive, a right to hoist The Corsican Flag; and I could not be justified in obliging them to wear any other.* Lord Hood was little aware that a secret negotiation, at this very juncture, had been actually agreed on between the Court of Madrid, and the French Convention.

During the time this was passing between the British, and Spanish admirals, Commodore Forteguerri, Commander in Chief of his Sicilian Majesty's ships, would not suffer his captains to obey Lord Hood's orders, though given in the most delicate manner, as acting under the authority of his Sicilian Majesty. Lord Hood, therefore, was under the disagreeable necessity of complaining of his conduct to the court of Naples: in consequence of this remonstrance, Commodore Forteguerri adopted half measures, and gave a feeble co-operation to the interests of the common cause; but the cordiality between the two commanders, so essential at this critical period, was thus destroyed.

On the evening of the 15th of November, the French vigorously attacked, with a large force, our post upon the Heights de Grasse, called Fort Mulgrave, and one of the most essential posts that covered the shipping in the harbour of Toulon. This attack was principally directed against that part which was occupied by the Spaniards on the right. General O'Hara, who was at dinner on board the *Victory*, lost no time in getting on shore. When he reached the Height, the French were close to the works; the Spaniards retreating, and firing their musquets in the air. The general instantly directed a company of the Royals to advance, who gallantly leaped the works, and put the enemy to flight, after leaving about 600 men dead and wounded in the field. The loss of the English amounted only to sixty-one. The British Admiral, in addition to what he had already experienced, since his taking possession of Toulon, had a fresh vexation towards the end of November, of the most serious and alarming nature; considering the augmented force of the surrounding enemy, and the critical situation of the extensive posts to be defended. After having been flattered with the most positive hopes of receiving, towards the middle of this month, 5000 Austrian troops; and when he had actually dispatched Vice Admiral Cosby, with a squadron of ships and transports to Vado Bay, to convey them, as previously concerted between himself and Mr. Trevor, his Majesty's minister at Turin; by letters received from Mr. Trevor, of the 18th of November, his Lordship's hopes were at once destroyed, and with them all expectation of the arrival of a single Austrian soldier at Toulon.

The enemy, at the close of November, having opened a battery against the post of Malbousket, near the arsenal, from which shells could reach the town, it was resolved to destroy it, and to bring off the guns; for this purpose General O'Hara digested a distinct and masterly plan of attack, which he communicated on the evening of the 29th of November, to the commanding officer of the troops of each nation. Accordingly, on the morning of the 30th, this plan was so far executed as to surprise the enemy's redoubt most effectually: -the British troops having obtained full possession of the Height and battery, their ardour and impetuosity was not to be restrained in this moment of success; but continuing to pursue the flying enemy in a scattered manner a mile beyond the works, the consequence was, that the latter collecting in great force, obliged our troops to retreat, and to relinquish the advantages they had at first obtained. General O'Hara arrived at the battery on the moment it was taken; and, perceiving the disorder of the troops, thus driven back, was hastening to rally them, when most unfortunately he received a wound in his arm, which bled so much as to render him incapable of avoiding the enemy; by whom he was made prisoner as he sat down under a wall, faint from loss of blood.

The French army before Toulon at this time amounted to 40,000 men; after the surrender of Lyons, this force, considerable as it already was, became daily augmented. The army of the coalesced powers never exceeded 12,000, and even these were composed of five different nations, and languages; consequently by no means formed to co-operate with each other. The greatest return of the British force, at any one period, was never more than 2360, out of which we had only 2100 rank and file; this was the case on the first of November: previous to the arrival of the first regiment of foot, (Royals) and the eighteenth regiment, there were only 1360 British soldiers at Toulon.[10] The circumference, necessary to be occupied for the complete defence of the town and harbour, extended fifteen miles, by eight principal posts, with several intermediate dependencies: with such a prodigious superiority as the enemy possessed, it will naturally excite the astonishment of every one, that they could be made tenable for so long a time as seven weeks.

Early on the 17th of December, by two in the morning, Fort Mulgrave, on the Height de Grasse, was stormed by an immense body of the enemy, after having kept up an incessant fire with shot and shells for 24 hours. The right occupied by the Spaniards soon gave way as before, by which means the French entered the works, and got entire possession of the Height: at the same time they attacked and carried the Heights of Pharon, immediately over Toulon.

In the forenoon of the 17th of December, a council of war was called, composed of

10 Return of the British Forces at Toulon on November the 1st, 1793, being the greatest number at any period: One lieutenant colonel, 3 majors, 31 captains, 53 lieutenants, 13 ensigns, 2 adjutants, 2 quarter masters, 1 surgeon, 2 mates, 106 serjeants, 57 drummers and fifers, 2100 rank and file fit for duty, 231 sick, 39 at Gibraltar and England recruiting. - Total, 2360. Return of Combined Forces on November the 4th, 1793: British: 2114, Spaniards: 6523, Neapolitans: 4332, Piedmontese: 1584, France: 1542 - Total, 16,095. November 10th arrived a Neapolitan polacre with troops: 500. At the same time a Spanish corps of artillery: 317 - Total 16,902. N.B. On the evacuation were embarked of British, Spanish, and Piedmontese, about 8000; the Neapolitans having in a panic embarked the preceding day.

the following members: Lord Hood, Admiral Langara, Admiral Gravina, General Dundas, General Valdes, Prince Pignatelli, Admiral Forteguerri, Sir Hyde Parker, Le Chevalier de Revel, and Sir Gilbert Elliot. After the most deliberate discussion, it was at length resolved, late in the afternoon, to retire from the different posts, and to evacuate Toulon at a fixed time; proper arrangements and regulations being made for that purpose. The resolutions were:

1. To send orders to the troops occupying the redoubt, and the lunette of Pharon, to retire to the posts of Artigues and St. Catherine's, and to maintain them as long as they can without being cut off.
2. To send orders to the posts of Great and Little Antoine, St. Andre, Pomet, and the Mills, to retire.
3. The posts of Malbousquet, and Mississi, must be held as long as possible.
4. The Committee General to make the necessary arrangements for informing the inhabitants of the intended evacuation; and that they should receive every possible assistance.
5. The sick and wounded shall be embarked without delay.
6. The French ships of war, which are armed, shall sail out with the fleet; *those which remain in the harbour, together with the magazines and the arsenal, shall be destroyed.* Measures shall be taken this night, if possible, for that purpose; but this resolution must not be put in execution until the last moment.

Admiral Langara undertook to deliver the necessary directions for destroying the ships, in the inner harbour or basin; and to scuttle and sink the two powder vessels, which contained all the powder of the different French ships, as well as that belonging to the distant magazines within the enemy's reach.

During the sitting of the Council, information was received that the Neapolitan troops had deserted their posts, and were stealing on board the ships with their baggage in great confusion and disorder; to which they had been encouraged by the Spaniards, as well as their own officers; and the next morning, December 18, the Neapolitan commanding officer on the post of Sepet, signified to the governor, that he would not remain there any longer: the retreat of the British troops, and the general evacuation of the place, could not therefore be now deferred beyond the ensuing night. Accordingly, during the night, the whole of the troops embarked without the loss of a single man; and 14,877 men, women, and children, of the loyal inhabitants of Toulon, were sheltered in the British ships. The Honourable Captain Elphinstone, in faithfully executing to the last moment the difficult service of embarking the troops, received high encomiums from Lord Hood, for his unremitting zeal and exertions in that important and dangerous duty.

The unaccountable panic which seized the Neapolitan troops during the deliberations of the Council, together with the shameful remissness of Don Langara, in not fulfilling what he had undertaken to perform, *prevented the complete execution of an admirable arrangement, for destroying all the French ships that lay in the Inner Road, the arsenal, and basin before the town; together with the magazine, the arsenal itself, and the various stores it contained.* Sir Sydney Smith having volunteered his services to burn the ships and arsenal, this hazardous duty was intrusted to his daring intrepidity, which he executed in a manner that justified his appointment to so arduous a task: by this means the treachery of the Spaniards was in a considerable degree counteracted. Ten ships of the line, with several frigates, in the arsenal and inner harbour, with the mast house, great store house, hemp house, and other buildings, were completely destroyed. Three ships of the line, three frigates, and seven corvettes, which had been manned and armed prior to the evacuation, accompanied the British fleet, with the French Rear Admiral Trogoffe: who nobly continued under Lord Hood's orders, notwithstanding the insidious attempts of Don Langara, to prevail upon him to put himself under *his* orders, and to follow the directions of the Spanish Court; as being more congenial with the interests of the Family Compact, which had formerly united their respective kingdoms.[11]

Sir Sydney Smith, and the officers immediately under his orders, surrounded by a tremendous conflagration of the ships and arsenal, had nearly completed the hazardous services assigned to them, when the loud shouts, and Republican songs, of the approaching enemy, were heard at intervals amid the bursting of shells, and firing of musquetry. In addition to the horror of such a scene, and which, for some minutes, had the good effect of checking the career, and arresting in awful contemplation, the minds of a vindictive enemy, the dreadful explosion of many thousand barrels of gunpowder, on board the *Isis* frigate, in the Inner Road, will ever be remembered. The concussion it produced shook the houses in Toulon like an earthquake, and occasioned the sudden crash of every window in them; whilst the scattered fragments of burning timber, which had been blown up, descending with considerable force, nearly destroyed all our officers and men who were employed in the discharge of their respective duties. This powder ship had been injudiciously, and we will hereafter prove treacherously, set on fire by the Spaniards, instead of scuttling and sinking her, as had been previously concerted. Sir Sydney having completed all the conflagration within his reach, to his astonishment first discovered that the Spaniards had not set fire to any of the ships in the basin before the town; he therefore hastened with the boats under his command towards the basin, that he might endeavour, though at so late a period, to counteract the perfidy of the Spaniards; when lo! to his great mortification, he found the boom at the entrance laid across, and was obliged to desist in his attempts to cut it, from the repeated volleys of musquetry directed towards his boats from the flag ship, and the wall of the Royal Battery. He therefore proceeded to burn the *Hero*, and *Themistocles*, prison ships in the Inner Road, after disembarking all the men. This service was scarcely effected; when *the explosion of the second powder ship took place*, by means equally unsuspected, and perfidious, with a shock even greater that the first; the lives of Sir Sydney Smith, and the gallant men who served under him, were providentially saved from the imminent danger in which they were thus a second time placed. Had Lord Hood's judicious and able plans been seconded by the Spaniards, not a single ship would have escaped.

When from analogy we reason on the above facts, and consider the motives which influenced the conduct of our allies, the Spaniards, throughout the whole of the transactions at Toulon, we clearly discern the different features of a foul premeditated treachery, whose limit was designed to extend to the destruction of the British admiral and his fleet. The facts themselves justify this assertion, without resorting to other evidence: yet in order to fix this historical truth by proofs that will not admit the possibility of a doubt, even in the mind of the most skeptical reader, we subjoin the following extract from a pamphlet, containing an account of the secret negotiations

11 A few days before the evacuation took place, Don Langara wrote a most pressing, and jesuitical letter to Rear Admiral Trogoffe, requesting him on various plausible pretexts, to put himself and the French ships under his orders; but Admiral Trogoffe very properly, and with great firmness, resisted this on the ground of recognising no Chief but Lord Hood, with whom only he had treated; and he transmitted to Lord Hood Don Langara's letter, together with his spirited answer on this occasion.

For the drawing from which the annexed engraving was copied we are indebted to John Theophilus Lee, Esq. only son of the late Captain Lee, R.N. It is an accurate representation of a Mortella Tower erected in St. Fiorenzo Bay, and celebrated for the defence made against an English line-of-battle ship, and three frigates. [Plate 290]

carried on under the direction of Robespiere, with several of the principal states of Europe, written and signed by his own hand.[12] Of this curious work, we intend taking further notice, in the Toulon Papers, which are preparing for the press,[13] and shall at present only insert what follows: "Arguments of weight, and especially of golden weight, says Robespiere, seldom fail of having some effect; *the Spanish admirals, and generals in the Mediterranean, had instructions sent them rather to watch, than to act with, the English*". In another part he adds, "It was therefore once determined to withdraw the army from before the town, (Toulon) and retreat to the other side of the Durance, *when fortunately the Spanish courier arrived, and every thing was settled between my brother*[14] *on our part, and Major S—— on the other, with respect to Toulon*".[14]

Robespiere then proceeds to remark - "The Spaniards, in consequence of this agreement, being attacked at an appointed time, *fled on all sides, and left the English every where to bite the dust; and particularly at a strong hold called by them Fort Mulgrave*. The ships which the Spaniards had to burn they did not set fire to. The British ships had however more than one escape at this period; *conformably to the agreement*, the Spaniards were to attempt the destruction of some of them, *by cutting the cables, and blowing up in the harbour some old French men of war laden with gunpowder: this indeed they did, but too late to cause any damage to the English; and in this instance alone we have any reason to complain of the Spaniards*".

12 Translated from the French, and published by Rivington.
13 No. XI.
14 Robespiere the younger was one of the commissaries attached to the French army before Toulon. Buonaparte at the same time commanded the artillery.

A view of the town and road of Bastia, the capital of the island of Corsica, with the *Victory*, Lord Hood's flag ship, and the rest of the fleet at anchor. A common trading vessel of the Mediterranean is also introduced at anchor in shore. This view was taken by Mr. Pocock from a large picture by Lieutenant Elliot, now in the possession of Lord Hood. [Plate 14] *[See Map of Corsica, Volume 3.]*

Everything therefore relating to Toulon may be considered as highly honorable to the British name, and to the noble admiral who so ably executed the trust which had devolved upon him. Actions of considerable merit, which embrace a variety of interests and are consequently perplexed, demand a considerable length of time, before they are clearly discerned, and duly valued. Great advantages were eventually derived to this Country by the blow which the naval power of the enemy thus early received. The republican hydra, though now writhing in all the anguish of despair, amid the last struggle of convulsive life, received her first mortal wound from the powerful arm of Lord Hood.

Early in the month of January (1794) whilst the British fleet lay in Hieres Bay, near Toulon, waiting for a convoy of transports and victuallers from Gibraltar, Sir Gilbert Elliot, one of the commissioners for Toulon, went to Corsica, accompanied by Colonel Moore, and Major Kochler, to consult with General Paoli upon a plan of operations for dispossessing the French of the different posts they held in Corsica. Lord Hood, on receiving a very favorable report from Colonel Moore, and Major Kochler, fully sensible of the importance which the conquest of the island of Corsica would be of to Great Britain, as containing several capital ports for the reception of his Majesty's ships in the Mediterranean, resolved to make every effort to drive the French from the island with the force entrusted to his command, aided by the troops brought from Toulon. The necessary preparations were accordingly made without delay; and on the 7th of February, the troops under the command of Lieutenant General Dundas were disembarked, from a division of ships and transports commanded by Commodore Linzee, in a Bay in the Gulph of St. Fiorenzo, to the westward of Mortello: by the incredible exertions of the

British seamen in dragging guns up precipices almost perpendicular, the Heights, which overlooked the tower of Mortella, were taken.

It was however judged advisable the next day to attack the tower from the Bay; and the *Fortitude*, Captain Young,[15] and *Juno*, Captain Samuel Hood,[16] were ordered against it: but after cannonading for two hours and upwards, they made no impression whatever on the prodigious thick walls of the tower; and the *Fortitude* having received much damage by red-hot shot, both ships hauled off in a masterly manner, as if nothing had happened. Captain Young received great credit for his cool and intrepid conduct during the attack, as well as in hauling off, and setting sail out of the Bay, when his ship was on fire in different places by the red-hot shot: considerable praise was also due to his first lieutenant Mr. Ross, who, though wounded, exerted himself with unsubdued spirit, and underwent incredible fatigue.

The *Fortitude* had several men killed and wounded. The tower was carried a few days afterwards by means of batteries erected on the Heights; and in the evening of the 17th of February, the enemy's works of Fornelli were stormed, and the town of St. Fiorenzo was taken.

Lord Hood, impatient to follow up the blow immediately, by attempting the reduction of Bastia, proposed a plan of co-operation to General Dundas, which he declined; deeming it impracticable, and visionary, without a reinforcement of 2000 troops which he expected from Gibraltar. Lord Hood therefore sailed on the evening of the 23d of February, to try what the appearance of his fleet alone off Bastia might produce. Here, with his usual cool perseverance, he cruised for a fortnight, gaining intelligence for his future plans; and, finding that the General remained inflexible, he determined to attempt *the reduction of Bastia with the naval force entrusted to his command*; he therefore demanded that the remains of the 11th, 25th, 30th, and 69th regiments, might immediately return to their duty, on board their respective ships, in which they had been originally ordered by his Majesty to serve as marines; and were consequently borne as part of the complements of these ships. After much delay, having received these troops, and also two officers of artillery and thirty men, with some ordnance stores, and entrenching tools, in the beginning of April Admiral Lord Hood commenced the siege of Bastia alone, by disembarking the seamen, and troops serving as marines, to the northward of the town; the guns, mortars, ammunition, and stores of every description, were landed, whilst the ships of the fleet were judiciously anchored in a semi-circular form, just without reach of the enemy's guns; so as effectually to prevent any boats from going into, or coming out from the town. On the 11th of April, our batteries on the Heights were ready to be opened, and on that morning Lord Hood sent a summons to the town; but the French General La Combe St. Michell would not receive his letter, and returned a vaunting message, that the only correspondence he should hold with an enemy on the Republican territory, would be from the mouths of his cannon charged with *red-hot shot*, and from the musquetry, and bayonets, of his brave companions.

When the officer returned on board the *Victory* with this message, Lord Hood made the appointed signal to the batteries on shore, to commence the attack; which, to the great consternation of La Combe Saint Michell, and the inhabitants, was immediately

15 Now Rear Admiral, and one of the Lords Commissioners of the Admiralty. Mr. Ross, at present first lieutenant of the *Impetueux*, was then Captain Young's first lieutenant.
16 Nephew to Lord Hood, who has distinguished himself on various occasions, particularly as commander of the *Zealous* in the Battle of the Nile.

done, by opening the batteries, consisting of five 24 pounders, two mortars of thirteen inch caliber, two of ten inch, and two heavy carronades, in different commanding situations, over the town, citadel, and out works.

The *Proselyte*, French gabarre, commanded by Captain Sericold,[17] having long French 12 pounders, was directed to be placed against part of the town, when the batteries opened their fire; but on getting under weigh, and coming to anchor, the swell cast her the wrong way, which prevented Captain Sericold from taking the precise station that had been allotted. The enemy fired nothing but red-hot shot at her, several of which struck between wind and water, lodging among the casks, and other craft in the hold. The signal of distress was immediately made; but Captain Sericold, notwithstanding his danger, continued to keep up an incessant fire, with fourteen guns, upon the town, until the boats of the squadron came to his assistance, and took the men out of his ship, which soon was in a blaze of fire.

The batteries, which opened so unexpectedly, had a powerful effect; as by information from the town, on the 24th of April, the enemy lost a great number of men; in the hospitals were near 300 wounded; at this time we had only four killed and twenty-one wounded. The loss of the British, owing to the skill of their Commander, was very trifling during the whole siege; but the service was extremely harassing, and dangerous.

Captain Nelson, of the *Agamemnon* (now Lord Nelson), commanded a brigade of seamen on shore, at the batteries, having three other captains under him, Hunt, Sericold, and Bullen: on this occasion, as on all others, he gave distinguished proofs of zeal and intrepidity.

At length, on the 21st of May, the town and citadel of Bastia, with the several posts on the Heights, surrendered to the arms of his Britannic Majesty, by articles of capitulation, drawn up and signed by the respective parties. The number of French and Corsican troops amounted to near 4,000; whilst the greatest return of the British force, employed during the siege, amounted only to 1,248.[18] A packet-boat, intercepted by the *Agamemnon*, Captain Nelson, two months previous to the commencement of the siege, contained the information, that from La Combe St. Michell's return of the French, and Corsican troops, then in Bastia, and for which he proposed subsistence in case of a siege, they amounted to 8,000. These facts completely contradict the vague assertions of M. Dumourier, in his pamphlet, entitled "A Speculative Sketch of Europe," wherein he affirms that the British are unequal to the toils, and delays of a siege; and have neither generals, engineers, nor a battering train: we need only, in refutation, apply the reasoning of the author of the *Strictures* upon Dumourier's pamphlet; "How was the strong and well fortified town of Bastia taken? *By a detachment of British seamen, and marines, or soldiers acting as such, inferior in number to the garrison of regularly disciplined troops; and who had no tents but such as were made of sails, and no other battering train than* THE LOWER DECK GUNS OF LINE OF BATTLE SHIPS." The vote of thanks to Lord Hood, for this astonishing exploit, which had been deemed impracticable, and visionary, by an able officer, General Dundas, was carried in both Houses of Parliament by a great

---

17 This gallant officer was afterwards killed on shore at the siege of Calvi.
18 Correct return of the British force employed at the siege of Bastia, commencing April 4, and ending May 21, 1794: 1 lieutenant-colonel, 4 captains of the navy, 1 major, 2 artillery officers, 1 engineer, 12 captains of the army and marines, 6 lieutenants of the navy, 21 lieutenants of the army, and marines, 5 ensigns, 2 surgeons, a commissary, and master's mate, 69 surgeon's mates, serjeants, and petty officers, 30 artillerymen, and 1092 soldiers, marines, and seamen. Total 1248.

majority. The Duke of Bedford, the Earls Albemarle, Lauderdale, Derby, and Thanet, entered their protests against it.

Whilst we are faithfully narrating the distinguished services of Admiral Lord Hood, we must not forget to notice that praise, which he gave so zealously, yet impartially, to those who fought, and conquered under his auspices. Few men have ever equaled his Lordship in the difficult task of rendering, with animated gratitude,

"The sufferage of the wise, the praise that's worth ambition!"

"I am unable (says Lord Hood in his letter to the Admiralty) to give due praise to the unremitting zeal, exertion, and judicious conduct of *Lieut. Colonel Villettes*, who had the honour of commanding his Majesty's troops; never was either more conspicuous. *Major Brereton*, and every officer, and soldier, under the lieutenant colonel's orders, are justly entitled to my warmest acknowledgments; their persevering ardour, and desire to distinguish themselves, cannot be too highly spoken of; and which it will be my pride to remember to the latest period of my life.

Captain Nelson, of his Majesty's ship *Agamemnon*, who had the command, and directions of the seamen, in landing the guns, mortars, and stores; and *Captain Hunt*,[19] who commanded at the batteries, very ably assisted by *Captain Bullen*, and *Captain Sericold*; and the *Lieutenants Gore, Hotham, Stiles, Andrews*, and *Brisbane*, have an ample claim to my gratitude; as the seamen under their management worked the guns, with great judgment, and alacrity; never was a higher spirit or greater perseverance exhibited; and I am happy to say, that no other contention was at any time known, than who should be most forward, and indefatigable, in promoting his Majesty's service: for although the difficulties they had to struggle with were many and various, the perfect harmony, and good humour, that universally prevailed throughout the siege, overcame them all. I cannot but express in the strongest terms the meritorious conduct of *Captain Duncan*, and *Lieut. Alexander Duncan*, of the Royal Artillery; and *Lieut. Debutts*, of the Royal Engineers; but my obligation is particularly great to *Captain Duncan*; as more zeal, ability and judgment, was never shewn by any officer, than were displayed by him; and I take the liberty of mentioning him as an officer highly entitled to his Majesty's notice.

I feel myself very much indebted for the vigilance, and attention of *Captain Wolseley*, of the *Imperieuse*, and of *Captain Hallowell*;[20] who became a willing volunteer, wherever he could be useful, after being superseded in the command of the *Courageux*, by *Captain Waldegrave*. The former kept a diligent watch upon the Island of Capreae, where the enemy have magazines of provisions, and stores; and *Captain Hallowell* did the same by guarding the harbour's mouth of Bastia, with gun-boats, and launches well armed, the whole of every night; whilst the smaller boats were very judiciously placed in the intervals between, and rather without the ships, which were moored in a crescent, just out of reach of the enemy's guns, by *Captain Young*, of the *Fortitude*, the center ship, on board of which every boat assembled at sun-set for orders; and the cheerfulness with which the officers and men performed this nightly duty is very much to be admired, and afforded me the most heartfelt satisfaction, and pleasure. The very great, and effectual, assistance I received from *Vice Admiral Goodall, Captain Inglefield*, and *Captain Knight*, as well as from every captain, and officer, of his Majesty's ships, under my command,

19 Captain Hunt died lately in the East Indies. (*Vide Naval Chronicle* p. 437, vol. I.)
20 Captain Benjamin Hallowell was afterwards re-appointed to the command of the *Courageux*, which was shipwrecked on the Barbary coast; and after this melancholy accident being taken on board the *Victory*, Sir John Jervis's flag ship, became a volunteer in the Spanish action of the 14th of February; he afterwards commanded the *Swiftsure* in the battle of the Nile.

has a just claim to my most particular thanks; not only in carrying into execution my orders afloat, but in attending to, and supplying, the wants of the little army on shore: it is to the very cordial and decided support alone I had the honour to receive from the whole, that the innumerable difficulties we had to contend with were happily surmounted.

Major Smith and *Ensign Vigoureuse*, of the 25th regiment, and *Captain Radsdale*, and *Lieutenant St. George*, of the 11th, embarking with their respective regiments, having civil employments on shore; — it is to their honour I mention, that they relinquished those employments, and joined their corps, soon after the troops were landed."

In addition to these testimonies of Lord Hood, issued in public orders, to the commanding officers of the respective corps, similar thanks to the following were addressed to Captain Nelson of the *Agamemnon*, and other naval officers:

"Victory, off Bastia, 22d May, 1794.
The commander in chief returns his best thanks to Captain Nelson, and desires he will present them to Captain Hunt, Captain Sericold, and Captain Bullen, as well as to every officer and seamen employed in the reduction of Bastia, for the indefatigable zeal and exertions they have so cheerfully manifested, in the discharge of the various laborious duties committed to them, notwithstanding the various difficulties and disadvantages they have had to struggle with; which could not have been surmounted but by the uncommon spirit, and cordial unanimity, that have been so conspicuously displayed; and which must give a stamp of reputation to their characters not to be effaced, and will be remembered with gratitude by the Commander in chief to the end of his life."

Lord Hood, having appointed Lieutenant Colonel Villettes, Governor of Bastia, until his Majesty's pleasure was known, and made other necessary arrangements, next proceeded to co-operate with Lieutenant General Stewart in the reduction of Calvi; while Vice Admiral Hotham, with a squadron, blocked up seven sail of French line of battle ships in the Bay of Gorjean. Without entering into a detail of the transactions attending the siege of Calvi, it is only necessary for us briefly to state, that the garrison surrendered to his Majesty's arms on the 10th of August; and that Lord Hood gave a just tribute of applause to Captain Nelson,[21] and Captain Hallowell, for their unremitting zeal, and exertions, in taking by turns, for twenty hours at a time, the command of the advanced batteries on shore.

Thus the conquest of the whole island of Corsica was completed by the skill, and perseverance, of a British admiral. Sir Gilbert Elliot, who had been an active spectator of the scenes going forward, since the evacuation of Toulon, was appointed by his Majesty viceroy of the island; his excellency having previously, on the 19th of June, in the character of commissary plenipotentiary, been specially authorized, accepted of the crown, and constitution of Corsica; as unanimously decreed in the general assembly of the Corsican nation, held at Corte, and signed in the assembly by all the members of which it was composed, consisting of upwards of 400 persons.

Lord Hood's health being much impaired by the fatigue, and anxiety, attending such a continuance of duty, and such a variety of harassing and perplexed service, returned to England for its re-establishment, in the month of December, 1794. In the month of May following, he had prepared to resume his command in the Mediterranean,

---

21 The gallant Lord Nelson lost the sight of his right eye at this siege, by a shot striking the battery near him, and driving some particles of sand with prodigious force into his eye.

with a reinforcement, when most unexpectedly, on the 2d of May, (1795), he was ordered to strike his flag, which has never been hoisted since.

This event is too recent to allow even the historian, much less an anonymous writer, to discuss it. We shrink not from our duty; but we respect the feelings, and the character, of our Superiors. Yet we contemplate with regret this distinguished veteran in his present retirement: - whilst the trumpet of a proud defiance thus continues to be sounded by a vindictive enemy, the energetic feeling of so brave a seaman, as the Governor of Greenwich Hospital, must have been difficult to repress . . .

Toulon: First Contact and Final Fight

A Letter from Lieutenant, now Captain Edward Cooke, to his Father-in-Law, General Smith, respecting the Negotiation at Toulon. II 378-384

Sept. 4, 1793
My Dear Sir, Before you receive this, my last will have reached you, which mentioned the Negotiation then depending. I have now the pleasure to announce its happy conclusion, and our being in full possession of Toulon, with all its forts and environs. My employments have been both civil and military. I hope I have acquitted myself to your satisfaction.

On our return here from the coast of Oneilla, we found there were two parties, one in support of the constitution of 1789, the other opposing it, in favour of equality and a republic. Marseilles was divided in the same manner; on the 29th past, two deputies arrived from the last place to treat with Lord Hood, respecting his taking that port under his protection for Louis XVII. They expected to have found deputies from the different sections of Toulon, charged with the same proposals, according to the agreement between the royalist party of these two places; but their not having arrived, and the uncertainty of the cause of this delay, induced Lord Hood to send me in a boat, bearing a flag of truce, to gain intelligence; and, as I might find it expedient to bring them off, or settle the business there; for which I was invested with full power.

My first difficulty was to pass their shipping, who were all of the other party; owing to their situation, I was obliged to pass within two hundred yards; but having, as you know, been in before, about a month ago, to treat for an exchange of prisoners, I had remarked their bad look out in the night, and from that circumstance I hoped for success.

I left the *Victory*, accompanied by a midshipman, at two in the afternoon, but delayed until it was ten o'clock before I got into the Harbour. The night was dark and windy, so I kept close under an high shore till abreast of their fleet, then boldly pushed off amongst them, conceiving they would not look for an enemy rowing between their ships. It answered perfectly, I passed unnoticed, or (what was the same to me) as one of their own boats; and I should have been on shore in their dock-yard unobserved, but for a strong chain laid across the narrow entrance of the pier. Here I was boarded by a gun-boat, but by great good fortune I had made an acquaintance with the man who commanded her when last in; so there was no noise made, and in a little time a deputation from the Committee General came down to receive my proposals: these I delivered, and said I would wait their answer.

Not being permitted to land, I remained all night in my boat, and next morning was conducted to the opposite side of the harbour, to a place called Lazaretto. It consists of an house and yard, surrounded by high walls, where all are put who are in quarantine. In the afternoon I received a letter, which induced me to send my boat off and remain alone. When it was nearly dark, the Committee sent me a guide, and an horse; which I immediately mounted, and following a bye path, in about two hours arrived at the city of Toulon. I was immediately conducted to a chamber, where the Committee General were sitting, and continued there till twelve o'clock. Every proposal that I made was accepted with joy; they were chiefly these – That we should immediately be put into full and entire possession of all the forts, with the city, and fortifications; that their fleets should remove without delay into the inner harbour; that all officers, both civil and military, would be at the disposal of Lord Hood; that they should immediately be supplied with grain, and also from time to time, equal to the consumption of the city, till peace was re-established, or till he heard from the court of Great Britain. I also further engaged that his Lordship should do his utmost to protect them from whatever force might be sent, and that all payment should be made in coin. Such were the chief articles.

It now became necessary to think of returning to the fleet; the mode of doing which being settled, and that I should be accompanied by two of their members, I left Toulon at one in the morning, and at day-light got to a village called Le Bruxe, on the sea coast, whence we embarked; but had scarcely got on board before we were arrested, and conducted on shore. The mob soon collected to a great number, and from their civility I was induced to enter into conversation with them; it had the desired effect, they liberated us, and the guard with difficulty escaped. Once more free, I made the best of my way to sea, and about noon got sight of the fleet, and soon after was on board. The fleet without delay bore up for a bay called Hieres (from some islands forming it) with an intention to anchor there; but it falling calm, we were obliged to stand off. The terms I had settled were such as Lord Hood approved, yet he did not like trusting them till the fleet that then lay in the outer harbour was removed to the inner one; this however could not be done, as they were of different sentiments: so I volunteered again to know the result of a deputation from all the sections to the fleets; the city before I left it having become unanimous respecting the English having possession of the place. I removed into a frigate about eight o'clock that same evening, and was in hopes to have landed somewhere on the coast that night; but finding it would inevitably, from the lightness of the wind, be day-light first, I determined to get as near Toulon as possible; and make another bold push. But I should tell you, when I had sent the boat off to the fleet, with an intention of remaining behind, to give them what information I had then gained, it being thought necessary she should return with a letter to me, she was seized, and carried on board the ship commanded by Rear Admiral St. Julian. He interrogated the midshipman who was in the boat, to discover what was become of me: how I had got to the city – what was my business – declaring if he caught me I should most certainly swing by the yard arm immediately (which for the matter of hanging I believed him most sincerely). My letter was opened, as the midshipman had not destroyed it, and it was read through in the whole fleet: but to return to my narrative.

At day-light in the morning, the Tartane in which I was embarked, being within three miles of the shore of Cape Brun, which is within their harbour's mouth; I requested Captain Freemantle to land me, which of course he complied with, and away I went in a nice little boat. A French frigate lay very much in my way; so to throw her off her guard, I stood towards her directly, till having neared the shore, so that her boat could not cut me off, I altered my direction, and rowed for the shore as fast as possible. The frigate immediately manned, and sent off her long boat, who kept up a constant fire of swivels at me the whole way; but they were too late, the shot all passed over my head, and I landed safe, though by no means without some small doubts; but that was no time for reflection. It was, from the nature of the shore, which is bounded by high rocks, absolutely necessary to pass the broadside of the frigate, who was anchored parallel with it; so stopping to take breath before I opened the vessel, I jumped from amongst the rocks, and ran for it. As I expected, she fired instantly; but I had not far to go, so only received her first fire before I got to the path that let up the cliff. Here the looseness of the ground, with the sand and dirt that the shot threw up, bothered me very much. Having at length gained the top, which though not high was exceedingly steep, I hid myself in the trees and fig-trees, till I again recovered my strength and breath; all which time the frigate kept up a constant fire; which, to be sure, made a confounded noise among the trees, but did me no harm. At length, quitting my post, I pushed forward for the city; and arrived about ten o'clock, amidst the acclamations of the greatest multitude I ever beheld.

The situation of things I found just the same; except that the shipping, having detained the deputies, had sent a letter to the Committee General, declaring their determination to do their utmost to preserve Toulon for the Republic. I recommended keeping a most watchful attention to the preservation of Fort la Malgue, and also one or two others; to cut off all communications with the shipping, who being the most numerous, and the strongest, had only to gain a footing on shore, to render themselves complete masters, which the Toulonese must be well aware their heads would pay for. I left Toulon at four, and at day-light next morning arrived at the sea-side about thirty-five miles from the town: here I remained until noon; when a small Genoese fishing boat coming on shore, with the assistance of my guide, and the deputy I was carrying off, I seized her and stood off immediately. About four o'clock in the evening I got on board the *Victory*, who had been driven a long way off the coast by a strong current. During the night Lord Hood held a council of war of all the admirals, at which I was present: after a long consultation, it was settled that I should be again dispatched, for the purpose of making signal to the fleet at the place they were to land, and to be ready to conduct them to Fort La Malgue.

When the council was broke up, and every one had returned to their ships, my orders were countermanded, and I was desired to hold myself in readiness to disembark with a body of sailors next morning. Signals were in consequence made, and every preparation completed before sun-rise. At nine in the morning, the ships directed to cover the landing stood in, and by two, the descent was made on the Fort of La Malgue, mounting forty-eight pieces of cannon; when the city of Toulon and all its fortifications were soon in our hands. Captain Elphinstone, of the *Robust*, commanded the troops, and myself the sailors. In the evening we received our appointments, he as governor, and myself as lieutenant governor. The moment the shipping found the fort in our possession, they stood in to the anchorage; the French had already quitted, in compliance with an order we had sent them, either to go instantly into the inner harbour, or we would sink them at their anchors. The Spaniards with their fleet bore in sight *some time afterwards*, and anchored the same evening. Next morning we regulated the numbers of them for each fort, and also the number for the city, which we found could be defended tolerably well by 5000 men; the number we have now on shore, composed of English and Spanish.

On the 30th we received intelligence of Carteaux's having advanced a part of his army within four miles of Toulon: Governor Elphinstone determined immediately to go out and fight them. At two he quitted Toulon with about 600 men (English and Spanish); having sent me an order to La Malgue, to advance with all the troops the fort could spare, to the defence of the city, and to be ready to support him in case of a defeat. I had scarcely got into the fort, and made the necessary arrangements for the night, when I heard a very heavy cannonading and discharge of musquetry, which lasted about fourteen minutes: you, I dare say, well know the anxiety with which I waited the result of this affair. At last, about ten o'clock, one of the people I had sent to gain intelligence, returned, and informed me our troops had carried a strong Post of the enemy's, and were in part on their march back. It had to me a bad appearance; but I was soon made easy by the arrival of Governor Elphinstone; who confirmed the account of their having possessed themselves of the enemy's cannon, which shortly after arrived; two sixes and a three pounder, brass, the most beautiful guns ever beheld. The place to which the enemy had advanced is called the Defiel of Ollioules; they were very strongly posted, so you cannot expect we should gain this success against 800 men, and that too without a single piece of cannon, but with some loss. We have to regret a very gallant officer; Captain Douglass, of the 11th regiment, was buried the day after the action, in Fort la Malgue, with every military honour. The inclosed copy of a letter from Carteaux to the commanding officer of that place, intercepted the day after, was printed for the amusement and information of the public; which will shew you the light in which they held Ollioules.[22]

September 5
Since my last we have remained quiet; but it is impossible we should continue so long, as the army of Carteaux, consisting of about 7000 men, is not above thirty miles off, waiting for the junction of that of Italy; which we have not received any certain account of, except that they have fallen back from Nice, marking their route by every cruelty the most degenerate of the human species could devise. From one of the Heights of Faron we frequently observe large bodies of the enemy in a wood below, where they appear to be throwing up some works; our intelligence places their number at 5000 men, 200 of which are peasants. Their commander was a *dancing master* at Toulon; since converted into a *General*. When combined, our present estimation of the French is at 12,000 men; our own at 5000, British and Spanish. Every road by which it is possible to attack us, is by nature no difficult matter to defend; added to which, the rains are coming on fast, which will distress the enemy much, as they laid their account to wintering in Toulon. I do not know if you have ever been here, but you know in some degree the strength of its situation; so I shall content myself with just mentioning the names of the different forts which are strongly garrisoned. La Malgue, commanding the harbour, city, and fortifications, is *head quarters*; next higher up, the Hill of Faron appears first, Saint Catherine's is between these two, on the road to Italy, in a hollow; Orligue of nine heavy guns still higher; and La Faron, nearly at the top to the mountain, commands more than half a mile beyond the village of La Vallette, to the east of St. Catherine, and the road to Italy. To the southward, at the top of the mountain, is a redoubt defended by a strong body of our troops, but without cannon; for this reason, that it is only accessible on this side, except a very small pass, up which cannon never can be brought, nor will it

22 *Vide*. Toulon Papers, page 110.

admit more than two men abreast, and may be defended by rocks and stones alone. Now were they to succeed by treachery, or any other means, in getting possession of this pass, so as to attack the redoubt, and we should allow them to carry it, they would only have the satisfaction of overlooking our forts, out of reach of musquetry, and of the possibility of dragging up a single piece of cannon, by any means whatever but by the side, whilst Faron could elevate so as continually to annoy them. Then, on the contrary, were they to get possession of any fort with cannon in it, I will not venture to say what might be the consequence.

The battle of Ollioules had produced us the effect we hoped it would create; obliging them to act rather more on the defensive, by which we gain time; it has also given confidence to our troops, whilst it has contributed to damp the spirit of our enemies, who conclude we must be in much greater force than we really are, from our venturing the attack of so strong a place.

I have now given you as minute an account, of what you will no doubt think a most extraordinary event, as my time will admit of, for you may easily believe I have not a moment to spare. Our want of officers makes the duty exceedingly severe. In addition to that of my station as lieutenant governor, I have hitherto taken upon me the charge as barrack master, and drilling of our seamen for garrison troops. I perceive you are laughing at me; but it requires solely *activity* and *inclination*.

September 8

I have only a minute to spare just to say I am made commander, and am this moment going off with dispatches to the King of Sardinia from Lord Hood.[23] I shall write to you from the King of Sardinia's army at Nice. It is evident Lord Hood has not thought my conduct undeserving a particular mark of his approbation by the post of honour I now hold; but that is not all, it has gained me (*nor would I part with this last for any thing this world could offer me*) the approbation and applause of every officer and man in the fleet, *nor shall they ever repent the opinion they have so publicly expressed of me.*

September 10

Our friends the Spanish gentlemen *look well and bold on a parade, but they will not stand a shot. The post of Ollioules, which we had so gallantly carried, they have lost for us.* It is very true that by keeping it we were extending too much, but that does not take from the disgrace attending its loss. It was defended by five hundred Spanish troops, with four pieces of cannon. The day before I left Toulon it was attacked by Carteaux. The garrison fled on the very first discharge, and but for one hundred sailors they would have lost the cannon, and many more men than they did; these brave fellows covered their retreat, and brought off the wounded with the loss only of two men. I expect to get on shore to-morrow, and two days after shall be able to deliver my dispatches. I cannot venture to inform you by letter what they are, being of the greatest consequence, of *course secret*. I left Toulon the day before yesterday in the *Lowestoffe*; but the *Bedford* and *Leviathan* of 74 guns, were sent after me with some additional orders; yesterday I received them, and removed into the *Bedford*. I hope to be back again in a fortnight.

EDWARD COOKE

---

23 Captain Cooke returned from the King of Sardinia with 1700 men; and 300 men which he raised himself going through the country.

Captain Edward Cooke, who has since so gallantly distinguished himself in the East Indies, was made Lieutenant in 1790, and after the date of the above letter, was appointed by Lord Hood to go on a secret expedition to Corsica. He was advanced Post in 1794; and was given the command of his Majesty's frigate *La Sybille* of 44 guns in 1796. The following are some particulars of his family: Captain Cooke's father, Colonel Cooke, married a sister of Admiral Bowyer's: after her husband's death she married General Smith, to whom the above letter is addressed, and who is Uncle to Sir William Sidney Smith.

The Fall of Toulon

From the 'Memoir of the Public Services of Sir Charles Brisbane, Knt.'
XX 86

[Lieutenant Brisbane had not been in Lord Hotham's flagship, *Britannia*] many days, before Lord Hood came on board; and we have some reason to believe, that the chief object of his lordship's visit was to satisfy himself with respect to the merits of Lieutenant Brisbane; as, shortly afterwards, he appointed him to the command of Fort Pomet, one of the most dangerous out-posts in the neighbourhood of Toulon, about five miles from the city.

This was an appointment extremely suitable to a display of his talents. - He assisted in repulsing the French at Fort Mulgrave, in November; and, after several other skirmishes on the heights of Phoron, he remained at Fort Pomet, till it was found necessary to destroy the enemy's ships, and to evacuate the town and harbour of Toulon. He was then ordered to make the best retreat in his power from the fort; but, although the French troops were pouring down in considerable force, and were within the distance of two musket shots, he stopped to set fire to a train, which communicated with five hundred barrels of gunpowder. The explosion blew the fort to atoms; and, from the situation of himself and his men, it was supposed, at a distance, that they had all perished. Amidst his ardour, however, Lieutenant Brisbane's judgment had not forsaken him. Himself and his men were safe; and, after surmounting many difficulties and dangers, they effected their retreat without loss.

Destruction of the French Fleet

Extracted from the 'Toulon Papers'
Sir Sidney Smith to Admiral Lord Hood, dated Toulon, 18 December 1793
XIX, II 290-295

Agreeable to your Lordship's orders, I proceeded with the *Swallow* tender, three English and three Spanish gun-boats, to the Arsenal, and immediately began making the necessary preparations for burning the French ships and stores therein; we found the dock gates well secured by the judicious arrangements of the Governor, although the dock-yard people had already substituted the three-coloured cockade for the white one; I did not think it safe to attempt the securing of any of them, considering the small force I had with me, and considering that a contest of any kind would occupy our whole attention, and prevent us from accomplishing our preparations.

The galley-slaves, to the number of at least six hundred, shewed themselves jealous spectators of our operations; their disposition to oppose us was evident; and being unchained (which was unusual) rendered it necessary to keep a watchful eye on them. I accordingly restrained them on board the galleys, by pointing the guns of the *Swallow* tender, and one of the gun-boats, on them, in such a manner as to enfilade the quay on which they must land to come to us; assuring them at the same time, that no harm should happen to them if they remained quiet. The enemy kept up a cross fire of shot and shells on the spot from Malbousquet and the neighbouring hills, which contributed to keep the galley-slaves in subjection, and operated in every respect favourably for us, by keeping the Republican party in the town within their houses, while it occasioned little interruption to our work of preparing and placing combustible matter in the different store-houses and on board the ships; such was the steadiness of the few brave seamen I had under my command. A great multitude of the enemy continued to draw down the hill towards the dock-yard wall; and as the night closed in, they came near enough to pour in an irregular though quick fire on us from the Boulangerie, and the heights which overlook it. We kept them at bay by discharges of grape shot from time to time, which prevented their coming so near as to discover the insufficiency of our force to repel a closer attack. A gun-boat was stationed to flank the wall on the outside, and two field-pieces were placed within against the wicket usually frequented by the workmen, of whom we were particularly apprehensive. About eight o'clock, I had the satisfaction to see Lieutenant Gore towing in the *Vulcan* fire-ship; Captain Hare, her commander, placed her agreeable to my directions, in a most masterly manner, across the tier of men of war, and the additional force of her guns and men diminished my apprehensions of the galley-slaves rising on us, as their murmurs and occasional tumultuous debates ceased entirely on her appearance; the only noise heard among them was the hammer knocking off their fetters, which humanity forbid my opposing as they might thereby be more at liberty to save themselves on the conflagration taking place around them. In this situation we continued to wait most anxiously for the hour concerted with the Governor for the inflammation of the trains. The moment the signal was made, we had the satisfaction to see the flames rise in every quarter. Lieutenant Tupper was charged with the burning of the general magazine, the pitch, tar, tallow, and oil store-houses, and succeeded most perfectly: the hemp magazine was included in this blaze. Its being nearly calm was unfavourable to the spreading of flames; but two hundred and fifty barrels of tar, divided among the deals and other timber insured the rapid ignition of that whole quarter which Lieutenant Tupper had undertaken.

The mast-house was equally well set on fire by Lieutenant Middleton of the *Britannia*: Lieutenant Pater of the *Britannia* continued in a most daring manner to brave the flames, in order to complete the work where the fire seemed to have caught imperfectly. I was obliged to call him off, lest his retreat should become impracticable: his situation was the more perilous, as the enemy's fire redoubled as soon as the amazing blaze of light rendered us distinct objects for their aim.

Lieutenant Ironmonger of the *Royals* remained with the guard at the gate till the last, long after the Spanish guard was withdrawn, and was brought safely off by Captain Edge of the *Alert*, to whom I had confided the important service of closing our retreat, and bringing off our detached parties, which were saved to a man. I was sorry to find myself deprived of the further services of Captain Hare: he had performed that of placing his fire-ship to admiration, but was blown into the water, and much scorched, by the explosion of her priming, when in the act of putting the match to it. Lieutenant Gore was also much burnt, and I was consequently deprived of him also; which I regretted the more from the recollection of his bravery and activity in the warm service

The annexed engraving, by Greig, from a design by Owen's, represents the
destruction of the French fleet at Toulon, by the boats under the command of
Captain Sir Sidney Smith. Plate 77

of Fort Mulgrave. Mr. Eales, midshipman, who was also with him on this occasion,
deserves every praise for his conduct throughout this service. The guns of the fire-ship
going off on both sides as they heated in the direction that was given them towards
those quarters from whence we were most apprehensive of the enemy forcing their way
in upon us, checked their career; their shouts and republican songs, which we could
hear distinctly continued till they, as well as ourselves, were in a manner thunderstruck
by the explosion of some thousand barrels of powder on board the *Iris* frigate, laying in
the inner road without us, and which had been injudiciously set on fire by the Spanish
boats in going off, instead of being sunk as ordered: the concussion of air, and the
shower of falling timber on fire, was such as nearly destroyed the whole of us. Lieutenant
Pater of the *Britannia*, with his whole boat's crew, nearly perished; the boat was blown
to pieces, but the men were picked up alive. The *Union* gun-boat, which was nearest to
the *Iris*, suffered considerably, Mr. Young being killed, with three men, and the vessel
shaken to pieces. I had given it in charge to the Spanish officers to fire the ships in the
basin before the town; but they returned and reported, that various obstacles had
prevented their entering it. We attempted it together as soon as we had completed the
business in the arsenal, but were repulsed in our attempt to cut the boom by repeated
volleys of musquetry from the flag-ship, and the wall of the Battery Royale. The cannon
of this battery had been spiked by the judicious precautions taken by the Governor
previous to the evacuation of the town. The rear of our column being by this time out
of the eastern gate, the horrid cries of the poor inhabitants announced that the villanous

part of the community had got the upper hand. Boats full of men, women, and children, pushed from the shore, even without oars, claiming our protection from the knife of the assassin by the most sacred of all ties, our professed friendship. We accordingly kept our station, for the purpose of affording them an asylum. Many straggling Neapolitan soldiers, whose undisciplined conduct had separated them from the main body, were among the number thus driven into the water. We received them as more particularly belonging to us, repulsing their pursuers by our fire; nor did we quit the shore till we had received all who were there to claim our assistance. The failure of our attempt on the ships in the basin before the town, owing to the insufficiency of our force, made me regret that the Spanish gun-boats had been withdrawn from me to perform other service. The Adjutant Don Pedro Cotiella, Don Francisco Riguelme, and Don Francisco Truxillo, remained with me to the last; and I feel bound to bear testimony of the zeal and activity with which they performed the most essential services during the whole of this business, as far as the insufficiency of their force allowed; it being reduced, by the retreat of the gun-boats, to a single felucca, and a mortar-boat which had expended its ammunition, but contained thirty men with cutlasses.

We now proceeded to burn the *Hero* and *Themistocles*, two seventy-four gun ships laying in the inner road. Our approach to them had been hitherto impracticable in boats, as the French prisoners which had been left in the latter ship were still in possession of her, and had shewn a determination to resist our attempt to come on board. The scene of conflagration around them, heightened by the late tremendous explosion, had, however, awakened their fears for their lives. Thinking this to be the case, I addressed them, expressing my readiness to land them in a place of safety if they would submit; and they most thankfully accepted the offer, shewing themselves to be completely intimidated, and very grateful for our humane intentions towards them, in not attempting to burn them with the ship. It was necessary to proceed with precaution, as they were more numerous than ourselves. We at length completed their disembarkation, and then set her on fire. On this occasion, I had nearly lost my valuable friend and assistant Lieutenant Miller, of the *Windsor Castle*, who had staid so long on board to ensure the fire taking, that it gained on him suddenly; and it was not without being much scorched, and the risk of being suffocated, that we could approach the ship to take him in. The loss to the service would have been very great, had we not succeeded in our endeavours to save him. Mr. Knight, midshipman of the *Windsor Castle*, who was in the boat with me, shewed much activity and address on this occasion, as well as firmness throughout the day.

The explosion of a second powder vessel, equally unexpected, and with a shock even greater than the first, again put us in the most imminent danger of perishing; and when it is considered that we were within the sphere of the falling timber, it is next to miraculous that no one piece of the many which made the water foam round us, happened to touch either the *Swallow* or the three boats with me.

Having now set fire to every thing within our reach, exhausted our combustible preparations, and our strength to such a degree that the men absolutely dropped on the oars, we directed our course to join the fleet, running the gauntlet under a few ill-directed shot from the forts of Balaqué and Aiguilette, now occupied by the enemy, but fortunately without loss of any kind. We proceeded to the place appointed for the embarkation of the troops, and took off as many as we could carry. It would be injustice to those officers whom I have omitted to name (from their not having been so immediately under my eye) if I did not acknowledge myself indebted to them all for their extraordinary exertions in the execution of this great national object, the quickness with which the inflammation took effect on my signal, its extent, and duration, are the best evidences that every officer and man was ready at his post, and firm under most perilous circumstances. I therefore subjoin a list of the whole who were employed on this service.

We can ascertain that the fire extended to at least ten sail of the line; how much farther we cannot say. The loss of the general magazine, and of the quantity of pitch, tar, rosin, hemp, timber, cordage, and gunpowder, must considerably impede the equipment of the few ships that remain.

I am sorry to have been obliged to leave any; but I hope your Lordship will be satisfied that we did as much as our circumscribed means enabled us to do in a limited time.

Discussion of Smith's Employment
From 'Correspondence'. "Philo-Nautus" to the Editor. ^{XXII 204-205}

Brighthelmstone, 10th September, 1809
Agreeing as I do with him [A.F.Y.] in many of the points he has touched upon in that letter [See the section on the Naval Service Volume III, appendix on *Naval Discipline*] he will, I hope, excuse the freedom with which I venture to criticise his extension of the epithet of "*interloper*" to a captain of the navy, for performing a service of great moment and peril, in the person of Sir Sidney Smith. . . .

When the last war with France broke out in 1792, Sir Sidney Smith was travelling in the Levant for amusement and improvement, and chanced to be at Smyrna, where there was collected at the same time a number of English seamen out of employ, some saved from shipwreck, and others straggling *along shore*. Sir S.S. being intent on returning home himself in obedience to the customary notice from the Admiralty Office, bethought himself of these men, as likely to be lost to their country at such a critical time; and, with equal patriotism and humanity, determined to reclaim them. He accordingly, *at his own risk*, purchased one of the lateen rigged small craft of the Archipelago, nicknamed by the Turks "*Kerlanghitch*," or (*Anglice*) swallows, from their swift sailing, and fitted her out under the English flag, under the name of the *Swallow Tender*. In which diminutive man of war, of between 30 and 40 feet keel, he shipped himself, with about as many turbulent fellows, and sailed down the Mediterranean in search of the English fleet, which he found at Toulon a week before the evacuation. Sir Sidney here delivered up his troublesome charge to the commander-in-chief, and was waiting for a passage to England, as a guest with his old commander, Lord Hood, on board the *Victory*, at the time it became necessary to decide upon the fate of the French fleet and arsenal, and when the extrication of the allied army was the principal object of solicitude, and absorbed almost the whole naval means of the combined English and Spanish squadrons. It was at this anxious moment Sir S.S. volunteered a service generally considered as impracticable with the slender means by which it was to be attempted, namely, the *Victory*'s pinnace in the first instance, to carry him round the fleet with the admiral's order in his hand, to put such other ships' boats in requisition as could be spared. To which was added the before mentioned *Swallow Tender*, with her crew of *desperadoes*: but fit men for a forlorn hope, and in some degree tamed under Sir Sidney's personal command. Besides which, his knowledge of Spanish enabled him to extract a couple of gun-boats from Admiral Gravina. And this was the whole force with which

Portrait of Commodore Sir
Samuel Hood, K.B. and K.S.F.
Engraved by Ridley from a print
published by Mr. Andrews at
Charing Cross by whose
permission the present engraving
was made. Plate 222

he started for the arsenal, then occupied by 700 convict galley-slaves, in a state of insurrection. He was followed by the *Windsor Castle*'s boat, under his friend Lieutenant (the late Captain) Miller, and the *Vulcan* fire-ship, it is true, was sent to him in the evening; by means of which four sail of the line were burnt: but previously to her arrival, and for the rest of the business, he had not a farthing candle to light the shavings with, and was besides positively ordered not to commence the work of destruction till the troops were all embarked. It is a singular fact, that from the circumstances of Sir Sidney Smith not being commissioned on full pay, though acting under the authority of Admiral Lord Hood, he was not considered as entitled to share prize-money, or rather head-money, *derived entirely from his own exertions*; and I am well assured never has received any pecuniary or other reward whatsoever for that service, any more than he has any *English* honour for all his services together.

A.F.Y.'s Reply. XXII 291

October 14, 1809

Philo-Naut is most perfectly correct in terming the word *interloper* a "slip of the pen," and if so used as to seem to apply to the gallant man whose cause he advocates, as an intruding adventurer, the expression deserves still higher censure. Philo-Naut, however, does not more admire the gallant Sir Sidney than I do, whether he considers his high military skill displayed at Acre, the conciliating wisdom evinced in the difficult association with a Turkish army, or his diplomatic abilities at El Arish. Since my last letter I have conversed with a very experienced officer, and a friend of Sir Sidney, who saw the whole of the service at Toulon. He says that the cause for regret on that occasion, should be, the error in not having coolly arranged a plan, and deliberately prepared for its execution, as soon as the accumulation of a French force in the neighbourhood rendered it *at least possible* that a retreat would be necessary. He agrees with me fully, however, that the execution of this plan should have been entrusted to an officer of the fleet, who was in commission, and who had seen the whole of the service. If that officer had not availed himself of the assistance of Sir Sidney as a volunteer, in every case in which an able adviser or gallant leader was wanted, he would not have merited success.

H.M.S. Juno in the Enemy Port

From the 'Biographical Memoir of Commodore Sir Samuel Hood, K.B. and K.S.F.' XVII 1, 10-13

It is recorded, on the sepulchral monument of a certain noble family, that "all the brothers were valiant, and all the sisters virtuous." With the female branches of the Hood family, we have not the honour of being acquainted; but, as far as our knowledge extends, respecting the males, we can with confidence assert them to be *all* "valiant.". . .

Captain Samuel Hood to the Right Honourable Lord Hood, Vice-Admiral of the Red, and Commander-in-Chief, &c.

Juno, Bay of Hierres, January 13, 1794
My Lord, I beg leave to enclose your Lordship a narrative of the fortunate escape of His Majesty's ship *Juno*, under my command, from the port of Toulon, after having run ashore in the inner harbour on the night of the 11th instant.

 The firm, steady, and quiet manner in which my orders were carried into execution, by Lieutenants Mason and Webly, in their respective stations; the attention of Mr. Kidd, the Master of the steerage, &c. with the very good conduct of every officer and man, were the sole means of the ship's preservation from the enemy, and for which I must request permission to give them my strongest recommendation.

Juno, Bay of Hierres, January 13, 1794
On the 3d instant I left the Island of Malta, having on board 150 supernumeraries, 46 officers and private marines of His Majesty's ship *Romney*; the remainder, Maltese, intended for the fleet.

 On the night of the 7th passed the S.W. point of Sardinia, and steered a course for Toulon; on the 9th, about 11 A.M., made Cape Sicie, but found a current had set the ship some leagues to the westward of our expectation; hauled the wind, but it blowing hard from the eastward, with a strong lee current, we could but just fetch to the westward of the above Cape. The wind and current continuing, we could not, till the evening of the 11th, get as far to windward as Cape Sepet; having that evening, a little before 10 o'clock, found the ship would be able to fetch into Toulon. I did not like to wait till morning, as we had been thrown to leeward before; and having so many men on board, I thought it my indispensable duty to get in as fast as possible. At 10 I ordered the hands to be turned up, to bring ship to anchor, being then abreast of Cape Sepet, entering the outer harbour. Not having a pilot on board, or any person acquainted with the port, I placed two midshipmen to lookout, with night glasses, for the fleet; but not discovering any ships, until we got near the entrance of the inner harbour, I supposed they had moved up there in the eastern gale: at the same time, seeing one vessel, with several other lights, which I imagined to be the fleet's, I entered the inner harbour, under the top-sails only; but finding I could not weather a brig, which lay a little way to the point, called the Grand Tower, I ordered the foresail and driver to be set, to be ready to tack when on the other side of the brig. Soon after the brig hailed us, but I could not make out what language; I supposed they wanted to know what ship it was; I told them it was an English frigate, called the *Juno*: they answered, *Viva*. After asking, in English and French, for some time, what brig she was, and where the British Admiral lay, they appeared not to understand me, but called out as we passed under their stern, *Luff!*

Luff! several times; which made me suppose there was shoal water near: the helm was instantly put a lee, but we found the ship was on shore before she got head to wind. - There being very little wind, and perfectly smooth, I ordered the sails to be clewed up, and handed: at this time a boat went from the brig towards the town. Before the people were all off the yard, found the ship went astern very fast, by a flaw of wind that came down the harbour: hoisted the driver and mizzen-stay-sail, keeping the sheets to windward, that she might get farther from the shoal. The instant she lost her way, the bow being then in 14 less 5, let go the best bower anchor, when she tended head to wind, the after part of the keel was aground, and we could not move the rudder. I ordered the launch and cutter to be hoisted out, and the ketch anchor [sic], with two hawsers, to be put in them to warp the ship farther off. By the time the boats were out, a boat came alongside, after having been hailed, and we thought answered as if an officer had been in her. The people were all anxious to get out of her, two of whom appeared to be officers. One of them said he was come to inform me, that it was the regulation of the port, and the Commanding Officer's orders, that I must go into another branch of the harbour, to perform ten days' quarantine. I kept asking him where Lord Hood's ship lay; but his not giving me any satisfactory answer, and one of the midshipmen having at the same instant said, "they wear national cockades," I looked at one of their hats more steadfastly, and by the moonlight clearly distinguished the three colours. Perceiving they were suspected, and on my questioning them again about Lord Hood, one of them replied, "*Soyez tranquille, les Anglois sont de braves gens, nous les traitons bien; l'Amiral Anglois est sortie il y'a quelque tems* [sic]."

It may be more easily conceived, than any words can express, what I felt at the moment. The circumstance of our situation of course was known throughout the ship. In an instant, and, saying we were all prisoners, the officers soon got near enough to know our situation. At the same time a flaw of wind coming down the harbour, Lieutenant Webly, third Lieutenant of the ship, said to me, "I believe, Sir, we shall be able to fetch out, if we can get her under sail." I immediately perceived we should have a chance of saving the ship; and at least if we did not, we ought not to lose His Majesty's ship without some contention. I ordered every person to their respective stations, and the Frenchmen to be sent below: they perceiving some bustle, two or three of them began to draw their sabres, on which I ordered some of the marines to take the half-pikes and force them below, which was soon done: I then ordered all the Maltese between decks, that we might not have confusion with too many men. I believe, in an instant, such a change in people was never seen; every officer and man was at his duty; and I do think, within three minutes, every sail in the ship was set, and the yards braced ready for casting: the steady and active assistance of Lieutenant Turner, and all the officers, prevented any confusion from arising in our critical situation. As soon as the cable was taught [sic], I ordered it to be cut, and had the great good fortune to see the ship start from the shore the moment the head sails were filled; a favourable flaw of wind coming at the same time, got good way on her, and we had then every prospect of getting out, if the forts did not disable us. To prevent being retarded by the boats, I ordered them to be cut adrift, as also the French boat. The moment the brig saw us begin to loose sails, we could plainly perceive she was getting her guns ready, and we also saw lights upon all the batteries. When we had shot far enough for the brig's guns to bear on us, which was not more than three ship's lengths, she began to fire, and also a fort a little on the starboard bow, and soon after all of them, on both sides, as they could bring their guns to bear. As soon as the sails were well trimmed, I beat to quarters, to get the guns ready, but not with an intention of firing till we were sure of getting out. When we got abreast of the centre part of the land of Cape Sepet, I was afraid we should have been obliged to make a tack; but as we drew near the shore, and were ready, she came up two points, and just weathered the Cape. As we passed very close along that shore, the batteries kept up as brisk a fire as the wetness of the weather would permit. When I could afford to keep the ship a little from the wind, I ordered some guns to be fired at a battery that had just opened abreast of us, which quieted them a little; we then stopped firing till we could keep her away, with the wind abaft the beam; when, for a few minutes, we kept up a very brisk fire on the last battery we had to pass, and which I believe must have otherwise done us great damage.

At half past 12, being out of reach of their shot, the firing ceased. Fortunately we had no person hurt; some shot cut the sails; part of the standing and running rigging shot away; and two French 36-pound shot, that struck the hull, is all the damage the ship sustained.

Sieges of Bastia and Calvi

From the 'Biographical Memoir of the Right Hon. Lord Nelson.' III 169-171

The unbounded confidence which the noble Admiral [Lord Hood] always reposed in Captain Nelson, manifests the high opinion which Lord Hood then entertained of his courage and ability to execute the arduous Services with which he was entrusted: if batteries were to be attacked; if Ships were to be cut out of their harbours; if the hazardous landing of troops was to be effected, or difficult passages to be explored; we invariably find Horatio Nelson foremost on each occasion, with his brave Officers, and his gallant Crew of the *Agamemnon*.[24] It was well observed in the Mediterranean at this time, that before Captain Nelson quitted his old Ship, he had not only fairly worn her out, but had also exhausted himself, and his Ship's company.[25] From habits of active service, however, his originally delicate constitution continued to support great fatigue; though his strength was visibly impaired previous to Lord Hood's coming to England.

At Toulon, and the celebrated victories achieved at Bastia, and Calvi, Lord Hood bore ample testimony to the skill, and unremitting exertions of Captain Nelson: during the memorable siege of Bastia, he superintended the disembarkation of troops and stores; and commanded a brigade of seamen, who served on shore at the batteries, having Captains Hunt, Sericold, and Bullen under his orders; in the execution of which duty, Captain Nelson gave eminent, and repeated proofs, both of skill as a Commander, and of personal intrepidity.

At the siege of Calvi (July and August 1794) he also distinguished himself in a conspicuous manner, when commanding an advanced battery of seamen on shore; and Lord Hood, on that occasion, as on every other, gave him a just tribute of applause. It was at this siege that Captain Nelson lost the sight of his right eye, by a shot from the

24 The greater part of the *Agamemnon*'s crew were raised in the neighbourhood of Burnham Thorpe.
25 When the *Agamemnon* came into Dock to be refitted, at the beginning of October, 1796, there was not a mast, yard, sail, nor any part of the rigging, but was obliged to be repaired - the whole being so cut to pieces with shot: her hull had long been kept together by cables served round.

enemy's battery striking the upper part of that which he commanded; and driving, with prodigious force, some particles of sand against his face.[26]

The following letter which he received, during the siege of Calvi, from Lord Hood, inclosing the resolutions of the two Houses of Parliament, was highly flattering to Captain Nelson's feelings, and shews the estimation in which his services were then held:

Victory, off Calvi, Aug. 8, 1794
Sir, Having received his Majesty's commands, to communicate to the respective Officers, Seamen, Marines, and Soldiers, who have been employed in the different operations which have been successfully carried on against the enemy in Corsica, a resolution of the two Houses of Parliament; which I have the honour herewith to inclose; and desire you will make known to all in the *Agamemnon*, and such other Officers and Seamen, as are with you, and were employed at Bastia, the sense that is entertained of their spirited and meritorious conduct.

Toulon Papers No. XXI

List of Ships, Frigates, and Corvettes, belonging to the Department of Toulon in August 1793, when Admiral Lord Hood took Possession of that Port, distinguishing such as were set fire to, burnt, and destroyed, or taken into his Majesty's Service, and brought away at the Evacuation; also those which have since that Period been captured, burnt, sunk, or destroyed. [II 297-303]

LIST (A)

In the Outer Road, and ready for sea, when Lord Hood entered with his Majesty's Fleet

Ships	Guns	Remarks
Le Commerce de Marseilles	120	Brought away from Toulon by Lord Hood – the
Le Pompee	74	Commerce de Marseilles is now a prison ship at Plymouth, and the Pompee (Captain Stirling) is in the Mediterranean.
Le Tonnant	80	Set on fire, but not destroyed so as to prevent
Le Hereux	74	being afterwards repaired. Both taken on the 1st of August 1798, by Lord Nelson, in the battle of the Nile.
Le Centaur	74	Burnt at Toulon on the 18th of December 1793, the night of evacuation, and destroyed.
Le Commerce de Bourdeaux	74	Set on fire, but not destroyed so as to prevent being afterwards repaired.

26 Lord Hood, in his official letter, says, "The journal I herewith transmit from Captain Nelson, who had the command of the seamen, will shew the daily occurrences of the siege; and whose unremitting zeal and exertion I cannot sufficiently applaud, or that of Captain Hallowell, who took it by turns to command in the advanced batteries twenty-four hours at a time; and I flatter myself they, as well as the other officers and seamen, will have full justice done them by the General: it is therefore unnecessary for me to say more upon the subject."

Le Destin	74	Burnt at Toulon on the 18th of December 1793, and destroyed.
Le Lys	74	Burnt at ditto, and destroyed.
Le Heros	74	"
Le Themistocle	74	"
Le Duguay Trouin	74	"
Le Patriote	74	These four ships being deemed in the worst state
L'Apollon	74	were sent to the ports of Brest, Rochefort, and
L'Orion	74	L'Orient, with 500 turbulent and disaffected
L'Entreprenant	74	seamen.
Le Scipion	74	Burnt by accident at Leghorn.
Le Genereux	74	Not destroyed; and escaped from the battle of the Nile; and afterwards captured the *Leander* of 50 guns.

In the Outer Road, total *17 Ships of the Line*

Frigates

La Perle	40	Brought away from Toulon, afterwards commissioned, and called the *Amethyst*; lost at Alderney 29th December 1795.
L'Arethuse	40	Brought away from Toulon, afterwards commissioned, and called the *Undaunted*; foundered on the Morant Keys, West Indies.
L'Aurore	32	Taken into his Majesty's service: now a prison ship at Gibraltar.
La Topaze	32	Brought away from Toulon; afterwards taken into the service, and commanded by Captain Church on the Halifax station.
L'Alceste	32	Given to the King of Sardinia as a compensation for the frigate taken by the French at Nice.

In the Outer Road, total *five Frigates*

Corvettes

La Poulette	26	Brought away from Toulon; afterwards commissioned, and burnt at Ajaccio, Corsica (20th October 1796), being unserviceable.
Le Tarleton	14	Brought away from Toulon, and afterwards taken into his Majesty's service.
La Caroline	20	Burnt at Toulon on the 18th of December 1793.
L'Auguste	20	"
La Bellisle	26	Taken into his Majesty's service at Toulon; Lieutenant Soccombe appointed Commander; and burnt at Ajaccio, Corsica (20th October 1796), being unserviceable.
La Proselyte	24	Taken into his Majesty's service at Toulon, and commanded by Captain Sericold; burnt by red-hot shot from the enemy's batteries (May 1794) at the siege of Bastia.

Le Sincere	20	Taken into the service at Toulon, and Lieutenant Shields appointed Commander.
La Mulet	20	Taken into the service at Toulon, and Lieutenant Bullen appointed Commander.
La Mozelle	20	Taken into the service at Toulon, Lieutenant Bennet appointed Commander; and on going into Toulon after the evacuation, she was taken by the French; since retaken by *L'Amiable*, Sir H. Burrard, in the Mediterranean, May 1794 - *La Mozelle*, Captain Brisbane, carried the first intelligence to Sir Geo. K. Elphinstone, at the Cape of Good Hope, respecting the destination of the Dutch Fleet under Admiral Lucas.
La Lamproye	20	Taken into the Neapolitan service.
La Petite Aurore	18	Taken into the Spanish service.

In the Outer Road of Toulon. In all, 17 Ships of the Line, 5 Frigates, and 11 Corvettes.[27]

LIST (B)

In Harbour, refitting, at the time Lord Hood entered Toulon

Le Triomphant	80	Burnt at Toulon on the 18th of December 1793.
Le Suffisant	74	"
Le Puissant	74	Brought away from Toulon; commanded by Monsieur Ferrand, who lay with this ship several weeks during the siege against a French battery of twenty-four guns, twenty-four pounders, at the head of *La Seine*, in Toulon Harbour, and conspicuously distinguished himself. He receives a pension of £200 a year from Government. - *La Puissant* is now a receiving ship at Spithead.
Le Dauphin Royale	120	This ship was entrusted to the Spaniards to burn; her name was first changed to the *Sans Culottes*, and afterwards to *L'Orient*; blown up in the memorable action of the Nile.
Frigate *La Serieuse*	36	Set on fire at Toulon 18th December 1793, but not destroyed so as to prevent her being repaired. - She was sunk on the 1st of August 1798, by Lord Nelson, in the battle of the Nile.

In the Harbour refitting. In all, four Ships of the Line and one Frigate.

27 It is to be remarked, that out of the above number of ships of the Line, Frigates, and Corvettes, which were ready for sea on our taking possession of Toulon, only three Line of Battle ships remaining were accidentally saved by the French at the evacuation from being totally destroyed by fire - the British Admiral deeming it of most consequence to burn or bring away such ships as had been recently fitted and ready for sea.

LIST (C)

In the Inner Harbour and Basin, and in want of complete repair.

Le Mercure	74	Set fire to at Toulon the 18th of December 1793, but not destroyed so as to prevent being repaired. Taken on the 1st of August 1798, by Lord Nelson, in the battle of the Nile.
La Couronne	80	Burnt at Toulon the 18th of December 1793.
Le Conquerant	74	Set on fire at Toulon, but not destroyed so as to prevent being repaired. Taken on the 1st of August 1798, in the battle of the Nile.
Le Dictateur	74	Burnt at Toulon the 18th of December 1793.
Le Censeur	74	Intrusted to the Spaniards to be burnt, consequently saved to the French; afterwards taken by Admiral Hotham's squadron; and since retaken by a French squadron off Cape St. Vincent's, October 1795.
Le Guerrier	74	Intrusted to the Spaniards to be burnt, consequently saved at Toulon – Taken on the 1st of August 1798, in the battle of the Nile.
Le Souverain	74	Intrusted to the Spaniards to be burnt, consequently saved at Toulon; afterwards called *Le Souverain Peuple*; and taken on the 1st of August 1798, by Lord Nelson, in the battle of the Nile.
L'Alcide	74	Deemed unserviceable, and intrusted also to the Spaniards to be burnt. In the action with Admiral Hotham's fleet (13th July 1795), she struck to the *Victory*, and soon after caught fire, and was blown up; and *only* three hundred of the crew saved.

Frigates

La Courageuse	36	Set fire to at Toulon on the 18th of December 1793, but not destroyed so as to preevent being repaired. Taken in July 1799, by the *Centaur*, Captain Markham.
L'Iphigenée	32	Set fire to at Toulon, but not destroyed so as to prevent her being repaired.
L'Isis	32	Powder magazines, intrusted to the Spaniards to be sunk, instead of which they were (as it is now believed with a diabolical intention) blown up, when the British Fleet was getting out of the harbour, and by the explosions some of our brave officers and seamen lost their lives.
Le Montreal	32	
La Lutine	32	Taken into his Majesty's service at Toulon as a bomb vessel, and Lieutenant J. McNamara (now

Captain of the *Cerberus*) first appointed
Commander; at present in the North Sea.

Corvettes

L'Alerte	16	Set on fire at Toulon the 18th of December 1793, but not destroyed so as to prevent her being repaired. Since run ashore by the *Flora*, off Brest.
La Bretonne	18	Intrusted to the Spaniards to be burnt, but saved to the French.

Total in the Inner Harbour and Basin wanting repairs, nine Line of Battle Ships, five Frigates, and two Corvettes.

Building

One ship of	74	Set on fire at Toulon the 18th of December 1793, but not destroyed so as to prevent her being repaired. Name unknown.[28]
One frigate of	40	Burnt at Toulon the 18th of December 1798. Name unknown.

LIST (D)

Ships in commission prior to Lord Hood's taking possession of Toulon, and which were then cruising in the Levant, or employed on various Services.

Le Duquesne	74	At first in the Levant, afterwards at Tunis, &c.
La Sybille	44	Up the Levant. Taken by the *Romney*, Captain Paget, at Miconi (17th June 1794); and Lord Hood appointed Captain E. Cooke to command her. She was paid off and repaired, and Captain Cooke re-appointed to the command. Now in the East Indies, where she has recently taken *La Forte*, of superior force, after a gallant action of one hour and a half.
La Sensible	36	Stationed in the Levant. Taken by the *SeaHorse*, Captain Foote, coming from Malta, June 1798.
La Melpomene	40	In the Levant and at Corsica. Taken the 10th of August 1794 by Lord Hood's squadron, at the surrender of Calvi, Corsica. Now in Channel Service, and lately commanded by Sir Charles Hamilton, Bart.
La Minerve (now *St. Fiorenzo*)	40	Stationed in the Levant and off Corsica. Taken by Lord Hood's squadron in the Bay of St. Fiorenzo, Corsica; having been sunk (19th February 1794) by the English batteries, and was afterwards weighed by the Ships of the squadron. Now commanded by Sir Harry B. Neale, in the Channel service.

28 *Query*, If the 74 be not the *Spartiate*, taken by Lord Nelson.

Fortunée	36	Stationed in the Levant and off Corsica; and when attacked by the English batteries, and Lord Hood's squadron, she was burnt by the enemy at her anchorage (19th February 1794), the crew having abandoned her, and escaped to Bastia.
L'Imperieuse	40	Taken on the 11th of October 1793, in the Bay of Especia, by the *Captain*, of 74 guns Captain Reeve, and *Speedy* sloop, Charles cunningham, Commander, having been detached from Lord Hood's squadron at Toulon. Captain Cunningham was first made Post into her: and she was afterwards commanded by Captain Wolsely till paid off – When re-commissioned, Lord Augustus Fitzroy was appointed to command her, and ordered to the Cape of Good Hope. She is now in the East Indies, commanded by J. Rowley.
La Modeste	36	Taken out of Genoa, on the 7th of October 1793, by the *Bedford*, Captain Man, and others of the squadron detached from Toulon under Rear Admiral Gell's orders. Captain T.B. Martin, now of the *Fishguard*, was first made Post into her. At present repairing at Portsmouth.
La Mignone	32	Stationed at Corsica, and taken by Lord Hood's squadron on the surrender of Calvi (10th August 1794) Lieutenant Ralph W. Miller (now Captain of the *Theseus*) was first appointed to command her, but was not confirmed Post till the beginning of 1796. This frigate was burnt at Ferajo, 31st July 1797, being unserviceable.
La Juno	40	Stationed in the Levant; and taken July 1799, by the *Centaur*, Captain Markham.
La Vestale	40	Stationed at Villa Franca. Taken by the *Terpsichore*, Captain R. Bowen, off Cadiz (13th December 1796); retaken next day.
Corvettes		
La Fleche	24	Stationed in the Levant. Taken by Lord Hood's squadron, 21st May 1794, on the surrender of Bastia. Lieutenant Came appointed to command her. Lost in St. Fiorenzo Bay, November 1795. Crew saved.
La Fauvette	24	Stationed in the Levant. Supposed still to exist in the French Navy.
L'Eclair	20	Stationed at Smyrna, and taken July 1793 by Lord Hood's Fleet, on her return to Toulon. Now at Sheerness in want of repair.
La Badine	24	Stationed at Villa Franca, and supposed still to exist in the French Navy.

Le Hazard	20 "
La Brune	24 "

In all cruising and employed in various Services prior to Lord Hood's taking possession of Toulon, one Ship of the Line, ten Frigates, and six Corvettes.

Total Ships in the foregoing Lists (A), (B), (C), (D), belonging to the Department of Toulon, August 1793.

Line of Battle Ships

120	80	74 guns	Total of the Line	Frigates	Corvettes
2	4	26	32	22	19

Recapitulation of the number of ships, Frigates, and Corvettes, in the Outer Road, Inner Harbour, Basin, and Arsenal of Toulon, in August 1793, and the number taken into the Service, disposed of, brought away, burnt, and destroyed, between the 1st of September and the 18th of December 1793 inclusive; together with those since taken, burnt, sunk, or destroyed.

	Ships of the Line	Frigates	Corvettes
Total Ships in Toulon - 2 of 120 guns, 4 of 80 guns, 25 of 74 guns, 12 frigates, and 13 corvettes or sloops.	31	12	13
Sent as cartels to Brest, Rochefort, and L'Orient, September 1793.	4		
Taken into his Majesty's service between the 3d of September and the 13th of December 1793, besides 11 armed zebecs, gun-boats, and galleys.		2	9
Taken into the service of the Spaniards, Neapolitans, and Sardinians.		1	2
Burnt and totally destroyed at the evacuation of Toulon.	10	3	2
N.B. Six others had been set fire to, but did not burn so as to prevent being repaired.			
Burnt by accident at Leghorn.	1		
Brought away from Toulon, and afterwards taken into his Majesty's service, including one ship of 120 guns.	3	3	2
Total disposed of, taken, burnt, and destroyed.	18	9	11
Ships remaining at Toulon on the 18th of December 1793, including six of the line considerably damaged from having been also set on fire.	13	3	2
Taken, burnt, sunk, or destroyed, of the above remaining Ships since the evacuation			

of Toulon, by Lord Nelson and others, as
mentioned in the foregoing list, including the
remaining ship of 120 guns, and one of 80
guns.   8   2   1
Supposed to exist in the French Navy of the
Ships left undestroyed at Toulon.   5   1   1

It is to be observed, that in addition to the ten sail of the line, three frigates, and two sloops, completely destroyed, the following ships were set on fire by Sir Sidney Smith, and the officers under his orders, viz. of the line, *Le Tonnant*, *Le Hereuse*, *Le Mercure*, *Le Conquerant*, *Le Commerce de Bourdeaux*, and a ship building, name unknown; also the frigates, *La Serieuse*, *Courageuse*, and *Iphigenie*[29] – And although it afterwards turned out that these Ships were not burnt so completely as the other ten sail of the line, &c. so as to prevent their being rebuilt and repaired; yet the damage they received was considerable; and as all the stores in the arsenal had been consumed or burnt, a long time elapsed before the enemy, with all his exertions, could get the Ships left undestroyed ready for service. It remained, therefore, only for the Spaniards to burn the seven ships of the line, which were in the Inner Harbour and Basin; and had they co-operated in the scene of conflagration in the manner pre-concerted, and which the Spanish Admiral had pledged himself to the British Admiral would have been done, every remaining Ship must have been completely destroyed.

Recapitulation of the number of Ships belonging to the Department of Toulon employed in the Levant, at the time Lord Hood entered that port, and the number taken while in possession, and since the evacuation, contained in List marked (D).

	Ships of the Line	Frigates	Corvettes
Total stationed in the Levant, Corsica &c.	1	10	6
Total taken, burnt, sunk, or destroyed, by Lord Hood's squadron, as named in list (D)		7	2
Taken by other cruizers		2	
Taken by Lord Hood's squadron and other cruizers		9	2
Supposed still to exist in the French Navy.	1	1	4
Total Ships of war taken, brought away, burnt, sunk, or destroyed, by Admiral Lord Hood, between the 11th of September 1793, and the 10th of August 1794, as named in Lists (A), (B), (C), (D)	14	16	13

29 The first named four sail of the line have been taken by Lord Nelson in the battle of the Nile; and as there is reason to suppose the Ship building was named the *Spartiate*, it will make five sail of the line since taken out of the six. *La Serieuse* frigate was sunk in the Bay of Aboukir; and the *Courageuse* has been recently taken by the *Centaur*.

Supplemental and Additional Notes to Toulon Papers, No. XXI in Volume II
page 297, of this Work. IV 478-480

LIST (A)

Ships	Guns	Remarks
Le Hereùx, should be Le Heureux	74	This ship was burnt after the battle of the Nile, by Lord Nelson's orders.
Le Commerce de Bourdeaux, since named Le Timoleon	74	Blown up in the battle of the Nile.
Le Dugay Trouin	74	Set fire to, but not destroyed; she has been detached to Brest by the French since the evacuation.
Le Genereux	74	Taken by Lord Nelson off Malta, Feb. 18, 1800, in attempting to escape from that island.
Le Belleisle, should be La Bellete	26	
La Lampraye, should be L'Empraye	20	Has been detached to Brest since the evacuation.

The two following Corvettes are omitted in this List:

Le Pluvier	20	Sent by Lord Hood with four sail of the line to Brest, with disaffected seamen.
La Sardine	22	Had been taken from the Sardinians at the commencement of the war, since taken by the *Egmont* off Tunis, March 1796.

LIST (C)

Le Mercure	74	This ship was burnt after the battle of the Nile, by Lord Nelson's orders.
La Couronne	80	She was not destroyed on the 18th of December, 1793; but was repaired, and taken in an action with Admiral Hotham's fleet off Corsica in 1794, under the name of *Ça Ira*, and was afterwards burnt by accident at St. Fiorenzo.
Le Dictateur	74	Not destroyed, but afterwards detached to Brest by the French.
Le Languedoc	80	Burnt and destroyed at Toulon the 18th of December 1793.
Le Censeur	74	Left at Cadiz in 1799, not being able to proceed with the combined fleet, the Spaniards giving them the *Saint Sebastian*, 74, in lieu, which they took with them to Brest.
Le Guerrier	74	Burnt by Lord Nelson's orders after being taken in the Battle of the Nile.

Le Souverain, now Called		
Le Guerrier	74	Cut down and employed as sheerhulk at Gibraltar.
L'Iphigenie	32	Destroyed on the 18th of December 1793.
L'Alert, brig, now called		
The Minorca	16	Taken by Lord Keith's fleet off Genoa, in July 1799. The ship ran on shore by the *Flora*, off Brest, must consequently be another of the same name.
La Bretonne	28	Now belonging to the Brest Department.

Building
One ship, named

Le Barras	74	Has been since detached to Brest.

For one Frigate read two Frigates

La Diana	48	Taken at the capture of Malta, 1800
La Minerve	44	Taken by the *Dido* and *Lowestoffe*, June 1795.

LIST (D)

Le Duquesne	74	Detached to Brest by the French since the evacuation.
La Junon, now called *Princess Charlotte*	40	
La Vestale	40	Taken by the *Clyde* off Bourdeaux, August 1799.

Recapitulation of the number of Ships belonging to the Department of Toulon, at the time Lord Hood entered that port; and the number taken and destroyed while in possession, and since the evacuation.

	Ships of the Line	Frigates	Corvettes
Total number of ships in Toulon when taken possession of	31	13	14
Total stationed in the Levant, Corsica, &c. including one corvette taken from the Sardinians.	1	10	6
	32	23	20

How disposed of

	Ships of the Line	Frigates	Corvettes
Sent as cartels to the ports in the Atlantic, September 1793.	4		1

Taken into the British service previous to the evacuation, besides eleven xebecs,

gun-boats, and galleys.		2	5
Taken into the Spanish service.			1
Given to the King of Sardinia, as a compensation for one taken from him; she was afterwards taken by the French, and from them again by the *Centaur*, June 1799.		1	
Brought away by Lord Hood at the evacuation.	3	3	2
Burnt and totally destroyed at the evacuation.	8	3	2
Burnt by accident at Leghorn.	1		
Taken, burnt, sunk, or destroyed since the evacuation (exclusive of *Le Censeur*, which has been since retaken and exchanged with the Spaniards for the *Saint Sebastian*, of 74 guns, now at Brest).	11	14	3
The above ship accounted for.	1		
Detached to Brest since the evacuation.	4		2
Supposed still to exist in the French service in the Mediterranean.			4
	32	23	20
Taken by Lord Hood's fleet previous to the capture of Toulon.			1
Still existing in the French service in the Mediterranean, and ports of the Atlantic..	8		7
Exchanged with the Spaniards.	1		
	9		7

1793-1794 – West Indies

AT THE OUTBREAK OF WAR resources were immediately earmarked for service in the West Indies, despite the known health hazard of operations. The economic importance of colonial production to the re-export commerce of European states ensured that there would be intense efforts to obtain possession of the French islands, which were in turmoil because of the French Revolution and its promise to give citizenship to the blacks and mulatos. That promise united French slave-owners into royalist factions, and was an additional reason for British colonial assemblies to urge the conquest of the French islands before the political contagion could spread. Naval officers were more interested in the rich prey to be found in French merchant shipping.

The action began when Vice-Admiral Sir John Laforey, who commanded the small British squadron at Barbados, carried a force of soldiers under Major-General Cuyler to recapture the island of Tobago which had been lost to the French in the American War. Rear-Admiral Alan Gardner, who had been hurried out to the Indies with seven of the line, and Major Bruce who brought with him two regiments, were less successful in an effort to bring Martinique to declare for the royalists. They were forced to evacuate the royalist insurgents who would certainly have been put to death. The commander of the Jamaica station, Commodore John Ford, was luckier when he responded to the requests from French colonists in Saint-Domingue for protection from the republicans, and the revolted mulatos. One of the best harbours in the islands, Nicholas Mole, guarded from the sea by a strongly sited battery, was thus closed to enemy privateers.

In the spring of 1794 Vice-Admiral Sir John Jervis and Lieutenant-General Sir Charles Grey were sent to capture Martinique, St Lucia and Guadaloupe. The decision was then made to send the soldiers not required for garrisoning the captured islands to secure the position on Saint-Domingue which had begun to deteriorate after initial, but incomplete, success. This proved less fortunate, perhaps because Grey and Jervis were too interested in plunder. The absence of a large part of the British force in Saint-Domingue had disastrous consequences when a small French force of two frigates and transports arrived at Guadaloupe. By the time Jervis and Grey learned of the development, the French had recovered Point-à-Pitre and moved their ships into harbour behind the guns of the batteries. They were able to depend on local support, of which commissioner Victor Hugues made certain by carrying the 'Reign of Terror' to the colony. The decimation of the British army by yellow fever eventually obliged it to evacuate the island on 10 December 1794.

The Naval Chronicle's coverage of operations in the Indies was extensive, but patchy, perhaps because so much of it was littoral operation. There is but a brief mention of Rear-Admiral Gardner's period of command at Barbados, and of his abortive effort against Martinique, in a biographical memoir published during the interval of peace following the conclusion of peace at Amiens in 1801, and an extract from a letter written by an officer in his squadron, published in the first volume, does nothing to amplify it. Another brief mention in the memoir of the public services of Lord Gardner adds a snippet. Commodore Ford's intervention in Saint-Domingue is better recorded, by his service letter to the Admiralty, and coverage of Vice-Admiral Jervis's operations in 1794 in Martinique, St Lucia and Guadaloupe is exhaustively reported. Only a brief excerpt from Jervis's biographical memoir is reprinted here, because much of the original is devoted to a very long letter from Jervis and Charles Grey to the Duke of Portland, 7 March 1795, disculpating themselves from the charge of peculation. In Volumes 17 and 18, however, was printed a very long journal, which even in the first edition was somewhat eluded, of the proceedings of the squadron by 'an officer' serving in it. This has been reproduced here much as it originally appeared, and is accompanied by *The Naval Chronicle*'s biographical memoirs of Captains Nugent and Faulknor commanding the *Veteran* and *Zebra*, respectively. The account of the death of *Zebra*'s pilot is a classic. Faulknor's own death acquired such a dramatic mystique in England that an 'Interlude' called 'The Death of Captain Faulknor' was performed at Covent Garden Theatre, and *The Naval Chronicle* reported that 'it also was selected by an eminent artist, as a subject well adapted to his genius.' The House of Commons voted funds for a monument, after a debate in which Faulknor's merits were greatly praised.

West Indian Operations
From the 'Biographical Memoirs of the Right Honourable Lord Gardner.' VIII 192-194

On the 19th of January 1790, Captain Gardner was appointed one of the commissioners for executing the Office of Lord High Admiral, which honourable and important situation he continued to hold during four successive commissions, till the month of May 1795, when he quitted the Admiralty Board. Some time in the year 1790, he was chosen one of the representatives in Parliament for the borough of Plymouth; and, at the general election in 1796, he was returned for the city of Westminister, which place he continues to represent, though not without some opposition at the late election, but of a nature too contemptible and ludicrous to merit observation in this place.

We now come to the services of Lord Gardner during the late war. The hostile disposition of France towards this country, on the subversion of her ancient government, being manifest, the most prompt and vigorous measures were taken by the British ministry to put the nation in a respectable state of defence. On the 1st of February 1793, immediately on the commencement of hostilities, a general promotion of naval officers took place, and Captain Gardner was advanced to the rank of Rear-Admiral of the Blue. On the 22d of February he had the honour to kiss his Majesty's hand, on being appointed to command the following squadron, then under sailing orders for the West Indies:

	Guns	Commanders
Queen	98	Rear-Admiral Gardner
		Captain Hutt
Orion	74	J.T. Duckworth
Hector	74	G. Montagu
Culloden	74	Sir T. Rich, Bart.
Heroine	32	A.H. Gardner
Andromeda	32	J. Salisbury
Rattlesnake	16	A. Mouat

Admiral Gardner hoisted his flag on the 6th of March, and the above squadron sailed from St. Helen's on the 26th of the same month. They arrived at Barbadoes on the 27th of April, without having met with any thing on their passage worthy of notice; and Admiral Gardner took the command on that station as successor to Sir John Laforey, Bart. The island of Tobago had surrendered a few days before his arrival, and an attack was meditated on Martinico; but the French unfortuately had reinforced the place; and Admiral Gardner not having with him a sufficient body of land forces to co-operate with the fleet, nothing of moment was effected during that season, against the possessions of the enemy in the Carribean Sea. In the autumn Admiral Gardner returned to England, and his squadron was immediately attached to the Channel Fleet, under the command of Earl Howe. On the 12th of April 1794, Admiral Gardner was advanced to be Rear of the White.

Extract of a Letter from an Officer belonging to Admiral Gardner's Fleet, dated Barbadoes, April 30 1793. [423-424]

We sailed from Spithead on the 24th of March, and arrived at Barbadoes on the 27th of April, but did not meet with any thing worthy of notice during our passage. We found Admiral Laforey had taken Tobago, and one of our frigates saw a French fleet consisting of ten sail of the line, and seven frigates, about ninety miles from us. Had we fallen in with them, a short action would have ensued. The French appeared to sail so much out of order, that I have little doubt we should have conquered, though we had only seven sail of the line, and two frigates. We supposed they were bound to Martinico, their principal island. The *Blanche* frigate arrived at Barbadoes yesterday, and says that the French had not reached Martinico on Saturday. We go very soon to see if it is practicable to get Martinico into our possession. Should the enemy's fleet be off there when we arrive, we must give them a defeat before we can carry our intentions into execution. As the island is very strongly fortified, it must depend on the strength of the royal party whether we are successful or not.

Additional material from the 'Memoir of the Public Services of the Right Honourable Alan Hyde Lord Gardner.' XXI 358

Rear-admiral Gardner succeeded Sir John Laforey in the command, on the Leeward Island station. Encouraged by the disputes which existed between the Royalists and Republicans, at Martinique, the expedition had been fitted out; and invited by the former, Admiral Gardner, and Major general Bruce, attempted a descent on the island. On the 16th of June, under cover of the ships of war, the General landed, with a body of about 3,000 British troops; but, finding the republican party too strong, he was obliged to reimbark, on the 21st, with considerable loss, particularly to the royalists, many of whom could not be taken on board the ships, and were unavoidably left to perish by the hands of their implacable enemies. The *Ferme*, a French ship of 74 guns, commanded by the Vicomte de Riviere, and the *Calypso* frigate, of 36 guns, put themselves under the orders of Admiral Gardner, and saved a number of their unfortuante countrymen from destruction, with whom they proceeded in Trinidad. The ships, commanded by French officers, were taken into the Spanish service. Martinique was taken in the following year, by Sir John Jervis and Sir C. Grey.

Operations on St Domingue, from 'Letters on Service'
Admiralty Office, December 9, 1793. XXXVII 339-341

Letters were this day received from Commodore Ford, commander-in-chief of his Majesty's ships and vessels at Jamaica, to Mr. Stephens [ie Philip Stephens, First Secretary of the Admiralty Board], of which the following are extracts, together with copies of papers therein referred to:

Europa, Mole of Cape St. Nicholas, September 26, 1793
In my letter of the 8th instant I informed their Lordships that I was proceeding to Jeremie with a detachment of troops, commanded by Lieutenant colonel Whitelocke, of the 13th regiment, to take a post at that place in the name of his Britannic Majesty, agreeable to a capitulation signed by General Williamson and Mons. Charmilly; and I have the satisfaction to add, that the squadron arrived there on the evening of the 19th, and that the troops landed the subsequent morning, and were received by the inhabitants with every demonstration of joy and fidelity, and the British colours hoisted under a royal salute, with the usual ceremonies on such occasions. No time was lost in landing the artillery and stores, and, as the weather was suspicious, the anchorage bad, and a heavy sea setting in, I judged it best to quit the bay in the evening, there being no danger to be apprehended from the naval force of the enemy; and in order to give Colonel Whitelocke an opportunity to secure himself as soon as possible, I directed Captain Rowley, of his Majesty's ship *Penelope*, to take the *Iphigenia*, *Hermione*, and *Spitfire* schooner, under his command, and proceed to Bay des Flamands, near St. Louis, on the south side of the island, and endeavour, by way of a diversion, to take or destroy some merchant ships that were to remain there during the hurricane months, and I proceeded myself with the *Europa*, *Goelan* brig, and *Flying Fish* schooner, towards the Mole with

Major Charles, a French officer belonging to the town of the Mole of Cape St. Nicholas, who had been captured and carried into Nassau by a Providence privateer, and afterwards sent by Lord Dunmore to Jamaica, where he arrived the day before the squadron sailed with letters to the governor and myself; upon examination of the major, it appeared that the garrison and inhabitants would surrender themselves to the arms of Great Britain, provided a certain number of troops could be sent to support them; and it was agreed that I should carry him up in the *Europa* to Jeremie, and, when the troops were landed, to send him in a flag of truce to the Mole to sound their dispositions, and then for him to return to Jamaica and fix on the plan; but as I found at Jeremie that a speedy attack on the Mole was mediated by the civil commissaries, I thought it would be most conducive to his Majesty's service to proceed there myself, in order to give all possible countenance to the mission; and in consequence I sent Major Charles, on the evening of the 21st, on board the *Flying Fish* schooner, to be landed in the night at a certain spot, and directed the *Goelan* to keep between the *Flying Fish* and *Europa* to give him support if necessary. Soon after daylight a signal, that an enemy was in sight, was discovered on board the *Flying Fish*, and upon the *Europa* opening the south point of the Mole, several armed vessels were seen in chase of her, but which returned to the town immediately, by which circumstances Lieutenant Prevost was enabled to join me, and from whom I was informed that the major, with three other French gentlemen, a midshipman, and boat's crew, had been taken in landing by an armed schooner, and carried to the town, from which I drew a conclusion not very favourable to our views, and the day passed in silent apprehension for the major's safety; but about five P.M. a gun was fired from Presqu'ille, and with joy I discovered a private signal which I had previously concerted with the French officer; on which I approached the battery as near as possible, under the necessary precautions, and about nine o'clock a boat came off with several officers belonging to Dillon's regiment, with professions of friendship and fidelity to the King of Great Britain; at the same time assuring me, that unless they received immediate support all would be lost; that the Blacks and Mulattoes at Jean Rabel, amounting to 8 or 10,000, were expected every hour to attack them; that the inhabitants, from severe duty and extreme misery, were divided, and relaxed into despondency, and in contemplation to fly to America, and that their goods were embarked in the vessels in the port for that purpose; that the troops of the line (through the intrigues of the civil commissaries) manifested strong symptoms of a general mutiny; and that they had sent fifty-five mutineers of Dillon's regiment to Charlestown the day before: from these circumstances I evidently saw that no time was to be lost, and I determined from that moment to try what could be done with the force of the squadron; to which end I sent the officers on shore to get the capitulation sighed (it being exactly the same as that of Jeremie, with the addition of the last article respecting the officers and troops of the garrison), with which they returned soon after daylight in the morning; and having publicly accepted it on the quarter-deck; with *Vive le Roi de Angleterre*, and three cheers on each side, I proceeded to the anchorage without hesitation, hoisted the British flag on several batteries, and took possession of the town and its dependencies (the parish of Bombarde and Platform included) in the name of his Britannic Majesty, with the marines of the *Europa*, commanded by Captain Robinson, an officer of distinguished merit and abilities in his profession, and whom I have directed to act as brevet-major for the present, in order to give him superior rank to the late commandant, till General Williamson can make the necessary arrangements, holding 200 seamen in readiness to land, if necessary, at a moment's warning; and I have the satisfaction of informing their Lordships, that we are

Platform Bay, Cape Nichola Mole, St. Domingo. Engraved by Hall, from a drawing by Hamilton, in the possession of the Right Honourable Earl of St. Vincent. ^{Plate 262}

in full possession of the finest harbour in the West Indies, guarded by batteries incredibly strong. An account of the ordnance, ammunition, and military stores in the magazines, you will receive herewith.

Europa, Mole of Cape St. Nicholas, October 27, 1793
In addition to my letter of the 26th ult. you will be pleased to inform their Lordships, that the *Flying Fish* schooner, which I sent to Colonel Whitelocke at Jeremie with a requisition for a small force for present, returned on the 28th ult. with the grenadier company of the 13th regiment; and his Majesty's ships *Penelope* and *Iphigenia* arrived on the 11th and 12th instant from Jamaica, with five companies of the 49th regiment, commanded by Lieutenant-colonel Dansey, whom Governor Williamson has appointed commandant of this district.

The annexed plate represents the *Magicienne*, Captain Ricketts, and the *Drake* brig, as engaged in dislodging a body of brigands, who had established themselves in Platform bay, about seven leagues to the westward of Cape Nicola Mole, St. Domingo. This action, so creditable to the officers of his majesty's ships, took place early in the year 1798; and is fully described in our "Memoir of the public services of the late Captain W.H. Jervis."

Martinique. At the suggestion of many of our Friends, and with the kind assistance of Mr. Arrowsmith, we intend *occasionally* to introduce such portions of hydrography as will correct the errors that have long existed in former maps and charts. Mr. Arrowsmith has favoured us with all the French West India Islands, on three plates; the first of which, Martinico, we now insert. The beauty and accuracy of the engravings speak sufficiently for themselves. Plate 180

Jervis's Command
From the 'Biographical Memoir of John Jervis, Earl of St. Vincent, K.B.'
IV 12-31

[In December 1793 John Jervis, then Vice-Admiral of the Blue,] accepted the command of a squadron equipped for the West Indies, and destined to act in conjunction with a formidable land force, sent thither at the same time, under Sir Charles Grey, against the French settlements in that quarter.[1]

The whole armament having rendezvoused at Barbadoes, operations were immediately commenced by an attack on the valuable island of Martinico. It fell after a short, but very vigorous contest: and this success proved the prelude to as speedy a reduction of the islands of St. Lucia and Guadaloupe. Thus did Great Britain, almost with astonishment, behold herself in possession of all the French colonies in that quarter, nor did there appear the smallest probability that any of them could ever be wrested back from her during the continuance of the existing contest. Strange, however, and almost incredible, are the events of war: a petty armament, not exceeding four ships of

---

1 On this occasion he vacated his seat in parliament. On the first of February in the preceding year, he had been advanced to the rank of Vice-Admiral of the Blue Squadron.

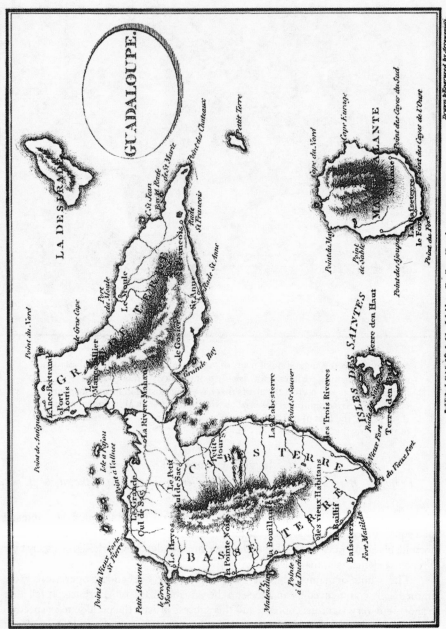

war, the largest mounting only fifty guns, and five transports having on board about 1500 troops, had the address and good fortune to elude the vigilance of the British commanders, and reach Guadaloupe in safety.

This event, so totally unexpected, gave a sudden and fatal turn to the issue of the campaign. But the reverse of fortune was not attributable in the slightest degree to any neglect or misconduct of the two gallant conquerors, whose exertions had hitherto been so uninterruptedly crowned with success. Not the smallest information had reached them that such a force was on its passage; not, considering the state of the French Navy at that time, contrasted with that of Britain, could it have been deemed probable, or perhaps possible, that France could have been rash enough to expose a squadron which, inconsiderable as it was, proved of no small public value, to the double risk of being captured the instant it quitted its own ports; or, should it escape that first danger, of being exposed to a second no less formidable, ere it could arrive at its place of destination. Its safe arrival, however, and subsequent success, may serve as a very useful and instructive lesson to mankind, that the events of war frequently defy the utmost human sagacity, being conducted and governed by the hand of Providence alone.

This reverse of fortune furnished an opportunity for various discontented persons, many of whom smarted under that rigid conduct of the Commanders in Chief towards them, which their own behaviour had occasioned, to join that description of people in England, which exists in all countries whatever, ready to seize every opportunity of aggravating misfortune, though by the most unjustifiable means.

Calumny repelled with honour and with effect, renders the character of the person against whom its envenomed shafts were unjustly directed, more brilliant, at least in the public eye, than it stood before the aera [sic] of the invidious attack. ... All ranks of men appearing as if ashamed of their first folly, vied with each other who should pay them the greatest honour. A public entertainment was given to the joint Commanders by the Grocers' Company; the freedom of which, as well as of several others, and above all, that of the city of London itself, was unanimously voted them.

Journal of the Proceeding of a Squadron of His Majesty's ships,[2] under the Command of Sir John Jervis, K.B., employed in conjunction with a Body of Troops, under the Command of Sir Charles Grey, K.B., to reduce the French Colonies in the Leeward Islands, 1794, and 1795. XVII 312-317, 388-393, 473-479, XVIII 45-47

From the MSS of a naval officer
After waiting nearly a month beyond the time expected for the fleet's sailing, we put to sea from St. Helen's, having left several of the ordnance vessels behind, with the *Quebec* frigate, Captain Rogers, who had orders to bring them out to join the squadron, with all possible dispatch.[3]

One cause, among others, which apparently stopped the early sailing of our squadron, was the expedition then on foot, and at that time ready to sail, under the command of Admiral M'Bride and Lord Moira, against the coast of France. Eight regiments, destined for the West India Expedition, were taken from the command of Sir Charles Grey, and sent upon that fruitless enterprize, so contrary to the known

An accurate map of the Island of Guadaloupe, in the West Indies. Drawn and engraved by Arrowsmith. Plate 198 interest of our country, according to the opinion of those persons who have known them best; and so constantly deprecated by the worthiest and wisest of the kingdom, who have had sense enough to perceive, that our genius and our situation were not fitted to continental wars, where the numbers of the enemy must always carry success with them; and that small expeditions against a country so peopled, and so warlike, must, according to all rational calculation, turn out to our disadvantage.

In our passage down Channel, we met Commodore Paisley in the *Bellerophon*, with two other ships of the line, who gave us intelligence that Lord Howe, with the British fleet, was to the westward; and that they had made an unsuccessful chase after four or five line of battle ships of the enemy, who had got into Brest, notwithstanding all his Lordship's exertions to prevent it, being favoured by the darkness of the night, and the wind.

When off Madeira, having foul winds, blowing very hard; Sir J. Jervis, with the *Boyne*, and several of the forty-gun ships, left us with the convoy under the command of Commodore Thompson, (who then hoisted a broad pendant,) to make our passage, by constantly standing to the westward, whilst he stood to the eastward. On our arrival at Barbadoes, the 10th day of January, 1794, we found Sir J. Jervis had arrived a few days before. Two or three days afterwards came in the *Irresistible*, with transports from Ireland: different frigates were dispatched to Tobago, and the other Islands, to collect all the troops which could be spared. The *Veteran*, Captain C.E. Nugent, was ordered to bring up the 9th regiment from Grenada, and St. Kitt's: on their arrival at Grenada, the *Ulysses* had just landed a part of the 9th, and was going to join Sir J. Jervis, with a part of another regiment, which they had relieved. The *Thetis*, and another transport, brought down the 56th regiment, very sickly, under convoy of the *Veteran*, with orders

2

Ships	Guns	Commanders			
Basse Terre					
Boyne	98	Vice-Admiral Sir John Jervis	*Dromedary*	44	S. Tatham
		Captain G. Grey	*Undaunted*	28	J. Carpenter
Irresistible	74	J. Henry	*Avenger*	18	Griffiths
Veteran	64	C.E. Nugent	*Nautilus*, sloop	18	Bowen
Roebuck	44	A. Christie	Point Petre		
Assurance	40	V.C. Berkley	*Experiment*	40	S. Miller
Woolwic	40	J. Parker	*Beaulieu*	40	E. Riou
Blanche	32	R. Faulknor	With Rochambeau		
Winchelsea	32	Lord Viscount Garlies	*Vesuvius*, bomb	8	
		(Gone to Mariagalante)	Gun-boats, with one 24-pounder		
Terpsichore	32	S. Edwards	*Spiteful, Venom, Spitfire, Teaser, Tickler*		
Rose	28	W.H. Scott	Gone with Expresses to England		
Reprisal	18	Young	*Blonde*	32	J. Markham
Inspector, sloop	18	Briger	*Rattlesnake*	18	D. Preston
Bulldog, ditto	18	E. Browne	*Sea Flower*	14	W. Pierrepoint
Fort Royal			To St. Thomas's		
Vengeance	40	Rear-Admiral C. Thompson	*Quebec*	32	J. Rogers
Asia	64	J. Browne	*Ceres*	32	R. Incledon

3 The squadron sailed from St. Helen's, November 27, 1794; and landed at St. Anne's Bay, February 5. Pidgeon Island surrendered four or five days afterwards; St. Pierre's taken, February 17; took possession of the heights of Soubrine, February 19; Fort Royal stormed, March 20; landed at St. Lucia, April 2; anchored at the Gozier, Guadaloupe, April 10; Fleur d'Epée stormed, April 12; landing of the troops and sailors at the Ance de vieux Habitants, April 15; taking of Morne Hoel, April 19; capitulation of Fort Charles, April 22; sailed from Guadaloupe in the Santa Margaretta, April 24.

to leave part at Grenada, and part at St. Kitt's. Having embarked that part of the 9th brought by the *Ulysses*, we returned again to join Sir John Jervis, and looked into Caz Navires Bay, Martinico, and into Gros Islet, St. Lucia, that we might join the squadron as soon as possible, if they were already arrived there; and finding they were in neither of those places, we hauled our wind for Barbadoes.

Next morning, then sixteen leagues to leeward of that island, we spoke a brig, and found that the fleet were already sailed. We then made sail again for Martinico; and, not meeting with the squadron, in the evening made all the sail we could for Barbadoes; and to our great joy, in the night, about 12 o'clock, we saw the Admiral's light, and soon after the fleet; but not being certain that it was our own, as they had been from Barbadoes already two days, we hauled in for St. Anne's Bay until day-light; and then found our fleet standing in for the land. All the next day we were working into the bay; and did not land the troops until late in the night of that day, being the 7th of February.

The 9th, under the command of Major Baillee, were landed earlier, to spike the guns of a battery which was very troublesome; and re-embarked in the *Veteran* as soon as that service was over. The troops under Sir Charles Grey marched along shore the next morning, to the Bourg de la Rivière Salée, and a large body invested Pidgeon Island, which surrendered two days afterwards. Sir John then went with the *Boyne* to the Grande Ance d'Arlef, for the sake of keeping up a more certain communication with the army; and the frigates, with the *Irresistible*, landed a large body of troops at Caz Navires.

Whilst these operations were going on, General Dundas, with Commodore Thompson, went round to [Gallion Bay][4] at the back of the island, and landed a large body of troops; which, after taking the posts and ports adjacent, marched and took possession of Gros Morne. General Dundas then marched to Port le Martre, to complete the investiture of Fort Bourbon; whilst Sir Charles Grey marched round the bay of Fort Royal, and Sir Charles Gordon from Caz Navires invested it on the other side. The fleet then pushed into Fort Royal Bay, and the seamen were landed, part at Caz Navires, and part at the Cul de Sac de Cohé, to get the cannons and mortars up the heights, meaning to besiege that important post.

Whilst these operations were carrying on, the *Veteran*, with the transports, &c. from St. Anne's Bay, arrived. Captain Nugent was immediately ordered, with the *Rattlesnake*, *Zebra*, and *Roebuck*, to run down to St. Pierre; and there take into the squadron, the *Blonde* and *Nautilus*, for the purpose of co-operating with General Dundas in the reduction of that place: the *Vesuvius* bomb was also sent with this detachment. The first day we were employed in cruising off the port, to prevent any of the vessels of the enemy from attempting to escape; and the next day passed in the same way. The squadron was soon reinforced by the *Asia*, Captain Brown; and in the evening Colonel Symmis came on board, who was to have the command of the troops, and seamen, intended for an attack to the westward of the town, to assist in drawing off the attention of the enemy from the ports, which were to be forced by General Dundas in his march towards St. Pierre's: another body of men were also expected, under Sir C. Gordon, from the eastward.

The *Veteran*, on going in to reconnoitre the enemy's batteries, received a fire from two batteries in the town, on the east side; one on the right; the other, called Corbet,

4 Here the MS cannot be deciphered, but a reference to our map of Martinico, (Vol. XIII, page 474,) points out Gallion Bay as the place where General Dundas landed.

was a gun and mortar battery, at some small distance from the town, to the eastward. She also reconnoitred a landing place to the westward, near the bed of a river, defended by a small battery, with two guns only, out of reach of point blank shot from Fort St. Marc, and also from a battery to the westward; and, besides, sufficiently secure for the landing of the troops, as was intended during the night.

On the night of the 16th, the troops having embarked in the flat-bottomed boats, the *Vesuvius* bomb was ordered in to bombard the town, under cover of the *Blonde*, and the *Santa Margaretta*; which service was performed by Captain Sawyer, as well as the nature of it would allow: it being impossible to approach the town sufficiently, or to come to an anchor near it, without great danger from the forts and batteries that lined the Bay, whose cross fire would soon have obliged her to sheer off. The captain of the *Vesuvius* was thus obliged to direct his fire as well as he could under sail, and as near as possible without the point blank range of their shot.

The three sloops of war, the *Zebra*, *Nautilus*, and *Rattlesnake*, were to cover the landing of the troops, at four o'clock, when the three-gun battery was silenced; but from some delay, they did not land until five. The *Veteran*, Captain Nugent, had silenced this battery early in the night; and soon after, being close off the west end of the town, the batteries ceased their fire, and a flag of truce was sent off for the purpose of capitulation; but the *Veteran* unluckily having fired several shot into the town, from her lower deck, the flag of truce returned, and did not come off again until the morning; when the *Veteran* and *Asia* came to, close within pistol shot of the town. An officer was sent to Fort St. Marc, and la Boutoile, to strike the French colours, and hoist English. It was some hours before Colonel Symms got into the town with the troops under his command. General Dundas did not arrive until the evening; and Sir C. Gordon not until next day.

A ludicrous incident occurred on this service. - As I was going from the municipality to visit the town, and the batteries to the westward, a flag of truce from General Dundas came in; and I was much astonished to find that the ships had anchored there five hours before. I forgot to mention, that the flag of truce which was sent off at day-break from the town, brought a letter to the commanding officer of the navy, desiring to capitulate; which was answered by saying, that they must surrender at discretion.

The *Veteran*, Captain Nugent, after remaining some time at this place, to regulate the business of the prizes, and the prisoners, returned to Fort Royal with the *Blonde*, carrying five hundred men, under General Dundas, to reinforce the besieging army under Sir Charles Grey: or rather to take post on the heights towards Mount Tartenson. It is impossible to do justice to the perseverance, and industry, of the troops and seamen, on this attack of Fort Bourbon, which lasted about six weeks. The seamen under the command of Captains Nugent and Rogers, were of so much use, in all the heavy work of dragging up cannon and mortars, through roads deemed before that event totally impracticable; that it has been frequently owned by the Commander in Chief, that it would have been impossible to succeed without their exertions. But great as those exertions were, it is doubtful what the event of this siege would have been, but for the change which latterly took place in the mode of attack; as, during the whole of the siege, notwithstanding the fire constantly kept up from all our batteries, very little impression had been made on the fort. They had lost, it is true, between three and four hundred men, before the storm of Fort Royal; but as long as they kept up the communication between Fort Bourbon and the town of Fort Royal, they had such constant supplies of arms and ammunition, of men and provisions, added to the advantage of casements, only open to fire from Fort Louis; that little success could be expected, without first cutting off the supplies which they obtained from this place. The event proves the truth of this conjecture; for as soon as our seamen got possession of Fort Royal, they sent out a flag of truce to capitulate: though, on marching out, they amounted to nine hundred men, who laid down their arms.

Monsieur de Sansi (a great friend of the Marquis de Bouelli, who had had the merit of superintending the plan formed by that able general in the attack of this island) was the first mover of the detail of this latter attack. A battery was formed under his direction, by the seamen, in which were mounted two 24-pounders; and another close to it, of one 24, and one eight inch howitzer. These two batteries having dismounted all the guns on this front of attack of Fort Louis, and another battery being raised in Mount Tartenson, of five 24's; and another close by the Prince's quarters,[5] which dismounted all the guns upon the [Not made out in the MS] at Fort Louis, and the upper batteries of that fort; the Asia and Zebra were ordered to prepare to enter the harbour, or careenage, close under the walls of the fort, to cover the boats which were already prepared to storm the place.

Commodore Thompson had the direction of this attack. The Asia, from unaccountable accidents, could not get in:[6] but the Zebra performed her part of the plan with great gallantry and judgment: and having placed herself under the wall, within pistol-shot; having first borne the fire from two or three guns before she went in; she covered the landing of the boats, commanded by Captains Nugent and Riou; which having for some time received the fire of grape, and round shot, from the Fort, before the Zebra got in, pushed across the Careenage, stormed the Fort, and took possession:[7] Captain Nugent, with the Veteran's people, hauled down the French colours, and hoisted the English. The admiral did Captain Nugent the honour to appoint him, with the consent of the general, to the command of the fort; and Captain Nugent employed himself in preparing two mortar batteries, of three thirteen-inch mortars each, in case the general should not agree to the terms of capitulation, to play into their casements, which were only open to that point of attack. - Three or four days after the capture of Fort Royal, the capitulation being signed, which gave the garrison the honours of war, and a passage to Europe; and to Rochambeau a passage to Rhode Island in America; the garrison marched out between a file of the troops, and seamen, which lined all the way from the Fort to the Parade, at Fort Royal. Captain Nugent had the honour of hoisting the English colours at Fort Bourbon, with General Whyte; as he had that of hoisting them himself at Fort Royal, or Fort Louis. The Veteran's seamen were placed next to

5 His Royal Highness Prince Edward, Major-General, since created Duke of Kent, who greatly distinguished himself. The town of Fort Royal was changed to Fort Edward, in honour of this prince.

6 According to Schomberg, the Asia failed of success, owing to the ci-devant Lieutenant of the port, M. de Tourelles, who had undertaken to pilot her in. See also our memoir of Captain Faulknor. Editor.

7 Sir John Jervis, in his public letter, mentions Captain Faulknor having taken possession of Fort Royal. It is true his sloop was the first which ran into the harbour, and served as a cover to the boats; but Captains Nugent and Riou stormed the fort with nearly twelve hundred men in boats, and they took possession of the fort. - This is directly contrary to received opinion. Captain Schomberg, in his Chronology, says, "that Captain Faulknor took the Fort at the head of his ship's company, before the boats could get on shore, though they rowed with all the force and animation, which characterize British seamen in the face of an enemy." - We, however, feel it our duty not to deviate from the MS, or to omit this passage; owing to the very respectable quarter whence it came to us. In the memoir of Admiral Nugent (Vol. X page 464) it is affirmed, that Captain Faulknor was the first person on the walls, and Captain Nugent the second, and that the Lieutenant of the cutter hauled down the colours. - Editor

the gate, and had the honour of taking possession of the fort, with the sixth regiment: this fort was taken possession of three days after the capture of Fort Royal, which was on the 20th day of March, 1794.

The prisoners being embarked in three transports, and set off for Old France; and Rochambeau being sent off in the *Vesuvius* bomb, which had landed her mortars; and the light infantry and grenadiers being embarked in the ships of war, the transports not being thought capable of getting to windward sufficiently to fetch Gros Islet, opposite which was meant to make the first landing; (General Prescot being left with the chief command of the island of Martinique, and a sufficient garrison for the defence of the chief forts of that island;) we set sail on the first of April, and on the second made several landings on St. Lucia: one under General Dundas near Gros Islet; another near the Islet du Choe, to windward of the Careenage; and another under the Prince, at the Cul de Sac des Roseaux. The same night another landing took place under Colonel Coote, at the Grand Cul de Sac; into which harbour the ships anchored next day. The next night Colonel Coote attacked a redoubt close to the fort; and having spiked the guns, and put all the guard, to the amount of forty men, to the bayonet, retired to the post which he had occupied near the Grand Cul de Sac. A summons was then sent to General Ricard, saying that it was meant to storm Mount Fortuné that night, and to desire him to deliver up the fort. The general, as governor of the island, refused this; and answered, *That he was determined to die in the defence of his post, and that all his garrison was equally determined.* The seamen were then ordered to be landed from the fleet, with the scaling ladders, which had been brought in the *Veteran* from Martinique: but the old general sent a flag of truce in the evening, to say, that his garrison had deserted him; and to demand what terms the commanders in chief would give *to an old man, who had served his king faithfully nearly forty years: whose troops had deserted him, and who then lay at their mercy.* As this old respectable man had an universal good character, had been a *Marechal du Camp* in the ancient government; and was respected by every class, to whom he had taken every opportunity of being kind; as he had prevented all sorts of licentious conduct whilst he had been governor, and had equally protected all parties; had borne himself with uncommon moderation in every particular; the commanders in chief were melted by his message, and gave him, and the small remnant of his garrison which had remained with him, all the honours of war; and leave for him to remain in the island, and even to go to England, if he chose; where the general promised to recommend him to the protection of the ministry.

Sir Charles Gordon being left with the 6th and 9th, as governor of St. Lucia; the admiral embarked the troops, and returned to Martinique, to put them into the transports, and to take with him, for the attack of Guadaloupe, some howitzers, and other light artillery, which probably might be found useful in the attack. Here the commodore remained with the *Vengeance* and the *Asia*; and the rest of the fleet, transports, &c. sailed for Guadaloupe. The *Quebec, Winchelsea,* and *Blanche,* were set to attack the Saints;[8] and in the morning, as we passed, we found they had got possession. On these islands were two forts commanding the anchorage, which is very good under the lee of them; and which was essential to possess, to shelter any transports, that in the passage from Martinique might not be able to fetch to windward of them, as the currents run very strong at times here; and they would in such cases, without that anchorage, be drawn totally to leeward of the Island of Guadaloupe.

8 Isle des Saintes. See Map of Guadaloupe, Vol XV page 136.

The *Boyne* and *Veteran* fetched into an anchor, with some others, chiefly forty-fours, very near the Gozier; where was a small fort of two guns. The *Winchelsea* being ordered to bring to before this fort, to cover the landing, Lord Garlies performed this service in a most masterly manner: under the cover of whose fire, we landed the troops upon a small piece of sand, on which there was such a surf, that it was with some difficulty we could preserve the boats from being stove to pieces. The *Veteran*'s pinnace, or barge, was totally lost: and a long boat and several of the flat boats were much damaged; but the landing was effected without any other loss. The enemy had spiked the guns in the Gozier battery before we got into it; and the principal inhabitants of the village had got off into the country. Our people were quartered in the town the whole of that night and the next day; and on the night following we marched against Fleur d'Epée.

But before I enter into a detail of this, I must make some remarks on the utility of the flannel clothing to the troops, and the sailors, on this expedition; so contrary to the ideas of most, who have not been much acquainted with a warm climate. It preserves from cold, and fever, and is the most beneficial clothing that can be provided for troops intended for expeditions against any places situated in a warm climate. The flux is kept off by it, and the rains are not so prejudicial, as they otherwise would be to the constitution. I must also make another remark before I go on: which is with respect to the very pernicious way of dealing out medicine to the seamen of His Majesty's fleet.[9] The surgeon of the ship pays for his medicines, and deals them out in scanty proportions to the sick under his care. We had fifty sick on board of the *Veteran* in fevers, and had it not been that the captain had luckily made a large provision of bark before he set off from England, many of those poor fellows would have died for want of medicine. Often has an application been made, for a small proportion of that bark bought by government, to be dealt out to the sick of the *Veteran*, but no attention was paid to our wishes on that point. Another subject of complaint is, that the officers who serve on shore have not the same advantages which the officers of the army have on such occasions. Beer or forage money, always given to the army on these occasions, has been refused to the navy; only because no precedent could be pointed out for it. . . . This is also a service which occasions an additional expense to the sailor: his shoes are worn out in a few days, which otherwise would last him many months: the fatigue is great, and the service is new; and as he performs it with cheerfulness, some little additional gratification should be given to him on such occasions, that he might not have reason to repine.

About twelve o'clock that night, being, as far as I remember, the 11th of April, General Dundas with the light infantry, joined by Captain Neville's fifty marines, and two hundred seamen from the *Veteran* and the *Winchelsea*, marched off in one column by the road which leads through the post, under which we had reconnoitred the preceding day, in order by day-light to get under the Fleur d'Epée; with two other columns, one under Colonel Symms, and the other under the Prince: the former marching by a road nearer to the sea coast, and the latter taking partly the road of one column, and turning off midway by another road between the two. On approaching the first post, the centinel alarmed the guard, and they were ready to receive us, as we advanced. The men had all the flints out of their muskets, and most of our seamen having nothing but pikes, there was no fear of giving too early an alarm; and they were soon upon the enemy, and in possession of their post; advancing in silence dead as the night, amidst a shower of

9 This is altered at present as the surgeons are allowed medicines by government.

The view which is here given, from a drawing by Mr. Pocock, of the attack upon the town and fortress of Basse Terre, in the Island of Guadaloupe, on the 23d of January, 1759, may be considered as illustrative of an interesting action in the life of the late Admiral Sir John Moore. [Plate 217]

musketry, into the battery. We lost fourteen or fifteen men, killed and wounded; but the enemy making off in good time, only three were taken. The order, discipline, silence, and perfect obedience of the men, never were more exemplified than in this little attack. Not a whisper was heard along the line of march: but every man watched his second, in order to keep close up; that they might, in case of need, be ready to succour those, who, from their situation in the column, were naturally the first in the attack. I never passed through such defiles; such a country so capable of defence: in which all owned, that fifty good and true men might have destroyed our little army on its march, long before they could have reached this post. Lieutenant Whitlock was left with the marines, and one company of seamen, to guard this post; and we pushed on with the general, and the rest of the column, to our destination under Fleur d'Epée. Just as we arrived there, and the day dawned, the storm began, amidst a most tremendous shower of musketry; some parts were more easy of ascent than others, but the part allotted to the seamen was scarcely practicable.

About one hundred and fifty men were killed and wounded, in the storm; most of them killed; their retreat being cut off by the fort's having been attacked in so many quarters: one man, apparently an officer, I shall ever remember; he seemed to have smiled as he died; to have had an infinite satisfaction in dying for his country, and his principles; 'twas dreadful that such bravery, and resolution, were not employed in a better cause. Strange as it may appear, all the features of this corpse had a smile upon them. I was mentioning this circumstance to Sansi; and Grand Pré, who was with us the whole of this campaign ever since the taking of Fort Royal, told me he had remarked the same thing of a corpse, and that it had fixed him to the spot some time as it were with admiration: this effect it had very strongly. I was lost in amazement for some minutes.

This was perhaps a very necessary piece of severity, with a view to the future conduct of the enemy which we had to encounter, in the other part of this double island: as they had, knowing the natural clemency and mildness of the English, defended themselves always to the last, with the hope of being able to save their lives at the very last extremity. We had thus a probability, by this example, of intimidating them, and preventing them from holding out; as the shortening of a business of this nature, prevents our own people from dropping off by sickness, which a much longer continuance of this campaign would have endangered. The ships' crews and troops were falling even at this time, the healthiest part of the year: and this may show what they had reason to expect in a later season of the rains.

Colonel Symms, just after the Fleur d'Epée was taken, went to drive the enemy from the town of Point à Petre, about four miles from the fort; and also from that, quite out of this part of the island, called Grande Terre, over the canal which separates it from Cabes Terre; and [I] found him with one of the *Veteran*'s companies under Lieutenant Conolly, and with the other under Lieutenant Cashman,[10] following at some distance. We pushed on to the town without any opposition. On arriving, I saw forty or fifty of the enemy in arms; pushing on, as I thought, to get into a battery commanding the town, of two or three guns: and then, having only twelve or fourteen men with me, I was forced to make the best of it, and hastening after them, we took possession of the. battery, and drove them entirely out of that part of the town . . . Colonel Symms and myself, immediately after this, collecting what few men we could, forced them down the road, where they had spiked two small field pieces, and drove them entirely out of the island. On both sides of this road is a morass almost impassable; though some I imagine had attempted to pass it, as we found a horse, belonging to some officer, sticking in the mud, though so deep, that with all our endeavours we could not extricate him. The enemy had just crossed the canal that separates the two islands, as we arrived; so that we had nothing to do but to return to Point à Petre, where we had a dinner with Sir Charles Grey, the Prince, Colonel Symms, and the whole corps. Mr. Herbert, of the *Veteran*, brought me the colours of the second battalion, the regiment de Guadaloupe, and which I gave to Sir Charles Grey: they were taken in the battery, which I mentioned before, by Mr. Herbert. Our seamen were re-embarked that night; and the day afterwards, the *Veteran*, under the command of Captain Harvey, with the *Irresistible*, and some frigates, with the light infantry in transports, under General Dundas, proceeded towards l'Ance des Vieux Habitants in Basse Terre; and on the night of the 15th of April, landed them, without opposition between that place and le Baillie; the ships being previously placed within pistol shot of the beach to protect the landing. The Prince, Sir Charles Grey, and Colonel Symms, had landed one day before this at the Petit Bourg; and luckily having marched along the coast to Troichien, a post capable of being defended by one hundred men against the whole army, they found it evacuated, and got an entrance into Basse Terre. In the mean while General Dundas, with a large body of seamen and marines, under the orders of Captain Nugent, who commanded the brigade of seamen, landed upon this expedition; by very fatiguing long marches, [they] got possession of the great and little Parks; whilst a battalion of infantry, detached the first night of our

---

10 This name perhaps not correct, being written very unintelligibly in the MS. *Vide Naval Chronicle*, Vol. III page 445. *et seq.*

landing, had secured the bridge, and the passes, which led to the Park, a post of as much consequence, and perhaps stronger, than the Palmiste; though not thought so by those who were then in the situation of defending the island.

The enemy had made *abattis* in every ravine at the passage over every river. - Two hundred men, with a good commander, might have rendered impassable many of the ravines in this march; and it would have been impossible even for General Dundas, who is reckoned the best officer we had on the service, to have found his way, with the small number of men he had under his command. . . . The only posts now remaining, were Morne Hoel, within half gun shot of the post we now occupied, and some posts on the Palmiste; which, when taken, it was supposed the Governor, who was not in Fort Charles, would capitulate. It grieved us much to see, as soon as we had surrounded the heights which commanded this fort and Basse Terre, that part of the town was set on fire: it continued to burn some time, and much of it was destroyed. We were led to believe that some negroes had done this; and it is true, that in passing through the town, soon after its surrender, I found some negroes lying in the street, who it was said had been shot [by the inhabitants] for having burnt the town: the Governor however was much suspected in this business. The night of April the 19th, 1794, the attack of Morne Hoel was determined. Colonel Blundell was to lead one column, and Captain Nugent was to command the other: the roads through which the troops and seamen marched, were very rugged, full of ravines, and in some parts almost impracticable: down one ravine particularly, thirty feet steep at least, and up another hill, which they were forced to climb up by the roots of trees for a great distance.[11] The battery l'Anglois was taken by Sir Charles Grey's column the night after the taking of Morne Hoel; and the next day all the forts upon the Palmiste, and Fort Charles, capitulated. On the 22d of April, 1794, the troops laying down their arms on the glacis, the Admiral, with the squadron, went into the road of Basse Terre; and Captain Nugent having joined his ship, removed all his goods and chattels into the Santa Margaretta, destined to go home with those who carried the expresses. He was superseded in the *Veteran* by a lieutenant from the *Boyne*, who had an acting order as captain. We took leave of our officers and ship's company with much regret; went on board the *Boyne* to receive orders from the Admiral, and immediately sailed for England, with the dispatches.

It was recommended by those most conversant with the situation of the French colonies, to endeavour to complete the reduction of those to windward, by the reduction of Cayenne: so that if the French should endeavour at any future period to arm against our new conquests, they would have no place to rendezvous for their squadrons: and another advantage, arising from this conquest, was the destroying a great nest of privateers, which would otherwise have been a great detriment to the trade of these, and the rest of our sugar colonies. Whether it was too late in the year, and that there were but troops sufficient to settle these conquests of the three islands of Guadaloupe, St. Lucia, and Martinique, and to garrison them afterwards; as indeed I believe is nearly the truth, the expedition was given up, at least I was made so to understand. St. Domingo also would have been embraced in the scheme of conquest, had there been any body of troops to be spared from these islands.[12] In my mind, two rules should have been laid

11 Colonel Blundell took possession of the fort at daylight.

12 After the reduction of these islands, General White was sent, with a body of troops, to assist in the conquest of St. Domingo: which was in a great measure the cause of the re-capture of Guadaloupe by the French, as it left so few troops to garrison that island.

down for our conduct there: - first, to admit none as emigrants, unless they could give a perfect and satisfactory account of the nature of their emigration; of their principles before they were driven off, and that they had at least some small property in the place: as many were driven off, not on account of their principles, which are as bad and as violent as those who remained; but from other motives totally unconnected with the great quarrel. The Noblesse of these Islands owed a great deal of money to the Bourgeoisie, whence originate the quarrel between the two; and this ended in those Noblesse being driven out. Another rule should have been adopted to drive out of these islands all those who had taken any active part: as the principles of their conduct are so rooted in their minds, that it is impossible that the mildest government will over eradicated them: and they will remain lurking in their haunts, ready to blaze forth, whenever the first spark of any future discord shall show itself.

The Mulattoes are the most dangerous of all; and the government will never be at peace, until they are totally driven out of the captured islands. The government have full powers to do this, notwithstanding the tenor of the manifesto, as very few came in before all their posts had been stormed; except the small garrisons who capitulated at two or three inferior posts.

To dwell on the scenes of horror that have been before us for four years in these islands, would require hearts as unfeeling as those which occasioned them: but I trust that the legislature will drain these conquests thoroughly of all the *Mauvais Sujets*; and that it will, by this means, root up the seeds of all future dissensions, and diminish the expenses of the government, by making it less necessary to leave large garrisons, which we can but ill afford for their protection.

Another thing should also be recommended in all these islands, as far as their situation might make it politic, or practicable: which is, to make a free port; and that should be as near the strong defences of the islands as it is possible; that, if attacked, the great mart, and all the richest magazines, might be within the protection of the strong posts. For instance, St. Pierre's was a free port, and it owes its consequence to that circumstance; whereas it would have been a much wiser policy, and will be so in us, to destroy that free port, and make a free port of Fort Royal, which is protected by Forts Bourbon and Louis. Thus, in case of invasion, when it would be necessary to concentrate the forces of the island; and it would be convenient to have only one port to defend, instead of two, very much detached from each other; (the communication from which, to each other, might be very easily cut off by an invading enemy;) less, much less would be sacrificed of the riches of the island, by withdrawing the troops from St. Pierre's; which would, if Fort Royal were a free port, dwindle into little more than a large village. At St. Lucie, Cartier [not plain in MS] seems to be the town fitted for a free port most of all others, being under the defence of Mont Fortuné, a post stronger by the nature of the ground than Fort Bourbon, being more difficult of approach; indeed scarcely to be approached at all: but on which there is now nothing but an unfinished redoubt; which indeed, if finished, would have been still the most miserable performance which the worst engineer ever devised; having no flank, or any line of defence, through the whole of it. And it seems to me, that no idea of throwing up defences in either island ever entered into their heads, until the alarm of Fort Bourbon being besieged took place in the rest of the islands: as we found that post, Fleur d'Epée, at Guadaloupe, and almost all the others, in every part unfinished, and so ill planned, that they seemed to have been recently formed by some engineer in a panic.

At Guadaloupe, Basse Terre is certainly a very proper place in which to concentrate the riches of that island: as the posts of the Palmiste, of Morne Hoel, and the Park, with the subordinate posts commanded by them, are near enough to command the town, and defend all the approaches to it: if also possessed of a pass leading from Cabes Terre to Basse Terre, without which an army can scarcely pass from one to the other; and which may be defended by a very small party, against a large army: these, with Morne Hoel, form the impracticable posts which defend Basse Terre: the Fleur d'Epée defends Grande Terre, and the approaches to Point à Petre: but an army might leave it behind, and burn that town, by proceeding through roads and passes, somewhat difficult; which may be passed, if we may judge from what we performed ourselves; but which certainly might be defended by a very small detachment of men, if they were conducted by able officers, against any numbers.

But certainly these posts are very, very much less capable of defence, than those of Basse Terre: so that I should choose, (to put it into the power of a small force to defend themselves, and as great a part of the riches of the island as possible, and as much of the magazines, &c.) to make Basse Terre also a free port; or to give that town some essential advantages over all the others in this island, to make it the interest of merchants to flock thither to establish their magazines.

I must also add, that on our passage to Barbadoes, and during the whole course of this expedition, we found that the people were much healthier, when they were served with wine, than when we gave them their allowance of spirits; which heated them, and made them much more liable to colds, and fevers, during the time they served in dragging up the guns; a very heavy work in the midst of frequent rains, which were very common during the siege of Fort Boubon; contrary to the general observations which I have had the opportunity of making of the weather, during five years I passed in the West Indies. At this season of the year, all the time of the rest of their service, we found that they endured much more fatigue, and were less liable to sickness, when served with wine, than grog: and double allowance of wine was generally given them during their heavy labours. We had a very good opportunity on our passage out, of observing the difference between the wine and the spirits; having received orders to serve alternatively wine and rum, a fortnight each. During the time the wine was served, the ship's company was in perfect good order, peaceable and laborious: but, on the contrary, when we served the rum, they were riotous and lazy; and punishment was necessary to keep them in good order. Whereas, it was unusual with us at other times to chastize any of them. The sick list, also, evidently increased on such occasions; and feverish complaints, and colds, were much more frequent: so much was this the case, that I broke through the order. The experience of the rest of the squadron justifies me in making this assertion; and I am well convinced, that government would do well to order wine sufficient for the companies of the different ships of the fleet, to be used instead of any thing else. If inducements may be wanting of the oeconomical kind, one might be alleged, that fewer men would be sent to the hospitals, and this saving would overbalance the additional expense: and now I am upon this subject, I must also say, that, according to my ideas, a small quantity of strong beer would be much more salutary to the people, than the immense quantity of bad small beer issued to the men on Channel service. And the same inducements might bring government into the measure: for I am well convinced, that the small beer issued to the men is very unhealthy, and particularly in cold weather, when they require something stronger to support themselves.

The companies of the ships of the squadron were also, whilst in the West Indies, served with cocoa and sugar, which made them a very comfortable breakfast, and must have conduced very much to the health of the people, as sugar is known to be a very great antiscorbutic. This was served them instead of butter and cheese; both which are very unwholesome in those hot climates, in the state in which they are served to the men, being generally very rancid and putrid: whereas the other both nourishes and dilutes, which is very necessary in the West Indies, where the heats are so excessive, and where the only safety is to keep up the perspiration.

The abilities of the French engineers appeared much greater, and more conspicuous, than our own: chiefly at Fort Bourbon, where they were most employed. And this occasion gratifies me much, as it recalls to my memory my very dear friend Sansi, whom I shall never forget . . . [13] The Commanders in Chief have every reason to recommend them to the government: Sir John Jervis has told me often, that they meant to do so. Sansi was the first mover of the Escalade of Fort Royal; and by thus changing the nature of the attack, which had been made originally in the nature of the siege of Fort bourbon, on which no impression had been made, though they had battered it for a month or nearly; and on which no impression would have been made, had they continued the fire from the batteries till now. He, as I said before, thus changing the nature of the attack, obliged Fort Bourbon to capitulate a day or two afterwards. His measures were bold beyond description, and full of energy.

At Fort Royal, during the siege of Fort Bourbon, several courts martial were assembled on board the *Vengeance*, Commodore Thompson; some on subjects of small moment, but others on crimes of a very serious nature: doubts arose about the legality of those courts; as none were summoned to sit, or did attend to take their seats, but the captains of such ships as were at Fort Royal; which were the *Vengeance*, the *Irresistible*, the *Boyne*, the *Veteran*, and the *Asia*; the commodore being president. But the objections were overruled: and, as little doubt was made that the strictest justice would attend the decisions of the court (though not composed strictly according to law), and as the exigencies of the service would have made it very unwise to call from their duties the captains of the different ships, who were detached from the flag, (though in sight at Cul de Sac, Cohè, and at Case Navire) the courts were holden without farther delay.

I myself cannot help thinking, that according to the meaning and interest of the statutes, the captains of these ships that were in sight at Case Navire, and the Cul de Sac de Cohè, should have attended. First they did not form (what is meant, in the articles of war, by the word detachments) any separate and distinct command, being within sight; and the admiral clearly did not understand or mean that they should be separated from him and his command, having frequently made their signals from the *Boyne*, which they repeated and answered, as they might very well, being within four or five miles of the flag. If ships in such a situation form detachments, the admiral has the power of *packing* a court martial whenever it pleases him; and I do not understand what is meant by the articles of war, which strictly limit the numbers, and point out the proper people who shall absolutely form such courts, and which seem intentionally to provide in such cases against the abuse of power which an admiral might assume, of forming courts martial of his own creatures and dependants only.

The articles say, that all the thirteen senior captains shall assist, and compose the court - the thirteen senior captains then present. - And now this brings to my memory an irregularity in the conduct of the commander in chief, which I always thought very

13 Sansi had a responsible situation given him in the island, as Superintendent of the Works, but it was taken away shortly afterwards, by the change of the Commander in Chief.

unwarrantable; though, in the midst of service, and till it was wholly fulfilled, I, as one concerned, did not choose to take notice of it: as, if any thing had happened to have rendered us unsuccessful in our attempts upon these islands, I know on such occasions the commanders are always ready to catch at any, the most trifling circumstances, to throw the blame of their own misconduct upon any one they find in their way. . . . A broad pendant was given to Captain Rogers at Case Navire, which was kept flying during the siege, in sight of the whole fleet; half of which were senior captains to him.

But to proceed to other subjects. When sailors are ordered upon this kind of service with the army, it would be proper, as already hinted, to have a very different species of slops issued to them, consisting chiefly of flannels, which in hot, as well as cold climates, are absolutely necessary. Flannel shirts, as well as drawers, worsted stocking, and strong course blue jackets, are the only clothing fitted for the nature of their service. I myself wore thick flannel in the midst of all the heats, and during the whole campaign on shore, as well as on board, and found that with it I could endure the greatest fatigue. I never found it immoderately hot, nor experienced any inconvenience from the flannel: on the contrary, I am convinced, that I was preserved by it from colds and fevers. Long marches in the heat of the day in a broiling sun never affected me; the flannel prevented the violent perspiration from being checked, and kept it up amidst dews and rains.

Our sailors were provided with flannel sheets, but unluckily they had only one each – a change would have been very necessary, and is almost indispensable.[14]

Two Accounts of Operations on Martinique and the Loss of Guadaloupe
From the 'Biographical Memoirs of Charles Edmund Nugent, Esq.' XX 462-467

We believe Captain Nugent remained unemployed till 1793, when the late war was commenced against the French Republic. On the 26th of December, in that year, Vice-Admiral Sir John Jervis sailed from Spithead, in the *Boyne*, of 98 guns, with a squadron of ships of war, having under his convoy a fleet of transports, with troops on board, commanded by General Sir Charles Grey, and destined for the West Indies. Captain Nugent sailed with this squadron, in the *Veteran*, a sixty-four gun ship. After a passage of nearly six weeks, the squadron arrived at Carlisle Bay, Barbadoes, whence they obtained a considerable reinforcement, and on the 3d of February 1794, proceeded to the attack of Martinico. Before the 16th of March, the whole island, excepting Forts Bourbon and Royal, was in possession of the English; and, it being determined to attempt the town and Fort Royal by assault, scaling ladders were prepared, and the *Asia*[15] and *Zebra*[16] were appointed to hold themselves in readiness "to enter the careenage, in order to batter the fort and to cover the flat boats, barges, and pinnaces under the command of Commodore Thompson, supported by Captains Nugent and Riou, while the grenadiers and light infantry from the camp at Sourierre, advanced with field-pieces along the side of the hill under Fort Bourbon, towards the bridge, over the canal, at the back of Fort Royal."[17] The result of this plan, which was successful in every part, excepting that of

14 This was written before the rainy season set in, which destroyed such numbers in despite of all precautions.
15 Of 64 guns, commanded by Captain Brown.
16 Of 16 guns, commanded by Captain Faulkner.
17 *Vide* Sir J. Jervis's Dispatches on the occasion.

the *Asia* getting into her station, will be seen by the following official letter from Commodore Thompson to Vice-Admiral Sir J. Jervis:

Fort Royal, March 20, 1794
Sir, I have the pleasure to acquaint you, that the only loss we have sustained in the capture of Fort Royal, is the pilot of the *Zebra* killed, and four seamen belonging to the same wounded. So soon as I perceived she could fetch in, I gave orders to Captains Nugent and Riou, who commanded the flat-boats, which, with the men embarked in them, were laying upon their oars, to push in and mount the walls; when every exertion was made, and the boats seemed to fly towards the forts. Captain Faulkner, in the mean time, in a most spirited and gallant manner entered the harbour through the fire of all their batteries and laid his sloop alongside the walls, there being deep water close to them; when the enemy, terrified at his audacity, the flat boats full of seamen pulling towards them, and the appearance of the troops from all quarters, struck their colours to the *Zebra*. A well-directed and steady fire from the gun-boats under Lieutenant Bowen, as also from our batteries, was of great service. The alacrity and steadiness of the Officers and seamen in general, under my command, was such, that I had not the least doubt of success against the whole force of the enemy, had they disputed our entrance.

The fort is full of ammunition and stores of all sorts; but the buildings are in a miserable condition, from the effects of our bombs, the gun boats, and batteries.

I have the honour to be, &c.

C. THOMPSON
Vice-Admiral Sir John Jervis, K.B. Commander in Chief, &c.

M. Rochambeau, who commanded in Fort Bourbon, having witnessed the success of the British arms at Fort Royal, sent out his aide-de-camp with a flag, offering to surrender on capitulation. Had this not been the case, however, the place must immediately have fallen by storm. Captain Faulkner, we believe, was the first person on the walls, and Captain Nugent the second. The Lieutenant of the latter hauled down the hostile colours; and during the negotiation, Captain Nugent held the command of the fort. The terms of surrender were adjusted on the 22d, and on the following day Captain Nugent, in conjunction with General Whyte, had the honour of hoisting the English colours, when the name of Fort Bourbon was changed to that of Fort George.

The whole of the loss sustained by the British Navy at Martinico amounted only to fifteen killed and thirty-two wounded.

To the reduction of Martinico immediately succeeded the capture of St. Lucia, without the loss of a single man.

The naval and military Commanders having left a sufficient number of troops for the protection of St. Lucia, returned thence to Fort Royal Bay, where they arrived on the evening of the 5th of April. On the morning of the 8th of the same month, Sir John Jervis, with the squadron, troops, &c. sailed to the reduction of Guadaloupe. For a clear and spirited detail of the particulars of this expedition, we must refer our readers to the following extract from Sir Charles Grey's dispatch to the Secretary of State, dated Point à Petre, April 12, 1794; briefly observing, that in the very desperate and hazardous service of carrying Fort Fleur d'Epée by storm, Captain Nugent, who, with Captain Faulkner, commanded a battalion of seamen, very eminently distinguished himself:

In my dispatch of the 4th instant, I had the honour to acquaint you with the success of his Majesty's arms in the conquest of the island of St. Lucia. Having left Sir C. Gordon to command in that island, I re-embarked the same day, and returned to Martinique the 5th instant, where we shifted the troops from the King's ships to the transports, took on board during the 6th and 7th, heavy ordnance and stores, provisions, &c. I sailed again in the morning of the 8th following. The Admiral detaching Captain Rogers with the *Quebec*, Captain Faulkner, with the *Blanche*; Captain Incledon, with the *Ceres*; and Captain Scott, with the *Rose*, to attack the small island called the Saints, which they executed with infinite gallantry and good conduct. Having landed part of the seamen and marines, and carried them in the morning without loss, the *Boyne* in which I sailed with the Admiral, and the *Veteran*, Captain Nugent, anchored off this place about noon, the 10th instant, and some more of the fleet, in the course of the afternoon; but a fresh wind and lee-current prevented most of the transports from getting in till yesterday, and some of them till this day. Without waiting, however, the arrival of all the troops, I made a landing at Grosier Bay at one o'clock in the morning of the 11th instant, under the fire of Fort Grosier and Fort Fleur d'Epée, with part of the first and second battalion of grenadiers, one company of the 43d regiment, and 500 seamen and marines detached by the Admiral, under the command of Captain George Grey, of the *Boyne*; the whole under the command of that able and vigilant Officer Colonel Symms, who had infinite merit in the execution of it; and the landing was covered by Lord Garlies, in the *Winchelsea*, his lordship having, with infinite judgment and intrepidity, placed his ship so well, and laid it so close to the batteries, that they could not stand to their guns, which were soon silenced. In effecting this essential service Lord Garlies was slightly wounded, and we did not suffer materially in any other respect. Some more of the troops arrived, and perceiving the enemy in considerable force and number at the strong situation of Fort Fleur d'Epée, I determined that no time should be lost in attacking them, and carried those posts by them at five o'clock this morning, under a heavy fire of cannon and musketry, although they were found infinitely strong, and changed the name of Fort d'Epée to Fort Prince of Wales; our troops being ordered, which was strictly obeyed, not to fire, but to execute every thing with the bayonet, having previously made the following disposition: The first division, under the command of his Royal Highness Prince Edward, consisting of the first and second battalion of grenadiers, and 100 of the naval battalion, to attack the Port in Morne Marigot. The second division, commanded by Major-General Dundas, consisting of the 1st and second battalion of light infantry, and 100 of the naval battalion, to attack the fort of Fleur d'Epée in the rear, and to cut off its communication with Fort Louis and Point à Petre. The third, commanded by Colonel Symms, consisting of the third battalion of grenadiers, and the third battalion of light infantry, and the remainder of the naval battalion, to proceed by the road on the sea-side, and to co-operate with Major-General Dundas. The detachments of the naval battalion, who were of the most essential service in those brilliant actions, were very ably commanded by Captains Nugent and Faulkner. The signal for the whole to commence the attack, was a gun from the *Boyne*, by the Admiral, at five o'clock this morning. The several divisions having marched earlier according to the distance they had to go, to be ready to combine and commence the attack at the same instant; and this service was perfected with much exactitude, superior ability, spirit, and good conduct, by the Officers who severally commanded these divisions, and every Officer and soldier under them, as to do them more honour than I can find words to convey an adequate idea of, or to express the high sense I entertain of their

Portrait of the late Captain
Robert Faulknor. Engraved by
Ridley, from a Miniature in the
possession of the Honourable
Elizabeth Stanhope. ^{Plate 208}

extraordinary merit on this occasion. The success we have already had, put us in possession of Grand Terre; also, with all possible expedition, to complete the conquest of this island. The return of the killed and wounded, and also a return of the killed and wounded, and prisoners taken, of the enemy, are transmitted herewith. The Commanding Officer of the Artillery had not brought the return of ordnance and ordnance stores taken, but they shall be transmitted by the next opportunity.

In this affair, the loss sustained by the English Army amounted to fifteen killed and forty-five wounded; by the Navy, two Midshipmen and eleven seamen wounded. The loss of the enemy was sixty-seven killed, fifty-five wounded and a hundred and ten prisoners.

The surrender of Basse Terre, by capitulation, comprehending the whole island of Guadaloupe, with its dependencies, immediately followed this successful achievement.

Captain Nugent was sent home with the dispatches, announcing the above event. He arrived in London on the 20th of May. In the letter from Sir John Jervis, of which he was the bearer, he is thus mentioned:

"Captain Nugent, who carries this dispatch, will recite many parts of the detail, which, in the various operations I had to concert, have escaped my memory. He served with the naval battalions at Martinique, St. Lucia, and in this island, and was present at many of the most important strokes."

Some time after Captain Nugent's return home, Captain Pakenham being extremely ill, and supposed to be dying, at Bath, he was appointed to his ship, the *Gibraltar*, of 80 guns; but about a fortnight after, to Captain Nugent's great surprise, Captain Pakenham came on board, perfectly well, and resumed the command.

During the suspension, and previously to the trial of Captain Molloy, in the spring of 1795, Captain Nugent commanded his ship, the *Caesar*, of 80 guns; after which, he was appointed to the *Pompee*, another eighty gun ship, which had been taken from the French at Toulon.

He proceeded with the *Pompee* to Spithead; but after he had seen her completely fitted, and after the Court-Martial on Captain Molloy had terminated, the First lieutenant of the *Caesar*, in compliance with the wishes of her crew, waited upon Captain Nugent, and solicited him to apply for the command of that ship. A stronger proof than this, of high respect and esteem for an Officer, can scarcely be given - a respect and esteem which Captain Nugent's conciliating conduct has ever entitled him to, and which he still holds in the service in an unabated degree. The flattering request was acceded to; Captain Nugent resigned the *Pompee*, and obtained the *Caesar*, in which ship he continued to be constantly employed in the Channel Fleet, until he received his flag, as Rear-Admiral of the Blue.

From the 'Biographical Memoir of the Late Captain Robert Faulknor.' XVI 27-45

On the 3d of February, 1794, Vice-Admiral Sir John Jervis, with his flag on board the *Boyne*, of 98 guns, Captain George Grey, sailed with a part of the fleet, and a large body of troops, under General Sir Charles Grey, to the attack of Martinico; and before the 16th of March, the whole of the island, excepting forts Bourbon and Royal, were in our possession. On the 17th, Lieutenant Bowen, of the *Boyne*, who had the command of the night guard, and gun-boats, nobly pushed into the careenage, and captured the *Bienvenu* frigate, under the severe discharge of grape shot and musketry from the ramparts and parapet of the fort. His gallantry, and the success which attended it, brought on an immediate attempt to take the town and Fort Royal by storm. Accordingly the *Asia*, of 64 guns, Captain J. Brown, and the *Zebra*, Captain R.W. Faulknor, were ordered to hold themselves in readiness to enter the careenage, and to cover the flat boats, barges, and pinnaces, that were under the command of Commodore Thompson, supported by Captains Riou and Nugent: a detachment from the army advancing at the same time along the side of the hill, under Fort Bourbon, towards the bridge over the canal, at the back of Fort Royal. Sir John Jervis in his dispatches adds as follows:

"This combination succeeded in every part, except the entrance of the *Asia*, which failed for the want of precision in the ancient Lieutenant of the port, Monsieur de Tourelles, who had undertaken to pilot the *Asia*. Captain Faulknor observing that ship baffled in her attempts, and the *Zebra* having been under a shower of grape shot for a great length of time, (which he, his officers and sloop's company, stood with a firmness not to be described, he determined to undertake the service alone; and he executed it with matchless intrepidity and conduct: running the *Zebra* close to the wall of the fort, and leaping overboard, at the head of his sloop's company, assailed and took this important post before the boats could get on shore, although they rowed with all the force and animation which characterize English seamen in the face of an enemy. No language of mine can express the merit of Captain Faulknor upon this occasion; but as every officer and man in the army and squadron bears testimony to it, this incomparable action cannot fail of being recorded in the page of history. The grenadiers and light infantry made good use of their field pieces and muskets; and soon after the surrender of the fort, took possession of the town, by the bridge over the canal at the back of it; while a strong detachment from the naval battalions at Point Negro, under the command of Captains Rogers, Scott, and Bayntun, in flat boats, barges, and pinnaces, approached the beach in front. Monsieur Rochambeau did not lose a moment, in requesting that Commissioners might be appointed to consider of terms of surrender; and the General and I named Commodore Thompson, Colonel Symes, and Captain Conyngham, to meet three persons named by him at Dillon's plantation, at nine o'clock on the 21st; and on the 22d the terms were concluded. The rapid success of His Majesty's arms has been produced by the high courage and perseverance of his officers, soldiers, and seamen, in the most difficult and toilsome labours; which nothing short of the perfect unanimity and affection between them and their chiefs could have surmounted. . . ."

The death of the pilot of the *Zebra*, which Commodore Thompson mentions . . ., was attended with some extraordinary circumstances, which have been preserved:

Captain Faulknor's collected mind, observing a visible confusion in the countenance of the pilot of the *Zebra*, when he received Captain Faulknor's orders to place the sloop close under the walls of Fort Royal; said to one of the officers - *I think Mr. _____ seems confused, as if he did not know what he was about. Was he ever in action before?* - "Many times Sir; he has been twenty-four years in the service." Captain Faulknor, however, being more convinced that his suspicion was well founded, went up to the pilot, and asked him some trifling question, to ascertain the real state of the case: when his agitation was such, as entirely to render him incapable of giving any answer. But he added in a low voice, and without raising his eyes to his noble Commander's face - *I see your honour knows me. I am unfit to guide her. I don't know what is come over me. I dreamt last night I should be killed; and am so afraid I don't know what I am about. I never, in all my life, felt afraid before.* Captain Faulknor, with that presence of mind which marked his character, and when all around was confusion and death, replied in a still lower tone: *the fate of this expedition depends on the helm in your hand - Give it me! and go and hide your head in whatever you fancy the safest part of the ship. But fears are catching: and if I hear you tell yours to one of your messmates, your life shall answer for it tomorrow.* -The poor fellow, panick struck, went away; and overcome with shame, sat down upon the arm chest; whilst Captain Faulknor seized the helm, and with his own hand laid the *Zebra* close to the walls of the fort: but before he had got upon them, at the head of his gallant followers, a cannon ball struck the arm chest, and blew the pilot to atoms. . . .

[Later, after serving with the squadron at Halifax, Captain Faulknor was to be a helpless spectator of the collapse of the British position on Guadaloupe.]

On leaving Halifax, His Royal Highness [Prince Edward] requested Captain Faulknor to send an account of the subsequent proceedings of the Army and Navy in the West Indies. The following is extracted from the fragment of a letter found amongst his papers; and will throw additional light on the history of a campaign, which has hitherto been very imperfectly given to the public.[18]

"Sir, In obedience to the commands of your Royal Highness, I embrace the earliest occasion of transmitting, as well as I have had the power to collect, the several events which have occurred since your Royal Highness left the West Indies.

The uncertain situation of a cruising frigate, and my being dispatched a few hours after the *Blanche*'s arrival to protect the north side of Guadaloupe, afforded me but little opportunity to make inquiry; and enables me still less to give a regular account, when such innumerable changes have arisen in so short a space of time. In reciting the unpleasing aspect of our affairs at this island, it will be impossible to prevent mentioning many painful circumstances: but when I contemplate the situation of this country in April last, where your Royal Highness had shone with such distinguished bravery and merit, and at the head of troops worthy of being thus led and inspired by the leader; what a sad reverse, now to behold the havoc of mortality, and the fruits of one unfortunate military error, which happened at Point à Petre, soon after the reinforcement had landed from France. That I may not, however, have reference to this out of its place, I will return to the period of my leaving Halifax, from whence I went in company with the *Alarm* to Boston; and being satisfied that the *Concorde* and *Perdrix* had not sailed, pursued

18 We have also a M.S. in our possession, drawn up by an officer who was present, which will be inserted in this Volume.

my orders from Admiral Murray, and made all the expedition in my power to join Sir John Jervis. But owing to contrary winds and calms, did not arrive at Guadaloupe until the 20th of October; and found the *Boyne* and *Terpsichore* at Basse Terre, the latter having joined the Admiral a short time before. The *Alarm* arrived two days after us, having parted company with the *Blanche* in the course of the passage.

I found the Admiral in good health and spirits. . . .

The Admiral had frequently written to America for the different frigates to return: but as he always put his signature at the corner of the letters, it was enough for the friendship and sagacity of the Americans; and if they were not opened, they were at least never allowed to be delivered. The *Terpsichore* got some intimation of this treachery, when she went into port; . . . and the other ships will soon be here. A short time previous to the *Blanche*'s arrival, our reduced camp near Petit Bourg, was obliged to capitulate, after sustaining many attacks from the enemy: the terms of this capitulaiton were such, I believe, as are usually given, except for the Royalists, for whom no proposition, or alternative could be obtained, or even listened to.

I pretend not to comment on these events: but I never understood that it was possible to extricate the small force Colonel ____ had with him, from the superiority of numbers, the advantage of situation, and the constitutional strength of the inhabitants and blacks, who are now become free, and armed throughout the island. The new French citizens have all the enthusiasm of freedom: and as if vindictive cruelty, and savage ferocity, were the consequence of a change of situation; these unhappy Royalists, of whom I have before spoken, when they were delivered up, experienced the most studied barbarity; being thrust into a ditch, and murdered in cold blood! Some were shot at; others staked; and the rest mangled in triumph, and unfeeling horror. Here the guillotine would have been an instrument of mercy.

At that season of the year, and thus situated, your Royal Highness must know the impossibility of another effort; and I conclude, in proportion as our abilities become enfeebled, the spirits of the enemy become elated: which, together with the mortality occasioned by the climate, and the depression mostly accompanying defeat, have produced the consequences I have already stated in the recent surrender of our camp in the vicinity of Petit Bourg; and left us no other possession on Guadaloupe, than the fort at Basse Terre, (Fort Matilda,) commanded by General Prescott, with a garrison of about 400 men; the Palmiste being entirely destroyed, and the guns and mortars burst, and rendered useless. The enemy opened their first battery of two guns, and a mortar from Morne Howel, the day after the *Blanche*'s arrival, and others were constructing on the hill which so immediately commands it . . ."

On the 10th of December, 1794, Fort Matilda, in consequence of the reinforcements which the enemy had received, was compelled to surrender to the republican arms. [Captain Faulknor was killed on 5 January, 1795, when his frigate, *Blanche* of 32 guns, engaged and eventually took *la Pique* frigate of 38 guns. On 4 April 1806 the House of Commons, despite the slight precedent for doing so in the instance of comparatively junior officers, voted to raise a monument to Captain Faulknor.

1794 – The Battle of the Glorious First of June

ECONOMIC COLLAPSE IN FRANCE, and the failure of the 1793 grain harvest, forced the French fleet to sea despite its problems with discipline and equipment. At Christmas 1793 Rear-Admiral Vanstabel sailed from Brest with two sail of the line and three frigates to escort home from Hampton Roads in Virginia a large convoy of grain ships and the West Indies trade. It took its departure again from America on 11 April, and on the same date Rear-Admiral Nielly sailed from Brest with five of the line to meet it. Finally, Rear-Admiral Villaret-Joyeuse sailed the main Brest fleet to bring the convoy safely in. Deputy Saint-André accompanied the fleet to ensure by his presence, and by the threat that any captain who failed to carry out his orders would be guillotined, that neither disaffection nor incompetence should imperil the convoy. The actions fought at the end of May and in the first days of June were a credit to the French National Marine and to the Royal Navy. It was Howe who was able to claim the tactical victory. His main concern was to prevent the French breaking away, which had been the preoccupation of a lifetime of tactical study. To secure his purpose he deliberately led the British fleet through the French line, first in line ahead, and then on the 1st, in line abreast. Strategically, on the other hand, the honours were less clear because the French did manage to deliver their convoy home.

The Naval Chronicle's lead report on the action formed the centrepiece of a biographical memoir of Earl Howe which was printed at the beginning of the first number in 1798. Later, biographical memoirs were inserted of many officers who had fought in the engagement, one of which, that of John Willett Payne, included a verbatim copy of a journal kept by an officer on board the *Russell*. Another journal was kept by John Thomas Duckworth, then commander of the *Orion*. From them can be seen Lord Howe's manner of employing the tactical signalling system he had done so much to develop. Many of the memoirs, however, merely repeated the material earlier inserted. The parts played in the battles by Sir Alexander

Hood, Lord Bridport, Sir Thomas Pasley, Bart, the Honourable George Cranfield Berkeley, Thomas Mackenzie, Esq, and by Cuthbert Lord Collingwood, are recorded in their biographical memoirs, but they add little to our understanding of events. Many notice the common complaint that Admiral Howe did not particularise their service in his official report (I 277-78, IV 362-64, XII 106-109, XV 361-364, XXXIII 368). This section closes with a letter to the editor by 'J.C.' written fifteen years later, when Admiral Lord Gambier faced a court martial for his conduct in Basque Roads, describing his earlier service.

List of Flag Officers in the Fleet, on the First of June 1794. [126]

Right Honourable Richard Earl Howe	Commander in Chief
Thomas Graves	Vice Admiral of the Red
Sir Alexander Hood	K.B. Ditto
George Bowyer	Rear Admiral of the White
Benjamin Caldwell	Ditto
Alan Gardner	Ditto
Thomas Pasley	Ditto
Sir Roger Curtis	First Captain to the Commander in Chief

British Line of Battle given by Lord Howe on sailing from St. Hellen's, May 2d, 1794

	Ships' Names	Guns	Captains
Niger, 32	Caesar	80	Captain Anthony James Pye Molley
Hon. A.K.	Bellerophon	74	Rear Admiral T. Pasley
Legge			Captain William Hope
(Repeater)	Leviathan	74	Rt. Hon. Lord Hugh Seymour
	Russel	74	Captain John Willett Payne
	Marlborough	74	Hon. George Berkeley
	Royal Sovereign	100	Admiral T. Graves, Captain Nicholls
	Audacious	74	Captain William Parker
	Defence	74	Captain James Gambier
	Impregnable	90	Rear Admiral B. Caldwell
			Captain George B. Westcott
	Tremendous	74	Captain James Pigott
	Culloden	74	Captain Isaac Schomberg
Latona, 32	Invincible	74	Honourable Thomas Pakenham
G. Thorn-	Barfleur	98	Rear Admiral G. Bowyer
borough			Captain Cuthbert Collingwood
	Arrogant*	74	Captain J. Hawkins Whitshed
Phaeton, 38	Theseus*	74	Captain R. Calder
W. Bentinck	Gibraltar	80	Captain T. Mackenzie

	Queen	100	Admiral Earl Howe
Southampton, 32	*Charlotte*		Captain Sir Roger Curtis, Knt
Hon. R. Forbes			Captain Sir And. Snape Douglas
	Brunswick	74	Captain John Harvey
	Valiant	74	Captain Thomas Pringle
Venus, 32	*Orion*	74	Captain John Thomas Duckworth
W. Brown	*Queen*	98	Rear Admiral Alan Gardner
			Captain John Hunt
Pegasus, 28	*Ganges**	74	Captain Truscott
R. Barlow			
(repeater)			
Aquilon, 32	*Ramillies*	74	Captain Henry Harvey
Hon. R.	*Bellona**	74	Captain George Wilson
Stopford	*Alfred*	74	Captain John Pazely
(repeater)	*Royal George*	100	Admiral Sir Alex. Hood, K.B.
			Captain William Domett
	Montagu	74	Captain James Montagu
	Majestic	74	Captain Charles Cotton
	Glory	90	Captain John Elphinstone
	*Hector**	74	Rear Admiral G. Montague
			Captain L.W. Halsted
	*Alexander**	74	Captain Richard Rodney Bligh
	*Thunderer**	74	Captain Albemarle Bertie

* These ships were detached to convoy the East India fleet on the 4th of May.

Accounts of the Action
From the 'Biographical Memoir of Earl Howe.' [1 19-23]

At length the moment arrived when such prudence and foresight, as his Lordship [i.e. Earl Howe] had firmly resolved to exercise, enjoyed the glorious regard which they merited. On the 19th of May 1794, he received the news, off Ushant, that the French fleet, under the command of Rear Admiral Villaret, with the representative of the people, Jean Bon St. André on board the Admiral's ship *La Montagne*, had left Brest.

The services which Lord Howe rendered his country, in the month of June 1794, give an added lustre to the evening of a life, that was early dedicated to the defence of Great Britain. We shall rather dwell on the predominant features of this great event, than enter into a minute detail of the action. Some parts have been misrepresented, and others have been indistinctly considered.

The bravery, and perilous situation of Lord Howe on the 29th of May, has been too much blended by the public, with his distinguished victory on the first of June. The future historian will be anxious to discriminate the various efforts of this intrepid spirit; that by viewing them in a separate light, he may justly appreciate their merit, and arouse posterity to an imitation of them.

Lord Howe,[1] about noon on the 29th of May, finding that the signal, which he had made for passing through the enemy's line, was not clearly understood by the headmost

1 From the notes of an officer on board a repeating frigate.

Portrait of the late Admiral Earl Howe, K.G. Engraved by Ridley, from an original painting. In the early part of our work, the Memoirs of several Naval Officers appeared, without any portrait annexed to them; but at the suggestion of several respectable subscribers, we have determined from time to time to give them, so as to form a regular series of British naval commanders. The portrait of Earl Howe, with whose memoirs our work commenced, is the first, and we are happy in this opportunity of presenting our readers with an elegant and accurate likeness of that illustrious character, to accompany the review which we have given of his life. Plate 124

ships, and being impatient to close with the enemy, tacked himself, at a quarter past two, P.M. and broke through the French line of battle, about six or eight ships from the rear; making the *Queen Charlotte* the leading ship:

"His bark was stoutly timbered, and his pilot[2]
Of very expert and approv'd allowance."

He continued alone on the weather side of the French line for a considerable time, cut off entirely from the rest of his fleet; and, heaving instantly about, stood unappalled on the same tack with the enemy: raking a French three decker, which had lost her fore topmast, and was edging down into the line.

The *Bellerophon*, who had tacked next in succession to the *Queen Charlotte*, resolutely followed so glorious an example; but could not penetrate the French line, until she came to the second ship, astern of the space, through which Lord Howe had passed: when bursting through, she passed so close to her opponent, as almost to touch, and totally unrig her; bringing down her top-masts and lower yards, with a starboard broadside; and raking the one leeward at the same time. The *Leviathan*, with the rest of the ships in the rear, also attempted passing the line; but they were so totally disabled as to be obliged instead to pass along the enemy's line to the rear.

From the 29th at night, until the 31st at noon, a fog prevented any thing decisive from taking place; at intervals only, when it cleared, could the enemy be discerned. The fog dispersed at half past one, and discovered the enemy in a line to leeward, seven miles distant. Lord Howe immediately formed the line; but the French ships keeping from the wind, prevented his closing with them. Seeing nothing could be effected that night, his lordship made the signal to haul the wind on the larboard tack. The enemy soon after did the same; and then the English van was abreast their center. The frigates in each fleet were placed in the middle, to observe the motions of their respective enemies; and the two fleets continued nearly in this situation during the night. The English carrying more sail in order to be abreast of the French by day light.

At length the eventful morning broke. The night had been passed by the English

---

2 Mr. Bowen, the distinguished master of the *Queen Charlotte* on this day, since deservedly raised to the rank of post captain, addressing Lord Howe frequently during the action by his title, was heard by the officers on board to receive from him this grateful and animated reply: "Mr. Bowen, you may call me My Lord! you yourself deserve to be a prince!"

Plate 1 represents the *Queen Charlotte*, on the 29th of May 1794, upon the starboard tack, under double-reefed topsails, having led through the French line of battle. This view is supposed to be taken from the eastward, in order to shew the extent of the enemy's line, which is on the larboard tack. The manner of passing through it is exemplified by the *Bellerophon*, Rear Admiral Paisley, whose ship is firing on both sides, as she passes. Plate 1

in firm, yet calm preparation for the approaching contest: by the French in drunkenness and gasconade. At five A.M. Lord Howe made the signal to bear down. At seven, being within three miles of the enemy, the English fleet hauled their wind. Lord Howe after making the signals, that he intended to pass through the enemy's line, and engage to leeward, and that each ship was to steer for, and to engage, independent of each other, the ship immediately opposed in the French line; his lordship bore away for the *Montagne*, a three decker, in the center of the enemy. The *Queen Charlotte* for some time desisted from firing, not being able to reach the *Montagne*, which endeavoured to draw ahead. At this critical moment Lord Howe, with his usual coolness and resolution, though fired at by several of the enemy, set his top-gallant sails, and dashed through the line, with the signal flying for closer action. The engagement continued very violent until near one o'clock, when the dismasted ships first seemed to emerge from the smoke.

During th.e action the sailors' wives, who were on board some of the English ships, fought with the most determined valour, at the guns; encouraging and assisting their husbands. After the action, seven ships of the line were in possession of the English; one of which, the *Vengeur*, sunk almost immediately on being taken.[3]

The number of the respective fleets, after the detachment from the English under Rear Admiral Montague, on the 4th of May, with the East India fleet; and the addition made to the French, by Admiral Nyelli's squadron, during the fog of the 31st, was nearly equal. According to Lord Howe's letter, dated at sea, June 2d, the French force,

View of Spithead, with Lord Howe's Fleet and the prizes (taken on the 1st of June 1794) in the state they appeared under jury masts, from the original sketch by Mr. Pocock. The Isle of Wight is represented in distant perspective. The ships are all correct portraits. Names of the Prizes: a *Impetueux* dd *Sans Pareille* b *L'Amerique* e *Le Juste* c *L'Achille* f *Le Northumberland*. The *Queen Charlotte*, Lord Howe's flag ship, is nearly in the centre of the fleet. Plate 4

consisting of 26 ships of the line, was opposed to his Majesty's fleet of 25, the *Audacious* having parted company, with the *Revolutionaire*.

Never had two fleets, met in those, or indeed in any seas, more resolutely determined to conquer, or to die. Victory or death, was emblazoned in gilt letters, on small white silk flags, which were distributed in different parts of the French ships. The French fleet was the strongest they had ever brought to sea: and it was their firm intention, had they succeeded, to have sailed immediately for the anchorage at Spithead. What a moment of national humiliation was averted by British valour! Every thing that could possibly tend to animate their sailors, even to a degree of phrenzy, had been ordered.

3 *Le Just*, 80 guns; *Sans Pareil*, 80; *L'Amerique*, 74; *L'Achille*, 74; *Northumberland*, 74; *L'Impetueux*, 74; *Vengeur*, 74; The *Mont Blanc*, 74; the *Montagnard*, 74; and *L'Audaciaux*, 74; were so completely disabled, as to founder on their return to port, the one after the action of the 29th of May, the others after that of the 1st of June. The *Revolutionaire* was also captured on the 28th of May, and struck to the *Russel*. Captain Parker, of the *Audacious*, who was detached from the fleet with her; would have had the honour of bringing the *Revolutionaire* into port, had not Admiral Nyelli's squadron of nine sail, five of them of the line, chased him on the morning of the 29th, and recaptured the prize. The *Audacious*, though harassed by the enemy's frigates, made her escape from a very superior force.

Brandy, in very liberal quantities, was served during the action between the guns; and some of the crews, in a state of savage ferocity, mixing it with gunpowder, drank in no very gentle terms destruction to Great Britain.[4]

Among the false reports that have prevailed, respecting this glorious action, is the fabricated story relative to the patriotic enthusiasm of the crew of the *Vengeur*.[5] We have been told that at the moment the ship was sinking, the air resounded with cries of *Vive la Republique! Vive la Liberte!* &c. Such an account but ill accords with the squalid and melancholy figures of those poor wretches, who were rescued from a watery grave by British humanity. If they uttered any shout, it was to thank their deliverers.

On the morning of June the 13th the fleet with the prizes were seen from Portsmouth in the offing. Crowds of eager spectators lined the ramparts and beach. When the *Queen Charlotte* had come to anchor, a salute was fired from the battery. About half past twelve his Lordship landed at [the] Sally Port, when a second discharge of artillery took place. He was received on his landing with military honours and reiterated shouts of applause, the band of the Gloucester regiment playing, "See the conquering hero comes!" It was a scene that baffles description! The surrounding spectators alternatively cheered and wept.

Their Majesties, with three of the Princesses, arriving at Portsmouth on the 26th, proceeded next morning in barges, to visit Lord Howe's ship the *Queen Charlotte* at Spithead.[6] His Majesty held a naval levee on board, and presented the veteran commander with a diamond hilt and sword, valued at 3000 guineas; and a gold chain, to which the medal, given on the occasion, is suspended.[7] His Lordship also received the thanks of both houses of Parliament, and of the Common Council of London, with the freedom of that city in a gold box. Lord Howe was obliged, on account of ill health, to resign the command in the Channel, in May 1795; on the 18th of March in the ensuing year, he kissed hands, being appointed General of Marines, vacant by the death of Admiral Forbes.

From the 'Biographical Memoirs of the Right Honourable Lord Gardner.'
VIII 194-195

In the spring of the year 1794, the French had fitted out a powerful armament for sea, with the express intention of invading these kingdoms. In the equipment of the ships that composed their fleet, the utmost care was taken to render them formidable antagonists to the enemy with whom they had to content. The seamen were the flower of the French marine, and the Commander in Chief, Villaret de Joyeuse, a man of acknowledged bravery, and long experience. On board the Admiral's ship were two of the representatives of the French people, delegated by the National Convention, to animate by their presence the operations of the fleet, and inspire the seamen with a more than ordinary portion of hostility against the British nation. England had not been threatened with so terrible an assault, since the days of the memorable *Armada*.

4 From the information of officers who were in the action.
5 Although this ship had struck to the *Brunswick*, the English would not acknowledge her submission, until the French had shewn it, in the most unequivocal manner, by hoisting the British Union.
6 Lord Howe, with the genuine modesty of a seaman, nobly transferred the compliments paid himself, to his crew, by saying with an emphasis that marks his character- " 'Tis not I! 'tis those brave fellows," pointing to the seamen, "who have gained the victory!"
7 How glorious would be an Order founded on such an origin, and devoted entirely to naval merit.

But the intentions of the enemy, in spite of all their measures, in spite of the bravery, bordering on desperation, with which they fought, and though almost determined on conquest or death, were, happily for the safety of the nation, averted by the splendid victory gained by Lord Howe, on the ever memorable 1st of June. The general bravery and good conduct displayed by the Admirals and Captains of the British fleet, on that glorious and important day, leaves no room for individual panegyric; nor would it be easy to select one Commander, on that never to be forgotten occasion, more distinguished than another. We can, therefore, only say, that Admiral Gardner was, not only not inferior in deeds of valour to his gallant "*brothers of the war*", but equaled in "*martial exploits*", the bravest of a host of heroes.

On board the *Queen* the number of slain was great. Captain Hutt lost a leg, and died on the 2d of July following; three Lieutenants, a Midshipman, and thirty-six men were killed, and sixty-seven wounded. In the action of the 29th of May, the *Queen* was in imminent danger. At one period of the engagement she lay totally disabled, and the enemy, after wearing, pointed their heads towards her, which would have endangered the *Royal George* and *Invincible* likewise; but Admiral Graves, in the *Royal Sovereign* gathered about him as many ships as he could, and placed himself between the enemy and them. The van of the enemy engaged this little phalanx as they came forward, and in succession bore away before the wind; by which means the *Queen*, and her gallant Commander and crew, were happily rescued.

On the return of the victorious fleet to port, Admiral Gardner received, with the other Flag Officers, various flattering marks of his Sovereign's favour. On the 28th of June, he was appointed Major-General of Marines, and received, on board the *Queen Charlotte*, from his Majesty's hands, a gold chain and medal, as a mark of his gracious master's royal approbation of his conduct in the actions of the 29th of May, and 1st of June. On the 4th of July, he was promoted to the rank of Vice-Admiral of the Blue, and on the 6th of the following month, was created an English baronet. In the official dispatches of Earl Howe, the services of Admiral Gardner were particularly noticed; he received also, with the other Commanders, the thanks of both Houses of Parliament, and addresses of congratulation from the city of London and other corporate bodies.

From the 'Biographical Memoir of Rear-Admiral John Willett Payne.'
III 31-33

We have been favoured with the following particulars relative to the Action of the 28th, and 29th of May, and first of June, 1794, by an officer who was on board the *Russell*.

May 28

At *seven* A.M. the advanced frigates made the signal to the Admiral for a strange sail, and at half past, for a strange fleet; Lord Howe immediately threw out the signal for the advanced squadron under Admiral Paisley, to reconnoitre the enemy - we being one of the advanced squadron immediately made all possible sail: between *nine*, and *ten*, A.M. discovered them to be the French fleet, consisting of twenty-six sail of the line, and five frigates; about *twelve* they brought to for a short time; then tacked, and formed their line: we had now all sail set, in chase of them. - About *three* the signal was thrown out to harass the enemy's rear: between *four*, and *five*, tacked ship, and fired at their sternmost Ships; about *six* they brought-to for us; and, in half an hour, we fetched up, with, and commenced firing upon their sternmost Ship, the *Revolutionaire*, a three decker - shortly

Position of the Van Squadron of the British fleet, at the close of the glorious action on the First of June, 1794. Taken from the windward side. The object of this sketch is to represent His Majesty's ship *Leviathan*, commanded by the Right Honourable Lord Hugh Seymour, in the exact situation in which she appeared after a most desperate engagement with *L'Amerique*. Plate 20

afterwards the *Bellerophon* commenced her fire upon the same Ship, and then the *Marlborough*, and *Leviathan*, came up, and fired at her. At *eight o'clock*, being almost dark, the *Audacious* came up, and brought-to upon the enemy's lee-quarter, and kept up a constant fire at her; the enemy also kept up a most tremendous fire from her tops - we still kept firing at the *Revolutionaire*, within half pistol shot, until *nine* o'clock, when she passed under our stern; her bowsprit, and mizzen mast, were gone, and her main-top seemed to be on fire: just as she passed under our stern, she struck her colours to the Fleet. The firing then ceased, and we kept sight of the enemy all night; being between the two lines.

May 29
The Admiral made the signal to form the line of battle ahead, as most convenient: we formed astern of the *Queen*, and were then the third Ship in the Van - the *Caesar* leading. The French Fleet, at this time, were going away to windward. At about half past *eight* A.M. they wore round to engage our Van. The *Royal George* commenced the Action, and soon afterwards we began firing; and kept engaging the enemy to the fourth Ship. - At *ten*, the Admiral threw out the signal to tack - the *Queen* wore; and when we got on her weather beam, we wore also, and hauled to the wind, on the other tack: in wearing, the foresail was cut from the yard; all the braces, and bow-lines, were gone, and the bowsprit was shot through; the Ship leaked very much, and we had above four feet

water in the Hold. We then passed down the French line, and left their sternmost Ship to leeward; the French Fleet now made sail, as if they wished to escape: on which The Signal was immediately thrown out by the Admiral for a general Chase: from the circumstances above-mentioned, we were obliged to make the Signal of Inability. Nothing but random fire continued during that afternoon; and we were employed in repairing our damages – the seamen at the rigging, and the marines at the pumps, as the water gained upon us, and continued doing so until *four* o'clock the next morning, when we succeeded in stopping the leaks. The *thirtieth*, and *thirty-first* of May, were so foggy, that we could not discern the enemy.

June the First

About *eight* o'clock A.M. saw the French fleet lying-to, main topsail to the mast; and The Admiral made the signal for each Ship to engage her opponent: a little before *nine* A.M. we bore down upon the enemy; the *Caesar* leading the Van, the *Leviathan* ahead of us, and the *Royal Sovereign* astern. About nine the action became nearly general on both sides. The *Russell* was the fourth Ship in the Van; we engaged briskly for an hour, when our opponent bore away, her masts and sails going as she advanced: we immediately bore up after her; but the French Ships coming up from to leeward, and astern, protected her. We then hauled up, and raked *L'Amerique*, who was already engaged with the *Leviathan*, within half pistol shot. The French Van were now totally dispersed, except two Ships that seemed inclined to engage us – we immediately hauled to windward, and favoured them with their wishes; but it was only for a short time: for on observing their fleet making off, they followed the example. I omitted to mention the going of our fore topmast about ten o'clock. About *one* P.M. all firing ceased – seven French Ships were at this time totally dismasted, one of which was observed to sink. In the afternoon we boarded *L'Amerique*, but quitted her by order of Admiral Graves, and took possession of *L'Impetueux*. Exchanged prisoners, and received 176 – officers, and men, included.[8]

During the three days action we had only eight men killed, and about twenty wounded; which is sufficient to prove our superiority of skill. Some of their Ships had about 150 men killed. Our brave Captain had many narrow escapes; but thank God! he weathered it out.

From the 'Biographical Memoir of Captain James Manderson.' XXX 97-98

[In May and June 1794 Manderson was junior lieutenant of H.M.S. *Queen*, and stationed in command of the quarter-deck guns.]

On the memorable 1st of June, the *Queen* broke through the French line, at 10 A.M.; when the eighth ship of the enemy, her opponent, hauled on board her fore and main tacks, and made sail; she therefore closed with the 7th, a ship of 84 guns, having 16 ports on a side on her lower deck: this ship (supposed to be the *Scipion*) also attempted to shake her off, by first making sail, and then running to leeward; her adversary, however, kept close upon her starboard quarter. The French captain's colours being twice shot away, he hoisted a jack at the mizzen-top-gallant mast head. At three quarters past 10, his mizzen-mast went by the board; and at 11, the *Queen*'s main-mast went over the lee side, carrying away the mizzen-yard, &c. fore part of the poop, and the barricading of the quarter-deck. In a quarter of an hour, the main-mast of her antagonist came down,

8 The prize, *L'Amerique*, was renamed *L'Impetueux*, and Payne, then a captain, was put in command of her.

and her foremast immediately after. At this time, the *Queen* falling round off, the French crew came upon deck, and waved submission with their hats, having been driven from their stations with great slaughter.

At half an hour past noon, it was perceived that twelve of the French ships, the *Mountain* being the headmost, were standing towards the *Queen*. The drum beat to quarters: it was a trying hour; all the sails that she had to set were the fore-sail and fore-top-sail, both torn in pieces by shot; and the fore-yard having been cut in two in the slings, in the affair of the 29th of May, that now in use was a jury, being a main-top-sail yard, and a studding sail hoisted on the mizzen-mast to keep her to the wind. In this state she met the French line. The *Mountain* passed without firing, perhaps from the slaughter on board; as did also her second astern; but when abreast of the third, the signal was made from the *Mountain* to engage, and nine ships opened their fire in succession, which was returned as vigorously as circumstances would permit. The *Terrible*, of 110 guns, with only her foremast standing, was the last ship in the line, towed by three frigates, two of which cast off and hauled to windward; no doubt, with the hope of giving the *Queen* a good drubbing (as the English fleet were lying to windward, spectators), and supposing that her guns were as much disabled as her masts; but as soon as they perceived the fire that she opened on their line, they up-helm and ran in great haste to leeward of the line-of-battle ships, without waiting to give or receive a shot.

When the firing had ceased, the situation of the French fleet was nearly as follows: ten two-decked ships totally dismasted, and which had struck, having English ensigns thrown over their sterns, to prevent their being fired into; among these, the *Republicain* of 110 guns, with only her foremast standing: three two-decked ships in flight to windward, about six miles S.E. of the *Republicain*: twelve sail in line-of-battle, one of which was the *Terrible*, of 110, mentioned before as having only her foremast standing. After these had engaged the *Queen*, when they came abreast of the ship which struck to her, they hove-to, and were joined by the *Republicain*, when they towed off three of the dismasted ships that had struck.

In the English fleet, the *Marlborough* and *Defence* were totally dismasted; the foremast of the *Royal George* was gone; the *Queen* had lost her main-mast, mizzen-top-mast, and mizzen-yard; the *Queen Charlotte* her top-masts; the *Brunswick* her mizzen-mast, being nearly out of sight to leeward, running before the wind: the other damages were not material to sight. At 2h. 20 min. the *Pegasus* took the *Queen* in tow: she had this day 14 men killed; and the second lieutenant (mortally) and 68 men wounded.

Proceedings of His Majesty's Ship the Orion,[9] *John Thomas Duckworth, esq.,*
Commander, and his Observations during the Actions of the 28th and 29th
of May, and 1st of June, 1794. [293-300]

May 28

At eight A.M. on the 28th of May, standing to the S.E. with the wind at S.S.W. a frigate, nearly ahead of the admiral, made the signal for a strange fleet; a few minutes after, the *Bellerophon* made the same signal, but could not distinguish the Compass

9 The *Orion*, since commanded by Sir James Saumarez, has been in all the principal actions of the present war, excepting that of Lord Duncan.

Flag. At ten minutes past eight, the admiral made the *Bellerophon*'s signal to reconnoitre the strange fleet in view; at twenty minutes, for seeing the enemy; at thirty minutes, for the fleet to prepare for action. About half past nine, the *Bellerophon*'s signal was made to shorten sail; at thirty-six minutes past ten, for the whole fleet to wear, and come to the wind on the larboard tack; and at ten minutes past eleven, that the ships companies would have time to dine.

May 29. P.M.

At fifty minutes past one, P.M. on the 29th of May, the signal was made to attack the rear of the enemy; at fifty-five minutes, for the fleet to chase. At two o'clock, to engage the enemy as arriving up with them; at five minutes past three, to tack in succession; at half past four, for each ship to carry a light during the night; at twenty minutes past six, to attack and harass the rear of the enemy; at twenty-five minutes, the same was repeated, with one gun; at five minutes past seven, to engage the rear of the enemy; at twenty minutes, to keep sight of them, and make known their motions; at twenty-three minutes, to assist ships engaged, - with one gun: - the *Russell*'s and *Marlborough*'s Pendants were now thrown out, and at half past seven, the signal was made to form the line of battle as most convenient; at forty-five minutes to recall from chase, the *Bellerophon* and *Marlborough* then firing at the enemy, as also several others, with a smart cannonading; but could not distinguish what ships they were, from our distance. Between nine and ten o'clock, intending to go ahead, was prevented by the admiral's hailing, and directing us to keep astern: hauled the main-sail up, and kept in the admiral's wake during the night.

May 29. A.M.[10]

At fifty-five minutes past three, A.M. on the 29th of May, the signal was made to form the line of battle, as most convenient. We accordingly made sail, and hauled to windward to go ahead of the admiral, and form the line: - formed in the van, the *Caesar* leading, the *Queen* second, the *Russell* third, and *Valient* fourth, the *Royal George* fifth, the *Invincible* sixth, the *Orion* seventh. At fifty-eight minutes past three, the signal was made to recall all cruisers; at seven, to prepare to tack in succession; at twenty minutes, to pass between the enemy's line to obtain the weather gage; at thirty minutes, the fleet at liberty to fire at the enemy on passing them, though not intending to bring them to a general action immediately. At fifteen minutes past eight, the signal was out for the *Caesar* to make more sail; at thirty-five minutes past eleven, the signal was made to tack in succession.

May 30. P.M.

At twenty-five minutes past twelve, P.M. (May 30) the signal was made to prepare to tack in succession; and at five minutes past one, the *Caesar* made the signal of inability. At twenty five minutes, the admiral made the signal to pass between the enemy's line to obtain the weather gage; and at twenty-two minutes after two, to tack in succession. - The *Caesar* wore, and went under our lee; the *Queen* tacked, and was followed by the *Russell*, who wore; the *Valiant* wore also, and passed under our lee; the *Royal George* tacked; the *Invincible* and *Orion* wore and followed, the *Queen* leading; the *Russell, Royal*

---

10 We inform such of our readers, as are not conversant with marine terms, that the day at sea begins at 12 o'clock at noon. From thence to 12 at night is consequently styled P.M. and from 12 at night, to the next day at noon, A.M.

George, *Invincible*, and *Orion*, passed part of the center, and the whole of the enemy's rear, excepting the last ship, which we passed to windward of. Observed the *Queen Charlotte* pass through the enemy's line to windward of us. At thirty-five minutes past two the *Queen*, *Royal George*, *Russell*, and *Invincible*, were to leeward; the two former made the signal to lie by to repair damages. At fifty minutes, the *Royal Sovereign*'s signal was made to tack in succession, and at fifty-five minutes for the fleet to chase. Being in too disabled a state to obey this signal, and observing a French line of battle ship in an ungovernable condition to leeward, bore down on her, and placing ourselves close on her lee quarter, with the main topsail aback, gave her two broadsides.

The *Barfleur* being ahead of us, and on the starboard tack, under full sail, I thought it necessary to bear up for her, which occasioned our getting too far astern to renew our attack. Observed the *Barfleur* firing into the line of battle ship we had left. Hauled our wind on the starboard tack, and began to reeve new braces, &c. &c. At thirty minutes past three, the signal was made to close round the admiral, or divisional commanders; at fifty-five minutes, to come to the wind on the starboard tack in succession; at five minutes past four, to form the line of battle as most convenient; at twenty minutes, ships to windward more particularly; at twenty-five minutes, the *Royal George* to come to the wind on the starboard tack, and form the line of battle as most convenient; at five, to recall ships chasing West; at five minutes past, to form the line of battle as most convenient, ships to windward more particularly; at twenty minutes past, to come to the wind on the larboard tack; at thirty-five minutes past five, to form the line of battle on the larboard line of bearing; at forty minutes past, the *Royal George*, *Queen*, and *Caesar*, to do the same; at forty-eight minutes to annul the same; at ten minutes past six, for the *Caesar* to form the line of battle on the larboard line of bearing; at twenty minutes past, for the whole fleet to do the same: the *Orion* answered with inability, having all her rigging cut to pieces.

May 30, A.M.
At ten o'clock, A.M. the fog clearing up, we saw the enemy broad to leeward. At four minutes past ten, the signal was made to form the order of sailing in two divisions; at thirteen minutes, the starboard division to keep in the admiral's wake; at twenty minutes past, the admiral's interrogatory whether the ships were in condition to renew the action: answered in the affirmative by all the fleet except the *Caesar*. At forty minutes past ten, the signal was made to prepare to come to the wind on the larboard tack; at fifty-five minutes, to come to the wind on the same; at eleven, the ships to keep in closer order to the van; at thirty-five minutes past, the *Russell* made the signal for having sprung a lower mast or yard; at twelve o'clock, the *Caesar* made the signal of ability to renew the action.

May 31, P.M.
Came on foggy again, and we lost sight of the enemy.

June 1, P.M.
Discerned the French fleet bearing N.N.W. At forty minutes past one, P.M. the admiral made the signal, for the fleet to make sail, after lying by; at forty-five minutes past one, to alter course to W.N.W. At ten minutes past three, to prepare to haul the wind on the larboard tack together; at thirty-two minutes past, to form the line of battle on the larboard line of bearing; at thirty-eight minutes past, the fleet to keep in closer order to

the van; at fifty minutes past, the larboard division to alter course to N.N.W. (at fifteen minutes past four, the *Royal Sovereign* made the *Caesar*'s signal to alter course to N.W.) at twenty-five minutes past four, the *Brunswick* to make more sail; at half past four, the fleet to alter course, two points to port, together. At fifty-five minutes past four, the signal was made for the van to prepare to engage the enemy's van; at five minutes past five, the center to prepare to engage the enemy's center; at fourteen minutes past, to alter course to N.W. by W. together; at twenty minutes past, for the rear to prepare to engage the enemy's rear. At half past six, the admiral made the signal for the *Venus* to come within hail; at forty-three minutes past, for each ship to carry a light during the night, and repeat signals; at fifty-five minutes, to come to the wind on the larboard tack; at twenty-two minutes past seven, for the rear to make more sail. At twenty-five minutes past seven, the *Southampton* hailed us, and informed, that the admiral would carry the same sail during the night, and desired us to keep a little to windward of his wake, and to carry as many reefs out of the topsails, as were consistent with safety. Observed the admiral at that time to be under single-reefed topsails, foresail, jib, and main topmast stay-sail.

June 1, A.M.
At four o'clock, A.M. the admiral made the signal for the van to close to the center; at ten minutes past four, the *Latona* made the signal for a strange fleet, bearing North. At half past four, the admiral made the signal for the fleet to alter course N.W. and at a quarter past six, the same to North; at twenty-five minutes past, for the fleet to close; at a quarter past seven, to haul the wind on the larboard tack together; at twenty-three minutes, that the admiral intended to pass through the enemy's line, and engage them to leeward; at five minutes past eight, the van to close to the center; at seventeen minutes, to make sail after lying by; at thirty-two minutes, for each ship to prepare to engage her opponent; at forty-six minutes past eight, for the *Gibraltar, Brunswick, Russell,* and *Culloden,* to make more sail; at fifty minutes past, the *Royal Sovereign,* and *Royal George,* made the signal to interchange places in the line, but could not distinguish the pendants with whom such change was to take place. At a quarter past nine, the admiral made the signal to engage close; at twenty minutes to make more sail, and at ten to chase.

When the signal for each ship to engage her opponent was made, the *Queen, Valiant,* and *Orion,* being close together, hailed each other, and agreed on the eighth, ninth, and tenth ships, as their proper opponents. At this time, the enemy's line filled, and made sail. The *Queen* hailed us, and though not distinctly heard, from the heavy fire, judged it was to make sail. Hauled on board the main tack, and found the main sheet shot away, which prevented our trimming. The enemy's line making sail, caused our taking the seventh ship from their rear. Bore down as close as possible without boarding, and observed the *Queen,* our second, bear up for the fifth, which was a three decker. Some time after, observed the *Brunswick* on our starboard bow, between two French line of battle ships, three were between us and the *Brunswick,* so that we could not cut the line to assist her. At half past ten, the two ships we were engaging bore up, when the masts of one went overboard; which enabled us to oppose our broadside to one coming up on our quarter. At this time our main topmast, which had gone some time before, was hanging over on the starboard side, and carried away half the main-top; and the main yard in the slings. The wreck much impeded three guns on each deck; we however continued firing until the enemy left us. As the smoke dispersed, we perceived the *Queen Charlotte,* with both her topmasts carried away, and otherwise much damaged;

hauled up to support her, observing two of the enemy's line of battle ships bearing down upon her, under full sail: but the *Gibraltar, Culloden*, and other ships, in apparent good order, hauling between us, prevented our intentions. Began to clear away the wreck, and to reeve new braces, and bowlines, to the few remaining sails. At eleven, the admiral made the signal to form the line of battle, as most convenient: endeavoured to keep near the admiral, not being in a state to take our station in the line with safety. At five minutes past eleven, the signal was made for the *Gibraltar, Culloden, Phaeton*, and *Latona*, to come within hail; at twenty-five minutes, for the *Montague, Majestic*, and *Culloden*, to form the line of battle as most convenient; at half past eleven, for the *Leviathan* to do the same; at forty-five minutes past, to wear, and come to the wind on the larboard tack.

June 2, P.M.

At fourteen minutes past twelve, P.M. the signal was made to close round the admiral, or divisional commanders; at half past twelve, for the *Culloden* to come within hail; at thirty-five minutes past, the *Defence* made the signal of needing assistance in battle, she being totally dismasted. At one o'clock, the signal was made to wear, and come to the wind on the starboard tack. Observed ten of the enemy's ships forming in line of battle to leeward. The *Brunswick*, from being to leeward, with her mizzen mast gone, was obliged to make sail away; discerned her some time after, with studding sails set. The *Queen*, being to leeward of our fleet, with her main-mast gone, passed the enemy's line to windward, keeping up a continual fire. Signals were now made for frigates, tenders, &c. to come within hail; at twenty-five minutes past two, to make sail after lying by, and form the line of battle as most convenient; at forty-five minutes, the *Gibraltar* and *Thunderer* to stay by prizes E.N.E. At eighteen minutes past three, the signal was made by the admiral for the *Royal Sovereign* to keep in the admiral's wake; and at half past three, to recall ships chasing east. Observing a French frigate standing up to some of their dismasted ships, the admiral made the signal to stay by prizes, and repeated the same at thirty-five minutes past four. At thirty-five minutes past five, the *Royal Sovereign* made the signal that the enemy's ships bearing W.N.W. were not secured. At half past six, the *Ramillies* made the signal for being in want of immediate assistance; at forty-six minutes past, the *Russell* made the signal for boats to tow, or assist in distress. At fifty-four minutes past six, the admiral made the signal for the fleet to bring to. At thirty-five minutes past seven, the *Aquilon* made the signal for boats to tow, or assist in the N.E.

Employed refitting our sails and rigging. Observed the enemy's fleet bear up with their dismasted ships in tow, which, we were prevented from following, by the scattered and disabled state of our fleet. We found in our possession seven sail of the line, totally dismasted, one of which sunk ten minutes after hoisting British colours, which she did on our firing a gun at her; she then also lowered a small sail she had set on the stump of her foremast. - The boats of the *Alfred*, and *Culloden*, employed in saving the crew of the ship which had sunk.

From the 'Biographical Memoir of the Late Captain John Harvey.' III 251-259.

At the commencement of the present eventful war, Captain John Harvey pressed forward in the path of naval glory, regardless of the bourne to which it sometimes leads: his daring spirit was roused at the awakening voice of insulted liberty:

Onn, Aella, Onn! - we longe for bloddie fraie;
Wee longe to here the raven synge yn vayne;
Onn, Aella, Onn! we certys gayne the daie,
Whanne thou doste leade us to the leathal playne!

                                                    Chatterton

Captain Harvey immediately addressed to the Admiralty, in the most anxious terms, his desire to be soon employed. The talents of such a man were too well known, to suffer any delay to paralyse his earnest wishes for active service: he was soon appointed to the *Magnificent*, but did not join her; as in consequence of the particular request of Lord Howe, he was appointed soon afterwards (February the seventh, 1793) to the *Brunswick*, a seventy four of a large and particular construction, with a complement of six hundred and fifty men. Lord Howe's sentiments on this occasion, will best appear from the following extract of a letter sent by Mr. Brett, his Lordship's confidential friend, to Captain Harvey:

"As his Lordship has an idea, occasions might arise, wherein it might be more convenient for him to shift his flag into a two decked Ship; in that case he would prefer the *Brunswick*, and therefore wishes to have a Captain in her with whom he is acquainted; and has authorised me to ask you whether it would be agreeable to you to be appointed to her in case he can get it done."

Lord Howe sailed from Spithead on the fourteenth of July 1793; but during that, and several subsequent cruises, no-thing particularly worthy of notice occurred until the memorable twenty-ninth of May, 1794; when the British and French fleets commenced that contest for the sovereignty of the ocean, which terminated with such glory to Great Britain on the First of June.[11]

The situation of the *Brunswick*, as commanded by Captain Harvey on this eventful day, rendered it impossible she could have been sufficiently noticed, in any of the accounts hitherto presented to the public: but as this ship had her full share in obtaining that victory, it would be injustice to withhold a narrative of her proceedings, which reflects so much honour on the conduct of her gallant officers and undaunted crew.[12]

On the twenty-ninth of May, 1794, the *Brunswick* being to leeward of the line, Captain Harvey, after using his utmost endeavours, found it impossible to take his proper station, as second to the *Queen Charlotte*; but resolving, as he said, *to have a berth somewhere!* he tried to get in between several of our ships; and hailing the *Culloden*, he desired the captain to shorten sail, when he pushed the *Brunswick* in between her and the *Montagne*, about the seventh ship from the rear; and in that station received the fire of the French line, as the fleets passed each other. Perceiving his friend, Captain Bazeley, in the *Alfred*, hard pressed by an eighty gun ship, Captain Harvey bore down to his assistance, and obliged the French ship to quit the *Alfred*, and follow her own fleet. On the thirtieth, and thirty-first, the weather being very thick and hazy, no engagement took place.

On the first of June, the *Brunswick* was in her station, and had continued close to the *Queen Charlotte*'s stern all night: the instant the signal was made for every ship to

11 Vol 1 pages 18, 19, 20. Vol II pages 365. Vol. III pages 31, 32.
12 *Narrative of the transactions on board his Majesty's ship the Brunswick - from which the subject of two pictures were taken by Mr. Nicholas Pocock.* The first represents the *Brunswick* grappled to, and engaging *Le Vengeur*, with her starboard guns, and totally dismasting *L'Achille*, in an attempt to board her on her larboard quarter. The second represents the sinking of *Le Vengeur*, with the disabled state of the *Brunswick* after the action.

bear down, and engage her opponent to windward, or leeward, as circumstances would admit, the Brunswick's helm was put up at the same time with the *Queen Charlotte*'s, and both ships ran down together for the center of the French line.[13] The signal being thrown out to make more sail, to shut in the angle of fire from the rear as soon as possible, both ships dropped their fore sails; and the *Brunswick*'s being first down, brought her rather ahead of the *Charlotte*, and covered that ship from the galling fire of the center, and rear of the enemy's fleet: but she suffered severely by it, for the cockpit was filled with wounded men, before a single shot was fired from the *Brunswick*.

Lord Howe cutting through the French line, close under the *Montagne*'s stern, raked the *Jacobin* ahead with his starboard guns; it was Captain Harvey's intention to pass between the *Jacobin*, and the next ship, that he might engage his proper opponent, as second to the Commander in Chief; but the enemy lay in such close order, that the *Brunswick* was obliged to bear up for an opening, which presented itself between *Le Patriote* the third, and *Le Vengeur* the fourth ship, from *La Montagne*. The former, endeavouring to frustrate this design, shot ahead; which being observed by Captain Harvey, he kept his helm a-port, and the two antagonists were immediately laid alongside each other - the starboard anchors of the *Brunswick*, hooking into the forechains of *Le Vengeur*.

When the Master informed Captain Harvey of this, and asked whether he should cut *Le Vengeur* clear, his animated reply was - *No! we have got her, and we will keep her!* So closely were they grappled, that the crew of the *Brunswick*, unable to haul up eight of her starboard ports from the third port abaft, were obliged to fire through them: thus situated they went off large from both fleets, hotly engaged - in an hour, and ten minutes, they were about a mile to leeward of the French fleet; when the smoke dispersing for a few minutes, they perceived a French line of battle ship, with her rigging and decks covered with men ready for boarding, and gathering upon their larboard quarter. Captain Harvey immediately ordered the lower deck to prepare for receiving her; the men from the five after starboard guns were instantly turned over to the larboard. The French ship being now within musket reach, a double headed shot was added to each gun, already loaded with single thirty-two pounders: the word was then given to fire, and reload as quick as possible; at the same time continuing to engage *Le Vengeur* with the starboard guns forwards. When about five or six rounds had been poured in, the gallant crew of the *Brunswick* had the satisfaction to behold first the fore mast, and then the other masts go by the board.[14] Many of the crew fell into the sea, and implored assistance; but *Le Vengeur* still required so much attention, that it was impossible to afford them any relief.

The joy which was experienced on board the *Brunswick*, from disabling their new assailant, may easily be conceived: but what words can express their glow of soul, when, in about an hour after this successful event, word was passed throughout the ship - *The brave Captain Henry Harvey*,[15] *in the Ramillies, is coming to the support of his gallant brother!!!* The air resounded with their cheers.

As the *Ramillies* stood towards the *Brunswick*, the crew of the former made signs,

13 The *Brunswick*'s fore-top-gallant mast was at this time shot away.
14 This ship proved to be *L'Achille* of 74 guns; the crew of which afterwards declared, that their capture was owing to the loss of masts, from the fire of the ship engaging *Le Vengeur*.
15 Now Vice-Admiral of the White, since created a Knight of Bath. This excellent Officer conducted, with Sir Ralph Abercrombie, the successful expedition against Trinidad, on the twelfth of February, 1797. *Vide*. Naval Anecdotes.

by waving, to cut *Le Vengeur* adrift, that she might drop, and receive the fire of the *Ramillies*.[16] A most tremendous broadside was poured into her, every shot of which seemed to take place; this was followed by a second equally animated; and then the *Ramillies* made sail for another French ship, bearing down upon them, and went off engaging her.

Previous to this, the rudder of *Le Vengeur* had been split, by some well-directed shot from the *Brunswick*; her sternpost had also been shivered; and such havoc made in her counter, that the water was rapidly pouring in. When the *Ramillies* left them, the *Brunswick* was lying across the bows of her opponent; and in that position kept up a steady raking fire, until the fore and main mast of *Le Vengeur* went by the board, dragging the head of the mizen mast with them. This dreadful conflict had now continued for two hours, and an half: the crew of the *Brunswick* with the greatest coolness, at one time driving home the *coins*, watching attentively the rising of the enemy's ship to fire below the water line; and at another withdrawing the *coins* to elevate the muzzles of their guns, and rip up the decks of *Le Vengeur*.

At length the French ship was obliged to confess the superiority of our professional skill, and to yield to British valour: her colours having been shot away, she hoisted an English Jack in token of submission, and implored assistance. The boats of the *Brunswick* had been shot to pieces; no relief therefore could by her be given to the vanquished opponent. *Le Vengeur* sunk between three and four o'clock; and though every exertion that humanity could dictate was made, only two hundred of the crew were saved - the remainder, in number about six hundred, went to the bottom in the ship.[17]

The *Brunswick* was now left a dismal wreck - her mizen, and fore-top-gallant masts gone; the bowsprit cut two thirds through, near the lower gammon; the main mast greatly crippled; the fore mast in a similar state, with a deep wound three feet below the tressel trees; all the running, and much of the standing rigging, shot away; the sails torn to shreds; eight ports on the starboard side wanting of their batteries; the starboard quarter-gallery entirely ground off; twenty-three guns dismounted.[18] Three anchors carried away from the starboard bow; the best bower, with the cat-head, towing under her bottom; and all the yards in a shattered state. The ship having been on fire three times, the hammocks taking fire on the gangway, were partly cut overboard; and the quick-work, [sic] just before the gangway, was much burnt and splintered. The loss she sustained in her crew, was considerable; forty-seven of them were killed, and one hundred and eighteen were badly wounded. Their wounds in general were peculiarly distressing and severe, being lacerated by langridge shot of raw ore, and old nails: stink pots were thrown into the port holes, which occasioned the most painful excoriations; burning and scalding the faces and arms of the British sailors in so shocking a manner, that they anxiously wished for death to terminated their agonies.

16 This was not done; but soon after the *Ramillies* had left them, the *Brunswick* swung clear of *Le Vengeur*, tearing away three anchors from her bow.
17 The crew of the *Vengeur* made frequent attempts to cut themselves clear of their opponent; but were as often prevented - being shot by the small arms of the British seamen and marines. They also attempted to board the *Brunswick* on the stern, but were repulsed by the brave 29th regiment, commanded by Captain Saunders.
18 In the account of the proceedings of his Majesty's ship *Orion* (*Naval Chronicle*, Vol. I. page 299) the *Brunswick* is mentioned as being seen with studding sails set; which, from the crippled state of her masts, must have been a mistake. One of the lower studding sails was indeed set forward, in order to make her steer; but all the rest were so completely destroyed, and rendered unfit for service, that it became necessary to bend an entire new suit.

In this forlorn state, the opinion of the officers was taken; when it was unanimously agreed that they could not possibly join the British fleet. They now perceived, at the extent of the French line, two ships in tolerable condition, that threatened to bear down to the *Brunswick*: next them lay all the dismasted ships, and those that had struck; and on the larboard, and weather quarter, appeared the remainder of the French ships, veering under each other. It was imagined also that these ships were preparing to attack the *Brunswick*, and the *Queen*, about two miles to windward of the former, in order to cut them both off. Captain Harvey, who was severely wounded, on being informed of the supposed intention of the enemy, gave his express commands, that the *Brunswick*, if attacked, should be defended to the last extremity; all his officers had but one sentiment on the occasion. The French, however, made no attempt upon the *Brunswick*; and therefore, finding it impossible to regain their station, it was judged necessary, in order to save the ship, to bear away for port: favoured by Providence, and good weather, she first made Cape Clear, in Ireland; and then coasting it up the Channel, anchored on the evening of the eleventh at St. Helens; and the next morning proceeded to Spithead.

As our biographical memoir draws towards its close, it will powerfully awaken the commiserating regard of every reader; and recall to the memory of the brave companions of Captain Harvey, that heroic fortitude, and patient endurance, which this illustrious officer displayed in his last moments.

He was wounded early in the action, by a musket ball, which tore away part of his right hand; but this he carefully concealed, and bound the wound up in his handkerchief. Some time after this he received a violent contusion in the loins, which laid him almost lifeless on the deck: from this severe blow he however rallied his strength of mind, and continued on the quarter-deck, directing and conducting the action; until a double-headed shot splitting, struck his right arm near the elbow, and shattered it to pieces: this seems to have been about half past eleven, just after his encounter with *L'Achille*. Growing faint through loss of blood, he was now compelled to retire; but when assistance was offered to conduct him below, he nobly refused it - *I will not have a single man leave his quarters on my account! My legs still remain to bear me down into the cockpit.* In this wounded, and shattered state, he essayed to go; when casting a languid, yet affectionate look towards his brave crew - *Persevere, my brave lads, in your duty! Continue the action with spirit for the honour of our King and Country; and remember my last words -* THE COLOURS OF THE BRUNSWICK SHALL NEVER BE STRUCK!

When he at length had reached the surgeon, surrounded by the maimed and dying, who were involved in smoke and sulphur; he displayed a fortitude that nothing could affect, and a tenderness of affection towards his crew, which all the anguish of his wounds could not diminish. About sun-set it was found necessary to amputate his arm above the elbow. On the *Brunswick*'s arrival at Spithead, Captain Harvey was the next morning conveyed on shore at Portsmouth; where, after bearing the most excruciating pain with Christian resignation, he was released from this world, and lost to his Country, on the thirtieth of June.

His lamented remains being carried to Eastry in Kent, were deposited with every respect, an affectionate sorrow could bestow, in a vault in that church; and the following inscription points out the hallowed spot to posterity.

"In a vault, near this place, are deposited the remains of Captain John Harvey, late Commander of his Majesty's ship *Brunswick*; who after gloriously supporting the honour of the British Navy, on the memorable first of June, 1794, under Earl Howe, died at

Portsmouth on the thirtieth of the same month, in consequence of the wounds he received in the engagement; aged fifty-three.

The House of Commons, to perpetuate his most gallant conduct on that day of victory, unanimously voted a monument to his memory in Westminster Abbey; his untimely death only, prevented his being honoured in the flag promotions which took place on that occasion.

In him his afflicted family, and numerous friends, have sustained an irreparable loss; his public character being only equaled by his private virtues."

> He there does now enjoy eternall rest
> And happy ease, which thou doest want and crave,
> And further from it daily wanderest:
> What if some little Payne the passage have,
> That makes frayle flesh to feare the bitter wave?
> Is not short Payne well borne, that brings long ease,
> And layes the Soul to sleepe in quiet grave?
> Sleepe after toyle, port after stormie seas,
> Ease after warre, death after life, does greatly please.
>
> Spencer

It is a singular coincidence of events, that Captain Harvey, and Captain Hutt of the *Queen*, were companions in a post-chaise from London, on joining their respective Ships, previous to their last cruise: they both lost a limb in the action; died on the same day; and are both recorded on the same national monument raised by a grateful Country to their memory.

Captain Harvey's widow is allowed a pension of one hundred pounds per annum: his two minor children, *Edward*, and *Sarah*, twenty-five pounds each; the former until he comes of age, and the latter until she marries.

Arms: Argent, on a chevron Gules, between three bears gambs erassed Sable, three crescents Or.

Crest: Two bears gambs erased Sable, supporting a crescent Or.

From the 'Memoir of the Public Services of the late Captain Sir Andrew Snape Douglas, Knt.' XXV 354; 358; 362-363

We shall, at this period of his professional life, introduce Captain Douglas's narrative of his services, as given in a letter which he afterwards addressed to his gallant patron and uncle, the present Sir Andrew Hamond, Bart. late comptroller of the navy. . . .[19]

"I continued upon that and other services, until Lord Howe proceeded to sea with the Channel fleet. This happened just at the time I had returned from Lisbon with a small frigate of the enemy, *la Prompte*, of 28 guns, and a privateer which I had taken; and I was then attached to the western fleet by the Admiralty. Lord Howe gave me a distinguishing pendant, and the command of all the frigates of the fleet formed into a separate squadron. This was the first appointment of the kind that had ever taken place; and, as such, I considered it as a very honourable one, although it was very fatiguing: for it might in some measure be considered in the same light as the flank corps of an army. I continued to serve in that situation, sometimes cruising separately, but in general with the fleet, until the captain of *Queen Charlotte*, Lord Howe's ship,

---

19 It is dated from on board the *Queen Charlotte*, when cruising off Ushant, November 23, 1796.

quitted the command of her, and went to be Commissioner of the Transport Board: when Lord Howe applied for me to be appointed to succeed him. I was accordingly nominated captain of the *Queen Charlotte*, on the 8th day of April, 1794.". . . .

Such was the modest letter of this great sea officer, to his intimate friend and relation; and it remains to be added, what is far from being generally known, that the glorious victory of what is called June the first, or rather the glorious termination of the battle which commenced on the 28th of May, and did not entirely terminate until the 1st of June, was much indebted to the great and painful exertions, of THE DOUGLAS, as Walter Scott might style this warrior. During the action on the first of June, and at a most critical moment in that memorable contest, a piece of grape shot forcibly struck Sir Andrew Douglas in the forehead, above the right eye. His face was covered with blood, and the pain was intense. Yet did that lamented officer, knowing the importance of the moment, order the tourniquet to be applied to what proved a mortal wound, even with a piece of the shot still remaining in it: and in that state, holding the tourniquet on with one hand, and grasping his speaking trumpet with the other, he instantly returned to the quarter-deck; where a gloominess and even a despair prevailed, which his activity and unparalleled exertions soon dissipated. Lord Howe, with his usual liberality, afterwards declared, that Sir A.Douglas was a prodigy; and that his admiral could never, as commander-in-chief, say enough of Sir Andrew's services during that action.

Later Reflections on Captain Gambier's Part in The Action, from 'Correspondence'
Letter to the Editor from "J.C.". XXII 102-103

Sunderland, August 13, 1809
Mr. Editor, I have waited with anxiety for the termination of the court martial on my old commander and friend Lord Gambier, not with any fear as to the result, as I felt confident that the more minute the enquiry, the more favourable would be the public impression of his conduct. It was many years since we sailed together, but I know him well, and notwithstanding the professional merit of almost every admiral and captain in the service is circumstantially known to his brother officers, yet having been an eye witness to his persevering intrepidity in the hour of danger, and his modest unassuming deportment on many triumphant occasions, I feel myself called upon to acknowledge his meritorious example and national worth. . . . At the commencement of last war, Captain, now Lord Gambier, commanded the *Defence*, of 74 guns; his regulation, discipline, and strict conformity in every particular to the articles of war, were notorious in the Channel fleet; for with great attention and judgment his exertions were adapted to promote the comfort and happiness of every officer and seaman in the ship: he may with truth be styled the seaman's friend. I could relate many instances of his unwearied attention in forwarding the deserving and friendless sailor, not only in promotion, but to the hurt and wounded, pecuniary assistance, when he conceived the smart money or Greenwich pension inadequate. To the idle and the dissolute his punishments were with vigilance directed, but in no instance attended with cruel severity; the old but now obsolete custom of the wooden collar and fine for swearing, was invariably adhered to, and no women were admitted to remain on board without possessing marriage certificates. The chaplain's attendance likewise on Sundays was never dispensed with when circumstances would admit, and rainy weather was not deemed a sufficient plea, whilst

the after part of the lower deck could be resorted to. This steady adherence to the instructions, and laudable endeavour to improve the morals of the seamen, were the only complaints I ever heard alleged against him. Could Lord Howe be now appealed to, whether the ship was or was not ever ready for any service, and whether on the 1st of June, 1794, she did not eminently prove the undaunted intrepidity of her commander; his venerable reply would at once fix the public favour. She was the first ship, by the *Queen Charlotte*'s log book, that cut through the enemy's line. When the signal was made in the morning for that purpose, the officers then present can report how far it was complied with, for the enemy, suspecting the intention, had closed, and formed in compact line to leeward, opening their fire from van to rear. Captain Gambier determined on fulfilling the signal, and passed between the 7th and 8th ship. The *Brunswick*, Captain John Hervey (who lost his life) hooked in the same attempt the head and sternmost ship of the enemy, which jammed her between two. The *Defence* had successively three or four ships engaging her; the men being almost from the first divided at their quarters to fight both sides of the ship; her masts all shot away; the main-mast falling inboard, with a great part of the lumber of the others fore and aft [on] the deck, the forecastle and quarter-deck guns disabled and useless, the helm lashed a-lee, and [the] ship no longer manageable, surrounded by the enemy, rendered it a scene only known to those who have experienced it. The marines stationed on the poop nearly all killed, and the officer at their head wounded. The master and boatswain killed, and the few remaining sent below to man the main and lower deck guns, (for it was his practice not unnecessarily to exposed the lives of the ship's company). Himself remained on deck. . . .

I appeal to Captain John Larkin, Captain Alexander Beecher, and Captain W. Roberts, the only surviving officers, (then lieutenants of the ship) to vouch for the truth of what I have asserted. The signal marks of attention and friendship shown him by Lord Howe are well known to every captain in that fleet; he considered him equal to any service, however hazardous and intricate; and with equal confidence may the country depend on his long tried ability, courage, and humanity.

I have the honour to be,

Yours, respectfully

J.C.

1794-1795 – Home Waters

DESPITE THE DEBILITATING EFFECT of the revolution on the French National Marine, and its tactical defeat on the 'Glorious First of June', it continued to have its successes. In November 1794 two British 74s, *Canada* and *Alexander*, were surprised by a superior force commanded by Rear-Admiral Neuilly, and after a running fight *Alexander* was captured. However, the fact that Sir Sydney Smith was able to sail right into Brest harbour to count the French fleet, and to get safely away, is indicative of its inefficiency.

In early 1795 Sir Alexander Hood, Lord Bridport, Admiral of the White, assumed command of the Channel Fleet, or 'Western Squadron', and was given orders to support landings by French royalist emigrés on the Quiberon peninsula. Vice-Admiral the Honourable William Cornwallis was detached with five ships to sweep the approaches to Quiberon prior to the arrival of the invasion force. There he encountered Rear-Admiral Vence who, with three ships of the line, was under orders to provide protection for the traffic along the southern coast of Brittany. Vence abandoned his convoy, and ran for the shelter of Belle-Isle. He sent a message overland for support, and Villaret-Joyeuse was ordered to sea with nine of the line. Having collected Vence's squadron, on 16 June Villaret-Joyeuse met Cornwallis. The numerical odds were heavily in favour of the French, but Cornwallis's ships' companies fought such a determined retreat that the French did not risk close action.

The sequal to Cornwallis's skirmish occurred when Admiral Lord Bridport, with fourteen ships of the line, of which eight were three-deckers, sailed to provide distant cover for the royalist landing, and encountered Villaret-Joyeuse with a squadron of nine ships, who set course for Isle de Groix off Lorient, hampered by the slow sailing of *Alexander*. She and *Redoutable* were put under tow, and he ordered his squadron to form line abreast on them, but his captains ignored the order. The next day when the British were coming into range he ordered the squadron to form line of bearing on *Alexander*, but only *Formidable* and *Tigre* obeyed. Those three ships became heavily engaged and were eventually taken. Doubting whether the remaining ships would put up any sort of fight, Villaret-Joyeuse took them into Lorient.

111

Bridport did not attempt to blockade them, but, because of shortage of supplies, Villaret-Joyeuse sent most of his crews to Brest by land. When the coast was clear, the ships were sailed back to Brest three at a time with the ferry crew returning by road for the second lot. He made no effort to interfere with the royalist invasion, but it defeated itself by its divided leadership, and by units of the army of the Republic commanded by the brilliant young General Lazare Hoche.

The transport of Princess Caroline of Brunswick from Cuxhaven to Greenwich under convoy of the Royal Navy, for her marriage to the Prince of Wales, the future George IV, was one of those great state occasions. A charming woman, known for her love of children, Caroline was to be made miserable by her marriage to which the Prince had only consented in return for the payment of his debts. He made no secret of his preference for his mistresses and eventually separated himself from Caroline, restricting her access to her child.

The capture of the *Alexander* is recorded in the biographical memoir of Richard Rodney Bligh, her captain. The conveyance of Princess Caroline was recorded by an officer onboard *Jupiter*. Somewhat unusually, the account of Sir Sydney Smith's reconnaissance of Brest was inserted in *The Naval Chronicle*'s biographical memoir of Sir Edward Pellew, who may have questioned why his own triumphs were not thought enough to retain people's interest. The operations in support of the French royalists were recorded as part of the biographical memoir of Sir John Borlase Warren who commanded the convoy escort and inshore force, with interesting supporting detail in the memoir of Joseph Ellison. Details of William Cornwallis's successful fighting withdrawal formed an important part of the biographical memoir of that officer, but his letter of thanks to his captains, officers and men was inserted years later in the memoir of Sir Erasmus Gower.

The Naval Chronicle's record of Lord Bridport's engagement consisted in the first place of a private letter from Lord Bridport which was placed in a biographical memoir appearing in the first volume, supported later by Bridport's official gazette letter which was inserted in the memoir of Sir John Borlase Warren. A narrative, constructed from interviews with two of the officers of the *Queen Charlotte*, was inserted in the memoir of the public services of Sir Andrew Snape Douglas, her commander. There is reference to this action in the Biographical Memoirs of the Right Honourable Lord Gardner (VIII 195-96) but it has been omitted because it adds nothing to our understanding.

Capture of the Alexander
From the 'Biographical Memoir of Richard Rodney Bligh, Esq.' XIII 425-430

At the commencement of the last War, Captain Bligh received a Commission for the

Excellent, of 74 guns; and in the early part of 1794, was removed to the *Alexander*, of the same force. In this ship, as he was returning on the 6th of November, to England, from Cape St. Vincent, whither he had escorted a convoy, in company with the *Canada*, he fell in with a French squadron, consisting of five ships of the line, three frigates, and a brig, commanded by Rear-Admiral Neuilly, having under him a *Chef d'Escadre*. By superior sailing, the *Canada* effected her escape, and the *Alexander* was left alone to combat this disproportionate force, which she most gallantly did for three hours, during the last of which she was attacked at once by every ship of the enemy. Yet, under these circumstances, she did not strike until great slaughter had been made among her crew, her masts and sails being utterly disabled, having eight feet water in her hold, and being dangerously on fire.

Captain Bligh's account of this desperate conflict, which was so bravely supported on his part, exhibits such an interesting specimen of British courage, accompanied by the most unassuming modesty, that we should deem ourselves guilty of injustice to his professional character, were we to withhold it from the readers of the *Naval Chronicle*. The following is his official letter, as it appeared in the *Gazette*, addressed to Mr. (now Sir Philip) Stephens [First Secretary of the Admiralty]:

On board the Marat, Brest, November 25, 1794
Sir, The arrival of the *Canada* must long since have informed their Lordships of my misfortune, in losing His Majesty's Ship *Alexander*, late under my command, having been taken by a squadron of French ships of war, consisting of five of 74 guns, three large frigates, and an armed brig, commanded by Rear-Admiral Neuilly. Farther particulars and details I herewith transmit you for their Lordship's information. We discovered this squadron on our weather bow, about half-past two o'clock, or near three, in the morning of the 6th instant, being then in latitude 48°25' north; 7°53' west, the wind then at west, and we steering north-east; on which I immediately hauled our wind, with the larboard tacks on board, and without signal, the *Canada* being close to us. We passed the strange ships a little before four, the nearest of whom at about half a mile distant, but could not discover what they were. Shortly after we bore more up, let the reefs out of the top-sails, and set steering-sails. About five, perceiving by my night-glass the strange ships stand after us, we crowded all the sail we could possibly set, as did the *Canada*, and hauled more to the eastward. About day-break the *Canada* passed us, and steering more to the northward than we did, brought her on her [our?] larboard bow. Two ships of the line and two frigates pursued; and three of the line and one frigate chased the *Alexander*. About half-past seven the French ships hoisted English colours. About a quarter past eight we hoisted our colours, upon which the French ships hauled down the English and hoisted theirs; and drawing up within gunshot, we began firing our stern chases at them, and received their bow chases. About nine, or shortly after, observing the ships in pursuit of the *Canada* drawing up with her, and firing at each other their bow and stern chases, I made the *Canada*'s signal to form a-head for our mutual support, being determined to defend the ships to the last extremity; which signal she instantly answered, and endeavoured to put it into execution, by steering towards us; but the ships in chase of her, seeing her intentions, hauled more to the starboard to cut her off, and which obliged her to steer the course she had done before. We continued firing our stern chases at the ships pursuing us till near eleven, when three ships of the line came up, and brought us to close action, which we sustained for upwards of two hours, when the ship was a complete wreck; the main-yard, spanker-

boom, and three top-gallant yards shot away; all the lower masts shot through in many places, and expected every minute to go over the side; all the other masts and yards were also wounded, more or less; nearly the whole of the standing and running rigging cut to pieces, the sails torn into ribbands, and her hull much shattered, and making a great deal of water, and with difficulty she floated into Brest. At this time the ships that had chased the *Canada* had quitted her, and were coming fast up to us, the shot of one of them at the time passing over us. Thus situated, and cut off from all resources, I judged it advisable to consult my officers, and accordingly assembled them all on the quarter deck; when, upon surveying and examining the state of the ship, (engaged as I have already described,) they deemed any farther resistance would be ineffectual, as every possible exertion had already been used in vain to save her, and therefore they were unanimously of opinion, that to resign her would be the means of saving the lives of a number of brave men. Then, and not till then, (painful to relate,) I ordered the colours to be struck; a measure which, on a full investigation, I hope and trust their Lordships will not disapprove. Hitherto I have not been able to collect an exact list of the killed and wounded, as many of the former were thrown overboard during the action, and, when taken possession of, the people were divided and sent on board the different ships, but I do not believe they exceed forty, or thereabout. . . .

I am, with great respect, &c.

R.R. BLIGH

The damage sustained by the French in the above action, was not less in proportion. They found both their prize and their own ships so shattered and unmanageable, that they were compelled to return immediately to Brest; and their departure from their cruising ground probably was the means of saving some very valuable English convoys from becoming their prey; for, at that moment, the Mediterranean trade under Admiral Cosby, and the Lisbon and Oporto trade under Captain Rodney, were within a distance of little more than twenty leagues from the scene of the action; and Lord Hood, in the *Victory* alone, was returning from Corsica, and believed to be very near; of all which circumstances the enemy were apprised.

Admiral Bligh's defence of the *Alexander* has never been surpassed in our naval annals; and, had it been his good fortune to have had with him, in that unequal conflict, such a force as might have attacked the French squadron with any fair estimate of success, the result will not be questioned by any one who is conversant with the superiority of British nautical skill and courage.

Sir Sydney Smith's Reconnoitre of Brest
From the 'Biographical Memoir of Sir Edward Pellew, Bart.' XVIII 449-450

On the 2d of January, 1795, in consequences of government having received accounts, that the French had sailed from Brest, with thirty-two sail of the line, and several frigates, the former commander [Sir J.B. Warren], accompanied by the latter [Sir Sidney Smith], sailed from Falmouth, with a squadron of frigates, to reconnoitre the port in question. Whether the *Arethusa*, Sir Edward Pellew's ship, was attached to this squadron, we are not certain; but we have some reason for thinking that she was. On the day following, Sir J.B. Warren detached Sir Sidney Smith, in the *Diamond*, to look into Brest harbour,

Chart of the Road and Port of Brest. Plate 48

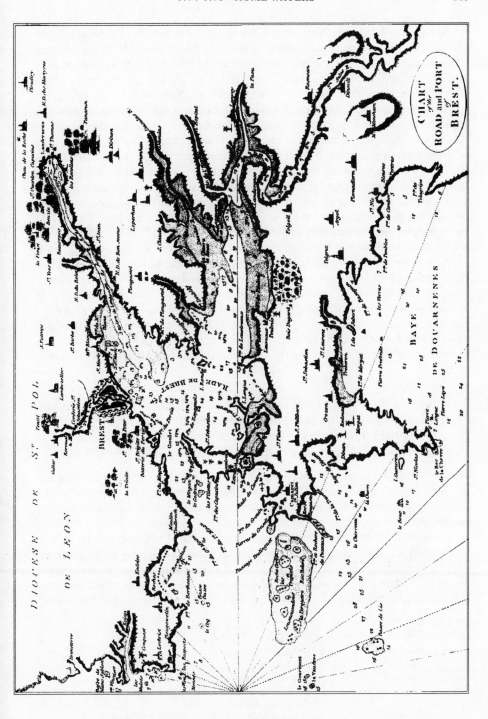

CHART of the ROAD and PORT of BREST.

whilst he remained at some distance with the rest of the squadron. The wind being to the eastward, the *Diamond* was obliged to beat up. About two, P.M. three sail were observed working up, which were soon perceived to be French men of war; and, shortly after, one of them anchored between Ushant and Brest. At five, the *Diamond* was also obliged to anchor within two miles of her, to wait for the flood tide. At eleven, Sir Sidney Smith weighed, and passed within half a mile of the Frenchman, which he distinctly discovered to be a ship of the line; under jury-top-masts, and much disabled. About two o'clock, on the morning of the 4th, the *Diamond* was well up with the entrance of Brest, where a frigate was lying at anchor. The ebb tide making down, before it was day light, Sir Sidney Smith was obliged to keep under sail, to prevent his getting to leeward, or creating suspicion; and he continued to stand across the harbour, often within musket shot of the enemy. At day-light he stood close in; and, having satisfied himself that the French fleet were at sea, he bore away to rejoin Sir John Warren. At this time, a corvette, which was coming out of Brest, hove to, and made a signal, which, not being answered by the *Diamond*, she hauled her wind, and worked in again. Soon after, Sir Sidney passed within hail of the line-of-battle ship, which was still at anchor. Apparently, she had no upper-deck guns mounted, and was very leaky. Sir Sidney asked her commander, in French, if he wanted "*any assistance.*" He answered, "*No; he had been dismasted in a heavy gale, and had parted with the French fleet three days ago.*" Some farther conversation passed, after which Sir Sidney crowded sail, and stood out to sea. He had so completely deceived the French men, by the manner in which he had disguised his ship, that they had not the slightest suspicion of her being an English man of war.

Narrative of the Proceedings of the Squadron Under the Command of Commodore John Willett Payne,[1] Appointed to Conduct Her Serene Highness The Princess Caroline of Brunswick to England
From the 'Minutes of an Officer on Board the Jupiter.' III 113-118

On the fourth of December (1794) Captain Payne, being appointed to conduct her Serene Highness the Princess Caroline of Brunswick to England, attended at the Admiralty, and received his commission, as Commodore of a Squadron of yachts ordered on that service.

Captain T. Larcom being in the mean time nominated to command the *Russell*, Commodore Payne hoisted his broad pendant on board the *Augusta* yacht. It being however thought expedient that a superior force should be sent, the Commodore shifted his broad pendant from the *Augusta*, to the *Jupiter* - a fifty gun ship, which had been lately repaired at Sheerness; commanded by Captain W. Lechmere, late of the *Saturn*.[2]

1 *Vid.* page 23.
2 Officers of His Majesty's Ship *Jupiter*, whilst on the above Service

Commodore	John Willett Payne
Captain	William Lechmere
Lieutenants	Jemmett Brown Mainwaring, George Irwin
	James Dunbar, Joseph Spear, Hon. Courtney Boyle
	George Barker, *Acting*
Marines	*Major* Robert Anderson, William Aldrige, *Lieutenant*
Warrant Officers	George Hermes, *Lieutenant*, Thomas Landseer, *Purser*
	Reverend James Stanier Clarke, *Chaplain*
	Francis Mason, *Commodore's Secretary*

At sun-rise, on the thirty-first of December, the Commodore saluted Vice Admiral Dalrymple, at Sheerness, with thirteen guns, which were returned.

On the second of January, 1795, at half past twelve P.M. made the signal to weigh; at half past five the squadron came-to, and moored at the Great Nore.

On the thirteenth of February, Commodore Payne struck his broad pendant, and went to London - returned on the twenty-sixth, hoisted the pendant, and the next day having unmoored, dropped with the squadron further to the eastward. On the *Jupiter's* coming to anchor, the rest of the squadron manned the shrouds and cheered the commodore, which was returned.[3]

On the *second* of March, at five A.M. made the signal to weigh: sailed in company with the *Phaeton* and *Latona* frigates; *Martin*, and *Hawke* sloops; *Cobourg, Active, Rose, Fly*, and *Princess Royal* cutters. At half past seven fell in with his Majesty's sloop *Lark*, hailed her, and she joined company. On the third, made the *Phaeton's* signal to look out: at noon saw the *Texel* bearing E.S.E. seven or eight leagues. *Fourth* - At one P.M. recalled the *Phaeton* by signal; at five Schelling Island S.E. by E. five leagues. *Fifth* - Fresh breezes and thick foggy weather; sent the *Cobourg* to make the land: at six A.M. made the signal with five guns to bring to on the starboard tack, hove-to, fired fog guns: at eight the *Cobourg* returned with a pilot; made the signal to bear up, and sail large: half past eleven made the signal to anchor; at noon came-to with the best bower, in five fathoms; veered an whole cable; repeated the signal to anchor with two guns. *Sixth* - Fresh breezes and thick foggy weather; A.M. clear weather; Heligoland[4] light, N. distant eleven, or twelve miles; sent the *Rose* cutter to the island for pilots: at six made the signal with a gun for pilots; half past, fired two guns shotted at a pilot boat to bring her to. All the squadron in company except the *Lark*. At noon two pilots came on board to carry the *Jupiter* into safe moorings, off Cuxhaven; which being the largest ship that had ever approached so near to that coast occasioned much anxiety: the *Lark* still missing; great apprehensions for her safety. *Seventh* - P.M. fresh breezes and thick weather with rain.: at one made the signal to anchor; and at half past two, with the best bower, came to in seven fathoms, abreast of New Work, Cuxhaven town bearing S.b.W. At ten A.M. threw out the signal to weigh; weighed and made sail with the squadron; at half past eleven threw out the signal to anchor; came-to off Cuxhaven, with the small bower in eight fathoms; made the signal for the squadron to moor: the *Lark* still missing.

The *eighth*, P.M. fresh breezes, and thick foggy weather. At half past one saluted by the fort with nine guns; an equal number returned. A.M. fresh gales, with snow; the river full of ice; which was driven out to sea with the tide in large masses, or whole fields at once: got the sheet anchor over the side: at six struck lower yards, and top-gallant masts; got the spritsail-yard in. At eight, the *Hawke*, who had suffered severely during the tempestuous night, parted, and with great violence drove foul of the *Jupiter*: the scene was particularly alarming, as the safety of both ships, from the violence of the tide, was at stake: providentially, with the assistance of day-light, and the skill of the officers on board, no material injury was occasioned: brought home the best bower anchor, got the spare anchor over the side, and double rounded the cables to secure them from the ice.

3 For a list of the squadron, *vid*. page 34.
4 Or Holy Island, is N.W. by N. about eight leagues from the mouth of the Elbe, which all ships endeavour to make, that are going to that river, or the Weser, and Eyder; it belongs to the King of Denmark. From the Monk Rock, which appears above water almost as high as the island, above a mile at S.S.E. there is a dangerous *sunken rock*; but the depth of eight or nine fathoms will keep a ship clear without it.

On the *ninth*, the severe weather, for a time, became more moderate - hove up the best bower; moored ship, and sent the stream anchor to the *Hawke*: and here we must notice an event, which was equally singular and interesting. During this day, a man who had been taken from off a piece of ice, that was floating out to sea, by one of the Blackeness pilot boats, was brought on shore a Cuxhaven, and gave the following account of his sufferings. "He had belonged to an Hambro' trading vessel, bound from London to that place, laden with groceries; during her passage she was lost, amid the ice, January 28th, on a sand off Cuxhaven. The master, with a boy, and the sailor above-mentioned, got upon the sand, at that time covered with ice, and preserved life with some wine, and biscuit, which they had saved from the wreck; at the end of eleven days, the master and boy died. The survivor, with an unshaken resolution and reliance on Providence, would not allow himself to despond; every night he laid down upon one of the dead bodies, and put the other over him; the intense cold keeping them from being offensive: in this forlorn and melancholy state he slept sound, and declared that he constantly received great consolation from dreams, which portended his future safety. The wine and biscuit being at length expended, he discovered some cockles on a part of the sand not covered with ice, upon which he existed until the ninth of March, and was thus miraculously saved. When he awoke that day, he found the mass of ice had separated, and was drifting out to sea - he then gave himself up for lost." On his first landing at Cuxhaven, having sufficiently recovered to make himself understood - for the warmth of the house caused an agony of pain, his relation found credit but with few; until they recollected that a vessel answering his description had been wrecked; and also saw the bills of lading which he produced.

On the *eleventh* of March, to the great joy of every one, who had imagined she was lost, the *Lark* rejoined. On the *fourteenth*, the weather again became squally, with snow: at four P.M. were obliged to strike lower yards, and top-gallant masts. At two A.M. a field of ice unusually large came with great violence athwart the *Jupiter*, and brought home the best bower anchor: the ship immediately drove towards the shore, and serious apprehensions for her safety were entertained; these the darkness of the night, the danger of the coast, and the peculiar severity of the weather, which covered the rigging with ice, and rendered it extremely difficult for the crew to perform their duty, greatly increased. The *Jupiter* was at length brought up by the best bower: hove short on the small bower, swayed up lower yards, and top gallant-masts; at half past eight weighed the small bower, shifted the birth [sic], and came-to with the small bower - veered to an whole cable. These precautions were hardly taken, and the crew by no means recovered from their great exertions during this dreadful night; when another field of ice came again athwart the *Jupiter*, and brought home the small bower. Without delay the best bower anchor was let go; when, notwithstanding its immense weight, to the great astonishment of everyone, it made no more effect on the impenetrable thickness of the ice than a log of wood: the situation of the ship during this interval of life and death, for such it appeared, was excessively precarious; at length meeting with some division in the ice, the cable to the joy of every one was heard to run out - a sound more delightful never charmed the ear of a mariner! On weighing the small bower one of the arms was found gone[5] - got the spare anchor over the side; cut the clinch of the small bower, and bent it to the spare anchor.

5 Surely the hemp, anchors, &c. for the Naval Service, on which the very lives of the crew depend, should not be furnished by contract: our enemies, in this respect, have a great advantage.

The annexed plate is a representation of the interior harbour of Brest. In the
distance, inclining to the left, is seen the dockyard, with the sheer-hulk, and vessels
of war in ordinary. Extending towards the right is the town with its fortifications.
To the left, approaching the fore-ground, is the guardship; and on the right a frigate
is seen proceeding to sea. ^{Plate 47}

The severe season continued, with but little intermission, until the *eighteenth* of
March, when the *Phaeton*, (who had made the signal of inability on the 16th, and put to
sea) again rejoined. A great quantity of ice still continued in the Elbe. On the twenty-
eighth, the hardships, and anxiety which the squadron had experienced were happily
terminated. The day had been unusually fine; the weather had become more genial;
and the whole scene had lost much of its gloom and dreariness; when, at half past four,
guns were heard in the offing; and soon the standard being discerned in a cutter standing
out of the Elbe, announced that the Princess of Brunswick was on board. What joy and
exultation pervaded the breast of every one! The preparative signal was immediately
made with one gun. The barge was dispatched with the First Lieutenant to steer,
accompanied with the boats of all the squadron: the scene which followed, had a peculiar
interest and grandeur. The procession of the boats, with their pendants flying, rowing
in order, and keeping time with their oars, had a fine effect. When the royal standard
was unfurled in the barge, the ships of the squadron were manned; and a salute of
twenty-one guns was fired from each of the ships. The evening continued remarkably
favourable: the sun seemed to linger in the horizon, and for a time, owing to the smoke,
had all the appearance of an eclipse; it then darted out with fresh lustre. On the sides of
the accommodation ladder of the *Jupiter* were placed midshipmen in their uniforms;
the officers, and guard of marines, were drawn up on each side the quarter-deck: the
moment her Royal Highness had ascended the first step, which was about six o'clock,
the standard was hoisted on the maintop-gallant mast-head of the *Jupiter*, and received
with customary marks of respect.

The favourable weather, with the exception of some foggy days, continued during
the remainder of the voyage. Her Royal Highness particularly endeared herself to the

crew, and shewed the utmost affability and attention to every one. The Princess was attended by Lord Malmesbury, and Mrs. Harcourt. An Admiral of high rank in the service of the Prince of Orange, was also on board. At half past four on the morning of the twenty-ninth, the signal to unmoor was thrown out, and afterwards the signal to weigh. At five the *Cobourg* cutter sailed for England; and at noon the chief pilot left the *Jupiter* abreast of the *Red Buoy.*

The twenty-ninth being Sunday, her Royal Highness at two o'clock had divine service performed on the quarter-deck of the *Jupiter*, by the Chaplain, the Reverend J.S. Clarke. On the *Thirtieth*, at seven in the morning, three strange sail were discovered in the southward; at half past, the *Latona, Lark,* and *Rose* cutter by signal were ordered to chase. At half past nine the *Martin*'s signal was made, to repeat between the *Jupiter*, and the chasing ships; who were soon recalled. The strange sail afterwards proved to be two French privateers with a prize, they had captured. At noon it came on thick foggy weather.

At half past seven, on the evening of the *third* of April, the *Jupiter* anchored at the Nore: and at sun-rise the next day, Vice-Admiral Buckner manned ship, and saluted the standard, as did the other ships under his flag. His Majesty's yachts the *Princess Augusta,* and *Mary,* came out, and joined company. At six the Commodore threw out the signal to weigh; and at seven for the squadron to part company. Accordingly his Majesty's ships *Phaeton, Latona, Hawke, Martin,* and *Lark,* parted company, and saluted the standard; as did vice-Admiral Buckner, and the ships at the Nore. Made sail standing up the river; at eleven came-to off Gravesend. At six P.M. Tilbury Fort saluted the standard.

Early on the fifth, her Royal Highness, attended by Lord Malmesbury, Mrs. Harcourt, and Commodore Payne, went in the barge on board the *Princess Augusta* yacht: when the standard was hoisted at the maintop, and Commodore Payne's broad pendant at the foretop. As the Princess passed Woolwich, the whole band of the royal regiment of artillery played God save the King, and the military cheered the standard - it was the first burst of loyalty her Royal Highness had heard on English ground, and it drew from her tears of joy. About noon the *Augusta* yacht reached Greenwich, when the Princess embarked in the barge, steered as before by Lieutenant Mainwaring, and landed on the right of the stairs, in front of the Hospital; where she was received by Sir Hugh Palliser, the Governor.

Cornwallis's Retreat
From the 'Biographical memoirs of the Honourable William Cornwallis.' VII 20-25

In November 1791, Commodore Cornwallis shifted his pendant to the *Minerva*, and shortly afterwards returned to Europe; he retained the command of his ship long after her arrival in England, and on the 1st of February, 1793, was promoted to the rank of Rear-Admiral of the White.

In May 1794, Admiral Cornwallis hoisted his flag on board the *Excellent*, and on the promotion in July the same year was advanced to the rank of Vice of the Blue; his flag was shifted to the *Caesar* in August, and in December it was flying on board the *Royal Sovereign.* There were few Officers to whom the country looked with greater confidence than Admiral Cornwallis, or from whose known gallantry and great experience higher expectations were formed, when occasion should call forth his abilities. Hitherto, although actively employed several years on the Channel station, no event had occurred in the course of his service of importance enought to attract the public attention; fortune at length gave him an opportunity of justifying the opinion the world had formed of him, and adding greatly to the naval glory of his country.

In the month of June 1795, Admiral Cornwallis commanded a detached squadron; cruising in the Bay of Biscay, and on the 7th he fell in with and chased three French line of battle ships and six frigates, the enemy being between the English and the land; the wind unfortunately carried them into Belleisle Road, where several large ships were at anchor, before the squadron could come up with them, although they were so near that the *Phaeton* exchanged some shot with the line of battle ships. The Admiral followed as far as was prudent, and then hauled his wind; in standing off they fell in with a convoy under the protection of three frigates, who pushed round the south end of Belleisle, eight of the convoy were taken, but the frigates saved themselves by running in shore among the shoals; the prizes were part of a convoy from Bourdeaux, laden with wine and naval stores, under the protection of three line of battle ships and eight frigates.

On the 16th, in the morning, standing in with the land, near the Penmarks, the *Phaeton* was sent ahead to look out, the Admiral standing after her with the rest of the squadron. At ten a signal was made by the advanced frigate for a fleet ahead, and afterwards that they were of superior force, upon which the signal was made to haul the wind on the starboard tack; at this period the hulls of the strange sails were not visible, they were to leeward on a wind, and thirty were counted from the *Royal Sovereign*; the Admiral continued to stand on the starboard tack, keeping the squadron collected. On ascertaining the enemy's force, by signal from Captain Stopford, it was found to be as follows: *thirteen* sail of the line, *fourteen* frigates, *two* brigs, and a cutter. To oppose which, the British squadron consisted of the

Royal Sovereign	100	Admiral Cornwallis
		Captain Whitby
Triumph	74	Sir Erasmus Gower
Mars	74	Sir Charles Cotton
Brunswick	74	Lord C. Gitzgerald
Bellerophon	74	Lord Cranston
Pallas and *Phaeton* frigates		Curzon, Stopford

In all *six* ships to cope with *thirty*. They might say with our immortal Bard, "God's arm strike with us! 'tis a fearful odds."

In the afternoon near one-half the enemy's force tacked and stood in shore; the wind fell very much, and coming round to the northward, brought these ships to windward of our force, the other ships at the same time laying up for them. They were discovered in the morning before daylight on both quarters of the English squadron.

About nine in the morning the enemy's frigates, one excepted, were all ranged abreast of, and to windward of the squadron, the attack was about this time began by one of the front line of battle ship on the *Mars*. The dispositions of the British force appear to have been thus: the *Brunswick* and *Bellerophon*, who were heavy sailing ships, and obliged to carry all their canvas, ahead of the Admiral, and *Mars* and *Triumph* being the rear ships,

> Slowly they mov'd, and wedged in firm array,
> The close compacted squadron won their way.

One of the enemy's frigates ranged up on the *Mars'* larboard quarter, they yawed and fired her broadside, which she frequently repeated; this was the only ship of that class which came down or attempted any thing during the day.

The line of battle ships came up in succession, and a teazing fire was kept up by them, with intervals, during the whole day, which the English ships returned from their stern chases; the Admiral proportioning his sail to the slowest of the squadron, and edging away to support them when it was requisite.

Towards the evening they appeared to have an intention of making a more serious attempt upon the *Mars*, which ship had fallen a little to leeward. The Admiral did not suffer her, however, to sustain the attack unaided, but immediately bore up to her assistance, on which the enemy drew back.

> On Ajax thus a weight of Trojans hung,
> The strokes redoubled on his buckler rung,
> Confiding now in bulky strength he stands,
> Now turns, and backwards bears their yielding bands;
> Now stiff recedes and hardly seems to fly,
> And threats his followers with retorted eye.
>
> Pope's *Iliad*

This was their last effort, if, as Admiral Cornwallis observes, any thing they had done deserved that appellation; they appeared to be drawing off, and before sunset the enemy's fleet had tacked and were standing from the British. No words can do more justice to the conduct of the fleet in general, than those of the commander in his public letter. Admiral Cornwallis observes, that

"The *Mars* and *Triumph* being the sternmost ships, were of course more exposed to the enemy's fire, and I cannot too much commend the spirited conduct of Sir Charles Cotton, and Sir Erasmus Gower, the captains of those ships. Lord Charles Fitzgerald also in the *Brunswick* kept up a very good fire from the after guns, but that ship was the whole time obliged to carry every sail. The *Bellerophon* being nearly under the same circumstances, I was glad to keep in some measure as a reserve, having reason at first to suppose there would be full occasion for the utmost exertion of us all, and being rather ahead of me was not able to fire much. I considered that ship as a treasure in store, having heard of her former achievements, and observing the spirit manifested by all on board when she past me, joined to the activity and zeal showed by Lord Cranston during the whole cruise. I am also much indebted to Captain Whitby for his activity and unremitting diligence on board the *Royal Sovereign*. The frigates showed the greatest attention and alertness; I kept the *Pallas* near me to repeat signals, which Captain Curzon performed much to my satisfaction. Indeed I shall ever feel the impression which the good conduct of the captains, officers, seamen, marines, and soldiers in the squadron has made on my mind; and it was the greatest pleasure I ever received to see the spirit manifested in the men, who, instead of being cast down at seeing thirty sail of the enemy's ships attacking our little squadron, were in the highest spirits imaginable.

I do not mean the *Royal Sovereign* alone, the same spirit was shewn in all the ships as they came near me; and although (circumstanced as we were) we had no great reason to complain of the conduct of the enemy, yet our men could not help repeatedly expressing their contempt of them. Could common prudence have allowed me to let loose their valour, I hardly know what might not have been accomplished by such men.

Little damage was sustained by the squadron in general. The *Mars* had twelve wounded, none killed, her masts and sails much cut and the *Triumph* shifted some of her sails, but the damage she received is so trifling, at least in her captain's eye, that Sir Erasmus Gower has not thought it worth reporting; indeed the cool and firm conduct of that ship was such, that it appeared to me the enemy's ships dared not to come near her."

We have no hesitation in pronouncing (and think our opinion will be seconded by those who are best able to appreciate naval merit), that such a retreat as the one we have just described, reflects as much honour on the abilities of the man who conducted it, as would the achievement of the most splendid victory. The retreat of the *Ten Thousand* has been more admired by judges of military merit than all the victories of Alexander.

Perhaps there never was a comparision more flattering to the naval prowess of our countrymen than the conduct exhibited by the different squadrons of the two nations from the 7th of June to the 17th; on the former day, Admiral Cornwallis fell in with three sail of the enemy's line and six frigates, they immediately fled in confusion to the cover of their batteries. On the latter day, when the English had to contend with more than treble their force, their retreat was so well conducted, and their squadron presented so imposing an aspect, that the enemy kept baying at a distance without daring to bring them to close action, although evidently in their power; sometimes they ventured to approach, but finding (if we dare take a liberty with Milton),

> How quick they turn'd; and retiring, behind them shot
> Sharp sleet of iron shower;

speedily bore up, and at length withdrew ingloriously, yielding the palm to a force so greatly inferior.

Nor should the gallantry of our noble tars pass without a comment; inspired with confidence by the steady conduct of their officers, they repeatedly encouraged each other during the whole of the day by animating cheers, which, we doubt not, had its due effect on the enemy.

We have heard it asserted, that at one period of this glorious day the *Phaeton*, being at a distance from the fleet, let fly her top-gallant-sheets (the signal for discovering a fleet), which is said to have given, if possible, additional spirits to the seamen. Allowing this to have been a preconcerted manoeuvre, it reflects great credit on the head that planned it; no conjectural circumstances, however, can add lustre to the fame Admiral Cornwallis acquired by this unparalleled achievement.

A promotion taking place in this month, the subject of our Memoir became Vice-Admiral of the Blue, and in the year 1796, was appointed to command on the West India station; in this year he was also appointed by his Majesty to the rank of Rear-Admiral of Great Britain.

During the *Royal Sovereign*'s passage to the West Indies a gale of wind so disabled her, that the Admiral thought it necessary to return to England; the Lords of the Admiralty doubting of the propriety of this measure, made it the subject of a Court Martial. Admiral Cornwallis was honourably acquitted, and shortly after, at his own request, struck his flag. This misunderstanding is the more to be regretted, as it deprived the country of the service of so valuable an Officer when much wanted. On the 14th of February 1799, he was promoted to the rank of Admiral of the Blue; and when the distinguished Nobleman, who now presides at the Admiralty [Earl St. Vincent], was appointed to that important station, Admiral Cornwallis succeeded him in the command of the Channel Fleet, and hoisted his flag on board the *Ville de Paris*, in February 1801.

The enemy kept so close in Brest harbour during the latter part of the war, that a

Commander destined to watch their motions could only exert his vigilance; however, should any future occasion demand his services, high as the reputation of the British flag has been raised of late years, it will not have its lustre diminished while led by a Cornwallis.

From the 'Biographical memoirs of Admiral Sir Erasmus Gower.' *XXX 298-99*

Sir Erasmus was next appointed acting captain for Lord Hugh Seymour, in the *Canada*, 74 guns, and afterwards to the *Triumph*, of the same force. In Admiral Cornwallis's celebrated retreat, the gallant captain and crew of the *Triumph* were amongst those who received the following spirited encomium of their noble commander-in-chief, dated June 18, 1795:

"Vice-admiral Cornwallis returns his sincere thanks to the captains, officers, seamen, and marines or soldiers, of the ships under his command, for their steady and gallant conduct in the presence of the French fleet yesterday; which firmness he has no doubt determined the enemy from making a more serious attack. - It would give the vice-admiral pleasure, to put the whole of their exertions in effect, meeting a more equal force; when the country would receive advantage, as it now does honour, from the spirit so strongly manifested by those brave men.

WM CORNWALLIS"

Fleet Under the Command of Lord Bridport on the 23d of June 1795. [290]

Ships	Guns	Captains
Royal George	100	Admiral Lord Bridport
		Captain W. Donnett
Queen Charlotte	100	Captain Sir Andrew SnapeDouglas
Prince of Wales	98	Rear Admiral Harvey
		Captain Bazely
London	98	Captain Griffith
Queen	98	Vice Admiral Sir A. Gardner
		Captain Bedford
Barfleur	98	Captain J.R.Dacres
Prince George	98	Captain W. Edge
Prince	98	Captain C.P. Hamilton
Sans Pareille	84	Captain Lord Hugh Seymour
		Captain Browell
Irresistible	74	Captain Grindall
Orion	74	Captain Sir James Saumarez
Colossus	74	Captain Monckton
Russell	74	Captain Thomas Larcom
Valiant	74	Captain Joseph Larcom
Frigates		
Revolutionaire	44	Captain Francis Cole
Thalia	36	Captain Lord H. Powlett
Aquilon	32	Captain R. Barlow
Astrea	32	Captain R. Lane
Babet	22	Captain Codrington

Charon hospital ship	44	Captain Lock	
Fire Ships			
Incendiary	14	Captain Draper	
Megaera	14	Captain Blackwood	
One lugger			

The French Fleet Consisted of

Ships	Guns	Ships	Guns
Le Peuple	120	*Le Formidable* (taken)	74
Le Nestor	80	*Le Jean Bart*	74
La Redoutable	80	*Les Droits de l'Homme*	74
Le Mutius	80	*Alexander* (taken)	74
Le Tigre (taken)	80	*La Voisténue*	74
Le Fougueux	80	*La Brave* (razée)	56
La Zélie	74	*La Scaevola* (razée)	56
Frigates			
La Virginie	*L'Insurgeante*	*La Régenerée*	*La Cocarde*
La Franternitée	*La Fidelle*	*La Fortitude*	*La Prosperpine*
La Nante	*La Rénard*	*La Dréade*	
Corvettes	Brigs	Cutters	
La Constance	*La Talente*	*La Peulterre*	
La Senseuse	*Le Papillon*	*La Montagne*	
		Le Dragon	

Account of Lord Bridport's Action
From the 'Biographical Memoir of Lord Bridport.' [1 278-282]

We shall give an account of this glorious action, from private letters which have not yet been published, and shall reserve the principal part of Lord Bridport's Gazette letter for its proper place, in our Historical Narrative of Naval Actions during the present war.

"We are now lying at single anchor at Spithead (June 12, 1795). The signal was made yesterday to prepare for sailing, and we unmoored this morning. Our fleet consists of fourteen sail of the line, five frigates, two fireships, one hospital ship, and a lugger. On the 22d, at four o'clock in the morning, being in latitude 47° 4' N. and longitude 4° 16' W. Belle Isle bearing E. by N. half N. 14 leagues, the frigates made the signal for a strange fleet, which we soon discovered to be the French. They were then right a-head of us, but the wind shifting in their favour, brought them on our weather bow. At six, the admiral made the following signals to chase: the *Sans Pareille*, *Colossus*, *Valiant*, *Russell*, *Irresistible*, and *Orion*; and at seven the signal was out for a general chase. The enemy at this critical moment had all sail set. We continued in chase all day, and the ensuing night, with very little wind, until three next morning, when, to our great joy, there sprung up a fine breeze. At four we discovered the Isle de Groais upon our lee bow; by six the *Orion* and *Irresistible* were well up with the *Alexander*, and began to engage. A short time afterwards the *Queen Charlotte* got up; when her gallant and since lamented commander, Sir A. S. Douglas, instantly opened a tremendous and well directed

Lord Bridport's action off L'Orient, 23d June 1795. The design of Mr. Pocock, in this engraving, is to give the public a clear idea of the situation of the British fleet, in Lord Bridport's glorious action off L'Orient; the particulars of which are detailed in the preceding memoir. The view is taken from the N.W. when the body of the enemy's fleet were got close in with Port Louis, and just before Lord Bridport made the signal to leave off chase.

In the centre is seen the *Royal George*, with the rest of the fleet continuing the chase. The *Tigre*, having struck her colours, and bore up, appears to the left: on the right, is the *Formidable* and the *Alexander*. The Isle de Groias, with Port Louis, and L'Orient, in distance. The English ships in this, as well as in succeeding designs, being taken from real sketches, may be considered as correct portraits. [Plate 7]

fire on both sides. The *Russell*, by a quarter past six, was also pretty well up, but did not begin to fire until she got abreast of the *Queen Charlotte*, to windward of her, when she opened a most spirited broadside. The *Russell*, as she passed, engaged several ships that were together, particularly the *Alexander*, who was to leeward. In about a quarter of an hour, one of the ships, which the *Russell* had engaged, took fire on the poop, and in a short time her mizen mast went overboard when she bore up and struck: this ship was the *Formidable*, of 74 guns. The *Sans Pareille* and *Collossus* had now been in action nearly twenty minutes. After the *Formidable* had taken fire, the smoke cleared up to leeward, and we perceived the *Alexander* had also struck. By this time we were got some distance into the Bay: all the braces, preventer braces, and rigging of the *Russell* were much cut; but we wore ship, and engaged about half and hour longer, when we were obliged to haul off to repair our damages, and reeve fresh braces. When we had got our good old ship into a manageable state, which we were not able to accomplish under a quarter of an hour, we made sail to renew the engagement. The *Royal George* passed us, and desired we would go to leeward of her, which we did, and then hauled up to fulfil our wishes: but before we could come into action, the *Royal George* had got close up alongside *Le Tigre*, and having engaged her about three minutes, she bore up and struck. Lord Bridport then advanced, with his usual spirit, and engaged again; firing at the same time at the French three decker, and keeping up an heavy fire on both sides. We also were by this time up, and engaging again; when the admiral, not thinking it prudent to advance any farther into the bay, as the enemy had already opened a battery upon us from the shore, bore up, and passing to leeward, whilst we were firing, gave us three cheers. About nine o'clock the firing ceased on both sides, when Admiral Gardner, in the *Queen*, made our signal to take possession of the *Tigre*. We accordingly hoisted out our boats and boarded her: but were obliged to make the signal to the Admiral of not being able to take her in tow, as our braces, preventer braces, and bowlines, were mostly shot away, and the sails and running rigging were again very much cut. The French fired red hot shot, and what they call *Langrage shot:* they fired very high, and aimed chiefly at the masts and rigging. We had only one man killed in the action; two died soon afterwards of their wounds. The *Tigre* had three hundred men killed and wounded; the others suffered in proportion. The remainder of the enemy's fleet made their escape into L'Orient. On the 14th of July our prizes, the *Tigre*, *Formidable*, and *Alexander*, arrived at Plymouth.[6] The *Alexander* received considerable damage; both her stern and sides are full of holes. Sir J. B. Warren's squadron of three line of battle ships and one frigate, were put into the order of battle by Lord Bridport, on his receiving intelligence of the force of the enemy, but could not come up until the action was entirely over. On the day after the action, Mr. Keith Stewart, a midshipman on board the *Queen Charlotte*, being induced by fatal curiosity to go over the ship's side to the carpenters, who were employed in stopping the shot holes, lost his hold and fell overboard. Every assistance was immediately given, but without success. He was the eldest son of the late Vice Admiral, the Honourable, Keith Stewart; a very promising young man, sincerely regretted by every one.

An action more to the credit of the noble admiral who conducted it, or of those officers, who fought under him, never was achieved; and, accordingly, this glorious victory is highly estimated by professional men. It certainly merits its due share of glory amid the victories of the present period, whose lustre can alone be abated by the injudicious comparisons of the ignorant, or those improper suggestions, which have in view to elevate a part above the rest. The column, that records the naval renown of the present war, should publish to all the world, the continued series of success we have experienced under the blessing of God, and should establish what is alone the truth: *that all in their consequences, and at the different periods in which they were gained, have equal claims upon this country: the accomplishment of each, in its order, had put the nation in a condition to attain the victory in succession.* The difference between the English and French fleets we have already stated in a preceding number.[7]

So near the coast was the British fleet during the above action, that the pilot on board the *Royal George* absolutely refused to proceed; when the gallant Lord Bridport, whose skill is alone equalled by his intrepidity, took charge of the ship himself. They

6 The *Tigre*, 80 guns, is at present [1798] commanded by Sir Sydney Smith. The *Formidable*, now the *Belleisle*, is repairing at Portsmouth. The *Alexander*, formerly taken from us by a French squadron in November 1794, was in the action off the Nile commanded by Captain A. J. Ball.

7 *Naval Chron.* No. ii. p. 157. Lord Bridport had fourteen sail of the line, opposed to twelve, and two razees of 56 guns each. Five English frigates to eleven of the French.

who know the peculiar dangers of the French coast, will best appreciate such an act of valour. Five of the French captains were broke for not taking the *Queen Charlotte*.

Lord Bridport, in his letter, says: - "I beg also to be allowed to mark my approbation, in a particular manner, of Captain Domett's conduct, serving under my flag, for his manly spirit, and for the assistance I received from his active and attentive mind. I feel likewise great satisfaction, in doing justice to the meritorious conduct of all the officers of every class, as well as to the bravery of the seamen and soldiers in the *Royal George*, upon this event, and upon former occasions."

Bridport's Report
From the 'Biographical Memoir of Sir John Borlase Warren, Bart. K.B.'
III 344-345

The following is the official letter from his Lordship, which we have not before inserted:

Royal George, at Sea, June 24th, 1795
Sir, It is with sincere satisfaction I acquaint you, for the information of the Lords Commissioners of the Admiralty, that his Majesty's squadron under my command attacked the enemy's fleet, consisting of twelve ships of the line, with eleven frigates and some smaller cruisers, on the twenty-third instant, close in with Port L'Orient. The ships which struck are the *Alexander, Le Formidable*, and *Le Tigre*, which were with difficulty retained. If the enemy had not been protected, and sheltered by the land, I have every reason to believe that a much greater number, if not all the line of battle ships, would have been taken or destroyed. In detailing the particulars of this service, I am to state, that on the dawn of day on the twenty-second instant, the *Nymph* and *Astrea* being the look out frigates ahead, made the signal for the enemy's fleet. I soon perceived there was no intention to meet me in battle; consequently I made the signal for four of the best sailing ships, the *Sans Pareil, Orion, Russel* [sic], and *Colossus*, and soon afterwards for the whole fleet to chase, which continued all that day, and during the night, with very little wind.

Early on the morning of the twenty-third, the headmost ships, the *Irresistible, Orion, Queen Charlotte, Russel, Colossus*, and *Sans Pareil*, were pretty well up with the enemy, and a little before six o'clock the action began, and near to some batteries, and in the face of a strong naval port; which will manifest to the public the zeal, intrepidity, and skill of the Admirals, Captains, and all other Officers, seamen, and soldiers, employed on this service; and they are fully entitled to my warmest acknowledgments.

I beg also to be allowed to mark my approbation, in particular manner, of Captain Domett's conduct, serving under my flag, for his manly spirit, and for the assistance I received from his active and attentive mind. I feel likewise great satisfaction in doing justice to the meritorious conduct of the Officers of every class, as well as to the bravery of the seamen and soldiers in the *Royal George*, upon this and upon former occasions.

I judged it necessary, upon the information I had received of the force of the enemy, to put the *Robust, Thunderer*, and *Standard*, into my line of battle; but their distance from my squadron, and under the circumstance of the little wind, they could not join me until after the action was over.

I shall proceed upon my station as soon as I have ordered a distribution of the prisoners and other necessary arrangements for the squadron. It is my intention to keep at sea to fulfil every part of my instructions.

I have judged it necessary to send Captain Domett with my dispatches, who will give their Lordships such farther particulars as shall have occurred to him on the victory we have gained.

You will herewith receive a list of the killed and wounded, with the ships they belonged to, and the Commanders names.

I am, Sir, &c.

BRIDPORT

Evan Nepean, Esq.

N.B. I am happy to find by the report made to me, that Captain Grindall's wounds are not dangerous.

Two Officers' Journals

From the 'Memoir of the Public Services of the late Captain Sir Andrew Snape Douglas, Knt.' XXV 363-370

If the services of Sir A.S. Douglas had been great, whilst he continued in Lord Howe's fleet during the year 1794, they were equally pre-eminent, and have certainly been much too unnoticed, in the memorable action which Lord Bridport had with the French fleet, on the 23d of June, 1795. The following narrative is given from some remarks by two of Sir A.S. Douglas's officers, on board the *Queen Charlotte*; beginning with the proceedings of Lord Bridport's fleet, from Friday, June 12th, 1795.

"Sailed from Spithead with a fresh breeze at east, the *Sans Pareil* (the *Prince* joined the day following) with *Colossus, Queen, London, Orion, Royal George, Queen Charlotte, Russel, Prince George, Valiant, Prince of Wales, Barfleur,* and *Irresistible,* of the line, frigates - *Thalia, Aquilon, Revolutionaire,* and *Astrea.* - *La Babet,* of 20 guns, *Charon,* hospital ship, *Incendiary* and *Megaera* fire-ships, with two cutters and two luggers. One Tuesday, June 16, after the clearing away of a thick fog, we saw a squadron under Sir John Warren, of three sail of the line, and six frigates, with several gun-boats and transports, consisting of about forty-five sail, and containing 5 or 6,000 French emigrants, with arms, provisions, and stores, to be landed in Quiberon Bay. On the 17th of June we saw Ushant, S.W. by W. four leagues. Spoke an American, who informed us that she had passed through the French fleet off the Penmarks, two days before, consisting of 27 sail.

Thursday, June 18th. At noon the Saints bore E. by S. three leagues. The wind N.N.E. We stood off to N.W. losing sight of Sir John Warren's fleet far to leeward standing to the eastward. By this it appeared, that the news obtained from the American had not been believed, or otherwise they would not have been thus exposed to the risque of being captured. On the next day, Friday, June 19th, the wind became violent from the N.E. At the dawn of day, a tender from Sir John Warren spoke the Admiral - bore down, and soon after his fleet hove in sight, bearing S.E. by S. and making the best of their way to rejoin; they seemed as if chased by an enemy. The admiral made the signal to prepare for battle. The *Galatea* came from Sir John, and sent a boat to the *Royal George.* The *Artois* hailed; and gave us to understand that she had seen the enemy's fleet. The next day, Saturday, June 20th, Sir John's fleet was in company, but much shattered by the gale.

Sunday, June 21st, began with strong gales from the N.E. The *Nymph* joined the fleet from to leeward; and one of the luggers sent us a boat, by which we were informed, that at the same time when the *Nymph* saw the English to windward, she saw the French fleet to leeward.

Monday, June 22, we had light variable airs and clear weather. At 25 minutes past 3 A.M. the *Astrea* made the signal for a fleet in the S.E. At 30 minutes past 3, saw them in that quarter from the *Queen Charlotte*, and Sir John Warren's fleet in the N.W. At 19 minutes past 4, the *Nymph* made the signal, that the strangers were enemies; and at 40 minutes, the admiral threw out the same signal. - During the night, the English fleet had been kept under very low sail; which, with the shift of wind, brought the French to windward.

The English fleet being on the larboard tacks, with a light air from E. by N. and their heads S.E. by S. - At 55 minutes past 5, the admiral made the signal to tack in succession. At 6, the *Queen Charlotte* tacked; and at half-past 6, the admiral made the signal for the *Sans Pareil, Orion, Colossus, Irresistible, Valiant,* and *Russel,* to chase to the eastward. At 45 minutes, the signal was out for a general chase in the same quarter. The body of the enemy bore at 8, E.S.E. 4 leagues. At noon they bore nearly the same, but not so distant. (Lat. 47°17' N. long. 4°11' W. Belleisle east, 10 leagues.)

Tuesday, June 23. Light airs, changing from E. by S. to south, S.W. by S. and back to S. by W. with smooth water. Continued in chase with every sail set that could prove of the least advantage. Gained fast ahead of all the English fleet, except the *Sans Pareil, Orion,* and *Irresistible,* and kept way with them. At the beginning of the chase, the *Royal George* was some distance ahead of the *Queen Charlotte.* At 15 minutes past 6 P.M. the admiral made the signal to keep sight of the enemy, and lead the fleet up to them. At half-past 6, the *Nymph,* which, with the *Astrea,* were close to the enemy's rear, signified that the French fleet consisted of 13 sail of the line, and 11 frigates. At 7 P.M. the admiral made the signal to attack or harass the enemy's rear. - At 25 minutes past 7, to engage as arriving up in succession. At midnight, the enemy were not more than 5 or 6 miles ahead of the *Queen Charlotte.* At 50 minutes past 3 A.M. the *London,* and *Nymph,* made the signal for land, N.N.E. At 4, we had light airs from S.W. by S. with the enemy about two miles ahead. The ship's head was E. by S. varying afterwards occasionally."

During the whole night, that preceded the morning of the 23d of June, Sir A.S. Douglas never left the deck; thus taking immediate advantage of every flaw of wind, and by his presence imparting additional promptness and energy to his judicious orders.

"By watching every breath of wind," (adds one of his officers) "that blew from the Heavens, and trimming incessantly to give it with the best advantage to the sails, Sir Andrew Douglas, soon after the morning broke on the 23d, had the satisfaction to find himself within two miles of the enemy's rear. Undismayed by the fire which they soon poured upon the *Queen Charlotte,* and the slender prospect of an essential support, he appeared willing, if necessary, to sacrifice his ship for the public benefit. She was seen to approach the enemy with a silent intrepidity, that at least deserved a pointed notice; and with even royals and steering sails set, she dashed amidst the thickest of the enemy. Sir A. Douglas thus received the broadsides of 5 or 6 of their ships, and the stern chasers of 3 of them at the same time; but closing with the nearest, four of them were brought into one point, by which the effect of their guns was greatly diminished.

Close as the French were to the shelter of their own coasts, it was only on such a display of gallantry that the British admiral could build a hope of checking their retreat: a gallantry that seldom failed to distinguish those officers, who had been led on under the auspices of an Howe. In this instance, however, it has scarcely been given to the discrimination of the public; and little or not distinction was afterwards made in the representation to the Admiralty, between those who boldly arrested the flight of the enemy, and others who were unable to mix in the battle.[8]

The *Queen Charlotte* had only a chance of support, from the *Orion, Irresistible, Sans Pareil, Russel,* and *Colossus,* and that not immediately from the three latter. - The *London, Queen,* and *Prince George,* appeared to be three miles astern, and the *Royal George* certainly not less than four; and the *Valiant, Prince of Wales, Barfleur,* and *Prince,* considerably astern of her. One distant ship might certainly have been taken for another, but such was in truth the general disposition: and these were the 14 sail of the line that composed the squadron, for three under the command of Sir John Warren, were too remote to be at all in question.

Let us now return to the *Queen Charlotte*, THE DOUGLAS of the battle. A little before six o'clock, the guns of this ship were opened from the starboard side, and their influence was such as is generally given to a cool reserve. At 20 minutes after 6 o'clock, the *Formidable,* which had received the greatest share of their effects, was disabled and on fire, and had surrendered. *Le Peuple,* formerly *le Montaigne,* became the next object: her shot were but ill directed, and soon feeling the warmth of her situation, she hauled her wind, sheered off, and was attacked by the *Sans Pareil,* and afterwards the *Colossus* or *Russel.* In the mean time *le Tigre,* supported by her friends, became the nearest in opposition; and sustained the contest until 14 minutes past seven.

Galled by the *Alexander* on the larboard side, the *Queen Charlotte* then bore a little away, to close with and silence her: *le Tigre* drew ahead, but the *Alexander* struck her colours. The freshening breeze had brought the *London* near enough to try a distant fire, and the rest of the squadron began to approach. At twenty minutes past seven, the main and foremasts being much wounded, fore-top-mast and bowsprit injured, part of the standing and all the running rigging cut, the sails full of holes, and rendered for a time totally useless, the *Queen Charlotte* lost her way, and ceased firing. Two or three minutes before eight o'clock, the *Royal George* passed her."

In another journal, Lord Bridport's ship, the *Royal George* is thus noticed-

"At 25 minutes past 7, the admiral made the *Russel*'s signal to engage closer. At 55 minutes, the signal for the ships having charge of the convoy to proceed. The *Royal George* soon after this passed on the starboard side in pursuit of the enemy, taking in her steering sails as she came abreast of the *Queen Charlotte.* At 30 minutes past 8, she made the *San Pareil*'s and *Colossus*' signals to discontinue the engagement; the first was now on the larboard, the second on the starboard bows of the *Queen Charlotte,* distant about a mile and a half. About this period, the *Royal George* began her fire.

The *Queen Charlotte* having knotted her ropes as well as the time would allow, hauled on board her fore and main tacks, in order to follow and give Lord Bridport the best support her state would admit. Twenty minutes after this, the *Royal George* bore up, and began by discharging her starboard guns at *le Peuple,* almost without any retort; and at half-past 8, she attacked *le Tigre,* now the lee ship, exhausted by the *Sans Pareil,* and latterly approached and fired at by the *Queen* and *London*: this ship had struck her colours, but unperceived by the *Royal George.*"

We have also the following additional information, in another journal: -

"At 35 minutes past 8, observed one of the enemy's ships with which the *Queen Charlotte* had been engaged strike, and which had drawn ahead when it became necessary

8 Lord Bridport's commendation certainly appears to have been restrained, and palsied, towards Sir A.S. Douglas.

to attack the *Alexander*.[9] - *The Royal George, Queen, Sans Pareil,* and *London,* being then near her. At 37 minutes past 8, the *Royal George* wearing, stood out, as did the rest of the fleet. The west point of the Isle of Groaix then bearing S.E. distant about two miles. The wind having drawn round to nearly that point in the course of the action, rendered it impossible for the enemy to get far enough to windward: they could not therefore obtain shelter between the island and the entrance of Port Louis, without making several tacks; for they did not stem higher than the mouth of the river Quimperlay: And as many of the English ships could weather the body of their Fleet, and had not been in action, the French might effectually have been cut off from their harbour, had it been judged right. But probably the risk was thought too great, and the Isle of Groaix might have been fortified. The first ship that surrendered proved to be *le Formidable*, the second the *Alexander*, and the third *le Tigre.*"

As the squadron under Sir John Warren rendered most essential service to Lord Bridport, on this occasion, by the information he thus received; and as probably no action would at that time have taken place, if Sir J. Warren had not passed by as he did; it is our duty in the next place to state his operations more amply than has hitherto been done. - The orders for the embarkation of the emigrant troops under Sir J. B. Warren, had been given on the 8th of June, (1795) and on the 11th, the whole were on board; having been completed under the direction of Captain Keates, and every despatch having been made that was possible. - On the 13th of the same month, June, the squadron and convoy had proceeded through the Needles; and on the 14th, the *Galatea*, Captain Keates, having been despatched to order a chasse marée out of Weymouth Road, and likewise another vessel of the same class, from Cawsand Bay, with the *Standard*, of 64 guns, and *la Concorde* - the ships and convoy had stood across the Channel in company with Lord Bridport's fleet, with whom they had continued until the 17th. When, having lost sight of them, the enemy's squadron were seen about 11 A.M. on the 18th, by the *Arethusa*, which ship Sir John Warren had sent in chase; whilst the *Anson*, which he had likewise stationed between her and the convoy, had repeated the signals of the enemy's force, amounting to 15 sail of the line, and seven frigates. Sir John Warren immediately made the signal to tack, and for the men of war to form in the rear of the merchantmen, and the *Concorde* to lead. He likewise sent the *Experiment* lugger, and also the *Thunderer*, to make signals to Lord Bridport's fleet.

On the next day, Captain Keates, in the *Galatea*, who had been directed to proceed into Quiberon Bay, with one of the chasse marées, joined Sir John Warren, and confirmed the account. Captain Keates had sent a chasse marée express, to find Lord Bridport's fleet. The next morning his Lordship appeared; and Sir John was then ordered to send down the three line-of-battle ships that were with him, which was done.

After the action of the 23d of June, and when the enemy's ships had got between the Isle of Groaix and the main, Sir John Warren, having left his convoy to windward under charge of a frigate, proceeded within a mile and a half of the S.E. point of that Island, to reconnoitre the position of the enemy. A large French frigate having been seen coming out of the eastern passage, most probably with the same view, the *Pomone* engaged her 25 minutes, in the expectation of cutting away some of her masts: the

9 At 16 minutes past seven the *Alexander* struck her colours; but firing two guns afterwards, orders were given to renew the action; on doing which she came round to, with her head to the southward. The *London* prior to this had arrived up, and had brought her guns to bear on the *Alexander*; but it did not appear that any return except from the stern chasers was made.

frigate, however, having lost her main-yard, veered and returned into port, it not being possible to intercept her. - We have certainly heard it very strongly reported, that signals were made by some of Sir John Warren's Squadron, that the remainder of the enemy were at anchor under Groaix, and had not entered the port of L'Orient. In Lord Bridport's official letter, these services of Sir John Warren appear to have been unnoticed.

We now return to the more immediate object of this biographical memoir. Sir A. Douglas, on going to the Admiral's ship, after the action, was received by Lord Bridport at the gangway, and thanked by him publicly for bringing the French fleet to action, and thereby retarding their design of getting into L'Orient. And these sentiments of Lord Bridport, were afterwards supported by Captain Domet, on his arrival in town, who expressed in very strong terms his Admiral's sense of Sir A. Douglas's services, of which he assured his friends, he could not say enough. Much as we respect Lord Bridport, we must candidly own, with some of the first officers in the service, that the tenor of his subsequent public letter, after all this, seems at variance with the general liberality of his conduct. It were surely sounder policy for a British seaman to commend a brother officer as he deserved, than to apprehend with cautious coldness, any jealousy which such liberality might produce. Public praise is food for professional valour, and when so justly merited, ought not to have been withheld.

Landing the Royalist Army
From the 'Biographical Memoir of Sir John Borlase Warren, Bart. K.B.' III 343-350

Sir John Warren in the month of June (1795) received orders to hoist his broad pendant in *La Pomone*, 44 guns, as Commodore of an expedition that had been planned against the French coast. Fifty sail of transports were attached to the squadron,[10] having on board nearly three thousand emigrant troops, under the command of Comtes De Puysaye, and D'Hervilly. The whole force sailed from Yarmouth Roads, Isle of Wight, and joined the western squadron off Ushant, under that gallant veteran Earl Bridport. Here they continued until they made the Penmarks; when the fleet hauled their wind to the northward, and the ships under Sir John Warren continued steering for the island of Belleisle. The ensuing evening the *Galatea*, Captain R. G. Keats, having been sent into Quiberon Bay, was chased by the French fleet under Admiral Villaret Joyeuse, who soon afterwards hove in sight. Commodore Warren immediately threw out the signal for the whole convoy to wear, and the *Concorde* to lead them; and for the line of battle ships, and frigates, to form in the rear.

A chasse marée that had accompanied the *Galatea*, having been ordered by Captain Keats to look out for the fleet under Lord Bridport, had been successful in joining; and

10 The squadron consisted of the following ships:

Robust	74 guns	Captain E. Thornborough
Thunderer	74	A. Bertie
Standard,	64	J. Ellison
La Pomone	44	Sir John Borlase, Warren, Bart.
Anson	44	P. C. Durham
Artois	38	Sir E. Nagle
Arethusa	38	M. Robinson
Concorde	36	A. Hunt
Galatea	32	R. G. Keats

With Six Gun Boats and Cutters.

thus communicated the important intelligence to the Commander in Chief: the *Thunderer*, and the *Experiment* lugger had also been detached by Sir John Warren, for the same purpose, and to acquaint the Admiral of the situation of the convoy.

Early on the following morning, Lord Bridport, with his usual zeal, was discerned under a press of sail. Sir John Warren detached, according to orders, the remaining line of battle ships from his squadron to join his Lordship: they however could not come up until the Action off L'Orient, on the twenty-third of June, 1795, had terminated with such an addition of glory to the British Navy.[11]

Commodore Warren pursued his course to Quiberon Bay; and notwithstanding the thick weather which came on, anchored between its entrance, and Belleisle. As the subsequent events of this expedition have been strangely misrepresented, and as it is of consequence to the history of the present war that they should be fairly stated; we shall now proceed to detail them from original documents, on which our readers may rely. On the twenty-first of June the convoy stood up the Bay, when several Royalist Chiefs came on board; and in the evening preparations were made to effect a landing, which took place soon after day-break the next morning, at the village of Saint Genes: where the whole emigrant force was landed, without the loss of a single man. Two hundred Republican troops, who made an appearance of opposing the disembarkation, were driven back with loss: in their retreat they fell in with a column of seven hundred Chouans, under the command of the Chevalier Tintiniac, by whom they were roughly treated. The naval force, under Sir John Warren, for the space of a fortnight was employed in landing arms and ammunition for sixteen thousand Royalists, who had joined the Army; and who were sent in different divisions up the country. Both the English, and the Emigrants, were received by the inhabitants with every mark of kindness and regard. A small expedition also took place up the river Vannes, under Captain A. Bertie, with four gun boats; which succeeded in destroying a sloop of war, and a cutter; some merchant vessels were also captured.

The Generals at length projected an attack on the Peninsula of Quiberon; a very strong and singular position. It runs southward from a point of the main land, between Port Louis, and Morbain; and is about three leagues from the east end of Belleisle. Commodore Warren, in consequence of this determination, disembarked two thousand Royalists, and five hundred emigrant troops, under Monsieur de Puysaye; to which three hundred British marines were added by the Commodore, with whom he himself landed. The whole force then moved towards the fort; which being invested on the other side by General D'Hervilly, with two thousand emigrant troops, and five or six thousand Royalists, newly armed and cloathed, the garrison surrendered prisoners of war to the amount of six hundred men, who were sent to England. The place was immediately garrisoned by the emigrant troops.

Stores, ammunition, and provisions, were landed without delay, in consequence of the very earnest requests from the Generals: the force of the Royalists, after penetrating to Vannes, Auray, Pentivi, and within a few miles of L'Orient, became contracted, on the approach of General Hoche; who was collecting two columns, of eight or nine

---

11 For particulars of this brilliant event, vid. *Nav. Chron.* Vol. I. pages 279, 280, 281-300. [Here was inserted Lord Bridport's official account of his action of 22 June 1795, but the present editor has transposed it to the account of that action which follows.]

Coast of France from Lorient to the Isle of Ré. ^{Plate 388}

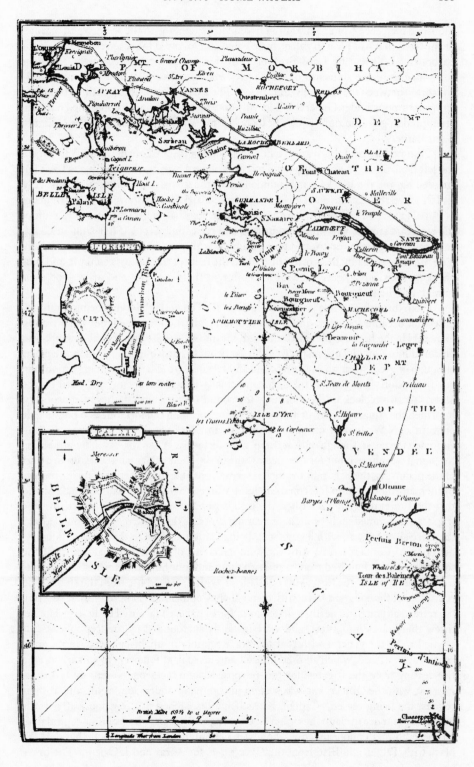

thousand men each from Nantz, and La Vendée; together with the seamen and marines of the fleet, that had been so gallantly defeated and followed into the very mouth of the harbour of L'Orient by Lord Bridport. In this position the force of the Royalists continued until the sixteenth of July, 1795; when another plan of attack, previously concerted between the Generals, took place. The garrison, consisting of three thousand emigrant troops under General D'Hervilly and a body of Chouans, marched out; and attempted to gain the right flank of Hoche's army, which was posted on the height of Saint Barbe.

Commodore Sir John Warren landed a second body of Chouans, under Vauban, on the left flank of the enemy; supported by two hundred marines: but the main object not succeeding, and the attack having commenced by the troops under Generals D'Hervilly, and Puysaye, the marines and Chouans were re-embarked, and drawn up in the trenches at Fort Penthievre. Sir John Warren then observing that the enemy was in pursuit of the emigrant troops, who appeared broken and retreating, brought five launches, each carrying an eighteen, or twenty-four pounder, within a small distance of the beach. The fire from the launches greatly distressed the flank of the enemy's column; and thus checking their career, gave time for the emigrant troops to rally, and make good their retreat into the fort.

From the unfavourable issue of this attack, the General D'Hervilly being wounded, desertion became frequent, and continued in an alarming degree among the troops. General Hoche had also obtained, through means of the deserters, or inhabitants who favoured him, intelligence respecting the garrison: in consequence of which the place, although of great strength, was surprised and taken by treachery after being a month in our possession - one part of the garrison actually joined the enemy, and fired on the other. At two o'clock in the morning, the sound of guns, and flashes of musquetry, informed the squadron that an attack had commenced on the fort; but as it blew a gale of wind at N.W. directly off shore, with rain and dark weather, it was impossible to approach the coast, though only at three miles distance. When the day at length broke, the signal was thrown out for the men of war to slip their cables, and work up to a part of the peninsula, the S. E. point, which it seemed possible to reach: but in their progress thither, an Aid de Camp informed Sir John Warren that the fort had been taken; and that the Emigrant General wished the troops to be disembarked. To effect this, the frigates were immediately brought as near the shore, as the depth of water would admit; the *Lark* sloop of war, with a gun-boat, being stationed close to the beach: under the direction of Captain Keats, with the joint exertions of the Officers and men of the squadron, eleven hundred troops, and two thousand four hundred Royalist inhabitants were brought off by the boats of the squadron, with a spirited fire from the ships. The remainder of the emigrant force, with their gallant Commander Sombreuil, after covering the retreat; although earnestly solicited to embark, and even favoured to do so by Hoche; threw themselves into a fort, and were instantly surrounded by the Republicans. It seemed to be the general wish that the brave Sombreuil might be saved: terms were accordingly offered, which allowed himself and his gallant followers to embark, on the fire ceasing from the frigates: for this purpose several messengers went on board *La Pomone*, with the Officer who was second in command under Sombreuil, and at their request the firing ceased. Captain Keats being dispatched in a few hours afterwards with a flag of truce to claim the emigrant Officers, and troops, who had thus capitulated, on the faith of Republicans, the whole was peremptorily denied: Hoche had left the place with Tallien and Blad from the *Convention*, for Auray and L'Orient. The brave and universally lamented Sombreuil, suffered by the orders of the miscreant Le Moine, a Republican General; notwithstanding his own grenadiers affirmed to the last, that the terms claimed had been agreed to. The whole was, however, disavowed by Le Moine; and owing to this notorious breach of national honour, many Officers and men were destroyed.

Thus terminated an Expedition, which at first promised to strengthen the cause of the Royalists, and to arrest the career of the general enemy. Every thing that valour or perseverance could effect, was attempted both by the British squadron, and the emigrant force; the event however was melancholy and unsuccessful: and consequently every exertion has been made, both by the great vulgar and the small, to cast an obloquy on the whole transaction; and to draw such inferences from it, as not only reflect disgrace on the original projectors, but even tend to tarnish the approved humanity, and integrity of the British character.

Commodore Sir John Warren next proceeded to take possession of the islands of Hedic, and Houac, in the Bay of Quiberon; in order to refresh the troops, and to continue his assistance to the cause of the Royalists by every means that offered. A body of two thousand Chouans who had been brought off from Quiberon, having been landed at their own request near L'Orient, penetrated into the adjacent country.

The British squadron was afterwards joined by several transports, with four thousand British troops on board commanded by General Doyle, and also the *Jason* frigate, 38 guns, Captain C. Stirling, having on board his Royal Highness Monsieur (Compt D'Artois) and suite, with the Duc de Bourbon. The whole force then proceeded to the Bay of Bourneauf, southward of the south point of the entrance of the Loire; and after examining the state of Noirmoustier Island, which is only separated from the main land by a narrow channel, they took possession of Isle Dieu, about five leagues at S. by W. from the Island of Noirmoustier. An high raging sea, which comes boiling and roaring up, as if it ascended from some subterraneous passage under the island, renders its roadsted a bad one: the troops however were disembarked, and communication was attempted to be opened with the Royalists in La Vendée. Here the British troops continued for near three months: when in consequence of orders from Rear-Admiral Harvey, the Commodore proceeded, late in the year 1795, with his squadron to Isle Dieu having been joined by some ships of the line, and brought off the whole of the army, and all the stores, with only the loss of six flat-bottomed boats: thus the island was evacuated, after destroying all the artillery on its coast.

From this period Sir John Warren was employed as Commodore in continual and successful cruises off the coast of France, from the port of Falmouth, under the immediate orders of the Admiralty. The situation of this port[12] at the entrance of the Channel, is of the utmost importance to the trade of Great Britain. The enemy's convoys destined to bring provisions, ammunition, and supplies for the French fleet in Brest, were thus continually intercepted: from the success of this squadron, and the division of ships under Sir E. Pellew, the French fleet were often kept in harbour for want of stores. *La Pomone, Galatea, Anson*, and *Artois*, at one time fell in with a convoy of no less than seventy sail going for provisions, under escort of *La Tribune, Proserpine, Thames, Coquille, Cygoin*, and *L'Etoile*; an engagement immediately ensued; but the enemy escaping through the Raz Passage, between the offing of Douarne-Nez Bay on the N.E. and Hodierne Bay on the S.E. the only ships taken were *L'Etoile*, and four merchantmen:

12 A view of this port is subjoined.

for the protection the trade and commerce of Great Britain had thus received from the squadron under Sir John Warren, the *Committee of Merchant Seamen for the Encouragement of the Capture of the Enemy's Privateers*, presented the Commodore with a sword of the value of one hundred guineas.

In consequence of a change which took place in the arrangement of the channel fleet, the ships under Sir John Warren were attached to it, and placed under the orders of the Commander in Chief Lord Bridport: after attending for some time the motions of the enemy in Brest, the Commodore's squadron became entirely dispersed. The following is a correct statement of the loss which the enemy sustained by the ships under Sir John Warren:

23 Neutrals detained, and part of each cargo condemned

87 Merchantmen captured

54 Merchantmen destroyed

25 Ships and vessels of war captured

12 Ships and vessels of war destroyed

19 Vessels recaptured (14 English, 3 Spanish, 1 Dane, 1 American)

220 - Total

From the 'Biographical Memoir of Captain Joseph Ellison.' XIX 18-25

[During his operations at Quiberon, Sir John Warren] sent the *Standard* to the great road of Belleisle, to blockade the island, and to endeavour to effect its surrender. Captain Ellison had two French royalist officers on board, Messrs. Puisaye and Suasse, of the engineers, who were authorised to treat, in conjunction with himself, with the governor of Belleisle. [An invitation to change his allegiance, however, was rejected by the governor of the garrison.] . . .

During the time that Captain Ellison remained before Belleisle, he received frequent presents of fruit and fish from the governor; two of whose *aides-de-camp* also once visited the *Standard*, with an invitation for him to go on shore; notwithstanding which, he was almost constantly annoyed by shot from the garrison. The British commander, it is scarcely necessary to say, declined the governor's polite offer.

Captain Ellison, who, it will be recollected, had been employed on a similar service, off the same place, with Sir Edward Hawke, kept his station for many weeks, in hopes of accomplishing the surrender of the island; after which, the object becoming hopeless, and his men suffering much from the scurvy, he was ordered to the island of Hedic; where, having landed them, he blew up the forts, pitched tents, and formed them into a little encampment, during their recovery.

In about six weeks, his ship's company having been restored to health, he received orders from Sir John Warren to sail with the *Thunderer*, Captain Bertie, to Noirmoutier, for the purpose of conducting the Comte d'Artois and his suite, who wished to take a survey of that island.

1795 – East Indies

A FRENCH ARMY OVERRAN the Netherlands in the winter of 1794-95, and on 15 May 1795 the Treaty of The Hague was signed, uniting in alliance France and the Netherlands, which was reformed into the Batavian Republic. In response, the British government ordered all Dutch property seized, and on 15 September general reprisals were ordered. Even before the Dutch signed the treaty, operations had commenced to seize Dutch overseas colonies and factories, starting with the despatch of a squadron under Rear-Admiral Elphinstone, Lord Keith, to take possession of the Dutch settlement at the Cape of Good Hope. Commodore Rainier commanding the East India Squadron deployed his forces to take Trincomalee and other posts in Ceylon.

The Naval Chronicle made only brief reference to the operation at the Cape in its memoir of Lord Keith, but provided a little more detail of the Ceylon expedition in its memoir of Lord Gardner.

Capture of the Cape
From the 'Biographical Memoirs of the Right Honourable Lord Keith, K.B.'
X 8-23

On the 11th of April 1794, our hero [the Right Honourable George Keith Elphinstone, later Lord Keith] received his first promotion as a Flag-Officer, by being made Rear-Admiral of the Blue; and on the 4th of July the same year, he was farther advanced to be Rear-Admiral of the White Squadron, and hoisted his flag on board the *Barfleur*, of 98 guns, one of the ships attached to the Channel fleet, which, on the glorious 1st of June, was commanded by Rear-Admiral Bowyer, but who, having unfortunately lost a leg on that memorable occasion, was obliged for a time to retire from the service. Our Admiral continued in the Channel fleet during the remainder of the year, in which nothing material took place; but early in 1795, the hostilities having broke out between Great Britain and the republic of Holland, he shifted his flag from the *Barfleur* to the *Monarch*, of 74 guns, and sailed from Spithead for the Cape of Good Hope, on the 2d of April, having the following ships under his command:

Monarch	74	Sir G.K. Elphinstone, K.B.
		Rear Admiral of the White
		Captain J. Elphinstone
Victorious	74	Captain W. Clark
Arrogant	74	Captain Richard Lucas
Sphynx	20	Captain George Brisac.
Rattlesnake	16	Captain J.W. Spranger

Capture of Trincomalee and Columbo

From the 'Memoir of the Public Services of the Right Honourable Alan Hyde Lord Gardner.' XXI 358-364

Remaining in the *Heroine*, he [i.e. Gardner] was soon afterwards ordered to India, where for some time he was actively employed in protecting the trade against the enemy's cruisers. Commodore (the late Admiral) Peter Rainier was, at this time, commander-in-chief on the India station. - In the month of July, 1795, the Cape of Good Hope was taken, by Admiral Keith's squadron; and, no sooner was Commodore Rainier[1] apprised of hostilities having been commenced against the Dutch, than he disposed of his ships[2] in such a manner as might most effectually annoy their trade; and, in conjunction with the Presidency of Madras, he adopted the most judicious plans for the reduction of their settlements. His first object, in the accomplishment of which Captain Gardner participated, was to secure the port of Trincomale [sic], and the other valuable possessions which the Dutch held in the island of Ceylon. This service occupies a portion of naval history, not yet, we believe, adverted to in our Chronicle; and, as Captain Gardner was engaged in nearly the whole of the proceedings, occasionally as a principal, the following summary sketch may not be thought unconducive to the general interest of this memoir.

The expedition against Trincomale having been determined on, Lord Hobart, the governor of Madras, and Commodore Rainier, despatched Captain Gardner in the *Heroine*, with Major Agnew, to Columbo, to explain its object to the governor-general of Ceylon. In the mean time, a body of troops, under the command of General Stuart, with ammunition and stores, were embarked on board the ships of war and transports. The expedition sailed from Madras on the 21st of July; and, at the same time, the

---

1 The commodore was promoted to the rank of rear-admiral of the blue squadron, in the month of June, 1795.

2 The following appear to have been the whole of the squadron at this time under Commodore Rainier's command:

Ships	Guns	Commanders
Suffolk[+]	74	P. Rainier, Esq. Commodore
		Captain R. Lambert
Arrogant[*]	74	Richard Lucas
Victorious[*]	74	W. Clarke
Centurion[+]	50	Samuel Osborne
Resistance[=]	44	Ed. Pakenham
Diomede[+]	44	Matthew Smith
Heroine[+]	52	A.H. Gardner
Orpheus[=]	32	Henry Newcome
Swift	16	J. Doling

* Joined in. [+] At the taking of Trincomale. [=] At the taking of Malacca.

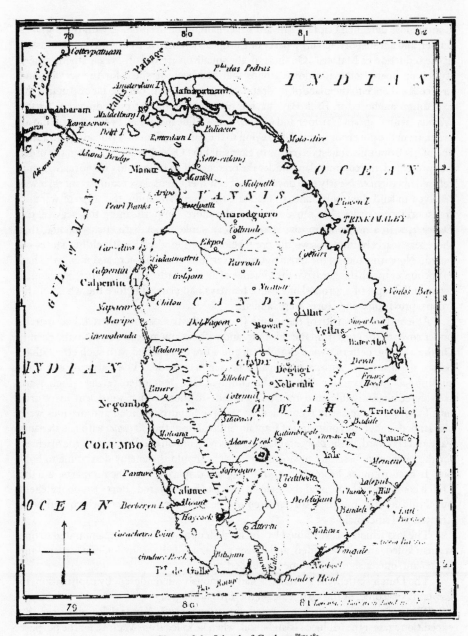

Chart of the Island of Ceylon. ^{Plate 385}

Commodore detached Captain Edward Pakenham, in the *Resistance*, with the *Suffolk's* tender, and a transport, having a party of European and native troops on board, to assist at the reduction of Malacca. On the 23d, the squadron arrived off Negapatnam, where it took on board some additional troops that had been destined for the service, and proceeded thence to the place of its destination, on the 25th. On the 1st of August, the expedition anchored in Back Bay; having been joined, on the preceding day, by the *Heroine*, with Captain Gardner and Major Agnew. The major had brought with him an order, from the governor general of Ceylon to the commandant of Trincomale, to admit 300 of his Britannic Majesty's troops to garrison Fort Ostenburgh; but, when the order was presented, the commandant, under the pretence of an informality in the instrument, refused obedience. Nearly two days having been spent in useless remonstrances, it was resolved to land the troops; and, to facilitate the disembarkation, the ships of war and transports were ordered to move nearer to the shore. In performing this service, the *Diomede*, with a transport in tow, struck upon a sunken rock with such violence, that there was scarcely time to save the crew before she foundered, with all her stores on board. Notwithstanding the most vigorous exertions of the officers and men, who had to encounter much danger from the violence of an extraordinarily high surf, occasioned by a continuance of a strong land wind, ten days had elapsed before the whole of the troops, provisions, and stores were landed.

At length, on the 18th of the month (August) the troops commenced their march, under cover of the guns from the shipping, and without any molestation from the enemy. On the 23d, the batteries were completed; and a fire was opened with such effect, that, before noon, on the 26th, a practicable breach was made. The garrison was then summoned to surrender; but, as the commandant demanded terms which were considered inadmissible, and refused to accede to those which were sent in return, hostilities were necessarily recommenced. Three hundred seamen and marines were also landed, under the command of Captain Smith, late of the *Diomede*, with Lieutenants Page and Hayward, of the navy, and Lieutenants McGibbon and Perceval, of the marines, for the purpose of assisting to storm the breach, should the enemy determine to hold out. In a few minutes, however, the white flag was displayed from the ramparts, and the Dutch commandant accepted the terms which had been offered. Fort Ostenburgh held out until the 31st; but then surrendered on the same terms as those which had been granted to Trincomale.

The loss which was sustained by the English upon this occasion, amounted to one seaman killed, and six wounded; and fifteen soldiers killed; one major, one captain, one lieutenant, one ensign, and 48 men wounded.

The Dutch settlement at Malacca had previously surrendered, by capitulation, to Captain Newcome, of the Orpheus, on the 17th of August.

The next service which occupied the attention of Admiral Rainier, was the expedition against the Molucca Islands; and, when he sailed from Madras, for the purpose of attacking those settlements, he left Captain Gardner as senior officer of his Majesty's ships and vessels on the coast of Coromandel and Malabar.[3]

3 On the 16th of February, 1796, Admiral Rainier reduced the settlement of Amboyna, and its dependencies; and, on the 8th of March, Banda was also delivered to him. In the treasury at Amboyna he found 81,112 rix dollars, and in store, 515,940 pounds weight of cloves. In the treasury at Banda, he found 66,675 rix dollars, 84,777 pounds of nutmegs, 19,587 pounds of mace, and merchandise and other stores of great value. Banda is the principal of a group of islands in the eastern sea, lying to the eastward of the Celebes. Their chief produce is nutmegs, with which they are thought to be capable of supplying the wants of all the world.

Captain Gardner had now the satisfaction of being entrusted with the conduct of the naval part of an expedition, though only on a small scale, himself. - Early in 1796, he was detached, with the following squadron, to co-operate with a body of troops, under Colonel Stuart, in the reduction of Colombo, on the island of Ceylon:-

Ships	Guns	Commanders
Heroine	32	Captain A.H. Gardner
Rattlesnake	16	Edward Ramage
Echo	16	Andrew Todd
Swift	16	J.S. Rainier
Bombay, frigate*	20	
Drake, brig	14	
Queen, ketch*	12	
Bombay Castle+	24	
Prince of Wales+	24	

* Belonging to the East India Company's Marine.   + East India ships.

On the 5th of February, this squadron having anchored off Negombo, about eighteen miles to the northward of Colombo, a small body of troops was landed, under Major Barbert, who immediately took possession of a fort which had been evacuated by the enemy. By the evening of the 6th, the whole army had disembarked. Colonel Stuart then proceeded, with a part of his force, against a strong post on the south bank of the Matual river, which he carried on the morning of the 12th; at which time, Captain Gardner brought the squadron to anchor, about two miles from the fortress of Colombo, where he landed some guns, stores, &c. with the view of commencing and carrying on the siege; and, on the 14th, in conjunction with Colonel Stuart, he summoned the governor to surrender. A capitulation was accordingly agreed to on the following day, by which Columbo, and the remaining possessions of the Dutch in Ceylon, submitted to his Majesty's arms.

1795 – Mediterranean

VICE-ADMIRAL WILLIAM HOTHAM, who succeeded Hood in command of the British squadron in the Mediterranean, encountered the Toulon squadron in March 1795, when on both sides together over a thousand men were killed or wounded in a passing action, and again in July. Both times he failed to make the most of his advantage, being glad enough to make no major mistake. Horatio Nelson, in command of *Agamemnon*, played his own part well, and was highly critical of his superior. He was subsequently employed on the Riviera attempting to intercept supplies for Napoleon's army in Italy.

The Naval Chronicle recorded these battles in the biographical memoirs of Sir Hyde Parker, who was Hotham's Rear-Admiral, in another in 1799 of Horatio Nelson who was by then the centre of attention following the battle of the Nile, and eventually, in 1803, in one of Lord Hotham which included his official reports of the action of 14 March and 14 July. Much later they were recorded in the biographical memoirs of Edward Grey, who had been lieutenant at the time in the frigate *Romulus*, and of John Holloway who was Hotham's flag captain.

Accounts of Hotham's Actions
From the 'Biographical Memoirs of Sir Hyde Parker, Bart.' V 302-06

The events which took place during the time Lord Hood and afterwards Lord Hotham, held that command are almost too recent to require recapitulation. The surrender of Toulon, and the different interesting events which took place during the time it continued in the possession of Great Britain and her allies, the invasion and complete reduction of the island of Corsica, and the two different encounters in which Admiral Lord Hotham almost fruitlessly endeavoured to engage the French fleet, first in the month of March, and secondly in the month of July 1795, were all of them occurrences extremely interesting to a man of gallantry and zeal for the service of his country, and it is but bare justice to observe, that Sir Hyde availed himself of those opportunities to the utmost of his power. The most material of those in which Sir Hyde had the power of displaying his exertions, was in the first encounter which took place between Mr. Hotham, and the remnant of the once formidable force which France had possessed in the port of Toulon.

The enemy's squadron, which consisted of fifteen sail of the line and five frigates, having ventured to sea, was so successfully pursued by the Vice-Admiral, that one of their ships was, on the 13th of March, brought to action by the *Inconstant* frigate, supported by the *Agamemenon*, commanded by Captain Nelson, and received so much damage, that nothing but the near approach of the rest of the enemy's ships, and the distance of the assailants from support, which was occasioned by their carrying a press of sail in chase, prevented that ship from falling into their hands. The disabled vessel was taken in tow, and the contest ceased during the remainder of that day; on the ensuing, the ship that had been engaged, together with that which had her in tow, were discovered at day-light so far to leeward, and separated from the rest of the squadron, as to afford a very probable chance of cutting them off; the proper measures were immediately taken to pursue this advantage, and made a proper use of it; the enemy were in consequence reduced to the alternative, either of abandoning them to the British fleet, or bearing down and hazarding an action in the hope of rescuing them.

Though the French Commander in Chief appeared to manifest every possible wish of avoiding an encounter, he appears to have thought it improper, wholly, to abandon his comrades, he accordingly formed his line, and bore down on the contrary tack to the British fleet, that he might at least have the credit of having made the attempt. The British advanced ships, the *Captain* and *Bedford*, had approached, however, so near, and were so well supported by the ships astern, that the enemy were completely cut off from all assistance, and surrendered, after making as good and as resolute a defence as circumstances would admit of. The conflict ended in a distant cannonade, for the van ships of the British were so much damaged, particularly the *Courageux* and *Illustrious*, each of which lost their main and mizen-masts, as to render it impossible to attempt any thing farther against an enemy, to windward, equal at least in force, and using every possible means in their power of avoiding an action. The French ships captured were the *Ça-Ira*, of 80 guns, having on board at the commencement of the action one thousand three hundred men, and the *Censeur*, of 74 guns, having one thousand men. Although the general result of the action was not so completely successful as it promised to have been, in case the enemy had been less cautious, yet an object far superior, considered in a nautical light, to the capture of two ships of the line, was attained by this partial encounter. The French ships were all crowded with men in a very extraordinary and unprecedented manner, for the purpose of carrying into execution some expedition, the object of which was either unknown, or at least not officially explained. Mr. Hotham therefore observed, that whatever might have been the enemy's design, the object of it was completely frustrated. They returned back into port wholly disappointed in their hopes and expectations, a circumstance not improbably more keenly felt by them than even their discomfiture.

Sir Hyde having been advanced on the 12th of April 1794, to be Rear-Admiral of the Red Squadron, and moreover on the 4th of July following, to be Vice-Admiral of the Blue, quitted his station of Captain of the fleet on board the *Victory*, and hoisted his flag on board the *St. George*, of 98 guns, as commander of a squadron or division of the fleet. He held that post at the time of the action just mentioned, and on the 1st of June subsequent to it, was promoted to be Vice-Admiral of the Red. No other material occurrence took place during the remainder of the time that Sir Hyde continued to command in the Mediterranean fleet, except the second skirmish, still more trivial than the first, which took place with the French fleet on the 13th of July succeeding his last promotion.

From the 'Biographical Memoir of the Right Hon. Lord Nelson.' [III 171]

Lord Hood having left the Mediterranean in the month of October, 1794; Admiral (now Lord) Hotham, on whom the command devolved, honoured Captain Nelson with equal confidence: he again distinguished himself in the actions with the French fleet of the thirteenth and fourteenth of March, and also on the thirteenth of July, 1795. Captain Nelson was afterwards appointed by Admiral Hotham to co-operate with the Austrian General, De Vins, at Vado Bay, on the coast of Genoa; in which service he continued during the whole time Admiral Hotham retained the command, until the month of November; when the latter was superseded by Sir John Jervis. - In April, 1796, the Commander in Chief so much approved of Captain Nelson's conduct, that he was directed to wear a distinguishing pendant; and in May he was removed from his old and favourite Ship the *Agamemnon*, to the *Captain*, 74 guns; after having buffetted the former about, in every kind of service, during three years and an half: on the eleventh of August a captain was appointed under him.

From the month of April until October, 1795, Commodore Nelson was constantly employed in the most arduous service, viz. the blockade of Leghorn, the taking of Port Ferajo, with the Island of Caprea; and lastly in the evacuation of Bastia: whence having convoyed the troops in safety to Porto Ferrajo, he joined the Admiral in St. Fiorenzo Bay, and proceeded with him to Gibraltar.

From the 'Biographical Memoirs of the Right Honourable William Lord Hotham.' [IX 351-357]

A general promotion of Naval officers taking place on the 24th of September 1787, Mr. Hotham was advanced to the rank of Rear-Admiral of the Red Squadron, but did not take upon him any command in consequence of this promotion, till the year of 1790, when a rupture with Spain being apprehended, he hoisted his flag on board the *Princess Royal*, of 98 guns, as Commander of the rear division of the Channel fleet. The dispute with Spain being accommodated, the fleet was dismantled, and Admiral Hotham struck his flag, having on the 21st of September in the same year, been promoted to the rank of Vice-Admiral of the Blue.

On the commencement of hostilities with France Mr. Hotham was advanced to the rank of Vice-Admiral of the White Squadron, on the 1st of February 1793, and in the month of April following was appointed second in command of the fleet ordered to the Mediterranean under Lord Hood, and hoisted his flag on board the *Britannia*, of 110 guns. This fleet sailed from Spithead in the beginning of May; but as we have already given a very ample account of its proceedings in our Memoirs of the Commander in Chief and in the Toulon Papers, we must refer our readers to them, to avoid unnecessary repetition.[1] On the 12th of April 1794, Mr. Hotham received a farther advance in rank, being promoted to be Vice Admiral of the Red Squadron. In the month of July following he was left by Lord Hood with a detached squadron, to block up some French ships of war which had escaped from Toulon, and were driven by the British fleet into the bay of Gourjean, where they were protected from an attack by batteries on shore. Admiral Lord Hood returning to England in the month of November, the command in chief of the Mediterranean fleet devolved on Mr. Hotham; but nothing of particular moment occurred till the month of March in the following year. Early in

1 *Vide* Memoirs of Lord Hood, Vol. II. page 24. Toulon Papers, Vol. II. pages 102, 192, 288.

that month the Admiral learned that a French squadron was at sea, and having gone in quest of them, he was so fortunate as to bring them to an action, the particulars of which will best appear from his official dispatch.

Britannia, at sea, March 16, 1795
Sir, You will be pleased to inform their Lordships, that on the 8th instant, being then in Leghorn road, I received an express from Genoa, that the French fleet, consisting of fifteen sail of the line and three frigates, were seen two days before off the isle of Marguerite, which intelligence corresponding with a signal made from the *Mozelle*, then in the offing, for a fleet in the north-west quarter, I immediately caused the squadron to be unmoored, and at day-break in the following morning we put to sea, with a strong breeze from the east-north-east.

The *Mozelle* previously returned to me, with the information, that the fleet she had seen were steering to the southward, and supposed to be the enemy; in consequence of which I shaped my course for Corsica, lest their destination should be against that island, and dispatched the *Tarleton* brig to St. Fiorenzo, with orders for the *Berwick* to join me with all possible expedition off Cape Corse; but, in the course of the night she returned to me with the unwelcome intelligence of that ship's having been captured two days before by the enemy's fleet.

To trespass as little as possible upon their Lordship's time, I shall not enter upon a detail of our proceedings until the two squadrons got sight of each other, and the prospect opened of forcing the enemy to action, every movement which was made being directed to that object, and that alone.

Although the French ships were seen by our advanced frigates daily, yet the two squadrons did not get sight of each other until the 12th, when that of the enemy was discovered to windward.

Observing them on the morning following still in that direction, without any apparent intention of coming down, the signal was made for a general chase; in the course of which, the weather being squally, and blowing very fresh, we discovered one of their line of battle ships to be without her top-masts, which afforded to Captain Freemantle, of the *Inconstant* frigate (who was then far advanced on the chase), an opportunity of shewing a good proof of British enterprise, by his attacking, raking, and harrassing her until the coming up of the *Agamemnon*, when he was most ably seconded by Captain Nelson, who did her so much damage as to disable her from putting herself again to rights: but they were at this time so far detached from our own fleet, that they were obliged to quit her, as other ships of the enemy were coming to her assistance, by one of which she was soon afterwards taken in tow.

Finding that our heavy ships did not gain on the enemy during the chase, I made the signal for the squadron to form upon the larboard line of bearing, in which order we continued during the night.

At day-light next morning, the 14th, being about six or seven leagues to the southwest of Genoa, we observed the enemy's disabled ship, with the one that had her in tow, to be so far to leeward, and separated from her own squadron, as to afford a probable chase of our cutting them off. The opportunity was not lost; all sail was made to effect that purpose, which reduced the enemy to the alternative of abandoning those ships, or coming to battle.

Although the latter did not appear to be their choice, they yet came down (on the contrary tack to which we were); with the view of supporting; but the captain of the

Bedford, whose signals were made to attack the enemy's disabled ship and her companion, were so far advanced, and so closely supported by the other ships of our van, as to cut them off effectually from any assistance that could be given upon our line as they passed with a light air of wind.

The two ships that fell proved to be the *Ça-Ira* (formerly the *Couronne*), of 80 guns, and the *Censeur*, of 74 guns.

Our van ships suffered so much by this attack, particularly the *Illustrious* and *Courageux* (having each lost their main and mizen-masts), that it became impossible for anything further to be effected.

I have, however, good reason to hope, from the enemy's steering to the westward, after having passed our fleet, that, whatever might have been their design, their intentions are for the present frustrated.

The French fleet were loaded with troops; the *Ça-Ira* having 1300 men on board, and the *Censeur* 1000, of whom, by their obstinate defence, they lost, in killed an wounded, between 300 and 400 men.

The efforts of our squadron to second my wishes for an immediate and effectual attack upon the enemy, were so spirited and unanimous, that I feel particular satisfaction in offering to their Lordships my cordial commendation of all ranks collectively. It is difficult to specify particular desert, where emulation was common to all, and zeal for his Majesty's service the general description of the fleet.

It is, however, an act of justice to express the sense I entertain of the services of Captain Holloway, of the *Britannia*. During a long friendship with that officer, I have had repeated proofs of his personal and professional talents; and on this recent demand for experience and information, his zeal afforded me the most beneficial and satisfactory assistance.

Herewith I transmit a list of the killed and wounded on board the different ships of the squadron, and have to lament of the loss of Captain Littlejohn, of the *Berwick*, who (I understand from some of her men that were retaken in the *Ça-Ira*), was unfortunately killed the morning of the ship's being captured; by which misfortune his Majesty has lost a most valuable and experienced officer; and I have only to add, that he has left a widow and four small children. I am, Sir, &c.

W. HOTHAM

A List of the British and French Fleets in the Action in the Mediterranean, on the 14th of March, 1795

British Order of Battle

Van Squadron, under the Commander in the Second Post
Starboard or Weather Division - Vice-Admiral Goodall

Ships	Guns	Men	Commanders	Killed	Wounded
Captain	74	590	Capt. Samuel Reeve	3	19
Bedford	74	590	Davidge Gould	7	18
Tancredi	74	600	Chev. Caraccioli	1	5
Princess Royal	98	760	S.E. Goodall, Esq. Vice-Adm. of the White, Capt. I.C.Purvis	3	8
Agamemnon	64	491	Horatio Nelson	0	13

Centre Squadron under the Commander in Chief
Vice-Admiral Hotham, and Rear-Admiral Linzee

Ships	Guns	Men	Commanders	Killed	Wounded
Illustrious	74	590	Capt. T. L. Frederick	20	70
Courageux	74	640	A. Montgomery	15	33
Britannia	110	859	W. Hotham, Esq. Vice-Admiral of the Red, Capt. John Holloway	1	18
Egmont	74	590	I. Sutton	7	21
Windsor Castle	98	755	Rob. Linzee, Esq. Rear-Admiral of the Red, Capt. John Gore	6	31

Rear Squadron under the Commander in the Third Post
Larboard or Lee Division Vice-Admiral Sir Hyde Parker

Ships	Guns	Men	Commanders	Killed	Wounded
Diadem	64	491	Capt. Charles Tyler	3	7
St. George	98	760	Sir H. Parker, Knt. Vice-Admiral of the Blue, Capt. Thomas Foley	4	13
Terrible	74	590	George Campbell	0	6
Fortitude	74	590	Wm. Young	1	4

The French fleet consisted of one ship of 120 guns, three of 80, eleven of 74, two of 40, two of 32, one of 20, and one of 18. The number of men on board the English line was 8896; that of the whole of the French fleet 18240. The unanimous thanks of both Houses of Parliament were voted to Vice-Admiral Hotham for his conduct on this occasion, and at the same time he was advanced to be Admiral of the Blue.

Nothing material took place on the Mediterranean station after this time, till the month of July, when the French fleet having again ventured to sea, and chased into St. Fiorenzo Bay, on the 7th, a small squadron under the command of Commodore Nelson, which had been dispatched by the Admiral on a cruise three days before, the British fleet, as soon as they could get ready for sea, sailed in pursuit of them, but did not get sight of the enemy till the 13th, then an indecisive encounter took place, the nature of which will best be explained by the following extract from the Admiral's dispatch to the Secretary of the Admiralty:

"You will be pleased to inform their lordships, that I dispatched on the 4th instant, from St. Fiorenzo, the ships named in the margin,[2] under the orders of Captain Nelson, whom I directed to call off Genoa for the *Inconstant* and *Southampton* frigates that were lying there, and to take them with him, if, from the intelligence he might there obtain, he should find it necessary.

On the morning of the 7th, I was much surprised to learn that the above squadron was seen in the offing, returning into port, pursued by the enemy's fleet, which by

2 *Agamemnon, Melcagar, Ariadne, Mozelle, Mutine* cutter.

General de Vin's letter (the latest account I had received), I had reason to suppose were certainly at Toulon.

Immediately on the enemy's appearance, I made every preparation to put to sea after them; and, notwithstanding the unpleasant predicament we were in, most of the ships being in the midst of watering and refitting, I was yet enabled, by the zeal and extraordinary exertions of the officers and men, to get the whole of the fleet under weigh that night, as soon as the land wind permitted us to move; from which we neither saw nor heard anything of the enemy till the 12th, when being to the eastward, and within sight of the Hieres Islands, two vessels were spoken with by Captain Hotham, of the *Cyclops*, and Captain Boys, of *la Fleche*, who acquainted them, that they had seen the French fleet not many hours before, to the southward of those islands: upon which information I made the signal before night to prepare for battle, as an indication to our fleet that an enemy was near.

Yesterday, at day-break, we discovered them to leeward of us, on the larboard tack, consisting of twenty-three sail, seventeen of which proved to be of the line. The wind at this time blew very hard from the W. N. W. attended with a heavy swell, and six of our ships had to bend main-top-sails, in the room of those that were split by the gale, in the course of the night.

I caused the fleet, however, to be formed with all possible expedition, on the larboard line of bearing, carrying all sail possible to preserve that order, and to keep the wind of the enemy, in hopes of cutting them off from the land, from which we were only five leagues distant.

At eight o'clock, finding they had no other view than that of endeavouring to get from us, I made the signal for a general chase, and for the ships to take suitable stations for their mutual support, and to engage the enemy as arriving up with them, in succession; but the baffling winds and vexatious calms, which render every naval operation in this country doubtful, soon afterwards took place, and allowed only a few of our van ships to get up with the enemy's rear about noon, which they attacked so warmly, that, in the course of an hour after, we had the satisfaction to find one of their sternmost ships viz. *l'Alcide*, of 74 guns, had struck; the rest of their fleet, favoured by a shift of wind to the eastward (that placed them now to windward of us), had got so far into Frejus Bay, whilst the major part of ours was becalmed in the offing, that it became impossible for anything farther to be effected; and those of our ships which were engaged, had approached so near to the shore, that I judged it proper to call them off by the signal.

If the result of the day has not been so completely satisfactory as the commencement promised, it is my duty to state, that no exertions could be more unanimous than those of the fleet under my command; and it would be injustice to the general merit of all, to select individual instances of commendation, had not superiority of sailing placed some of the ships in an advanced situation, of which they availed themselves in the most distinguished and honourable manner; and amongst the number was the *Victory*, having Rear-Admiral Mann on board, who had shifted his flag to that ship upon this occasion.

I am sorry to say, that the *Alcide*, about half an hour after she had struck, by some accident caught fire in her fore-top, before she was taken possession of, and the flames spread with such rapidity that the whole ship was soon in a blaze; several boats from the fleet were dispatched as quickly as possible, to rescue as many of her people as they could save from the destruction that awaited them, and three hundred of them were in consequence preserved, when the ship blew up with the most awful and tremendous explosion, and between three and four hundred people are supposed to have perished.

Commodore Nelson's Squadron, skillfully manoeuvering against a superior French
force, in 1795. Engraved by Baily, from a drawing by Pocock.

The annexed plate, with the subjoined explanatory communication [below], from a
correspondent, will be found illustrative of the services of the late Admiral Lord
Nelson,[3] Captain Sir Charles Brisbane, Knt.[4] and Admiral Lord Hotham:[5]

London, 20th February 1811

Mr. Editor, If you think the accompanying sketch worthy a place in your interesting
Chronicle, I have much pleasure in offering it, as a tribute to the memory of the hero,
whose brilliant achievements have immortalized the naval annals of England.
Perhaps the coolness and intrepidity of Nelson were never more conspicuous, than
on the occasion alluded to, when, with a single ship of the line, two small frigates, a
sloop, and a cutter, he manoeuvred so skillfully, as to prevent one of his squadron
from capture, although hard pressed by five sail of the line, (French) which, under
Spanish colours, endeavoured to decoy the British Commodore, and afterwards
declined bringing him to action, although the two headmost ships of the enemy had
it in their power.

Early in July, 1795, Captain Nelson was detached with ships named in the margin,[6]
to co-operate with the Austrian army at Vado, which the French getting intelligence
of, sent five sail of their best sailing ships of the line, to take the English squadron.
Fortunately they were discovered on the evening of the 6th July, and signals were
immediately made by Captain Nelson, to return, and join Admiral Hotham, at St.
Fiorenzo. At day-light next morning, the enemy had gained considerably on us, and
the two headmost ships were within gun-shot. The *Moselle* had lost her main-top-
gallant-mast in the night, which obliged the *Agamemnon* to shorten sail repeatedly to
support her, and the enemy were so intimidated by the daring behaviour of the

3 *N.C.* III 171.
4 *Ibid.* XX 89.
5 *Ibid.* IX 355.
6 British force, *Agamemnon*, 64; *Meleager*, 32; *Ariadne*, 24; *Moselle*, 18; *Mutine*, 12. French Force, four
ships of 74 guns, and one of 80 guns.

Commodore, that they did not open their fire, till the British ships were close in with Cape Corse, which the *Agamemnon* very fortunately weathered by about half a mile. The *Meleager*, *Ariadne*, and *Mutine* were well to windward; but *la Moselle* (the dullest sailer) being to leeward of the Cape, had no alternative but to strike, run on shore, or attempt the almost impracticable passage between the rocks off Cape Corse, and the little islet, at a short distance from it. Captain Charles Brisbane, with his ususal intrepidity, having decided upon trying the passage, *la Moselle* bore up, and the Frenchmen knowing it was impossible to follow her, opened their fire in succession upon us; but Captain Brisbane had previously placed all her spare sails between decks, with a quantity of tar, and every thing else inflammable, being determined to run her on shore, and set fire to her, rather than let her fall into the hands of the enemy. The *Agamemnon* was prepared for a similar fate, had she not weathered the point. The Frenchmen finding themselves in danger, tacked and stood towards the coast of France, when the *Agamemnon* communicated, by signal to the Admiral, the force of the enemy, and immediately tacked also to watch their motions; and was subsequently engaged with them, when *l'Alcide*, the headmost ship, was burnt:

I am, Sir, your obedient Servant,

W.H.R.

Had we fortunately fallen in with the enemy any distance from the land, I flatter myself we should have given a decisive blow to their naval force in those seas; and although the advantage of yesterday may not appear to be of any great moment, yet I hope it will have served as a check upon their present operations, be they what they may."

The loss sustained by the British ships in this encounter amounted to ten killed, and twenty-four wounded. Towards the close of the year Admiral Hotham resigned the command of the Mediterranean fleet, and returned to England. On the 7th of March 1797, in reward of his long and meritorious services, the Admiral was raised to he dignity of a Peer of Ireland, by the title of Baron Hotham; and on the 14th of February 1799, he was promoted to the rank of Admiral of the White Squadron, but had not taken upon him any command. His Lordship is the descendant of an ancient and respectable family in Yorkshire; and some of his near relations have distinguished themselves at the bar, and in the army.

From the 'Naval Biography of Edward Grey, Esq.' XXVI 184-185

No ships were ever more gallantly defended than these [the *Censeur* and the *Ça-Ira*]; especially the *Ça-Ira*. When she struck, she had not a stick standing but her bowsprit: her hull was a perfect riddle; she had a great number of shot-holes under water; several of her ports, and all her anchors, were disabled; and she had upwards of 400 men killed and wounded. - The *Ça-Ira* was taken possession of by the *Courageux*, Captain B. Hallowell. Before day-light, on the morning after the action, Captain Hope, without orders, bore down to the disabled ships, with the view of affording them such assistance as their distressed state might require. On hailing the *Ça-Ira*, he was answered in bad English, by one of the French officers, that she was sinking, and in extreme want of immediate aid. It was now the dawn of day. Captain Hope, with the utmost promptitude, ordered the stern-boat to be lowered, and despatched Lieutenant Grey, and Mr. Anderson (the carpenter of the *Romulus*) to inspect and ascertain the real state of the ship. When the boat approached the *Ça-Ira*, the number of Frenchmen who pressed forward to jump into her was so great, that it was not safe to venture alongside. Lieutenant Grey, therefore, went under the counter, got on board by the rudder pendants, and ordered the boat to lie off on her oars. He now found, that the officer of the *Courageux*, who had taken charge of the prize, and as many of his men as he could collect, had abandoned her in the night, conceiving her to be in a sinking state. On sounding the well, there appeared seven feet water in the hold. The first step, therefore, that Lieutenant Grey took was, to set all the pumps to work - seven in number; an object which he accomplished, with considerable difficulty, chiefly by French soldiers, as the seamen, on the plea of being prisoners, would not work. The French officers declined all exertion of their influence, on the same ground. With the assistance of his own carpenter, and the carpenter and gunner of the *Ça-Ira*, who rendered every assistance in their power, Lieutenant Grey then inspected the ship, with all the minuteness of which his time would allow. She was in a most alarming state. The water was forcing its way in, through the shot-holes under water, fore and aft; several of the lower ports, in the gun-room, rendered useless in the action, were obliged to be filled up with deal plank; many of the bolts in the sides, for securing the lower-deck guns, had been shot away, and others so much damaged as to render it scarcely possible to secure the guns, which were French 36-pounders.

Apprised of this, and of other serious damages, the commander-in-chief immediately ordered Captain Hope to have the *Ça-Ira* more particularly surveyed, and to report to him, whether it would be more advisable to keep possession of, or to abandon her, after taking out the prisoners. - The result of a farther examination was, that Lieutenant Grey conceived the ship might be saved, provided he could have a sufficient number of carpenters, and of men from the fleet, to work at the pumps, and to give the necessary assistance in repairing the damages, &c. Arrangements were made accordingly, by sending a certain number of men on board the *Ça-Ira*, from each ship in the fleet, to the amount of more than a hundred; and upwards of 400 of the *Ça-Ira*'s crew, (officers and men) were, at the same time, distributed amongst the English ships. Still, more than 600 remained; but, by unremitting exertion, the *Ça-Ira* was got into Porto Espetice, near Genoa, on the afternoon of the 17th.

Thanks of the Viceroy of Corsica, and the July Battle
From the 'Biographical Memoir of John Holloway, Esq.' XIX 368-369

Admiral Hotham's fleet, with their two prizes, arrived safely, after a severe gale, in the Gulf of Spezia on the 18th, and the *Courageux*, dismasted, reached Leghorn the same day. On the 19th the *Bombay Castle* and *Blenheim*, with the convoy from England, arrived also at Leghorn; a circumstance of the utmost importance to the fleet, since, besides the seasonable reinforcement of two ships of the line, all kinds of stores had been sent out for repair.

Admiral Hotham and his officers had the satisfaction to receive the following from the Viceroy of Corsica [Gilbert Elliot]:

Bastia, April 6, 1795
Sir, I have the honour to transmit to you a letter from the president of the parliament of Corsica, enclosing the vote of thanks of the chamber of parliament to you, sir, and to the officers and men under your command, for the signal and important victory obtained over the French fleet on the 14th of March.

I am happy in this opportunity of expressing to you, and entreating you to convey to the fleet, my own exalted sense of the lustre added to his Majesty's arms, and of the honour acquired to our country, by the gallantry and good conduct displayed on the 13th and 14th of March.

I am not less sensible of the deep and solid obligations which this country, and all who have a regard for its security and happiness, owe to the important events of those days.

GILBERT ELLIOT

Vice-Admiral Hotham, &c.

Nothing of any importance occurred in the operations of the fleet, from the above action, to the succeeding month of July, 1795; when, the French fleet having again ventured to sea, another engagement took place, which is thus detailed by the admiral in his official letter. . . .

[The extract from Admiral Hotham's dispatch of July 14, which has been printed in full above, need not be repeated here.]

The prompt manner in which the admiral put to sea with his squadron, to follow the French fleet, and his conduct throughout the action [of the 4th July], was certainly honourable to his professional character: and although navy officers were offended at the discontinuance of the partial action which had commenced with some of the flying ships of the enemy (whence an opinion, too hastily formed, was encouraged by a party at home, hostile to the long and meritorious services of Admiral Hotham), that gallant officer, on his return, was deservedly honoured by a distinguished mark of his sovereign's favour, and raised to the dignity of an Irish peer, by the title of Baron Hotham. Thus much is due from us, as honest chroniclers, to assert; and more particularly in this place, as Captain Holloway was so intimately and eminently concerned in the whole of these proceedings. . . . [Of Captain Holloway, his biographer wrote:] Such is the general outline of the services and characer of this naval officer; who by plain sailing, and keeping a steady course, has gained a high character in his profession, and preserved the confidence of government, amidst the vicissitudes and cabals of party. Truer than the compass, he has throughout life displayed no variation. As the anonymous author of the Atlantis, already cited, said, "John Holloway comprises the genuine character of a true British tar, and a gallant officer. Honest without disguise, brave without ostentation, and independent without being assuming, he merits every thing that can be said in his favour, as a deserving naval commander."

1796-1797 - Home Waters: Ireland

OPERATIONS IN HOME WATERS, and in the Mediterranean, during 1796 and 1797 were to be dominated by the fear of invasion of the British Isles orchestrated by Irish patriots. In March 1795 Prussia had made peace, thus ending the threat to France's northern frontier, and in June 1795 Spain had been forced to conclude peace. In August 1796, by the Treaty of San Ildefonso, the Spanish king, the imbecile Charles IV, was committed to war against Britain and Portugal. Hostilities were actually precipitated in October after Pitt sanctioned an ill-conceived attempt to seize the homecoming Spanish treasure ships. The Spanish fleet, although woefully badly manned, was large enough to make it a highly dangerous strategic force which Paris could commit in support either of the Toulon or of the Brest fleet. The revolutionary government of France was replaced in October 1795 by a bourgeois administration under the control of a 'Directory' which put French finances on a firmer basis and so enabled the navy to begin to address its supply and pay problems, and also to begin the reestablishment of discipline, but reconstruction was to take some time.

Howe's resignation in April 1797 finally put an end to Bridport's uncertain position as acting commander of the Channel, or Western, Squadron which he had occupied since late 1794. Bridport formally succeeded him, and Vice-Admiral Sir Alan Gardner became second in command.

In October 1796 Villaret-Joyeuse was ordered to fit out the Brest fleet to land a French army under General Hoche at Bantry Bay in southwestern Ireland, with the ultimate objective of invading England. When he complained of the poor supplies and discipline of the fleet, he was replaced by Admiral Morard de Galles, who sailed his fleet of seventeen of the line, and nineteen light craft with seven transports and a powder ship.

However, *Séduisant*, 74 guns, ran on a rock leaving harbour, and the frigate *Fraternité*, onboard which were the Admiral and General Hoche, became separated from the rest of the squadron, which made its way under Admiral Bouvet but missed its proper landfall and spent days beating against gale-force easterlies into Bantry Bay. The log of *Kangaroo*, an 18-gun brig, recorded how she sailed right through the French fleet which was manoeuvring to enter Bantry Bay. *Kangaroo* beat back to Plymouth with the news, arriving 1 January 1797, and forwarding a despatch to the Admiralty. The fleeting opportunities which occurred to put the army ashore were missed by General Grouchy acting, or failing to do so, in the absence of Hoche. The continued easterly wind, and shortage of supplies, made it unhealthy to remain long in the Bay when Bridport could be expected to appear with the Channel Fleet. The inadequacy of Spithead as an operational base, however, was made abundantly clear by the difficulty Bridport experienced in getting to the westward when ordered to sea by the Admiralty.

Rear-Admiral Kingsmill, who commanded the Irish station, continued at his post into 1798, and was thus the man who thwarted a second invasion attempt made that year, this time directed at northern Ireland. A small crack army was landed at Killala Bay in August, but another squadron carrying essential support was intercepted in the Irish Sea in October. *Hoche* and four frigates were captured. Wolfe Tone, the Irish revolutionary leader who was captured in the *Hoche*, later killed himself to avoid execution.

A straggler from the French fleet of 1796-1797, *Droits de l'Homme*, was engaged in heavy weather by Vice-Admiral Sir Edward Pellew with two frigates, the 44-gun *Indefatigable* and the 28-gun *Amazon*. In the murk, navigation became inexact. When land was sighted close under their lees all three ships broke off their fight to claw themselves clear, but only *Indefatigable* saved herself from the rocks in Audierne Bay. The shipwrecks of the *Droits de l'Homme* and *Amazon* at the end of 1797, as the explosion of *Amprion* in September 1796, mark the dangers of a life in the navy. The captain of the *Amprion* was Israel Pellew, brother of the *Indefatigable*'s captain.

The Naval Chronicle's account of the explosion of *Amprion* was reported as a separate news item even though published over three years after the event. The accounts of both Irish invasion attempts, that of 1796 and that of 1798, formed parts of the biographical memoir of Sir Robert Kingsmill, and it has been decided to reproduce it intact despite the violence done thereby to chronology. The log of the *Kangaroo* was inserted in the biographical memoir of Captain Courtney Boyle, published in 1813. A narrative of the engagement with the *Droits de l'Homme*, closely based on the official action report, formed part of the biographical memoir of Sir Edward Pellew. An excerpt from that letter is nonetheless included here, and is balanced with an account by a British prisoner onboard the French ship.

Bridport Assumes Command
From the 'Biographical memoir of Lord Bridport.' [1282]

On the 31st of May 1796, Lord Bridport was made a peer of Great Britain. Since Lord Howe finally resigned the command in the Channel, in 1797, he has continued to hold it with great credit to himself and his country. The hardships he has endured, and still continues to endure [in 1798], on that station, can only be known to those who have experienced the painful fatigue of so arduous a service. But it behooves his countrymen in general to remember, that the salvation of the city and port of London, the security of its commerce, and the immediate safety of its inhabitants, all arise from the patient watchings, and continued skill of this distinguished veteran.[1]

Loss of the Amprion. [III 197-202]

Ha! total night, and horror, here preside;
My stunn'd ear tingles to the whizzing tide,
It is the funeral knell! and gliding near,
Methinks the phantoms of the Dead appear.
But lo! emerging from the watery grave,
Again they float incumbent o the wave;
Again the dismal prospect opens round,
The wreck, the shores, the dying, and the drown'd.

Falconer's Shipwreck

A more authentic account, than has yet been published, of the loss of His Majesty's Ship Amphion, of 32 guns, blown up in Hamoaze, September 22, 1796. Communicated by a Correspondent, who was at Plymouth when the dreadful event took place

The *Amphion* frigate, of 32 guns, Captain Israel Pellew, after having cruised some time in the North Seas, had at last obtained an order to join the squadron of frigates, commanded by Sir Edward Pellew. It was on her passage, that an hard gale of wind occasioning some injury to the fore-mast, obliged her to put into Plymouth, off which place she then was: she accordingly came into the Sound, anchored there on the nineteenth of September, and went up into harbour the next morning about seven A.M. On the twenty-second, at about half past four P.M. I felt, whilst at Stonehouse, a violent shock like an earthquake; which extended as far off as the Royal Hospital, and the town of Plymouth. The sky towards Dock appeared red, like the effect of a fire: for near a quarter of an hour no one could discover what was the occasion; though the streets were crowded with people running different ways in the greatest consternation. When the alarm, and confusion, had a little subsided; it first began to be known, that the *Amphion* was blown up! Several bodies and mangled remains were found and picked up by the boats in Hamoaze; whose alacrity on this melancholy occasion was particularly remarked, and highly commended. The few who remained alive of the crew were conveyed, as fast as their mangled situations would permit, to the Royal Hospital: as the frigate was

---

1 On the 15th of March 1796, Lord Bridport succeeded Earl Howe in the civil office of Vice Admiral of Great Britain; and on the 1st of June, in the same year, was advanced Admiral of the White.

originally manned from Plymouth, the friends and relations of her unfortunate ships's company mostly lived in the neighbourhood; it is dreadful to relate what a scene took place - arms, legs, and lifeless trunks, mangled and disfigured by gunpowder, were collected and deposited at the hospital, having been brought in sacks to be owned. Bodies still living, some with the loss of limbs, others having just expired as they were conveying there; men, women, and children, flocking round the gates, and entreating admittance, whose sons, husbands, and fathers, were amongst the unhappy number. During the first evening nothing was ascertained concerning he cause of this event, though an hundred reports instantly circulated. The few survivors, who by the day following had in some degree regained the use of their senses, could not give the least account. One man who was brought alive to the Royal Hospital died before night; another before the following morning: the boatswain[2] and one of the sailors appeared likely, with great care, to do well. Three or four men who were at work in the tops were blown up with them, and falling again into the water were picked up very little hurt; these, with the two before mentioned, and one of the sailor's wives, were supposed to be the only survivors, except the Captain, and two Lieutenants.

The following particulars were however collected from the examination of several people, before Sir Richard King, the Port Admiral; and the information that could be procured from those who saw the explosion from Dock.

The first person known to have observed any thing, was a young midshipman in the *Cambridge* guard ship, lying not far distant from the place where the *Amphion* blew up; who having a great desire to observe every thing relative to a profession he had just entered upon, was looking at the frigate through a glass, as she lay close alongside of the sheer-hulk, and was taking in her bowsprit. She was lashed to the hulk; and an old receiving ship, the *Yarmouth*, was lying on the opposite side, quite close to her; and both within a few yards of the Dock-Yard jetty. The midshipman said, the *Amphion* suddenly appeared to rise altogether upright from the surface of the water, until he nearly saw her keel - the explosion then succeeded: the masts seemed to be forced up into the air, and the hull instantly to sink - all this passed before him in the space of two minutes.

The man who stood at the Dock Yard stairs said, that the first he heard of it was a kind of hissing noise; and then the explosion, when he beheld the masts blown up into the air. It was very strongly reported, and erroneously inserted in many newspapers, that several windows were broke at Dock by explosion, and that in the Dock Yard there was much mischief done by the *Amphion*'s guns going off when she blew up; but though the shock was felt as far as Plymouth; and at Stonehouse enough to shake the windows; yet it is a wonderful and miraculous fact, that surrounded as she was in the harbour with ships, close alongside of the jetty, and lashed to another vessel, no damage was done to any thing but herself. It is dreadful to reflect, that owing to their intention of putting to sea the next day there were nearly one hundred men, women, and children, more than her complement on board, taking leave of their friends; besides the company at two dinners that were given in the ship; one of which was by the Captain.

Captain Israel Pellew, and Captain William Swaffield, of his Majesty's ship *Overyssel*, who was at dinner with him, and the First Lieutenant, were drinking their wine: when the first explosion threw them off their seats, and struck them against the carlings of

2 Mr. Montandon, who had not long before been promoted into the *Amphion*, from the *Russel*, by Admiral Macbride in the North Seas.

the upper deck, so as to stun them. Captain Pellew, however, had presence of mind sufficient to fly to the cabin windows; and seeing the two hawsers, one slack in the bit, and the other taut, threw himself with an amazing leap, which he said afterwards nothing but his sense of danger could have enabled him to take, upon the latter; and saved himself by that means from the general destruction; though his face had been badly cut against the carlings, when he was thrown from his seat. The First Lieutenant saved himself in the same manner, by jumping out of the window, and by being also a remarkable good swimmer; but Captain Swaffield being, as supposed, more stunned, did not escape: his body was found on the twenty-second of October with his skull fractured, appearing to have been crushed between the sides of two vessels. He was conveyed in an hearse, and buried at Stonehouse chapel.

The sentinel at the cabin door happened to be looking at his watch; how he escaped no one can tell, not even himself; he however was brought on shore, and but little hurt: the first thing he felt was the having his watch dashed out of his hands, after which he was no longer sensible of what happened to him. The boatswain was standing on the cat-head; the bowsprit had been stepped for three hours; the gammoning and every thing on; and he was directing the men in rigging out the jib boom; when suddenly he felt himself driven upwards, and fell into the sea; he then perceived he was entangled in the rigging, and had some trouble to get clear; when being taken up by a boat, belonging to one of the men of war, they found that his arm was broke. One of the surviving seamen declared to an officer of rank, that he was preserved in the following astonishing manner: he was below at the time the *Amphion* blew up, and went to the bottom in the ship: that he had a knife in his pocket, which he recollected; and taking it out cut his way through the companion of the gun-room (which was shattered already with the explosion); then letting himself up to the surface of the water, swam unhurt ashore. He shewed the knife to the officer who heard this, and declared he had been under the water full five minutes.

I also heard in the Dock Yard, that one of the sailor's wives had a young child in her arms; the fright of the shock made her take such fast hold of it, that though the upper part of her body alone remained, the child was alive, locked fast in her arms, and likely to do well.

Mr. Spry, an auctioneer, who had long lived in great respectability at Dock, with his son, and godson, had gone on board to visit a friend: they were all lost.

The man at the Dock Yard stairs said, that about half an hour before the frigate blew up, one of her Lieutenants, and Lieutenant Campbell of the Marines (nephew to Colonel Campbell), and some of the men, got into the boat at the stairs, and went off to the ship. Lieutenant Campbell had some business to transact at the marine barracks in the morning; and continuing there some time, was engaged by the Officers to stay dinner, and spend the evening with them; he thus would have escaped: but somebody who came from the *Amphion* said, there were letters on board for Lieutenant Campbell; as they were some he was very anxious to receive, he left the barracks about half an hour before dinner to fetch them, meaning to return again directly: during the short interval he was on board, the ship blew up. He was a young man universally respected, and lamented by the Corps, and indeed by every one who knew him. One of the Lieutenants who lost his life was the only support of an aged mother and sister; who at his death had neither friend nor relation left to protect and comfort them. The numbers of people who afterwards were daily seen at Dock in deep mourning for their lost relatives was truly melancholy. Captain Pellew was taken up by the boats, and carried to Commissioner

Fanshaw's house in the Dock Yard, very weak with the exertions he had made; and so shocked with the distressing cause of them, that he appeared at first scarcely to know where he was, or to be sensible of his own situation: when he was a little recovered, in the course of a day, or two, he was removed to the house of a friend, Dr. Hawker of Plymouth.

Sir Richard King had given a public dinner in honour of the Coronation. Captain Charles Rowley of the *Unite* frigate, calling in the morning, was engaged to stay; and put off dining, as he had previously intended to do, on board the *Amphion*. Captain Darby of the *Bellerophon* was also to have dined with Captain Pellew, and had come round in his boat from Cawsand Bay; but having some business concerning his ship to transact with Sir Richard King, it detained him about half an hour longer at Stonehouse than he intended; and he was just gone down to the beach, and getting into the boat to proceed up Hamoaze, when he heard the fatal explosion. Captain Swaffield was to have sailed the next day; so that the difference of twenty-four hours would have saved this much lamented, and truly valuable Officer. His brother, Mr. J. Swaffield of the Pay Office, being asked to the same dinner, had set out with him from Stonehouse; but before he had reached Dock, a person came after him on business, which obliged him to return; and thus saved him from sharing his brother's untimely fate.

Many conjectures were formed concerning the cause of what had happened: some thought it was owing to neglect; that the men were employed drawing the guns, and contrary to rule had not extinguished all the fires, though the dinners were over: this however the First Lieutenant said was impossible, as they could not be drawing the guns, the key of the magazine being to his certain knowledge hanging up in his cabin at the time. Some of the men indeed declared that the guns were drawn in the Sound, before they came up Hamoaze. It was also insinuated that it was done intentionally, as several of the bodies were afterwards found without any clothes on, as if they had prepared to jump overboard before the ship could have time to blow up. As no mutiny had ever appeared in the ship, it seems unlikely that such a desperate plot should have been formed, without any one who survived having the least knowledge of it; and it is a well known fact, that in almost every case of shipwreck, where there is a chance of plunder, there are wretches, so far destitute of the common feeling of humanity, as to hover round the scene of horror; in hopes of stripping the bodies of the dead, and seizing whatever they can lay their hands on in the confusion, to benefit themselves.

It was the fore magazine which took fire; had it been the after one much more damage must have ensued. The moment the explosion was heard, Sir Richard King arose from dinner, and went in his boat on board the hulk, where the sight he beheld was dreadful: the deck covered with blood, mangled limbs, and entrails, blackened with gunpowder; the shreds of the *Amphion*'s pendant, and rigging, hanging about her, and pieces of her shattered timbers strewed all around. Some people at dinner in the *Yarmouth*, though within a very small distance, declare that the report they heard did not appear to be louder than the firing of a cannon from the *Cambridge*, which they imagined it to be, and had never even rose from dinner, till the confusion upon deck led them to think some accident had happened! This may appear astonishing: I can only say, it was told me by very respectable people at the time.

At low water, the next day, about a foot and an half of one of the masts appeared above water; and for several days the Dock Yard men were employed in collecting the shattered masts and yard, and dragging up what they could procure from the wreck. On the twenty-ninth, part of the fore-chains was hauled up, shattered and splintered, and all the bolts forced out; also the head and cutwater. On the third of October, it was intended that an attempt should be made to raise the *Amphion* between two frigates, the *Castor* and *Iphigenia*, who were accordingly moored on each side of her; but only a few pieces of the ship could be got up, one or two of her guns, some of the men's chests, chairs, and part of the furniture of the cabin. Some bodies floated out from between deck, and amongst the rest a midshipman's; these and all that could be found, were towed round by boats through Stonehouse Bridge up to the Royal Hospital stairs, to be interred in their burying ground. Indeed the sight for many weeks was dreadful; the change of tide washing out the putrid bodies, which were towed round by the boats when they would hardly hold together. It is needless to enlarge on such a subject; any one may be able to form an idea of it, when told that bodies continued to be found even as late as the *thirtieth of November*, 1796, when the *Amphion* having been dragged round to another part of the Dock Yard jetty to be broke up, the body of a woman was washed out from between decks. A sack was also dragged up, filled with gunpowder at bottom, and just topped with biscuit; which in some measure confirmed an idea that had before gained ground, that the gunner had been stealing the powder to sell, and had concealed what he could get out by degrees in the above manner; and that thinking himself safe on a day when every one was entertaining their friends, he had carelessly been amongst the gunpowder without taking the necessary precautions. As he was said to have been seen at Dock very much in liquor in the morning, I think it seems probable that this might be the cause of a calamity as sudden as it was dreadful.

Invasion of Ireland
From the 'Biographical Memoirs of Sir Robert Kingsmill, Bart.' V 206-212

The conclusion of the year [1796] was productive of an event and plan of operations set on foot by the enemy, which had in its intention nothing less than the reduction of all Ireland. A very formidable armament, consisting of no less than seventeen ships of the line, with twenty-seven frigates, cutters, or other vessels, having a considerable body of troops on board, sailed from Brest in the hopes of effecting an immediate descent on the south of that island. This formidable force consisted of the following ships. The list of them, together with their fate, will in all probability prove considerably interesting:

Ships of the Line

L'Indomptable	80	Les Droits de L'Homme,	74
Le Redoutable	74	driven on shore by the	
Le Patriote	74	Indefatigable, and Amazon	
L'Ecole	74	Le Tourville	74
Le Trajan	74	Le Watigny	74
Le Cassard	74	La Constitution	74
Le Nestor	74	Le Seduisant, lost	74
Le Pluton	74	Le Pegase	74
Le Fougeux	74	La Revolution	74
Le Mucius	74		

Ship cut down

Scaevola, foundered	40

Frigates

La Fraternite	L'Impatiente, lost
L'Immortalite	Le Tortu, taken

Portrait of Sir Robert Kingsmill,
Bart., Admiral of the Blue
Squadron. Engraved by Ridley,
from an original painting by L.F.
Abbot, Esq. ^{Plate 55}

La Resolue	*La Bravoure*
La Bellone	*La Fidele*, run down
La Surveillante, scuttled	*La Romain*
La Syrene	*La Charente*

Corvettes

L'Atlante, taken	*Le Renard*	*La Mutine*, taken
Le Voltigeur	*La Vautour*	*L'Affronteur*

Ships armed en flute

Le Suffrein, taken	*Le Nicomede*
La Ville de L'Orient, taken	*L'Allegre*, taken
La Justine, taken, afterwards lost	*L'Experiment*

Corsairs

Le Patriote   Lazare Hoche

It were a needless waste of time to enter into any other particular detail of the disasters that attended this ill-fated armament. The moment was critical, and, though succoured by Providence, as the arms of Britain appeared to be, it certainly required the most consummate intelligence and share of ability to enable a commander, at the head of no greater force than that which was commanded by Mr. Kingsmill, to stem, or hold himself in readiness to oppose even the shattered remains of that armament, which, after all its misfortunes, still threatened him with attack. The discomfiture of this expedition naturally procured a cessation from any similar attempt for several months; and Mr. Kingsmill's cruisers were of necessity compelled to be content with resuming their former less interesting occupation against privateers, or such casual cruisers, as in despite, not only of their want of success, but the still more serious misfortunes that attended them of being almost constantly captured, still maintained sufficient hardiness to attempt a continuance of their predatory war.

Few periods more momentous than the preceding have ever existed in the history of any country in the universe, and it was singularly fortunate, without meaning the smallest reflection on any other of the noble, and brave persons his contemporaries, who were then in the service, that Mr. Kingsmill should at that time hold the command on that station. As a native of the country he was dear to them as a brother; and by his conduct as an officer, placed among them in a situation not highly unlikely to have created disgust and dislike, he had universally endeared himself to them as a friend and protector. All these qualities and qualifications were, it must be universally admitted, peculiarly necessary at so critical a period as that alluded to. Ireland passed without experiencing the smallest inconvenience, into a state of perfect tranquillity, and continued so for a considerable space of time subsequent to the invasion, unmolested by foreign, and unvexed by internal foes.

The duties and attention of Vice-Admiral Kingsmill did not, however, cease or relax in consequence of the lately impending danger being completely averted; repeated captures continued still to add as well to the reputation of the Commander in Chief, as of those who immediately acted under his instructions. For a period of more than twelve months, public affairs continued to flow in the same regular channel; at length the perturbed and seditious spirits of those domestic enemies whose hopes had on the former occasion been crushed, having acquired new vigour from the extensive promises of assistance held forth to them by France, burst forth at once with all the violence of a volcano, the effects of which appeared as threatening to shake the whole country, even to its very foundation.

Difficulties and political dangers appeared consequently to rise, in dreadful climax above each other. Although no force belonging to the enemy was sufficient to contend even with the light cruisers which Mr. Kingsmill had the direction of, yet his situation was evidently more irksome than it would have been provided he had been under the necessity of entering into a fair and regular conflict against a foe far superior to him in force. In the latter instance, his own abilities might have been called into action in their fullest extent; and, aided by the bravery of his followers, might have promised every reasonable hope of effecting the most extensive success, which, allowing for the disproportion of force, could possibly have been gained; but, circumstanced as he stood at that awful moment, he had to contend against a numerous and treacherous host of foes, not formidable, perhaps in point of real strength, but capable of effecting the deepest mischief. Aided as the arrival of succour was, by the encouragement which the discontented held forth, it became necessary to guard with the most scrupulous attention every creek, every inlet, throughout a long extent of coast; and the casual or unavoidable omission with respect to any of those points at which it was possible to introduce support, might have occasioned the long, if not the fatal, prolongation of that system of warfare which actually deluged a considerable part of the country, and appeared to threaten the desolation of the whole.

Sixteen months afterward, however, France resumed her project, and exposed herself a second time to the gallantry of the British navy. The *Hoche*, a ship of the line, eight frigates, a schooner, and a brig, found an opportunity of clearing Brest harbour. They had on board nearly 5000 troops, together with great quantities of arms and stores of all kinds; so that they were well prepared to make a powerful effort. Captain Countess, in the *Ethalion*, to whose judicious management the fortune of the day ought, perhaps, in a great measure to be attributed, kept the enemy continually in sight, from the moment of its leaving its port, on the 17th of October 1798, when Lord Bridport was driven off his station. This excellent officer had been detached by Captain Keats of the *Boadicea*, to watch the motions of the squadron, with the *Anson*, and *Amelia* frigates, together with the *Sylph* brig under his orders. He continued watching the enemy's ships till the 10th of November, when, having ascertained their real situation, he ordered Captain Herbert of the *Amelia*, to go in quest of some of the divisions of the British fleet, which he knew were off the northern coast of Ireland. On the 11th Captain Countess himself fell in with Sir John Borlase Warren, whom he acquainted with the approach of the enemy. Happily, meanwhile, the vigilance of the Board of Admiralty had procured the most accurate information of the ultimate destination of the Brest squadron, and nothing could have been better directed than the stations of the British fleet.

No sooner had the enemy's ships appeared off the Irish coast, than Admiral Kingsmill was made acquainted with their situation, and his cruisers displayed the utmost activity in intercepting such of the French as escaped from the general action, the glory of which fell to the share of that gallant officer Sir John Borlase Warren. When that action commenced, the wind was at N.W. As the frigates that had troops on board, though they fought valiantly when once engaged, avoided coming into the action as much as lay in their power, no regular line was preserved; and as the British ships were very much dispersed in the chase of the enemy, only a part of them could get into action. The *Robust*, of 74 guns, Captain Thornborough, bore the brunt of the engagement with the *Hoche*, which ship was fought in a very gallant manner for upward of three hours. She was the finest ship of her rate in the French navy, almost new, and fitted out with uncommon care. Beside the *Hoche*, four frigates were taken, two of which were the *Immortalite* and the *Coquille*. Three frigates that escaped, anchored in Donegal Bay on the following day, and one of them sent a boat on shore with sixty men, who, in attempting to land, were repulsed by the Mount-Charles yeomanry, commanded by Captain Montgomery. At the time these frigates escaped, they, steering to the southward, were chased by the *Canada*, the *Foudroyant*, and the *Melampus*, which ships, however, except one captured by the *Melampus*, they out-sailed.[3]

When the circumstances which preceded this event are seriously considered, the mind of every well-wisher to his country sinks back as if in dismay from an abyss of danger, which he had, as it were miraculously, escaped. To the already inflamed minds of the seditious, the most trivial addition of assistance became, as was manifested by the forlorn hope landed a short time before under the orders of General Humbert, the most material encouragement. When it is reflected that the number of troops intended to be introduced into Ireland by the armament whose discomfiture has just been related, amounted to five times that number which had just before alarmed Ireland, from the centre to the utmost extremities, on all sides, it cannot remain a wonder to every lover of peace and every well-disposed member of society, that its discomfiture should cause a universal joy. The delay of a few hours, whether occasioned by accident or want of diligence, would inevitably have proved of the utmost consequence, and Britain had to felicitate herself that Providence, in conjunction with the bravery of the officers and seamen whom she employed, had, to speak least consequentially of the event, prevented a most dreadful effusion of blood.

Warned by experience, intimidated by facts, and rendered totally averse to any repetition of the same species of event, France, and its temporary Government, appeared to rest satisfied that the discomfiture just experienced was an insurmountable barrier to all future hopes. Devoid of the more potent antagonists, the Admiral was again compelled to confine his views against those whose utmost efforts might indeed irritate, and partially injure individuals belonging to the community, but whose direful attacks need never be apprehended, on a national ground, as in the slightest degree consequential. Mr. Kingsmill continued occupied on the same station, industriously employing the same means which he had before exerted, and with so much effect, against the enemies of his

3 For farther particulars respecting this action, see vol. iii. p.352.

Entrance into Cork harbour. Engraved by Baily, from a drawing by Pocock. The
view of the harbour was taken when it bore N.N.E. by the compass. In that
direction the harbour appears open; but in others, and in hazy weather, it is (as the
phrase is) a blind harbour, without any apparent opening, the land being of nearly
an equal height along the coast. ^{Plate 283}

country, till toward the conclusion of the year 1800, when he resigned his command to
Sir Alan, now Lord Gardner, and has never accepted of any subsequent naval
employment.

A recapitulation of the honours and compliments repeatedly paid to this gentleman[4]
by the most respectable corporate bodies and the noblest individuals, would far exceed
those limits which necessity prescribes to this species of biography. Suffice it to say, the
frequent repetition of them, and the warmth exultingly displayed by the parties in
paying what was considered as bare tribute of justice to the worth of their protector,
were sufficient to prove that few men could have been fortunate enough to equal him in
their esteem, and none to exceed him.

Heraldic Particulars

Arms: Argent a chevron ermines between three Fers de Moline pierced and seme of
cross crosslets fitchy sable, a chief of the second.

Crest: On a wreath, a cubit arm vested argent, cuff ermines, in the hand proper a
Fer de Moline, as in the Arms.

Motto: Do Well, Doubt Naught.

4 See vol. iv. page 247.

Log of H.M.S. Kangaroo
From the 'Biographical Memoir of the Hon. Captain Courtney Boyle.' XXX 11-12

Thursday, December 22, 1796, Cape Clear E.S.E. four leagues. At one P.M. made sail in chase of a sloop. At two, brought-to the chase; proved from Bristol, bound to Galway. At four, from the masthead, saw several sail to the southward, under the land. Half-past four, counted 19 sail of large ships working into Bantry Bay. At five, tacked to the northward, took in top-gallant-sails, rove steering sail geer, fore and aft, and got the sails on the lower and top-sail yards. At a quarter before six, tacked to the southward. At six, the Bull Rock S.W. two miles. At eight, observed the fleet tack, by signal from the admiral - *viz.* two lights, one under, the other at mizen-peek [sic], and two at the spritsail yard arms. At ten, tacked to the northward. At eleven tacked to the southward. At two A.M. passed within hail of a frigate. Half-past two, passed and hailed a lugger, who made no reply; tacked, in order to speak her again, when she bore up for the admiral. At half-past four, set top-gallant-sails. At five, passed close to a line-of-battle ship and two frigates. At a quarter past eight tacked. At nine, to windward of the fleet. At half-past nine, the weathermost ship hoisted a cornet pendant, white with a red fly, a Dutch flag and yellow one at her mizen-peak; when the lugger in company with her, hoisted a white pendant, with a red fly, white flag with blue border, and half blue half white, at her main-top-mast head. Two ships to leeward shewed large French pendants at their mizen-top-mast heads. Counted 22 sail, some well into the Bay. At noon, counted 9 sail of the fleet standing in-shore, and a brig (apparently on the look-out), standing to the southward.

December 22. At three P.M. hove-to off Crookhaven harbour, and despatched Mr. Talbot, the second lieutenant, with a letter to Vice-admiral Kingsmill, at Cork.

Engagement of H.M. Frigates Indefatigable and Amazon, with Les Droits de L'homme
From the 'Biographical Memoir of Sir Edward Pellew, Bart.' ·XVIII 454-457

On the 13th of January, whilst cruising in the *Indefatigable*, accompanied by the *Amazon*, Captain Reynolds, about fifty leagues south-west of Ushant, he [Sir Edward Pellew] discovered a large ship in the north-west quarter, steering under an easy sail, towards the coast of France. This was about half-past twelve, in the day; the wind blowing hard at west, with thick hazy weather. Chase was immediately given; and, at four P.M. Sir Edward's ship had gained sufficiently upon the enemy, for him to perceive that she had no poop. At a quarter before six, Sir Edward came up with the chase, and brought her to close action, which was well supported, on both sides, for nearly an hour, when, as in the case of her contest with *la Virginie*, the *Indefatigable* unavoidably shot a-head. The *Amazon* now appeared astern, and gallantly supplied her place; but, as the eagerness of Captain Reynolds to second his friend had brought him up under a press of sail, his ship also, after a well-supported and close fire for a short time, unavoidably shot a-head. The enemy, deriving courage from the latter circumstance, made an attempt to board the *Indefatigable*. The effort failed; but she kept up a constant and heavy fire of musketry till the end of the action, frequently engaging both sides of the ship at once.

Sir Edward, with the utmost possible exertion, replaced some of the disabled rigging, and brought his ship under proper sail; and, Captain Reynolds having reduced the sail of the *Amazon*, a second attack was commenced; the consorts placing themselves, after some raking broadsides, one upon each quarter, frequently within pistol shot. After continuing the engagement, without intermission, for five hours longer, the *Indefatigable* was obliged to sheer off, to secure her masts.

About twenty minutes past four in the morning, the moon opening rather brighter than before, Lieutenant Bell, who was keeping a vigilant look-out on the forecastle, descried a glimpse of the land; and he had scarcely reported the discovery to Sir Edward Pellew, before the breakers were seen. At this critical moment, the *Indefatigable* was close under the enemy's starboard bow, and the *Amazon* was as near to her on the larboard. Not an instant was to be lost. Every life depended upon the prompt execution of orders; and, to their credit, nothing could surpass the activity of the brave crew of the *Indefatigable*, who, with astonishing alacrity, hauled the tacks on board, and made sail to the southward. Before day-light, they again saw breakers upon the lee bow, and wore to the northward. Not knowing exactly on what part of the coast they were embayed, the approach of morning was most anxiously looked for; and, soon after it opened, the land was seen very close a-head: the ship was again wore, in twenty fathoms water, and stood to the southward. A few minutes afterwards, the *Indefatigable* discovered, and passed within a mile of, the enemy who had so bravely defended herself. She was lying on her broadside, a tremendous surf beating over her. She was afterwards found be *les Droits des Hommes*, of 74 guns, commanded by Captain, *ci-devant* Baron, le Cross; with 1,600 men, seamen and soldiers, on board; 170 of whom perished, exclusive of those killed in the action.

The miserable fate of these brave men was, perhaps, the more sincerely lamented by the crew of the *Indefatigable*, from the apprehension of their experiencing a similar misfortune, their ship having, at that time, four feet water in the hold, the sea rolling heavily, and the wind being dead upon the shore.

Sir Edward Pellew now ascertained his situation to be that of Audierne Bay; and perceived that the fate of himself, ship, and crew, depended on the chance of weathering the Penmark rocks. This, by the uncommon exertions of the men, notwithstanding their fatigued and almost exhausted state, in making all the sail that they could set, was happily accomplished at eleven o'clock; the *Indefatigable* passing about a mile to windward of the Penmarks.

The *Amazon* was less fortunate. When the *Indefatigable* had hauled her wind to the southward, she had hauled hers to the northward; and Captain Reynolds, notwithstanding every effort, found his masts, yards, rigging, and sails, so miserably cut and shattered, with three feet water in the hold, that it was impossible to work off the shore. In this condition, a little after five in the morning, the *Amazon* struck the ground; and, almost at the same moment, the enemy was also stranded. The crew of the *Amazon* - excepting six, who stole away the cutter and were drowned - were saved by making rafts; but, upon their landing, they were made prisoners.

In this gallant and hardly-fought action, which commenced at a quarter before six, P.M. and lasted, with the exception of short intervals, until half-past four, A.M. the sea ran so high, that the men, in the respective ships, were up to their waists in water, on the main-deck. Some of the guns of the *Indefatigable* broke their breechings four times; others drew the ring-bolts from their sides; and many, from getting wet, were repeatedly obliged to be drawn, immediately after loading.

The loss which the *Indefatigable* sustained was only nineteen wounded, amongst whom was Mr. Thompson, the first lieutenant. - The *Amazon* had three men killed, and fifteen badly wounded.

Sir Edward Pellew to the Secretary of the Admiralty, 17 January 1797.
VIII 466-467

I have the honour to make known to you, for the information of the Lords Commissioners of the Admiralty, that on Friday last, the 13th instant, at half past noon, in latitude 47 deg. 30 min. N. Ushant bearing N.E. fifty leagues, we discovered a large ship in the N.W. quarter, steering under easy sail for France; the wind was then at west blowing hard, with thick hazy weather.

At about twenty minutes past four, the moon opening rather brighter than before, showed to Lieutenant George Bell, who was watchfully looking out on the forecastle, a glimpse of the land; he had scarcely reached me to report it, when we saw the breakers. We were then close under the enemy's starboard bow, and the *Amazon* as near her on the larboard; not an instant could be lost, and every life depended upon the prompt execution of my orders; and here it is with heartfelt pleasure I acknowledge the full value of my officers and ship's company, who with incredible alacrity hauled the tacks on board, and made sail to the southward. The land could not be ascertained, but we took it to be Ushant, and in the Bay of Brest, crippled as we were, I had no particular fears, but before day we again saw breakers on the lee bow; the ship was instantly wore to the northward; and being satisfied that the land we had before seen was not Ushant, the lingering approach of day-light was most anxiously looked for by all, and soon after it opened, seeing the land very close ahead, we again wore to the southward in twenty fathoms water, and a few minutes after discovered the enemy, who had so bravely defended herself, laying on her broadside, and a tremendous surf beating over her. The miserable fate of her brave but unhappy crew, was perhaps the more sincerely lamented by us, from the apprehension of suffering a similar misfortune. We passed her within a mile, in a very bad condition, having at that time four feet water in our hold, a great sea, and the wind dead on shore, but we had ascertained, beyond a doubt, our situation to be that of Hodierne Bay [sic], and that our fate depended upon the possible chance of weathering the Penmark Rocks. Exhausted as we were with fatigue, every exertion was made, and every inch of canvas set that could be carried, and at eleven A.M. we made the breakers, and by the blessing of God, weathered the Penmark Rocks about half a mile.

Narrative of the dreadful Shipwreck of Les Droits de L'Homme, a French ship, of 74 guns, driven on Shore on the 14th of January 1797, after a severe Action with the Indefatigable and Amazon Frigates, under the Command of Sir Edward Pellew and Captain Reynolds. By Elias Pipon, Lieutenant. 63d Regiment. VIII 465-469

On the 5th of January 1797, returning home on leave of absence for the recovery of my health, from the West Indies, in the *Cumberland* letter of marque, saw a large man of war, off the coast of Ireland, being then within four leagues of the mouth of the river Shannon. She hoisted English colours and decoyed us within gunshot, when she substituted the tri-colour flag, and took us. She proved to be *Les Droits de L'Homme*, of 74 guns, commanded by *ci-devant* Baron, now Citoyen La Crosse, and had separated from a fleet of men of war, on board of which were 20,000 troops intended to invade Ireland; on board of this ship was General Humbert, who afterwards effected a descent in Ireland, with 900 troops, and 600 seamen.[5] On the 7th of January went into Bantry Bay to see if any of the squadron was still there, and on finding none, the ship proceeded to the southward; nothing extraordinary occurred, until the evening of the 13th, when two men of war home in sight, which proved afterwards to be the *Indefatigable* and *Amazon* frigates. It is rather remarkable that the Captain of the ship should inform me that the squadron which was going to engage him, was Sir Edward Pellew's, and declared, as was afterwards proved by the issue, "that he would not yield to any two English frigates, but would sooner sink his ship with every soul on board;" the ship was cleared for action, and we English prisoners, consisting of three infantry officers, two captains of merchantmen, two women, and forty-eight seamen and soldiers, were conducted down to the cable-tier, at the foot of the fore-mast.

The action began with opening the lower-deck ports, which, however, were soon shut again, on account of the great sea (I must here observe that this ship was built on a new construction, considerably longer than men of war of her rate, and her lower-deck, on which she mounted thirty-two pounders, French, equal to forty pounders English, was two feet and a half lower than usual), which occasioned the water to rush in to that degree, that we felt it running on the cables. The situation of the ship before she struck on the rocks, has been fully elucidated by Sir Edward Pellew, in his letter of the 17th of January 1797, to Mr. Nepean; the awful task is left for me to relate what ensued.

At about four in the morning, a dreadful convulsion at the foot of the fore-mast, aroused us from a state of anxiety for our fate, to the idea that the ship was sinking! It was the fore-mast that fell over the side; in about a quarter of an hour an awful mandate from above re-echoes from all parts of the ship, "*Pauvres Anglais! pauvres Anglais! Montes bien vite, nous sommes tous perdues!*" Every one rather flew than climbed up. Though scarcely able before to move, from sickness, I now found an energetic strength in all my frame, and soon gained the upper-decks, but oh, what a sight! dead, wounded, and living, intermingled in a state too shocking to describe: not a mast standing, a dreadful loom of the land, and breakers all around us. The *Indefatigable*, on the starboard quarter, appeared standing off in a most tremendous sea, from the Penmark Rocks, which threatened her with instant destruction. To the great humanity of her Commander those few persons who survived the shipwreck, were indebted for their lives, for had another broadside been fired, the commanding situation of the *Indefatigable* must have swept off at least a thousand men. On the larboard side, was seen the *Amazon*, within two miles, just struck on the shore - our own fate drew near. The ship struck, and immediately sunk! shrieks, horror, and dismay were heard from all quarters, whilst the merciless waves tore from the wreck many early victims. Day light appeared, and we beheld the shore lined with people who could render us no assistance. At low water, rafts were constructed, and the boats got in readiness to be hoisted out. The dusk arrived, and an awful night ensued. The dawn of the second day brought with it still severer miseries than the first, for the wants of nature could hardly be endured any longer, having been already near thirty hours without any means of subsistence, and no possibility of procuring them. At low water a small boat was hoisted out, and an English captain and eight sailors succeeded in getting to the shore. Elated at the success of these men, all thought their deliverance at hand, and many launched out on their rafts, but ah! death soon ended their hopes.

Another night renewed our afflictions. The morn of the third day, fraught with

5 Sir Edward Pellew has told me since, that the official account from France, on which he has received head-money, amounted to 1750 souls, at the time of the shipwreck.

greater evils than ever, appeared; our continued sufferings made us exert the last effort, and we English prisoners, tried every means to save as many fellow-creatures as laid in our power. Larger rafts were constructed, and the largest boat was got over the side. The first consideration was to lay the surviving wounded, the women, and helpless men, in the boat, but the idea of equality, so fatally promulgated among the French, lost them all subordination, and nearly one hundred and twenty jumped into the boat, in defiance of their officers, and sunk it. The most dreadful sea that I ever saw, seemed at that fatal moment to add to the calamity, nothing of the boat was seen for a quarter of an hour, when the bodies floated in all directions; when appeared, in all the horrors of sight, the wreck, the shores, the dying, and the drowned! Indefatigable in acts of humanity, an Adjutant-General (Renier) launched himself into the sea, to obtain succours from the shore, and was drowned in the attempt.

Already near one-half of the people had perished, when the fourth night renewed its horrors, all our miseries. Weak, distracted, and wanting every thing, we envied the fate of those lifeless corpses [which] no longer wanted sustenance. The sense of hunger was already lost, but a parching thirst consumed our vitals. Recourse was had to urine and salt water, which only increased the want; half a hogshead of vinegar indeed floated up, and each had half a wine glass, which gave a momentary relief, yet soon left us again in the same state of dreadful thirst. Almost at the last gasp! every one was dying with misery, and the ship, which was now one-third shattered away from the stern, scarcely afforded a grasp to hold by, to the exhausted and helpless survivors.

The fourth day brought with it a more serene sky, and the sea seemed to subside, but to behold from fore to aft, the dying in all directions, was a sight too shocking for the feeling mind to endure. Almost lost to a sense of humanity, we no longer looked with pity on those who were the speedy forerunners of our own fate, and a consultation took place, to sacrifice some one to be food for the remainder. The die was going to be cast, when the welcome sight of a man of war brig renewed our hopes. A cutter speedily followed, and both anchored at a short distance from the wreck. They then sent their boats to us, and by means of large rafts about one hundred and fifty, of near four hundred who attempted it, were saved by the brig that evening. Three hundred and eighty were left to endure another night's misery, when, dreadful to relate, above one half were found dead next morning.

I was saved at about ten o'clock on the morning of the 18th, with my two brother officers, the captain of the ship, and General Humbert. They treated us with great humanity on board the cutter, by giving us a little weak brandy and water every five or six minutes, after which a basin of good soup. I fell on the locker in a kind of trance for near thirty hours, swelled to that degree, as to require medical aid to restore my decayed faculties. We were taken to Brest almost naked, having lost all our baggage, where they gave us a rough shift of clothes, and in consequence of our sufferings, and the help we afforded in saving many lives, a cartel was fitted out by order of the French Government, to send us home without ransom or exchange. We arrived at Plymouth on the 7th of march following.

To that Providence, whose great working I have experienced on this most awful trial of human afflictions, be ever offered the tribute of my praise and thanksgivings!

1797 – Mediterranean:
Cape St Vincent, Cadiz, Tenerife

THE THREAT IN HOME WATERS, and the impossible odds in the Mediterranean, necessitated a change of operational focus for the Mediterranean Squadron from the Gulf of Lyons to Cadiz. Corsica was evacuated, and the fleet, now commanded by Admiral John Jervis, sailed to Gibraltar. Storm damage reduced his command to ten of the line, but the Admiralty was able to reinforce him with another five ships under Rear-Admiral Sir William Parker when winter weather put an end to any immediate threat to Ireland. Nelson, promoted Commodore, had been sent back in a frigate from Gibraltar to withdraw the garrison at Elba, and at the end of January 1797 he steered for the rendezvous off Cape St Vincent. West of Gibraltar, in the dark, he passed through the Spanish fleet, now commanded by Admiral Don José de Cordova, which had sailed from Cartagena to escort home a convoy of four mercury ships. When it appeared out of the mist the next morning, it greatly outnumbered the British, but it was in poor order, and there was a wide gap between the convoy with its close escort and the twenty or twenty-one ships of the main force. Jervis signalled: 'The admiral means to pass through the enemy's line,' in order to give the Spaniards no time to reform their line. His consummate qualities as an admiral included a strong grasp of tactical possibilities, and his thinking may have owed something to the work of John Clerk of Eldin whose *Essay on Naval Tactics* was not to be published until 1797, but who had circulated his manuscript amongst 'his friends.' (See the review of his book in Appendix I of this volume: Naval Strategy and Tactics.)

The action which followed makes it evident that Jervis's discipline and training had created a highly effective force. At a critical moment Nelson, on his own initiative, his flag now flying in the 74-gun *Captain*, wore out of the British line, and blocked the Spanish movement to reunite their fleet. His ship faced tremendous odds, but was quickly supported. Only four Spanish ships were captured, two of which struck to Nelson, but the evident capacity of Jervis's command, and his victory against such

171

apparent odds, made possible the close blockade of the greatly superior Spanish fleet at Cadiz, and discouraged French forces at Brest seeking action in the Channel. Nelson was put in command of the inshore squadron, where he set a personal example for bravery which helped to stem the spread of mutiny from the Channel Fleet.

He was then given command of a raid to capture a treasure ship at Tenerife in the Canaries, which went badly wrong. The notion that the Spanish governor was taken in by Hood and Troubridge's threat to burn the town is entirely fanciful. The withdrawal of the British survivors is to be attributed more to the dislike Spaniards had for the French alliance. The editor's conviction that the defeat was not the result of any British failure cannot be accepted. Clearly the planning was inadequate.

As these events occurred only in the year preceding the publication of the first number of *The Naval Chronicle*, and because of the interest in Nelson which had been stimulated by the events of 1798, reportage of the Battle of Cape St Vincent and the Canaries operation was extensive. The most important of these were the biographical memoirs of Admiral Jervis and Commodore Nelson, the former of which included Jervis's official dispatches, and several supporting documents by officers in the fleet. Nelson also wrote an account of his part in the battle for the Duke of Clarence, which was signed by himself and Captain Miller and Lieutenant Barry. A narrative of the action from a different perspective, that of Sir James Saumarez, was also published, and some details were added in biographical memoirs of Edward Berry, Cuthbert Collingwood, Robert Calder and George Murray. In 1809 a correspondent, Lieutenant 'H', added to the record by supplying a copy of Rear-Admiral William Parker's protest to Nelson that the contribution of his own ship, the *Prince George*, had been ignored. Nelson's dismissive reply was included.

The Naval Chronicle recorded its version of events at Tenerife primarily in two extended biographical memoirs, of Thomas Troubridge and Samuel Hood, and the action at Tenerife formed the concluding passages in another on Richard Bowen who was killed there. In the Troubridge memoir were inserted Nelson's service letter to Jervis planning the raid, and his correspondence with Troubridge.

This section closes with Nelson's application for a pension, which required a statement of his service record, and with the report in late 1799 of Admiral Cordova's disgrace.

Withdrawal from the Mediterranean, and the Battle of Cape St. Vincent
From the 'Biographical memoir of John Jervis, Earl of St. Vincent.' IV 32-41

In the first edition that we printed of the life of the illustrious character now under our consideration, we in this part of our memoir stated that Sir John, whose health had

Portrait of the Right Honourable
Earl of St. Vincent. Engraved by
Ridley, from a painting by J.F.
Abbot, Esq. Plate 36

been considerably impaired, as well by disease as [by] the fatigue which both his mind and body had undergone, during the time he was absent on the West India station, having been somewhat restored after his return to his native country: he seized, with all the enthusiasm of a hero in the highest vigour of youth, the earliest opportunity .his convalescent state afforded, of soliciting one of the most active employments which the state of warfare at that time afforded. We are now however happy at having it in our power to correct any misstatement that formerly appeared, and can assure our readers, from authority, that Sir John *never solicited a command, or applied for any particular service*, but was invested, as soon as his health was sufficiently re-established, with the Mediterranean command in a few days after that honourable and public testimony just related had been borne to his merit by the House of Commons.[1] He proceeded to the Mediterranean on board a frigate; and immediately on his arrival, Admiral Hotham, his predecessor, resigned to him this important trust. Notwithstanding the very severe blow the French marine in that quarter had sustained, in consequence of the partial destruction of the arsenal, as well as the fleet, at Toulon, the exertions of the enemy, so extraordinary and unprecedented as to seem almost incredible, had refitted and collected a force of nearly twenty ships of the line. During the period of Admiral Hotham's command, this fleet had been hardy enough to venture out; and though two slight discomfitures had served in some measure to prevent a repetition of the same presumption, yet that very circumstance rendered the future operations in the same quarter much more irksome to the British Commander in Chief than a situation attended with more danger, and requiring far superior exertions, would have been.

The French armament lay ready for sea, in as good a state of equipment as the resources possessed by the enemy could put it. The inattention of a few hours might enable this foe, rendered almost desperate by calamity, to escape from the state of durance in which he was held, and effect considerable mischief on some vulnerable territory belonging to the allies, and friends of Britain, before sufficient discovery could be made of his route to render pursuit politic, or effectual. The unremitting attention of Sir John operated very successfully to the prevention of any such disaster, and the British commerce was consequently extended over the face of the whole Mediterranean, without

1 On the first of June he was advanced to the rank of Admiral of the Blue, as he had been, on the twelfth of April in the preceding year, to that of Vice-Admiral of the White.

experiencing any other interruption than some few casual depredations committed on vessels entirely, or at most, nearly defenceless, which the French corsairs, equipped from their petty ports, were fortunate enough to fall in with. The French directory having, by insinuations, by threats, and other artifices of terror or persuasion, contrived, towards the end of the year 1796, to detach the Court of Spain from the alliance of Great Britain; the situation of the fleet in that quarter, under the orders of Sir John, was suddenly rendered extremely critical. Though the state of the Toulon squadron was insufficient to create any disquiet in his mind: yet the fleet at Cadiz alone, in the most perfect condition for service, more that doubled the force he commanded. The political situation of his country, at that time, rendered the greatest exertions necessary - a formidable combination was raised against her; and the fleets of her opponents, Holland, France, and Spain, had they all been permitted to unite, would have composed an immense armament, consisting of nearly one hundred ships of the line. The internal commotions which had for some time pervaded Ireland, appeared to afford these confederated foes the greatest hopes of success, provided it were possible for them to put on shore any body of regular troops sufficiently numerous to countenance the rebellious insurgents in their open avowal of that treason, which owing to the insidious representations of those among their own countrymen who possessed most influence, and were considered as the leaders of their party, had long been cherished in their bosoms. At this period it had attained an height truly formidable and alarming.

An attempt was made by France, immediately after Spain became an ally to the cause of republicanism, to carry this project into execution; and though it had completely failed, there was little reason to expect that the want of success on that occasion would so far intimidate the enemy as to prevent a repetition of it. Regarding therefore the general posture of public affairs, it must appear evident, that very urgent necessity peremptorily demanded the immediate execution of some grand and decisive measure, which might, by its consequential success, contribute to dispel that tremendous cloud which appeared on the point of bursting over her. Of this situation, together with all the circumstances which led to it, Sir John was perfectly well acquainted: but very little relief could be expected, highly as the abilities of its commander might be estimated, from a squadron consisting of *twenty-six* ships of the line *and ten frigates*,[2] which, putting the French force at Toulon totally out of the question, had to contend with an enemy of three times its own force.

This disparity of numbers was in some degree reduced by the arrival of Rear-Admiral Parker from England, who formed a junction with Sir John on the sixth of February. Still, however, his force was so very unequal to that of the enemy, that nothing but the existing case could have warranted the attack, nor any thing short of the greatest exertions in regard to professional knowledge and gallantry which the human mind is perhaps capable of making, could have rendered its event successful. Independent of that superiority which the enemy possessed in respect to force, they had the additional satisfaction of being so near to their own ports, that even in case of discomfiture, they could retire without dreading the consequence of pursuit, and moor in safety under the cannon of their own fortress, in a less space of time than would be required to refit the rigging of a frigate, after an hour's contest with a vessel of equal force. The magnitude of the object, a firm reliance on the intrepidity, as well as activity of those whom he

2 Don Juan Langara came up the Mediterranean with twenty-six ships of the line and ten frigates, and appeared off Cape Corse when Sir John Jervis was in the act of evacuating the island of Corsica.

commanded, and a proper confidence in his own judgment, contributed to make the British Admiral despise all the surrounding difficulties, and determined him to attempt a new mode of attack which he had long arranged in his own mind as practicable, should fortune ever favour him with an opportunity of carrying it into execution. He had long entertained very sanguine hopes it would be crowned with the most brilliant success, and the instant he received the augmentation of force by the junction of Mr. (now Sir William) Parker, as well as became apprised of the situation of the enemy, he delayed not a moment in making known to those whom he commanded, his resolution to engage them, and the peculiar manner in which he intended to arrange his attack. The event is known to all, and the leading particulars will be best explained by the official narrative of Sir John himself.

Victory, in Lagos Bay, Feb. 16
Sir, The hopes of falling in with the Spanish fleet expressed in my letter to you of the thirteenth instant, were confirmed that night by our distinctly hearing the report of their signal guns, and by intelligence received from Captain Foote, of his Majesty's ship *Niger*, who had, with equal judgment and perseverance, kept company with them for several days on my prescribed rendezvous, which from the strong south-east winds, I had never been able to reach; and that they were not more than three of four leagues from us. I anxiously awaited the dawn of day; when being on the starboard tack, Cape St. Vincent bearing east by north eight leagues, I had the satisfaction of seeing a number of ships extending from south-west to south, the wind then at west by south. At forty minutes past ten, the weather being extremely hazy, *la Bonne Citoyenne* made the signal that the ships were of the line, twenty-five in number, his Majesty's squadron under my command, consisting of the fifteen ships of the line named in the margin,[3] were happily formed in the most compact order of sailing, in two lines. By carrying a press of sail, I was fortunate in getting in with the enemy's fleet at half past eleven o'clock, before it had time to connect and form a regular order of battle. Such a moment was not to be lost; and confident in the skill, valour, and discipline of the officers and men I had the happiness to command, and judging that the honour of His Majesty's arms, and the circumstances of the war in these seas, required a considerable degree of enterprise, I felt myself justified in departing from the regular system, and passing through their fleet in a line formed with the utmost celerity, tacked, and thereby separated one third from the main body, after a partial connonade, which prevented their rejunction till the evening, and by the very great exertions of the ships which had the good fortune to arrive up with the enemy on the larboard tack, the ships named in the margin[3] were captured,[4] and the action ceased about five o'clock in the evening. I enclose the most correct list I have been able to obtain of the Spanish fleet opposed to me, amounting to twenty-seven sail of the line, and an account of the killed and wounded in His Majesty's ships, as well as in those taken from the enemy.[5] The moment the latter, almost totally dismasted, and His Majesty's ships the *Captain* and *Culloden* are in a state to put to sea, I shall avail myself of the first favourable winds to proceed off Cape St. Vincent, in my way to Lisbon. Captain Calder, whose able assistance has greatly contributed to the public service during my command, is the bearer of this, and will more particularly describe to the Lords Commissioners of the Admiralty the movements of the squadron on the fourteenth, and the present state of it. I am, &c.
Evan Nepean, Esq. &c.

J. JERVIS

3 Comparative View of the Force of the British and Spanish Fleets

British Line of   Spanish Fleet opposed to
    Battle as Formed   the British

Ships	Commanders	Ships, Guns
Culloden	Captain T. Troubridge	*Santissima Trinidada*, 130
Blenheim	J. L. Frederick	*Conde de Regla*, 112
Prince George	Rear-Admiral W. Parker	*Salvador del Mundo*, 112
	Captain J. Urwin	*Mexicana*, 112
Orion	Sir James Saumarez	*Principe de Asturias*, 112
Colossus	George Murray	*Conception*, 112
Irresistible	George Martin	*San Josef*, 112
Victory	Admiral Sir J. Jervis KB	*San Genaro*, 74
	Captain Sir R. Calder Kt	*San Firmin*, 74
	G. Grey	*San Ildefonzo*, 74
Egmont	J. Sutton	*San Juan Nepomuceno*, 74
Goliath	Sir C. Knowles, Bart.	*San Francis de Paulo*, 74
Britannia	Vice-Admiral C. Thompson	*San Ysidro*, 74
	Captain John Foley	*San Antonio*, 74
Barfleur	Vice-Admiral Waldegrave	*San Pablo*, 74
	Captain J. R. Dacres	*Atlante*, 74
Captain	Commodore Nelson	*Glorioso*, 74
	Captain R. W. Miller	*Conquestador*, 74
Namur	J. H. Whitshed	*San Nicholas*, 84
Diadem	G. H. Towry	*Oriente*, 74
Excellent	C. Collingwood	*Infanta de Pelayo*, 74
		Firme, 74
		Soberano, 74
Frigates		*San Domingo* (flute), 58
La Minerva	Captain Geo. Cockburn	*San Juan*, 74
Southampton	James McNamara	Names unknown, 74
Lively	Lord Garlies	74
Niger	Samuel Foote	Frigates
Bonne Citoyenne	Lord Mark Kerr	*Perla*, 34
Raven	William Prowse	*Ceres*, 34
Fox Cutter	Lieutenant Gibson	*Matilde*, 34
		Paz, 34
		Mercedes, 34
		Diane, 34
		Antiocha, 34
		Brigida, 34
		Dorotea, 34
		Vigilante (brig), 18

4 *Salvador del Mundo*, 112 guns; *San Josef*, 112; *San Nicholas*, 84; *San Ysidro*, 74.

5 *English officers killed and wounded*
Mr. Joseph Wixon, Master's Mate, wounded
Captain Major William Norris, Marines, killed
Mr. James Godench, Midshipman, killed
Commodore Nelson bruised, but not obliged to quit the deck
Excellent - Mr. Peffers, Boatswain, killed.
Culloden - Mr. G. A. Livingstone, Lieutenant of marines, killed
Mr. Wm. Balfour, Midshipman, wounded
Total killed and wounded on board the Spanish ships taken by the squadron under Sir John Jervis
Killed, 261 - Wounded, 342 - Total, 603
Among the killed is the General Don Francisco Xavier Winthuysen, Chef d'Escadre.

In addition to those circumstances already related, there are several, scarcely less consequential, which the confined limits of a report hastily drawn up immediately after this splendid encounter, prevented the insertion of.[6] When the Spanish reconnoitring vessels were distinctly perceived, several British ships were immediately ordered to chase: so that, on the appearance of the enemy's van, it became necessary to form the line ahead and astern of the Admiral, as most convenient, without respect to the order of battle. This was done by signal at five minutes past eleven. The signal to cut through the enemy's line was made by the Admiral at thirty-five minutes past eleven; and this was immediately followed by that to engage. These signals were obeyed with equal ardour and celerity by Captain Troubridge, in the *Culloden*, followed by *Blenheim, Prince George,* and the other ships, as they had formed.

The moment the enemy's line was broken, all the ships to windward wore; some in succession, others two or three together, as their fears or necessity compelled them. The signal was then given for the British fleet to tack in succession. This was immediately done by the greater part of the line; but the *Captain,* bearing the broad pendant of Commodore Nelson, being in the rear, wore and pushed on, with a view to support the *Culloden,* and prevent the seventeen Spanish ships already cut off, from rejoining their van. This manoeuvre completely succeeded. He was soon followed by the *Excellent,* and presently after by the *Diadem* and *Namur.* At one o'clock, the *Britannia's* signal

6 The following remarks on this splendid victory are furnished by an anonymous hand:

"If a daring spirit of enterprise ever manifested itself in any character, it surely never shone more conspicuous, than in the unparallelled attack made by Admiral Sir John Jervis on the Spanish fleet on the fourteenth of February. What is, however, if possible, still more worthy admiration, is the judicious close of that glorious action, which evinces the gallant Admiral's judgment to be equal to his valour: for had the signal to bring to, been delayed even five minutes longer, our trophies must not only have remained very insecure, but possibly, with the *Captain* man of war, might have fallen into the hands of the enemy. Owing to the situation of both the fleets, the British ships could not have formed without abandoning the prizes, and running to leeward, the enemy at this time having at least eighteen or nineteen ships that had not suffered in the slightest degree by the action. At this period the *Captain* was lying a perfect wreck on board the *San Nicholas* and *San Josef* Spanish ships, and many of the other ships were so shattered in the masts and rigging, as to be wholly ungovernable."

The following are instances of the singular interposition of Divine Providence in favour of the British in the late action:

Extract from an Officer's Journal of Sir John Jervis's Squadron

Feb. 1.   The *Culloden* parted company in chase.

Feb. 4.   An American vessel came into the squadron, consisting then of only nine sail of the line, which intelligence he afterwards communicated to the Spanish Admiral.

Feb. 6.   Rear-Admiral Parker joined the squadron with five sail of the line.

Feb. 9.   The *Culloden* and a cutter joined the squadron.

Feb. 13. Commodore Nelson joined the squadron.

Feb. 14. A fog concealing the British force, enabled fifteen ships of the line to attack the Spanish fleet, consisting of twenty-seven, among which were seven three-deckers. *La Santissima Trinidada,* of 130 guns, was so disabled in the action, that she was obliged to be towed off for Cadiz in the night.

Feb. 16. The squadron was forced into Lagos Bay, to secure the prizes, and repair the damages it had sustained in the action. A few days after it experienced the tail of a gale of wind: had this blown home, every ship and man must have perished, as from the badness of the ground most of the ships drove, or cut their cables. The *Victory, Irresistible,* and *Salvador del Mundo,* parted their cables.

On the twenty-third sailed without accident, and arrived at Lisbon on the twenty-eighth, after passing near Cape St. Vincent's, which station the Spanish fleet, consisting of twenty-two sail of the line, had quitted the evening before.

However incredible it may appear, it is a positive fact, that in the action of the fourteenth of February, Commodore Nelson, in the *Captain* of 74 guns, and Captain Troubridge, in the *Culloden,* of the same force, turned the whole van of the Spanish fleet, consisting of three first rates, and four 74 or 80 gun-ships.

was made to tack, the headmost of the British ships having so much damaged the Spanish van, that it began to move off, and the principal force becoming, in consequence, necessary for the succour of the *Captain* and the *Culloden*, with the other ships that were then commencing their attack upon the enemy. On the *Britannia*'s putting her helm a-lee, the *Barfleur* instantly wore, and, as being a faster sailer, soon reached within a cable's length of the *Victory*, directly in her wake, which station she maintained till the end of the action,[7] about a quarter of an hour's interval excepted, when the *Namur*, from her swift sailing, was enabled to push between her and the *Victory*. The Spanish ships being thus cut off, and prevented from rejunction during the battle, by the quick and well-directed fire of the *Prince George*, the *Culloden, Blenheim, Orion, Irresistible,* and *Diadem*; the rest of the British squadron fought with the others, and, before sun-set, took possession of the *Salvador del Mundo*, and *San Josef*, of one hundred and twelve guns, the *San Nicholas* of eighty-four , and the *San Ysidro* of seventy-four; the *Santissima Trinidada*, the Spanish flag-ship, escaping with considerable difficulty, and in the most shattered condition.

At this period, nine or ten of the Spanish ships that had been separated, and, therefore, unengaged during the whole contest, having at length effected a junction with their van, were preparing to come down and renew the action. It was now that the great merit of Sir John Jervis displayed itself to advantage. With the most prompt resolution he brought to, and made so able a disposition for the defence of the ships under his care, that, though still superior in number, they thought proper to leave their friends, and avoid the danger with which they were threatened.

The consequences of this victory were as happy, as the circumstances which attended it were glorious. The arrangements made by the enemy, in all the pride of expected triumph, were completely disarranged; and the British fleet, though for a long time inferior in numbers, as well as force, exhibited the singular and wonderful spectacle to the rest of the world, of the power it possessed, in being capable of confining a fleet stronger that itself, within the harbour of the principal port belonging to Spain, and insulting that port itself, by every act an enemy elated with victory could devise. The joy with which the news of this success was received in England, was in no degree inferior to the magnitude and consequence of it; nor did the public gratitude keep an unequal pace with the general exultation. Sir John received from his Sovereign, exclusive of other inferior honours, the more consequential elevation to the dignity of a Baron, and Earl of Great Britain, by the titles of Baron Jervis, of Meaford, the place of his birth, and Earl of St. Vincent, the scene of his glory. A pension of three thousand pounds a year was also bestowed on him by the unanimous vote of Parliament. These honours and rewards posterity can never think unmerited; they in some measure become necessary, in an historical light, to put the cause of gratitude out of the question, for they stand an established proof to the latest moment of recorded time, that on the fourteenth of February 1797, *fifteen British ships of the line engaged and defeated a Spanish fleet, consisting of twenty ships, the smallest of them carrying 74 guns, and seven others mounting 112 to 130 guns each!*

His Lordship continued during the space of the two succeeding years, uninterestingly for himself, but gloriously for his country, occupied in the blockade of Cadiz, or such services as the depressed spirits of his antagonists rendered it necessary for him to undertake, either in his own person, or by proxy. Among the latter may be

---

7 See the plate [number 37 in the first edition].

reckoned the victory obtained by Lord Nelson in the Bay of Aboukir, the fame of which is too great, and too recent, to need the smallest eulogium or account from the pen of the historian.

Finding, however, his health considerably impaired by the fatigue of his very labourious service, he was compelled to return to England in the month of July 1799, and after a long struggle with disease, was fortunate enough to overcome the only enemy of whom he could stand in dread. He recovered his health in so great a degree, as to enable him in the month of May, 1800, to take upon himself the command of the fleet which was sent from the shores of Britain in earnest search of that armament which now comprises nearly the whole of that marine force possessed by her combined enemies; but which, formidable as its numbers may seem, appears to shrink from the contest, and consider itself happy in the safety it derives from the batteries of Brest, which have hitherto defended it from the effects of his Lordship's terrestrial thunder.

Account of Nelson's Actions at St. Vincent, Cadiz and Tennerifa
From the 'Biographical memoir of the Right Hon. Lord Nelson. III 172-180

During the month of December, 1796, Commodore Nelson hoisted his broad pendant on board *La Minerve* frigate, Captain George Cockburne, and was dispatched with that ship, and *La Blanche*, to Porto Ferrajo, to bring the naval stores left there to Gibraltar; which the fleet at the time much wanted. On the passage thither, in the night of the nineteenth of December, 1796, the Commodore fell in with two Spanish frigates; he immediately attacked the ship which carried the poop-light, and directed the *Blanche* to bear down to engage the other: at forty minutes past ten at night, the Commodore brought his ship to close action, which continued, without intermission, until half past one; when *La Sabina*,[8] of 40 guns, 28 eighteen-pounders on her main deck, and 286 men, commanded by Captain Don Jacobo Stuart, struck to *La Minerve*. Captain Preston in *La Blanche* silenced the ship he had engaged; but could not effect possession, owing to three more ships heaving in sight.

Commodore Nelson's letter to Sir John Jervis, respecting the above action, dated December the twentieth, 1796, may be considered as a noble example of that generous and modest spirit, which pervades the minds of great men: he assumes no merit to himself, but gives the whole to Captain Cockburne, his Officers, and crew.

"You are, Sir, so thoroughly acquainted with the merits of Captain Cockburne, that it is needless for me to express them: but the discipline of *La Minerve* does the highest credit to her Captain and Lieutenants, and I wish fully to express the sense I have of their judgment, and gallantry. Lieutenant Culverhouse, the First Lieutenant, is an old officer of very distinguished merit; Lieutenants Hardy,[9] Gage and Noble, deserve every praise which gallantry, and zeal, justly entitle them to; as does every other officer, and man in the ship.

You will observe, Sir, I am sure with regret, amongst the wounded, Lieutenant James Noble, who quitted the *Captain* to serve with me; and whose merits, and repeated

8 *La Sabina* had one hundred and sixty-four men killed, and wounded: she lost her mizen mast during the action, with the main, and fore-masts. *La Minerve* had seven killed, and thirty-four wounded; all her masts were shot though, and her rigging much cut.

9 This same excellent officer commanded the *Mutine* brig, on the first of August, 1798 - and was afterwards Captain of the *Vanguard*.

wounds received in fighting the enemies of our country, entitle him to every reward a grateful nation can bestow."

On the twenty-ninth of January, 1797, Commodore Nelson sailed in *La Minerve*, from Porto Ferrajo, on his return to join Sir John Jervis; having on board Sir Gilbert Elliot (now Lord Minto), late Viceroy of Corsica, with Lieutenant Colonel Drinkwater, and others of Sir G. Elliot's suite; after reconnoitring the principal ports of the enemy in the Mediterranean, the Commodore arrived at Gibraltar a few days after the Spanish fleet had passed through the Straits from Carthagena. Impatient to join Sir John Jervis, the Commodore remained only one day at Gibraltar; and on the eleventh of February, in proceeding thence to the westward to the place of rendezvous, he was chased by two Spanish line of battle ships, and fell in with their whole fleet off the mouth of the Straits. The Commodore fortunately effected his escape, and joined the Admiral off Cape St. Vincent, on the thirteenth of February; just in time to communicate intelligence relative to the force, and state of the Spanish fleet; and to shift his pendant on board his former ship the *Captain*, 74 guns, Ralph W. Miller, Esq. Commander.

Commodore Nelson had not removed from *La Minerve*, to the *Captain*, many minutes, when on the evening of the same day, the signal was thrown out from the British fleet to prepare for action; the ships were also directed to keep in close order during the night.

As the Gazette Letters afford but an imperfect idea of the exploits of Commodore Nelson on this memorable day; we shall, in addition to the valuable manuscript already published,[10] refer to such documents as throw considerable light on his brilliant achievements of the fourteenth of February.

An officer who was on board the *Lively* repeating frigate, commanded by Lord Viscount Garlies, has since published a letter to a friend, which was originally intended for a private circle: this gentleman had an opportunity of observing the manoeuvres of both fleets; and by comparing his own minutes afterwards, with those of others, and conversing with the principal characters, he had been enabled to give the public, a most correct and interesting account of this glorious action; which is illustrated with eight plans, shewing the different positions of the two fleets.[11]

"When Sir John Jervis on the fourteenth of February had accomplished his bold intention of breaking the enemy's line, the Spanish Admiral, who had been separated to windward with his main body, consisting of eighteen ships of the line, from nine ships that were cut off to leeward, appeared to make a movement, as if with a view to join the latter. This design was completely frustrated by the timely opposition of Commodore Nelson, whose station in the rear of the British line afforded him an opportunity of observing this manoeuvre: his ship, the *Captain*, had no sooner passed the rear of the enemy's sips that were to windward, than he ordered her to wear, and stood on the other tack towards the enemy.

In executing this bold, and decisive manoeuvre, the Commodore reached the sixth ship from the enemy's rear, which bore the Spanish Admiral's flag, the *Santissima Trinidada*, of 136 guns; a ship of four decks, reported to be the largest in the world.

10 Vol. II. page 500. *Remarks relative to myself in the Captain.* [Re-published below.]
11 Lieutenant Colonel Drinkwater, who was Secretary at War at Corsica, author of the journal of the Siege of Gibraltar. Having accompanied Sir Gilbert Elliot on his passage to England in *La Minerve*, from Porto Ferrajo to Cape St. Vincent, they were afterwards removed into the *Lively*; and through Sir G. Elliot's particular solicitation the frigate was allowed to wait the result of the action. This interesting narrative in published by Johnson, St. Paul's Church-yard.

The annexed view of Gibraltar is taken from the westward. The portrait of a
bomb-ketch on the old construction is introduced, with the fleet under the
command of Admiral Sir George Rooke, standing into the Bay. [Plate 45]

Notwithstanding the inequality of force, the Commodore instantly engaged this colossal
opponent; and for a considerable time had to contend not only with her, but with her
seconds ahead and astern, each of three decks. While he maintained this unequal combat,
which was viewed with admiration, mixed with anxiety, his friends were flying to his
support: the enemy's attention was soon directed to the *Culloden*, Captain Troubridge,
and in a short time after to the *Blenheim*, of 90 guns, Captain Frederick, who opportunely
came to his assistance.

The intrepid conduct of the Commodore staggered the Spanish Admiral, who
already appeared to waver in pursuing his intention of joining the ships cut off by the
British fleet; when the *Culloden*'s timely arrival, and Captain Troubridge's spirited
support of the Commodore, together with the approach of the *Blenheim*, followed by
Rear-Admiral Parker, with the *Prince George, Orion, Irresistible*, and *Diadem*, not far
distant, determined the Spanish Admiral to change his design altogether, and to throw
out the signal for the ships of his main body to haul their wind, and make sail on the
larboard tack.

Not a moment was lost in improving the advantage now apparent in favour of the
British squadron: as the ships of Rear-Admiral Parker's division approached the enemy's
ships, in support of the *Captain* (Commodore Nelson's ship) and her gallant seconds,
the *Blenheim* and *Culloden*, the cannonade became more animated and impressive. In
this manner did Commodore Nelson engage a Spanish three decker, until he had nearly
expended all the ammunition in his ship; which had suffered the loss of her fore-top
mast, and received such considerable damage in her sails and rigging, that she was

almost rendered *hors du combat*. At this critical period, the Spanish three decker having lost her mizen mast, fell on board a Spanish two decker of 84 guns, that was her second: this latter ship consequently now became the Commodore's .opponent, and a most vigorous fire was kept up for some time, by both ships, within pistol shot.

It was now that the Commodore's ship lost many men, and that the damages already sustained, through the long and arduous conflict which she had maintained, appearing to render a continuance of the contest in the usual way precarious, or perhaps impossible. At this critical moment, the Commodore, from a sudden impulse, instantly resolved on a bold and decisive measure; and determined, whatever might be the event, to attempt his opponent sword in hand: the boarders were summoned, and orders given to lay his ship on board the enemy.

Fortune favour the brave! Nor on this occasion was she unmindful of her favourite. Ralph Willett Miller,[12] the Commodore's Captain, so judiciously directed the course of his ship, that he laid her aboard the starboard quarter of the Spanish eighty-four; her spritsail yard passing over the enemy's poop, and hooking in her mizen shrouds: when the word to board being given, the officers and seamen, destined for this perilous duty, headed by Lieutenant Berry,[13] together with the detachment of the sixty-ninth regiment commanded by Lieutenant Pearson, then doing duty as marines on board the *Captain*, passed with rapidity on board the enemy's ship; and in a short time the *San Nicholas* was in the possession of her intrepid assailants. The Commodore's ardour would not permit him to remain an inactive spectator of this scene. He was aware the attempt was hazardous; and he thought his presence might animate his brave companions, and contribute to the success of this bold enterprise: he therefore, as if by magic impulse, accompanied the party in this attack; passing from the fore chains of his own ship, into the enemy's quarter gallery, and thence through the cabin to the quarter deck; where he arrived in time to receive the sword of the dying Commander,[14] who had been mortally wounded by the boarders.

He had not been long employed in taking the necessary measures to secure this hard earned conquest, when he found himself engaged in a more arduous task. The stern of the three decker, his former opponent, was placed directly amidships of the weather-beam of the prize, *San Nicholas*; and, from her poop and galleries, the enemy sorely annoyed with musquetry the British, who had boarded the *San Nicholas*. The Commodore was not long in resolving on the conduct to be adopted upon this momentous occasion: the two alternatives that presented themselves to his unshaken mind, were to quit the prize, or instantly board the three decker. Confident in the bravery of his seamen, he determined on the latter. Directing therefore an additional number of men to be sent from the *Captain* on board the *San Nicholas*, the undaunted Commodore, whom no danger ever appalled, headed himself the assailants in this new attack; exclaiming, WESTMINISTER ABBEY! OR GLORIOUS VICTORY!

Success in a few minutes, and with little loss, crowned the enterprize. Such indeed was the panic occasioned by his preceding conduct, that the British no sooner appeared on the quarter deck of their new opponent, than the Commandant advanced; and asking

12 This gallant officer afterwards lost his life in the *Theseus*, under Sir Sydney Smith, by the explosion of some shells on the quarter deck. He was in the battle of the Nile, where he gained great honour. *Vid Nav. Chronicle* Vol. II. page 580.

13 Now Sir Edward Berry; Lord Nelson's Captain in the *Vanguard* in the battle of the Nile.

14 This sword the Commodore afterwards presented to the city of Norwich.

for the BRITISH COMMANDING OFFICER, dropped on his knee, and presented his sword; apologising at the same time for the Spanish Admiral's not appearing, as he was dangerously wounded. For a moment Commodore Nelson could scarcely persuade himself of his second instance of good fortune: he therefore ordered the Spanish Commandant, who had the rank of a Brigadier, to assemble the officers on the quarter deck, and direct means to be taken instantly for communicating to the crew the surrender of the ship. All the officers immediately appeared; and the Commodore had the surrender of the *San Josef* duly confirmed, by each of them delivering his sword.

The coxwain of the Commodore's barge (John Sykes, since dead) had attended close by his side throughout this perilous attempt. To him the Commodore gave in charge the swords of the Spanish officers, as he received them; and the undaunted tar, as they were delivered to him, tucked these honourable trophies under his arm, with all the coolness imaginable. It was at this moment also, that a British sailor, who had fought under the Commodore, came up in the fullness of his heart; and excusing the liberty he was taking, asked to shake him by the hand; to congratulate him upon seeing him safe on the quarter deck of a Spanish three decker.

This new conquest had scarcely submitted, and the Commodore returned on board the *San Nicholas*, when the latter ship was discovered to be on fire in two places. At the first moment appearances were alarming; but the presence of mind, and resources of the Commodore and his officers, in this emergency, soon got the fire under.

A signal was immediately made by the *Captain* for boats to assist in disentangling her from the two prizes; and as she was incapable of further service until refitted, the Commodore again hoisted his pendant for the moment, on board *La Minerve* frigate; and in the evening shifted it to the *Irresistible*, Captain Martin; but as soon as the *Captain* was refitted, he re-hoisted his pendant on board the latter ship.

For such distinguished gallantry on the fourteenth of February, he received the insignia of the Bath, and the gold medal, from his Sovereign; and was also presented with the freedom of the city of London in a gold box."

In the month of April, 1797, Sir Horatio Nelson hoisted his flag, as Rear-Admiral of the Blue, and was detached to bring down the garrison of Porto Ferrajo. On the twenty-seventh of May he shifted his flag from the *Captain*, to the *Theseus*, and was appointed to the command of the inner squadron at the blockade of Cadiz. During this service his personal courage, if possible, was more conspicuous than at any other period of his former services. In the attack on the Spanish gun-boats (July the third, 1797) he was boarded in his barge; with only its usual complement of ten men, and the coxwain, accompanied by Captain Freemantle.

The Commander of the Spanish gun-boats, Don Miguel Tyrason, in a barge rowed by *twenty-six oars, having thirty men, including officers*, made a most desperate effort to overpower Sir Horatio Nelson, and his brave companions. The conflict was long, and doubtful, they fought hand to hand with their swords: his faithful coxwain JOHN SYKES was wounded in defending the Admiral; and twice saved his life, by parrying several blows that were aimed at him. and mortally wounding his adversaries. Eighteen of the Spaniards being killed, the Commandant and all the rest wounded, the Rear-Admiral, with his gallant barge's crew, succeeded in carrying this superior force.

Sir John Jervis, in his letter to the Admiralty, dated the fifth of July, 1797, says:

"The Rear-Admiral, who is always present in the most arduous enterprises, with the assistance of some other barges, boarded and carried two of the enemy's gun-boats, and a barge launch belonging to one of their ships of war, with the Commandant of the flotilla. *Rear-Admiral Nelson's actions speak for themselves; any praise of mine would fall very short of his merit!"*

During the night of the fifth of July, Sir Horatio Nelson ordered a second bombardment of Cadiz; which produced considerable effect on the town, and among the shipping.

On the fifteenth of July he was detached, with a small squadron,[15] to make a vigorous attack on the town of SANTA CRUZ, in the Island of Teneriffe. The Rear-Admiral, on his arrival before the town, lost no time in directing a thousand men, including marines, to be prepared for landing from the ships, under the direction of the brave Captain Troubridge of his Majesty's ship *Culloden*,[16] and Captains Hood, Thomson, Freemantle, Bowen, Miller, and Waller, who very handsomely volunteered their services. The boats of the squadron were accordingly manned, and the landing was effected in the course of a dark night. The party were in full possession of the town of Santa Cruz for about seven hours. Finding it impracticable to storm the citadel, they prepared for their retreat, which the Spaniards allowed them to do unmolested, agreeable to the stipulations made with Captain Troubridge. Although this enterprise did not succeed, his Majesty's arms acquired by the attempt a great degree of lustre; and as the Rear-Admiral himself handsomely expresses it in his letter to Earl St. Vincent, *more daring intrepidity never was shewn, than by the Captains, Officers, and men, he had the honour to command.* Sir Horatio Nelson in this attack lost his right arm by a cannon shot;[17] and no less than two hundred and forty-six gallant officers, marines, and seamen, were killed, wounded, and drowned.

The life of Sir Horatio Nelson was providentially saved by Lieutenant Nisbet, his son-in-law, on this disastrous night: the Admiral received his wound soon after the detachment had landed, and while they were pressing on with the usual ardour of British seamen: the shock caused him to fall to the ground, where for some minutes he was left to himself; until Mr. Nisbet missing him, had the presence of mind to return; when after some search in the dark, he at length found his brave father-in-law weltering in his blood on the ground, with his arm shattered, and himself apparently lifeless. Lieutenant Nisbet having immediately applied his neck handkerchief as a tournequet to the Admiral's arm, carried him on his back to the beach; where, with the assistance of some sailors, he conveyed him into one of the boats, and put off to the *Theseus* under a tremendous, though ill-directed fire from the enemy's battery.

The next day after the Rear-Admiral had lost his arm, he wrote to Lady Nelson; and in narrating the forgoing transactions, says, "I know it will add much to your pleasure, in finding that your son Josiah, under God's providence, was instrumental in saving my life."

The painful operation of the amputating the arm being performed on board, in the night, by some mistake in taking up the arteries, the Rear-Admiral afterwards suffered the most excruciating pains, and was obliged to come to England for advice.

It was the thirteenth of December before the surgeons, who attended him, pronounced him fit for service. On Sir Horatio Nelson's first appearance at Court, his

15 Consisting of the *Theseus, Culloden, Zealous, Seahorse, Emerald, Terpsichore*, and *Fox* cutter: the *Leander* afterwards joined.

16 Since created, for his distinguished services, a Baronet.

17 The same night at ten o'clock the Admiral's arm was amputated on board the *Theseus*; he immediately after began his official letter, and finished it by eleven.

View of Santa Cruz in the Island of Teneriffe. Engraved by Wells, from a drawing taken in 1791, by G.T.

To the editor of the *Naval Chronicle*.

July 5, 1805

Sir, The view of Santa Cruz was taken when about three miles eastward of it, in the month of September.

The peak was clothed in snow, forming a fine contrast with the dark mountains below it. But from the account given by Glass, it appears that the summit of Teneriffe is never free from snow; for he says, "This island was named Thenerife, or the White Mountain, by the natives of Palma . . . Small vessels anchor near the town; but men of war in thirty, forty, and fifty fathoms, about a mile from it. The bottom being foul in may parts of the road, the Spaniards usually buoy their cables, that they may receive no injury. Vessels are open to the effects of eastern gales, but it is said they seldom happen. . . .

Your humble servant,   "Half-Pay." Plate 134

Sovereign received him in the most gracious and tender manner; and when, with deep sensibility of condolence, the King expressed his sorrow at the loss the noble Admiral had sustained, and at his impaired state of health, which might deprive the country of his future services; Sir Horatio replied with dignified emphasis - "*May it please your Majesty, I can never think that a loss which the performance of my duty has occasioned; and so long as I have a foot to stand on, I will combat for my King and country!*"

Previous to the issuing of a grant, which secured to this gallant officer some public remuneration for the hardships he had endured, a positive custom required that a memorial[18] of service should be drawn up: one more brilliant never met the eye of the

18 Vol. I. page 29. [Re-published below.]

Sovereign of a brave nation. Sir Horatio had actually been engaged against the enemy upwards of one hundred and twenty times! and during the present war had assisted at the capture of seven sail of the line, six frigates, four corvettes, and eleven privateers of different sizes; and taken, or destroyed, near fifty sail of merchant vessels.

On the nineteenth of December, 1797, the ship that was intended for Sir Horatio Nelson's flag not being ready, the *Vanguard* was for this purpose commissioned. On the first of April, 1798, he sailed with a convoy from Spithead; but at the back of the Isle of Wight, the wind coming to the westward, he was forced to return to St. Helen's. On the ninth, he again sailed, with a convoy to Lisbon; and on the twenty-ninth of April, joined Earl St. Vincent off Cadiz.

'A Few Remarks Relative to Myself in the Captain, in which my Pendant was Flying on the most Glorious Valentine's Day, 1797,' signed by Nelson, Ralph Willett Miller, and Edward Barry. [II 500-501]

[The wording of this copy differs slightly from that sent to H.R.H. the Duke of Clarence, and published in the Despatches and Letters of Lord Nelson, II pp. 340-43.]

At one, P.M. the *Captain* having passed the sternmost of the enemy's Ships, which formed their van and part of their centre, consisting of seventeen sail of the line; they on the larboard, we on the starboard tack; the Admiral made the signal to tack in succession, but perceiving all the Spanish ships to bear up before the wind, evidently with an intention of forming their line, going large, joining their separate divisions, at that time engaged with some of our centre ships, or flying from us, - to prevent either of their schemes from taking effect, I ordered the ship to be wore [sic], and passing between the *Diadem* and *Excellent*, at a quarter past one o'clock was engaged with the headmost, and of course leewardmost, of the Spanish divisions. The ships, which I knew, were the *Santissima Trinidada* [sic], 126; *San Josef*, 112; *Salvador del Mundo*, 112; *San Nicholas*, 80; another first rate, and a 74, names unknown.

I was immediately joined, and most nobly supported, by the *Culloden*, Captain Troubridge: the Spanish Fleet, not wishing, I suppose, to have a decisive battle, hauled to the wind on the larboard tack, which brought the ships above mentioned to be the leewardmost, and sternmost ships, in their Fleet. For near an hour, I believe (but do not pretend to be correct as to time), did the *Culloden*, and *Captain*, support this apparently, but not really, unequal contest; when the *Blenheim* passing between us, and the enemy, gave us a respite, and sickened the Dons.

At this time the *Salvador del Mundo*, and *San Isidro*, dropped astern, and were fired into, in a masterly style, by the *Excellent*, Captain Collingwood, who compelled the *San Isidro* to hoist English colours; and I thought the large ship, *Salvador del Mundo*, had also struck: but Captain Collingwoood, disdaining the parade of taking possession of a vanquished enemy, most gallantly pushed up, with every sail set, to save his old friend and messmate, who was to appearance in a critical state; the *Blenheim* being a-head, the *Culloden* crippled and astern. The *Excellent* ranged up within two feet of the *San Nicholas*, giving a most tremendous fire. The *San Nicholas* luffing up, the *San Josef* fell on board her; and the *Excellent* passing on for the *Santissima Trinidada*, the Captain resumed her station a-breast of them, and close alongside: - at this time the *Captain* having lost her foretop-mast, not a sail, shroud, nor rope left; her wheel away, and incapable of further service in the line, or in chace; I directed Captain Miller to put the helm a starboard, and calling for the Boarders ordered them on board.

The soldiers of the 69th Regiment with an alacrity which will ever do them credit, and Lieutenant Pierson of the same Regiment, were among the foremost in this service: - the first man who jumped into the enemy's mizzen chains was Captain Berry, late my First Lieutenant; (Captain Miller was in the very act of going also, but I directed him to remain;) he was supported from our sprit-sail yard, which hooked into the mizzen rigging. A soldier of the 61st regiment having broke the upper quarter-gallery window, I jumped in myself, and was followed by others as fast as possible. I found the cabin door fastened, and some Spanish officers fired their pistols: but having broke open the doors, the soldiers fired; and the Spanish Brigadier (Commodore with a distinguishing pendant) fell, as retreating to the quarter deck. I pushed onwards for the quarter-deck, where I found Captain Berry in possession of the poop; and the Spanish ensign hauling down. I passed with my people, and Lieutenant Pierson, on to the larboard gangway, to the forecastle, where I met two or three Spanish officers prisoners to my seamen: - they delivered me their swords. A fire of pistols, or muskets, opening from the admiral's stern gallery, of the *San Josef*, I directed the soldiers to fire into her stern; and calling to Captain Miller, ordered him to send more men into the *San Nicolas*, and directed my people to board the first-rate, which was done in an instant, Captain Berry assisting me into the main chains. At this moment a Spanish officer looked over from the quarter-deck rail and said they surrendered. From this most welcome intelligence, it was not long before I was on the quarter-deck, where the Spanish Captain, with a bow, presented me his sword, and said the Admiral was dying of his wounds. I asked him on his honour, if the ship were surrendered? he declared she was: on which I gave him my hand, and desired him to call his officers, and ship's company, and tell them of it - which he did; *and on the quarter-deck of a Spanish first rate, extravagant as the story may seem, did I receive the swords of the vanquished Spaniards; which, as I received, I gave to William Fearney, one of my bargemen, who put them, with the greatest sang froid, under his arm.* I was surrounded by Captain Berry, Lieutenant Pearson, of the 69th regiment, John Sykes, John Thompson, Francis Cooke, all OLD AGAMEMNONS, and several other brave men, seamen, and soldiers. - Thus fell these ships!

N.B. In boarding the *San Nicholas*, I believe we lost about seven killed, and ten wounded, and about twenty Spaniards lost their lives by a foolish resistance. None were lost, I believe, in boarding the *San Josef*.

Other Perspectives on the Battle of Cape St Vincent
'Further Remarks, made during the memorable Action off Cape St. Vincent,
Feb. 14, 1797; on board his Majesty's Ship Orion, Sir James Saumarez,
Commander.' II 502-503

February 14, at three A.M. heard the report of several guns, from the Spanish fleet, in the south-east quarter; wind, west. At seven, hazy weather. At eight, being more clear, saw several large ships bearing south by west on the starboard tack. At half past eight, found them to be the Spanish fleet: our fleet at this time being in close order of sailing, with a press of sail to get up with them. At ten, the haze clearing up, discovered the enemy's force to be twenty-seven sail of the line, with many frigates, armed ships, &c.

At half past ten, the *Fox* cutter captured a Spanish merchant brig: the enemy's fleet at this time endeavouring to form, in line of battle, on the starboard tack. At half past eleven, our van ships, *Culloden*, *Orion*, *Prince George*, and *Colossus*, being up with their rear ships, opened their fire; which became general in short time. At noon, the fleet in close action with the enemy's fleet. At half past noon, the body of the Spanish fleet, consisting of nineteen sail of the line, wore, and formed their line on the larboard tack: part of their fleet being at a small distance a-head, in action, with part of our fleet, our Admiral made the signal to tack, and cut through the enemy's line; which was effected by several of our ships: the rest of our fleet still in action with the separated ships of the enemy, to prevent their joining their fleet.

At one, the *Colossus* lost her fore-yard, and fore top-sail-yard, being shot away by the enemy; a Spanish three decker perceiving this, bore down to rake her: backed our main-topsail to support her; preparing at same time to take her in tow. The Spanish ship seeing us determined not to quit her, they [then?] wore ship, and stood from us. Several of our ships tacked, that were in action with the separated ships of the enemy: we filled our main-topsail, and made sail a-head. At two, his Majesty's ship *Captain* began the action of the larboard tack; followed close up by the *Culloden, Blenheim, Prince George, Orion,* and *Diadem,* which were soon in action; the body of our fleet coming up with all possible sail set. At half past two P.M. the action became general: the Admiral made the signal to engage the enemy closer. At three, observed one of the enemy's two-decked ships had struck her colours, and had hoisted an English jack over Spanish colours. At half past three, the Spanish ship *Salvador del Mundo,* which we were engaging, struck her colours, and hoisted an English jack: lowered down the cutter from the stern, and sent our First Lieutenant to take possession of her; then made sail a-head, and renewed the action.

At four, the Spanish Ships *San Josef* and *San Nicholas,* being much disabled, fell aboard of each other; his Majesty's ship *Captain,* at that time in close action with the *San Nicholas,* boarded and took her: a short time after, the three-decked ship *San Josef* struck also. At ten minutes past four, we got abreast of the Spanish Admiral, the Commander in Chief, a four-decked ship: opened a heavy fire on her; as also did the *Blenheim* soon after, the fore and mizen masts of the Spanish ship went over her side; and being otherwise totally disabled, at fifty-five minutes after four she struck her colours, and hoisted English ones: but we could not take possession of her, as several of their heavy ships, which had been but little in action, came down to her assistance; and the day being far spent, we discontinued the action, and brought to on the starboard tack, in close order of battle, with the four Spanish men of war prizes to leeward - the Spanish fleet in a line a-head, on the larboard tack, to windward of our line. Observing several of their large ships bearing down, as we supposed to rake the *Britannia,* both of us opened an heavy fire on them: which obliged them to haul off. At six, both English, and Spanish fleets, lying to, on different tacks: ship's company employed all night repairing our damages, to be ready to renew the action at day-light, next morning.

February 15. At day-light, the enemy's fleet, consisting of twenty-two sail of the line, to windward of ours, in a line of battle a-head, and on the larboard tack. The Spanish Admiral's ship almost out of sight to leeward, with a Spanish frigate towing her. Our prizes in company. People employed repairing and splicing the rigging, in expectation of the Spanish fleet coming down to renew the engagement: got all clear for battle, but the Spaniards kept to windward. At two P.M. took one of the prizes in tow. At three, anchored with the fleet, and prizes, in Lagos Bay; where next day we put on shore about 3000 Spanish seamen and soldiers - the Spanish fleet then out of sight.

From the 'Biographical Memoir of Captain Sir Edward Berry, Knt.'
XV 178-179

Mr. Berry's very conspicuous merit attracted the observation of Earl St. Vincent and

Commodore Nelson, two of the first officers of the age, with whom he had the satisfaction of forming a lasting and honourable friendship. By Lord Nelson, whose skill in selecting of officers, and in appreciating their talents, was equalled only by his own consummate professional excellence, he was particularly distinguished. He served under him as first Lieutenant, in the *Captain*, on the memorable 14th of February, 1797; and, by his extraordinary activity in boarding the *San Nicholas* and *San Josef*, both of which yielded to the superior prowess of Nelson, he acquired the honest eulogium of every officer in the fleet. Lieutenant Berry was the first man who jumped into the mizzen chains of the *San Nicholas*, whither he was followed by a party of seamen and marines destined for the service. When Commodore Nelson reached the quarterdeck, he found his Lieutenant in possession of the poop, and one of his men hauling down the Spanish ensign. The Commodore, having secured the *San Nicholas*, gave the word for boarding the *San Josef*, when Lieutenant Berry assisted him into the main-chains of the latter ship, and had afterwards the satisfaction of attending him on the quarter-deck, at the moment of his receiving the sword from the Spanish Commander. The assistance which he afforded, and the spirit which he displayed, throughout the whole of this important encounter, greatly endeared him to his superiors in naval rank, and fixed him so firmly in the friendship of the gallant Commodore, that their mutual attachment terminated but with the lamented death of the latter.

In the course of the year 1797 Mr. Berry was made Post, and appeared at Court with his friend Sir Horatio Nelson. When His Majesty was condoling with that hero on the loss of his arm, which had been shattered at the attack upon Santa Cruz, Sir Horatio pointed to Captain Berry, observing, that *he had still his right arm left!*

From the 'Biographical Memoir of Cuthbert Lord Collingwood.' XV 366

So well did the Hero of the Nile know his [i.e. Collingwood's] value, that when the ship which Captain Collingwood commanded was sent to reinforce this squadron, he exclaimed with great joy and confidence in the talents and bravery of her Captain, "See here comes the *Excellent*, which is as good as two added to our number." And the support which he in particular this day [i.e. February 14, 1797] received from this ship, he gratefully acknowledged in the following laconic note of thanks:

"*Dear Collingwood! A friend in need is a friend indeed.*"

And in a short detail of the transactions of his own ship, sent home, as it since appears from one of his letters to Captain Locker,[19] to be, if he approved, inserted in the papers, we have this best of all authorities, from the best of all judges, Commodore Nelson's own account of what his friend Collingwood did on that memorable day. "At this time the *Salvador del Mundo* and *San Isidro* dropped astern, and were fired into in a masterly style by the *Excellent*, Captain Collingwood, who compelled the San Isidro to hoist English colours; and I thought the large ship *Salvador del Mundo* had also struck; but Captain Collingwood disdaining the parade of taking possession of a vanquished enemy, most gallantly pushed up with every sail set to save his old friend and messmate, who was to appearance in a crippled state. The *Barfleur* being a-head, the *Culloden* crippled and astern, the *Excellent* ranged up within two feet of the *San Nicholas*, giving a most tremendous fire. The *San Nicholas* luffing up, the *San Joseph* fell on board her, and the *Excellent* passing on for the *Santissima Trinidada*, the Captain resumed her station a-head of them, and close alongside."

19 Published in the appendix to Charnock's *Biographical Memoirs of Lord Nelson*, page 67.

From the 'Biographical Memoir of George Murray, Esq.' $^{XVIII\ 187}$

In the course of the ensuing year [1796], Captain Murray was appointed to the *Colossus*, of 74 guns, and joined Sir John Jervis, in the Mediterranean. During the blockade of Cadiz, he commanded the advanced squadron; and, so much was his conduct admired by the enemy, [that] the Spanish admiral, under a flag of truce, sent him an invitation to be present at a bull fight; offering to leave his nephew on board of the *Colossus*, as a pledge for his safe return. This honour, however, Captain Murray thought proper to decline.

In the memorable action of the 14th of February, 1797, from which Earl St. Vincent derives his title, the *Colossus* was ordered by his lordship to lead the van of the fleet; but, carrying away her fore-top-sail-yard, and, of course, falling to leeward, she lost her portion of the honour of that day. It was but upon one tack that the *Colossus* could carry sail at all; and, being extremely defective in other respects, Lord St. Vincent, as soon as he could spare her, sent her home. This, however, was not until the close of the following year.

When Captain Murray sailed for England, he was the bearer of a particular request, from the commander in chief to Lord Spencer [First Lord of the Admiralty], that his lordship would give him a better ship, and return him to the fleet as soon as possible.

St. George's Part
From 'Correspondence'. $^{XXI\ 300-306}$

Mr. Editor, As you profess to be a faithful chronicler of naval events for the future historian, you should candidly insert, as indeed you have often done, the different naval documents that have circulated amongst us in manuscript, but are in general little known to the public. In your second volume, page 500, you inserted Lord Nelson's remarks on his ship the *Captain*, February 14, 1797, which first appeared in the *Sun*: but you have never inserted the letter which those remarks produced from Admiral W. Parker, of the *St. George*. I have therefore sent you a copy.

LIEUTENANT H

Blenheim, off Cadiz, September 1, 1797
Dear Bingham, I have heard some time back, by some of my friends in England, that from a statement of the action of the 14th February, by then Commodore Nelson, I had not that credit that properly belonged to me.

I have had no power to do myself the justice I might be entitled to, for want of a sight of that letter, which I did not get until the 20th of July.

It is of no moment to me to make any observations further than concerns myself; I have written to him upon the subject, which, lest any of my friends may not have considered me in the situation I really stood, in the success of that day from that cause also, I here send you the copy of what I have written, with his answer.

He was absent from the fleet at the time I wrote, and when he returned had lost his arm. I had no immediate answer; it was left with the commander-in-chief, by whom he desired it to be delivered to me after he was gone to England, as I was told to prevent a rejoinder; but with assurances that no offence was meant by him to me, and that he never thought it could be understood that both ships had struck to him.

This answer is little to the purpose, though after what he had written it could not be much otherwise. He has got my observations as far as respects myself; and I receive in words what I suppose was thought he should not commit to paper, for I believe he had advice upon the occasion.

I have no other object or wish than to be considered by my friends in the way I am entitled, or any intention of making comments upon Admiral Nelson's letter, but what concerned my own situation, and the ships he did not mention.

Dear Bingham, Your friend and well-wisher

W. PARKER

P.S. You may shew this, with its enclosure, to any of my friends whom you may suppose have read Admiral Nelson's letter.

Blenheim, off Cadiz, 25 July, 1797
My Dear Sir, It was not until the 21st of this inst. July, that I saw the letter in the *Sun*, dated the 20th March, with remarks upon the proceedings of his Majesty's ship the *Captain*, in the action of the 14th February, to the whole of which, from a near situation, I was an eye witness.

I very readily admit that you have all the credit that belongs to an able officer and a brave man; but in support of myself, the officers of the *Prince George*, and *Orion* (and *Blenheim*, previous to your acknowledging her) I cannot but express my surprize at the statement contained in your letter.

You say, after wearing, that at a quarter past one o'clock you were engaged, and immediately joined, and most nobly supported by the *Culloden*, Captain Troubridge, for near an hour. Did the *Culloden* and *Captain* support this apparently, though not really, unequal contest, when the *Blenheim* passing between you and the enemy, gave you a respite, &c.

I must here take the opportunity of pointing out to you, that after passing through the enemy's disordered line upon the starboard tack, viz. the *Culloden, Blenheim, Prince George, Orion,* and *Colossus,* the *Culloden* and *Colossus* more to windward than the other three ships, which were in an exact line close to each other, tacked per signal in succession, and stood after the enemy upon the larboard tack in the following order, viz. *Culloden, Blenheim, Prince George,* and *Orion,* the *Colossus* having lost her fore and fore-top-sail yards, missed stays, and remained astern; during the progress towards the enemy upon the larboard tack, you were observed to wear from the rear of our line, and stand towards the enemy also, the *Culloden* by the minutes on board the *Prince George,* began to engage first, viz. twenty minutes past one o'clock, and you fell in ahead of her some time after, and began to engage at half-past one. Soon after you began, the *Blenheim* was advanced upon the *Culloden*'s larboard quarter as far ahead as she could be, keeping out of her fire, and began also; and not long afterwards the *Prince George* was the same with respect to the *Blenheim,* and *Orion* with respect to the *Prince George.* The *Prince George* began at thirty-five minutes past one, but for some time could not get advanced enough to bring her broadside to bear without yawing, occasionally; the *Orion* in the *Prince George*'s rear began as soon as she could get sufficiently advanced; therefore, so different to your statement, very soon after you commenced your fire, you had four ships pressing on, almost on board of each other, close in your rear; but the ships thus pressing upon each other, and the two latter not far enough ahead to fire with proper effect, besides having none of the enemy's ships left in the rear for our succeeding ships, at thirty minutes past one I made the signal, No. 66 (fill and stand on), the most applicable as I thought to the occasion, which, though occasionally shot away, was re-hoisted, and kept flying the greater part of the action.

From the time stated that the *Prince George* began to engage the enemy upon the larboard tack, until the *San Josef* struck her colours (say about five or ten minutes past four), after falling on board the *San Nicholas*, the fire of the *Prince George* was without intermission, except a small space of time, edging under your lee when dividing from the *San Josef*, her then antagonist, not being able to pass to windward of your ship, and the *San Nicholas*, then on board each other, viz. your larboard bow upon her lee quarter, the *San Josef* mizen-mast being gone, and main-top-mast head below the rigging shot away, fell on board the *San Nicholas* to windward, the *Prince George* in the mean time edging to leeward of you and the *San Nicholas*, and advancing sufficiently ahead of the *Captain* to fire clear of her, re-commenced her fire both upon the *San Nicholas* and *San Josef*, from receiving shot from the *San Nicholas* upon passing ahead of the *Captain*, then on board of her; this continued pretty heavy eight or ten minutes, until the *San Josef* struck her colours; then, upon ceasing to fire, we were hailed from the *Captain*, saying both ships had struck. The *Prince George* endeavoured to proceed on ahead, leaving the *San Josef*, as also the other, to be taken possession of by you, assisted by such succeeding ships as the commander-in-chief, who had arrived up, might direct.

The first ship that came within my observation, except the five ships alluded to, was the *Excellent*, whose captain neither requires your testimony or mine in proof of his bravery and good conduct; he closed with the *San Isidro* at twelve minutes past three, and she soon struck: he had all his sails set, passing on ahead; the *Namur* some time after came up, fired at some ship in the rear, and passed on ahead also; and about this time the *Orion*, in my rear, lowered her boat down to take possession of a three-decker (the *Salvador*), which she had been some time opposed to, after the *Prince George* had passed her; this was, I think, about the time the *Prince George* was edging under your lee, and the commander-in-chief arriving up.

Of this action, my dear Sir, I felt conscious at the time, and feel so now, that every exertion was used on my part as a flag officer, and by the captain and officers, and company of the *Prince George*, in which I was embarked, to take and destroy the enemy, and believe me, neither they or myself expected to meet an account so different to the real statement of that action, as is observed in your letter. I am well aware that people in action know but little of occurrences in their rear, yet when a letter is written to be exposed to public view, positive assertions should be made with great circumspection.

I observed nothing but gallantry and good conduct in every ship that came under my observation, from first to last, and think myself equally entitled to an acknowledgment of a proportion of the success of that day, with any man present at it.

I feel much concern at the occasion of this letter, but remain, &c.

W. PARKER

Rear-Admiral Nelson's answer, written with his left hand: August 19
Dear Sir, I must acknowledge the receipt of your letter of the 25th July; and after declaring, that I know nothing of the *Prince George* till she was hailed from the forecastle of the *San Nicholas*, it is impossible I can enter into the subject of your letter, &c.

HORATIO NELSON

Dispatches
From the 'Biographical Memoir of Sir Robert Calder, Bart.' XVII 97

Captain Calder was the bearer of Sir John Jervis's dispatches to Government on the occasion; for which, and for the service which it had been his lot to render to his country, he received the honour of knighthood from His Majesty, on the 3d of March, 1797. He also, in common with his brother officers, received the thanks of Parliament, and was presented with a gold medal, emblematic of the victory in which he had participated.

In the following year, the royal favour was still farther extended towards him; as, on the 22d of August, he obtained a patent of baronetage, as Sir Robert Calder, of Southwick, in the county of Hants.

St. Vincent and Tenerife
From the 'Memoir of the Public Services of the Late Sir Thomas Troubridge, Bart.' XXIII 8-16

On the 16th of February . . . with his official despatch, Sir John Jervis transmitted the following private letter to Earl Spencer, at that time First Lord of the Admiralty, respecting the conduct of certain officers concerned in the engagement:

"My Lord, The correct conduct of every officer and man in the squadron on the 14th instant, made it improper to distinguish one more than another in my public letter, because I am confident that had those who were least in action been in the situation of the fortunate few, their behaviour would not have been less meritorious. Yet to your lordship it becomes me to state, that Captain Troubridge, in the *Culloden*, led the squadron through the enemy in a masterly style, and tacked the instant the signal flew; and was gallantly supported by the *Blenheim, Prince George, Orion, Irresistible,* and *Colossus.* The latter had her fore and fore-top-sail yards wounded, and they unfortunately broke in the slings in stays, which threw her out and impeded the tacking of the *Victory.* Commodore Nelson, who was in the rear on the starboard tack, took the lead on the larboard, and contributed very much to the fortune of the day, as did Captain Collingwood; and, in the close, the *San Josef* and *San Nicholas* having fallen foul of each other, the *Captain* laid them on board, and Captain Berry, who served as a volunteer, entered at the head of the boarders, and Commodore Nelson followed immediately, and took possession of them both."

We have copied the above valuable and important document from Clarke and M'Arthur's splendid *Life of Lord Nelson*, from two motives: that of shewing the estimation in which Captain Troubridge's services were holden by his commander-in-chief; and that of endeavouring to do away a misconception which has prevailed, respecting that veteran chief, Earl St. Vincent himself. In consequence of his lordship having omitted specifically to notice the exertions of such officers as most effectually contributed to the success of the action, he has been accused of an avarice of praise, of wishing to monopolize the glory of the day, and of a sordid aim to deprive merit of its most gratifying meed - the applause of a grateful nation. The above letter, coupled with the preceding notice of his lordship's general thanks to the officers of the fleet, will, we presume, be thought sufficient to clear the conduct of the noble Earl from any imputation, derogatory to his public or private character, on the point in question.

Captain Troubridge, with the rest of the officers of the fleet, had the honour of receiving the thanks of both Houses of Parliament, and of being presented with a gold medal, emblematic of the victory, to be worn in uniform.

Very soon after the battle off Cape St. Vincent, the commander-in-chief had reason to suspect, that the Viceroy of Mexico, with an immense treasure, had taken shelter in the harbour of Santa Cruz, in the island of Teneriffe, and that the town of Santa Cruz

Portrait of Sir Thomas
Troubridge, Bart. Rear-Admiral
of the White Squadron.
Engraved by Cook, from a
painting by Drummond. Plate 301

itself was an assailable object. He accordingly detached the *Terpsichore* and *Dido* off Santa Cruz, to reconnoitre, and adopted every other means within his power to obtain the requisite information. Commodore Nelson, too, who was ultimately appointed to command the attack, was indefatigable in his exertions to acquire all possible intelligence relating to the subject. The interest which he took in the affair, the comprehensive energy of his mind, and the enthusiastic *amor patriae*, by which he was at all times inspired, will best be seen by the following letter, bearing the date of April 12, 1797, which he addressed to Sir John Jervis:

"My Dear Sir, Troubridge talked to me last night about the Viceroy at Teneriffe. Since I first believed it was possible that his Excellency might have gone there, I have endeavoured to make myself master of the situation and means of approach by sea and land. I shall begin by sea. The Spanish ships generally moor with two cables to the sea and four cables from their stems to the shore; therefore, although we might get to be masters of them, should the wind not come off the shore, it does not appear certain we should succeed so completely as we might wish. As to any opposition, except from natural impediments, I should not think it would avail. I do not reckon myself equal to Blake; but if I recollect right, he was more obliged to the wind coming off the land, than to any exertions of his own: fortune favoured the gallant attempt, and may do so again. But it becomes my duty to state all the difficulties, as you have done me the honour to desire me to enter on the subject.

The approach by sea to the anchoring place is under very high land, passing three valleys; therefore the wind is either in from the sea, or squally with calms from the mountains. Sometimes in the night a ship may get in with the land wind and moderate weather. So much for the sea attack, which if you approve I am ready and willing to look at, or to carry into execution. But now comes my plan, which could not fail of success, would immortalize the undertakers, ruin Spain, and has every prospect of raising our country to a higher pitch of wealth than she ever yet attained: but here soldiers must be consulted, and I know from experience, excepting General O'Hara, they have not the same boldness in undertaking a political measure that we have; we look to the benefit of our country, and risk our own fame every day to serve her: a soldier obeys his orders and no more. By saying soldiers should be consulted, you will guess I mean the army of 3,700 men from Elba, with cannon, mortars, and every implement now embarked; they would do the business in three days, probably much less. I will undertake with a very small squadron to do the naval part. The shore, although not very easy of access, yet is so steep that the transports may run in and land the army in one day. The water is conveyed to the town in wooden troughs: this supply cut off, would probably induce a very speedy surrender: good terms for the town, private property secured for the islanders, and only the delivery of public stores and foreign merchandise demanded, with threats of utter destruction if one gun is fired. - In short the business could not miscarry.

Now it comes for me to discover what might induce General de Burgh to act in this business. All the risk and responsibility must rest with you. A fair representation should also be made by you of the great national advantages that would arise to our country, and of the ruin that our success would occasion to Spain. Your opinion besides should be stated, of the superior advantages a fortnight thus employed would be of to the army, to what they could do in Portugal; and that of the six or seven millions sterling, the army should have one half. If this sum were thrown into circulation in England what might not be done. It would insure an honourable peace with innumerable other blessings. It has long occupied my thoughts.

Should General de Burgh not choose to act, after having all these blessings for our country stated to him, which are almost put into our hands, we must look to General O'Hara. The Royals, about 600, are in the fleet with artillery sufficient for the purpose. You have the power of stopping the store-ships; 1000 more men would still insure the business, for Teneriffe never was besieged, therefore the hills that cover the town are not fortified to resist any attempt of taking them by storm; the rest must follow - a fleet of ships and money to reward the victors. But I know with you, and I can lay my hand on my heart and say the same, *It is the honour and prosperity of our country that we wish to extend.*"[20]

On the 15th of July, after the attack had been fully determined on and arranged, [but as a strictly naval operation without the assistance of the army] Rear-admiral Nelson was detached to Santa Cruz, with the following squadron:

Ships	Guns	Commanders
Theseus	74	Sir Horatio Nelson, K.B., Rear-admiral of the Blue
		Captain R.W. Miller
Culloden	74	Thomas Troubridge
Zealous	74	Samuel Hood
Leander	50	Thomas B. Thompson
Seahorse	38	T.F. Freemantle
Terpsichore	32	Richard Bowen
Emerald	36	J. Waller
Fox, cutter	12	J. Gibson

Captain Troubridge was fixed upon to command the seamen and marines who were to be landed at Teneriffe; and, on the 20th of the month, when the squadron was within thirteen leagues of the island, he received the following orders:

20 *Vide* Clarke and M'Arthur's *Life of Nelson.*

To Thomas Troubridge, Esq. Captain of His Majesty's Ship Culloden, and
Commander of the Forces ordered to be landed for taking Santa Cruz, dated Theseus,
at Sea, July 20, 1797

"Sir, I desire you will take under your command the number of seamen and marines named in the margin,[21] who will be landed under Captains Hood, Miller, Freemantle, Bowen, and Waller, and the marines under Captain Thomas Oldfield, and a detachment of the royal artillery under Lieutenant Baynes, all of whom are now embarked on board his Majesty's frigates *Seahorse, Terpsichore,* and *Emerald.* With this detachment you will proceed as near to the town of Santa Cruz as possible, without endangering your being perceived; when you will embark as many men as the boats will carry, and force your landing in the north east part of the bay of Santa Cruz, near a large battery. The moment you are on shore, I recommend you first to attack the battery; which when carried, and your post secured, you will either proceed by storm against the town and mole-head battery, or send in my letter, as you judge most proper, containing a summons, of which I send you a copy; and the terms are either to be accepted or rejected in the time specified, unless you see good cause for prolonging it, as no alternation will be made in them: and you will pursue such other methods as you judge most proper for speedily effecting my orders, which are to possess myself of all cargoes and treasures which may be landed in the island of Teneriffe. Having the firmest confidence in the ability, bravery, and zeal of yourself, and of all placed under your command, I have only heartily to wish you success, and to assure you that I am your most obedient and faithful servant, Horatio Nelson." [22] . . .

To facilitate the enterprise, and to render every person concerned perfectly acquainted with his intended duty, Rear-admiral Nelson, whose heart and soul seem to have been engaged in the affair, recommended the following judicious regulations:[23]

"First, that the boats of each ship should be kept together by towing each other, which will keep the people of each ship collected, and the boats in six divisions will be nearly got on shore the same moment. Secondly, The marines of each ship of the line to be put in their launches, which will carry them. Thirdly, The moment the boats are discovered by a firing being made on them, the bomb-vessel to commence her fire on the town, and to keep it up till the flag of truce is hoisted from either the enemy, or from us. Fourthly, That a captain should be directed to see the boats put off from the beach, that more men may be speedily got on shore with the field pieces. Fifthly, Frigates to anchor as soon as possible after the alarm is given, or the forces are ashore, near the battery in the N.E. part of the bay. Sixthly, Immediately as the forces are ashore, they are to get in the rear of the battery marked S. in the N.E. part of the bay, and to instantly storm it, and also to take post on the top of the hill which is above it. Every ship to land the number of men as against their name expressed, with a proper proportion of officers: and the captains are at liberty to send as many more men as they please, leaving sufficient to manage the ship, and to man the launch and another boat. Every captain that chooses is at liberty to land and command his seamen, under the direction of Captain Troubridge.

21						
	Theseus	200	Exclusive of	*Terpsichore*	100	
	Culloden	200	commissioned	*Emerald*	100	The *Leander* had
	Zealous	200	officers and	total	900	not then joined
	Seahorse	100	servants			

22 *Vide* Clarke and M'Arthur's *Life of Nelson.*
23 *Ibid.*

It is recommended to put on the seamen as many marine coats or jackets as can be procured, and that all should have canvas cropbelts. The marines to be all under the order of Captain Oldfield, the senior marine officer, and he is requested to put himself under the direction of Captain Troubridge, as is Lieutenant Baynes, of the royal artillery, with his detachment."

Copies of the above regulations having been sent to the respective captains, they, on the afternoon of the 20th, repaired on board the admiral, by signal, to receive their final orders, as follows:

July 21. The *Culloden*'s officers and men, with only their arms, to be ready to go on board the *Terpsichore* at one P.M. this day, to carry with them four ladders, each of which is to have a lanyard four fathoms long, a sledge hammer, wedges, and a broad axe. The boats' oars to be muffled either with a piece of canvas or kersey. H.N.

Memorandum The *Culloden* and *Zealous* each to make a platform for one eighteen-pounder, the *Theseus* a sleigh for dragging cannon. Each ship to make as many iron ram-rods as possible, it being found that the wooden ones are very liable to break when used in a hurry. The *Seahorse* to make a platform for one nine-pounder.

The unfortunate failure of this expedition, occasioned by a variety of unforeseen circumstances, is well known; but it redounds highly to the credit of every officer and man concerned, that the failure resulted not from any defect in the plan of attack, or from any error or incapacity of execution. In addition to the dreadful surf which the men had to encounter in landing, the extraordinary great force with which they afterwards had, unexpectedly, to contend, was such as defied every hope or possibility of success; and nothing but an uncommon adroitness and presence of mind, could have prevented every individual or the party from being made prisoners. Captain Troubridge, as will appear from the following letter, had a most arduous and delicate duty to perform:

Captain Troubridge to Sir Horatio Nelson, K.B. dated Culloden, July 25, 1797
Sir, From the darkness of the night I did not immediately hit the Mole, the spot appointed to land at, but pushed on shore under the enemy's battery close to the southward of the citadel; Captain Waller landed at the same time, and two or three other boats. The surf was so high many put back; the boats were full of water in an instant, and stove against the rocks, and most of the ammunition in the men's pouches was wet. As soon as I had collected a few men, I immediately advanced with Captain Waller to the square, the place of rendezvous, in hopes of there meeting you and the remainder of the people; and I waited about an hour, during which time I sent a sergeant, with two gentlemen of the town, to summon the citadel. I fear the sergeant was shot on his way, as I heard nothing of him afterwards. The ladders being all lost in the surf, or not to be found, no immediate attempt could be made on the citadel; I therefore marched to join Captains Hood and Miller, who I had intelligence had made good their landing, with a body of men, to the S.W. of the place I did. I then endeavoured to procure some account of you and the rest of the officers, but without success. By day-break we had collected about eighty marines, eighty pikemen, and one hundred and eighty small armed seamen; these I found were all who remained alive that had made good their landing; with this force, having procured some ammunition from the Spanish prisoners we had made, we were marching to try what should be done with the citadel without ladders, when we found the whole of the streets commanded by field pieces, and upwards of 8,000 Spaniards and 100 French under arms, approaching by every avenue. As the boats were

all stove, and I saw no possibility of getting more men on shore, the ammunition wet, and no provisions, I sent Captain Hood with a flag of truce to the governor, to declare, "I was prepared to burn the town, which I should immediately put in force, if he approached one inch farther;" and at the same time I desired Captain Hood to say, "It would be done with regret, as I had no wish to injure the inhabitants; that if he would come to my terms I was willing to treat;" which he agreed to.[24] I have the honour to send you a copy of them by Captain Waller, which I hope will meet with your approbation, and appear highly honourable. The following parley was sent with the flag of truce: "*Santa Cruz. July 25th.* That the troops, &c. belonging to his Britannic Majesty shall embark with all their arms of every kind, and take their boats off, if saved, and be provided with such other as may be wanting; in consideration of which, it is engaged on their part, that they shall not molest the town in any manner, by the ships of the British squadron now before it, nor any of the islands in the Canaries, and prisoners shall be given up on both sides. Given under my hand and word of honour, Sam. Hood. Ratified by T. Troubridge, and J. Antonio Gutierrez."

The concluding passage of this letter is as follows:

"From the small body of men, and the greater part being pike and small armed seamen, which can be only called irregulars, with very little ammunition in the pouches but what had got wet in the surf at landing, I could not expect to succeed in any attempt upon the enemy, whose superior strength I have before mentioned. The Spanish officers assure me they expected us, and were perfectly prepared with all the batteries and the number of men already mentioned under arms. This, with the great disadvantage of a rocky coast, high surf, and in the face of forty pieces of cannon, will shew, though we were not successful, what an Englishman is equal to; and I have the pleasure to acquaint you, that we marched through the town on our return with the British colours flying at our head.

P.S. I beg also to say, that when the terms were signed and ratified, the governor in the handsomest manner sent a large proportion of wine, bread, &c. to refresh the people, and shewed every mark of attention in his power."

Rear-admiral Nelson, in referring Earl St. Vincent to the above letter of Captain Troubridge, for the proceedings of that officer, observes: "I cannot but express my admiration of the firmness with which Captain Troubridge and his brave associates supported the honour of the British flag."

From the 'Memoir of the Public Services of the Late Captain Richard Bowen.'
XXIII 375-376

On the 24th of July, every necessary arrangement having been made, Captain Bowen had the glorious, but eminently hazardous post assigned to him, of leading the rear-admiral to the attack. At the head of forty or fifty of his crew, he landed at the Mole Head of Santa Cruz, stormed the battery, spiked the guns, and was proceeding towards the town, in pursuit of the fugitive Spaniards, when a tremendous discharge of grape, from some field pieces in his front, brought him to the ground, with his first lieutenant, and many of his brave followers, at the moment that Nelson received his wound on landing.

24 The particulars of the conversation which took place on this occasion, between Sir Samuel Hood and the Governor of Santa Cruz, are interestingly related in our biographical memoir of Sir Samuel, *Naval Chronicle*, Vol. XVII page 19.

Thus fell Captain Richard Bowen! than whom, says the immortal Nelson, *a more enterprising, able, and gallant officer, does not grace his Majesty's naval service!* - The failure of this enterprise, by the other boats mistaking their direction in the darkness of the night, is too well known, for a repetition of the painful details to be at all necessary. The body of Captain Bowen, covered with wounds was discovered in the morning, under those of his first lieutenant and his whole boat's crew, who had been his faithful companions in many hazardous and successful enterprises; had been the witnesses, and humble imitators, of his gallantry, in many triumphs over the enemies of his country; and who had sealed their attachment to their lamented leader, by participating in his glorious fate. His body was committed to the deep, with the honours of war, on the 27th of July. The dark wave rolls over the remains of the hero; the tears of his friends and of his shipmates embalm his memory; and the fame of his gallant actions shall endure, when the marble shall have mouldered into dust!

From the 'Biographical Memoir of Commodore Sir Samuel Hood, K.B. and K.S.F.' XVII 18-20

In the month of April, 1796, Captain Hood was appointed to command the *Zealous*, of 74 guns; in which, during that year, he was actively employed under Sir John Jervis, off Toulon; and, in 1797, off Cadiz. In the summer of the latter year, he was with Lord Nelson, at Teneriffe, when his Lordship had the misfortune of losing his arm. By his spirited and judicious conduct, in effecting the return of the British troops and seamen from their disastrous attack, he had the satisfaction of endearing himself to that great commander and lamented hero, whose loss we can never cease to deplore. After Rear-Admiral Nelson had been wounded, and carried back to his ship; after all the boats had been either sunk by the dreadful fire from the enemy's batteries, or swamped in the surf, Captain Hood and Sir Thomas Troubridge [who had assumed command after Nelson was wounded] found themselves in the heart of the town of Santa Cruz, at the head of a few seamen and marines, armed with pikes, but surrounded by some thousands of Spaniards. Their situation was most critical. It was dark; and, for the present, the enemy were kept in check, from not being acquainted with the position, or number, of the invaders; but, by day-light, their miserable force must inevitably be discovered! They deliberated; and

"*Decision followed, as the thunderbolt the lightning's flash!*"

Captain Hood immediately waited on the Spanish Governor, Don Juan Antoine Gutterry [sic], with the following laconic message: "*I am come, Sir, from the commanding officer of the British troops and seamen now within your walls, and in possession of the principal strutto, to say, that as we are disappointed in the object which we came for, (alluding to specie,) provided you will furnish us with boats - those we came in being all lost - we will return peaceably to our ships; but, should any means be taken to molest or retard us, we will fire your town in different places, and force our way out of it at the point of the bayonet.*" Taking out his watch, he added: "*I am directed to give you ten minutes to consider of this offer.*"

The Governor was astonished at the proposal, made with such confidence, on the part of men whom he conceived to be already in his power. He observed, "*that he had thought they were his prisoners; but, as it was not so, he would hold a council with his officers, and let the British commander know the result in the course of an hour.*" To this Captain Hood cooly replied, "*that he was limited to a second, and that his friends were anxiously awaiting his return, to re-commence hostilities should not his demand have been complied with.*" He was about to take his leave; when the Governor, alarmed at the probable consequences of driving Englishmen to extremity, acceded to his proposal. He accordingly provided boats, and sent all the English off to their ships, where they had ceased to be expected, laden with fruit, and various other refreshments. - The conduct of the Spanish Governor was indeed eminently noble and generous. Previously to the embarkation of the invaders, he furnished them with a ratio[n] of biscuit and wine; and gave orders, that such of the British, as had been wounded, should be received into the hospital. He also intimated to Admiral Nelson, that he was at liberty to send on shore, and purchase whatever necessaries the squadron might be in need of, whilst it remained off the island.

Nelson's Service Record. [129]

Lord Nelson. At the latter end of last year, this gallant officer received a pension of a thousand pounds per annum, in consequence, as was said, of the loss of his arm, but in fact as a small recompence for a whole life of danger, hardship, enterprize, and service. Previous to the issuing of the grant, a positive custom required, that he should distinctly state his services to his Majesty. The following is the memorial which was delivered in upon the occasion:-

> *To the King's most excellent Majesty, the Memorial of Sir Horatio Nelson, K. B. and a Rear-Admiral in your Majesty's Fleet.*

That, during the present war, your Memorialist has been in four actions with the fleets of the enemy, viz. on the 13th and 14th of March 1795; on the 13th July 1795; and on the 14th of February 1797; in three actions with frigates; in six engagements against batteries; in ten actions in boats employed in cutting out of harbours; in destroying vessels, and in taking three towns. Your Memorialist has also served on shore with the army four months, and commanded the batteries at the sieges of Bastia and Calvi. That during the war, he has assisted at the capture of seven sail of the line, six frigates, four corvettes, and eleven privateers of different sizes; and taken and destroyed near fifty sail of merchant vessels; and your Memorialist has actually been engaged against the enemy upwards of ONE HUNDRED AND TWENTY TIMES. In which service your Memorialist has lost his right eye and arm, and been severely wounded and bruised in his body. All of which services and wounds your memorialist must humbly submit to your Majesty's most gracious consideration.

Cordova's Disgrace
From the 'Monthly Register of Naval Events.' [II 440-41]

4 October 1799. Letters from Spain say, the conduct of the commander and captains of the Spanish fleet, in the engagement with Admiral Jervis off Cape St. Vincent, having been referred to a Council of War, the council has come to a decision, which is confirmed by his Catholic Majesty. The following is the result:

The Commander, Don Joseph Cordova, is deprived of all his offices, declared incapable of ever serving in any rank, and prohibited from appearing at court, or in any of the chief towns of the maritime coasts.

The next in command, Count Morales des Los Rios, is deprived of his rank.

The Captains, Don Gonzale Vallejo, Don Juan De Agairre, and Don Joseph De Torres, are to suffer the same punishment; and Don Augustine Villavicienze, independently of degradation, is declared incapable of holding any other in future.

Several other Captains and Officers are, by the same judgment, deprived of their offices for a limited time of six, four, and two years, according to the degree of their criminality.

Several Captains, Lieutenants, and Ensigns, are only condemned to be reprimanded in public.

This sentence has made a strong impression at Madrid, particularly what relates to Don Joseph De Cordova, who is treated with so much severity.

1797–1798 – West Indies

IN RESPONSE TO THE FRENCH RECAPTURE of Guadaloupe, 30,818 soldiers, virtually half of the active British army, were sent out to the West Indies between December 1795 and March 1796, but because of severe storms in the Channel, they did not succeed in reaching the islands until April and May 1796 and were thereby condemned to go on service in the rainy season. General Abercrombie and Rear-Admiral Christian overcame stiff resistance to recapture St Lucia, and the revolts in St Vincent and Grenada were suppressed. The Dutch colonies were also occupied without resistance. Although Nicholas Mole in Saint-Domingue was held until 1798, its hinterland was difficult to defend against the military genius of Toussaint l'Ouverture. The warfare in the Windward and Leeward Islands served to prevent any serious attempt by the French to act offensively against Jamaica.

The entry of Spain into the war on the side of France diverted attention to the easier prospect of seizing her possessions, although Spain also attempted its own offensive. In February 1797 General Abercrombie received the surrender of Trinidad with little resistance. Three Spanish ships of the line were destroyed by their own crews in the harbour, and a fourth was captured virtually undamaged. In the late summer of 1798 a Spanish army sent to occupy the British settlements in Honduras was defeated by British forces based on Jamaica. Letters from the Earl of Balcarras, Governor of Jamaica, and from Vice-Admiral Sir Hyde Parker, C-in-C Jamaica station, transmitting reports of the successful defence of Belize in late September 1798 were received in London early in 1799.

Of these extensive operations, only the gazette letter from the naval commander on the Trinidad expedition, Rear-Admiral Henry Harvey, and the accounts of operations in Honduras have been reproduced here.

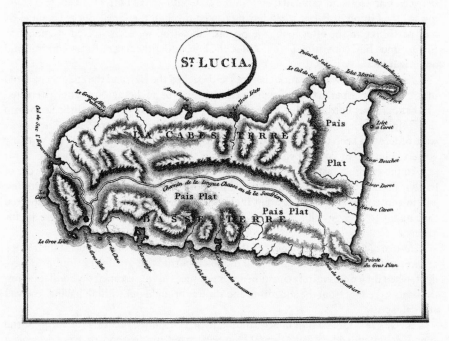

An accurate map of St. Lucia. Drawn and engraved by Arrowsmith. ^{Plate 206}

The Capture of Trinidad
From 'Naval Anecdotes.' ^{III 259-261}

Official Letter from Rear-Admiral Henry Harvey (Brother to the late Captain John Harvey), Commander in Chief of His Majesty's Ships and Vessels at Barbadoes, and the Leeward Islands, dated off Port d'Espagne, in the Gulph of Paria, February 21, 1797, to Mr. Nepean [Admiralty Secretary]

Sir, I have the honour to acquaint you, for the information of their Lordships, that it having been determined an attack should be made on the Island of Trinidad, both with a view to that colony, and to the Spanish squadron which had been there for some time past, the troops intended for this expedition from Martinique were accordingly embarked in the ships of war, and transports, and I sailed from Fort Royal bay, the twelfth instant, with the ships and vessels of his Majesty's squadron under my command. Lieutenant-General Sir Ralph Abercrombie embarked with me in the *Prince of Wales*.

The *Invincible* had previously sailed for Barbadoes, with two transports, to embark a part of the fourteenth regiment; and the *Thorn* and *Zebra* were ordered to receive the detachment from Tobago. The *Favorite* was sent to St. Vincent to collect some troops from that island; and the whole were ordered to rendezvous at the island of Cariacou, one of the Grenadines, on or before the thirteenth; and on my arrival at that island, the fourteenth, I found all the ships and transports were assembled.

On the fifteenth, in the morning, I sailed with the squadron and transports, passing between Cariacou and Grenada; and on the sixteenth arrived off Trinidad, and stood toward the Gulph of Paria; when having passed through the Great Bocas Channel, at half-past three in the afternoon, the Spanish squadron were discovered at anchor in Shagaramus Bay, consisting of four sail of the line, under the flag of Rear-Admiral, and one frigate.

As the day was well advanced before I approached the Bay, and the enemy appeared in strength on Gasparaux Island, which commanded the anchorage, by batteries erected for that purpose; I ordered the *Arethusa, Thorn*, and *Zebra*, to proceed a little farther up the Gulph, and anchor with all the transports. The *Alarm, Favorite*, and *Victorieuse*, were ordered to keep under sail above the transports during the night, and prevent any vessels sailing from Port d'Espagne.

In the evening, just before dark, I anchored with the ships of the line, in order of battle, opposite the enemy's squadron, within random shot of their ships and batteries, and in constant readiness to prevent their escape during the night; which I suspected they might attempt, as all their sails were bent, and they appeared perfectly ready for sailing.

At two o'clock in the morning of the seventeenth, we discovered one of their ships on fire, and soon after three others, all of which burnt with great fury until near daylight, when they were entirely consumed. One of them having escaped the conflagration, the boats were sent from the squadron, and she was brought out without having received any damage.

I have great satisfaction in acquainting their Lordships, that this squadron of the enemy, commanded by Rear-Admiral Don Sebastian Ruiz de Apodaca, were destroyed or captured, according to the list I herewith inclose; and although this service was effected without any other act on the part of his Majesty's squadron under my command, than being placed in such a situation as to prevent their escape; I am fully convinced, that had they remained at their anchorage until the next day, the Officers and men whom I have the honour to command would have completed, by their exertion and zeal, the capture of the whole; notwithstanding the advantage of their situation, under the cover of about twenty pieces of cannon and three mortars, which were mounted on Gasparaux Island, and had been placed there for the sole purpose of defending the ships in the bay: that island, which like the ships, had been abandoned during the night, was taken possession of soon after day-light by a party of the Queen's regiment.

General Abercrombie, early in the morning, joined the *Arethusa*; and the troops were all landed, in the course of the day, under the direction of Captain Woolley, covered by the *Favorite* sloop, about three miles from the town, without opposition: the General took possession of the town the same evening, and [on] the eighteenth the Governor desired to capitulate for the whole island, and the articles were agreed to, and signed the same day; a copy of which I herewith transmit.

Captain Harvey, of his Majesty's ship *Prince of Wales*, will have the honour to deliver this dispatch, from whom I have always experienced the greatest zeal and attention to his Majesty's service.

I have the honour to be, Sir,

Your most obedient humble servant,

HENRY HARVEY

List of the ships of war burnt and captured in Shagaramus Bay, in the Gulph of Paria, February 17, 1797, by the squadron under the command of Rear Admiral H. Harvey

Burnt

San Vincente	84 guns	Rear-Admiral Don Sebastian
		Ruiz de Apodaca
		Captain Don Geronimo Mendoza
Galliardo	74	Don Gabriel Sorendo
Arrogante	74	Don Raphael Benesa

Captured

San Damaso	74	Don Toref Jordan

Burnt

Santa Cecilia	36	Don Manuel Urtesabel

Operation in Honduras
From 'Gazette Letters.' [1 245-248]

Whitehall, January 22 [1799]

Letters, of which the following are Copies, were received from the Earl of Balcarras [Governor of Jamaica], by his Grace the Duke of Portland, one of his Majesty's Principal Secretaries of State [Home Secretary].

Jamaica, 7 November 1798

My Lord, On the 31st of October I received a dispatch from the Bay of Honduras.

Lieutenant-Colonel Barrow informs me, that the settlers had been attacked by a flotilla consisting of 31 vessels, having on board 2000 land troops and 500 seamen: Arthur O'Neil, Governor General of Yucatan, and a Field Marshal in the service of Spain, commanded in person. I have great satisfaction in transmitting the letter of the Lieutenant-Colonel, by which your Grace will be informed, that this armament has been repulsed, and the expedition entirely frustrated.

The Lieutenant-Colonel speaks in the handsomest manner of the conduct of Captain Moss, of his Majesty's ship *Merlin*, and of the wonderful exertions of the settlers and their negro slaves, who manned the gun-boats.

The conduct of Lieutenant-Colonel Barrow, and of the settlers, in putting the port of Honduras Bay into a respectable state of defence, as well as the gallant manner in which it was maintained, gives me entire satisfaction, and it is with pleasure that I report their services to your Grace.

I have the honour to be, &c. &c

BALCARRAS

To his Grace the Duke of Portland

Honduras, September 23, 1798

Lord, . . . Our fleet was drawn up with his Majesty's ship *Merlin* in the centre, and directly abreast of the Channel: the sloops with heavy guns, and the gun-boats in some advance to the northward, were on her eastern and western flanks.

The enemy came down in a very handsome manner, and with a good countenance, in a line abreast, using both sails and oars. About half after two o'clock Captain Moss made the signal to engage, which was obeyed with a cool and determined firmness, that to use his own expression to me on this occasion, would have done credit to veterans. The action lasted about two hours and a half, when the Spaniards began to fall into confusion, and soon afterwards cut their cables, and sailed and rowed off, assisted by a great number of launches, which took them in tow.

Captain Moss, on seeing them retreat, made the signal for our vessels to chase; but night coming on, and rendering a pursuit too dangerous in a narrow channel and difficult navigation, they were soon after recalled.

At half after three in the afternoon, I received a letter from Captain Moss, stating that the enemy was preparing to attack him, and requiring all the assistance which I could give. I immediately ordered as many men to embark and proceed to his assistance, as small craft to carry them could be procured. The alacrity shewn on this occasion was great indeed; but as a requisition of this nature was by no means expected, the necessary arrangements had not been made for so speedily embarking the troops; and of consequence some irregularity ensued; for the cannonade being distinctly heard, and a certainty of an engagement having taken place, it became impossible to restrain the eagerness of the colonial troops, who possessing canoes, dories, and pit pans, without thought or retrospect of those left behind, hastened with impetuosity to join their companions, and share their danger: hence arose difficulty and disappointment to the regular troops, who being under arms, and anxious to proceed with all expedition, suffered delay from want of the necessary boats and craft to embark in.

As soon as I saw seventeen craft of different descriptions, having on board two hundred men, set off with orders to rally round the *Merlin*, I immediately joined them in hopes of assisting Captain Moss and harrassing the enemy; but although we were only two hours in getting on board the *Merlin*, a distance of three leagues and a half, in the wind's eye, we were too late to have any share in the action. But I am of opinion, that the sight of so many craft full of men coming up with velocity, hastened the return of the enemy, and that their appearance on the following day, as well as the junction of two armed ships, the *Juba* and *Columbia*, which I had ordered round to St. George's Key on the 9th, induced the fleet to prepare for returning to their respective posts. The Spaniards remained under Key Chappel until the 15th; on the morning of which they made various movements, and in the course of the day some of them anchored under Key Caulker. On the morning of the 16th, it was discovered that they had stolen off; eight of their largest vessels got out to sea, and stood to the northward; the remainder, being twenty-three in number, shaped their course for Baccalar.

We have every reason to believe that the enemy suffered much in the action of the 10th, as well in killed and wounded, as in the hulls and rigging of the vessels engaged; and I am happy to inform your Lordship that we had not a single man hurt, and that no injury was done to any of our vessels deserving of notice.

It would be unjust, my Lord, to mention the names of any officers, either of the military, or militia, on account of any particular service performed by them; for the conduct of all being such as to merit my best thanks, no particular distinction can be made.

It is also unnecessary for me to say any thing respecting Captain Moss: his penetration in discovering, and activity in defeating the views of the enemy; his coolness and steady conduct in action, point him out as an officer of very great merit. He first suggested to me the very great use which might be made of gun boats against the enemy, and gave me much assistance by the artificers belonging to his ship in filling them out. I am happy to say, that the most cordial co-operation has always existed between us. On the 13th inst. I sent out two scout canoes, well manned, with orders to pass the Spanish fleet in the night; and, proceeding to the northward, to board the first small vessel they could fall in with. On the 16th they captured a small packet-boat with five hands, when, taking out the prisoners, letters, &c. and destroying the boat, they returned here on the 17th. At day-light of that day the canoes were entangled with the retreating Spanish fleet near Savanna-Qay, and escaped with difficulty.

The expedition was commanded by Arthur O'Neil, a field-marshal in the armies of Spain, and Captain General of the Province of Yucatan. The Campeachy fleet was commanded by Captain Bocca Negra: two thousand soldiers were embarked and distributed in proportion to the dimensions of the vessels, on board of the fleet, which consisted of:

The vessels which made the attack, in number - 9

Reserve of equal force - 5

A very large sloop of equal force, and six schooners not so large but armed in the same manner as those which came down to the attack, and drawing too much water remained with the transports and victuallers - 7

Transports, victuallers, &c. all carrying bow and side guns of different calibres - 11

Total - 31

and navigated by 500 seamen, principally from the Havanna and Campeachy.

I am, &c

THO. BARROW

Lieutenant-Colonel Commandant

BALCARRAS

(True Copy) To the Earl of Balcarras

Admiralty Office, January 22 [1799]

Extract of a letter from Vice-Admiral Sir Hyde Parker, Knt. commander of his Majesty's ships and vessels at Jamaica, to Evan Nepean, Esq. dated on board his Majesty's ship Abergavenny, in Port-Royal Harbour, the 6th November, 1798

Sir, You will be pleased to acquaint the Right Honourable the Lords Commissioners of the Admiralty, that I have received dispatches from Captain Moss, of his Majesty's sloop *Merlin*, dated Honduras, 27th September, a copy of which, describing the defeat of the Spanish flotilla is herewith enclosed.

Merlin, St. George's Key, September 27, 1798

Sir, My letters by the *Swift* schooner, which sailed from Honduras express on the 21st of last August, have informed you of the enemy's force intended for the reduction of this settlement, and their situation at that time; since which our look-out canoes have watched them so closely, that all their movements were made known to me as they happened. On the 4th of this month they were visible from our mast-heads at Belize, and look outs reported to me thirty one sail of all descriptions; but their exact force by no means certain. The next day six of their heaviest vessels attempted to force their passage over Montego-Key shoals, by putting their provisions and stores into other vessels; had they effected this, it would have secured them all a passage to Belize over

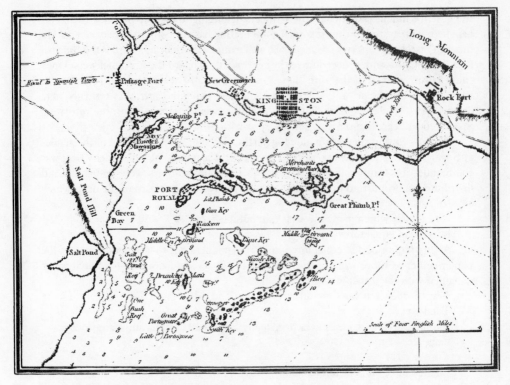

Port Royal Harbour, in the Island of Jamaica, is situated in latitude 17° 41' north, longitude 75° 34' west from London. ^{Plate 299}

shoal-water, where I could by no means act. I ordered three of our armed vessels to annoy them in their endeavours, which succeeded so far as to occasion their removal at dark, and a small channel they had marked by driving down stakes was also taken up by our canoes. I now clearly saw that their next effort would be to get possession of St. George's Key, from which place (only nine miles from Belize) they might go down through the different channels leading to it, and continue to harrass the inhabitants and destroy the towns at their leisure, and drive me from my anchorage there; this determined me to gain the Key before them, if possible; I therefore left Belize on the evening of the 5th, and secured this place, at the instant twelve of their heaviest vessels were attempting the same; they hauled their wind and returned to Long Key, on my hauling my wind towards them. They continued working and anchoring among the shoals until the 11th, at the distance of three or four miles; when having made their arrangements, at one P. M. nine sail of sloops and schooners, carrying from twelve to twenty guns, including two twenty-four and two eighteen pounders each had in prow and stern, with a large launch a-stern of each full of men, bore down through the channel leading to us in a very handsome cool manner; five smaller vessels lay to windward out of gun-shot, full of troops, and the remainder of thier squadron at Long Key Spit to wait the event, each of which carried small prow guns, with swivels fore and aft. At half past one P.M. seeing their intention to board the two sloops, and that they meant to come no nearer, but had anchored, I made the signal to engage, which began and continued near two hours; they then cut their cables and rowed and towed off by signal in great confusion over the shoals. I had placed the *Merlin* as near the edge of them as possible, and nothing that I had was equal to follow them, unsupported by the *Merlin*. At dark they regained their other vessels, and continued in sight till the 15th at night, when they moved off with a light southerly wind: some are gone to Baccalar, and some prisoners taken, report others are gone to Campeche. I am happy to add that the service was performed without a man killed on our side. The enemy I think must have suffered much from the great number of men on board, and the precipitate manner they made their retreat. This armament was commanded by General O'Neil, Governor of the province; troops and sailors included, about 2500 men; and so certain were the Spaniards of success, that the letters found in a canoe taken, were actually directed to Belize and St. George's Key.

The behaviour of the officers and crew of his Majesty's ship gave me great pleasure, and if we had had deep water to follow them in, I think many of them would have fallen into our hands. The spirit of the Negro slaves that manned the small crafts was wonderful, and the good management of the different commanders does them great credit.

Our force, besides the *Merlin*, is as follows:

Two sloops, with one eighteen-pounder and 25 men.

One sloop with one short nine-pounder and 25 men.

Two schooners with 6 four-pounders and 25 men each.

Seven gun-flats, with 1 nine-pounder and 16 men each.

I have the honour to be, Sir, &c.

JNO. R. MOSS

1797 – Spithead Mutiny

ON 17 APRIL 1797 the seamen and marines at Spithead refused to sail until their grievances about pay, victuals and treatment of the sick and wounded were met. Against this well-organised collective action the government was powerless, and to his credit Earl Spencer, the First Lord since December 1794, did not compound the problem by attempting the use of force. Lord Howe was called out of retirement to meet the seamen's delegates and respond to their demands. Parliament rushed through a bill on 10 May authorising the changes, and the King signed a pardon for all the sailors involved. Freshly printed copies were rushed down to Portsmouth. About half of the officers whom the seamen had sent ashore were relieved of their duty.

The embers of mutiny continued to smoulder, however, and burst out from time to time on foreign stations as ships were sent out as reliefs. In October the ships' companies at the Nore were to embark on a more violent, and treasonable, mutiny.

The Naval Chronicle was reluctant to dwell on events which it, and its readership, considered disgraceful. Although the sailors conducted themselves with masterly self-control, and made it clear that they would sail the fleet if the French threatened invasion or attack on a convoy, the whole episode frightened a generation which had watched the excesses of the French Revolution. Reportage, accordingly, was confined to brief, tight-lipped, passages in a number of biographical memoirs.

The Great Mutiny
From the 'Biographical Memoirs of Sir John Colpoys, K.B.' XI 269-272

Early in the following year, 1797, symptoms of mutiny and discontent displayed themselves in his Majesty's fleets at Portsmouth and Spithead. In the month of February, petitions were sent from all the line of battle ships at Portsmouth, to Lord Howe; but as they were considered to be only the products of a few factious individuals, they were wholly disregarded. This neglect, however, tended to a more extensive dissemination of mutinous principles; and, on the 15th of April, when Lord Bridport ordered the

This marine view from Spithead, by Mr. Pocock, represents a sloop of war lying-to, with her head-sails to the mast; on the fore-ground an oyster smack is introduced, and in distance to the left a galliot gun-vessel: beyond this is seen Fort Monkton, a favourite design of the Duke of Richmond: the south part of it occupies the place where the *Gillkickers* used to stand, as a mark for coming through the narrows into Spithead from the seaward. To the right of the mouth of the harbour are seen Portsmouth church, the platform, and flag staff. . . .

"This sea road between the Isle of Wight and the continent of Hampshire, from Cowes to St. Helen's, is near 20 miles in length, and in some places three miles broad: it is capable of receiving with ease more than a thousand sail of shipping. The anchoring ground is kept exceeding good by the flux and reflux of the water, from east to west twice ever tide. It is thus rendered so safe, that seamen call it *The King's Bed-chamber*. Even the sands contribute to its safety: the spit, or bank of sand lying to the north, breaks the sea on that side; the Horse's bank, does the same to the east, and Norman's land, and the Mother bank, the same on the south."

Mottley, *History of Portsmouth*, 1802 Plate 149

signal for the fleet to prepare for sea, the seamen of the *Queen Charlotte*, instead of weighing anchor, ran up the shrouds and gave three cheers, as the notice for disaffection, which was immediately answered by every ship in the fleet. Astonishment, on the part of the Officers, succeeded this sudden and violent act of disobedience: they used every means in their power to induce a return to duty; but all their exertions were ineffectual; and, on the following day, two delegates were appointed from each ship to represent the whole fleet, the Admiral's cabin in the *Queen Charlotte* being fixed upon as the place for their deliberations.

On the 18th of April, a Committee of the Board of Admiralty arrived at Portsmouth, and made propositions to the mutineers, all of which, however, were ineffectual. On the 21st of the month, Vice-Admiral Colpoys, accompanied by Admirals Gardner and Pole, went on board of the *Queen Charlotte*, in order to confer with the delegates; but these men assured the Admirals, that no arrangement would be considered as final until it should be sanctioned by the King and Parliament, and guaranteed by a proclamation for a general pardon.

After much time had been spent in negociation, the wishes of the men were in a great measure acceded to; and it was concluded that loyalty and subordination had resumed their seats. Unfortunately this was not the case. On the 7th of May, when Lord Bridport made the signal to weigh and put to sea, every ship in the fleet refused to obey. For this second act of disobedience, the seamen alleged, as a reason, the silence which Government observed of the subject of their complaints. The idea, that the promised redress of their grievances would not be carried into effect, was strengthened by the distribution of a number of seditious hand bills among the ships, and the seamen therefore resolved to hold a convention of delegates on board the *London*, at Spithead. In pursuance of their intention, they proceeded in their boats alongside of that ship; but Vice-Admiral Colpoys, determined to oppose their coming on board, cautioned them against acting as they had formerly done; told them that they had asked a great deal, and had obtained much; that he would not suffer them to proceed to demand more; that they ought to be contented; and that, if they offered to meet in convention, he would order the marines to fire on them. The delegates, however, persisted, and the Admiral ordered the marines to level their pieces at them. In this situation, the Admiral again admonished them, but without effect; a slight scuffle ensued, and one of the delegates, all of whom were armed, fired at Lieutenant Sims, of the marines, and wounded him. At the command of the First Lieutenant of the ship, the marines then fired, and killed five seamen, two of whom were delegates. The whole crew of the *London* now declared open hostility against the officers and marines, turned the guns in the fore part of the ship towards the stern, and threatened to blow all aft into the water unless they surrendered. Circumstances as they were, to this imperious menace there was no alternative but submission.

In consequence of the death of their comrades, by the firing of the marines, the seamen were proceeding to hang the Lieutenant, by whom the orders had been given; but, at this trying moment, Admiral Colpoys rushed forward, alleged his own responsibility, and assured them, that his Lieutenant had acted only by his orders, agreeably to instructions received from the Admiralty. The seamen instantly demanded these instructions, which were immediately produced. The mutineers then confined Admiral Colpoys, Captain Griffiths, and the officers, to their cabins, and made the marines prisoners. On the 11th of May, four days after the renewed symptoms of mutiny had appeared, the crew of the *London* expressed a wish that Admiral Colpoys and Captain Griffiths should go on shore, which they accordingly did, accompanied by the Reverend Mr. Cole, the Chaplain.

The fleet remained in this mutinous state till the 14th of the month, when Lord Howe arrived at Portsmouth, invested with full powers for settling the different points in dispute. As he also brought with him an Act of Parliament, which had been passed on the 9th, in compliance with the wishes of the seamen, and a Proclamation of pardon for all who should immediately return to their duty, affairs were, for a time,[1] adjusted to

---

1 It must be fresh in the recollection of our readers, that, towards the end of the month, a mutiny, still more alarming than the one above mentioned, broke out on board the ships at the Nore in the North Sea fleet, under a pretence of redress of other grievances, besides what related to pay and provisions. This was the mutiny for which Parker and several others afterwards suffered.

the satisfaction of the sailors; the flag of disaffection was struck, and, two days after, the fleet put to sea to encounter the enemy.

Vice-Admiral Colpoys, we believe, did not return on board of the *London*; but, sometime in the course of the year, as a distinguishing mark of his Majesty's favour, he was invested with the Noble Order of the Bath.

From the 'Biographical Memoir of Lord Howe.' [123]

The conduct of Lord Howe, during the mutiny in 1797,[2] was as commendable as it was arduous. The difficulties he had to encounter, would almost baffle the exertions of the human mind. The kingdom contemplated, with a degree of unusual anxiety, this venerable character, whose head was silvered o'er with age and long service, struggling at the close of life, to withstand the insidious artifice of the enemy, which threatened to lay the proudest honours of Great Britain in the dust. He felt humanely for those who were infected by the noxious poison, and strove with parental tenderness in their behalf. He stood like the guardian genius of his country, between the dead and the living, and stayed the plague.

From the 'Biographical Memoirs of the Right Honourable Lord Gardner.'
VIII 196-197

From this time, the shattered remains of the French Navy having kept close to their harbours, Sir Alan Gardner, who continued attached to the Channel Fleet, and had removed his flag, in the course of the year 1797, from the *Queen* to the *Royal Sovereign*, of 110 guns, had no farther opportunity of adding to the splendid reputation he had so honourably acquired. In the spring of the year 1797, an alarming mutiny broke out in the Channel Fleet, and Sir Alan Gardner was one of the Officers who contributed eminently to suppress it. Accompanied by Admirals Colpoys and Pole, he went on board the *Queen Charlotte*, to confer with the delegates of the fleet, and at no small personal risk, remonstrated with them on the impropriety of their conduct. His firmness had like to have produced disagreeable consequences, but happily the respect due to his character preserved him from the violence of the mutineers; nor were his conciliatory propositions altogether without effect. To dwell on transactions like these is highly offensive to our feelings; but in justice to the seamen of the Channel Fleet, we must observe, that their mutiny was unattended with those acts of violence and treason, which distinguished a similar proceeding at the Nore; and that their demands were not altogether improper, may be gathered from the circumstance, that most of them were acceded to by the Lords of the Admiralty, and afterwards confirmed by Parliament.

On the 14th of February 1799, Sir Alan Gardner was advanced to the rank of Vice-Admiral of the Blue, and on the 30th of August 1800, he was appointed Commander in Chief of his Majesty's ships and vessels employed on the coast of Ireland. The brilliant successes of Admiral Kingsmill's cruisers on that station, we have already noticed in our Memoirs of that gentleman,[3] and if Sir Alan Gardner's were not as successful, the fault did not lie with him, but resulted from the impoverished state of the enemy's marine, which prevented them from sending any vessels to sea. We have only to record the capture of two vessels during the short period of Sir Alan's command; the one a

2 On the 2d of June 1797, Earl Howe was invested with the insignia of the garter.
3 Vol. V. p.206. [See above]

privateer, of 16 guns, the other of 14; and the termination of hostilities in the month of October 1801, necessarily suspended the further prosecution of offensive measures.

Containing the Spreading Infection
From the 'Biographical Memoir of the Honourable Captain Courtenay Boyle.'
XXX 13

On the 24th of April, the *Kangaroo* anchored in Dublin Bay, and on the 9th of May in the River Shannon. On his arrival at Cork, Captain Boyle received the admiral's orders to proceed with convoy to Portsmouth; but, when off the coast of Cornwall, being again informed of the mutinous state, in which were several of the men of war at Portsmouth, he determined to take the convoy chiefly laden with provisions, to Plymouth, where he came to anchor on the 4th of June. He there, however, found the same alarming spirit to prevail in several of the ships; notwithstanding which, he contrived to preserve his own ship's company quiet and orderly. Admiral Sir R. King directed him to anchor close to the *Magnanime*, lying in the Sound, and to be prepared to act against her should they proceed to greater violence. In this painful situation, the *Kangaroo* remained several days, and kept off the mutinous delegates from boarding her. By repeatedly urging the crew of the *Kangaroo* to proper conduct, Captain Boyle actually induced them to offer their services against the ships that were in a state of mutiny at the Nore; which was thankfully received, and the co-operation of himself and officers was immediately promised. This highly praise-worthy conduct of the *Kangaroo*'s ship's company, was conveyed through the port admiral to government; when Captain Boyle was directed to make known the approval of the Lords Commissioners of the Admiralty on that occasion, and several of the men were afterwards selected to make them petty officers.

From the 'Biographical Memoir of Captain Joseph Ellison.' XIX 26-29

The *Marlborough*'s crew had committed the most daring outrages, and had evinced a spirit of disaffection, in a greater degree than that of any other ship; notwithstanding which, when Captain Ellison took the command, he was received by them with marked approbation. They gave him three cheers; said they had heard that he was the seaman's friend; and that they would go round the world with him. - As a proof of the satisfaction which he had reason to expect from them, it is worth mentioning, that, on their expressing a wish to have leave to go on shore, he gave sixty of them liberty at once, and not one staid beyond the time which had been fixed for their return. . . .

[However, in 1798, when ordered to join Lord St. Vincent's squadron off Cadiz,] the spirit of disaffection, which had been only quelled for the moment, amongst the crew of the *Marlborough* again broke forth. Their intention, as it afterwards appeared, was to put Captain Ellison, and his officers, to death, though without any cause of complaint, and to carry the ship into Brest. Fortunately, their schemes were frustrated by one of the seamen; who, having overheard their conversation, got in at the quarter-galley window, at midnight, and, awakening the captain, who was in his cot, made the discovery. "For God's sake, Captain Ellison, get up," said he; "the ship is in a state of mutiny; you and your officers are to have your throats cut, and the ship is to be taken possession of!" - On receiving this alarming intelligence, Captain Ellison immediately went upon the quarterdeck; and, looking around, he saw a number of men assembled on the poop, *more* than the *watch*. On asking the officer of the watch the reason of this, the men, perceiving that they were detected, returned, in the greatest confusion, over the quarters, and along the muzzles of the guns, to the main-deck, and got into their hammocks. Captain Ellison then summoned all the officers upon deck; where, accompanied by them, he continued during the remainder of the night. At eight o'clock in the morning, the hands were turned up, in order to discover the ringleaders, but without effect. However, in the course of the day, a seaman came forward, and mentioned two who had been the most active in the business, and they were immediately put in irons. On joining Lord St. Vincent's fleet, they were tried by a court martial, condemned, and executed on board the *Marlborough*. - A public letter was subsequently received by Captain Ellison, from the Admiralty, expressing their lordships' approbation of his conduct, and that of his officers on this trying occasion.

From the 'Memoir of the Public Services of Sir Charles Brisbane, Knt.'
XX 90-91

[Whilst at St. Helena in command of the *Dortrecht*, Captain Brisbane's] fortitude and presence of mind were put to a severe test. The news of the general mutiny of 1797 having reached that island, the crew of the *Dortrecht*, inspired by the same baleful spirit which had diffused itself throughout the Royal Navy, rose upon their officers, and menaced them with general destruction. The utmost promptitude and vigour became necessary; and, seizing one of the ring-leaders, Captain Brisbane placed a halter about his neck, and, apparently, was proceeding to immediate execution. His object, however, being only to inspire terror, and to convince the crew that he was not to be intimidated, he relaxed from the threatened infliction of justice; but, while the cord was yet round the culprit's neck, he solemnly declared to him, that, if he ever again ventured to open his mouth against his king or country, or in disobedience to the commands of his officers, the yard-arm should inevitably be his portion.

The imperative proceeding, on the part of Captain Brisbane, shook the guilty resolutions of the mutineers; and, by a continued firmness, they were happily reduced to a sense of their duty.

The mutiny having also broken out at the Cape, Admiral Pringle sent a 20-gun ship down to St. Helena, expressly to request the return of Captain Brisbane, that he might take the command of the *Tremendous*; the crew of that ship having risen upon their officers, and turned their captain on shore.[4]

For a time, the mutineers, having obtained a pardon, returned to their duty; but the flame having been only smothered, not extinguished, it burst forth again with redoubled violence, extending to the *Sceptre*, and to some other ships. A council was immediately held on shore, wherein it was wisely determined by Lord Macartney, the governor, Admiral Pringle, and General Dundas, to use force, and the most decisive measures, for quelling it, and bringing the ringleaders to punishment: all the batteries were instantly manned, and upwards of 100 pieces of cannon were loaded and pointed at the *Tremendous*, the admiral's ship, on board which the mutiny was at the greatest

---

4 It was on board the *Tremendous* that the mutiny first made its appearance at the Cape of Good Hope. The crew, charging Captain Stephens, her commander, with cruelty and misconduct, at first threatened to bring him to a court-martial, composed of members chosen from amongst the mutinous delegates. Captain Stephens, feeling this as an imputation upon his honour and character as an officer, afterwards requested a court-martial upon his conduct, which was accordingly held on board the *Sceptre*, in Table Bay, and he was honourably acquitted.

height: the furnaces were heated, and red hot balls were prepared to fire on her as she lay at anchor off the Amsterdam battery, if the mutineers should refuse to deliver up the delegates, with the ringleaders, and not return to obedience. A proclamation was issued at seven o'clock in the morning, and only two hours were allowed for the mutineers to deliberate whether they would accept the terms offered. Ten minutes before the expiration of the time granted, the mutineers finding that it was positively determined to sink the *Tremendous*, in case of refusal; hoisted the flag of submission on board that ship, which was immediately followed by all the others. The delegates were given up, many of them were executed, others were severely flogged, and good order and discipline were once more restored on board the fleet.

1795-1797 – North Sea Operations The Mutiny at the Nore, and the Battle of Camperdown

NAVAL OPERATIONS IN THE NORTH SEA at the beginning of the war had been concerned primarily with the escort of trade and pursuit of privateers, but had become more demanding when the Dutch were overrun and concluded a military alliance with the French. The Russian deployment in 1796 of a squadron to cooperate with the British introduced complicated issues of diplomacy for the station commander, Admiral Adam Duncan, and the violent sequel to the mutiny at Spithead which broke out at the Nore on 12 May 1797 and spread to the North Sea Squadron at Yarmouth was a matter of the greatest alarm. The mutineers stopped merchant shipping entering or leaving the Thames in the hope of forcing the government's hand. Eventually the supply of victuals to the fleet was cut off, the forts at Tilbury, Gravesend and Sheerness were prepared to fire red hot shot, and the buoyage in the estuary was removed to deter attempts to take the ships to the Texel where Duncan was maintaining with token forces the blockade of the Dutch fleet. Gradually the ships' companies turned against their leaders, fights broke out, and finally one by one the ships sailed away to surrender. Parker, who had allowed himself to be identified as leader of the mutineers, and twenty-eight delegates were hanged, and others were flogged round the fleet.

Despite the bitterness left behind the mutiny, when the Dutch sailed in October as part of the general plan of operations which included the attempted invasion of Ireland, the crews of the Nore ships delivered a stunning and hard-fought victory at the battle of Camperdown. Duncan's tactics, an attack in two divisions in line abreast on the enemy van and rear, seeking to cut through the Dutch to prevent their withdrawal to leeward, was a logical development on those employed by Howe at the First of June, and was a foreshadowing of those used by Nelson at Trafalgar.

The Naval Chronicle's reportage of these events was largely incorporated in a substantial biographical memoir of Admiral Duncan.

From the 'Biographical Memoirs of Adam Duncan, Lord Viscount Duncan.'
IV 94-97

On the fourteenth of September, 1789, Captain Duncan was promoted to be Rear Admiral of the Blue, as he moreover was, to the same rank in the White Squadron, on a second advancement of flag-officers, which took place on the twenty-second of September, 1790. He was raised to be Vice Admiral of the Blue, on the first of Feb. 1793; of the White, on the twelfth of April, 1794; to be Admiral of the Blue, on the first of June, 1795; and, lastly, to be Admiral of the White, on the 14th of Feb. 1799. During all these periods, except the two last, singular as it may appear to posterity, the high merit Admiral Duncan possessed, continued either unknown, or, to give the treatment he received what may perhaps be a more proper term, unregarded. Frequently did he solicit a command, and as often did his request pass uncomplied with. It has even been reported, that this brave man had it once in contemplation to retire altogether from the service, on a very honourable civil appointment, connected with the Navy; but, as this circumstance has no better foundation than mere rumour, it cannot be given to the world as an anecdote to be implicitly credited.

At length, however, his merit burst through the cloud which had so long obscured it from public view. He received, in the month of February, 1795, an appointment, constituting him Commander in Chief, in what is called the North Seas, the limits of his power extending from the North Foreland, even to the *Ultima Thule* of the ancients, or as far beyond, as the operations of the enemy he was sent to encounter, should render necessary. He accordingly hoisted his flag on board the *Prince George*, of 98 guns, at Chatham; but that ship being considered too large for the particular quarter to which the Admiral was destined to act, he removed soon afterwards into the *Venerable*, of 74 guns, and proceeded to carry into execution the very important trust which was confided in him.

When the patience and unwearied constancy with which this brave officer continued to watch a cautious and prudent enemy, during the whole time he held the command, a period of five years, are considered, it becomes a matter of difficulty to decide, whether those invaluable qualities just mentioned, or the gallantry, as well as the judgment, he displayed on the only opportunity the enemy afforded him of contesting with them the palm of victory, ought most to render him the object of his country's love and admiration. The depth of winter, the tempestuous attacks of raging winds, the dangers peculiarly attached to a station indefatigably maintained off the shoals and sands which environ the coasts of the United Provinces, added to many dark and comfortless nights, all united to render the situation, even of the common seaman, peculiarly irksome; what then must have been the situation of the Commander in Chief? Yet, in the midst of these discouraging inconveniences, surrounded, as he stood, on every side, by perils of the most alarming kind, he never shrunk, even for a moment, from his post, during the whole time he held the very consequential command allotted to him. There does not appear to have been a single month in which he did not shew himself off the hostile coast he insulted; though he was, through necessity, compelled to be content with the secondary consideration, of having dared a foe to a contest, which they very wisely, prudently, or timidly, shrunk from.

Portrait of the Right Honorable
Lord Viscount Duncan.
Engraved by Ridley, from a
Painting by J.S. Copley, R.A.
Plate 38

The effects, politically, though differently impressed on the minds of the whole human race, of that event known by the name of the French Revolution, are still too recent to require much description. Never will they be forgotten, not only on account of their execrable motives and mischievous tendency, but the pains, almost amounting to incredibility, which had been taken to disseminate similar principles over the face of the whole country. They had very justly excited the greatest agitation in the minds of all men; for those who were the friends of peace, were racked by the apprehensive tortures of anxiety, while such as were not ashamed to profess a contrary mode of thinking, were on the tiptoe of expectation and hope, that anarchy would annihilate all good and regular government, leaving the needy, the daring, and the ambitious, to fatten on the spoils of their country, and triumph in its ruin.

In counteraction of this impending storm, different alliances were prudently formed by Britain; and in 1796, a formidable Russian squadron arrived in the Downs, with instructions that its Admiral should put himself totally under the orders of the British Commander in Chief, in the same quarter. To command a body of men whose manners, whose customs, whose discipline was totally dissimilar to those of his own people, must have required no common share of judgment, patience, benevolence, and every other good quality that can form an ingredient in the character of what may be called a perfect man; and though we by no means wish to be so fulsome in the rage of panegyric, as to attribute infallibility to Admiral Duncan, it must be evident that he actually possesses, in a very eminent degree, those qualities just alluded to. So highly did he acquire the love and the respect of his foreign associates, that in consequence of a representation made by their Admiral to the Empress Catherine, of the satisfaction he felt in acting under the orders of Mr. Duncan, she thought proper, though unsolicited, to honour him with the Imperial Order of Alexander Newski, being the second, in point of rank, among the degrees of Russian knighthood.

It were too tedious a detail to enter into the minutiae of those numerous services he rendered his country during the more early part of his command. They were, at least, proofs of his diligence; though the inferior force of the many prizes made by the ships he commanded,¹ might render any exertion of gallantry on his part unnecessary. A sad, a dreadful occurrence, however, which took place in the month of May, 1797, called forth all those powers which had so long laid dormant: the urgency and peculiarity of the case might be said far to exceed, in difficulty and danger, any situation in which an

Correct Portraits of Two Russian Men of War, each of 64 guns, as they lay at anchor off Sheerness, in the year 1796. The Russian ships differ little in their construction from ours: the stern is generally plain, and snug, without much carving; their masts are nearly at equal distances. Their ships are also easily known from the bowsprit's steeving much more than those of the English. In the captain's barge, the Russian sailors row with short oars, two men on each thwart. Nothing can exceed the coarse fare with which they are contented; even the bread and broth of Sparta, must be considered as delicacies to the train oil, which the Russian mariner receives as his repast. [Plate 19]

officer could be thrown, who had to contend with only the public and avowed enemies of his country. It is almost needless to say we advert to that dreadful mutiny, or commotion among the seamen, which, after having raged some time with tremendous fury on board the Channel fleet at Portsmouth, had spread its deleterious contagion through the ships employed under the orders of Admiral Duncan.

Fain would the historian pass over, in the strictest silence, an event, the recital of which brands with shame that character, which, till then, stood foremost in the ranks of honour, and whose very failings fascinated beholders, till they were almost induced to

1 Among which may be reckoned the capture of the Dutch Commodore, Vanderkin; the *Argon*, of 32 guns, taken by Captain Halstead, in the *Phoenix*, May, 1796; and the *Mercury*, of 16 guns, a brig sloop of war, taken by the *Sylph* on the same day; the *Echo*, of 18 guns, and *De Gier*, of 14; two sloops of war were driven on shore by the *Pegasus* at the same time. To these we may add a considerable number of very valuable trading vessels, as well as others of inferior consequence. From the French, the *Victorieuse* and *Suffisante* French national brigs, mounting 14 guns each, were captured in August, 1795, soon after he put to sea. The *Pandora*, a vessel of the same force and description, in the month of December following. The *Jalousie* corvette, mounting 18 guns, in the month of May, 1796.

consider them virtues. Fain would we ourselves banish the recollection of it from our minds, and consign to everlasting oblivion an act, which, by comparison, raises rebellion almost into a venial offence, and effaced from the treasons committed by our ancestors, the charge even of impropriety. Desperate was the situation of the country; but the firmness and intrepidity of those noble-minded persons who preferred a loyalty, though dangerous to themselves, to any situation in which appeared a single particle of dishonour, saved it from the abyss of destruction. No one contributed more eminently to effect this excellent service, than Admiral Duncan. The dangers, the difficulties, he had to encounter, were new and unprecedented; and never did the conduct of any man burst forth with more conspicuous lustre. Foreign to the present purpose would be any attempt at tracing the primary cause of this grand convulsion to its fountain-head; suffice it to say, the seeds of sedition had been widely and most industriously scattered, and on such soils as appeared best appropriated to the succour and maintenance of the deleterious plant. A governmental measure, honestly suggested, and not unwisely though perhaps incautiously carried into execution, contributed very materially to aid the dreadful conspiracy. In aid of those necessities, in respect to the want of seamen, which the continuance of the war had, at that time, brought on Britain, every parish or district throughout the kingdom was, by law, compelled to send, in proportion to their extent and population, a certain number of persons to serve on board the fleet.

The consequence had nearly proved fatal; among the quota of men, as they were called, were a number of persons, bankrupts as well in character as fortune, who had before figured in what was considered an higher sphere of life, having been either petty merchants or attornies. These men, not contented with the iniquities they had been guilty of, and the depredations they had committed on society, in their former occupations, joyfully accepted the prodigious bounty of thirty guineas, or upwards, per man, offered by different parishes, who were anxious to be rid of a business which they considered as an incumbrance, and entered into the Navy, in the certainty of obtaining a better maintenance than they had, many of them, been for some time accustomed to. They entertained also the hope that their introduction would afford some opportunity of disseminating those principles, which, if once established in any degree of force, would render them an opportunity of becoming more dissolute, abandoned, and mischievous, than even their former situations in society had permitted them to be.

Their views were, in not inconsiderable degree, furthered, by the privilege they enjoyed of sending and receiving all their letters free of postage; by these means the conspiracy found means to extend itself unseen; cherished and encouraged by those equally dangerous characters whom they had left on shore, to act their part in a different quarter, a chain of correspondence was formed, and the flame of rebellion, smoking in dangerous concealment, was daily acquiring strength, while its source was undiscovered, and its extent unknown.

The hidden fire received no small encouragement from the serious cause of discontent which the enrollment of these mischievous characters, and the circumstances attending it, was supposed to have occasioned among those who were justly esteemed British seamen. These valuable persons, many of whom had been compelled to enter into the King's service, had received no higher bounty than five pounds per man, and had been obliged, at the same time, to relinquish an employment, the pay of which amounted to three or four pounds per month, for the King's pay of twenty-two shillings and six-pence. These hardships, which the situation of the country required should be submitted to with patience by those whose service was required, were eagerly emblazoned in all the disgusting colours sedition could paint, through the hopes of acquiring proselytes to her hellish purpose: but though expectation was sanguine, and that expectation in all probability, promoted the eagerness with which the dangerous and hellish emissaries just alluded to, engaged in a service completely incompatible with their former situations in life, yet the event proved, in great measure, contrary to their hopes. The thorough bred seamen, notwithstanding the disadvantages under which they laboured, nearly without an exception, were steady in their conduct, and uniform in their loyalty. As it had been quaintly though truly remarked, the core of the mutiny was formed of land lubbers, or half and half sailors, who, in a gale, are almost impediments to the honest and spirited exertions of good and practical seamen.

The tumour, however, having burst, it required the most consummate skill to prevent its fatal effects from overpowering and corrupting the whole body. As an officer bearing command, no person had ever more endeared himself to those whom he was appointed to conduct, than Admiral Duncan; for, while benevolence and good humour had acquired him the universal love of all who knew him; a regularity of government of discipline, unalloyed by severity, and unmixed with the smallest portion of that species of conduct which too often appears in very humane well-disposed men, perpetually reminding those over whom they are put in authority, of the great inferiority of their station, had rendered him revered, as well as adored.

On the instant the baneful influence of this disease made its appearance, he visited every ship in the fleet; his presence had the temporary effect of Ithuriel's spear; it compelled the daemon of discord to quit the more pleasing shape which it had taken, and resume its natural one, disgusting, loathsome, and terrific; its idolatrous worshippers became, for a short space, ashamed of their deity, and returned to their duty without apparent reluctance. The disease, however, was only checked, not cured; for when the fleet put to sea, it renewed its appearance, attended by all its former virulent symptoms, the *Venerable* and *Adamant* appearing the only ships that were not thoroughly tainted with the infection. On the evening before the Admiral himself intended to put to sea, he made the signal for the *Trent* frigate to get under weigh: his commands were not complied with; and on inquiring into the cause, it was found that the crew peremptorily refused obeying their officers, on pretence that the regulation established immediately before, by Act of Parliament, in respect to the weight and measure of provisions, had not been adopted with respect to them. The fact really was, the augmentation had so very recently passed into law, that the particulars of it had not been at that time officially notified to the officers whose particular duty it was to attend to it. The fomenters of dissention, eagerly snatching at the only existing chance of exciting farther tumult, had set fire to the train, by merely suggesting the hardship, and the conflagration spread to the utmost of their wishes.

The Admiral, on this alarming occasion, ordered all hands to be called upon deck; he publicly made known to them the delinquency of their companions; he informed them of his intention to go alongside the frigate early in the ensuing morning, and compel the rebellious crew to return to their duty. "Who is there," said he, "that on this occasion will desert me?" The question was immediately answered in the negative; his people, with one accord, declaring their utmost abhorrence of such conduct, and their assurance of support, to the utmost of their power, in the punishment of it. In the course of the evening, however, a letter, couched in the properest terms possible, was transmitted to him from his ship's company; they offered, by way of satisfying the discontent which pervaded the crew of the *Trent*, and to shew them they fared no worse than all others embarked in the same cause did, to deliver to him the different weights and measures used by the Purser[2] in the allotment of their provisions, and depend entirely on his justice and candour, far as regarded their own allowances. This offer convinced the mutineers of the impropriety of their conduct; the effusion of British blood, and by the hands of Britons, was happily prevented; for before the ensuing morning, the frigate proceeded on the service whither she was ordered by her Commander in Chief.

Towards the end of May, Admiral Duncan quitted Yarmouth Roads by order of the Admiralty Board, with instructions to cruise off the back of those sands which at some distance environ that anchorage, till he should be reinforced. The *Nassau* and *Montague*, one of 64, the other of 74 guns, refused to put to sea, under pretence that they were in the course of payment, though there were at that time scarcely ten shillings due to each man on board. This sad example induced the rest of the ships to pursue the same line of conduct; so the *Venerable* and *Adamant*, whose crews, as already observed, never relaxed from their duty, were left to proceed by themselves off the Texel, whither the Admiral, unattended as he was, immediately repaired.

Stratagem supplied, on this occasion, the place of numbers; for the Admiral, by making a variety of signals as to ships in the offing, effectually duped Admiral De Winter, as he himself afterwards confessed, into the belief that the Channel of the Helder was blocked up by a force superior to that he himself commanded. At this critical period, the only symptom of mutiny that ever was observed on board the *Venerable*, made its appearance. It becomes, indeed, rather a matter of wonder, considering how prevalent is the force of example, that it should have been so tardy, or so languid, as it fortunately proved: a plot, however, was actually on foot, and was happily discovered by some truly valuable men belonging to the Gunner's crew. The Admiral, as he had before been frequently compelled to do, during the critical period alluded to, ordered all hand to be turned upon deck. He immediately addressed them in the firmest, and, at the same time, the coolest terms: after a few minutes, six men, among the stoutest in the ship, and who were charged with being the ringleaders of the conspiracy, were brought before him. It was, at that time, impossible to say what height the disease had reached; the moment was more than critical; it was awful; and, while the delay of an instant might have rendered it fatal, a strong measure, too hastily or unadvisedly taken, might have been equally injurious to the cause of tranquillity.

"My lads," said the Admiral, "I am not, in the smallest degree, apprehensive of any violent measure you may have in contemplation; and though I assure you I would much rather acquire your love than incur your fear, I will, with my own hand, put to death the first man who shall presume to display the slightest symptom of rebellious conduct." Turning round immediately to one of the mutineers; "Do you, Sir," said he, "want to take the command of this ship out of my hands?" - "Yes, Sir," replied the fellow, with the greatest assurance. The Admiral immediately raised his arm, with an intent to plunge his sword in to the mutineer's breast: he was prevented by the Chaplain and Secretary, who seized his arm, from executing this summary act of justice; an act rendered, at least, justifiable, if not necessary, by the particular situation in which not only himself, but the greatest part of those whom he commanded, were at that time placed.

The blow being prevented, the Admiral attempted not to make a second, but

2 Mr. Hore, whose honour and character could not possibly receive any greater panegyric than they did, from the unforced and natural conduct of the *Venerable*'s people on this occasion.

immediately called to the ship's company with some agitation: "Let those who will stand by me, and my officers, pass over immediately to the starboard side of the ship, that we may see who are our friends, and who are our opponents." In an instant the whole crew, excepting the six fomenters of the disturbance, ran over with one accord. The culprits were immediately seized, put in irons, and committed to the gun-room; from whence they were afterwards liberated, one by one, after having shewn those signs of real penitence, which induced the Admiral, by well-timed acts of lenity, to endear himself, if possible still more to a faithful crew, who, in the midst of tumult, had stood faithful to their trust, uncorrupted in the very focus of seditious seduction.

The instance of mild forbearance of forgiveness just related, may not impossibly be thought censurable by the stern and rigid disciplinarian; when, however, the existing complexion of the times, added to the very exemplary conduct of the remaining part of the crew, are considered, together with the little danger that was to be apprehended from any disturbance that could be excited by six headstrong persons, surrounded as they were, by as many hundreds, who revered their Commander as a father, and loved him as a friend, it certainly was worth making the experiment, whether even dissolute morals might not be reclaimed by lenity. The motive was benevolent, and the effect happy; for, except in the slight instance already related, not the smallest symptom of discontent ever appeared on board the *Venerable*.

Let us now turn our minds from a most disgusting subject, and hasten to the account of one of those events which will, to the latest posterity, continue to grace, with the utmost splendour, the page of British Naval History - the engagement with the Dutch fleet off Camperdown. The fleet of the enemy had long been in a complete state of equipment for actual service; it consisted of fifteen ships of the line, six frigates, and five sloops of war; the wind was favourable for their putting to sea; and nothing but the ingenious artifice already related, in all probability prevented it. At length the Admiral, in the hope of annoying them very materially, if they attempted to come out, the channel being so narrow as not to admit of more than one ship passing at a time, anchored, having the *Adamant* in company, at the outer buoy of the Texel, both ships having springs on their cables. What the event of so unequal a contest would have been, is now of little consequence; but whatever it might have proved, the measure certainly reflected the highest honour on the man whose gallantry not only projected it, but made every possible preparation in his power to carry it into execution in the most advantageous manner possible.

The crew were at their quarters for three days and three nights, almost in momentary expectation that the enemy would come out. Their Admiral even made the preparative signal for sailing; but a few hours before the time when their intention was to have been executed, the wind came round to the westward, and prevented it. During the eight following days, the Admiral and his consort were on the tiptoe of expectation, waiting for a reinforcement, when at length, to their great joy, they were joined by the *Sans Pareil*, of 84, and the *Russel* [sic], of 74 guns. Other ships coming in soon afterwards, the disparity of numbers so far decreased, as to annihilate all anxiety for the event of the expected contest. The *Venerable* herself kept the sea during eighteen weeks and three days, without intermission, in which time many of the ships which had joined the Admiral after the mutiny, had been compelled to make a temporary return into port, either on account of a want of provisions, or the damage they had received in the gales of wind which happened about that period.

At length the Commander in Chief, in spite of all the care and economy he could

Representation of the action off Camperdown, between the English and Dutch
fleets, on the 11th of October 1797, engraved by Dodd. The particular period which
it represents of the action, is about four o'clock in the afternoon, not long before the
contest ceased. The flag ship of Admiral de Winter, which was the last of the enemy
that surrendered, is seen nearly in the centre, returning the fire of the *Venerable* very
feebly; while the *Hercules*, a Dutch ship of 64 guns, on fire abaft, is drifting across
the bows of both those ships. On the right hand are seen, in the back ground, some
of the enemy's ships which had then surrendered; and on the left is the *Monarch*,
together with her prize the *Jupiter*. Plate 39

contrive, found himself under the necessity of returning to port, to revictual and procure
a supply of stores, the *Venerable* being in want of nearly every species of necessary
requisite to a ship employed on so active a service. The Dutch Admiral, who had
accurate information from small vessels, which were kept out as scouts, of all the motions
which the British fleet made; wearied by his long confinement in port, urged by the
representations made from his own Executive Government, and stimulated by the
influence of the French faction in Holland, ventured at last to put to sea. Though a
man inferior to no one, perhaps, in personal courage, he knew too well the superiority
of the British ships, and the crews which navigated them, both in respect to equipment
and nautical knowledge, to suppose that the event of an action would be conformable to
the wishes or interests of his countrymen, unless he outnumbered his antagonists far
higher than he could expect or hope. But by putting to sea, he considered that he
should at least quiet the minds of his countrymen for a time; and that calm he hoped to
produce, without putting his armament to the risk of a defeat: this he was induced to
flatter himself with, under the reflection that the same wind which wafted his enemy

from the British shore, would render his return into port so easy, that he might avoid an action.

The activity of Admiral Duncan rendered these expectations futile. Having previously dispatched orders to Yarmouth for the preparation of the different articles he stood in need of, so that as little time as possible might be lost, the fleet had no sooner got to an anchor, than the vessels employed in victualling, were alongside. The Commander in Chief setting the first example of assiduity, quitted not his ship for a moment; he continued almost constantly on deck, encouraging the men, and promoting every possible exertion, insomuch, that the *Venerable* herself was ready for sea in four days, and the whole of the fleet in less than eight. He lost not a moment in getting out to his station, having received early intelligence that the event he had so long wished for, had actually taken place.

Fortune propitiously decreed that the zeal and unremitting perseverance of the Admiral should not pass without acquiring the reward of victory, which he had so long and so diligently laboured to win. On the eleventh of October, at nine o'clock in the morning, the headmost ships of the fleet made the signal of having discovered the enemy, and after a pursuit of three hours, succeeded in the well-judged operation of cutting through the enemy's fleet, by which means they were cut off from their own ports. The subsequent events of the glorious victory obtained on that occasion, and the minute, though highly interesting particulars with which the contest abounded, will be best explained by the annexed extract from the log-book of the *Venerable*:

1797, October 11

British North Sea Fleet

No.	Ships	Captains	Guns	Divisional Commanders
1	*Russel*	Henry Trollope	74	
2	*Director*	William Bligh	64	Richard Onslow, Esq.
3	*Montague*	John Knight, Vice Admiral of the Red	74	
4	*Veteran*	Geo. Gregory	64	
5	*Monarch*	Vice Adm. Onslow Edw. Obryen, Capt.	74	
6	*Powerful*	Wm. O'Drury	74	
7	*Monmouth*	James Walker	64	
8	*Agincourt*	Jo. Williamson	64	
9	*Triumph*	W. H. Essington	74	
10	*Venerable*	Admiral Duncan Wm. G. Fairfax Admiral of the Blue	74	Adam Duncan, Esq., Commander in Chief, &c. &c. &c.
11	*Ardent*	R. R. Burges	64	
12	*Bedford*	Sir Thes. Byard	74	
13	*Lancaster*	John Wells	64	
14	*Belliqueux*	John Inglis	64	
15	*Adamant*	Wm. Hotham	50	
16	*Isis*	Wm. Mitchel	50	

Repeaters: *Beaulieu, Circe, Martin* Sloop, *Black Joke* Lugger, *Rose* and *Active* cutters, and another.

Dutch Fleet

No.	Ships	Captains	Guns	Divisional Commanders
1	Vryheld	Adm. De Winter	74	Commander in Chief - Taken
2	Jupiter	V Adm. Reynties	74	Second in command - Taken
3	Brutus	R Adm. Bliss	74	- Escaped
		Van Treslong	74	
4	States General	Rear Adm. Storey	74	The first ship drove out of the line by His Majesty's ship Venerable - Escaped
5	Hercules	Ryscost	64	- Taken
6	Adm. D. Vries	Zegu	68	- Taken
7	Gleikheid	Rysch	68	- Taken
8	Leyden	Masqustein	68	- Escaped
9	Ceroerus	Jacobson	68	- Escaped
10	Wassenaar	Holland	64	- Taken
11	Haerlem	Wiggotts	68	- Taken
12	Delft	Verdoom	56	- Taken
13	Batavia	Souters	56	- Escaped
14	Alkmaar	Kraffe	56	- Taken
15	Beschermer	Kengett	56	- Escaped
16	Mars*	Koff	44	- Escaped
17	Monikendam	Lancaster	44	- Taken
18	Heldin	Desnionil	32	
19	Ambuscade	Hays	32	- Taken
20	Waakzaniheid	Vearop		
21	Minerva	Elbriachts		
22	Galatea	Revery		
23	Ajax	Akanboath		
24	Althelante	Piats		
25	Daphne	Frederick		
26	Harige	Harhiufied		

* Taken into the line

Memorandum The Dutch had ten guns more in their line of battle than the British, and eighty-eight guns besides in their frigates and brigs. Several of their ships carried thirty-six and twenty-four pounders on their lower and on their main decks.

N.B. The British ships only thirty-twos and eighteens.

1797 October 11th, Signals

Hrs.	Min.	By whom made	To whom addressed	Number and Signification
9	0	Venerable	General	10. Prepare for battle
9	15	Ditto	Circe	47. Come within hail
9	20	Ditto	Russel	101. Close with the Admiral

Hrs.	Min.	By whom made	To whom addressed	Number and Signification
9	22	Ditto	General	48. Line on starboard bearing.
9	26	Ditto	General	17. Alter the course to port, and steer S.S.E.
9	38	Ditto	General	48. With compass signals to form the line on starboard, bearing N.E. and S.W.
9	50	Ditto	General	67. Make more sail
9	58	Ditto	*Isis* and *Lancaster*	67. To make more sail
10	–	Ditto	*Russel*	16. To steer more to starboard
10	4	*Venerable*	*Isis*	67. To make more sail
10	5	Ditto	General	16. With compass signals, the fleet to steer S.
10	15	Ditto	General	7. With two guns, general chase
10	24	Ditto	General	35. To engage the enemy as arriving up with them
10	33	*Venerable*	*Beaulieu*	67. To make more sail
10	38	Ditto	*Belliqueux*	67. To make more sail
10	45	Ditto	*Monarch* and *Montagu*	69. To shorten sail, but hauled down before answered
11	–	Ditto	Van	71. Van to shorten sail
11	2	Ditto	General	66. Take in one reef of the topsails
11	8	*Venerable*	General	48. Starboard line of bearing
11	11	Ditto	Ditto	81. With preparative, come to the wind on the starboard tack
11	17	Ditto	General	95. To take stations in the line as ships' pendants are thrown out, after ninety-five was answered, countermanded
11	29	Ditto	Particular	87. Ships to windward to come down
11	30	Ditto	General	36. Each ship to engage her opponent in the enemy's line.
11	35	Ditto	General	14. Bear up and sail large
11	40	Ditto	Van	41. The van to attack the enemy's rear
11	53	*Venerable*	General	34. To pass through the enemy's line, and engage them to leeward. P.M.
12	5	Ditto	General	5. With red pendant over, for close action
12	30	The Action commenced		
3	–	The Firing ceased		
3	20	*Venerable*	General	101. Close round the Admiral
4	10	Ditto	General	10. Prepare for battle

N.B. The wind veering round, and blowing upon the shore, made the signal from the *Venerable* to the ships of our fleet not disabled, to tow off the *Prizes*.

October 11, 1797. Remarks

At seven A.M. saw three large ships to leeward, standing to the squadron [*Wind N.W. by N.*]; on nearing them, found they had each a red flag flying at the main top gallant-mast-head, being the signal for an enemy. These ships proved to be Captain Trollope's squadron, consisting of the *Russel*, *Adamant*, and *Beaulieu*, frigate, who had kept sight of the Dutch fleet, and watched their motions. His Majesty's ship *Circe*, likewise one of that squadron, joined us afterwards. [*Fresh Breeze and squally weather.*] At half past eight o'clock A.M. saw the Dutch fleet to leeward; made the signal, bore up with the fleet, and stood towards them. At fifty minutes past nine, made the signal for the fleet to make more sail. On approaching the enemy's fleet, saw them forming their line of battle on the larboard tack; their force consisting of sixteen sail of the line, three stout frigates, and two smaller ones, with five brigs, having four flags flying, viz. one blue at the main, one white at the mizen, one blue at the mizen, and one blue at the fore-top-gallant-mast-head. Their frigates and brigs drawn up to leeward of their line of battle ships, and placed opposite to the intervals, which rendered them a great annoyance to our ships; especially while passing through their line, and during the greatest part of the action. [*N.W. by N.*] At eleven A.M. made the signal for the van to shorten sail, to let the sternmost ships come up, and connect our line as well as time would permit. The enemy at this time in a line of battle on the larboard tack, with their main-top-sail yards square, but keeping them shivering, and sometimes full, by which their line was gradually advancing towards their own shore, which, at this period, was not seven miles distant. [*Squally weather with Rain.*] The land in sight was situated between the village of Egmont and Camperdown. By the inequality of sailing of several of our ships, the squadron was unavoidably going down towards the enemy in no regular order of battle. Brought to for a short time on the starboard tack, in order to form them; but the enemy being still advancing towards their own shore, it was determined by our Admiral to get between them and their own land, at all events, to prevent their escape. The signal for bearing up was therefore made before our ships could possibly get into any regular order of battle. Had our time been lost in making regular distribution of our ships, the Dutch fleet must have got so near their coast, it would have been impossible to follow them with any view of advantage. At fifty-three minutes past eleven, made the signal to pass through the enemy's line, and engage them to leeward. Soon after the signal was made for close action, and repeated by the *Monarch* and *Powerful*; it was kept flying on board the *Venerable* near an hour and a half, when it was shot away. About thirty minutes past twelve, the action commenced by Vice Admiral Onslow, in the *Monarch*, who broke through the enemy's line, passed under the Dutch Vice Admiral's stern, and engaged him to leeward. The *Venerable* intending to engage the Dutch Commander in Chief, was prevented by the *States General*, of 76 guns, bearing a blue flag at the mizen, shooting close up with him; we therefore put our helm aport, run under his stern, engaged him close, and soon forced him to run out of the line. The *Venerable* then fell alongside the Dutch Admiral De Winter, in the *Vryheid*, who was for some time well supported, and kept up a very heavy fire upon us. At one o'clock, the action was pretty general, except by the two or three van ships of the enemy's line, which got off without the smallest apparent injury. About half an hour after the commencement of the action on the part of the *Venerable*, who began only five minutes later than our own Vice Admiral, the *Hercules*, a Dutch ship of 64 guns, caught fire ahead of us; she wore, and drove very near our ship to leeward, while we were engaged, and very roughly handled, by four ships of the enemy. A little before three o'clock, while passing to leeward of the Dutch Admiral and Commander in chief, on the opposite tack, our starboard broadside was fired, which took place [effect?] principally among the rigging, as all her masts came immediately by the board: soon after he struck his colours, all farther opposition being vain and fruitless. Admiral Duncan dispatched the *Rose* cutter with a note to the Secretary of the Admiralty, containing account of his having obtained a victory over the Dutch fleet. During the greatest part of the action, the weather was variable, with showers of rain, till half past two o'clock, when it fell almost calm. On its clearing up, we perceived nine ships of the enemy's line, and one stout frigate, had struck. About four o'clock P.M. Admiral De Winter was brought on board the *Venerable* by Mr. Charles Richardson, first Lieutenant of the *Circe*, in the boat of that frigate, whose signal had been made for that purpose. The *Venerable* wore with the fleet, turning our heads off shore which was not then distant above five miles. Began repairing the rigging, which, with the sails, mast, and yards, had suffered much in the action. The people likewise constantly at the pumps, having received a number of shot-holes below our water line. Made the frigates and undisabled ships signals to take possession of prizes. During the battle, the *Venerable* was gallantly supported by the *Ardent* and *Triumph*, Admiral Duncan's seconds, and afterwards by his Majesty's ship *Powerful*, who had taken her opponent, then run up, and rendered effectual assistance to us, while surrounded by enemies. The *Powerful* and several others showed by their gallant conduct, that they perfectly understood the signal for close action. Could a doubt remain in the minds of any person in the fleet, about the meaning of any signal or manoeuvre, they could not possibly mistake the gallant example of the two English Admirals, and several others, who entered completely into the meaning of the signal No. 34, and immediately pushed through the enemy's line, as the only method of defeating the Dutch fleet in the situation in which they wore. It was perfectly in the power of the whole British fleet to have put signal 34 into execution. The enemy was directly to leeward, and openings to pass through their line in several parts of it; but some of our ships, it is said, did not put No. 34 into execution. Notwithstanding, the 11th of October, 1797, will be remembered with pleasure by our friends, and regretted by our enemies.

The foregoing account is so full that it requires no addition or remark; suffice it, that we briefly state the action commenced between twelve and one o'clock in the afternoon, and after continuing rather more than three hours with unceasing violence, was at last closed by the surrender of nine ships of the line, with two frigates; the remainder, though not without much difficulty, succeeding in effecting their escape.

It has been remarked, and with some truth, that the laconic manner in which the gallant Admiral first announced his success to the Admiralty Board, in no small degree resembled the celebrated letter of Captain Walton, written in consequence of his having attacked, taken, or destroyed, a detachment of the Spanish fleet off Syracuse. "We have taken," said that brave officer, "and destroyed all the Spanish ships and vessels that were upon the coast; the number as per margin. Yours, &c. G. Walton." That which we bring into comparison with it, was to the following purport:

Venerable, off the coast of Holland, the 12th of October, by log (11th) three P.M.
Camperdown E.S.E. eight mile. Wind N. by E.

Sir, I have the pleasure to acquaint you, for the information of the Lords Commissioners of the Admiralty, that at nine o'clock this morning, I got sight of the Dutch fleet; at half past twelve I passed through their line, and the action commenced, which has been very severe. The Admiral's ship is dismasted, and has struck, as have several others, and one on fire. I shall send Captain Fairfax with particulars the moment I can spare him. I am,

ADAM DUNCAN

The Admiral, as a public and proper reward for his very brilliant conduct on the foregoing occasion, was raised by patent bearing date October the thirtieth, to the dignity of a Baron and Viscount of Great Britain, by the titles of Baron Camperdown and Viscount Duncan. The *Venerable* had received so much damage, and had become so leaky, owing to the number of shot she had received in her hull, that she was, with the greatest difficulty, brought into port; and being found unfit for further service, without previously undergoing thorough repair, was, of course, ordered to be dismantled for that purpose. His Lordship, who continued to retain his command, shifted his flag into the *Kent*, a new ship of 74 guns, then just launched. Soon as the ships destined to remain under his orders were refitted, he returned again to his station; and by his continued vigilance, the Dutch trade was almost annihilated: their vessels, whenever any were found hardy enough to attempt putting to sea, were captured in sight of their own ports; for the whole coast was so completely blockaded, that instances very rarely occurred of their being able to elude the extreme vigilance of the British cruisers.

A very singular proof of this fact took place about twelve months after the Camperdown fight; two Dutch frigates, the *Furie*, of 36, and the *Waakzamheid*, of 26 guns, had been lying in the Texel many weeks with troops on board. Eager to seize the first probable opportunity of escape, in order to effect a desultory descent on some part of the British dominions, being at last favoured by a strong eastern gale, which they flattered themselves had blown the English cruisers off their coast, they ventured out to sea on the twenty-third of October, 1798, under cover of a thick fog, but were both captured on the following day, by Captain King, in the *Sirius*. His Lordship continued to retain the same command till the commencement of the present year, but the extreme caution of the enemy prevented him from finding any second opportunity of completing the destruction of the Dutch maritime power; and the surrender of their ships at the Texel, in the month of August, 1799, has, to a certainty, removed to a more remote period, the possibility of acquiring in the same quarter similar honours to those gained off Camperdown.

Heraldic Particulars relative to Lord Viscount Duncan

On the sixth of June, 1777, he married Miss Dundas, daughter of Robert Dundas, Esq. Lord President of the Court of Session in Scotland.

On the twenty-third of December, 1787, his eldest son, Mr. Henry Duncan, died at Edinburgh.

Arms: In the centre of his paternal coat (being Gules, two cinque foils in chief, and a bugle horn in base, stringed Azure), pendant by a ribbon Argent and Azure, from a naval crown Or, a gold medal, thereon two figures, the emblems of Victory and Britannia; Victory alighting on the prow of an antique vessel, crowning Britannia with a wreath of laurel; and below, the word "Camperdown".

Crest: A first rate ship of war, with masts broken, rigging torn and in disorder, floating on the sea, all proper; and over the motto "Disce pati".

Supporters: On the dexter side an Angel, mantle purpure; on the head a celestial crown; the right hand supporting an anchor proper; in the left a hand supporting a staff, thereon hoisted a flag azure; the Dutch colours wreathed about the middle of the staff.

Motto: "Secundis dubiisque rectus."

Royal Thanksgiving
From the 'Biographical Memoir of Sir Henry Trollope, Knt.' ^{XVIII 362-363}

On the 19th of December, 1797, his Majesty and all the royal family, attended by all the officers of state, and both houses of parliament, went in procession to St. Paul's cathedral, to return thanks for the glorious victories which had been achieved, and to deposit the colour which had been taken from the French, on the 1st of June, 1794; from the Spaniards, on the 14th of February, 1797; and from the Dutch, on the 11th of October, in the same year. Sir Henry Trollope was one of the officers who walked in this memorable procession.

1798 – Coastal and Commerce Warfare

DESPITE THE VICTORIES AT Cape St Vincent and Camperdown, the need to counter the danger of invasion was to be a major factor in British defence planning until in 1805 that option was decisively closed for the enemy. At the end of 1797 the government of France again took up the idea of invading Britain, and General Buonaparté, back from Italy, was put in command of the Army of England. He surveyed the embarkation ports and ordered the construction of troop-carrying gunboats, but his advice to Paris was that invasion was impossible without command of the sea.

Captain Sir Home Popham was to play a considerable part in anti-invasion efforts. An account of his attempt in 1778 to destroy the Bruges Canal formed part of *The Naval Chronicle*'s biographical memoir.

The account of Captain Edward Cook's raid on the merchant shipping of the Philippines, and that of Captain John Skinner's defence of the *Princess Royal* against a French privateer, are typical of the stories of the incessant and brutal war on commerce which, by its impact on the capacity of nations to pay for the war, was the basis of sea power.

Raid on the Bruges Canal
From the 'Biographical Memoir of Sir Home Riggs Popham, K.M. and F.R.S.' XVI 273–277

We must now revert to the early part of 1798; at which period government, having received intelligence that the enemy had collected a great number of gun-boats, and transport schuyts, at Flushing, with the view of sending them to Dunkirk and Ostend, by the Bruges canal, formed a plan for destroying the basin gates and sluices. From his intimate acquaintance with the topography of maritime Flanders, where he had for some time resided, and from his well-established reputation for enterprise, Captain Popham was fixed upon for conducting the expedition. Accordingly, the following squadron was ordered to assemble at Margate, and there to take on board a body of about 2000 troops, under the orders of Major-General Coote:

Ships	Guns	Commanders
Expedition	26	Captain H.R. Popham
Circe	28	R. Winthorpe
Vestal	28	Charles White
Ariadne	20	J. Bradby
Champion	20	H. Raper
Hebe	14	W. Brichall
Minerva	14	J. Mackeller
Druid	12	C. Apthorpe
Harpy brig	16	H. Bazeley
Savage	16	N. Thompson
Dart	16	R. Ragget
Kite brig	16	W. Brown
Tartarus bomb-ketch	8	T. Hand
Hecla bomb-ketch	8	J. Oughton
Wolverene gun-vessel	16	L.M. Mortlock
Blazer do.	12	D. Burgess
Tarrier do.		T. Lewen
Vesuve do.	4	W. Elliot
Craish do.	12	B.M. Praed
Boxer do.	12	T. Gilbert
Aurte do.	12	J. Sewer
Asp do.	12	J. Edmonds
Furnace do.	12	M.W. Suckling
Vigilant do.		
Biter do.	12	J.D. de Vitré

This flotilla having been completed, it sailed from the coast of Kent on the 14th of May, but did not appear off Ostend until the morning of the 19th, at which time it cast anchor. The wind soon after shifted to the west, and became so boisterous that Captain Popham and the General entered in to a consultation upon the propriety of standing out to sea, and deferring the debarkation till a more favourable opportunity. At this moment, a vessel was brought alongside of Captain Popham, which had been cut out from the Lighthouse battery by the *Vigilant*; the report from which was, that the force in the garrisons of Ostend, Nieuport, and Bruges, was but slight. On the receipt of this intelligence General Coote proposed to land immediately, even if the surf, which broke with much violence on the shore, should make his retreat doubtful. To this spirited proposal, Captain Popham acceded, and instantly ordered the troops to be landed, without waiting for the regular order of debarkation. Such was the alacrity displayed upon this occasion, that many of them actually reached the shore, under protection of the gun-boats, before they were discovered. It was one o'clock in the morning when the squadron first came to an anchor; by four, a considerable number of the troops was landed; and it was not until a quarter past, that the enemy's batteries opened on the ships. Their fire was immediately returned, in a most spirited manner, by Captain Mortlock of the *Wolverene*, Lieutenant Edmonds of the *Asp*, and Lieutenant Norman of the *Biter*. From the precision with which the *Hecla* and *Tartarus* bombs threw their shells, the town was several times on fire, and the ships in the basin were much damaged. As a feint to cover the operations of bringing up the materials, and of destroying the sluices, a summons was sent to the Commandant of Ostend to surrender the town and its dependencies to His Majesty's forces; to which he returned an answer, that the council of war had unanimously resolved not to surrender the place, until they should have been buried under its ruins.

At length, by five o'clock, the whole of the troops were landed, together with a body of sailors, and all the necessary implements for destroying the sluices, covered by the gunboats.

The fire from the batteries having much damaged the vessels opposed to them, Captain Popham called them off, and directed the *Dart, Harpy*, and *Biter*, to take their stations; but, it being low water, they were incapable of getting sufficiently near to produce much effect. At half-past nine, the *Minerva* transport, which had parted company, joined; but, from the circumstance of the surf running very high, it was impossible for the troops which she had on board to participate in the military operations.

The party which had landed marched directly to the sluice-gates; and, at twenty minutes past ten, a great explosion was seen, which indicated their destruction.

The canal, which it was the object of the assailants to destroy, was a grand national work, which had cost the States of Bruges an immense sum of money, and had taken the labour of five years to complete. The sluice-gates were indeed demolished, and several boats were burnt, but the explosion failed in its intended extent. That failure, however, was by no means attributable to Captain Popham. His activity and skill throughout the affair, reflected on him the highest credit.

The author of the *History of the late War*, in his account of this expedition, states, that "after having thus, as was supposed, rendered the canal of Bruges unserviceable, and prevented, for a time at least, the conveyance of naval or military stores, the Commander in Chief attempted about noon to retreat on board the shipping; but he soon discovered that the wind was so high, and the surf so much increased, that this operation became impracticable. Upon this it was deemed proper to occupy a position upon the sand-hills at a distance from the beach, and, by way of gaining time, the Governor of Ostend was summoned (again) to surrender; but this fate was unhappily reserved for the invaders themselves, as that officer found means in the course of the night to assemble a great force, with which he hemmed in the English early in the morning; and all resistance being in vain, they surrendered after a gallant defence, in the course of which Major-General Coote was wounded - Captain Popham," it is added, "endeavoured without effect to obtain an exchange of prisoners; and it appears at first to have been the intention of the French government to oblige the troops to labour at the reparation of the works they had demolished: but it was soon found, on inspection, that the damage was but trifling, every thing being restored to its former state in the course of a few weeks." [1]

When, in 1790, a treaty had been entered into between Great Britain and Russia, by which the latter was to furnish a certain number of ships and men, for the projected expedition against Holland, Captain Popham was sent to Cronstadt, in the *Nile* lugger,

---

[1] The loss sustained in this expedition amounted to two Midshipmen and eleven seamen killed; three wounded, doing duty on shore: on board the *Wolverene*, one seaman killed, and ten wounded. 23d Regiment - one killed and five wounded. On board the *Asp*, one seaman killed, and Lieutenant Edmonds wounded. In the army, about 60 were killed and wounded. The number taken prisoners, exclusive of Captain McKellar and some seamen belonging to the Navy, amounted to 58 officers, 77 non-commissioned officers, and 999 rank and file.

in the capacity of a British Commissary, to superintend and facilitate the embarkation
of the Russian troops.

Commerce Warfare

*The Late Captain Edward Cooke's Expedition in His Majesty's Frigate La
Sybille, in 1798. (From the Letter of an Officer then on board).* [III 119-122]

On the 4th of January we left Macao, apparently convoying the Europe and Country
Trade; but designedly on a cruise, to reconnoitre the Spanish force in the Phillipines,
and, if possible, cut out from under the batteries of Manilla, the *Rey Carlos*, of 800 tons,
belonging to the Spanish company, and the *Marquesetta*, an Amoy trader, reported to
have on board 500,000 dollars; to attack all their armed dependencies, and annoy them
as much as possible as we passed through the Archipelago.

On the 11th of January we made Luconia, ran along shore, and on the 12th captured
a coaster; took out of her only the cash, 4000 dollars, then liberated the vessel and
people, desiring they would proceed on their voyage, and apprehend no further
molestation. Next day we saw, and could have taken, several vessels of the same
description, and, it is doubtless, equally valuable; but Prudence, which seems to guide
all our operations, would admit no hazard to the grand object for a trivial consideration;
hence this part of the cruise is not so brilliant in number of prizes, nor so lucrative as
some people would have made it; but I think it highly honourable and praise worthy,
particularly as Captain Cooke seemed to feel much the distress that might accrue to
individuals to whom the cash and vessels were consigned, although they were subjects,
and under the banner of our enemies; his lenity is only equaled by good manoeuvres;
and I respect him for his feelings as much as his bravery.

On the 13th, in the evening, we entered the Bay of Manilla, passing their signal-
house on Corregidore, as French frigates, and anchored as necessity made expedient.
Next day stood towards Manilla Town; and by well-conceived, and well-conducted
manoeuvres, captured the following vessels belonging to His Catholic Majesty, without
hurting a single man on either side:

> A gun-boat, No. 31, carrying one thirty-two pounder, four swivels, thirty
> oars, fifty-two officers and men
> A gun-boat, No. 33, carrying one twenty-four Pounder, four swivels, twenty-
> eight oars, fifty officers and men
> A gun-boat, No. 34, carrying one twenty-four pounder, four swivels, thirty
> oars, fifty officers and men
> A guard-boat, rowing twelve oars, with fifteen officers and men
> A felucca, rowing twenty oars, with twenty-three officers and men
> Admiral Don Martin Alaba's barge, rowing twenty oars, with twenty-one
> officers and men

In all - seven boats, about 232 men, 3 great guns, 12 swivels, 27 muskets, 34 cutlasses, 18
half pikes, 13 pistols, 153 round shot, 137 grape shot, and 100 shells.

This was performed in broad day-light, between eleven and three o'clock, in view
of all the people of Manilla and Cavita, and managed with admirable address. The
guard-boat came first, with the second Captain of their frigate, *Maria de Cabega*. The
second boat was Admiral Alaba's barge, with the Governor's nephew. The third boat,
a felucca, with one of Admiral Alaba's Aid-de-Camps, bringing compliments of

congratulation on our arrival, and information that all we could wish, or want, would be ready for us; and that boats were getting ready, with anchors and cables, to assist us into their ports. These officers were so completely deceived, and entertained for an hour and half, that they had no suspicions they were on board an English ship; and, therefore, opened their hearts freely on every subject. While this was transacting in the cabin, the boat's crews were handed into the ship, and our sailors changed clothes with their boatmen, and then rowed up in their boats, in company with our own, and boarded and carried all their gun-boats that were out of the river. The people in the gun-boats finding it impossible to resist the impetuosity of our boarders, surrendered immediately. This being perceived, and thought rather unaccountable on shore, the fourth boat was dispatched with the Captain of the port, for a categorical answer, why the boats were detained; and to say, that if they were not immediately sent on shore, they should conceive us to be enemies. This officer and his crew were handed into the ship, and then they were all entertained with dinner, and their boat's crew with fresh China beef and grog: in this manner we passed an interval of vexatious calm, that left no alternative but this amusement. After this we had an unsuccessful breeze that facilitated discovery, and prevented all further attempts in the bay. From these officers we ascertained the *Rey Carlos* was in the Cavita, and most likely aground there, and that the *Marquesetta* had relanded her money again, in consequence of a suspicious ship appearing off the Islands some days ago (supposed to be the *Resistance*). Hence the most lucrative part of this enterprize was frustrated, but the other was completely accomplished; that is, correct information of their Naval force, viz. *Europa*, of 74 guns; *San Pedro*, of 74; *Montaneger*, of 74; *Maria de Cabega*, of 36; and *Lucia*, of 36; all under equipment at the arsenal, but at that time nearly ready; with a number of gun-boats, all new and coppered, and apparently very well appointed for the intended purpose.

Had the wind been propitious, that we could have kept *incog.* a little longer, I am induced to believe we could have burnt not only their ships of war, but the arsenal, on the night of the 14th January: in short, it is impossible to say what might not have been done, if we could have effected a nocturnal approach. By four o'clock in the afternoon we were discovered to be enemies, so as to cause general alarm round the bay. It was then time to be off, and execute plans laid further to the southward; and, if possible, precede information that we were amongst the Islands. The kind usage to the prisoners while on board, and giving them the guard-boat, barge, and feluccas, to return on shore in, without even obliging their officers to give their paroles; must afford them, and the natives in particular, an high idea of British generosity and at the same time positive contradiction to the doctrine of their Priests and Alcaldies, who have taught them to believe the English to be a very barbarous enemy.

At this season of the year, in the supposed security the Spaniards thought themselves from the monsoons, a very few more such ships, and men, would have taken the place with ease.

On the 15th of January we left the Bay, in company with the three prize gun-boats, one of which was unfortunately lost on the night of the nineteenth, in an hard squall; it is supposed she filled and foundered - there were in her Lieutenant Rutherford of the *Fox*, and Mr. Nicholson, midshipman, from the same ship, and eleven seamen. From hence we coasted Mindora, Panay, Negros, and Majindanas, without our meeting any thing worthy attention, until the 23d, when we arrived off Samboangan; when we were determined to attack the Spaniards; and anchored accordingly off their fort at a quarter past one o'clock, and found them vigilantly upon their guard, ready to repel all our efforts: as soon as the ships and gun-boats were placed, a smart cannonading was kept upon them, which they returned in a well-directed fire upon us. At three o'clock, observing our shot had done their fortifications very little hurt, the landing party was ordered into the boats, to attempt carrying the place by storm and escalade: on approaching the shore, the enemy were perceived in such numbers, and so well armed to contest the landing, and others in ambush ready to annoy and to cut off the retreat, that it was judged imprudent to hazard the attempt; the boats were therefore recalled, the cables cut, and the enterprize given up as impracticable with our little force. in the two hours we engaged the fort, Mr. Standings, Master of the *Sybille* was killed, and one marine; and another wounded, and sixteen seamen and marines; the small spars and rigging of both Ships were much cut, and a great number of shot in each Ship's hull. We anchored about three miles from the fort to repair the damages, and break up the gun-boats, &c, until the 26th, when it seems Captain Cooke's attention was called to China by the convoy that would be ready about the time we could arrive. This not admitting further delay in the Archipelago, particularly as there seemed little to be done but against stone walls, we sailed for Pollock Harbour to complete our water, in performing which we unfortunately lost twelve seamen, who were attacked by the armed Illanos from ambush amongst the Mangroves, who killed two on the spot, and took ten prisoners, which they carried off instantaneously. Every effort was made to recover them without success. Their deserted village was therefore burnt, and every injury done them in our power; we only caught one of the Illanos, who was mortally wounded in being taken. From hence we went to Mindanas, and interested the Sultan as much as possible to recover the unfortunate prisoners, and restore them to some British ship or British Settlement. This he has promised most faithfully to perform, if he can by any means obtain them. From thence we sailed on the 9th February, and arrived in port on 3d of March.

Defence Against a French Privateer
From 'Correspondence.' III 126-128

Extract of a letter from a passenger on board the Princess Royal Packet, Captain John Skinner, during her voyage with the June Mail from Falmouth to America

New York, 25 August 1798
I have at last the pleasure to inform you of my arrival here, the 14th instant, after a very tedious passage: we left Falmouth on the 12th of June, in company with the *Grantham* packet, bound to Jamaica, which kept with us five days. Four days after, on the morning of the 21st of June, we fell in with a French privateer; at five o'clock, she made sail after us; we had light airs and a smooth sea - all sails set. At mid day, we triced up our boarding nettings and made clear for action, with our courses up. The privateer, towards the afternoon, came up with us fast, by the assistance of her sweeps. At seven P.M. our men were all at quarters; she hoisted English colours, firing a shot, which we returned, and she answered by a gun to leeward. At this time, she was within cannon shot, but it growing dark, kept in our wake; and we turned in, not expecting an attack till next morning. However, before day-light, at half past three in the morning, she came within pistol-shot, and fired a broadside of great guns, swivels, &c. which we immediately returned, and kept up a general fire with our cannon and small arms. Our force was only two six-pounders, and four four-pounders; of which six guns we got five on one side to bear on them; we mustered thirty men and boys, exclusive of Captain Skinner

and his Master, besides thirteen passengers and four servants, in all forty-nine. The privateer was a low brig, apparently mounting twelve or fourteen guns, and full of men. Our guns were extremely well plied; a Lieutenant going to join the *St. Alban's* man of war was Captain of one of our six-pounders, and the rest of us passengers plied the small arms with much effect. The engagement continued, without intermission, for two hours, when she out with her sweeps, left off firing, and rowed off, for it was near calm, there not being wind enough to carry us a knot through the water. As she was rowing off, we got our two stern chasers, the six-pounders, to bear upon her, and hit her twice in her counter, which must have gone through and through, for it caused great noise and confusion on board, (and soon after we saw two men at work over her stern.) At six o'clock, being out of cannon-shot, we ceased firing, and set about repairing our damage, she had some swivels fixed on her tops, which would have done us considerable mischief, had they not been drove from them early in the action, which was Captain Skinner's first objective at the beginning of the engagement. Thank God! we had no one killed, most of their shot went above us; the boarding nettings, directly over our quarter-deck, were shot away, as their principal force seemed to aim at the passengers, who plied fourteen muskets to some advantage, and annoyed the privateer much.

Captain Skinner conducted himself well: it was no new business to him; his orders were given coolly, and every thing done with great precision and regularity. I believe you know that he lost his right arm in an engagement on board of a frigate last war.

I cannot omit mentioning, that a Lady (a sister of Captain Skinner) who with her maid were the only female passengers were both employed in the bread-room during the action making up papers for cartridges; for we had not a single four pound cartridge remaining when the action ceased.

Our sails were shot through, rigging very much cut, our spars and boat upon deck shot through, several grape and round shot in our bows and side, and a very large shot (which must have been a nine or twelve pounder) in our counter. The Ship proved a little leaky after the action, but she got pretty tight again before our arrival. Captain Skinner was slightly wounded, but is now well.

In addition to the foregoing extract, we have the following information from a respectable American gentleman (lately arrived from Bourdeaux) who was a prisoner on board this privateer when she engaged the *Princess Royal* packet:

He states her force to have been fourteen long French four-pounders, and two twelve-pounders; that she had eighty-five men on board at the time, of whom two were killed and four wounded in the action. That all her masts were shot through, her stays and rigging very much cut; that when she got to Bourdeaux she was obliged to have new masts, and a complete set of new rigging. They supposed on board the privateer that there was not a single shot fired from the packet that did not take effect; which seems probable; for though so low in the water, she had ninteen shot in her bottom under her wale. At the time, there were on board thirty English and American prisoners. She was so peppered that she certainly would have been made a prize of, could the packet have pursued her; and was so cut to pieces by the action that she afterwards ran from every thing, until she got into Bourdeaux to refit: the shots that raked her as she rowed off went quite through, and caused much confusion,

She is called *L'Aventure* privateer of Bourdeaux, has been running all the war, and done much mischief; so that her not being captured is the more to be regretted: was formerly the American brig *Adventure*, of Baltimore.

1798 – Battle of the Nile

THE BRITISH NAVAL WITHDRAWAL from the Mediterranean had led to Austria seeking peace with France, and it looked as though Naples would have to do so as well. London, in consequence, was eager after Cape St Vincent to return to the theatre, and was especially stimulated to do so by intelligence that a French expeditionary force commanded by General Buonaparté was preparing in Toulon and the ports of northern Italy. Its real objective, unknown in London, was Malta, which Buonaparté captured from the Knights of St John, and Egypt, with a possible ultimate goal of India. Nelson was sent with a small squadron, which was reinforced to fourteen ships, and after a prolonged search, caught up with the French fleet anchored in Aboukir Bay near Alexandria. It was already late in the day, but Nelson attacked immediately, and before dawn had destroyed or captured eleven French ships and two frigates. The scale of his victory was entirely new, and was greeted with wild applause in Naples, and throughout Europe. This battle established Nelson as a national hero, and, suffering from a head wound as he was, the adulation effectively undermined his self discipline.

The Naval Chronicle's lead account of the battle of the Nile was a narrative written by Sir Edward Berry, his flag captain. In his extended piece, Berry described the pursuit of the French, and Nelson's battle planning, before he recorded the details of the action itself. Nelson's service letter to his chief, Earl St Vincent, follows, along with the English and French lines of battle, and the returns of killed and wounded. A year later *The Naval Chronicle* published its biographical memoir of Nelson, which of course included an extended description of the action at the Nile. A review of the book by the Reverend Cooper Willyam, *Swiftsure*'s chaplain, about her voyage in the Mediterranean, was published in 1803. In it was quoted his account of *Swiftsure*'s part in the battle. In 1807 another account was included in Samuel Hood's biographical memoir, and twelve years after the battle appeared the biographical memoir of Thomas Troubridge, in which were inserted several contemporary letters which were now available after the appearance of Clarke and M'Arthur's biography of

Nelson. In the Consolidated Edition, two accounts of the battle written by French officers have been placed next, and the last major entry is the biographical memoir of Thomas Thompson who commanded *Leander* in the battle. The memoir includes an account of her later defeat by the *Genereux*, one of the few French to escape from Aboukir Bay, when taking despatches to London. Shorter entries include a letter Nelson wrote to Fanny Nelson, his wife, describing the dismasting of *Vanguard* during the pursuit, one from the Queen of Naples describing Nelson's triumphal return after the victory, and one from his father expressing the hope that, if victory went too much to Horatio's head, people would forgive him.

Horatio Nelson: "Upon officers going into action, I would have every man believe, I shall only take my chance of being shot by the enemy, but if I do not take that chance, I am certain of being shot by my friends."
To Captain Thomas Bertie, January 4th, 1798. XXVI 10-11

Engagement of the Nile
An Authentic Narrative of the Proceedings of His Majesty's Squadron under the Command of Rear Admiral Sir Horatio Nelson, From its Sailing from Gibraltar to the Conclusion of the Glorious Battle of the Nile. Drawn up from the Minutes of an Officer of Rank in the Squadron [Captain Sir Edward Berry] I 43-60

The glorious victory achieved by Rear-Admiral Sir Horatio Nelson, off the *Mouth of the Nile*, on the 1st and 2nd of *August* last, has received, and must ever continue to receive, the warmest tribute of admiration and applause. It has not only filled every British bosom with the proudest exultation, but foreign nations have participated in our feelings, and have hailed the British conquereor as the hero and saviour of Europe. No naval, or perhaps any other battle, ancient or modern, ever had so much depedant upon its consequences - consequences which have even surpassed the anticipations of the most experienced statesmen and profoundest politicians in Europe; and no battle that ever was fought, was perhaps conducted, in its progress, with so much judgment, or contest, to its issue, with so much ardent and perservering courage.

The account of the general result of this action, even the best historians that shall hereafter record it, will be proud to borrow from the simple and eloquent letter of the admiral himself: but in every transaction of the kind, after the first tumult of national exultation shall have in some degree subsided, a thousand circumstances remain to be supplied for the satisfaction of the enquiring mind, and which are essential to gain a just and perfect impression of the actual merit of the great services which have been performed. The hero, like every other man, is best known and remembered by minute traits of character. Great and brilliant events dazzle and astonish, while the deliberations and turns of mind in a great man, that produce such events, attract our attention, awaken all our admiration, and permanently fix our esteem.

To supply what the British nation have long anxiously wished for, an authentic detail of all the operations of the British squadron, previous to the battle, and of its particular conduct in the grand crisis which ensued, we are happy that we can, through the kindness and indulgence of an officer who bore a most distinguished share in that great event, now present a Narrative, at once minutely circumstantial and studiously accurate.

Narrative

Sir Horatio Nelson had been detached by the Earl St. Vincent into the Mediterranean, with the *Vanguard* of 74 guns, the Rear Admiral's flag ship, the *Orion* and *Alexander* of 74 guns each, the *Emerald* and *Terpsichore* frigates, and *la Bonne Citoyenne* sloop of war.

Nothing material occurred to the squadron from the day it sailed from Gibraltar, which was on the 9th May, till the 22nd, when, being in the Gulph of Lyons, at two A.M. a most violent squall of wind took the *Vanguard*, which carried away her topmasts, and at last her foremast. The other ships experienced the fury of the gale, but not in the same degree as the *Vanguard*, a stronger vein of the tempest having taken that ship. The three line of battle ships lost sight of the frigates on the same day, and at the moment of the misfortune which befel the *Vanguard*, the British squadron was not many leagues distant from the French fleet, under Buonaparte, which had on that very day set sail from Toulon.

The squadron hove up for Sardinia, the *Alexander* taking the *Vanguard* in tow, and the *Orion* looking out a head to endeavor to get a pilot, for the purpose of gaining St. Pierre's Roads.

On the 24th, with very great difficulty we reached that anchorage, where we were in great hopes of meeting with a friendly reception, which our distressed situation seemed to demand from a neutral power; the Governor of St. Pierre, however, had orders from the French not to admit any British ship; but their utmost hostility could not prevent us from anchoring in the Road. - The resources which the British seamen always have within themselves, availed us much upon this occasion. Captain Berry, with the very great assistance received from Sir James Saumarez and Captain Ball, was enabled with great expedition to equip the *Vanguard* with a jury fore mast, jury main and mizzen topmasts, and to fish the bowsprit, which was sprung in many places; and on the 4th day from our anchoring in St. Pierre's Road, we again put to sea with top-gallant yards across.

It is proper here to observe, that altho' the Governor of St. Pierre, in consequence of peremptory orders from the French, denied us a public reception, he yet privately acted in a friendly manner, giving us in an underhand way every assistance in his power.

The Admiral, eager to execute the orders he had received, did not think of sailing to Naples, or any other port where he could have received the most open friendly assistance, in getting the ship properly refitted, which her condition evidently required, but immediately steered for his appointed rendezvous; nor did he ever express the smallest intention of shifting his flag to either of the other ships, which to many officers the peculiar circumstances of his own ship might have seemed to render desirable. - The Admiral and officers of the *Vanguard* indeed had the happiness to find that the ship sailed and worked as well as the other ships, notwithstanding her apparently crippled condition.

The squadron reached the rendezvous on the 4th June, and on the following day was joined by *la Mutine*, Captain Hardy, who was charged with orders to the admiral, and who brought the highly acceptable intelligence, that Captain Troubridge had been detached with ten sail of the line, and a 50 gun ship, to reinforce us. This intelligence was received with universal joy throughout our little squadron; and the admiral observed to Captain Berry, that he would then be a match for any hostile fleet in the Mediterranean, and his only desire would be to encounter one.

June 6. - The squadron was spread, anxiously looking out for the unexpected reinforcements. By a vessel spoke with on that day, we were informed that several sail then in sight, were Spanish ships richly laden; but prize money was not the object of the admiral - all selfish consideration was absorbed in his great mind by that of the honour and interests of his country, and his attention and anxiety were solely engrossed by his desire to meet his promised reinforcement, that he might pursue the enemy, of the sailing of whom from Toulon, he had certain intelligence. The *Alexander* being on the look out, stopped one of those ships; finding she had on board eighty or ninety priests, driven by the French persecutions and cruelties from Rome, he thought it would be an act of humanity to permit her to pursue her voyage; and he accordingly released her, and rejoined the Admiral bringing with him a few volunteers from the Spanish vessel, chiefly Genoese, who were desirous of the honour of serving in the British fleet, expressing at the same time their detestation and resentment at the ill usage which they had experienced from the French.

On the 8th at noon, we had the happiness to discover from the mast head ten sail, and it was not long before we recognized them to be British ships of war, standing upon a wind in close line of battle, with all sails set. Private signals were exchanged, and before sunset the so much wished for junction was formed, an event which was certainly facilitated by the great professional ability, judgment and zeal of Captain Troubridge.

The admiral had received no instructions what course he was now to steer, and no certain information respecting the destination of the enemy's fleet; he was left, therefore, entirely to his own judgment. He had the happiness however, to find, that to the captains of his squadrons he had no necessity to give directions for being in constant readiness for battle. On this point their zeal anticipated his utmost wishes, for the decks of all the ships were kept perfectly clear night and day, and every man was ready to start to his post at a moment's notice. It was a great satisfaction to him, likewise to perceive that the men of all the ships were daily exercised at the great guns and small arms, and that every thing was in the best state of preparation for actual service.

The admiral knew that the enemy had sailed with a N.W. wind, which naturally led him to conclude that their course was up the Mediterranean. He sent *la Mutine* to Cevitta Vechia, and along the Roman coast, to gain intelligence, and steered with the fleet for Corsica, which he reached on the 12th June. Several vessels had been spoken with on the passage thither, but no intelligence whatever was obtained from them. He continued his course on the 13th between Corsica and Elba, and between Pianosa and Elba, through the latter of which passages large ships or fleets had not been accustomed to pass. We made the Roman coast, and were joined by *la Mutine*, without gaining any intelligence, notwithstanding the active exertions of Captain Hardy. The Admiral now determined to steer towards Naples, in the hope of some satisfactory information. It had been reported that the plundering Algiers was the object of the French armament; but the account was too vague to warrant the admiral in implicitly adopting it. We saw Mount Vesuvius on the 16th and detached Captain Troubridge, in *la Mutine*, to obtain what information he could from Sir William Hamilton. He returned with a *report* only, that the enemy had gone towards Malta. The admiral now lamented that even a day had been lost by visiting the bay of Naples, and determined, by the shortest cut, to make the Faro di Messina, which the fleet passed through on the 20th, with a fair wind. The joy with which the Sicilians hailed our squadron, when it was discovered by them

View of the north-west entrance to the straight, or Faro de Messina. Engraved by
Baily, from a drawing by Bennet. ^{Plate 324}

to be British, gave the most sincere satisfaction to every one on board of it. A vast
number of boats came off, and rowed round it with the loudest congratulations, and the
sincerest exultation, as they had been apprehensive that the French fleet was destined
to act against *them* after the capture of Malta. Here we gained intelligence from the
British Consul, that Malta had actually surrendered. We had now hope of being able to
attack the enemy's fleet at Goza, where it was reported they had anchored, and the
admiral immediately formed a plan for that purpose.

We were now steering with a press of sail for Malta, with a fresh breeze at N.W. On
the 22nd of June, *la Mutine*, at day light in the morning, spoke a Genoese brig from
Malta, which gave intelligence that the French had sailed from thence on the 18th, with
a fresh gale at N.W. The admiral was not long in determining what course he should
take, and made signal to bear up and steer to the S.E. with all possible sail. At this time
we had no certain means of ascertaining that the enemy were not bound up the Adriatic.

From the day we bore up, till 29th of June, only three vessels were spoken with, two
of which had come from Alexandria, and had not seen any thing of the enemy's fleet;
the other had come from the Archipelago, and had likewise seen nothing of them. This
day we saw the Pharos tower of Alexandria, and continued nearing the land with a press
of sail, till we had a distinct view of both harbours; and, to our general surprize and
disappointment, we saw not a French ship in either. *La Mutine* communicated with the
Governor of Alexandria, who was as much surprised at seeing a British squadron there,
as he was at the intelligence that a French fleet was probably on its passage thither.

It now became a subject of deep and anxious deliberation with the admiral what
could possibly have been the course of the enemy, and what their ultimate destination.
His anxious and active mind, however, would not permit him to rest a moment in the
same place; he, therefore shaped his course to the northward for the coast of Caramanea,

Fort Ricasole and entrance to the harbour of Valetta, in the island of Malta.
Engraved by Baily, from a drawing by Bennet. ^{Plate 279}

to reach as quickly as possible some quarters where information could most probably be obtained, as well as to supply his ships with water, of which they began to run short.

On the 14th of July we made the coast of Caramanea [Turkey]; steering along the south side of Candia [Crete], carrying a press of sail both night and day with a contrary wind, on the 18th we saw the Island of Sicily, when the admiral determined to enter the port of Syracuse. With this harbour no person on board the fleet was acquainted - but by the skill and judgment of the officers, every ship safely got in, and immediately proceeded to get in water, &ca. with all possible expedition. This was the first opportunity the *Vanguard* had of receiving water on board from the 6th May, so that not only the stock of that ship, but of several others of the squadron, was very nearly exhausted. Although there was no proper or regular watering place, yet the great exertions of the officers and men enabled us to complete this necessary service in five days, and on the 25th the squadron again put to sea.

We received vague accounts while at Syracuse, that the enemy's fleet had not been seen in the Archipelago nor the Adriatic, nor had they gone down the Mediterranean; the conclusion seemed to be, that the coast of Egypt was still the object of their destination, therefore neither our former disappointment, nor the hardships we had endured from the heat of the climate, though we were still to follow an uncertain pursuit, could deter the Admiral from steering to that point where there was a chance of finding the enemy.

Now that it is ascertained by events that Alexandria was the object of the enemy, it may seem strange that they should have been missed by us both in our passage thither and our return to Syracuse; but it appears that the French steered a direct course for

Candia by which they made an angular passage towards Alexandria, whilst we steered a direct course for that place, without making Candia at all, by which we of course very considerably shortened the distance. The smallness of our squadron made it necessary to sail in close order, & therefore the space which it covered was very limited; and as the Admiral had no frigates that he could have detached upon the look out, added to the constant haze of the atmosphere in that climate, our chance of descrying the enemy was very much circumscribed. The distance likewise between Candia and the Barbary coast, about thirty-five leagues, leaves very sufficient space for more than two of the largest fleets to pass without mutual observation, particularly under the circumstance described.

On our return to Syracuse, the circumstance of our steering up to the northward, while the enemy kept a southern course for Alexandria, makes it obvious that our chance of falling in with them was still less than before.

On the 25th July we left Syracuse, still without any positive information respecting the enemy; but it occurred to the admiral, that some authentic intelligence might be obtained in the Morea. We steered for that coast, and made the gulph of Coron [Koroni] on the 28th. Captain Troubridge was again employed on that important service of obtaining intelligence and was dispatched in the *Culloden* into Coron, off which place, by the great exertions of that able officer, the fleet was not detained above three hours. He returned with intelligence from the Turkish Governor, that the enemy had been seen steering to the S.E. from Candia about four weeks before. Captain Troubridge had the peculiar satisfaction of observing during his very hurried visit to Coron, that the inhabitants there entertained the most serious apprehensions from the French armament, and the most perfect detestation against that people.

Upon the information obtained by Captain Troubridge, the admiral determined again to visit Alexandria, and carried all sail steering for that place, which we had the pleasure to descry on the 1st of August at noon; but not as before, it now appeared full of vessels of various kinds! and we soon had the satisfaction of perceiving the French flag flying on board some of the ships. The utmost joy seemed to animate every breast on board the squadron at the sight of the enemy; and the pleasure which the admiral himself felt, was perhaps more heightened than that of any other man, as he had now a certainty by which to regulate his future operations.

The admiral had, and it appeared most justly, the highest opinion of, and placed the firmest reliance on the valour and conduct of every captain in his squadron. It had been his practice during the whole of the cruize, whenever the weather and circumstances would permit, to have his captains on board the *Vanguard*, where he would fully develope to them his own ideas of the different and best modes of attack, and such plans as he proposed to execute upon falling in with the enemy, whatever their position or situation might be by day or by night. There was no possible position in which they could be found that he did not take into his calculation, and for the most advantageous attack of which, he had not digested and arranged the best possible disposition of the force which he commanded. With the masterly ideas of their admiral, therefore, on the subject of naval tactics, every one of the captains of his squadron was most thoroughly acquainted; and upon surveying the situation of the enemy, they could ascertain with precision what were the ideas and intention of their commander, without the aid of any further instructions; by which means signals became almost unnecessary, much time was saved, and the attention of every captain could almost undistractedly be paid to the conduct of his own particular ship, a circumstance upon which, on this occasion, the advantages to the general service were almost incalculable.

It cannot here be thought irrelevant to give some idea of what were the plans which admiral Nelson had formed, and which he explained to his captains with such perspicuity, as to render his ideas their own. To the naval service at least they must prove not only interesting but useful.

Had he fallen in with the French fleet at sea, that he might make the best impression upon any part of it that might appear the most vulnerable, or the most eligible for attack, he divided his force into three sub-squadrons, viz.

Vanguard	*Orion*	*Culloden*
Minotaur	*Goliath*	*Theseus*
Leander	*Majestic*	*Alexander*
Audacious	*Bellerophon*	*Swiftsure*
Defence		
Zealous		

Two of these sub-squadrons were to attack the ships of war, while the third was to pursue the transports, and to sink and destroy as many as it could.

The destination of the French armament was involved in doubt and uncertainty; but it forcibly struck the admiral, that, as it was commanded by the man whom the French had dignified with the title of the "Conqueror of Italy," and as he had with him a very large body of troops, an expedition had been planned, which the land force might execute without the aid of their fleet, should the transports be permitted to make their escape, and reach in safety their place of rendezvous; it therefore became a material consideration with the admiral so to arrange his force, as at once to engage the whole attention of their ships of war, and at the same time materially to annoy and injure their convoy. It will be fully admitted, from the subsequent information which has been received upon the subject, that the ideas of the admiral upon the occasion were perfectly just; and that the plan which he had arranged, was the most likely to frustrate the designs of the enemy.

It is almost unnecessary to explain his projected mode of attack at anchor, as that was minutely and precisely executed in the action which we now come to describe. These plans, however, were formed two months before an opportunity presented itself of executing any of them, and the advantage now was, that they were familiar to the understanding of every captain in the fleet.

It has been already mentioned that we saw the Pharos of Alexandria, at noon, on the first of August. The *Alexander* and *Swiftsure* had been detached a-head on the preceding evening to reconnoiter the ports of Alexandria, while the main body of the squadron kept in the offing. The enemy's fleet was first discovered by the *Zealous*, Captain Hood, who immediately communicated by signal, the number of ships, sixteen, lying at anchor in line of battle in a bay upon the larboard bow, which we afterwards found to be Aboukir Bay. The admiral hauled his wind that instant, a movement which was immediately observed and followed by the whole squadron; and at the same time he recalled the *Alexander* and *Swiftsure*. The wind was at this time N.N.W. and blew what seamen call a top-gallant breeze. It was necessary to take in the royals when we hauled upon a wind.

The admiral made the signal to prepare for battle, and that it was his intention to attack the enemy's van and centre as they lay at anchor, and according to the plan before developed. His idea, in this disposition of his force, was first to secure the victory, and then to make the most of it as circumstances might permit. A bower cable of each ship

Plate 2 gives, what is termed, a bird's eye view of Lord Nelson's action with the
French fleet, in Aboukir Bay, on the 1st of August 1798. ^{Plate 2}

was immediately got out abaft, and bent forward. We continued carrying sail and standing
in for the enemy's fleet in a close line of battle. As all the officers of our squadron were
totally unacquainted with Aboukir bay, each ship kept sounding as she stood in.

The enemy appeared to be moored in a strong and compact line of battle, close in
with the shore, their line describing an obtuse angle in its form, flanked by numberous
gun-boats, four frigates, and a battery of guns and mortars on an island in their van.
This situation of the enemy seemed to secure to them the most decided advantages, as
they had nothing to attend to but their artillery, in their superior skill in the use of
which the French so much prided themselves, and to which indeed their splendid series
of land victories was in general chiefly to be imputed.

The position of the enemy presented the most formidable obstacles; but the admiral
viewed these with the eye of a seaman determined on attack, and it instantly struck his
eager and penetrating mind, *that where there was room for an enemy's ship to swing there
was room for one of ours to anchor*. No further signal was necessary than those which had
already been made. The admiral's designs were as fully known to his whole squadron,
as was his determination to conquer or perish in the attempt.

The Goliath and *Zealous* had the honour to lead inside, and to receive the first fire

Chart of Bay of Aboukir, as illustrating the narrative of Lord Nelson's action, which
was inserted in our first number.
    We waited until a correct Chart of this Bay was in our possession, before we
presented one to our readers that might tend to give a clear idea of the situation of
the English and French fleets, on the first of August.

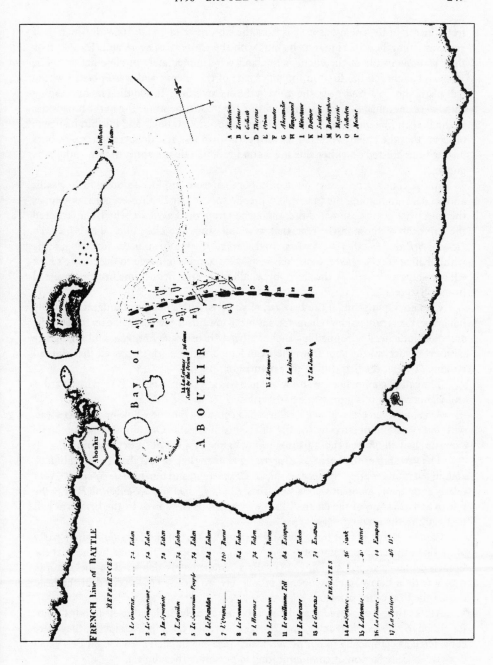

FRENCH Line of BATTLE

REFERENCES

1 Le Conorix. .... 74 Taken
2 Le Conquerant .... 74 Taken
3 La Spartiate .... 74 Taken
4 L'Aquilon .... 74 Taken
5 Le Souverain People .... 74 Taken
6 Le Franklin .... 80 Taken
7 L'Orient. .... 120 Burnt
8 Le Tonnant .... 80 Taken
9 L'Heureux .... 74 Taken
10 Le Timoleon .... 74 Burnt
11 Le Guillaume Tell ... 80 Escaped
12 Le Mercure .... 74 Taken
13 Le Genereux .... 74 Escaped

FRIGATES

14 La Sérieuse .... 36 Sunk
15 L'Artemise .... 40 Burnt
16 La Diane .... 14 Escaped
17 La Justice .... 40 D.º

A Audacious
B Zealous
C Goliah
D Theseus
E Orion
F Leander
G Alexander
H Vanguard
I Minotaur
K Defence
L Swiftsure
M Bellerophon
N Majestic
O Culloden
P Mutine

from the van of the enemy, as well as from the batteries and gun boats with which their van was strengthened. These two ships with the *Orion*, *Audacious* and *Theseus*, took their stations inside of the enemy's line and were immediately in close action. The *Vanguard* anchored the first on the outer side of the enemy, and was opposed within half pistol shot to *le Spartiate*, the third in the enemy's line. In standing in, our leading ships were unavoidably obliged to receive into their bows the whole fire of the broadsides of the French line until they could take their respective stations, and it is but justice to observe, that the enemy received us with great firmness and deliberation, no colours having been hoisted on either side nor a gun fired, till our van ships were within half a gun shot.

At this time the necessary number of our men were employed aloft in furling sails, and on deck, in hauling the braces, &c. preparatory to our casting anchor. As soon as this took place, a most animated fire was opened from the *Vanguard*, which ship covered the approach of those in the rear, that were following in a close line. The *Minotaur*, *Defense*, *Bellerophon*, *Majestic*, *Swiftsure* and *Alexander*, came up in succession, and passing within hail of the *Vanguard*, took their respective stations opposed to the enemy's line. All our ships anchored by the stern, by which means the British line became inverted from van to rear.

Captain Thompson, of the *Leander*, of 50 guns, with a degree of judgment, highly honorable to his professional character, advanced towards the enemy's line on the outside, and most judiciously dropped his anchor athwart hause of *le Franklin*, and raking her with great success, the shot from the Leander's broadside which passed that ship all striking *l'Orient*, the flag ship of the commander in chief.

The action commenced at sun set, which was at 31 min. past six P.M. with an ardor and vigour which it is impossible to describe.

At about seven o'clock total darkness had come on; but the whole hemisphere was, with intervals, illuminated by the fire of the hostile fleets. Our ships, when darkness came on, had all hoisted their distinguishing lights, by a signal from the admiral.

The van ship of the enemy, *le Guerrier*, was dismasted in less than twelve minutes: and, in ten minutes after, the second ship, *le Conquerant*, and the third, *le Spartiate*, very nearly at the same moment were also dismasted. *L'Aquilon* and *le Souverain Peuple*, the fourth and 5th ships of the enemy's line, were taken possession of by the British at half past eight in the evening.

Captain Berry, at that hour, sent Lieutenant Galwey of the *Vanguard* with a party of marines, to take possession of *le Spartiate*, and that officer returned by the boat the French captain's sword, which Captain Berry immediately delivered to the admiral, who was then below in consequence of a severe wound he had received in the head during the heat of the attack.

At this time it appeared that the victory had already declared itself in our favour, for although *l'Orient*, *l'Heureux*, and *Tonnant*, were not taken possession of, they were considered as completely in our power, which pleasing intelligence Captain Berry had likewise the satisfaction of communicating in person to the admiral.

At ten minutes after nine, a fire was observed on board *l'Orient*, the French admiral's ship, which seemed to proceed from the after part of the cabin, and which increased with great rapidity, presently involving the whole of the after part of the ship in flames. This circumstance Captain Berry immediately communicated to the admiral who, though, suffering severely from his wound, came upon deck, where the first consideration that struck his mind was concern for the danger of so many lives, to save as many as possible of whom he ordered Captain Berry to make every practicable exertion. A boat, the only one that could swim, was instantly dispatched from the *Vanguard*, and other ships that were in a condition to do so immediately followed the example, by which means, from the best possible information, the lives of about seventy Frenchmen were saved.

The light thrown by *l'Orient* upon the surrounding objects, enabled us to perceive with more certainty the situation of the two fleets, the colours of both being clearly distinguishable. The cannonading was partially kept up to the leeward of the centre till about ten o'clock, when *l'Orient* blew up with a most tremendous explosion. An awful pause and death like silence for about three minutes ensued, when the wreck of the masts, yards, &ca. &ca. which had been carried to a vast height, fell down into the water, and on board the surrounding ships. A port fire from *l'Orient*, fell into the main royal of the *Alexander*, the fire occasioned by which was however extinguished in about two minutes, by the active exertions of Captain Ball.

After this awful scene, the firing recommenced with the ships to leeward of the centre till twenty minutes past ten, when there was a total cessation of firing for about ten minutes, after which it was revived till about three in the morning, when it again ceased.

After the victory had been secured in the van, such British ships as were in a condition to move, had gone down upon the fresh ships of the enemy.

At five minutes past five in the morning the two rear ships of the enemy, *le Guillaume Tell* and *le Genereux* were the only French ships of the line that had their colours flying.

At fifty-four minutes past five a French frigate *l'Artemise*, fired a broadside and struck her colours; but such was the unwarantable and infamous conduct of the French captain, that after having thus surrendered, he set fire to his ship, and with part his crew, made his escape on shore.

Another of the French frigates, *la Serieuse*, had been sunk by the fire from some of our ships; but as her poop remained above water, her men were saved upon it, and were taken off by our boats in the morning.

The *Bellerophon*, whose masts and cables had been intirely shot away, could not retain her situation abreast of the *l'Orient*, but had drifted out of the line to the lee side of the bay, a little before that ship blew up. The *Audacious* was in the morning detached to her assistance.

At eleven o'clock *le Genereax* and *Guillaume Tell* with the two frigates, *le Justice* and *le Dianne*, cut their cables and stood out to sea, pursued by the *Zealous*, Captain Hood, who, as the admiral himself has stated, handsomely endeavoured to prevent their escape; but as there was no other ship in a condition to support the *Zealous*, she was recalled.

The whole day of the second was employed in securing the French ships that had struck, and which were now completely in our possession, *le Tonnant* and *Timoleon* excepted, as these were both dismasted and consequently could not escape, they were naturally the last of which we thought of taking possession.

On the morning of the third the *Timoleon* was set fire to, and *le Tonnant* had cut her cable and drifted on shore, but that active officer, Captain Miller, of the *Theseus*, soon got her off again, and secured her in the British line.

The British force engaged, consisted of twelve ships of 74 guns, and *Leander*, 50.

From the over anxiety and zeal of Captain Troubridge to get into action, his ship the *Culloden*, in standing in for the van of the enemy's line, unfortunately grounded upon the tail of a shoal running off from the island, on which were the mortar and gun batteries of the enemy; and notwithstanding all the exertions of that able officer and his ship's company, she could not be got off. This unfortunate circumstance was severely felt at the moment by the admiral and all the officers of the squadron; but their feelings were nothing compared to the anxiety and even anguish of mind which the captain of the *Culloden* himself experienced, for so many eventful hours. There was but one consolation that could offer itself to him in the midst of the distresses of his situation, a feeble one it is true - that his ship served as a beacon for three other ships, viz. the *Alexander, Theseus,* and *Leander*, which were advancing with all possible sail set close in his rear, and which otherwise might have experienced a similar misfortune, and thus in a greater proportion still have weakened our force.

It was not till the morning of the 2d, that the *Culloden* could get off, and it was found she had suffered very considerable damage in her bottom; that her rudder was beat off, and the crew could scarcely keep her afloat with all her pumps going.

The resources of Captain Troubridge's mind availed him much, and were admirably exerted upon this trying occasion. In four days he had a new rudder made upon his own deck, which was immediately shipped; and the *Culloden* was again in a state for actual service, though still very leaky.

The admiral, knowing that the wounded of his own ships had been well taken care of, bent his first attention to those of the enemy. He established a truce with the commandant of Aboukir, and through him made a communication to the commandant of Alexandria, that it was his intention to allow all the Frenchmen to be taken ashore to proper hospitals, with their own surgeons to attend them; a proposal which was assented to by the French, and which was carried into effect on the following day.

The activity and generous consideration of Captain Troubridge were again exerted at this time for the general good. He communicated with the shore, and had the address to procure a supply of fresh provisions, onions, &ca. which were served out to the sick and wounded, and which proved of essential utility.

On the 2d the Arabs and Mamlukes, who during the battle had lined the shores of the Bay, saw with transport that the victory was decisively ours, an event in which they participated with an exultation almost equal to our own; and on that and the following nights, the whole coast and country were illuminated as far as we could see, in celebration of our victory. This had a great effect upon the minds of our prisoners, as they conceived that this illumination was the consequence not entirely of our success, but of some signal advantage obtained by the Arabs and Malmelukes over Buonaparte.

Although it is natural to suppose that the time and attention of the admiral, and all the officers of the squadron, were very fully employed in repairing the damages sustained by their own ships, and in securing those of the enemy, which their valour had subdued, yet the mind of that great and good man felt the strongest emotions of the most pious gratitude to the Supreme Being, for the signal success which, by his divine favour, had crowned his endeavours in the cause of his country; and in consequence, on the morning of the 2d, he issued the following memorandum to the different captains of his squadron:

MEM. Vanguard, off the Mouth of the Nile, 2d day of August, 1798
Almighty God having blessed His Majesty's Arms with victory, the admiral intends returning public thanksgiving for the same at two o'clock this day, and he recommends to every ship doing the same as soon as convenient.

To the respective Captains of the Squadron.

At two o'clock accordingly on that day, public service was performed on the quarter deck of the *Vanguard*, by the Reverend Mr. Comyn, the other ships following the example of the admiral, though perhaps not all at the same time.

This solemn act of gratitude to heaven seemed to make a very deep impression upon several of the prisoners, both officers and men, some of the former of whom remarked, "that it was no wonder we could preserve such order and discipline, when we could impress the minds of our men with such sentiments after a victory so great, and at a moment of such seeming confusion."

On the same day the following memorandum was issued to all the ships, expressive of the admiral's sentiments of the noble exertions of the different officers and men of his squadron:

Vanguard, off the mouth of the Nile, 2nd day of August, 1798
The admiral most heartily congratulates the captains, officers, seamen and marines of the squadron he has the honour to command, on the event of the late action; and he desires they will accept his most sincere and cordial thanks for their very gallant behaviour in this glorious battle. It must strike forcibly every British seaman, how superior their conduct is, when in discipline and good order, to the riotous behaviour of lawless Frenchmen.

The squadron may be assured the admiral will not fail with his dispatches, to present their truly meritorious conduct in the strongest terms to the Commander in Chief.
To the Captains of the Ships of the Squadron.

The praise expressed in this memorandum, could not fail to be highly acceptable and gratifying to every individual in the squadron; and the observation which it endeavoured to impress upon the minds of all, of the striking advantages derived from discipline and good order, was so much the effect of recent experience, that every heart immediately assented to its justice.

The benefit of this important truth will not we trust, be confined to any particular branch of the British Navy; the sentiment of the hero of the Nile, must infuse itself into the heart of every British seaman, in whatever quarter of the globe he may be extending the glory and interest of his country, and will there produce the conviction that *courage* alone will not lead him to conquest, without the aid and direction of exact discipline and order. Let those who desire to emulate (as every British seaman must) the glory acquired upon this signal occasion, pursue the same means which principally led to its acquisition. Let them repose the most perfect reliance in the courage, judgment, and skill of their superior officers, and let them aid the designs of these by uniformly submissive obedience and willing subordination - so shall the British navy continue to be the admiration of the world, till time shall be no more!

Immediately after the action, some Maltese, Genoese, and Spaniards who had been serving on board the French fleet, offered their services in ours which were accepted; and they expressed the greatest happiness at thus being freed, as they themselves said, from the tyranny and cruelty of the French.

On the fourth day after the action, Captain Berry of the *Vanguard*, sailed in the *Leander* of 50 guns, with the admiral's dispatches to the commander in chief, Earl St. Vincent, off Cadiz, containing intelligence of the glorious victory which he had obtained.

[Later the editor added:] In the chief commander upon this occasion [Nelson], it is evident that the high gallantry of his spirit is the least striking qualification for the command with which he had so judiciously been invested. To fight and to conquer had been familiar to him; but he was now called upon for the exercise of qualities which raise the true hero above the level of the general mass of mankind, and constitute the character of *a great commander*. These, it has been seen, he not only fully possessed, but most admirably exerted. He pursued to every point in which there seemed the best chance of finding his enemy - he suffered incertitude and disappointment with unshaken firmness; and the delay which occurred in the gratification of his wishes, only added to the heroic feeling from which they arose.

An idea has gone abroad, that the attack in Aboukir Bay was directed by accident. No idea can be more unfounded, or more derogatory to the professional character of the gallant admiral. It is proved from this Narrative, that his mode of attack was the result of deep and deliberate cogitation; and so clearly had he explained himself to those who were to bear their respective shares in the execution of his plans, that when they discovered their enemy, little remained to be done but to commence the premeditated attack.

Nelson's Account of the Loss of Vanguard's Masts
From 'Naval Anecdotes.' XIV 472

The subjoined extract of a letter from Admiral Nelson to his Lady, dated *Vanguard, St. Peter's Island, off Sardinia, May 24, 1798*, is one of the many instances which have been adduced of the religious tendency of the writer's mind. It relates to the storm, in which Admiral Nelson's detached squadron was separated and much damaged, while in quest of the French fleet:

"My Dearest Fanny, I ought not to call what has happened to the *Vanguard* by the cold name of accident; I believe firmly it was the Almighty goodness to check my consummate vanity. I hope it has made me a better officer, as I feel it has made me a better man; I kiss with all humility the rod. Figure to yourself on a Sunday evening, at sun-set, a vain man walking in his cabin, with a squadron around him, who looked up to their Chief to head them to glory, and in whom their Chief placed the firmest reliance, that the proudest ships of equal numbers belonging to France would have lowered their flags; and with a very rich prize lying by him. - Figure to yourself on Monday morning; when the sun rose, this proud conceited man, his Ship dismasted, his fleet dispersed, and himself in such distress that the meanest frigate out of France would have been an unwelcome guest. But it has pleased Almighty God to bring us into a safe port, where, although we are refused the rights of humanity, yet the *Vanguard* will, in two days, get to sea again as an English man of war."

Nelson's Victory Dispatch
From 'The London Gazette Extraordinary,' Tuesday, October 2, 1798. I 62-63

Admiralty Office, October 2, 1798
The Honourable Captain Capel, of his Majesty's sloop *Mutine*, arrived this morning from Rear Admiral Sir Horatio Nelson, K.B. to Evan Nepean, Esq. Secretary of the Admiralty, of which the following are copies: . . .
[Covering letter to Nepean, enclosing:]

Rear-Admiral Nelson to Admiral the Earl of Saint Vincent, Commander in Chief, &c. &c. &c. off Cadiz

Vanguard, off the Mouth of the Nile, Aug. 3, 1798

My Lord, Almighty God has blessed his Majesty's arms in the late battle, by a great victory over the fleet of the enemy, whom I attacked at sun set on the 1st of August off the mouth of the Nile. The enemy were moored in a strong line of battle for defending the entrance of the Bay (of Shoals), flanked by numerous gun-boats, four frigates, and a battery of guns and mortars on an Island in their van; but nothing could withstand the squadron your Lordship did me the honour to place under my command. Their high state of discipline is well known to you, and with the judgment of the captains, together with their valour and that of the officers and men of every description, it was absolutely irresistible.

Could any thing from my pen add to the characters of the captains, I would write it with pleasure, but that is impossible.

I have to regret the loss of Captain Westcott, of the *Majestic*, who was killed early in the action; but the ship was continued to be [sic] so well fought by her first lieutenant Mr. Cuthbert, that I have given him an order to command her till your Lordship's pleasure is known.

The ships of the enemy, all but their two rear ships, are nearly dismasted; and those two, with two frigates, I am sorry to say, made their escape: nor was it, I assure you, in my power to prevent them. Captain Hood most handsomely endeavoured to do it, but I had no ship in a condition to support the *Zealous*, and I was obliged to call her in.

The support and assistance I have received from Captain Berry cannot be sufficiently expressed. I was wounded in the head, and obliged to be carried off the deck, but the service suffered no loss by that event. Captain Berry was fully equal to the important service then going on, and to him I must beg leave to refer you for every information relative to this victory. He will present you with the flag of the Second in Command, that of the Commander in Chief being burnt in the *l'Orient*.

Herewith I transmit you lists of the killed and wounded, and the lines of battle of ourselves and the French.

I have the honour to be, &c

HORATIO NELSON

English Line of Battle

Ships' Names	Captains	Guns	Men
Culloden	T. Troubridge	74	590
Theseus	R.W. Miller	74	590
Alexander	Alexander J. Ball	74	590
Vanguard	Rear-Ad. Sir H. Nelson, K.B.		
	Edward Berry	74	595
Minotaur	Thomas Louis	74	590
Leander	T.B. Thompson	74	590
Swiftsure	B. Hallowell	74	590
Audacious	David Gould	74	590
Defence	John Peyton	74	590
Zealous	Samuel Hood	74	590

Orion	Sir James Saumarez	74	590
Goliath	Thomas Foley	74	590
Majestic	Geo. B. Westcott	74	590
Bellerophon	Henry D.E.Darby	74	590
La Mutine, Brig			

HORATIO NELSON

Vanguard, off the Mouth of the Nile, August 3, 1798.

French Line of Battle

Ships' Names	Captains	Guns	Men	
Le Guerrir		74	600	*Taken*
Le Conquérant		74	700	*Taken*
Le Spartiate		74	700	*Taken*
L'Aquilon		74	700	*Taken*
Le Souverain Peuple		74	700	*Taken*
Le Franklin	Blanket First Contre-Admiral	80	800	*Taken*
L'Orient	Brueys, Admiral and Commander in Chief	120	1010	*Burnt*
Le Tonnant		80	800	*Taken*
L'Heureux		74	700	*Taken*
Le Timoléon		74	700	*Taken*
Le Mercure		74	700	*Taken*
Le Guillaume Tell	Villeneuve Second Contre Amiral	80	800	*Escaped*
Le Généreux		74	700	*Escaped*

HORATIO NELSON

Vanguard, off the Mouth of the Nile, August 3, 1798

Frigates			
La Dianne	48	300	*Escaped*
La Justice	44	300	*Escaped*
L'Artemise	36	250	*Burnt*
La Sérieuse	36	250	*Sunk*

HORATIO NELSON

Vanguard, off the Mouth of the Nile, August 3, 1798

A Return of the Killed and Wounded on board His Majesty's Ships under the Command of Sir Horatio Nelson, K.B. Rear Admiral of the Blue, in Action with the French, at Anchor, on the 1st of August 1798, off the Mouth of the Nile

	Killed			Wounded			
Ships	Off.	S.M.	Mar.	Off.	S.M.	Mar.	Total
Theseus	0	5	0	1	24	5	35
Alexander	1	13	0	5	48	5	72

	Off.	S.M.	Mar.	Off.	S.M.	Mar.	
Vanguard	3	20	7	7	60	8	105
Minotaur	2	18	3	4	54	6	87
Swiftsure	0	7	0	1	19	2	29
Audacious	0	1	0	2	31	2	36
Defence	0	3	1	0	9	2	15
Zealous	0	1	0	0	7	0	8
Orion	1	1	1	5	18	6	42
Goliath	2	12	7	4	28	9	62
Majestic	3	33	14	3	124	16	193
Bellerophon	4	32	13	5	126	17	197
Leander	0	0	0	0	14	0	14
Total	16	156	46	37	562	78	895

Off. *Officers*   S.M. *Seamen*   Mar. *Marines*

Ships' Names	Officers' Names	Rank
Officers Killed		
Vanguard	Taddy [sic], William Faddy	Captain of Marines
	Thomas Seymour	Midshipman
	John G. Taylor	Midshipman
Alexander	John Collins	Lieutenant
Orion	Baird	Captain's Clerk
Goliath	William Davies	Master's Mate
	Andrew Brown	Midshipman
Majestic	George B. Westcott	Captain
	Zebedee Ford	Midshipman
	Andrew Gilmore	Boatswain
Bellerophon	Robert Savage Daniel	Lieutenant
	W. Launder	Lieutenant
	George Joliffe	Lieutenant
	Thomas Ellison	Master's Mate
Minotaur	J.S. Kirchner	Master
	Peter Walters	Master's Mate
Officers Wounded		
Vanguard	N. Vassal	Lieutenant
	J. Adye	Lieutenant
	J. Campbell	Admiral's Secretary
	M. Austin	Boatswain
	J. Weatherston	Midshipman
	George Antrim	Midshipman
Theseus	Hawkins	Lieutenant
Alexander	Alexander J. Ball, esq.	Captain
	J. Cresswell	Captain of Marines
	W. Lawson	Master
	G. Bully	Midshipman
	Luke Anderson	Midshipman
Audacious	John Jeans	Lieutenant
	Christopher Font	Gunner

Orion	Sir James Saumarez	Captain
	Peter Sadler	Boatswain
	Philip Richardson	Midshipman
	Ch. Miell	Midshipman
	Lanfesty	Midshipman
Goliath	William Wilkinson	Lieutenant
	Law. Graves	Midshipman
	P. Strachan	Schoolmaster
	James Payne	Midshipman
Majestic	Charles Seward	Midshipman
	Charles Royle	Midshipman
	Robert Overton	Captain's Clerk
Bellerophon	H.D. Darby, Esq.	Captain
	Ed. Kirby	Master
	John Hopkins	Captain of Marines
	Chapman	Boatswain
	Nicholas Betson	Midshipman
Minotaur	Thomas Irwin	Lieutenant
	John Jewell	Lieutenant of Marines
	Thomas Foxten	Second Master
	March Wills	Midshipman
Swiftsure	William Smith	Midshipman

Later Accounts of the Battle

Nelson's Character

From the 'Biographical memoir of the Right Honourable Lord Nelson.' [III 180-189]

On the nineteenth of December, 1797, the Ship that was intended for Sir Horatio Nelson's flag not being ready, the *Vanguard* was for this purpose commissioned. On the first of April, 1798, he sailed with a convoy from Spithead; but at the back of the Isle of Wight, the wind coming to the westward, he was forced to return to St. Helen's. On the ninth, he again sailed, with a convoy to Lisbon; and on the twenty-ninth of April, joined Earl St. Vincent off Cadiz.

On the thirtieth of April, the day following, Sir Horatio Nelson was detached from Earl St. Vincent,[1] with the *Vanguard*,[2] *Orion*, and *Alexander*, of 74 guns each, the *Emerald* and *Terpsichore* frigates, and *La Bonne Citoyenne* sloop of war; and was afterwards joined by the brave Captain Troubridge of the *Culloden*, with ten sail of the line.

The subsequent actions of this great man's life, are traced in such indelible characters on the hearts of Britons, that they need little from his biographer but the grateful tribute

1 Vol. I. page 43.
2 List of the Officers who served under Rear Admiral Sir Horatio Nelson in the *Vanguard*, at the glorious victory of the Nile: *Captain*: Sir Edward Berry. *Lieutenants*: 1. Edward Galway - wounded; 2. Nathaniel Vassell - wounded; 3. William Standway Parkinson; 4. Henry Compton; 5. J. Adye - wounded; 6. Bladon Capell. Marines: *Captain*: William Faddy - *killed*. *Lieutenants*: 1. Christopher Noble; 2. - Young; 3. Ivey Hare. *Master*: Wales Clod. *Chaplain*: Reverend Mr. Comyn. *Purser*: Alexander Sheppard. *Surgeon*: Michael Jefferson. *Adm. Sec*: Mr. J. Campbell - *wounded*.

of admiration and respect. The interesting narrative of the proceedings of his Majesty's squadron under the gallant Admiral, from its first leaving Gibraltar to the conclusion of the glorious victory of the Nile, August the first, 1798, has been already inserted from the minutes of an officer of rank, who was present. To this some brief observations shall be added; with a correct detail of events subsequent to that glorious and ever memorable day.

> By my hopes –
> This present Enterprise set off his head!
> I do not think a braver gentleman,
> More active, valiant, or more valiant young;
> More daring, or more bold, is now alive
> To grace this latter Age with Noble Deeds!

Shakespear

The consummate judgment, with which the plan of attack was immediately formed and executed by Rear Admiral Nelson, on an enemy's fleet moored in a compact line of battle; protected in the van by a battery, and flanked by four frigates, and many gunboats; was worthy of the great and intrepid mind of this distinguished officer. He deservedly received the most public and eminent praise:[3] his Majesty, in the speech from the throne, styles it – *this great, and brilliant victory!*

The French fleet was first discovered by Captain Samuel Hood of the *Zealous*; the action commenced at sun-set. The *Goliath*, Captain T. Foley, and the *Zealous*, Captain Hood, had the honour to receive the first fire of the enemy. The shores of the Bay of Aboukir were soon lined with spectators, who beheld the approach of the English, and the awful conflict of the hostile fleets, in silent astonishment.

Sir Horatio Nelson, as Rear Admiral of the Blue, carried the blue flag at the mizen; but from a standing order of Sir John Jervis, the Commander in Chief, the squadron wore the white, or St. George's ensign in the action;[4] and it is remarkable, that this occasioned the display of the cross, upon the renowned, and ancient coast of Egypt.

A most animated fire was opened from the *Vanguard*, which ship covered the approach of those in the rear: in a few minutes, every man stationed at the first six guns in the fore-part of the *Vanguard*'s deck, were all down, killed or wounded; and one gun in particular was repeatedly cleared.[5] Sir Horatio Nelson was so entirely resolved to conquer, or to perish in the attempt, that he led into action, with six ensigns or flags, viz. red, white, and blue, flying in different parts of the rigging: he could not even bear to reflect on the possibility of his colours being carried away by a random shot from the enemy.

According to the information we have been able to collect from the officers who were present, it appears, that the flag ship of Admiral Bruyes, *L'Orient*, was certainly subdued before she blew up; and we insert this, as an important fact; it was even the opinion of many, that she had previously struck.

The severe wound which Sir Horatio Nelson received, was supposed to have proceeded from langridge shot, or a piece of iron: the skin of his forehead being cut with it at right angles, hung down over his face. Captain Berry, who happened to stand

3 Debrett's Debates, 1798, vol. vii. pages 4, 51, 60, 65.
4 The St. George's ensign is white, with a red cross; the first quarter bearing the Union.
5 One of the midshipmen that fell in the *Vanguard*, had but just remarked the escapes he had experienced; when a shot came, and cut him in two.

near, caught the Admiral in his arms. It was Sir Horatio's first idea, and that of every one, that he was shot through the head. On being carried into the cockpit, where several of his gallant crew were stretched with their shattered limbs, and mangled wounds the surgeon with great anxiety immediately came to attend on the Admiral. *No*, replied the hero, *I will take my turn with my brave followers!* The agony of his wound increasing, he became convinced that the idea he had long indulged of dying in battle, was now about to be accomplished. He immediately therefore sent for his Chaplain, the Reverend Mr. Comyn, and begged of him to remember him to Lady Nelson; and having signed a commission appointing his friend the brave Hardy, Commander of the *Mutine* brig, to the rank of Post Captain in the *Vanguard*, Admiral Nelson took an affectionate leave of Captain Louis,[6] who had come by his desire on board; and then with the utmost composure resigned himself to death.

When the surgeon came to examine the wound, it evidently appeared that it was not mortal: this joyful intelligence quickly circulated through the ship. As soon as the painful operation of dressing was over, Admiral Nelson immediately sat down, and that very night wrote the celebrated official letter, that appeared in the Gazette.[7] He came on deck just time enough to behold the conflagration of *L'Orient*.

The Bay of Aboukir was covered for a week with the floating bodies of the slain, exhibiting a most painful and horrid spectacle; and though men were continually employed to sink them, many of the bodies, having slipped off the shot, again appeared on the surface. It was a great mercy to our brave countrymen, considering the excessive heat of the weather, that some pestilential disorder did not take place in consequence.

Captain Benjamin Hallowell, of the *Swiftsure*, who had ever been on terms of the most intimate friendship with Sir Horatio Nelson, finding his brother officers eager to outvie each other in sending various presents to the Admiral, that had been made from the wreck of *L'Orient*, actually ordered his carpenter to make a Coffin, solely from the wreck, both as to wood and iron. His orders were punctually obeyed; and one being finished with considerable elegance from the materials of *L'Orient*'s main mast, it was presented to the Admiral with an affectionate and polite letter.[8] Sir Horatio Nelson highly appreciated the present of his brave officer; and for some months had it placed upright in his cabin. At length, by the tears and entreaties of an old servant, the Admiral was prevailed on to allow its being carried below: when he afterwards shifted his flag to the *Foudroyant*, and in expectation of meeting the French fleet, the coffin was carefully conveyed on board; where it now remains, and will probably accompany Lord Nelson to his grave.

The limits of our work only allow us, in the further prosecution of this interesting tack, to give a correct summary of Lord Nelson's life subsequent to his glorious victory of the Nile.

On the twenty-second of September, 1798, he arrived at Naples, and was received as a deliverer by their Majesties and the whole kingdom. December the twelfth, the blockade of Malta took place, which has since continued without intermission: on the twenty-first his Sicilian Majesty, and family, embarked in the *Vanguard*, and were carried

---

6 Vol. I. page 287. - The anecdote inserted at this page, is perfectly correct, except in what relates to a boat being hoisted out from the *Vanguard*. Captain Berry hailed the *Minotaur* as she passed.

7 Vol. I. page 63. beginning with "ALMIGHTY GOD has blessed his Majesty's arms in the late battle, by a great victory," &c.

8 This letter we may probably at some future opportunity lay before our readers.

to Palermo, in Sicily. In March he arranged a plan for taking he Islands in the Bay of Naples, and for supporting the Royalists who were making head in the kingdom: this succeeded in every part. In May he shifted his flag to the *Foudroyant*, being advanced to be Rear Admiral of the Red; and was obliged to be continually on his guard against the French fleet. In June and July, he went to Naples, and, as his Sicilian Majesty was pleased to say, *reconquered his kingdom, and placed him upon his throne*. On the ninth of August Lord Nelson brought his Sicilian Majesty back to Palermo, having been upwards of four weeks on board the *Foudroyant*. On the thirteenth, his Sicilian Majesty presented him with a sword most magnificently enriched with diamonds, conferred on him the title of Duke of Bronti; and annexed to it the feud of Bronti, supposed to be worth 3000l. per annum. On the arrival of the Russian squadron at Naples, Lord Nelson directed Commodore Troubridge to go with the squadron, and closely blockade Civita Vecchia; and to offer the French most favourable conditions if they would evacuate Rome, and Civita Vecchia;[9] which terms the French General Grenier complied with, and they were signed on board the *Culloden*: thus a prophecy made to Lord Nelson on his arrival at Naples was fulfilled, that HE SHOULD TAKE ROME by his ships.

The life of Lord Nelson forcibly illustrates the remark, which he has often been heard to make, *that perseverance in any profession will most probably merit its reward, without the influence of any contingent interest.* The noble Admiral, who had thus attained to such high honours in his profession; may justly say to those, who love the service, and like him have its honour continually at heart - GO! AND DO THOU LIKEWISE!

In whatever light we consider the Character of this illustrious Mariner, its brilliancy dazzles the eye with an endless variety. It shews us what diligence may accomplish, and what indolence has often lost; it gives new energy to the desponding mind, and supplies the persevering with fresh hope. Yet whilst we draw such conclusion we must remark, that LORD NELSON'S SEVEREST TRIAL IS YET TO COME! his present elevation has drawn upon him, the eyes of all men; and those of envy ever wakeful will steadily observe, whether the great Conqueror of the modern hydra, excels the demigod of Greece, by rising superior to the delusive snares of Prosperity.

Like Aristides, and his contemporary the Roman hero Cincinnatus, it is to be hoped, Lord Nelson will give equal proofs of justice, and moderation, when elevated to the highest stations of honour and power, as he did in the various vicissitudes of a perilous profession, and through the trying scenes of adversity. Thus tempering ambition with humility, and firmness with mildness, may the proud wishes of his country be in every respect accomplished:

> Still rising in a Climax, till the last,
> Surpassing all, is not to be surpass'd.

Granville

Lord Nelson's character, and military exploits, may be put on a parallel with those of Agrippa, in a few words: *eminent merit, attended with remarkable modesty.* Like this Roman, he had been victorious in both hemispheres, and with the fleets of France and Spain. Like Agrippa also, Lord Nelson's glory has not been confined to one element. He has triumphed both by sea and land. Agrippa could boast of the splendid trophies of the rostal crown, and the seagreen standard; Lord Nelson can likewise boast of similar honours.[10] The same figure with which Virgil has so beautifully distinguished Agrippa

---

9 A sea-port of Italy, in the patrimony of St. Peter, where the Pope's gallies [sic] were stationed.

in his description of a sea-fight, may be thus rendered and justly applied to Lord Nelson in the battle of the Nile -

> Next with kind gales, the care of every god,
> Nelson leads on his squadron through the flood.
> A *Naval Crown* adorns the warrior's brows,
> And fierce he pours, amid the embattled foes!''

The noble Admiral's humanity in private life has been long felt by the poor of Burnham Thorpe, and its vicinity. His firm and steady attachment to his friends has been not less conspicuous than his benevolence and bounty to the poor, so far as he possessed the means of rendering service. Lord Nelson's character in the humble and private walks of life, like that of his professional one, will excite equal admiration: as Delany said of Swift, "*They will both bear to be reconsidered, and re-examined with the utmost attention; and will always discover new beauties and excellencies, upon every examination. They will bear to be considered as the sun; in which the brightness will hide the blemishes: and whenever petulance, ignorance, pride, malice, malignity, or envy interpose to cloud or sully his fame, I will take upon me to pronounce, that THE ECLIPSE WILL NOT LAST LONG*".

Presents to Lord Nelson for his Services in the Mediterranean, between October the First, 1798, and October the First, 1799

From his King and County, a Peerage of Great Britain, and the Gold Medal.
From the Parliament of Great Britain, for his own life, and two next heirs, per annum, £2000
From the Parliament of Ireland, not exactly known, but supposed to be the same as given Earl St. Vincent, and Lord Duncan, per annum, 1000
From the East India Company, 10,000
From the Turkey Company, a piece of plate of great value.
From Alexander Davidson, Esq. a gold medal.
From the City of London, a sword of great value.
—, to the Captains who served under his orders in the battle of the Nile, a sword.
From the Grand Signior, a diamond aigrette, or Plume of Triumph, valued at, 2000
From the same, a rich pelice, valued at, 1000
From the Grand Signior's mother, a rose, set with diamonds, valued at, 1000.
From the Emperor of Russia, a box, set with diamonds, and a most elegant letter, value, 2500
From the King of the Two Sicilies, a sword richly ornamented with diamonds, and most elegant and kind letter, 5000
Also the Dukedom of Bronti, with an estate, supposed, per annum, 3000
From the King of Sardinia, a box set with diamonds, and a most elegant letter, 1200

10 Refer to Lord Nelson's arms at the end. *Navali rostrata corona.* The Naval Crown bestowed by the ancients, on such as had signalized their valour, in an engagement at sea, was set round with figures like the beaks of ships. The Roman Admirals after their death, had their sepulchres ornamented with sculptured rostral crowns, and festoons of sea-weeds.
11 Parte alia ventis, et Diis Agrippa Secundis,
   Arduus, agmen agens; cui Lelli Insigne superbum,
   Tempora navali fulgent rostrata corona.
                    AEn. lib. viii. I. 682.

From the Island of Zante, a gold headed sword and cane, as an acknowledgment, that had it not been for the battle of the Nile, they could not have been liberated from French cruelty.

From the City of Palermo, a gold box and chain, brought on a silver waiter. Also the freedom of the City of Palermo, which constitutes him a Grandee of Spain.

The family of Nelson has been long resident in the county of Norfolk. His Lordship's grandfather was rector of Hilborough in that county, of which living the Nelsons for many years have been, and still are, the patrons. His father is the Reverend Edmund Nelson, Rector of Burnham Thorpe, and married May 11, 1749, Catherine, daughter of Maurice Suckling, D. D. Rector of Barsham in Suffolk, Woodton in Norfolk, and one of the Prebendaries of Westminster, by whom (who died December 24, 1767) he had issue eight sons and three daughters; three sons and two daughters are now living.

1. Maurice, born May 24, 1753; in the Navy Office; married and no issue.

2. William, in holy orders, Rector of Hilborough; born April 20, 1757; married in November 1786, Sarah, daughter of the Reverend Henry Yonge, of Great Torrington, in Devonshire, cousin to the Right Reverend Philip Yonge (late Bishop of Norwich), and has issue a son and daughter - Charlotte Mary, born September 20, 1787; Horatio, born October 26, 1788.

3. Horatio, the present Peer, born September 29, 1758; married March 11, 1787, Frances Herbert (descended from the Herberts, Earls of Pembroke and Montgomery), daughter and coheir of William Woodward, Esq. Senior Judge of the Island of Nevis, and relict of Josiah Nisbit, M.D. of Nevis aforesaid, by whom she had issue of Josiah, a Captain in the Royal Navy. By Lord Nelson, no issue.

His Lordship is related to the noble families of Walpole, Cholmondely, and Townsend, his mother being the grand daughter of Sir Charles Turner, Bart. of Warham, in the county of Norfolk, and of Mary, daughter of Robert Walpole, Esq. of Houghton, and sister to Sir Robert Walpole, first Earl of Oxford, and to Horatio first Lord Walpole of Wolterton, whose next sister Dorothy was married to Charles, second Viscount Townsend. His maternal ancestors, the Sucklings, have been seated in Woodton, in Norfolk, near three centuries.

Arms: The arms first granted to Lord Nelson, were, Or, a cross flory sable, a bend gules surmounted by another engrailed of the field, charged with three bombs fired proper.

And for the crest, a wreath of the colours, the stern of a Spanish man of war proper, thereon inscribed, "San Josef".

Supporters: On the dexter a sailor, armed with a cutlass and a pair of pistols in his belt proper, the exterior hand supporting a staff, thereon hoisted a Commodore's flag Gules. On the sinister a lion rampant reguardant proper, in his mouth a broken flag-staff, therefrom flowing a Spanish flag, Or and Gules.

Augmentation[12]

Arms: A chief undulated argent, thereon waves of the sea, from which a palm tree issuant between a disabled ship on the dexter, and a ruinous battery on the sinister, all proper.

12 The above augmentation was granted by Royal Sign Manual, dated the fifteenth of November, 1798, and the motto was chosen by his Majesty.

Crest: On a Naval Crown Or, the Chelengk, or plume of triumph, presented to him by the Grand Senior, with the motto, "Palmam qui meruit ferat."

Supporters: In the left hand of the sailor a palm branch, and another in the paw of the lion, both proper, with the addition of a tri-coloured flag and staff in the mouth of the latter.

The following anecdote was forwarded to use by an officer in the action off the Nile, and we believe has not been communicated to the Public. [1 287; XVI 186-187]

On the 1st of August, when the *Vanguard* anchored alongside *Le Spartiate*, she became exposed to the raking fire of *L'Aquilon*, the next ship in the enemy's line; by which the *Vanguard* had between fifty and sixty men disabled in the space of ten minutes. Owing, however, to the gallant and judicious manner, in which Captain Louis took his station ahead of the *Vanguard*, the *Minotaur*, not only effectually relieved her from this distressing situation, but overpowered her opponent. Lord Nelson felt so grateful to Captain Louis for his conduct, on this important occasion, that about nine o'clock, while yet the combat was raging with the utmost fury, and he himself was suffering severely in the cockpit, from the dreadful wound in his head; he sent for his first lieutenant Mr. Capel, and, ordering him to go on board the *Minotaur*, in the jolly boat, desired Captain Louis would come to him; for that he could not have a moment's peace, until he had thanked him for his conduct: adding, *this is the hundredth and twenty-fourth time I have been engaged, but I believe it is now nearly over with me.* The subsequent meeting which took place between the admiral, and Captain Louis, was affecting in the extreme. The latter hung over his bleeding friend in silent sorrow. - "Farewell, dear Louis," said the admiral, "I shall never forget the obligation I am under to you, for your brave and generous conduct; and now, whatever may become of me, my mind is at peace."[13]

Swiftsure's Battle
From 'Naval Literature'. [VIII 226-38; 387-97]

A voyage up the Mediterranean in his Majesty's Ship the Swiftsure, one of the Squadron under the command of Rear-Admiral Sir Horatio Nelson, K.B. now Viscount and Baron Nelson of the Nile, and Duke of Bronte, in Sicily. With a Description of the Battle of the Nile on the 1st of August 1798, and a Detail of Events that occurred subsequent to the Battle, in various Parts of the Mediterranean. By the Reverend Cooper Willyams, A.M. late of Emmanuel College, Cambridge; Vicar of Exning, Suffolk; Chaplain of his Majesty's Ship the Swiftsure; and Domestic Chaplain to the Earl of St. Vincent. 4to. 309 pages, and forty-three plates

We have to thank the author of the agreeable and elegant volume before us, for the pleasure which we have derived from the perusal of his work; and we are glad to find a Chaplain of the Navy employing his leisure to so much advantage as this gentleman has done.[14] In the event of a future war, we hope his example will not want imitators, and

---

13 In the later version a correction is made to the story: instead of Lieutenant Capel going onboard the *Minotaur* Captain Berry hailed her.
14 Our author formerly published an "Account of the Campaign in the West Indies, in 1794."

that the Chaplains of the Navy will become the historiographers of the squadrons to which they may belong. . . .

We proceed to extract, with pleasure, our author's account of the glorious battle of the Nile. The time of the occurrences during the action, he informs us, was corrected from the minutes of Mr. Gamble, Purser of the *Swiftsure*, who was employed in the honourable post of Signal Officer during the combat, and marked the events as they occurred; and further assistance was afforded him by Captain R.W. Miller, of the *Theseus*, so that the accuracy of the account may be very safely relied on.

"At a quarter past three p.m. the Admiral made the signal 'to prepare for battle, and we (in the *Alexander* and *Swiftsure*) had not bore up more than an hour, before we also descried the French fleet at anchor, in a line of battle, in the Bay of Aboukir. Towards them we stood with the enthusiastic ardour of men bent on conquest, and who knew there could be no alternative between that and death. By standing so far in towards Alexandria, we were left far astern. This was at first regarded as a most unfortunate event, but we had reason to think otherwise. At four p.m. the Admiral made the signal to prepare to anchor with springs on the cable, and that it was his intention to engage the van and centre of the enemy. At five the *Alexander* made a signal to the *Swiftsure*, that of standing into danger; and immediately tacked. Captain Hallowell luffed up to avoid the danger, and we had the mortification to perceive that the *Culloden* was aground on a reef of hidden rocks. These rocks extend a considerable way from the island, which forms the north-west point of the Bay of Aboukir. In his eager desire to gain a forward station in the glorious contest, the gallant commander had with crowded sail borne down towards the enemy. No one in the fleet had the least knowledge of the bay; nor was any known chart of it existing, except an ill drawn plan found on board the vessel captured on the 29th of June, which had been presented to the Admiral, but from that nothing certain could be made out. Captain Troubridge had kept constantly sounding as he proceeded, and, just before he struck, had found ten fathoms of water; before the lead could again be hove, the *Culloden* was fast aground on the rocks. Warned by his disaster, several other ships, standing into the same danger, were preserved from a similar fate. The evening was now closing in, the bay quite unknown, and the enemy ready to receive us, drawn up in a close line from north-east to south-west, forming an obtuse angle at the centre. . . .

The *Alexander* and *Swiftsure* now came in for their share of glory. Having been (as I before observed) prevented assisting at the commencement of the battle, by bearing down to reconnoitre Alexandria, and afterwards being obliged to alter course, to avoid the shoal that had proved so fatal to the *Culloden*, it was eight o'clock before they came into action, and total darkness had enveloped the combatants for some time, which was dispelled only by the frequent flashes from their guns; the volumes of smoke now rolling down the line from the fierce fire of those engaged to windward, rendered it extremely difficult for the rest of the British ships who came in last to take their station: it was scarcely possible to distinguish friend from foe. To remedy this evil, Admiral Nelson directed his fleet to hoist four lights horizontally at the mizen-peak as soon as it was dark. The *Swiftsure* was bearing down under a press of sail, and had already got within range of the enemy's guns, when Captain Hallowell perceived a ship standing out of action under her fore-sail and fore-top-sail, having no lights displayed. Supposing that she was an enemy, he felt inclined to fire into her; but as that would have broken the plan he had laid down for his conduct, he desisted: and happy it was that he did so; for we afterwards found the ship in question was the *Bellerophon*,[15] which had sustained such serious damage from the overwhelming fire of the French Admiral's enormous ship *L'Orient*, that Captain Darby found it was necessary for him to fall out of action, himself being wounded, two lieutenants killed, and near two hundred men killed and wounded.[16] His remaining mast falling soon after, and in its fall killing seven officers and men, (among the former was another of his lieutenants,) he was never able to regain his station. At three minutes past eight o'clock the *Swiftsure* anchored, taking the place that had before been occupied by the *Bellerophon*; and two minutes after began a steady and well directed fire on the quarter of the *Franklin* and bows of *L'Orient*. At the same instant the *Alexander* passed under the stern of the French Admiral, and anchored withinside on his larboard quarter, raking him and keeping up a severe fire of musketry on his decks. . . ."

Zealous's Battle
From the 'Biographical Memoir of Commodore Sir Samuel Hood, K.B. and K.S.F.' XVII 20-23

In 1798, Captain Hood was employed in blockading the port of Roch[e]fort. He was recalled from this station, for the purpose, it was said, of commanding a secret and remote expedition; and was only waiting to be relieved by Captain Keats, when some of the enemy's frigates, attempting to escape by night, afforded him another opportunity to displaying his vigilance and skill, in preventing the accomplishment of their object.

Instead, however, of being appointed to the command of an expedition, Captain Hood, in the *Zealous*, (with Sir Thomas Troubridge, in the *Culloden*, and nine other ships,) was dispatched to reinforce the squadron of Lord Nelson.

On the memorable 1st of August, 1798, Captain Hood, having the look-out, first discovered the French fleet in the Bay of Aboukir, and was ordered, by signal, to reconnoitre their position. When Admiral Nelson, about six in the evening, arrived off the Bay of Shoals, he hove to, and hailed Captain Hood, to ask him, "*What he thought of attacking the enemy that night?*" His answer was, "*We have now eleven fathoms water; and, if the Admiral will give me leave, I will lead in, making known my soundings by signal, and bring the van ship of the enemy to action.*" Late as it was, the firmness of this answer decided the Admiral, who said, "*Go on, and I wish you success.*" During this conversation, the *Goliath* passed, and took the lead, which she kept; but, not bringing up alongside the first ship, went on to engage the second. On this, Captain Hood exclaimed to his officers: "*Thank God! my friend Foley has left me the van ship.*" He soon after took such a position on the bow of *le Guerrier*, the ship in question, as to shoot away all her masts,

---

15 Captain Hallowell being aware of the difficulty of breaking men off from their guns when once they have begun to use them, determined not to suffer a shot to be fired on board the *Swiftsure*, till the sails were all clued up, and the ship anchored in her station. As the British fleet bore down towards the scene of action, they were first saluted by a shower of shot and shells, from two batteries on the island, and were then obliged to receive the whole fire from the broadsides of the French line full into their bows. The men being employed aloft in furling sails, and below hauling the braces, ranging the cables, and preparing every thing for placing the ships in the best situation at anchor, it is a providential circumstance that greater slaughter was not the consequence; especially, as it is but justice to observe, that the French received us with cool deliberate courage, and did not open their fire till we were within half-gun-shot distance of them, when both sides hoisted their colours. A shot striking the larboard bow of the *Swiftsure* several feet below the water mark, was a considerable annoyance; the chain-pumps were obliged to be kept constantly at work, nor could the leak be kept completely under; she had four feet water in the hold from the commencement to the end of the action.

16 The lights which had been hoisted, must have gone overboard when the mizen-mast fell.

and effect her capture, in twelve minutes from the time that the *Zealous* commenced her fire. This was achieved without the loss of a man, or the slightest injury to Captain Hood's ship.

The *Zealous* afterwards engaged, alone, the four French ships which escaped,[17] until called off by signal. The total loss which she sustained in the conflict amounted to only one seaman killed, and seven wounded.

For the service which Captain Hood rendered, in this glorious and important engagement, he was subsequently honoured with the thanks of Parliament; and was also presented with a sword by the City of London.

After the victory of Aboukir, Admiral Nelson proceeded to Naples, and left Captain Hood with the command of the following squadron, on the coast of Egypt:

Ships	Guns	Commanders
Zealous	74	Captain Samuel Hood
Goliath[18]	74	Thomas Foley
Swiftsure	74	Benjamin Hallowell
Emerald	36	T.M. Waller
Alcmene	32	George Hope
Fortune, polacre	18	
Bonne Citoyenne	20	
Seahorse[19]	38	Ed. J. Foote
La Torride, advice boat		
La Legere, ditto		

With this force, Captain Hood kept the port of Alexandria closely blockaded. He also contributed, in a material degree, to the interests of this country, by his amicable communications with all the Pachas and Governors under the Grand Seignior; and particularly with Jezzar, Pacha of Acre, whose friendship he succeeded in acquiring.

While on this station, Captain Hood took, and destroyed, upwards of thirty of the neutral transports, which had carried the enemy's troops to Egypt; and, as an honourary reward for his services, was presented, by the Grand Seignior, with a handsome snuff-box, set with diamonds.

In the month of February, 1799, he joined Lord Nelson at Palermo, and was employed in reducing His Sicilian Majesty's subjects to obedience, and in driving the French out of the kingdom of Naples. At Salerno,[20] with only forty marines belonging to the *Zealous*, Captain Hood kept in check a force of 3000 men, who were attacking that place, until the few Neapolitans that had taken up arms had time to escape. The enemy attempted to surround the little band of Neapolitan royalists; but, favoured by the exertions of Captain Hood, they had the good fortune to effect a retreat, with the loss of only two killed, nine wounded, and six prisoners. Twice also Captain Hood drove the French out of Salerno, by the fire from the *Zealous*.

Captain Hood was afterwards employed on shore at Naples, in taking charge of

17 *Le Guilliaume Tell*, of 80 guns; *le Genereux*, 74; *la Diane*, 48; and *la Justice*, 44.
18 Returned to join the fleet under Admiral Nelson.
19 Joined afterwards.
20 Salerno is a sea-port town of Italy, in the kingdom of Naples, and capital of the province of Principato Citra. It has a good harbour, fortified, and defended by a castle. It is situated at the distance of twenty-six miles, E.S.E. from Naples.

Castel Nuovo;²¹ and kept the city perfectly quiet, during the siege of St. Elmo,²² and of Capua,²³ until the period of their reduction. His Sicilian Majesty acknowledged these services, by presenting him with a snuff-box, enriched with diamonds; and at the same time conferring on him the rank of Commander of the Order of St. Ferdinand and of Merit.

This honour was confirmed to Captain Hood, by his own Sovereign's royal license and permission.

Troubridge's Frustration
From the 'Memoir of the Public Services of the Late Sir Thomas Troubridge, Bart.' XXIII 17-28

Sir Horatio Nelson, as may more fully be seen, by referring to the earlier volumes of our Chronicle,²⁴ had been for some time unsuccessfully employed in quest of the French squadron, which had sailed from Toulon with Buonaparte. Captain Troubridge joined him at sun-set, on the 8th of June. Without any other information, than that the enemy had sailed with a north-west wind, which induced him to conclude that his course had been up the Mediterranean, Admiral Nelson now set la Mutine to Civita Vecchia, and along the Roman coast, to gain intelligence, and proceeded with the fleet to Corsica, where it arrived on the 12th, and, on the 13th, was rejoined by la Mutine, the commander of which had been unable to obtain any information respecting the French. The admiral then sailed for Naples; and, on the 16th, when in sight of Mount Vesuvius, he sent Captain Troubridge in la Mutine, to communicate with Sir William Hamilton and General Action. Sir William, who had previously corresponded with Admiral Nelson, thus wrote to him, by Captain Troubridge, on the following day:

"My Dear Nelson, I have just received your letter from Captain Troubridge; I went with him directly to General Action, and Captain Troubridge has an order to the commanders of all the Sicilian ports, that will fully answer your purpose. The official answer of the Marquis de Gallo, Secretary of State for Foreign Affairs, to my written demand for the King's ships to be admitted into all the ports of the Two Sicilies, without any limitation, and there provide themselves with provisions and stores, of which I have given a copy to Captain Troubridge, will show you on what grounds we stand here at this moment. It is very tantalizing to see, as we do, your ships at a distance, and to have no communication with you; but we hope in God soon to see you in this bay with the Sans Culotte, &c. and that Buonaparte, with all his Sçavants and Astronomers [sic]. Adieu, my brave dear friend."²⁵

21 Castel Nuovo was taken possession of on the 26th of June, the French having previously evacuated the City of Naples. This is one of the five castles which protected the city. It has a communication with the royal palace, and on one side is contiguous to the sea. Its arsenal formerly contained 50,000 complete stand of arms.

22 The French, when they evacuated Naples, retained possession of the fort of St. Elmo, or St. Eramo, which is hewn out of a rock, towards the west of the city. Its subterraneous works are wide, lofty, and bomb-proof; and it has eight reservoirs of water. The harbour is spacious, with a canal and a mole nearly 500 paces in length; and, on the whole, it is a place of great strength. On the present occasion, it held out eight days, during which time our heavy batteries were advanced within 130 yards of the ditch. Sir Thomas Troubridge, assisted first by Captain Ball, and afterwards by Captain (now Admiral) Hallowell, commanded the forces which were landed from the English squadron.

23 Capua is situated fifteen miles north of Naples.

24 Vide Vol. I page 44; and Vol. III page 131.

25 Vide Clarke and M'Arthur's Life of Nelson.

After the receipt of the above letter, Admiral Nelson took the nearest cut to Malta, which, he had the mortification to find, had surrendered to the French. He then sailed to Alexandria; after which, not finding the enemy, he shaped his course for the coast of Caramania, steered along the south side of Candia, made the island of Sicily on the 18th of July, and entered the port of Syracuse. Having watered, he sailed thence on the 25th; and, still under the prepossession that a descent upon Egypt was the object of the French, he steered for the Morea, where he thought it probable that some authentic information might be obtained. On the 25th, the fleet being off the Gulf of Coron, Captain Troubridge was despatched in the *Culloden*, to collect what intelligence he could from the Turkish governor. Without detaining the squadron, he returned in a few hours, with a French brig prize in tow, with the information, that the enemy had been seen steering to the S.E. from Candia about four weeks before. This determined the admiral once more to visit Alexandria, which he accordingly reached, at noon, on the 1st of August, and discovered that the harbours were full of shipping, which proved to be the long-sought-for French fleet. The result is well known.[26] In happened most unfortunately for Captain Troubridge, that his ship, the *Culloden*, in standing in for the van of the enemy's line, grounded upon the tail of a shoal, running off from the island, on which were the mortar and gun-batteries of the enemy; and, notwithstanding all the efforts of her gallant commander and crew, she could not be got off till the morning of the 2d of August; when it was found that she had suffered considerable damage, and that she could scarcely be kept afloat, with all pumps going. Captain Troubridge, in a letter to Earl St. Vincent, dated August 16, 1798, thus relates the particulars of this unfortunate event:

"Your lordship will have heard by Sir H. Nelson's letters, and Captain Berry, of the misfortune that befell the *Culloden* just as I got within gunshot of the enemy. As we had no knowledge of the place, and the soundings continuing regular as we stood in, I did not conceive the smallest danger; the man at the head calling out eleven fathom when she struck. The only consolation I have to support me in this cruel case is, that I had just time to make the signal to the *Swiftsure*, and *Alexander*, which saved them, or they must inevitably have been lost, as they would have been further on the reef from their hauling considerably within me. Every exertion in my power was used to save his Majesty's ship; but it was long doubtful whether I should be able to keep her afloat after I had got her off; the rudder was gone, and she was making seven feet water an hour. However, by great labour, on the third day we got a new rudder made and hung, and with thrummed sails reduced the leak considerably. The false keel is gone, and probably part of the main, as she struck very hard for nine hours with a heavy swell. All the gripe I can see is off. I shall use every exertion to patch the poor *Culloden* up again, and I flatter myself I can still fight a good battle in her, if opportunity offers. . . ."

The generous sympathy of the hero of the Nile is well depicted in the following passage, from the work to which, in the composition of this memoir, we are so much indebted.[27] It also serves to shew the high estimation in which Captain Troubridge was deservedly holden by his admiral:

"In the first interview which Nelson had with his early shipmate and friend, Captain Troubridge, after the action, he thus endeavoured to cheer the mortified spirit of that

---

26 A note in the First Edition lists the various documents published in its volumes on the Battle of the Nile, most of which have been reproduced in this chapter.
27 Clarke and M'Arthur's *Life of Nelson*.

great and intrepid officer: 'Let us, my dear Troubridge, rather rejoice that the ship which got on shore was commanded by an officer, whose character is so thoroughly established in the service as your own.' "

The unfortunate circumstance of the *Culloden* getting on shore, proved, however, a source of much subsequent uneasiness and vexation to her commander. In common with the other officers concerned in the action, Captain Troubridge received the thanks of both Houses of Parliament; and also the gold medal, presented by his Majesty on the occasion; but it appears, by the following letter from Lord Spencer to Lord Nelson, that, respecting the latter honourary token, there was some difficulty:

Admiralty, December 25, 1799
I am happy to find that the *Culloden* was capable of being continued in service, as I well know the value you so deservedly set on Captain Troubridge's assistance. In the strict execution of the King's orders, respecting the medals to be given on occasion of the battle of the Nile, Captain Troubridge, not having actually been in action, would have been excluded; but I am very happy to tell you, that I have been expressly authorized by his Majesty to present him with a medal, as well as all the other captains in the line on that day, for his services, both before and since, and for the great and wonderful exertions he made at the time of the action, in saving and getting off his ship.[28]

A more serious difficulty, though not immediately relating to Captain Troubridge, arose from the *Culloden*'s going on shore. The first lieutenants of all the line-of-battle ships *engaged* were promoted to the rank of master and commander; but, from the accident of the *Culloden*, she was not actually in the engagement, and her first lieutenant was consequently, by the etiquette of the service, excluded from the promotion. On this mortifying subject, Lord Nelson, after his return from Leghorn, where Captain Troubridge had also been actively employed, thus urgently expressed himself, in a private letter to Earl St. Vincent:

"I received yesterday a private letter from Lord Spencer, of October 7, declaring that the first lieutenants of all the ships *engaged* would be promoted. I sincerely hope this is not intended to exclude the first lieutenant of the *Culloden*; for heaven's sake, for my sake, if it be so, get it altered. Our dear friend Troubridge has endured enough, his sufferings were in every respect more than any of us; he deserves every reward which a grateful country can bestow on the most meritorious sea officer of his standing in the service. I have felt his worth every hour of my command; and had before written to you my dear lord on this subject, therefore I place Troubridge in your hands."

The liberal-minded interference of the commander-in-chief (Earl St. Vincent) on this occasion, appears, from the following passage in a letter of Lord Spencer to Lord St. Vincent, dated October 9, 1798, to have ultimately led to the most satisfactory result:

"The exception of the first lieutenant of the *Culloden* was necessary, on account of that ship not having got into action from the circumstance of being aground; I am,

28 Clarke and M'Arthur's *Life of Nelson.* The resources of Captain Troubridge's mind availed him much, and were admirably exerted upon this trying occasion. In four days he had a new rudder made upon his own deck, which was immediately shipped; and the *Culloden* was again in a state for actual service, though still very leaky. . . . The activity and generous consideration of Captain Troubridge were again exerted at this time for the general good. He communicated with the shore; and had the address to procure a supply of fresh provisions, onions, &c. which were served out to the sick and wounded, and which proved of essential utility. *Vide Naval Chronicle* Vol. i page 58.

however, so fully convinced of the merit both of Captain Troubridge and his officers on all occasions, that I beg you would be so good as to give the first vacancy of commander that arises, to the first lieutenant of the *Culloden*."

[For his services to the Neapolitan Crown following the battle of the Nile, Troubridge was presented with the Sicilian order of St. Ferdinand and of Merit, and on 23 November 1799 he was created a Baronet of Great Britain. He was promoted Rear-Admiral of the Blue on 23 April 1804, but was presumed drowned when the *Blenheim* was struck by a hurricane in March 1807 off Mauritius.]

Two French Accounts of the Battle. I 149-154; III 192-195

Account of the Engagement off the Nile by a French Officer
The following very curious and original Paper was communicated to us from the most respectable authority. It was written in French on board the Alexander, on her passage to Naples, by Monsieur C-2, Adjutant-general to Admiral Blanquett

The 1st of August 1798, wind W.N.W. light breezes and fair weather, the second division of the fleet sent a party of men on shore to dig wells, every ship in the fleet sent twenty-five men to protect the workmen from the continual attacks of the Bedouins and vagabonds of the country. At two o'clock P.M. the *Heureux* made the signal for twelve sail W.S.W. which we could easily distinguish from the mast-heads to be ships of war. The signal was then made for all the boats, workmen, and guards to repair on board their ships, which was only obeyed by a small number. At three o'clock the Admiral, not having any doubt but that the ships in sight were the enemy, ordered the hammocks to be stowed for action, and directed *L'Alerte* and *Ruillier* brigs of war to reconnoitre the enemy, which we soon perceived were steering for Bequier Bay, under a crowd of canvass, but without observing any order of sailing. At four o'clock, we saw over the fort of Aboukir two ships apparently waiting to join the squadron:[29] without doubt they had been sent to look into the port of Alexandria. We likewise saw a brig with the twelve ships, so that they were now fourteen sail of the line and a brig. *L'Alerte* then began to put the Admiral's orders into execution, viz. "To stand towards the enemy until nearly within gun-shot, and then to manoeuvre and endeavour to draw them towards the outer shoal lying off the island," but the English Admiral, without doubt, had experienced pilots on board, as he did not pay any attention to the brigs tract [track?], but allowed her to go away, hawling well round all the dangers. At this time a small boat dispatched from Alexandria to Rosetta, voluntarily bore down the English brig, which took possession of her, notwithstanding the repeated efforts of *L'Alerte* to prevent it, by firing a great many shot at the boat. At five o'clock the enemy came to the wind in succession; this manoeuvre convinced us that they intended attacking us that evening. The Admiral got the top gallant yards across, but soon after made the signal that he had not seamen enough to engage under sail (for he wanted at least 200 good seamen for each ship). After this signal each ship *ought* to have sent a stream cable to the ship astern of her, and to have made a hawser fast to the cable about twenty fathoms in the water, and passed the opposite side to that intended as a spring; *this was not generally executed.* Orders were then given to let go another bower anchor, and the broadsides of

29 *Alexander, Swiftsure.*

the ships were brought to bear upon the enemy, having the ships head S.E. from the island of Bequier, forming a line about 1300 fathoms N.W. and S.E. distant from each other eighty fathoms, and with an anchor out S.S.E. At a quarter past five, one of the enemy's ships.[30] that was steering to get to windward of the headmost of the line ran on the reef E.N.E. of the island;[31] she had immediate assistance from the brig and got afloat in the morning. The battery on the island opened fire on the enemy, and their shells fell ahead of the second ship in the line. At half past five the headmost ships of our line, being within gun-shot of the English, the Admiral made the signal to engage, which was not obeyed till the enemy was within pistol-shot and just doubling us. The action then became very warm; the *Conquerant* began to fire, then *Le Guerrier, Le Spartiate, L'Aquilon, Le Peuple Souverain,* and *Le Franklin.* At six o'clock the *Serieuse* frigate the *Hercule* bomb cut their cables, and got under way to avoid the enemy's fire: they got on shore; and *Serieuse* caught fire and had part of her masts burnt. The *Artimise* was obliged to get under way, and likewise got on shore. The two frigates sent their ships companies on board the different line of battle ships. The sloops of war, two bombs, and several transports that were with the fleet were more successful, as they got under weigh and reached the anchorage under the protection of the fort of Aboukir. All the van were attacked on both sides by the enemy, who ranged close along our line. They had each an anchor out astern which facilitated their motions, and enabled them to place themselves in the most advantageous position at a quarter past six. The *Franklin* opened her fire upon the enemy from the starboard side; at three quarters past six she was engaged on both sides. the *L'Orient* at this time began firing from her starboard guns, and at seven the *Tonnant* opened her fire. All the ships from the *Guerrier* to the *Tonnant* were now engaged against a superior force; this only redoubled the ardour of the French who kept up a very heavy fire. At eight o'clock at night the ship which was engaging the *L'Orient* on the starboard quarter,[32] notwithstanding her advantageous position, was dismasted, and so roughly treated that she cut her cables and drove farther from the line. This event gave the *Franklin* hopes that *L'Orient* would now be able to assist her, by attacking one of the ships opposed to her, but at this very moment the two ships that had been observed a stern of the fleet, and were quite fresh, steered right for the centre;[33] one of them anchored on *L'Orient*'s starboard bow, and the other cut the line astern of *L'Orient,* and anchored on her larboard quarter. The action in this place then became extremely warm. Admiral de Brueys, who at this time had been slightly wounded in the head and arm, very soon received a shot in the belly, which almost cut him in two. He desired not to be carried below, but to be left to die on deck. He only lived a quarter of an hour. Rear Admiral Blanquett, as well as his aid de camp, were unacquainted with this melancholy event until the action was nearly over. Admiral Blanquett received a severe wound in the face, which knocked him down: he was carried off the deck senseless. At a quarter past eight o'clock the *Peuple Souverain* drove to leeward of the line, and anchored a cable's length abreast of *L'Orient*; it was not known what unfortunate event occasioned this. The vacant space she made placed the *Franklin* in a more unfortunate position, and it became very critical from the manoeuvre of one of the enemy's fresh ships, which had been to the assistance of the ship on the shore:[34]

30 *Culloden.*
31 See Plate II. No. 1.
32 *Bellerophon.*
33 *Alexander, Swiftsure.*
34 *Leander.*

she anchored athwart the *Franklin*'s bows, and commenced a very heavy raking fire. Notwithstanding the dreadful situation of the ships in the centre, they continually kept up a very heavy fire. At half past eight o'clock the action was general from the *Guerrier* to the *Mercure*. The Admiral de Bruey's death, and the severe wounds of Admiral Blanquett, must have deeply affected the people who fought under them, but it added to their ardour for revenge, and the action continued on both sides with great obstinacy. At nine o'clock the ships in the van slacked their fire, and soon after totally ceased, and with infinite sorrow, we supposed they had surrendered. They were dismasted very soon after the action began, and so much damaged that it is to be presumed that they could not hold out any longer against an enemy superior by an advantageous position in placing several ships against one. At a quarter past nine o'clock the *L'Orient* caught fire in the cabin; it soon afterwards broke out upon the poop; every effort was made to extinguish it, but without effect, and very soon it was so considerable that there was no hopes [sic] of saving the ship. At half past nine, Citoyen Gillet, Capitaine de Pavillon of the *Franklin*, was very severely wounded, and was carried off deck. At three quarters past nine, the arm chest filled with musket cartridges blew up, and set fire to several places in the poop and quarter deck, but was fortunately extinguished. Her situation however was still very desperate; surrounded by enemies, and only 80 fathoms to windward of *L'Orient* entirely on fire. There could not be any other expectation than falling a prey either to the enemy or flames. At ten o'clock, the main and mizen masts fell, and all the guns on the main deck were dismounted. At half past ten the *Tonnant* cut her cables to avoid the fire of the *L'Orient*. The English ship that was on *L'Orient*'s larboard quarter, so soon as she had done firing at her, brought her broadside upon the *Tonnant*'s bow, and kept up a very heavy raking fire. The *Heureux* and *Mercure* conceived that they ought likewise to cut their cables. This manoeuvre created so much confusion amongst the rear ships, that they fired into each other, and did considerable damage. The *Tonnant* anchored ahead of the *Guillaume Tell*. The *Genereux* and *Timoleon*, and other two ships, got on shore. The ship that engaged the *Tonnant* on her bow, cut her cables; all her rigging and sails were cut to pieces, and she drove down and anchored astern of the English ship, that had been engaging the *Heureux* and *Mercure* before they changed their position. Those of the etat major and the ship's company of the *L'Orient* who had escaped death, convinced of the impossibility of extinguishing the fire, which had got down on the middle gun deck, endeavoured to save themselves. Rear Admiral Ganteaine saved himself in a boat, and went on board the *Salamine*, and from thence to Aboukir and Alexandria. The Adjutant General Motard, although badly wounded, swam to the ship nearest *L'Orient*, which proved to be English.[35] Commodore Casabianca, and his son only ten years old, who during the action gave proofs of bravery and intelligence far above his age, were not so fortunate; they were in the water, upon the wreck of *L'Orient*'s masts, not being able to swim, seeking each other until three quarters past ten, when the ship blew up, and put an end to their hopes and fears. The explosion was dreadful, and spread the fire all around to a considerable distance. The *Franklin*'s decks were covered with red hot seams, pieces of timber, and rope on fire. She was on fire, but luckily got it under. Immediately after the tremendous explosion the action ceased every where, and was succeeded by the most profound silence. The sky was darkened by clouds of black smoke, which seemed to threaten the destruction of the two fleets. It was quarter of an hour before the ship's crew recovered from the kind of

35 *Alexander.*

stupor they were thrown into. Towards eleven o'clock the *Franklin*, anxious to preserve the trust confided to her recommenced the action with a few of her lower deck guns. All the rest were dismounted; two thirds of his ship's company were killed and wounded; and those who remained most fatigued. She was surrounded by enemy's ships, who mowed down the men every broadside. At half past eleven o'clock, having only three lower deck guns that could defend the honour of the flag, it became necessary to put an end to so disproportioned a struggle, and Citoyen Martinet, captain of a frigate, ordered the colours to be struck.

The action in the rear of the fleet was very trifling, until three quarters past eleven o'clock, when it became very warm. Three of the enemy's ships were engaging them, and two were very near. The *Tonnant*, already badly treated, who was nearest the ships engaged, returned a very brisk fire. About three o'clock in the morning she was dismasted and obliged to cut her cables a second time; and not having any more anchors left, she drove on shore. The *Guillaume Tell*, *Le Genereux*, and the *Timoleon*, shifted their births, and anchored further down, out of gunshot; these vessels were not much damaged. At half past three o'clock the action ceased throughout the line. Early in the morning the frigate *La Justice* got under weigh, and made several small tacks to keep near the *Guillaume Tell*, and at nine o'clock anchored; an English ship having got under weigh, and making short tacks to prevent her from getting away. At six o'clock two English ships joined those which had been engaging the rear,[36] and began firing on the *Heureux* and *Mercure*, which were aground: the former soon struck, and the latter followed the example, as they could not bring their broadsides to bear upon the enemy. At half past seven the ship's crew of *L'Artimise* frigate, quitted her and set her on fire: at eight o'clock she blew up. The enemy without doubt had received great damage in their masts and yards, as they did not get under weigh to attack the remains of the French fleet. The French flag was flying on board four ships of the line and two frigates.[37] This division made the most of their time, and at three quarters past eleven *Le Guillaume Tell*, *Le Genereux*, *La Diane*, and *La Justice* were under weigh and formed in line of battle. The English ship that was under sail stood towards her fleet, fearing that she might be cut off:[38] but two other enemy's ships were immediately under weigh to assist her.[39] At noon the *Timoleon*, which probably was not in a state to put to sea, steered right for the shore under his foresail; and as soon as she struck the ground her foremast fell. The French division joined the enemy's ships, which ranged along their line on opposite tacks, within pistol shot, and received their broadsides, which it returned: they then each continued their route. The division was in sight at sun-set. Nothing remarkable passed during the night of the 2d. The 3d of August in the morning, the French colours were flying in the *Tonnant* and *Timoleon*. The English admiral sent a flag of truce to the former to know if she had struck; and upon being answered in the negative, he directed two ships to go against her.[40] When they got within gun-shot of her she struck, it being impossible to defend her any longer. The *Timoleon* was aground too near in for any ship to approach her. In the night of the second they sent the greatest part of their ship's company on shore; and at noon the next day they quitted her and set her on fire."

36 *Theseus* and *Goliath*.
37 *Timoleon, Tonnant, Genereux, Guillaume Tell, Justice, Diane.*
38 *Zealous.*
39 *Audacious, Leander.*
40 *Theseus* and *Leander*.

Thus ends the journal of the 1st, 2d, and 3d days of August, which will ever be remembered with the deepest sorrow by those Frenchmen who possess good hearts, and by all those true republicans who have survived this melancholy disaster.

The following curious letter from Lachavardiere, the French Consul at Palermo, gives a circumstantial account, in the French style, of Lord Nelson's engagement in the Mediterranean. It is highly animated, but much tinctured with national partiality.
From 'Naval Anecdotes.'

Naples, 20 Sept. 1799
The day before yesterday two English vessels arrived, and NELSON himself is expected to-morrow in a third. To give you some idea of the favour in which the enemies of our Country are held here, you must know, that with my own eyes I saw the King of Naples go more than two leagues to sea, to meet the English, to applaud and congratulate them. The two vessels which are arrived have brought two French Officers with them - one of them is Rear-Admiral Blanquet. They were both in the action of the first, second, and third of August. You may depend upon the correctness of the following account of that dreadful event.

Our fleet, after having effected a disembarkation, and having left the transports in Alexandria, went to anchor at Rosetta, about fifteen leagues from Alexandria. There they anchored about four leagues from land. On the first of August a signal was made for the English fleet being in sight. They reconnoitred our position, and seeing a considerable space between the shore and our vessels, they caused six of their Ships to pass between the shore and our fleet. It was then five o'clock in the evening; the English fleet was composed of fourteen Ships, and ours of thirteen.

At a quarter past five the firing commenced, when the fleets were in the following position: Our thirteen Ships were formed in a single line, six English Ships were between us and the land, seven others were on the opposite side, and the fourteenth having cut our line in half, hindered by that manoeuvre six French vessels from taking a share in the action. The fleets cannonaded each other with the utmost vivacity the remainder of the day, and the whole of the night. When the day appeared on the second, the advantage was equal. The ships were within pistol-shot of each other, and every possible means of destruction were mutually used by both fleets. It was in this situation of affairs that Admiral Brueys was wounded in the head and the hand, nevertheless he continued to command, till a cannon ball *cut him in two: he lived a quarter of an hour afterwards*, and would expire upon his deck. A moment afterwards the Captain of the Admiral's ship, Captain CASSA BIANCA, formerly a deputy, was mortally wounded by a splinter: this beautiful vessel then took fire, and every effort to extinguish it proved ineffectual. The young Cassa Bianca, a boy of ten years old, who during the action had performed prodigies of valour, refused to escape in a boat, being unwilling to leave his wounded father: nevertheless he afterwards put his father upon a mast which was thrown into the sea; himself and the Commissary of the fleet were upon it when *L'Orient*, of 120 guns, blew up with a most horrible noise, and destroyed these unfortunate persons. The explosion was so dreadful, that the town, which was four leagues distance, was shaken with it. The two squadrons thought for ten minutes they would be destroyed with the showers of fire, red-hot cannon, &c. which fell. For ten minutes they waited in silence the moment of their destruction: but Englishmen and Frenchmen were in the presence of each other, and again the cannons thundered, and the battle became more bloody than ever.

One circumstance is worth notice: while the Admiral's ship remained, the French had the advantage, and an English ship, of 74 guns, which was forced to run aground, had struck her colours: but the disorder which the blowing up of the Admiral's ship occasioned, all the officers being either killed or wounded; Vice Admiral Blanquet weltering in his blood from a wound which he received in the face; the Captain of the *Franklin*, rendered incapable of fighting by having received three wounds; Du Petit Thouars and another Captain killed; all these circumstances soon changed the face of affairs. Several of our vessels without masts and without the capability of motion, and with their cannon dismounted, became a prey to the enemy. Nevertheless, on the third, the action still continued between some of our vessels and the English. On that day, the crew of the *Timoleon*, sooner than surrender, set fire to the vessel, and saved themselves. This then is the result of the battle. The *L'Orient*, of 120 guns, is blown up; the *Timoleon*, of 74, is burnt; the *William Tell* is at Malta, with the frigates the *Diana* and the *Justice*; the frigate *L'Artemise* was burnt in the action; and the *Serieuse* sunk, and the crew saved. All the crew of *L'Orient* were saved on shore [sic!]. We are afraid that the *Genereux*, of 74, which retired with the *William Tell*, is sunk in the Canal of Malta. Our nine other vessels are taken, viz. *Le Guerrier, Le Conquerant, Le Spartiate, L'Aquilon*, and *Le Peuple Souverain*, of 74 guns each; *Le Franklin, Le Tonnant, Le Mercure*, and *L'Heureux*. Three of these vessels were in so bad a condition, that the enemy burnt them in the roads. All the prisoners were sent to Alexandria, because the English were in want of provisions; they will be a useful reinforcement to the army. The loss of the English was 1000 killed and 1800 wounded, by their own account. Nelson is severely wounded in the head! Several of their vessels are in a very bad state.

The unfortunate issue of this action is attributed to two causes: first, the suffering the English to get between us and the land; and the second and principal one is, the having engaged at anchor. However that might be, the calamity has happened, and it must not be thought of any more. If the Government act properly, in my opinion, they will honour the memory of Admiral Brueys, of young Cassa Bianca, and all those brave men who died fighting. It will do more, it will recompence the surviving Officers. Rome, after the battle of Cannae, thanked Varro: but this is not like the battle of Cannae; we have no Hannibal to encounter. The English squadron is cruising before Alexandria, where they wish to burn our transports; but we are assured they cannot effect it. Seven of their vessels are conducting the six French Ships to Gibraltar.

Neapolitan Celebration

The following is an extract from the Queen of Naples' letter to the Marquis de Circello, the Neapolitan Ambassador at London, after Admiral Nelson's arrival at Naples. XIV 473-74

I write to you with joy inexpressible! The brave and enterprising British Admiral Nelson has obtained a most signal and decisive victory. My heart would fain give wings to the courier who is the bearer of these propitious tidings, to facilitate the earliest acknowledgments of our gratitude. So extensive is this victory in all its relative circumstances, that were it not that the world has been accustomed to see prodigies of glory achieved by the English on the seas, I should almost question the reality of the event. It has produced among us a general spirit of enthusiasm. It would have moved you much to have seen my infant boys and girls hanging round my neck in tears, expressing their joy at the happy tidings, made doubly dear to us by the critical period at which they arrived. This news of the defeat of Buonaparté's Egyptian fleet has made many disaffected persons less daring, and improved the prospect of the general good. Make my highest respects acceptable to their Majesties of England. Recommend the gallant hero, Nelson, to his Royal Master. He has raised in the Italians an enthusiastic reverence for the English nation. Great expectations were naturally found on his enterprising talents, but no one could look for so total an overthrow of the enemy. All here are frantic with excess of joy.

Leander's Two Battles
From the 'Biographical Memoirs of Sir Thomas Boulden Thompson, Knt.'[XIV 5-13]

For a full and circumstantial account of the glorious Battle of the Nile, on the 1st of August, we must refer our readers to the earlier volumes of our work.[41] Instead therefore of entering into detail, we shall simply offer a few brief observations, relating more immediately to the subject of the present Memoir - the enemy had taken a station which they supposed, and not without probability, would secure to them the most decided advantages. The situation in which they were moored was such as might be expected to afford full play to their artillery to the force and dexterous management of which the splendid series of their land victories was in a great measure to be imputed. Our officer's ship, the *Leander*, though but of 50 guns, was stationed in the line of battle. By an instantaneous exertion of that powerful genius which, with the rapidity of thought, conceives and executes new measures for cases of untried emergency, Admiral Nelson immediately decided on the movement which determined the event of the day; and thus early prevented the effectual co-operation of the French batteries with their line.

In a narrative of this illustrious victory of Admiral Nelson, which was published at a shortly-subsequent period, the achievements of our officer are mentioned in terms of the highest praise - "Captain Thompson," says the writer, "of the *Leander*, of 50 guns, with a degree of skill and intrepidity highly honourable to his professional character, advanced towards the enemy's line on the outside, and most judiciously dropped his anchor athwart the hauser of *le Franklin*, raking her with great success, the shot from the *Leander*'s broadside, which passed that ship, all striking *L'Orient*, the flag-ship of the French Commander in Chief."

Thus did Captain Thompson, with a ship of inferior force, succeed in that noble achievement peculiar to British bravery and skill; the cutting through the enemy's line.[42]

On the 5th of August, the *Leander* sailed, with Captain, now Sir Edward Berry, of the *Vanguard*, as the bearer of Admiral Nelson's dispatches to the Commander in Chief. In the course of the *Leander*'s passage, Captain Thompson had an opportunity of exerting his Naval abilities, which, though unfortunate in the result, as fully and gloriously manifested the heroism of his character, and vigour of his genius, as any of his previous or subsequent exploits. Disabled by the late battle, and far short of her complement of men, on the 18th of August the *Leander* was fallen in with by *le Genereux*, a French 74 gun ship, with her full complement of men. Under these circumstances, Captain

41 Brought together in the preceding pages.
42 The total loss which the *Leander* sustained was that of 14 seamen being wounded.

Thompson, as wisdom directed and duty required, endeavoured to avoid an engagement; but the state of his ship rendering it impossible to escape without a contest, he instantly prepared for action; and, notwithstanding the inferiority and disadvantages under which he laboured, he maintained an obstinate combat for *six hours and a half*. At length, finding his ship entirely a wreck, he consulted with Captain Berry on the propriety of holding out any longer; and, with the concurrence and advice of that able officer, he found it expedient to yield to the circumstances of the moment, and reluctantly surrendered.

The *Leander* was carried into Corfu, whence the unfortunate captives were sent to Trieste. Immediately on his arrival at the latter place, Captain Thompson wrote to Admiral Nelson, apprising him of the loss of his Majesty's ship *Leander*, in the following terms; a duplicate of which was also dispatched, under cover, to Evan Nepean, Esq., for the information of the Lords Commissioners of the Admiralty:

Trieste, October 13, 1798
It is with extreme pain I have to relate to you the Capture of his Majesty's Ship *Leander*, late under my command, by a French 74 gun ship, after a close Action of six hours and a half. On the 18th of August last, being within five or six miles of the west end of Goza, near the Island of Candia, we discovered at day-break a large Sail on the S.E. quarter, standing directly for the *Leander*; we were then becalmed, but the stranger bringing up a fine breeze from the southward, we soon made him to be a large Ship of the Line. As the *Leander* was in Officers and Men upwards of 80 short of their complement, and had on board a number which were wounded on the 1st, I did not consider myself justified in seeking an Action with a Ship which appeared of such considerable superiority in point of size, and therefore took every means in my power to avoid it: I, however, soon found, that an inferiority of sailing made it inevitable; and I therefore, with all sail set, steered the *Leander* a course which I judged would receive our Adversary to the best advantage, should he bring us to battle. At 8 o'clock the strange Ship (still continuing to have the good fortune of the wind) had approached us within a long random shot, and had Neapolitan Colours hoisted, which he now changed to Turkish; but this deception was of no avail, as I plainly made him to be French. At nine he had ranged up within a half gun-shot of our weather quarter; I therefore hauled the *Leander* up sufficiently to bring the broadside to bear, and immediately commenced a vigorous cannonade on him, which he instantly returned. The Ships continued nearing each other till half-past ten, keeping up a constant and heavy firing. At this time I perceived the Enemy intending to run us on board, and the *Leander* being very much cut up in rigging, sails, and yards, I was unable , with the light air that blew, to prevent it. He ran us on board on the larboard bow, and continued alongside us for some time. A most spirited and well-directed fire, however, from our small party of Marines, (commanded by the Serjeant,) on the poop and from the quarter-deck, prevented the enemy from taking advantage of his good fortune, and he was repulsed in all his efforts to make an impression on us. The firing from the great guns was all this time kept up with the same vigour; and a light breeze giving the Ships way, I was enabled to steer clear of the Enemy, and soon afterwards had the satisfaction to luff under his stern, and passing him within ten yards, distinctly discharged every gun from the *Leander* into him. As from thenceforward was nothing but a continued series of heavy firing within pistol-shot, without any Wind, and the Sea as smooth as glass, I feel it unnecessary to give you the detail of the effects of every shot, which must be obvious from our situation.

I shall therefore content myself with assuring you, that a most vigorous cannonade was kept up from the *Leander* without the smallest intermission, until half-past three in the afternoon. All this time the Enemy having passed our bows with a light breeze, and brought himself on our starboard side, we found that our guns on that side were nearly all disabled by the wreck of our own spars, that had all fallen on this side. This produced a cessation of our fire, and the enemy took this time to ask us if we had surrendered? The *Leander* was now totally ungovernable, not having a thing standing but the shattered remains of the fore and main-masts, and the bowsprit; her hull cut to pieces, and the decks full of killed and wounded; and perceiving the Enemy, who had only lost his mizen-top-mast, approaching to place himself athwart our stern; in this defenceless situation I asked Captain Berry if he thought we could do more? He coinciding with me that farther resistance was vain and impracticable, and indeed all hope of success having for some time vanished, I therefore now directed an answer to be given in the affirmative, and the Enemy soon took possession of his Majesty's Ship. I cannot conclude this account without assuring you how much advantage His Majesty's Service derived during this action from the gallantry and activity of Captain Berry, of the *Vanguard*. I should also be wanting in justice if I did not bear testimony to the steady bravery of the officers and seamen of the *Leander* in this hard contest, which, though unsuccessful in its termination, will still, I trust, entitle them to the approbation of their Country. The enemy proved to be the *Genereux*, of 74 guns, commanded by M. Lejoille, *chef de division*, who had escaped from the Action of the 1st of August, and being the rearmost of the French line, had received little or no share of it, having on board 900 men, about 100 of whom we found had been killed in the present contest, and 188 wounded. I enclose a list of the loss in killed and wounded in the *Leander*, and have the honour to be, &c.

T. Thompson

A Return of Officers and Men Killed and Wounded on board His Majesty's Ship Leander
Officers killed - Mr. Peter Downes,[43] Midshipman; Mr. Gibson, Midshipman of the *Caroline*; Mr. Edward Haddon, Midshipman; 24 Seamen killed; Marines killed - Serjeant Dair, and 7 Privates. Total: 3 Officers, 24 Seamen, 1 Serjeant, 7 Marines.
Officers wounded - Capt. Thompson, badly; Lieutenant Taylor; Lieutenant Swiney; Mr. Lee, Master; Mr. Mathias, Boatswain, badly; Mr. Lackey, Master's Mate; Mr. Nailor, Midshipman; 41 Seamen; 9 Marines. Total: 7 Officers, 41 Seamen, 9 Marines, wounded.

The circumstance of their being taken prisoners was not the only inconvenience which Captain Thompson and his officers sustained; for no sooner had they arrived on board of *le Genereux* that they were plundered of every article belonging to them excepting the clothes which they wore. They expostulated with the French Captain on the harshness of this treatment, but their remonstrances were in vain; and when they reminded him of the situation of the French officers who had been made prisoners by Admiral Nelson, in comparison with those now taken in the *Leander*, he coolly replied:

---

43 This gentleman was the younger son of the ancient family of Downes, of Shrigley, in Cheshire. He was only in his 20th year, but had served in the most active scenes during the whole of the war, with the highest honour to himself, the most distinguished approbation of his commanding officers, and the universal esteem of his comrades. Towards the conclusion of the defence of the *Leander*, he received a fatal shot, of the wound from which he lingered, with the greatest resignation, till the following morning. *Ed.*

"J'en suis faché, mais le fait est, que les Francois sont bons au pillage".[44] Captain Berry expressed a wish to have a pair of pistols returned to him, of which he had been plundered. On their being produced, however, by the man who took them, the French Captain immediately secured them for himself, telling Captain Berry that he would give him a pair of French pistols to protect him on his journey home. It is proper to add, that the promise was never performed.

Various other acts of cruelty were experienced by Captain Thompson and his gallant crew, from these worshippers of liberty and equality, which would have disgraced a Bombay Corsair, or an American Savage. Their inhumanity was even carried to such an extreme, that, at the very moment when the Surgeon of the *Leander* was performing the chirurgical operations, he was robbed of his instruments; and the wound which Captain Thompson had received was nearly proving fatal by their forcibly withholding the attendance of his surgeon. The barbarous treatment inflicted on these brave men was continued even after their arrival at Corfu, as is evident from the following letter on this subject addressed by Mr. Stanley, the British consul at Trieste, to the Lords of the Admiralty:

Trieste, 3d December, 1798
My Lords, Thirty seamen of the *Leander*, which was taken and carried into Corfu, arrived here from that Island the 20th ult: these poor men were forced away in three small inconvenient vessels, ten in each, some of them badly wounded, and in a very weak state, being obliged to lie on the decks, exposed to the inclemency of the season, seventeen days. On Friday ten more arrived from the same place. The first thirty, having finished their quarantine of thirteen days, came out this morning much recovered from the attention to their health and food. The last ten have suffered more than the others, being twenty-three days on their passage, and so short of provisions, that, had not some passengers taken compassion on them, they must have perished. I am sorry to observe the French behaved very badly to them in the shortness of provisions. I hope, by proper care, to restore these valuable meritorious men to their Country and families. I have the honour to be, &c.

EDWARD STANLEY
British Consul at Trieste
Right Hon. Lords Commissioners of the Admiralty

By comparing the following ridiculous and bombastic epistle from the Captain of the *Genereux*, with the plain unvarnished statements of the British officers who were concerned, our readers will be enabled to judge of the *veracity* with which Frenchmen *write*, as well as of the *superior gallantry* with which they *fight*.

Corfu, September 8, 1798
I have the pleasure to announce to you my arrival at Corfu. I have been here for some days past, having brought in the English ship *Leander*, of *seventy-four* guns, which I met near the Isles of Goza and Candia, about a league from the shore. This ship had been sent to carry dispatches from Bequiers Road,[45] where the English had attacked us on the 1st of August. We were at anchor, but in a position certainly not very secure for our

44 I am sorry for it; but the fact is, that the French are expert at plunder.
45 Meaning Aboukir.

squadron: of this bad situation they took advantage, and having placed us between two fires, a most dreadful slaughter took place, the ships not being at a greater distance than pistol shot, and at anchor. From the circumstance of the wind, with relation to the English ships, we should have been superior in the contest, if *L'Orient*, our Admiral's ship, had not blown up in the air, which threw us all into disorder; as, to avoid the flames that had already reached *le Tonnant*, every Vessel was obliged to shift its station. Having, however, placed my Ship in a situation favourable to the direction of its cannon, I fought her until three in the morning of the following day to that in which, at ten in the evening, *L'Orient* blew up.

By a singular accident I missed having a broadside at Captain Darby, who sailed with us in the last war from the Cape of Good Hope to Cadiz. His ship, the *Bellerophon*, of 74 guns, sailed past me about half-past ten in the evening, having lost her main-mast and mizen-mast. I fired three of our shots at her, which carried away the mast she was hoisting, and struck away one of the lanthorns off the poop.

I immediately ordered one of my officers to *go in pursuit of, and to bring on board of my ship the Captain of this ship*; but in half an hour afterwards, when I was about to send my boat on board her, the fire from several English ships being directed against me, compelled me rather to think of answering their guns than of taking possession of the other Ship; and the slow manner in which the officer whom I had dispatched proceeded to execute my orders, was the cause of my failing to take possession of this other Ship.

As to the *Leander*, I was obliged to fight with her for nearly four hours and three quarters. She carries *seventy-four guns*, 24 and 30 pounders on her lower deck, and 12 pounders on her upper. I should have made myself Master of her in less than an hour, had we been at close fighting. During the Engagement we boarded her; and I should have succeeded in making prize of her by boarding, if I had had a more active Crew.

LEJOILLE, jun.

On the 17th of December, 1798, Captain Thompson having been regularly exchanged, a Court Martial was held on board his Majesty's ship *America*, at Sheerness, to inquire into his conduct, and into that of the officers and men who served under him, when the *Leander* was taken. The requisite forms having been gone through, the court delivered the following honourable sentence of acquittal:

"The Court having heard the evidence brought forward in support of Captain Thompson's narrative of the capture of the *Leander*, and having very maturely and deliberately considered the whole, is of opinion, that the gallant and almost unprecedented defence of Captain Thompson, of the *Leander*, against so superior a force as that of the *Genereux*, is deserving of every praise this Country and this Court can give; and that his conduct, with that of the officers and men under his command, reflects not only the highest honour on himself and them, but on their Country at large; and the Court does therefore *most honourably* acquit Captain Thompson, his officers, and ship's company; and he and they are hereby most honourably acquitted accordingly."

The President of the Court, after the sentence had been read, addressed Captain Thompson in the following words:

"Captain Thompson - I feel the most lively pleasure in returning to you the sword with which you have so bravely maintained the honour of your King and Country: the more so, as I am convinced, that when you are again called upon to draw it in their defence, you will add fresh laurels to the wreath which you have already so nobly won."

Soon after this period, his Majesty was pleased to confer the honour of Knighthood on Captain Thompson, and to reward his services with a pension of 300l. per annum.

In the following Spring, 1799, he was appointed to the *Bellona*, of 74 guns, and joined the fleet under the command of Admiral Lord Bridport, off Brest, between the 30th of April and the 12th of May. From this station he was dispatched, to reinforce Earl St. Vincent, with whom he remained, in the Mediterranean, till the month of August, and then returned to England.

In the course of the year 1799, Sir Thomas had the satisfaction of hearing, that his old ship, the *Leander*, was taken at Corfu, by the Russians and Turks; and that the Emperor of Russia had ordered her to be restored to his Britannic Majesty.

In the early part of 1800, Captain Thompson was employed in the Channel and in Soundings; whence he returned with Admiral Sir Alan Gardner, to refit, in the month of March.

We are not aware that our officer was engaged in any farther service, until the period of the memorable Baltic Expedition, which sailed from Yarmouth Roads, under the command of Sir Hyde Parker, in March 1801.

From 'The Monthly Register of Naval Events.' *I 83-85*
The Nile Medal

Medals, in honour of Lord Nelson's victory, are in circulation, with the following designs:

OBVERSE - Religion supporting the Bust of Admiral Nelson, with her right hand resting upon a cross and scull; by her is the British Lion, defending the Irish Harp. In the back ground a Pyramid and Palm Tree, to mark the country where the victory was obtained. Legend - "Nothing can oppose Virtue and Courage."

REVERSE - An Anchor, with a Shield, on which is the Royal Arms of England, surrounded with a Laurel, and a Scroll entwining it, with this Motto, "Praise be to God," November 29th, 1798; above, the Eye of Providence, denoting its influence and Favour. Legend - "Under this Sign you shall conquer."

Navy Board Purchase Prices

Dec. 14. The Navy Board has purchased the hulls of the following prizes, taken by Lord Nelson, at the sum of £117,000 viz. *Le Franklin* and *Tonnant*, of 80 guns; *Le Spartiate, Aquilon, Conquerant*, and *Souverain Peuple*, of 74 guns. The two last ships were only valued at £5000 each; the *Franklin* at £30,000.

The name of *Le Franklin* is to be changed to the *Canopus*; the *Aquillon*, to the *Aboukir*; and *Le Souverain Peuple*, to *Le Guerrier*. The last is to be the sheer-hulk at Gibraltar.

The Hopes of the Reverend Nelson
From 'Naval Anecdotes.' *III 192*

NANTES IN GURGITE VASTO!

The following letter was written by the venerable father of Lord Nelson, to the Rev. B. Allot, in answer to that gentleman's congratulations on the ever-memorable victory of the Nile

My great and good Son went into the world without fortune, but with a heart replete with every moral and religious virtue. These have been his compass to steer by; and it has pleased God to be his shield in the day of battle, and to give success to his wishes to be of service to his Country. His Country seems sensible of his services; but should he ever meet with ingratitude, his scars will cry out, and plead his cause - for, at the siege of Bastia, he lost an eye; at Teneriffe, an arm: on the memorable fourteenth of February, he received a severe blow on his body, which he still feels; and now a wound on the head. After all this, you will believe his bloom of countenance must be faded; but the spirit beareth up yet as vigorous as ever. On the twenty-ninth of September he completed his fortieth year; cheerful, generous, and good; fearing no evil, because he has done none: an honour to my grey hairs, which, with every mark of old age, creep fast upon me.

1798 – Ireland, Malta and Minorca

NELSON'S VICTORY AT THE NILE did not have an immediate impact on the situation in northern Europe, where two small French squadrons had embarked forces to support an uprising of the United Irishmen. The first of these had succeeded in effecting a landing in August of 1798 at Killala Bay in northern Ireland, but they were unable to keep the field on their own when a much larger British army was brought against them. In September another attempt was made, by Rear-Admiral Bompart with *Hoche* of 74 guns, and eight frigates, but this squadron was intercepted at sea by Rear-Admiral Sir John Warren with three 74s and five frigates before he could get to Lough Swilly.

In the Mediterranean, the impact of the Nile was more immediate. British forces were landed on Malta to co-operate with the Maltese resistance to French occupation, and at the end of the year a squadron under the command of Commodore Sir John Duckworth landed an expeditionary force on Minorca. It quickly succeeded in capturing the island which was ideally positioned for the Royal Navy base of operations against the French coast.

The final act of the year was to be the wreck in the Scilly Islands of the *Colossus* of 74 guns, which was carrying in its hold the priceless antique vases which had been collected by Sir William Hamilton, the British envoy to Naples, whose wife, Emma, had become Horatio Nelson's lover. Only part of this collection was recovered. On board also was the body of Admiral Shuldham.

The principal account of the 1798 Irish invasion attempt was inserted in the memoir of Sir John Warren. A briefer passage has been published above as part of the memoir of Vice-Admiral Kingsmill who commanded at Cork. The account of the operations at Minorca formed part of the biographical memoir of Sir John Duckworth, and Duckworth's official letter was also printed from the *Gazette*. The account of events on Malta was provided by Captain Alexander Ball's official letter, forwarded by Nelson to Admiral the Earl of St Vincent, who forwarded it to Evan Nepean, Secretary of the Admiralty. Report of the loss of the *Colossus*

The *Hoche*, under Jury Masts, towed by the *Doris*, 36 guns, Captain Lord Ranelagh, into Lough Swilly. Plate 27

was recorded in the first of *The Naval Chronicle*'s 'Monthly Register of Naval Events', as well as in the biographical memoir of *Colossus*'s captain, George Murray.

Capture of the Hoche
From the 'Biographical Memoir of Sir John Borlase Warren, Bart. K.B.'
III 351-358

At the close of the glorious year 1798, Sir John Warren received orders from Vice-Admiral Sir Alan Gardner in Cawsand Bay, to proceed with the *Foudroyant*, 80 guns, Captain Sir T. Byard, and *Robust*, 74 guns, Captain E. Thornbrough, and *Magnanime*, 44 guns, Captain the Honourable M. de Courcy, in search of the enemy's squadron, that had escaped from Brest. The Commodore immediately sailed; and struggling with unfavourable weather, arrived with his squadron off the coast of Ireland, without falling in with a single vessel of war: he then proceeded with a press of sail to the N. W. along shore.

Intelligence of the probability of the enemy's appearance off Black Sod Harbour, having been communicated by the *Kangaroo* brig, 18 guns, Captain E. Brace, the Commodore remained for some days off the harbour and Achile Head; when standing further to the northward, on the eleventh of October, the squadron under Monsieur Bompart, consisting of one ship of the line, the *Hoche*, and eight frigates, a schooner, and a brig, with troops and ammunition on board destined for Ireland, at length appeared in sight. The following is the official account as sent to Vice-Admiral Kingsmill:

Canada, Lough Swilly, Ireland, 16th October 1798

Sir, In pursuance of the orders and instructions I received by the *Kangaroo*, I proceeded with the ships named in the margin (*Canada, Robust, Foudroyant, Magnanime*) off Achile Head; and on the tenth instant I was joined by his Majesty's ships *Melampus* and *Doris*; the latter of whom I directed to look out for the enemy off Tory'Island and the Rosses: in the evening of the same day the *Amelia* appeared in the offing; when Captain Herbert informed me he had parted with the *Ethalion, Anson*, and *Sylph*, who with great attention had continued to observe the French squadron, since their sailing on the seventeenth ult. In the morning of the eleventh, however, these two ships also fell in with us; and at noon the enemy were discovered in the N. W. quarter, consisting of one ship of 80 guns, eight frigates, a schooner, and a brig. I immediately made the signal for a general chase, and to form in succession as each ship arrived up with the enemy; whom, from their great distance to windward, and an hollow sea, it was impossible to come up with before the twelfth.

The chase was continued in very bad, and boisterous weather, all day of the eleventh, and the following night; when, at half past five A. M. they were seen at a little distance to windward, the line of battle ship having lost her main top-mast.

The enemy bore down and formed their line in close order upon the starboard tack; and from the length of the chase, and our ships being spread, it was impossible to close with them before seven A. M. when I made the *Robust*'s signal to lead, which was obeyed with much alacrity, and the rest of the ships to form in succession in the rear of the van.

The action commenced at twenty minutes past seven o'clock A. M. the Rosses bearing S. S. W. five leagues, and at eleven, the *Hoche*, after a gallant defence, struck; and the frigates made sail from us: the signal to pursue the enemy was made immediately, and in five hours afterwards three of the frigates hauled down their colours also; but they, as well as the *Hoche*, were obstinately defended, all of them being heavy frigates, and, as well as the ship of the line, entirely new, full of troops and stores, with every necessity for the establishment of their views and plans in Ireland.

I am happy to say, that the efforts and conduct of every officer and man in the squadron seemed to have been actuated by the same spirit, zeal, and unanimity in their King and Country's cause; and I feel myself under great obligations to them, as well as the officers and men of this ship, for their exertions upon this occasion; which will, I hope, recommend them to their Lordship's favour.

I left Captain Thornbrough, after the action, with the *Magnanime, Ethalion*, and *Amelia*, with the prizes; and am sorry to find he is not arrived; but trust they will soon make their appearance.

I have the honour to remain, Sir,

Your most obedient humble servant,

JOHN BORLASE WARREN

P.S. The ships with us in the action were the *Canada, Robust, Foudroyant, Magnanime, Ethalion, Melampus*, and *Amelia*.

The *Anson* joined us in the latter part of the action, having lost her mizen mast in chase the day before.

I have sent my First Lieutenant Turquand to take the command of the *Hoche*.

The following states some particulars not mentioned in the Gazette:

Extract from a Letter from Sir John Borlase Warren, to Lord Viscount Castlereagh, dated from his Majesty's ship the Canada, in Lough Swilly, the 16th instant

Dublin Castle, Oct. 18, 1798
My Lord, I take the liberty of communicating to you, for the information of his Excellency the Lord Lieutenant, that I fell in with the enemy's squadron on the twelfth instant, the Rosses bearing S. S. W. five leagues, and, after an action which continued most of the day, four of their ships struck their colours.

I believe a brig, with Napper Tandy on board, was in company, as she left the French at the commencement of the business. The enemy's ships had numbers of troops on board, arms, stores, and ammunition; and large quantities of papers were torn and thrown overboard after they had struck.

I am of the opinion that few of the frigates which escaped will arrive in France, as they had received much damage in their masts and rigging; and, from the violent gales that followed the next day, they must be in a crippled state, and may in all probability be picked up by some of the squadrons on the coast of France, or by Admiral Kingsmill's cruisers. They had thrown everything overboard, boats, spars, arm-chests, &c.

I left the prizes with the *Robust, Magnanime, Ethalion*, and *Amelia*. The *Hoche*, of 80 guns, was one of the ships taken

I am, &c.

J. B. WARREN

As the letters of Captains Moore and Countess afford a further account of this victory, and are referred to by Sir John Warren in a subsequent dispatch, they are next subjoined:

Captain Graham Moore, Commander of his Majesty's ship Melampus, to Sir John Borlase Warren, dated at sea, off Lough Swilly, the 16th October, 1798
Sir, I have the honour to inform you, that on the thirteenth instant, at midnight, being well up towards St. John's Point, we discovered two large ships close to us on our weather beam: on seeing us, they hauled up on the opposite tack. As I had not the least doubt of their being two of the enemy's frigates, we tacked, and closed with the nearest in an hour, going ten knots. After hailing and ordering her to bring-to without effect, she trying to get away athwart our stern, we opened such a fire upon her, as completely unrigged her in about twenty-five minutes, and forced her to bring-to and surrender: she proved to be *La Resolue* French frigate, commanded by Jean Pierre Barqueau, mounting 40 guns, and 500 seamen and troops on board; the other frigate was *L'Immortalite*, of 44 guns, twenty-four pounders, on the main-deck, and 600 seamen and soldiers. She made several signals whilst we were occupied with her consort, but gave us no disturbance.

Both on this occasion and during the action of the twelfth, the officers, seamen, and marines, of his Majesty's ship under my command displayed the utmost degree of zeal, alacrity, and gallant spirit; Mr. Martin (the First Lieutenant, an old and good officer), with Lieutenants Price, Ellison, and Hole, of the marines, conducted themselves much to my satisfaction; and I experienced very great assistance from the steady good conduct of Mr. Emory, the Master.

As a very heavy gale of wind came on immediately after our boarding *La Resolue,* the Second Lieutenant, Mr. John Price, with twenty-one men, were all that could be thrown on board of her, with the loss of our two cutters. That officer deserves very great credit for his active exertion in clearing her of the wreck of her mast and rigging, and in keeping company in so violent a storm; as our object was to disable our antagonist before her consort could assist her. *La Resolue* had only ten men killed, and a great number wounded; but I am inexpressibly happy to add, that in the action of the twelfth we had only one man wounded; and the affair of the thirteenth did not deprive their country of the services of a single man of the brave crew of the *Melampus*.

I have the honour to be, &c.

GRAHAM MOORE

Captain George Countess, Commander of his Majesty's ship Ethalion, to Evan Nepean, Esq

Plymouth Sound, November 8, 1798
I have to request you will be pleased to inform my Lords Commissioners of the Admiralty, that since my letter of the twenty-second of September, by Captain White, of the *Sylph*, I continued to watch the motion of the French squadron in his Majesty's ship under my command (having with me the *Anson*, and *Amelia*) until the fourth of October at noon; when an hard gale of wind coming on, we lost sight of them in lat. 53 deg. 13 min. north, and long. 16 deg. 15 min. west, Sligo Bay bearing north 77 east, distance ninety-one leagues.

The wind being off shore, we carried sail to get in with the land, to give the necessary information. The *Amelia* separated on the night of the eighth: I had previously desired, in case of separation, each ship to make the best of her way to give the alarm. On the eleventh we fell in with the squadron under Sir John B. Warren; but it blowing strong, could not get on board to communicate any intelligence; but seeing the *Amelia* with him, I was satisfied he had all the information I could give.

Soon after our joining the above squadron, the *Anson* made the signal for the enemy, whom we discovered coming down: but they hauled to the wind on observing us. We chased, and kept close to them during the night; and next morning the attack commenced, which no doubt you have been fully informed of by Sir J. B. Warren. After the *Hoche* struck, we pursued the weathermost frigate, who was making off, and sailed very fast. After a considerable chase we came up with and engaged her: she made an obstinate resistance for an hour and fifty minutes after we got abreast of her, when she struck her colours, most of her sails having come down; and five feet water in her hold. She proved to the *Bellone*, of 36 guns, twelve pounders; having 300 soldiers on board besides her crew. The squadron chased to leeward; and of course we separated, being obliged to remain by the prize; and have been under the necessity of keeping the sea ever since.

I cannot speak too highly of the bravery and conduct of all my officers during the action, as well as of their extreme vigilance in watching them for seventeen days. Mr. Sayer, First Lieutenant, is in the prize; and I can with pleasure say, his Majesty has not a more zealous or better officer. We had one man killed, and three wounded. The enemy appear to have had twenty killed.

I have the honour to be &c.

GEORGE COUNTESS

On the sixteenth of October, the *Mermaid*, 32 guns, Captain Newman, fell in with *La Loire*, pierced for 50 guns, and mounting 46, one of the French frigates that had escaped from Sir John Warren; and though not successful in capturing her, the brave Commander and crew of the *Mermaid* particularly distinguished themselves.[1] The *Loire*, after being thus crippled by the *Mermaid*, fell in with the *Anson*, 44 guns, Captain P. C. Durham; and after a second spirited resistance was by him taken.

On the eighteenth of November 1798, the following dispatch was forwarded by Sir John Warren to the Admiralty, dated from on board the *Canada*, Plymouth Dock.

Sir, I have been waiting with great anxiety the arrival of the *Robust*, and *La Hoche* at this port, to enable me to make a return of the killed and wounded in the different ships under my orders, upon the twelfth of October last; but as I understand those ships may be still further detained by repairs at Lough Swilly,[2] I send the inclosed, which it was impossible for me to obtain before the present moment, as the whole squadron was separated in chase of the flying enemy, and have successively arrived at this port; it was impracticable, therefore, to communicate the particulars to their Lordships sooner, or to state the very gallant conduct of *Captains Thornbrough, and De Courcy*, in the *Robust* and *Magnanime*; who, from their position in the van on that day, were enabled to close with the enemy early in the action; and were zealously and bravely seconded by every other ship of the squadron; as well as by the intrepidity displayed by the *Anson* in the evening in obeying my signal to harass the enemy, and in beating off their frigates.

For further particulars, I refer their Lordships to the letters they may have received from Captains Countess and Moore of the *Ethalion* and *Melampus*.

I am happy in reflecting that so many advantages to his Majesty's arms have been purchased with so inconsiderable a loss in the ships of the squadron.

I have the honour to remain, &c.

JOHN BORLASE WARREN

Sir John Warren, on his return from the coast of Ireland, was honoured with the freedom of the cities of London and Derry;[3] and received the thanks of the Houses of Lords and Commons of Great Britain, with those of the Irish Parliament. When the promotion of Admirals took place in 1799 on the memorable fourteenth of February, this distinguished officer was advanced to the rank of Rear-Admiral of the Blue; and, for the first time during the present war, remained unemployed until the twenty-seventh of July in the same year; when he received orders to hoist his flag on board the *Temeraire*, 98 guns, lying at St. Helens. He sailed thence in a few days; and beat down Channel against a westerly wind to join the fleet in Torbay: apprehensions being entertained that the French had escaped out of Brest.

On the second of August 1799, Rear-Admiral Warren being off Ushant, under Lord Bridport, and standing down with the advanced squadron to the Passage du Raz, discovered the Spanish ships from Roch[e]fort, on the other side of the Saints: having made the signal, the wind not allowing the British ships to go through the passage (although it was favourable for the Spaniards, who thus would soon have gained Brest, or joined the French squadron, then under weigh in *Bertheaume Road*) the *Temeraire* stood round the Saints, after the enemy, who had hauled their wind, and made sail. Although Rear-Admiral Warren was afterwards detached by the Commander in Chief

1 For an account of this action, vid. page 42 of the present volume.
2 View of the coast of Lough Swilly, and the *Hoche* in tow of the *Doris* frigate, page 129, Plate 28.
3 He was also elected a member of the Salters Company.

in search of the Spanish ships, they escaped; and arrived at Ferrol two days prior to the appearance of the British squadron off that port.

Sir John Warren on the return of the Channel fleet to Torbay, in the month of October, 1799, shifted his flag to the *Renown*, a new ship, of 74 guns; and except an absence of a few weeks, has been with a division of the WESTERN SQUADRON, under Sir Alan Gardner, during the whole of the preceding winter.

To delineate the character of Rear-Admiral Sir John Borlase Warren in a few words: he early entered into the glorious service of the BRITISH NAVY through inclination; and the same zeal which first induced him to encounter the perils of the ocean, had throughout animated his mind to overcome them. He possesses the sincerity of a seaman, without any of the roughness of the old school; and displays the elegance of a man of fashion, without dissipation, or duplicity. To strangers he has sometimes the appearance of a distant reserve; to his friends his manner is open, and impressive. He feels the honest ambition that impels the Brave, without the parade or boast of vanity: he commands without asperity; and gains obedience and respect, without the influence of terror: his courage proceeds from a mind that is improved, and is therefore uniform; his principles are founded on the basis of Christian Faith, and are therefore steadfast:

Operations to Liberate Malta
From 'Gazette Letters.' [1 162]

Admiralty Office, December 25 1798
Captain Alexander John Ball to Rear-Admiral Horatio Nelson, Alexander off
Malta, October 30 1798
Sir, I have the honour to acquaint you, that the commandant of the French troops in the castle of Goza, signed the capitulation the 28th instant, which you had approved. I ordered Captain Creswell, of the marines, to take possession of it in the name of his Britannic Majesty, and his Majesty's colours were hoisted. The next day the place was delivered up in form to the deputies of the island, his Sicilian Majesty's colours hoisted, and he acknowledged their lawful sovereign.

I embarked yesterday all the French officers and men who were on the island of Goza, amounting to near 217.

I enclose the articles of capitulation, and an inventory of the arms and ammunition found in the castle, part of which I directed to be sent to the assistance of the Maltese, who are in arms against the French. There were 3200 sacks of corn in the castle, which will be great relief to the inhabitants, who are much in want of that article. I have the honour to be, &c.

Duckworth's Occupation of Minorca
From the 'Biographical Memoir of Sir John Thomas Duckworth, K.B.'
XVIII 8-10

In 1797, he [Duckworth] returned to England; in the early part of the 1798, he was employed in the Channel fleet, under the command of Admiral Lord Bridport; and, in the month of August following, having joined Earl St. Vincent, in the Mediterranean, he again hoisted his broad pendant in his old ship, the *Leviathan*.[4]

---

4 On this occasion, H. Digby, Esq. was the captain under him.

Mahon harbour. The anxiety with which the public mind is at present directed towards the Mediterranean, made us wish to gratify our readers as soon as possible with a correct view of this commodious and excellent harbour; now, when most wanted, in our possession. The design was made by Mr. Pocock, from a large and most accurate drawing, done at Mahon in 1773, by Joseph Chiesa, for the late General James Johnstone, when Governor; now in the possession of the Right Honourable Lady Cecilia Johnstone, by whose permission two different views have been copied for the *Naval Chronicle*. Plate 16

The reduction of Minorca being deemed an object of considerable importance, Commodore Duckworth was, about this time, appointed to the command of the following squadron, for the purpose of effecting it:-

Ships	Guns	Commanders
Leviathan	74	J.T. Duckworth, Esq. Commodore
		Captain H. Digby
Centaur	74	John Markham
Argo	44	J. Bowen
Aurora	28	J.G. Caulfield
Cormorant	20	Lord Mark Kerr
Calcutta, armed frigate	24	R. Plouden
Coromandel, ditto	24	R. Pressland
Ulysses, ditto	24	Lieutenant W. Simmons
Peterel	16	
Constitution cutter	14	Whisten

With this force, accompanied by the late General Stuart, brother to the Marquis of Bute, as Commander of the troops, Commodore Duckworth arrived off Minorca, on the 9th of November. He immediately landed a body of troops at Addaya Creek, near Fournella, without opposition from the enemy, who blew up their magazines, spiked their guns, and evacuated the fort. The troops proceeded on their march to Mercadal,

View of Quarantine Island, Port Mahon. Engraved by Baily, from a drawing by R.S.
Plate 421

which they entered without resistance, the enemy having retired to Ciudadela, and thence to Mahon; the squadron, in the mean time, blocking up the different bays and creeks, to prevent supplies being thrown into the island, from Majorca. - In the course of the same day, a detachment of 300 men, under the command of the Honourable Colonel Paget, arrived at Mahon, and compelled Fort Charles to surrender; by which the Colonel was enabled to remove the boom which obstructed the entrance of the harbour, and to open a free passage for the *Aurora* and *Cormorant*, which Commodore Duckworth had ordered upon that service.

On the evening of the 12th, four Spanish frigates were observed standing over from the island of Majorca;[5] on the receipt of which intelligence, the Commodore instantly put to sea, with the *Leviathan, Centaur, Argo, Calcutta, Ulysses*, and *Coromandel*, in quest of them. At day-break the next morning, five sail were seen standing for Ciudadela, and the signal was made for a general chase; but the enemy observed it, and immediately hauled their wind for Majorca. The pursuit was continued, with little wind, till eleven at night, by which time the Commodore had arrived within three miles of the sternmost frigate; but, fearful lest he might be drawn too far from Minorca, he directed Captain Markham, in the *Centaur*, to pursue the enemy, and return off Ciudadela, to co-operate with the army, if necessary. On his arrival off that place, he received the agreeable intelligence from General Stuart, that the whole island had surrendered to His Majesty's arms, by capitulation, on the 15th.

On the same morning, Commodore Duckworth was joined by the *Argo*, Captain Bowen, who, in the chase on the 13th, had re-captured the *Peterel*, which had been taken on the preceding day by the Spanish frigates. - Captain Markham also rejoined the Commodore, but without having had the good fortune to come up with the enemy.

During the proceedings at Minorca, a detachment of 150 seamen was landed, to assist and to co-operate with the army, under the direction of Captain Bowen; but, other essential service rendering it necessary that that officer should return to his ship,

5 The *Flora, Casilda, Pomona*, and *Proserpine*, of 40 guns each.

the command of the seamen devolved on Mr. William Buchannan, the second Lieutenant of the *Leviathan*, whose general conduct on the occasion was entitled to much praise.[6] Indeed, all the captains, officers, seamen, and marines, who were employed, either on shore, or in covering the landing of the troops and military stores, displayed the greatest zeal and activity.

Thus the conquest of Minorca was effected, without the loss of a single man; although the Spanish troops, including officers, amounted to between three and four thousand; and had the means, in every respect, of making a stout resistance. - A great quantity of ordnance of military stores was taken in the forts. In the arsenal, at Mahon, was found abundance of naval stores; the keel and stern-frame of a man of war brig on the stocks, with her timbers, part of her stores, rigging, &c. fourteen gun-boats, hauled up, with all their rigging complete; and thirteen other large boats, from twenty to thirty-six feet [at the] keel, with their rigging in good order, and fit for service. Two large merchant ships, a zebeck, and four tartans, were taken in the harbour.

Commodore Duckworth's Dispatch
From the 'Monthly Register of Naval Events.' [177-80]

Gazette Letters

Admiralty Office, December 23, 1798
Lieutenant Jones, of his Majesty's ship *Leviathan*, arrived here this afternoon with a dispatch from Admiral the Earl of St. Vincent to Mr. Nepean, of which the following is a copy:

Le Souverain, Gibraltar, December 6, 1798
Sir, I enclose a copy of a letter from Commodore Duckworth, with other documents relating to the conquest of the Island of Minorca; upon which important event I request you will congratulate the Lords Commissioners of the Admiralty.

Lieutenant Jones, First of the *Leviathan*, is the bearer of this dispatch, who, from the report of Commodore Duckworth, and my own observation when my flag was on board that ship, is highly deserving their Lordship's favour and protection. I am, Sir, &c. &c.
St. Vincent

Leviathan, off Fournelles, Minorca, 19th Nov. 1798
My Lord, In pursuance of your Lordship's instructions to me of the 18th and 20th of October, I proceeded with the ships under my orders, and the troops under the command of the Honourable General Charles Stuart, to the rendezvous off the Colombrites; and, after having been joined by his Majesty's sloop *Peterel*, and the arrangements for landing had been completed, on the 5th in the afternoon I stood for Minorca, but in consequence of light winds I did not make that island till day-break on the 7th, then within five miles of the Port of Fournelles, where finding the wind directly out of that harbour, and the enemy prepared for our reception, I (having previously consulted the General) made the signal for Captain Bowen, of the *Argo*, accompanied by the *Cormorant* and *Aurora*, to assist in covering the landing, to lead into the Creek of Addaya, there not being water

6 [General Stuart's letter to Lieutenant Buchannan is quoted in the First Edition.]

or space enough for the line of battle ships; which he executed in a most officer-like and judicious manner; and in hauling round the Northern point a battery of four twelve-pounders fired one gun: but, on seeing the broadside, the enemy left it, blowing up their magazines, and spiking the guns, when the transports were got in without damage, though there was scarcely room for stowing them in tiers. During this service, which was rapidly executed, the *Leviathan* and *Centaur* plied on and off Fournelles, to divert the attention of the enemy; but knowing an expeditious landing to be our greatest object, as soon as I observed the transports were nearly in the creek, I bore away, and anchored with the *Leviathan* and *Centaur* off its entrance, to see that service performed. One battalion was put on shore by eleven o'clock, and directly took the height, which proved fortunate, as the enemy very quickly appeared in two divisions, one of which was marching down towards the battery before mentioned, when I ordered the covering ships to commence a cannonade, which effectually checked their progress, and the General kept them at bay with the troops he had; and by six o'clock in the afternoon the whole were on shore, with eight six-pounders, field-pieces, and eight days' provisions, as also two howitzers. On the same evening, after ordering the *Cormorant* and *Aurora* to proceed off Port Mahon, with seven transports, to form a diversion, I got under weigh with the *Leviathan* and *Centaur*, and turned up to Fournelles with an intent to force the harbour; but on my entering the passage, I found the enemy had evacuated the forts, and the wind throwing out caused me to anchor when I made the *Centaur*'s signal (which was following me) to haul off, landed the marines of the *Leviathan*, took possession of two forts of four guns each and one of six: but soon after the General requesting I would not enter this port, I ordered Captain Digby to embark the marines, and to put to sea, and cruize under the command of Captain Markham, who was employed in covering the Port of Fournelles and Addaya, and preventing succour being thrown in, whilst my pendant was hoisted on board the *Argo*, where I continued two days, aiding and directing the necessary supplies for the army. In this I was ably assisted by Captain Bowen. During these two days I visited head-quarters to consult with the General, when it was decided, as the anchorage at Addaya was extremely hazardous, and the transports in hourly risque of being lost, to remove them to Fournelles; which was executed under cover of the *Leviathan* and *Centaur*. On the 11th, I ordered the Centaur off Ciudadella to prevent reinforcements being thrown in, and anchored the *Leviathan* at Fournelles, landed some twelve-pounder field-pieces and howitzers, the sailors drawing them up to the army, shifted my pendant to the *Leviathan*, and left the *Argo* at Addaya, ordering Captain Bowen to continue there till all the depots were re-embarked and removed, which was effected that day. Late that evening I received information from the General that four ships, supposed to be of the line, were seen between Minorca and Majorca. In the middle of the night, the General sent me another corroborating report from the look-out man, of the four ships seen being of the line. I instantly put to sea (though one-fifth of the crews were on shore) with two ships of the line, a forty-four, and three armed transports, and stood towards Ciudadela; when at day-light the next morning, that place bearing S. E. by S. eight or nine miles, five ships were seen from the mast-head standing directly down for Ciudadela. I instantly made the signal for a general chace, when I soon observed the enemy haul their wind for Majorca; but I continued the pursuit to prevent the possibility of their throwing in succour to Minorca; and at noon I discovered the enemy from the fore-yard to be four large frigates and a sloop of war; this latter keeping her wind, I made the *Argo*'s signal to haul after her, and Captain Bowen, by his letter of the 15th, informs me he took her at half past three in the afternoon, and proved to be his Majesty's sloop *Peterel*, which had been captured the preceding forenoon by the squadron of frigates I was in chase of. For further particulars on that head I shall refer you to Captain Bowen's letter, where I am convinced you will observe with great concern the very harsh treatment the officers and crew of the *Peterel* met with when captured: and he has since added, that one man, who resisted the Spaniards plundering him of forty guineas, was murdered and thrown overboard. I continued the chase till 11 o'clock that night, when I was within three miles of the sternmost frigate; but finding the wind become light, I feared it would draw me too far from the Island of Minorca; I therefore hailed the *Centaur*, and directed Captain Markham to pursue the enemy, steered directly for Ciudadella, which I made the subsequent afternoon (the 14th), with the *Calcutta* and *Ulysses*. The next morning (the 15th) at day-break, the *Argo* joined us off Ciudadela. Having had no communication from the General, I sent the First Lieutenant, Mr. Jones, though a very hazardous night, in the ship's cutter, with a letter to the General, proposing to cannonade Ciudadella if it would facilitate his operations. In the morning of the 16th, Lieutenant Jones returned with duplicates of two letters I had previously received by Captain Gifford, the general's Aide-de-Camp, acquainting me that he had summoned the town on the 14th, and that Terms of Capitulation were agreed upon on the 15th to surrender to his Majesty's arms. When I went on shore, I signed the Capitulation the General had made, on which fortunate event I most truly congratulate your Lordship. The *Centaur* joined, not having been so fortunate as to capture either of the Spanish frigates, though within four miles of the sternmost. Captain Markham being apprehensive the continuance of the chace would carry him to a great distance from more essential service. From the 10th in the morning, when Fort Charles was put into our possession, and Lord Mark Kerr in the *Cormorant*, with the *Aurora*, Captain Caulfield, entered the port, those ships have been employed for the defence of the harbour, guarding the prisoners; and I have the pleasure to assure your lordship, in the performance of the various services incident to the movements I have stated, I cannot pass too high encomiums on the Captains, Officers, and Seamen under my command. From Captains Poulden and Pressland, agents of transports, I received every possible assistance in their departments; and when it was necessary I should proceed to sea to bring to action a reputed superior force, they shewed great spirit, and used every exertion to accompany me in their armed transports, as did Lieutenant Simmonds, the other agent, in his. I must now beg leave to mention my First Lieutenant, Mr. George Jones, who, in the various and hazardous services he had to undergo during the attack of the Island, has proved highly deserving my praise; I have therefore put him to act as Commander of the *Peterel*, which ship I have presumed to recommission to convey the present dispatches. There is also high merit due to my Second Lieutenant, Mr. William Buchanan, whom I landed as second in command under Captain Bowen, with more than 210 seamen. There were likewise the *Leviathan's* and *Centaur's* marines with the army, to the number of 100; but the other essential service calling Captain Bowen on board his ship, the command of the seamen devolved on Lieutenant Buchanan, and, as will appear by the strongest accompanying testimony given him from the Commander in Chief of the Army, he performed the services with the army with the greatest ability and exertion. I should feel myself remiss were I to close this without noticing to your Lordship the particular exertions, activity, and correctness of Lieutenant Whiston, of the *Constitution* cutter, in the various services and messages he had to execute.

The General having signified his wish that his dispatches should be sent without delay, I have not yet been able to visit the port of Mahon, to obtain a return of the state of the dock-yard or vessels captured in that place; but I understand, from Captain Lord Robert Mark Kerr, that there are no ships of war, and only one merchant ship of value; the particulars of which I will transmit by the earliest opportunity. I have the honour to be, my Lord, with the highest respect, &c.

From the 'Monthly Register of Naval Events'. [1 250-251]

The importance of Minorca
25th January 1799. The acquisition of the Island of Minorca to this Country is of considerable importance. Its naval hospital (built by the English), and its accommodation for heaving down the largest ships, are extraordinary good. The harbour is no less commodious - it is also safe, but somewhat difficult to enter, and extremely liable to damage the copper on ship's bottoms, from the rocky sides, against which large vessels are often pressed, when coming in, by eddy breezes from an irregular hilly shore. Fresh meat at Minorca is neither very plentiful nor very good, if we except pork, which, in most hot climates, is excellent. Vegetable[s] are neither raised in profusion, [n]or remarkable for great delicacy. Its honey is famous; its wine almost the reverse.

Minorca Opened to Trade
From 'Gazette Letters.' [1 337]

Saturday, February 16, 1799
At the Court at St. James's, the 13th of February, 1799 - Present the King's Most Excellent Majesty in Council
Whereas the Island of Minorca has been surrendered to his Majesty's arms, and the territory and forts of the same are delivered up to his Majesty, and the said island is now in his Majesty's possession: His Majesty is thereupon pleased to order and declare, and it is hereby ordered and declared, that all his loving subjects may lawfully trade to and from the said island of Minorca, subject nevertheless to the duties, rules, regulations, conditions, restrictions, penalties, and forfeitures, required by law. And the Right Honourable the Lords Commissioners of his Majesty's Treasury, and the Lords Commissioners of the Admiralty, are to give the necessary directions herein as to them may respectively appertain.

W. FAWKENER

Wreck of the Colossus
From the 'Monthly Register of Naval Events.' [1 86]

Scilly, Saturday, December 15, 1798
It is with much concern I acquaint you with the loss of the *Colossus*, of 74 guns, Captain G. Murray, on the night of Monday the 10th inst. on St. Mary's Road, Scilly.

On Friday the 7th inst. the above ship came in with a direct contrary wind, having under her convoy eight vessels from Lisbon, that arrived at the same time, the rest of the fleet having parted two days before for Ireland and the northern ports. In the evening, the wind increasing to a gale, her cable parted, and all attempts to secure the ship failing, she drifted on a ledge of rocks, called Southern Wells, near the Island of Sampson, from eighteen to twenty-four feet under water, all the convoy riding in safety then and since, notwithstanding the wind had risen to a perfect tempest. Most fortunately not a life was lost, save Quarter-master Richard King, who dropped overboard in the act of sounding. The inhabitants of the island exerted themselves to the utmost of their ability in cutters and open boats, and by Tuesday evening every person was taken out and safely landed, the sick and wounded first, whereof many were from the battle of the Nile, the most worthy Captain, and most to be commiserated, remaining to the very last. The following night the ship fell on her starboard beam ends; and so violent was the persevering gale, that no crafts could attempt to approach the ship, and at present little prospect offers of any stores, property, or even the officer's baggage being saved, or hereafter recovered, to any extent. The ship is said to have been distressed, in order to supply other vessels of his Majesty's fleet, and also to have been in a bad state before, and worse since she left Lisbon.[7]

From the 'Biographical Memoir of George Murray, Esq.' *XVIII 187-188*

The *Colossus* had a convoy from Lisbon in charge; and on board of her were the remains of Admiral Lord Shuldham, which were coming to England for interment.

On entering the Channel, Captain Murray found the wind blowing strong from the north-eastward; and, being in a very crazy vessel, with but little provision on board, he thought it best to take the *Colossus* into Scilly. She had been but a short time in the road, when the gale increased to such a degree, that, although completely land-locked, she was forced from her anchors, and driven upon a ledge of rocks, called Southern Wells, where she was totally lost. With the exception of one man, however, who fell overboard in the act of sounding, the whole of the crew were saved.

A court martial sat, on the 19th of January following, to inquire into the loss of the *Colossus*, when the captain and all the officers were honourably acquitted.

Death of Admiral Shuldham. [188]

Admiral Lord Shuldham died lately at Lisbon at a very advanced age. His Lordship's name stood first on the List of Admirals of the White Flag, being junior only to Lord Howe, who is Admiral of the Fleet. He was made a Post Captain in the year 1746, and an Admiral in 1787. His body, on coming to England for interment, went down with the *Colossus* man of war, off Scilly [7 December 1798]. We understand he died without issue, in which case the title becomes extinct. He was son to the Rev. Samuel Shuldham, a resident in the diocese of Ossory.

7 [The *Colossus* was transporting to England the second of the great collections of Greek vases made by Sir William Hamilton, diplomat at the Court of Naples and husband of Emma Hamilton. Eight cases were lost, but sixteen were rescued to form part of the collection in the British Museum.]

APPENDIXES

Appendix 1 – Papers on Naval Strategy and Tactics

APART FROM THE EVIDENCE of tactical ideas which may be gleaned from reading the Sailing and Fighting Instructions, and signal books, there was little official discussion of matters of tactics and strategy. At least since the sixteenth century, however, there existed a body of private writing on questions of the strategic employment of sea power. By the end of the eighteenth century there was fairly general agreement that the British navy was needed, first for defence against invasion, and then for defence of the maritime trade, which was the life of Britain and also the economic basis for its defence capability, and finally for the movement of British forces to defend a world empire and to carry the war to the enemy. The economic strategy was primarily a mercantilist one, directed at the increase of British economic resources, with little discussion of the strategic utility of attack on enemy trade beyond the advantage to captors of prize taking. It was British maritime trade which paid for the coalition armies which eventually defeated Napoleon Buonaparté.

During the war against the French Revolution and Empire, and later against the American Republic, discussion of operational and administrative strategy, and of fleet tactics, was growing. The papers included in this Appendix fall almost entirely into these categories. The fact that matters of the greatest professional importance were published in a generally available forum, some of which were translations of important papers first appearing in the French *Moniteur*, is in striking contrast to the official secrecy which characterised the conduct of war in the twentieth century.

The first entry is a review of Clerk of Eldin's 'Essay on Naval Tactics', which was the first important English monograph study of tactics. *The Naval Chronicle* warmly endorsed it. To the list given in the review, of naval commanders who praised the work, should be added Horatio Nelson who liked to have it read aloud. The letter which follows is somewhat critical of Clerk's analysis, but agrees that it is an important book for naval officers to study. Apparently some of the servicemen who wrote to *The Naval Chronicle* on professional subjects were paid for their work, which must therefore be considered as expressing ideas which the editors believed contributed usefully to the development of naval science, but probably this letter did not fall into that category.

Subsequent to the Clerk review, *The Naval Chronicle* did not devote space specifically to papers on fleet evolutions intended to bring an enemy to battle on satisfactory terms, but tactics inevitably must be based on the capabilities of the principal weapon system employed. Gunnery was to prove a major interest of *The Naval Chronicle*, so much so that it has been convenient to devote another appendix entirely to matters of gunnery and pyrotechnics. Readers are invited to pursue their interest in fleet tactics by referring to the papers in the appendix on gunnery in Volume IV.

The second group of papers in this appendix is Captain Home Popham's organisation plan for the Sea Fencibles for defence of the English south and east coasts, and analysis of possible invasion routes. This amounted to a government plan, and certainly would not have been published a century later.

The third group of papers is concerned with the question of the propriety of mounting a continuous blockade of enemy fleet bases. Although Howe's and Bridport's distant blockade of Brest had been criticised at the beginning of the war, these letters to the editor were written after St Vincent established a permanent blockade of Brest. Experience of the wear and tear inflicted by blockade operations on ships and their companies, and of the impossibility of ensuring that the enemy had no opportunity to escape when bad weather drove off the inshore squadrons, made their authors critical of the experiment.

The fourth set of papers is concerned with the problems of trade defence. Both were written in 1813 when American privateers were operating on the coast of France and in the English Channel with orders, unusual in the age, to destroy British shipping. Traditional trade defence had been able to concentrate on the approaches to enemy harbours where captured British ships might be retaken, but the American policy demanded interception of the raiders before they made their kill. 'J. M.' had a plan for a cruiser line across the Bay of Biscay, and Captain Manderson detailed a tactical plan for patrols in the English Channel.

The fifth paper is an account of the origins of telegraphic signals. Popham's system greatly increased the ability of commanders to give tactical instructions, and to receive intelligence from scouts.

The last document included in this appendix is from *The Naval Chronicle*'s biographical memoir of William Budge, who had become a career civil servant when lack of influence ended his hopes in the navy. In July 1804 he became private secretary to Viscount Melville, First Lord of the Admiralty. The first excerpt from the memoir contains his thoughts on why British efforts to blockade the French coast achieved only limited success. Other excerpts précis Budge's thoughts about the importance to Britain of her mercantile marine, and about the cost to the navy of building ships under contract in mercantile yards.

Document List

Clerk of Eldin's 'An Essay on Naval Tactics'
Review, from 'Naval Literature,' 1799 [I 32-42; 137-140]

An Essay on Naval Tactics, systematical and historical, with explanatory Plates. In Four Parts. Part I. By J. Clerk, Esq. Fellow of the Society of Scottish Antiquaries, and of the Royal Society of Edinburgh. 4to. 10s.6d. Cadell. P. 165

The glorious victories with which our arms have been crowned at sea in the course of the present war, have given frequent occasion to mention Mr. Clerk of Eldin, the author of the new system of naval tactics; it may therefore be agreeable to our readers to lay before them a short state of the merits of a work that has been productive of such unexampled benefits to this country.

In the beginning of the year 1782, when the nation was depressed by the disasters of our arms and the want of naval success during the American war, Mr. Clerk printed and distributed among his friends a few copies of this work, which threw such a new light upon the subject of sea engagements, that no doubt can be entertained of the happy change which (since that period) has taken place in the naval affairs of Britain, is to be attributed to this ingenious and scientific work. When we look back to our naval transactions, before the adoption of the present system, the contrast is so striking, as to fill us with regret that it had not been sooner known.

The disappointment which the nation suffered with regard to our great naval armaments, induced Mr. Clerk to study to find out, if possible, the cause of these disappointments, and to publish his ideas on the subject. Though he never was at sea, he had always attended very much to maritime affairs, and had observed that during the greater part of the three last wars, when British single ships met with single ships of equal force belonging to any other nation, they always were an overmatch for the enemy; or that even in the rencountre of small squadrons, our seamen never failed to exhibit the most skillful seamanship, intrepidity, and perseverance, attended with uninterrupted success. Yet when large fleets were assembled, no proper exertion had ever been made, nothing memorable had been achieved, more particularly with the French, whose system was to batter and destroy our rigging, and then escape unhurt themselves, leaving the British fleet too much disabled to follow them; in fine, to use the author's own words when speaking of general engagements, "The result has always been the same, namely, that in such actions our fleets in the two last wars and the present,[1] have been invariably baffled - nay, worsted, without having ever lost a ship, or almost a man." Yet our officers and men were as brave as they are now, and our ships were equally as good; but experience has proved that we were defective in tactics. As our mode of attacking was then to range along the line of the enemy, until the van of our fleet came opposite to the rear of his; thus our ships ran the gauntlet of the enemy's whole fleet, giving them an opportunity to cripple each ship as it passed, of which the French never failed to take advantage. But the happy genius of an individual, by pointing out a superior mode of attack, has been the means of enabling us to carry our naval glory to a pitch hitherto unrivalled in any age or nation.

The leading principle of Mr. Clerk's system is, to force an enemy's fleet into close engagement, whatever efforts he may make to avoid it, and the breaking through his line of battle, and cutting off one division of his fleet from another, so as to prevent the enemy from being able to extricate himself, is recommended as a certain means of either capturing the division you have cut off, or of bringing on a general engagement. The uniform success of this manoeuvre, now so well known, leaves no room to doubt the infallibility of Mr. Clerk's system. Of this the victories of Lords Rodney,[2] Howe, St. Vincent,[3] and Duncan,[4] who all read and approved his work and adopted his system, are most brilliant examples.

In the instance of the battle of the Nile, the French had formed themselves in a line, which they very naturally deemed impregnable, but which certainly deprived them of the power of retreating. In this fixed position they remained to wait our attack, and consequently the superior skill which Lord Nelson has exhibited, was not in *forcing* them to fight, but in his manner of commencing the action. And here it is easy to discern the spirit of the new system in his mode of attacking the van of the enemy's fleet, to which the rear could give no assistance until it was become too late; while the brave Captain Thompson in the *Leander*, by *cutting their line*, completed their confusion

1 This was written during the American war.

2 Lord Rodney being asked by a mutual friend of his and Mr. Clerk's, what he thought of Mr. Clerk's essay on naval tactics, replied, "You shall see what I think of it whenever I am so happy as to meet the French fleet again; for I am determined to follow it." And he had the magnanimity to acknowledge afterwards in every company, that the victory gained over the French fleet on the 12th of April 1782, was fought upon Clerk's system. A peace was the immediate consequence of this memorable victory.

3 General Debbieg, an officer well known from his superior genius in his own profession, and naturally an admirer of works of genius, having read Mr. Clerk's essay, lent it to Lord St. Vincent, then Sir John Jervis. Sir John after reading it, enquired of the general where he might buy a copy for himself: "It is not to be bought," answered the general; "I had this copy from the author, who is a particular friend of mine; he had but a few copies printed, all of which he has given away among his friends." "Since that is the case," said Sir John Jervis, "you shall not have this copy back again; it is too good a thing for you, who are a landsman; I will keep it to myself."

4 Lord Duncan having received one of the few copies of this essay first printed, soon after wrote to advise Mr. Clerk to reprint it, as he said it was very much approved of by all the navy officers, many of whom, not being able to procure printed copies, had copied it over in writing. When Lord Duncan returned to Edinburgh, after the battle of Camperdown, he waited on Mr. Clerk, complimented him upon his works, and in a liberal and handsome manner, acknowledged that he and the other admirals had been much obliged to him.

and defeat. There is a degree of masterly boldness, as the French observe, in Lord Nelson's manoeuvres, and a dauntless intrepidity in the execution of them, that must ever command the admiration of the whole world.

This action is a flattering proof of the superiority of our seamen, a topic much insisted on by Mr. Clerk, and from which he promises certain success whenever our fleets can be brought into close engagement with the enemy.

We believe there are few of our readers who, after perusing the above, will not be touched with one common sentiment, that while the nation pays the tribute of applause, so justly due to the skill and bravery of our naval commanders, it ought not to forget the gratitude no less justly merited by the ingenious author of *Naval Tactics*.

The above account of Mr. Clerk's work, having appeared in a morning print,[5] with such considerable testimony in favour of our author, we thought it too interesting not to be inserted.

Mr. Clerk has since published the remaining parts, an account of which will appear in our second number.

This essay on naval tactics, strange as it may appear, was the first original scientific treatise published on that subject in this kingdom; all the other treatises that appeared in Great Britain prior to it, being either translations from the French, or remarks upon French authors. Some of the principal French treatises on naval tactics are the following:

1. *L'Art des Armées Navales, ou traité des Evolutions Navales*, par Paul L'Hoste, 1 vol. folio, printed at Lyons, 1727. This book was translated and published by Christopher O'Bryen, Esq. in 4to. in 1762.

2. *Tactique Navale, ou traité des Evolutions et des Signaux*, par M. le Vicomte de Morogues, 4to. Paris, 1763.

3. *Le Manoeuvrier*, par M. Bourdé de Villehuet.

4. *L'Art de Guerre en Mer, ou tactique Navale*, &c. par M. le Vicomte de Grenier.

Translations of the two last have appeared in English in 4to. in 1788, under the name of the Chevalier de Sauseuil, and a translation of parts of the three last is in the second volume of the *Elements and Practice of Rigging and Seamanship*, published in 1794. Other books on evolutions and tactics are:

Théorie de la Manoeuvre des Vaisseaux, Paris, 1689. Pilot's *Theory of Working Ships applied to practice, &c*, translated by Stone, 1743. *De la Manoeuvre de Vaisseaux, ou Traité de Mechanique et de Dynamique, &c.*, par M. Bouguer. *The British Mars, &c.* by William Flexney, 1763. *A Sea Manual*, by Sir Alexander Schomberg, 1789. *A View of the Naval Force of Great Britain, &c.* by an Officer of Rank, 1791, &c..

The order of battle, which was first formed in the last century by the Duke of York, and has been continued in use to the present day, the Viscount de Grenier thinks extremely defective. Various causes may conspire to render the task of breaking it not difficult. Its great extent must make it no easy matter for the admiral to judge what orders are proper to be issued to the ship's stations in its extremities; whilst his signals, however distinctly made, are liable to be mistaken by the commanders of those ships. The extremities of a long line are necessarily defenceless, especially if it be to leeward; because, after it is formed, the enemy may throw himself with a superior number, on its van or rear, and put that squadron to flight before assistance can be sent to it from the other squadrons. These defects the Viscount de Grenier thinks may be remedied by never presenting to the enemy any part of a fleet without its being flanked; so that were

5 *True Briton.*

the commander of the adverse fleet to attack those parts which hitherto have been reckoned weakest, he might find himself defeated when he looked for conquest. With this view the viscount proposes a new order of battle; in which the fleet, composed of three divisions, instead of being drawn up in one line as usual, shall be ranged on the three sides of a regular lozenge, formed by the intersecting of the two close-hauled lines. It is obvious that one of the divisions of a fleet ranged in this manner will always be formed in the order of battle; whilst the two others, resting upon the first ship ahead, and the last astern of that division, will be formed on the close-hauled line opposite, and will stand on chequerwise on the same tack with the ships which are in the line of battle serving to cover the headmost and sternmost of those ships, and thereby prevent the enemy from penetrating the line or doubling the rear.

The vicomte thought it a great mistake, though very generally fallen into, that the weather-gage is of any advantage to a fleet equal in force to its enemy, and willing to engage. To him the great art of war at sea appears to consist in drawing or keeping to *windward a part of the adverse fleet*, and collecting all one's forces against that part; and it is chiefly to effect this purpose that he proposes his new system of tactics. The reader, who would understand his principles, must never lose sight of this evident truth, that each ship of a fleet necessarily occupies at all times the centre of an horizon; which the author divides into two unequal parts, calling the greater the *direct and graduated space*, and the less, the *indirect, crossed, and ungraduated space*. The reason of these appelations is, that on the greater segment of the horizontal circle there are twenty different points, which may be marked by degrees from one of the close-hauled lines to the other, and to which a ship may sail from the centre by so many direct courses without tacking; whereas to the other twelve points, including that from which the wind blows, she cannot arrive but by steering cross courses, which must necessarily delay her progress.

Having introduced the Viscount de Grenier to the notice of our readers, the celebrated precursor of Mr. Clerk, an attentive perusal of whose work would afford considerable improvement to the seaman, we return to our author.

The first part, to which our attention is at present directed, is confined to the attack from the windward. This is accompanied with thirty geometrical plates; in which the British ships are distinguished by a red colour, and letters of reference beginning with the alphabet and ending at E. The ships of the enemy are distinguished by a black colour, with letters beginning at F.

Mr. Clerk concludes his demonstrations in this volume with the following striking reflections:

"If, then, after a proper examination of the late sea engagements, or rencounters, it shall be found that our enemy, the French, have never once shown a willingness to risk the making of the attack, but, invariably, have made choice of, and earnestly courted a leeward position: if, invariably, when extended in line of battle, in that position they have disabled the British fleets in coming down to the attack: if, invariably, upon seeing the British fleet disabled, they have made sail, and demolished the van in passing: if, invariably, upon feeling the effect of the British fire, they have withdrawn, at pleasure, either a part, or the whole of their fleet, and have formed a new line of battle to leeward: if the French, repeatedly, have done this upon every occasion: and, on the other hand, if it shall be found that the British, from an irresistible desire of making the attack, as constantly and uniformly have courted the windward position: if, uniformly and repeatedly, they have had their ships so disabled and separated, by making the attack, that they have not once been able to bring them to close with, to follow up, or even to detain one ship of the enemy for a moment; shall we not have reason to believe, that the French have adopted, and put in execution, some system, which the British either have not discovered, or have not yet profited by the discovery?"

The following general observations are extracted from some very judicious ones, which conclude the article of examples cited, with Mr. Clerk's opinion of their merit.

"From these examples it appears, that the attack, in every one of them, without variation, has been made by a long extended line, generally from the windward quarter, by steering or directing every individual ship of that line upon her opposite of the enemy, but more particularly the ships in the van.

That the consequences of this mode of attack have proved fatal in every attempt; that is, our ships have been so disabled, and so ill supported, that the enemy have been permitted not only to make sail and leave us, but to complete the disgrace have, in passing, been permitted to pour in the fire of their whole line upon our van, without a possibility of retaliation on our part.

Another reflection will naturally occur: that, by the great destruction of rigging, the consequence of this mode of attack, the nation has been thrown into a most enormous expence of repair; while our enemy, by their cautious conduct, preserving their ships often unhurt, has been enabled not only to protract the war, but, if persisted in, will, without doubt, ensure the possession, perhaps, of a superior navy, complete and entire to the conclusion.

Having now demonstrated, from evidence which should be satisfactory, that the mode or instructions hitherto followed for arranging great fleets in line, so as to be able to force an enemy to give battle on equal terms, must be somewhere wrong, it will be required to show whether any other mode may be devised, or put in practice, that will have a better effect."

Mr. Clerk then proceeds to *the mode of attack proposed*, which he divides into sections. The clear and concise manner in which throughout he treats his subject, are deserving of great praise.

In these sections, the attack from the windward upon the rear of the enemy, the leading subject of the volume is treated of at large.

"Suppose[6] a fleet of ten, twenty, or more ships, extended in line of battle, endeavouring to avoid a close engagement, but at the same time keeping under an easy sail, with the intention of receiving the usual attack from another fleet of equal number, three or four miles to windward, sailing in any form; but let it be *in three lines or divisions*: it is required by what method shall *the latter* make the attack on *the former* with advantage.

The improbability, or rather impossibility, of attacking and carrying the enemy's whole line of ships having already been demonstrated; the next consideration will be, how many ships may be attacked and carried with advantage? Let it be supposed that the three sternmost ships only, and not exceeding the fourth, are possible to be *carried*; let a sufficient strength be sent down to force an attack upon these three ships, disposed and supported according to the judgment of the admiral, while in the mean time, he should keep to windward with the rest of his fleet, formed into such divisions as might best enable him to attend to the motions of the enemy, and the effect of his attack; being himself so far disengaged from action, as to be able to make his observations, and give his orders, with some degree of tranquillity."

Mr. Clerk in the second section considers the *attack upon the enemy's three sternmost*

6 In this extract we are obliged to leave out the references to the plates.

ships more particularly, and, in the succeeding sections, pays attention to the supposed attempts of the enemy to support the attacked ships. The author in this part of his work shews considerable ingenuity, and appears particularly to have studied it. We can only lament that so much nautical knowledge, and of so original a stamp, has arisen without the pale of a profession, that would have been so greatly adorned by its author. . . .

That Mr. Clerk's work will be of considerable service to the Navy of Great Britain, the commendation it has already received from some of the most distinguished officers in it, is a sufficient proof. Yet still he certainly gives too little credit to the enemy's fleet for their exertions in repelling the attack: he too much supposes them, as has been observed, to be helpless, and claims the victory. This, however, is a fault which it certainly is easier to point out, than to avoid. The judicious and able reflections he has made with such boldness and originality, demand the attention and gratitude of his Country. We trust he will continue his naval labours, as much still remains for so able a writer to elucidate. A more general account of naval actions, from the accession of the house of Hanover, with judicious commentaries upon them, is a work Mr. Clerk is fully competent to perform, and would prove very acceptable to naval men.

[Plates illustrating Grenier and Clerk's tactical ideas can be found in Brian Tunstall and Nicholas Tracy, *Naval Warfare in the Age of Sail*, Conway Maritime Press, 1990.]

Letter commenting on Mr. Clerk's Essay
From 'Correspondence.' [1 233-4]

Mr. Editor, As in the first number of your work, you dwell particularly on the merits of Mr. Clerk's *Naval Tactics*; I enclose the criticism of an officer, which I have had permission to copy, from his own memorandums on a blank leaf of the book: the communication may possibly be acceptable to your readers.

This essay is certainly to be regarded as a very extraordinary effort of genius in the author; who, being without any practical knowledge in the profession, must form all his deductions from the powers of his own fertile mind, in the discussion of the subject. I think many of his remarks on general actions are very just; but his idea of them, being solely taken from the public correspondence of the different commanders, cannot give opportunity, in the desired degree, for the improvement of officers anxious to perfect themselves in naval tactics: first, because of the want of a more minute, or particular recital of the various incidents, occurring on either side in general engagements: and secondly, on account of the limited extent, to which the observation of the chief commanders, on such occasions, is almost unavoidably confined. The author grounds the system he would establish, for that he supposes to have been the only one before in practice, on a presumption, that the enemy has always meant (and ever intends) to avoid being engaged in a general action: but I cannot perceive that he assigns the enemy the movements, which they would naturally adopt, on such an attack as he describes may be [*sic*, being?] made on their rear. Mr. Clerk appears to claim the merit of having *first suggested* that peculiar mode of attack. He nevertheless takes notice of the admitted insufficiency of the only *established code of signals* (the general sailing and fighting instructions instituted by Admiralty authority towards the end of the last century), as having required material additions to be made to them by the commanders in chief at later periods. Had Mr. Clerk examined such documents, he would have found provision was therein made for the same manner of attack occasionally, more (if I mistake not) than thirty years antecedent to his first publication in 1782: viz. by a signal in substance *to engage the ships of the enemy as arriving up with them in succession.* On recurring to those documents and explanatory instructions, he would have been better enabled to judge of the ideas, which prevailed in later times, both preparatory to, and for the government of fleets in battle. Why such abovementioned provision was not adverted to in the instances he details, I do not pretend to account. The author appears to have been much seduced by the pleasing belief of being the original proposer of a perfect, or more improved system of naval tactics; but being deficient in practical knowledge, he has been induced, from his earnestness to cause the adoption of it, into many erroneous conclusions in different parts of his work.

I never, Mr. Editor, before heard of *the curve of pursuit*, on which Mr. Clerk largely comments. If it ever was in the contemplation of any flag-officer to apply it, as the author insinuates, such commander must have forgotten, that the chord, or what Mr. Clerk terms the *oblique line of approach*, is the shortest distance; as it is the most advantageous, and easily to be traced in steerage, between the two extreme points of an arch; and must also have entirely disregarded, what I conceive to be the ordinary rule of practice, on the cruising service, when ships to leeward, keeping their wind, are to be joined by those chacing from a windward position, A simple demonstration of this will be found, I think, in P. Hoste.[7]

Before Mr. Clerk had been led to imagine, that the idea of *forcing the enemy's line* was a late suggestion, he should have remembered, that this mode of attack is recorded in the *earliest* relation of naval actions extant; and has been more recently brought into notice, by the practice of it, even from the commencement of the Dutch wars in the last century. It is not however my intention by these reflections to discountenance the circulation of Mr. Clerk's *Naval Tactics.* On the contrary, I highly recommend an attentive perusal of the work (and indeed of all similar publications, whether in French or English) to every officer, who is anxious to acquire an habit of adverting readily to opposite expedients, in different situations; when the arduous trust of a squadron, or the more important and serious charge of a fleet, suspends for a time, on a trembling balance, that reputation, which the service of many years had acquired.

Your very humble servant

X.Z.

Plan Proposed by Captain Popham, R.N., for Raising the Sea Fencibles - 1799. [480-487]

When the British Nation was roused in all its energy, to guard against the invasive threats of the kingdom that styles itself Great, it behoved every one, and especially professional men, to propose such plans, as their own judgment and experience suggested. Among these, the one drawn up by Captain Popham deserves particular notice, as having been acted on, though not to the full extent. We have received the following outline of it, from a friend, which we hasten to communicate to our readers.

Captain Popham's sentiments on the possibility of an invasion, at the period alluded to, was detailed at length in his letters to officers, and men of considerable rank, and was duly appreciated: the substance of this is subjoined, as having a relation to the following outline:

7 Clerk's 'curve of pursuit' was a hyperbolic course supposedly followed by a ship to windward when closing with an enemy. X.Z.'s criticism is certainly valid.

Captain Popham raised a corps of Sea Fencibles at Nieuport, in Flanders, in November 1793, by an order from his royal Highness the Duke of York, through Sir James Murray (now Pulteney), Adjutant General. This corps was composed of the fishermen of the place. Sir Charles Grey bore ample testimony to Major General Thomas Dundas of their steady conduct at the first siege of Nieuport. They were afterwards under the command of Captain Wiltshire Wilson, of the Royal Artillery, who has likewise borne testimony that no men could behave better than they did at the second siege of Nieuport. From this Captain Popham thought the adoption of a similar Corps in England would be of great service.

Outline of a Plan as an Auxiliary Defence of the Coast of England against Invasion, by the Establishment of Sea Fencibles. Submitted to the consideration of the Right Honourable the Lords Commissioners for executing the Office of Lord High Admiral of Great Britain, &c.

In carrying this plan into effect, the seamen and fishermen present themselves as a great and valuable resource to the nation; they are competent to many essential services, more particularly afloat, for which the other inhabitants of the coast are not so well calculated; and as they are for the great part fathers of families, have a proportionate interest in the security and protection of the kingdom from invasion; they would be among the first to experience its horrors from the particular situation of their towns, and consequently will feel it their duty to be foremost in offering their exertions in the common cause.

The mode which is about to be suggested, while it calls forth all their energy, and puts them in a condition to be eminently useful, secures certain advantages which government is always forward in offering to zeal and merit.

It is accordingly proposed to enroll the seamen and seafaring men resident in the towns and villages on the coast, and train to artillery, with a positive assurance that they are never to be called out, unless for actual service, or for the purpose of exercising.

It is intended that each of the sea-coast counties should be divided into a certain number of districts, each consisting of a proportionate number of beaches; that the Sea Fencibles of each county shall be commanded by a captain of the navy; and a commander be stationed in each district to quarter the men on the beaches, to exercise them occasionally, and to have the beaches watched whenever the weather is favourable for the enemy to attempt a landing.

The commander of each district is to establish an office in the most convenient or central town in his district, for the purpose of enrolling such seamen or seafaring men as voluntarily offer themselves for this laudable service.

The Sea Fencibles are to be exercised once every week in such batteries as may already be on the coast, or hereafter directed to be made by order of government.

Each man so enrolled will be allowed one shilling per day on the days he is called to exercise, if he attends, or when he is employed on actual service; this pay to be paid on the last day of every month, at the office of the commander of each district, and in the presence of the mayor or chief magistrate of the town where the office is established.

The commander of each district will also have authority to grant a protection to the men[8]

---

8 *Alteration by the Admiralty* - Protections will be granted under such restrictions as the Admiralty may judge proper to those men who enroll themselves as Sea Fencibles, &c.

who enroll themselves as Sea Fencibles, and this protection will be an exemption from any other military duty while they actually belong to the Corps of Sea Fencibles.

The commander will be authorised to grant any reasonable leave of absence to the men of his district to enable them to follow their lawful occasions; but they will be required to apply for a ticket of leave, to the end that the commander may be at all times enabled to ascertain the number of men on whose service he can depend; exclusive of which the protections will not be respected without the district of the commander who has granted them, unless accompanied by such a ticket of leave.

In case the Lords Commissioners of the Admiralty shall deem it expedient to place armed row galleys[9] on any of the beaches, such Sea Fencibles as come forward to man them, whether to attack or annoy small privateers, or retake any vessels that may have fallen into the enemy's hands, will, independent of the pay already stated, be supplied with provisions whilst they are on board of those galleys, or any other armed vessels or boats that may be sent for the protection of the sea coast; exclusive of which they will be entitled to prize money for any privateers or other vessels they may take belonging to the enemy.

In case there should not be any provisions on board of such vessels as they may embark in, then they will be allowed subsistence from the time they are on board, at the rate of eightpence per day per man.

The Sea Fencibles are not to be forced to serve out of the district they undertake to defend, unless the enemy make good a landing, when they will in course follow their commanders, who will be furnished with half pikes to arm the men of his district, and these pikes will be made longer than a musquet with its bayonet fixed, that the Sea Fencibles may have an opportunity of charging the enemy with advantage in any general action, or of storming such redoubts as the French may throw up, or any other work they may presume to make in England.

In case it should be necessary for the Sea Fencibles to act as pioneers, for the purpose of retarding the progress of the French, the proper implements will be supplied them for that service; as well as for the construction of bridges for the advantage of the army.

When the Sea Fencibles are thus employed, they will be paid and subsisted in the same manner as if actually embarked.

The chains of communication which this body of men will establish between the sea and the interior will afford the means of assembling our troops from all parts to the place of attack, and thus give a confidence and security from surprise, and an additional strength to the commander in chief, by all the number of troops he is now obliged to detach for the purpose of manning the established batteries along the sea coast; and I have no doubt but in a short time after their enrollment, they will not only embark very cheerfully on any service that may be required of them, but always hold themselves ready for any active enterprise that it may be though expedient to undertake.

If there is to be a part of field artillery kept in reserve in any interior part of the sea coast counties, I really am of opinion that two or three pieces ought to be attached to each division of Sea Fencibles, for them to take charge of when it is necessary to quit their batteries on the coast, and join the army. They would by this means form a most respectable train of artillery.

It has been submitted for consideration, whether two gun batteries along the coast

9 Galleys, 60 to 70 feet long: 12 to 12 1/2 broad. To carry an 18-pounder, or 42 carronade. Row 36 to 40 oars. May cost £320 building.

of Sussex, from Hastings to the westward, might not be of very great service; not only in annoying the enemy in his attempt to land, but also to give protection to the coasting trade. The guns proposed for these batteries are the French and Dutch prize guns, 42 pounders; they are to be on their ships carriages and trucks, consequently only a platform will be required. The reasons for proposing these heavy guns are, that when an enemy gets possession of them, he will not be able to move them without the greatest difficulty; and they are seldom made use by us, except sometimes in batteries.

It is also proposed that the gunners of such ships in ordinary as are not likely to be immediately wanted, shall be attached to the batteries, to exercise the men and take charge of the stores.

Districts for the Commanders of the Sea Fencibles between Bristol and the Firth of Forth. The Captain of the Country will in Course fix on the most Central Spot in the District for the Commander to establish his Office at

			Post Capt.	Cmdr
Sommersetshire	Bristol	Bridgwater	1	3
	Minehead			
Devonshire, North and South	Ilfracombe	Barnstaple	2	8
	Saltash district	Plymouth district		
	Kingsbridge	Dartmouth		
	Teignmouth	Exmouth		
Cornwall	Padstow	St. Ives	1	8
	Penzance	Helford Harbour		
	Falmouth	St. Maw's		
	Fowey	Cawsand		
Dorsetshire	Sidmouth	Lyme	1	6
	Weymouth	St. Alban's Head district		
	Wareham district	Poole district		
Hants	Christchurch	Lymington	1	8
	Isle of Wight 2*	Southampton 2*		
	Gosport	Portsmouth		
Sussex	Chichester	Arundel	1	8
	Shoreham	Brighton		
	Seaford	Eastborne		
	Hastings	Rye		
Kent	Kent	Hythe	1	8
	Folkstone	Dover		
	Deal	Margate		
	Whitstable	Faversham		
Essex	Malden	Colchester	1	3
	Harwich			
Suffolk	Ipswich	Orfordness	1	4
	Thorpwell	Lowestoffe		
Norfolk	Yarmouth	Foulness	1	3
	Lynn			

Lincolnshire	Boston Deeps and to the Humber 3*		1	3
Yorkshire	Hull	Flamborough	1	5
	Bridlington	Scarborough		
	Whitby			
Durham	Stockton	Hartlepool	1	4
	Sunderland to South Shields			
Northumberland	Newcastle, Shields, Tinmouth		1	3
Berwick	Including the Firth 4*		1	4
		Total	16	78

* [The number of commanders appointed to those districts.]
Each post captain, including office, &c. per month (calendar)
exclusive of travelling charges   £ 49-7-0
Ditto commander　ditto   £ 33-12-0
　16　　Total amount of post captains   £ 789-12-0
　78　　Ditto　commanders   £ 2,620-16-0
18,800 Ditto　men   £ 3,760-0-0
        Total £ 7,170-8-0

If the half-pay is not allowed, exclusive of the daily allowance herein
stated, there will be a deduction from the aggregate of per month £ 846-0-0

It is impossible to make any calculation of the number of men that may be raised without visiting all the places, but supposing that each officer raises 200 men, the numbers raised in the above line of coast will be 18,800; and stating the expence of those men at the first idea of 4s per month, it will be per month £3,760; but when it is necessary to embark them, or to march them out of their district, then the estimate of subsistence, at the rate of 8d per day per man must be added.

Having sketched this outline of a plan of defence for the sea coast, it remains only to remark, that with motives such as these to exertion [sic]; with duties at once so imperious and important to discharge; with such private and public advantages attending the discharge of those duties; with the gratitude and acknowledgment it must excite, and the retribution it must ensure, from those of rank and property in their neighbourhood, it is impossible but that one universal spirit of emulation must be kindled in every bosom on our coasts.

Under such an impression, those who shall not be able to render personal service, will unquestionably endeavour to evince their ardour, by considering how great an inducement it may be to serve, if those who may be killed or wounded on this service, could look forward to the possibility of obtaining some support for their families or themselves from the district to which they belong: and this may probably make the defence so strong and so formidable, as to awe the enemy; who, far from putting the exertion of our Sea Fencibles to the proof, will deem it more prudent to remain at home, and desist from an enterprise which can promise them nothing but ruin and confusion.

Heads of a Letter from Captain Popham to a General Officer on the Subject of the Sea Fencible Plan

Dear Sir, I took the liberty of suggesting the annexed plan,[10] on a conviction that the

10 Sea Fencibles.

French, in their present state of unreasonable enmity to this country, would attempt any enterprise, however desperate and sanguinary in its execution, which might tend to irritate the people against the existing government, or cause a momentary depreciation of the public credit; and I now presume to offer you my opinion on their arrangements for this serious threat or intended attack. But in offering this opinion I take it for granted, they have many thousand men who they wish to provide for in the most plausible manner, who are pampered up with the hopes of plunder, and enthusiastic to a degree of maniasm [sic].

These troops will be cantoned along their extensive sea coast from Ostend to Brest.

The coast will be divided into three grand or principal districts of Picardy, Normandy, and Brittany, and to these may be added the departments of Brest; I will proceed to show the capability of the first district Picardy, from which comparative calculations of the others may be drawn. This district shall extend to part of Flemish Flanders, shall have in its view the invasion of the coast of Sussex, and that part of the south-west coast of Kent that is comprehended between Dungeness and the South Foreland.

I will now take it for granted, that they have built a certain number of flat vessels, which I believe to be the case; that these vessels carry two heavy guns, with field pieces on board, and that they will make use of the fishing boats for auxiliary transport vessels; as I know the places in the district I am now writing upon, have as many vessels of that description as can be wanted.

Having supposed that the French have troops and vessels sufficient for the enterprise, and are desperate enough to undertake it; let us for a moment allow them system and experience sufficient to conduct, at a proper time, and in a proper manner, the embarkation of the troops in this district, which should be finished in two hours with southerly or easterly winds, and ought to take place at the setting in of a frost; when the best informed philosophers predict its continuance from the observations they have made on the appearance of weather, and its effect on mercury in different situations.

I will annex the places of embarkation in this district, with the least number of men which may be embarked, their respective destinations and the distances from their own coast:

Ostend	6000	Folkstone, Hythe, and to Dungeness	18-22 leagues
Nieuport	2000		
Dunkirk	4500		
Gravelines	2500		
Calais	3000	Rye and Hastings	18-20 leagues
Boulogne	4000		
Estaples	2000	Hastings to Beachy	Ditto
Rue	2000		
Crotey	2000		
Treport	2000		
Dieppe	8000	Brighton	
St. Vallery de Caux	2000	Brighton to Arundel	20-25 leagues
Fecamp	4000		
Havre	12000		
Total	56000		

Having now embarked the troops, they are thrown on the calculation of chances; therefore let us allow that one third will be lost in getting across; nearly that number in effecting their landing and concentrating their men; and the remainder may probably exist a few days before they are taken or destroyed.

I do not apprehend the Directory[11] predicts a better fate for their troops. Their object will be answered in some respects: they will have provided for their idle soldiers; they will have made a commotion in England; and oblige this country to victual such as escape, which ought to be few indeed.

The district of Normandy is well checked by the islands of Guernsey and Jersey, particularly the latter, which is so well situated to watch the operations of St. Maloes, that I wonder an attempt has not been made on these islands preparatory to the invasion of England.

Should the Directory be really and seriously bent on the invasion of this country, I think it will be preceded by strong expedition from Brest to Ireland, and at the same time probably to the Bristol Channel and coast of Wales.

If the *soit nommé Armée d'Angleterre* is not ready, and the necessary arrangements made, it will not astonish me to hear that the enterprise is put off till next year, and that we shall be kept in a continued state of alarm by their practising the embarkation and disembarkation of troops.

I think the fishing boats ought to be seized, and if it can be managed to make the *coup* general, it will not only deprive the enemy of a number of transports, but the best pilots they have for the coast of Sussex, which I suppose are principally in the Dieppe vessels. There are belonging to Ostend, Nieuport, Dunkirk, Gravelines, Calais, Boulogne, and Dieppe, at least eight hundred vessels; indeed I should think many more. From this information you will best judge of the expediency of the measure, and the advantage that may result from its being carried into effect.

I am, dear Sir, &c..   H.P.

N.B. Further hints on the possibility of invasion, and the mode of defence to be adopted, will be given in a subsequent number.

Popham's Further Consideration of the Sea Fencibles
II 52-55. See also XVI 379-382

The following Letter from Captain Popham of the Navy, to General Sir Charles Grey, was written at the Time the former was employed to establish Sea Fencibles on the Coast of Sussex. It contains some useful hints for the Mode of Defence, had the Enemy put his Threats of Invasion into Execution

[Dover, 6 April 1798]
Considering my appointment as commanding the Sea Fencibles from Beachy Head to Deal inclusive, I feel it not only my duty, but very much my inclination, to submit to you such ideas as have suggested themselves to me, on the practicability of the enemy's landing in the above district; to which, although it may be correct to confine a public

---

11 The adminstrators of the French government.

report, yet I hope I shall not be marked as impertinent in cases, where I presume to make any observation beyond the limits of my station.

It cannot be supposed that a predatory incursion, or partial invasion, will have any effect on this Country beyond the first moments of its operation; consequently it is necessary to determine with what wind a general invasion may be made, so as to comprehend the coasts of Essex, Sussex, and Kent, which are all the coasts that can be possibly estimated as within the narrow seas: but to make the combination complete, it must also be considered what wind will permit the transports to sail out of every port in Holland, Flanders, and France, to the eastward of Havre de Grace, and at the same time insure the smoothest water on the coast of England; because they can have no covering navy, and must very much depend on small vessels for the advantage of beaching.[12]

The wind from E. to E.N.E. will enable them to sail from the Brille, Helvoetsluys, and Flushing, for the southern part of Suffolk, and the coast of Essex; that is, from Orfordness to Malden river. The distance across the sea may be about thirty-five leagues.

From Sluys, Ostend, Nieuport, and Dunkirk, the same wind will carry them through the Queen's Channel, and South Channel, up the Swale; and the distance from Sluys, which is the easternmost port to Faversham, will not exceed 30 leagues; and I believe it will scarce be necessary for me to say, that they have more schoots and bilanders in Holland, than they can have occasion for on such an expedition; and that the turbot men are as well acquainted with the coasts of Kent and Essex, and the channels leading to the Thames, as our own pilots.

Taking it for granted that the invasion will be confined to the narrow seas, unless an attempt is made on Guernsey or Jersey, previous to its commencement, I have named in the margin[13] the number of places, from whence an embarkation may be made, between Gravelines and Havre; and I shall now proceed to offer a few remarks on the coast between the South Foreland and Beachy, which is the western limit of my district; at the same time, Sir, I assure you I shall be much flattered to be asked an opinion of any other part of the coast, where my local knowledge may enable me to assist you.

The fleet in the Downs, with the Goodwin Sands, are such securities to the coast, between the two forelands, that little is to be apprehended in that space.

In Eastware Bay, which is about a mile and a quarter long, a landing may be effected; but it is so surrounded with cliffs, that I think the attempt would be very dangerous, as the enemy cannot expect any immediate support from the eastward.

From a little westward of Folkstone, to the sea wall near Dymchurch, there is a fine bay of six miles, in which infantry may land at any time, and cannon and cavalry may be landed at half tide; and in many places, particularly near Sandgate Castle, it is so bold a shore, that large ships may anchor within half a mile, in case the enemy mean to use any of the Dutch men of war to cover their landing.

To the westward of Dymchurch the land begins to trench to the southward, and consequently the E.N.E. wind, which I hold out as the best wind for a general invasion, would make so much sea from thence to the Ness Point, that it would be impossible to

12 In severe frosts, with light moderate S.E. winds, it is remarked that there is by no means so much surf on the coast, as with the same portion of wind in open weather.

13	Gravelines	St. Vallery	Distance from these
	Calais	Triport	places to the S.W.
	Boulogne	Dieppe	coast of Kent and coast
	Etapelles	Fecamp	of Sussex, 15-25 leagues.
	Crotoy	Havre de Grace	

attempt a landing; independent of which, the shore is so flat at and near Romney, that under the most favourable circumstances of wind and weather, the enemy could only land infantry in small boats, except at high water.

From the Ness Point to the entrance of Rye Old Harbour, there is a fine shingle beach, steep too, and with an easterly wind it is as smooth as possible. From Rye Old Harbour to Hooksledge, or the end of Pitlevel, a distance of five miles, there is an uncommon fine beach of sand and shingle, on which, with an easterly wind, a debarkation to any extent may be made. In this space there is an harbour of more consequence than people are in general aware of; it is formed by a natural beach thrown up parallel to the shore, and at right angles with the entrance of Rye New Harbour; it is called Providence Harbour, and the sketch, which I have the honour to lay before you, will give you some idea of it, till I have an opportunity of completing a survey of it for the information of government: - but in the interim I have reported to the Admiralty in a few words, that I have seen fifteen square-rigged vessels lie there; that large cutters drawing eleven feet water use it; but as there is not more than two feet at low water over a muddy bottom, any vessels they chuse to send there must take the ground. The tide runs on the springs from eleven to eighteen feet; and with a very trifling expence, and a little exertion, vessels of ten feet drought of water may be got out, and in, at half tide; but unless it is thought an object to give the harbour some protection, I left it for their superior judgment to decide, whether it would not be more politic to block it up than to open it. I believe the harbour would be completely under the range of mortars from Winchelsea Terrace; but of this, Sir, you must be the best judge, nor should I now have presumed to touch on this subject, had I not observed mortars dismounted lying on the coast.

From Hooksledge, to Hastings, there is an inaccessible cliff of five miles, having only two narrow passes, Ecclesbourne and Govers: from Hastings to Bowpeep Barracks the shore is rocky, and a landing would be attended with some risk at low water; but from Bowpeep to Bulverhithe, a distance of two miles, there is probably as fine a beach as any in the world to land inflantry, cavalry, or cannon; and large ships may anchor within half a mile of the shore.

From Bulverhithe Point about four miles to the westward, the shore is rocky, and cannot be used at low water; from thence to Beachy Head, there is in general so fine a beach, that a landing may be made at any time of tide; but an E.N.E. wind would make a considerable sea from Pevensey to Laugney Point, as the coast trenches there much to the southward; but from Langney Point nearly to the pitch of Beachy Head, the water would be perfectly smooth.

Although I have pointed out some spots between Hastings and Beachy, that are rocky, yet they are not to be considered as barriers to a general debarkation in this bay, which certainly presents itself as a very spacious one, with the advantage of having been used with success on a former occasion: but you, Sir, must be the best judge of the back country, and the opposition an enemy may meet in this extent of eighteen miles.

From Beachy Head to Selsey Bill, there are some partial spots that are rocky, but an E.N.E. wind makes such smooth water along the coast, that the rocks can scarcely be said to prevent any part of it being made use of for the purpose of debarkation; but I take it for granted that the commanding officer of that district will send you a report as to the coast, harbours, &c. &c.

I am now building at Dover a Row Galley, to carry one heavy gun, and I think the Admiralty will give orders for others of the same description to be built; indeed they have applied to the Treasury at my instance, to order three smuggling vessels, lately taken by the custom-house cutters, to be delivered over to me for the purpose of being lengthened and fitted as galleys; and when I get these vessels under my orders, I think I shall be able to prevent the French row boats from coming near this coast, either to reconnoitre, or annoy our trade.

I hope, Sir, in a few days, to be able to wait on you with a return of the number of men, we are likely to obtain as Sea Fencibles, and to take your orders as to their disposition.

Discussion of the Blockade of Brest
'Z.E.' to the Editor of the Naval Chronicle, January 10, 1804. XI 12-13

Sir, As I am aware that your valuable publication circulates through every department of the navy, I have been induced to trouble you with a few observations on a subject which has for some time past occupied a considerable portion of the public attention. I allude to the general system of blockade which has been adopted by us during the present war. For nearly eight months, I believe, the gallant Admiral Cornwallis, whose well-merited praise is the theme of every tongue, has closely and incessantly watched the motions of the French fleet in Brest harbour. Compelled by stress of weather, he indeed recently quitted his station; but, with that promptitude, vigour, and perseverance, which so eminently distinguish his character, he almost immediately returned. More fears, however, have, in my opinion, been entertained relative to the escape of the Brest fleet than that even would justify. My observations will apply to future periods as well as to the present. Should the Brest fleet escape, the probability is in our favour, that it would be met by some of our cruising squadrons. It is worthy of notice, however, that the same wind at W.S.W. which would drive the English fleet for shelter into Torbay, would prevent the French from coming out of Brest. Admitting, however, that a shift of wind occurred, and that the French were thus enabled to effect their escape; the same shift of wind would also be fair for the British fleet to sail from Torbay in pursuit of them; and, though the enemy would have the start, it is not unlikely that they might be overtaken, or indeed find themselves between two fires.

In the prosecution of a war, our grand objects unquestionably are - to protect our commerce, and thereby enrich the nation, both collectively and individually, rendering our finances more competent to support the necessary expenditure of a state of warfare; to reduce the naval force of our enemy, that we may be enabled to shorten the contest, and ultimately to command peace on more advantageous terms; and, finally, to preserve our island from invasion, and its concomitant, slavery. By keeping the fleets of the enemy in their ports, we may indeed protect our commerce, and defy the menaces of invasion; but we cannot by this achieve the important object of crushing their naval force. The enemy may even derive material advantage from the system of blockade; for, while their ships are safely moored in port, ours are exposed to all the risk of storms and hurricanes; may thus be disabled, and rendered incapable of either offence or defence, after which the hostile fleet may fearlessly venture out and accomplish its purpose unmolested.

A long blockade is objectionable also in other respects: it fatigues, harasses, and deadens the enterprising spirit of our sailors. The wear and tear of our shipping, too, is a consideration of importance.

Our naval superiority is such that an attempt to calculate on the result of an action with any of the present French flotillas would be justly ridiculed for its absurdity. Be it remembered, however, that it is only by suffering them to come out of harbour that we can have an opportunity of engaging them; it is only by engaging that we can hope to conquer them; it is only by conquering them that we can insure our own permanent safety. I am, Sir, Yours, &c.

Z.E.

Letter on Blocade Methods from 'A.F.Y.'
Present Management and Discipline of the Navy, Letter II. 1808. XIX 286-289

One of the prominent points in the management of the navy, has been, of late years, the blockading the enemy's fleets in Brest, Toulon, Rochefort, or Cadiz; and much difference of opinion subsists respecting the manner in which this service is performed, or whether it should be performed at all. It has been my lot to have assisted at the blockade of two of the above ports: Toulon I have only seen a little of; but though never concerned in blockading an enemy's fleet in the harbour at Cadiz, I am well acquainted with it, and the coasts near it, and am of opinion, that it is the only port, of those above mentioned, which can be blockaded to advantage. Ships in this service have for the greatest part of the year a fine climate and good anchorage; though this latter advantage, I understand, has not been made much use of by the present commander in chief; but the monotony of tacking and wearing, kept up for a long series of months, to the infinite injury of masts, yards, rigging, sails, and ships, is truly vexatious. I will not descend to particulars, because I have them only from hear-say evidence, but I believe one three-decker was more than twelve months under sail, while a fever was prevalent on board her a considerable part of the time. However, I think an enemy's fleet may be blockaded in Cadiz without our own ships suffering any thing, but from mismanagement.

Toulon stands next in order, in point of ease of blockade, but I am not competent to speak of it from experience.

From Brest, I conceive that a fleet which can patiently endure the insult of an equal or inferior fleet cruising off the harbour, till a convenient opportunity to sail, will very frequently find such an offer. For instance - upon the coming on of a strong S.W. or western gale, the British fleet bear up for Torbay, with the chance of some masts, yards, and sails being damaged. Suppose the French fleet, which has no such risk, prepared to make the first use of the change of wind, it starts with all the advantage of its distance to the westward, and a fair wind out of the harbour, while the British fleet has often to beat to windward out of Torbay; and when the intelligence arrives of the sailing of the French fleet, the same measures exactly must be taken, as if there had been no blockade at all. I would not advise that our Channel fleet should lie always in Torbay, or elsewhere, till the enemy has sailed; but I would discontinue the rigid system of blockading by a fleet of ships of the line in winter, and only pay a visit off Brest occasionally, in such weather as did not afford probability of much risk to our ships. I believe the officers who have been used to the Channel fleet, all wonder at the "hair-breadth escapes" they have had, in going in and out of Torbay in the winter gales. In the summer time I should suppose that the anchorage outside Falmouth harbour might be used to good effect in taking in water, fresh provisions, &c. The present mode of doing so much with boats at sea, is attended with great danger, labour, and expence, besides the infinite waste that attends many articles, by victuallers joining the fleet in weather when they cannot be unloaded, or when by some change of position of the fleet, they are for some time missed. I rather believe that the noble earl [St Vincent], who with much skill and perseverance blockaded the port of Cadiz for some time, occasioned the experiment to be made of managing the fleet of Brest in the same way; but those who know the different circumstances attending the two services, will wonder that the same means of executing them could ever have been thought of. The risk, trouble, anxiety, expence, waste, and danger, of victualling a fleet at sea, should never be incurred but in case of extreme necessity; and, with respect to the fleet stationed to watch Brest, I think a very little management in the arrangement of the ships would be ever preclude such necessity. I conclude that there are obstacles which have always prevented our possessing ourselves of Ushant during a war, or it would have been done, as its possession would render the watching of Brest so very easy, with a few frigates or sloops of war, to communicate from that island to the Lizard, from whence signals or telegraphs might convey the intelligence when necessary. There is a great danger, under the present system, of a whole fleet wanting repair at the same time, and such repairs as will occupy a great deal of time.

The noble earl before alluded to is possessed of very peculiar talents, which have borne him through a system of discipline and management, for which, when he began it, perhaps there was a good deal of reason, as he found a lax sort of command the order of the day. But when occasion has once put power in the hand of man, it is I believe only a Washington who has known how to relinquish it. At present I shall allude only to that part of his plan which made him force labours of extreme difficulty and danger on officers and men in boats; and in this he has, unfortunately, been imitated by many who could not judge so well of the exact service which they could perform. I offer this remark to every officer who may honour this with a perusal.

One great error which has crept in through the same channel, is the short space of time allowed the ships to refit when they come into port, a measure by which the country is far from being benefited. After the heavy service of the blockade of Brest, or Rochefort, for a year or more, a ship is allowed perhaps eight or nine days to refit in Cawsand bay, when the distance from the dock-yard alone occasions a very severe labour to the officers and boat's crews, and the short time occasions every thing to be done in a hurry; and some repairs have been ordered to be completed there, which could not possibly be well done. Perhaps it might have been intended to make the stay of a ship in harbour so very uncomfortable, as to occasion a desire even for a cruise off the Black Rocks in preference. I am of opinion, that three weeks at least should be allowed for such refitting, as eight days have been allotted for, and during that time, every officer and man should have leave to go on shore, unless confined on board for bad conduct. - *This is the way to prevent desertion.* - A squadron of six or seven sail of the line should always be ready in Torbay, or off Falmouth, according to the season, to start in any pursuit. This service should be taken in succession by the ships as they have been refitted; and, as one joins, the longest on that employ should join the squadron off Rochefort, and release the ship longest on that station, which ship should join the grand fleet.

A squadron should in general be kept off Rochefort, while it is the fashion for the chosen flying squadron of the enemy to make it their station; though perhaps it would be cheaper to keep a stronger force ready to meet them on our foreign stations, than to watch them in so tempestuous a sea as the Bay of Biscay, and where the same ease of escaping, as I have mentioned to be the case at Brest, takes place. Experience is, I believe, fully on my side in this assertion.

I remain, Sir, your humble servant

A.F.Y.

Origin of Telegraphic Signals, 1812. XXVII 457

The following statement, which has been transmitted to us by a correspondent, will, we doubt not, prove interesting to many of our readers:
Captain Thompson,[14] of the Royal Navy, better known to the public as poet Thompson, who died some years ago in his command on the coast of Guinea, contrived, while a lieutenant, a set of alphabetical signals, which, there is every reason to supposed, furnished the idea of the telegraphic signals now in use. They were literal; that is, they served for the expression of single letters, instead of the words and short sentences expressed by the telegraphic signals. The "y" was, as well as the "j" and "v", omitted. The five vowels were denoted by simple flags of different colours, and the eighteen consonants by party colour flags diversified in their shape. At that time a double intrigue subsisted in the fashionable world, between the late Duke of Cumberland and Lady Grosvenor on the one hand, and, on the other, between Captain Hervey[15] and the notorious Miss Chudleigh, afterwards Duchess of Kingston. In the conduct of this joint intrigue, the alphabetical signals were eminently useful, as they enabled each of the gallants to further the views of the other, on all occasions which might present themselves, for carrying on the amorous correspondence.

That the telegraphic signals now employed in the navy, originated in this way, may be inferred from this circumstance, that Sir Home Popham,[16] to whom the service is directly indebted for them, was a midshipman under Captain Thompson, when the latter acted as commodore on the coast of Guinea station; as was also the late Captain Eaton, who preserved a copy of the above literal signals until his death. Sir Roger Curtis,[17] who has, with much ingenuity, contrived a plan of nautical correspondence, similar to that introduced by Sir Home Popham, but who has not been equally successful in its adoption, likewise served under Captain Thompson.

Thus did the literal signals, which among other uses, had the singular application described above, apparently lead to the telegraphic signals, the utility of which is now so generally acknowledged. The latter were, at the glorious battle of Trafalgar, the medium by which the memorable sentence "England expects every man to do his duty," the conception of the greatest hero our naval annals record, was re-echoed throughout the fleet, already prepared to "conquer or to die."

Manderson's Proposal for Improving the Security of Trade in the Channel

From the 'Biographical Sketch of Captain James Manderson,' 1813. XXX 103-109

We are now about to conclude this article by observing, that Captain Manderson, having long conceived a mode to be practicable, for more effectually clearing, by destruction

14 Sir Home Popham's portrait and memoir are given in the XVIth Volume of the *Naval Chronicle*, pages 265 and 353.

15 A portrait and memoir of Sir Roger Curtis, appear in our VIth Volume, page 261.

16 For a portrait and biographical memoir of this distinguished officer, *vide Naval Chronicle*, Vol. VI page 437, and Vol. Vii page 94. A portrait and memoir of his nephew, Captain Sir T.B. Thompson, the present Comptroller of the Navy, will be found in the XIVth Volume, page 1, *et. seq.*

17 This gentleman, who afterwards became Earl of Bristol, and was the elder brother of the late Earl, the celebrated virtuoso and collector, commanded a ship of the fleet in which the Duke of Cumberland was embarked. A strong intimacy subsisted both between them and the ladies.

and capture, the English channel of enemy's cruisers, than by any method at that time practised, submitted a plan to the consideration of Mr. Yorke (then at the head of the Admiralty), which he thought (and our readers shall have an opportunity to judging how justly he thought) would bear to be examined. It was, simply, to arrange a number of cruisers in lines of connection, which would command a certain space, according to their numbers. There could, it was presumed, be no difficulty in the execution, to any one who understood the import of a signal, and what angle one point of the compass makes with another. It has, indeed, been sometimes lamentably perceptible, in the manoeuvring of fleets at sea, how much the study of naval tactics has been neglected; but the arrangements necessary in this case were not liable to so many intricacies as the evolutions of fleets. The following plan, we transcribe, as explained by writing and delineation:

"The havoc committed but too successfully by French privateers on the trade of the United Kingdom in the English Channel, and close to our own shores, notwithstanding the great superiority of the British navy, and the number of cruisers employed for the protection of trade, manifestly proves that there is some radical error in the distribution of these cruisers; and that to render their services and efforts more effectual, some system of operation is wanting, hitherto unthought of perhaps, and evidently unpractised.

The system of detached cruisers has been long tried; but experience has proved the mode to be inadequate, in any considerable degree, to the capture and destruction of the enemy's privateers that infest different parts of the Channel, particularly to the westward of the Downs. It does not appear, that ever a system of combination and extension has been tried, which can command a certain space of sea, or coast, in which, all enemies, cruizers included, would have little chance of escaping.

Notwithstanding the superior seamanship of the British navy, when compared, generally, with that of other nations, yet it must be allowed, there is some defect in the knowledge of combined evolution, arising, most assuredly, from the want of study and practice.

Without farther remark, I shall proceed to shew, what would be the effects of the combination of a number of vessels employed in the channel, in various ways, for the capture of the enemy's cruizers.

Let it then be supposed, that 21 vessels were selected for this purpose - cutters, gun-brigs, and such others as could be spared; what arrangement, or arrangements, ought to be practised, to render their operations and services as effectual as possible?

They shall first be considered as designed to come upon and enclose a certain portion of the English coast, so as every vessel within the area of their arrangement, should have little, or no chance of escaping. Let it be farther supposed, that the wind is either westward or eastward, to enable privateers to sail across the Channel both ways, which is the most favourable time for their operations, the arrangement should begin to form off the windward part of the coast designed to be enclosed. If the wind were at west, and 21 vessels sailed from Spithead with the design of enclosing a portion of the coast eastward, any where between Selsey Bill and the South Foreland, they ought to sail so far into the offing, so as not to give alarm to any of the enemy's cruisers that might be near the shore; and when at a proper distance, 9 or 10 miles, so many vessels ought to keep that position, as would be wanted to complete a line to within two or three miles of the shore; the remainder to execute the proposed arrangement as fast as possible.

The most favourable disposition of the squadron to effect the end in view, may probably be a centre and two wings, formed in straight lines; the wing vessels to be three miles from each other, and the centre four, for reasons which will hereafter appear. It has been observed, that as soon as the squadron arrived off that part of the coast, on which the western line was to form, and being 6 or 9 miles distant from the shore, one or two vessels ought to keep that position designed to extend it to within two or three miles of the coast, as should be judged prudent. This line should be formed N.W. by N. and S.E. by S. to consist of 7 vessels, at three miles distance from each other; the centre to form on its outward extremity E. by S. to consist of 7 vessels, at four miles distance from each other; and the starboard, or eastern wing, being the same number as the western or larboard wing, to form N.E. by E. on the east end of the centre: the vessel, or vessels, directed to keep their position of the western wing, and designed to complete it, to do this after a reasonable time.

When this arrangement was completed, the position of the squadron would be according to the figure No. 1; the centre extending 24 miles, each wing 21 miles, and the extent of coast enclosed, on the approach of each van of the wings to the shore, would be 57 miles, or 19 leagues; and the area of sea included between the three lines and the land would be 738 square miles; at which time the centre would be 5 leagues from the line of coast, if the vans of the wings were about three miles from the shore; and an enemy, or enemies, enclosed, might at first feel very little alarm at this situation, from the great distance of the wings.

The enclosing of the coast being effected, the next object would be, the securing the area of sea so enclosed. As the centre would be every moment drawing nearer to the shore, the wings would be shortened, and the vessels composing them come closer to each other. The proper manoeuvre of the van of starboard, or leeward wing, would be to heave to; that of the centre to steer parallel to the line of the eastern wing, or N.E. by E.; and the larboard, or weather wing, to steer on the same point of the compass; one, two, and three, if necessary, making all sail along the shore to drive out any vessels that might be near it. After the centre had run 15 miles on the last course, the position of the fleet would then be 5, 8, 19, 21 as in figure No. 2. 1, 2 and 3 being advanced in shore; and as Nos. 4, 14, 15, 16, 17 and 18 would be thrown out of the order, the centre vessels ought to close to the westward, to make room for some of those thrown out to form into their line, by which it would become more compact; and if 18 took the place of 19, the latter and 20 could close on 21, to prevent any enemies, as *n*, *m*, and *o*, standing any chance of escaping through the van of the lee wing or centre.

It will be evident to every impartial observer, that by such a disposition of the number of vessels proposed, any enemies enclosed in the area of sea between the three lines and the land, would be captured almost to a certainty.

If the wind were more southerly than west, the same evolution could be performed, unless it were so far to the southward, and blew so strong, as to render a near approach to the cast dangerous; in which case it would also be dangerous for an enemy, who would have to choose between running close in with a lee and hostile shore, or attempting to break through one of the lines.

If the wind were easterly, and the squadron had sailed from the Downs, the starboard, or eastern wing, would then have to perform the movement supposed to be done by the larboard wing, or division, with a westerly wind, and the latter that of the former.

If the wind blew off shore, it would not be advisable for those vessels that are to form the advance of the wings, to run farther off the shore than absolutely necessary,

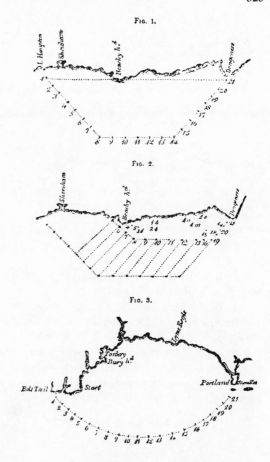

FIG. 1.

FIG. 2.

FIG. 3.

whether the fleet came from the eastward or westward. If it came from the eastward, and the wind were at N. or N.N.E. and the fleet at *A* in figure No. 4, those that were to form the outer part of the starboard, or eastern wing, could easily assume their stations; but if those designed to form the western wing run so far to leeward as the outer part of the eastern, with the wind at N. they would have to ply again to windward to get into their stations; therefore, they should sail from *A*. W. by N. by compass,[18] until arriving at *B*.

As the distance between the vans of the wings, according to the proposed plan, would be 56 miles; the extension of the centre 24; the difference 32 divided by 7 will give 4 1/2 miles, and 1/14 of a mile, for the difference of distance between every two opposite ships in the wings, and those next to them; subtracted successively from the van towards the centre; and added to the extension of the centre to obtain the distance between 7 and 15; and to that again to obtain the distance between 8 and 16; and so likewise of every successive distance. Now as it is supposed to be the second line from the van, leaving out the fractional part, two distances will give 9 miles, which subtracted from 56, the distance between the vans, will leave 47 miles, the distance No. 3 must run W. by N. to get into her station; 2 and 1 forming N.W. by N. from her, 4, 5, 6, 7, and 8

18 In this case it is supposed the centre is formed E. by S. and W. by N.

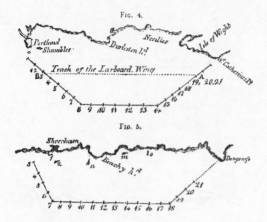

S.E. by S. at the appointed distance. At any time judged convenient, 20 and 21 could form N.E. by E. from *A*. or 19.

To perform the same service, the fleet could be formed into the segment of a circle, at three miles distance, the radius of which circle would be 37 miles, and the depth of the segment 12, as in figure No. 5.

As it canot be supposed, that such a disposition as a perfect segment could be attained, to form from either wing, the following arrangements would bring the fleet, in some manner, into the proposed order, the two vans supposed to bear east and west of each other.

To form from the eastern or starboard van		To form from the western or larboard van	
20 19	S.W. from 21	2 3	S.E. of 1
18 17	S.W. 3/4 W from 19	4 5	S.E. 3/4 E. of 3
16 15	S.W. by W. 3/4 W. from 17	6 7	S.E. by E. 3/4 E. of 5
14 13	W.S.W. 3/4 W. from 15	8 9	E.S.E. 3/4 E. of 7
12	from 18, W. 1/2 S.	10	from 9, E. 1/2 S.
11	from 12, West	11	from 10, East
10	from 11 W. 1/2 N.	12	from 11, E. 1/2 N.
9 8	from 10, W.N.W. 3/4 W.	13 14	from 12, E.N.E. 1/4 E.
7 6	from 8, N.W. by W. 3/4 W.	15 15	fm 14, N.E. by E. 3/4 E.
5 4	from 6, N.W. 3/4 W.	17 18	from 16, N.E. 3/4 E.
3 2 1	N.W. from 4	19 20	21 from 18, N.E.

To form from the centre in this order, as 11 would be the centre, those from 11 to 21 would take their stations as mentioned, to the north eastward; those from 11 to 1, north westward, as pointed out. If judged necessary to make the curve more perfect, where two numbers are mentioned as taking the same bearing from a third, the middle number could place herself a little without the line of bearing.

Thus it has been shewn, how an extent of 20 leagues of coast may be suddenly enclosed by 21 vessels of war of any description; either by three lines, forming a centre of 7 vessels, at 4 miles distance from each other; and two wings, of 7 vessels each, at 3 miles distance from each other; or by forming into the segment of a circle, the depth of which shall be 12 miles.

The first arrangement appears preferable, because it is less intricate; but more especially because it encloses a greater area of sea, and the centre being farther from the coast, would not immediately alarm any enemy's cruizers that might be within it.

By such a disposition, or arrangement, the coast in the Channel might be enclosed from the South Foreland to two leagues west of Beachy Head; or from two or four leagues west of the South Foreland, to four or six leagues west of Beachy Head. From Beachy Head to St. Catherine's Point, on the Isle of Wight; from St. Catherine's Point to four leagues west of the Bill of Portland; from the Bill of Portland to the Bolt Head; from the Rame Head to the Lizard.

The advantages such a system of combination would have over many detached cruizers, must be evident, and therefore needs no arguments to support its claims to attention; as a view of the arrangement must be convincing to the beneficial effects that might be expected to follow the practice against the swarms of privateers in the English Channel.

The combination might form on the French coast as well as the English; extending its two wings towards the latter, and sailing on in that direction, when the wind permitted, by which every vessel within the two vans would be enclosed. The centre could be formed across the Channel, and sail either eastward or westward, according to the state of the winds, and on any cruizer, or cruizers, being perceived within the wings, their vans could be directed by signal to shape such a course towards each to her, as might be judged necessary to prevent them escaping.[19]

I shall now proceed to shew, how the coast might be swept, if the expression be allowable, to any extent, during a wind that would allow the vessels to sail along the shore, either eastward or westward. This certainly would be a most desirable object.

Let it then be supposed, that 21 vessels sailed from Spithead, Plymouth, or *Falmouth*, to sweep the English coast eastward; perhaps, the best arrangement would be, in some manner, according to that in figure No. 5. 1 and 2 take their stations in shore; and supposing the direction of the coast to be E. by N. 3, 4, 5, 6 and 7 form 6 points from it, or S.E. by S. S by E. by compass; then the next numbers to 18 form parallel to the coast, E. by S. by compass; and 19, 20 and 21, form 4 points within this line, that is, N.E. by E. all at three miles distance from each other; than will the line parallel to the coast be 16 miles off, and the van ship, or vessel, about 9. This may, perhaps, be supposed a sufficient distance not to alarm any cruizers that may be in shore. The line of coast, Nos. 3 and 21, would be about 15 leagues. Any cruizers that might be near the coast would be forced out by 1 and 2. Upon their being perceived, and attempting to escape along the shore, the same ought to be immediately communicated to the van, by flags and guns, when clear, the latter to draw immediate attention, and by guns alone when hazy; the leading ship to alter her course from E. by S. to N.E. or N.N.E. as circumstances might require, each successive number following, and keeping the former distance, until 21 came as near the shore as might be judged prudent, when all the vessels in the van ought to heave to, and wait for the rear closing on the enemy or enemies within the line,

19 We have been informed, that Captain Manderson, some years since, had made considerable progress in detailing a similar mode of cruizing in any part of a sea or ocean frequented by enemies' cruisers. If our information be correct, we should be thankful to Captain M. for such communication on that subject as it may be agreeable to him to make. We have also heard, that he lately submitted to Lord Melville a plan for the more effectual carrying on war with America.

by which time, probably 18, 17, and 16 might be drawn into the N.E. by E. line. But upon the signal being made for an enemy in shore, perhaps the best manoeuvre would be for the line parallel to the coast, to sail directly towards it, as it would draw all the fleet closer together, by the rear continually shortening this line, and the van after 21 hove-to; and this would give the whole an opportunity of drawing closer together, to prevent any escape.

If it were judged better to have the line parallel to the coast at a greater distance from it, the rear line could form at 4 miles distance, which would take the parallel to 6 leagues distance."

Although the Board of Admiralty does not appear to have honoured these patriotic suggestions of Captain Manderson with its sanction, we consider them entitled, by something more than their good intention, to be recorded in a work like "The Naval Chronicle."

Trade Defence
*Letter to the Editor from 'J.M.' [James Manderson?], Cornwall,
1 September 1813.* ^{XXX 204-08}

Mr Editor, Although the system of blockading the principal ports of her maritime enemies, has been in some measure successfully adopted by Great Britain; yet the forming of a plan to blockade an extent of coast does not appear to have suggested itself as a practicable effort. If such a measure could be executed with any tolerable degree of certainty, the advantages must be apparent, if the space invested be the haunt of numerous privateers and vessels of war, that issue forth to attack her commerce; and especially, if, added to this consideration, it be also the resort of commerce carried on by any of her enemies.

That an object of such magnitude would be liable to interruptions in the execution, must be acknowledged; nevertheless, it must also be allowed to comprehend particular advantages. I shall, therefore, proceed to explain in what manner it may be effected.

When outward-bound fleets are on the point of sailing, or convoys expected from distant parts, the cruizers sailing at such times from the ports of France, have been but too successful in making captures, notwithstanding our numerous cruizers employed in looking after them. But if many of these cruizers, at such times, had been arranged in connection, ready for offence and defence, it is very probable, that such cruizers would have suffered so severely, as to have rendered this mode of warfare far more hazardous than it is at present, besides cutting off their captures.

Let it be supposed that a valuable fleet is about sailing into the Atlantic; or that one is expected from that ocean; how is it possible to guard all the French coast along the Bay of Biscay, so that cruizers and their captures may have little chance of escaping?

In considering the proposition without a plan, it may be thought that it would require a vast naval force to effect such a purpose; but when viewed, as reduced to a system, much of the imagined difficulty disappears.

From Ushant to Cape Ortegal, the distance is about 99 leagues; suppose a vessels stationed three or four leagues from Ushant, and so a chain continued in the line of bearing of Cape Ortegal, which is nearly S.S.W. 1/4 W. each ship, or vessel, at three leagues distance, to within the same distance of the southern Cape, this would require *thirty-one ships and vessels of war*; and the arrangement would be as exhibited in the sketch annexed. In executing such a plan, it would not be necessary that the vessels

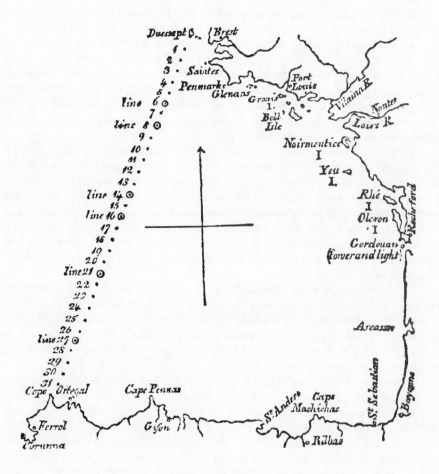

Biscay cruiser line. XXX 208

should be all frigates, or even sloops of war; yet every other alternate vessel ought to be of force, ready to assist against a superior enemy. Between two frigates might be placed a sloop of war, an armed brig, or a cutter; and on the appearance of any number of hostile cruizers, part of the chain could soon draw together by signal to make head against them. A line of ships and vessels of war thus stationed, would prove a formidable barrier against cruizers issuing from ports in the bay of Biscay; the greatest distance any vessel could pass in hazy weather, or during night, would be four miles and a half; and this distance would be altogether accidental.

In clear weather, a signal might be communicated from Ushant to Cape Ortegal in a short time. If something similar had been practised when squadrons of the enemy were expected to sail on distant services, they could not have passed without being observed, and their situation communicated to the commander-in-chief off Brest, or any other of the naval stations in the Bay.

Should it be said, that such an arrangement would be liable to many objections, on account of blowing and hazy weather, when the vessels would be uncertain of their real situation with respect to each other, and be unable to keep their proper stations; it is answered, the same objections apply to every naval operation, particularly those embracing objects of magnitude and extension. Ships of war cannot be expected to keep post like a body of troops on the land; during hazy weather they cannot ascertain their positions like military bodies directed by fixed objects at hand; but they can do all that can be reasonably expected from good seamen and navigators; and that is all men will require who are conversant in naval affairs.

If a line, thus formed, were only in very indifferent order at the season when large and valuable convoys were expected from the West Indies, or any other quarter, the difficulty the enemy's cruizers would find in getting into the ocean from the Bay of Biscay, or from the ocean into the Bay, must be apparent to every impartial mind. In the night the danger might be as great as in the day, on account of the probability of falling on one side of the intermediate spaces. The same might be observed of the danger during hazy weather, as the vessels could not be so disunited as not to admit of a great probability of many of those belonging to the enemy, whether cruizers or captures, coming in view.

When by chase any part of the arrangement might be broken for a time, the other vessels should continue in their proper stations, or extend their distances two or three miles to fill up the vacancy, as otherwise some hostile vessel might pass unnoticed. To prevent a great opening being left, not above two vessels should chase at a time, unless the object were of magnitude. When no probability appeared of closing with the chase, it ought to be immediately relinquished.

On the return of any vessel thus drawn off, or on the clearing away of thick hazy weather, there could be no difficulty in ascertaining on what part of the line such vessel had fallen, or the positions of the whole; as by an immediate display of number signals, each shewing that of her station, the discovery would be at once made, one being next to Ushant, and so on to thirty-one off Cape Ortegal. If fifteen and sixteen were to chase, either towards the coast or the ocean, on their return to the line, without depending on the knowledge of any vessel by sight, by shewing their numbers, 15 and 16, and seeing them answer by 10 or 18, they would immediately ascertain their position, and the course to their proper stations. This line could not be supposed to preclude cruizers from being employed in harassing and capturing the enemy on his coast.

The adopting of such a measure might, perhaps, be found more efficacious in cooping up the enemy, than any that has yet been practised. And when long-practised modes have been proved to fall far short of expectation, by the experience of many years, dearly purchased, why should not others be executed by way of experiment? If, indeed, the mind of man is arrived at its *ne plus ultra* in naval tactics, if it is to be chained down by the belief that nothing new can be discovered, then indeed the country ought to sit down contented under all her losses and disasters as remediless; but until this can be proved by the testimony of experience, she has a right to expect that her power shall be tried in all possible shapes for her benefit, and not to be fettered by old prejudices, which time has established into overbearing assumptions. Has not the mode of warfare of fleets undergone a modern revolution? What has been the consequence of the 12th of April, 1782? Let the battles of the first of June, 1794, of Aboukir, and Trafalgar, bear witness. It would once have been thought the height of arrogance, and daring ignorance, to have proposed any such modes of attack.

When it was intended to execute such a plan, it might be necessary that those to be employed on the service should have no knowledge of the intention, until in a situation whence it could not be communicated to the public, and so to the enemy, who would be particularly guarded when it was known that such an arrangement was to take place.

It must not be supposed this precaution alludes to those in the service, otherwise than by incautiously communicating such information; by which means it might find its way into the public prints, which always give the maritime enemies of Great Britain, near her, timely notice when convoys are to sail, or are expected, and every likely operation of her fleets and squadrons. A source of information to an enemy, pregnant with greater evils than may be imagined, and which the benefit of the country certainly requires to be in a great degree restrained.

A squadron might be sent to sea with sealed orders, to open them in such a latitude and longitude, directing it to extend itself northward from Cape Ortegal, and another at the same time in like manner from Ushant southward; and if the numbers were not complete, it could be filled up in a few days, all having their numbers particularly specified; and therefore there could be no mistake of station. To prevent the enemy having any knowledge from appearance, those next the land might be placed at a greater distance, or to cruize off and on, as at other times.

Opposite the enemy's naval ports ought to be ships of force, and the 5 first numbers might be occupied by ships and vessels attached to the Channel Fleet.

Were the blockade designed to be continued for any considerable time, the vessels to compose the line could be victualled accordingly; or a plan of relief might be necessary, which would take about twelve more in number. After the first had been stationed six weeks or two months, relieve the twelve next Cape Ortegal; in a fortnight these may be supposed ready to relieve the next twelve; then there would only remain the six next to Ushant, which could be done occasionally, more especially if they were chiefly attached to the squadron designed to cruize off Brest. Thus the whole might be relieved every nine or ten weeks; or in a shorter period, if judged necessary.

It might be objected, that the number of ships and vessels of war it would require, could not well be spared; but surely the magnitude of the object ought to be allowed considerable weight; and more so as it would now render the American commerce extremely hazardous. It might, however, be asked, whether a portion of the British navy could be in any manner more beneficially employed for the advantage of the country? It would require, including the numbers mentioned for relief, about the eighteenth part of the ships and vessels of war in commission, employed, or designed for active service.

The whole coast of France might be thus blockaded. From Ushant to Calais is about 102 leagues; but Jersey and Guernsey lying in the track, about 23 vessels would be sufficient. From Calais to the Elbe, the distance is about 100 leagues, and at four leagues distance from each other (as well as those from Ushant to Calais), would require 24. As the greater part of the 47 between Ushant and the Elbe would be near our own ports, their relief could be effected by about 16 more; thus requiring about the 7th part of the British navy to blockade our enemy's coast from Cape Ortegal to the Elbe. Appearances at present give the nations of Europe reason to hope, that such an extent of sea-coast will not long remain under the control of one gigantic power.

But without grasping at such an immense object, it will appear that it is practicable to blockade the Bay of Biscay, or even a greater extent of coast, with a small part of the British naval force in commission. This system could be transferred from one place to another, as existing circumstances might require.

If something similar had been adopted off the American ports, where their navy frequent, could they have reigned so long without chastisement?

What might be the effects of such an arrangement on an important extent of an enemy's coast, cannot be truly ascertained, unless experimentally put in execution; but perhaps its beneficial consequences might prove more than imagined, and give privateering a more fatal blow than any it has yet received.

That a part of the British navy could be better employed may appear doubtful; as the arrangement comprises in itself the advantages of several detached squadrons; and commands a space of sea to which, according to the general mode of cruizing, they are altogether inadequate, although their aggregate number may be equal.

The advantages of thus commanding the Bay of Biscay at particular times are so manifest, that it would be superfluous to add more upon the subject. While this was effected, a line reaching from the Lizard to Ushant would prevent any cruizers from entering, or getting out of, the Channel of England.

The distance being about thirty-one leagues, and the ships and vessels being stationed within two leagues of each other, would require about 14, which would leave very little probability of any hostile vessels, or their captures, passing the space, unless of superior force. Man cannot, indeed, command the elements; and a gale of wind might, at times, cause the space to be left partly open; but in general it would be impassable but by a superior force.

If this last measure had been put in execution during former wars, great advantages would have been derived from it. The vicinity of the secure harbour of Falmouth, to the Lizard and Bay of Biscay, would render the plan much easier in execution, than if the vessels had to run further eastward for supplies, or in any exigency that might occur, which obliged them to seek refuge in port.

Should the French privateers, to evade the line, run further into the ocean, it could be suddenly transferred to the suspected haunt, stretching itself on a given meridian from one prescribed latitude to another. When the Baltic fleets are expected home, a line could be extended from Flamboro' Head to the Elbe, or in any other manner that might be judged safe and beneficial.

J.M.

William Budge's Papers on Economic Blockade and Ship Construction by Contract
From the 'Naval Biography of the Late William Budge, Esq.' 1816. XXXV 1-16; 93-97

Reasons for our Cruizers failing to Block the Trade of France
Although they have been sometimes interrupted, the coasting trade of France was carried on much in the same manner, until the termination of the war in 1814. For this there may be assigned various reasons. Notwithstanding the immense naval force of Great Britain, it does not appear that it has ever contained a description of vessels properly adapted for cutting off and destroying the coasting trade of France; and the formidable appearance of *Proctor's bills* has tended much to damp the ardour of such hazardous service, under the fire of batteries and such murderous musketry, where the fruit of danger, blood, and wounds, has gone to enrich those in office on shore.

But it is certainly high time that the nation should look seriously into this subject, and place before her eyes the immense incomes which individuals have derived from the toils of the British navy; and set bound to the expense of condemnation. One per cent out of the whole captures during a war would be immense; but when we hear of men receiving thirty thousands per annum, it must be allowed to be a shameful violation of justice. Do they talk of their duties? What are they to those of men who are continually in the midst of dangers and death? who are upon an enemy's lee shore, amidst the horrors of the tempest, and the blackness of night? who are continually exposed to all the dangers inseparable from warfare carried on upon the enemy's coast, where the combatants are exhausting the vigour of youth, many of them to close their eyes for ever, many to return maimed and mutilated, and many to be pierced to the quick, at finding all their prospects blasted by the paralyzing and fleecing effects of a *Proctor's bill*. No wonder such a stand is made against the officers of the navy choosing their own Proctors: but is justice at the bottom of this objection? - So those may tell us who reap the fruits of the present oppressive system of gain. The condemnation of every vessel ought to be limited in expense to a certain per centage, and this only to amount to a certain value on vessels that may be richly laden. The system by which the enemies of Great Britain have found so great a protection to their commerce in neutral bottoms, ought to be probed to the quick; and no perjured person allowed to appear the second time in court; no firm covering a fraud of millions; an extent of wealth which no firm ever has possessed, or ever will posess; the nursery of perjury and deception. - Nothing in the nation calls louder for investigation and reform than the subjects mentioned. It is sincerely to be wished, that this Augean stable may be cleansed before it becomes more intolerable.[20]

The Strategic Importance of British Mercantile Shipping
In September, 1801, Mr. Budge published in the Antijacobin Magazine, "A Review of the Political State of Europe." ... After noticing St. Domingo as the principal source of the mercantile navigation of France, and therefore of her military marine, he observes:

"Indeed, it is owing to the wonderful extent and magnitude of our mercantile marine, that we are at this moment enabled to maintain our ground, and thereby prevent the entire subversion of every establishment in Europe."

After mentioning the various branches of British commerce, he says:

"There are collectively employed and registered, according to the most unquestionable authority, 17,295 British vessels, amounting in burthen to 1,666,481 tons; and (allowing one man to every twelve tons), navigated by 138,873 men. This is by far the greatest *mercantile marine* that ever belonged to any one nation; and from this grand source our *military marine* is consequently supplied. France has so fully felt the effect of this, that she will make every effort to reduce our maritime power and commercial prosperity."

Transports and Ship Construction under Contract
In 1810, under the signature of *Amicus Patriae*, he published a letter to the late Viscount Melville, on the subject of his speech in the House of Lords, respecting the employment of ships of war in transporting troops, of which measure Mr. Budge highly approved.

Speaking of the transports taken up in 1809, he said: - it would be seen, that 173 ships and vessels were taken up the preceding year for the transport service, the aggregate

20 See Mr. Brown's Letter to the King of Prussia, *N.C.* Vol. XXXI p. 288.

burthen of which amounted to thirty-four thousand four hundred and sixty tons. Comparing this number with that of troop-ships employed previous to the peace of Amiens, he says:

"Their number was fifty-five; the tonnage of which amounted to fifty thousand one hundred and forty-seven tons: therefore, upon an average, each ship may be reckoned at nine hundred and twelve tons. But, on a comparative average, according to the number of vessels taken up last year, and the amount of their tonnage, it would require nearly five times the number, or *two hundred and fifty sail*, at two tons per men, to convey *twenty-five thousand men.*"

And then justly observes:

"The object of the service would be liable to be defeated, from the causes which must naturally arise in conducting and keeping together, for any length of time, such a number of vessels, many of them possessing the worst qualities, subject to no discipline, and upon the whole, unfit for the service in which they might be employed.

The more, therefore, the proposition for appropriating a certain number of ships of war, for the reception and conveyance of troops shall be investigated, the more clearly will be seen the wisdom, advantages, and economy of the measure."

In speaking of ships building from 1802 to 1807, specifying the ships launched, and ordered to be built each year, he remarks, that, "in 1807, eight ships of the line were launched, and *twenty-three* were ordered to be built; and of these, no less than *nineteen by contract*.

After noticing the ships launched, and ordered to be built in 1808, in 1809, and 1810, the year in which he was writing, he says:

"Since the first of July, 1802, to this time, *thirty-seven* ships of the *line* have been launched, and *fifty-five* ordered to be built; twelve of which form a part of those launched, and *forty-four* remain to be completed, of the latter number, *twenty-seven are building by contract*.

If, then, in addition to the *thirty-seven ships* launched since 1802, there be brought to account the *sixty-six* French, Dutch, Spanish, and Danish captures, the difference in our favour, and against France, is, ninety-four sail of the line, after allowing eight sail of British ships lost through casualties at sea. Upon what grounds, then, or even upon what pretext, can this unprecedented and ruinous system of building be pursued? Since it appears, from the appendix to your Lordship's Speech, that there are now *one hundred and five* ships of the line in active employ, and *thirty-nine* British [ships] in ordinary, four-fifths of which may be fairly considered as repairable, &c &c."

On the repairs of the ordinary, he remarks:

"Unless a well-digested and regular system be laid down and pursued, it will be *impossible* to repair the fleet.

In corroboration of this observation, I beg to state the following facts, from a return laid before the House of Lords, of the number of docks in the King's yards, at Deptford, Woolwich, Chatham, Sheerness, Portsmouth, and Plymouth. In that return it is stated, that the *Tremendous*, of 74 guns, has been in dock ever since the 9th of February, 1807, being *three years and four months*; and there is reason to fear, that she will yet be detained some months longer. The *Prince of Wales*, of 98 guns, appears also to have been in dock since the 9th of March, 1809, about fifteen months.

In the same return, it is stated, that two small frigates, the *Southampton* and the *Aquilon*, are occupying *first-rate docks* at Portsmouth; the *Southampton* since the 27th of

May, 1809, and the *Aquilon* since the 8th of July; the one twelve months and other eleven."

This latter fact forcibly points out how advantageous it would be in promoting the interests of the country, through the rapidity of the movements of her squadrons and cruisers, into the Bay of Biscay and Atlantic Ocean, did she possess a naval establishment near the Lizard, where all frigates employed to the westward could be docked and repaired. . . .

[*Budge advocated a naval establishment at Falmouth.*]

Mr. Budge, after mentioning that ships which have been long in a state of ordinary are liable to be forgotten, and ultimately passed over as unserviceable, proceeds to make a comparison between the value of contract-built ships, and those built in the King's yards, as it relates to original cost and durability, as follows:

"I have endeavoured to ascertain the probable difference, and I find that a seventy-four gun ship, of seventeen hundred and forty-one tons, is estimated in the King's yards at £28 10s per ton; which is *five pounds* per ton less than is paid in the merchants' yards; or *eight thousand seven hundred and five pounds* upon the ship: so that, if this estimate be correct, the Crown will pay *two hundred and thirty-five thousand, and thirty-five pounds* more for the *twenty-seven seventy-fours* yet building in the merchant's yards, than would be paid for building the same number in the king's yards. Besides the difference of the expense in the prime cost of the ship, whether it be more or less than what is here stated, there is a point connected with the measure of even still greater importance, and that is, the difference in the construction and durability of the ship, which I am told may be fairly reckoned at *five pounds* per ton, *at least*, in favour of the king's-built ship."

After some farther observations, he concludes from these premises, that the loss to the country, on twenty-seven seventy-fours, of 1741 tons each, is "*four hundred and seventy thousand and seventy pounds.*" Let John Bull chew this quid . . .

[*Budges's most telling argument was that five years after Trafalgar, the new ships were not needed:*]

"In truth, it seems as if we were determined, notwithstanding our *immense superiority*, to build two ships to one of the enemy."

Appendix 2 – Ship Design and Ship Gear

THE FIRST GROUP OF PAPERS is concerned with the fundamentals of ship design. It begins with a general treatise on the design of ships of the line, and an address by Gabriel Snodgrass on his shipbuilding experience in East India Company service. Unfortunately, it has not been possible to include any of the appendices in the Consolidated Edition. Following are statistics of the weights involved in the 80-gun ship, and a note on the longevity of the *Royal William* which had first entered the service in 1679. In 1813 a plate was published showing the new use of diagonal riders and diagonal decking which enabled nineteenth-century shipwrights to extend the length of ships of the line well beyond eighteenth-century limits. There is also a brief note about irregularity of numbers in the complements of British ships of the line. Stimulated by the experience of the American War, it appeared that the Admiralty were determined to lay down super-frigates capable of matching those in the United States Fleet. A correspondent wrote to protest at the idea that they might be built of materials which would not stand the strain of protracted service, and of course would have provided their men with little protection.

Approximately half the papers selected for this appendix are concerned with new technologies. Of considerable long-term utility was the development, by Richard Hall Gower, of a new five-masted schooner, which was eventually built and given sea trials. This ship is the subject of the second group of papers. Other papers pursuing this interest, which could not be included, are: 'Arguments tending to illustrate what ought to be the proper Shape of a Vessel intended to sail with Celerity,' IV 135-39; and *Transit*'s speed trial against HM Sloop *Osprey*, 24 July 1801, VI 48.

The third group of papers is concerned with the development of new, or improved, gear for use in the fleet. Included are papers on emergency anchors, on improvement in sail design, and on a new design of landing craft or 'batteau'.

The papers in the fourth group are all concerned with special duty vessels. Included are papers on a floating battery, one on an iron caisson for use as a floating dock, one of 1805 on a French praam designed specifically for escorting invasion barges across the English Channel, and another of 1815 on an American design for a torpedo boat.

The fifth group focuses on steam propelled ships. The first paper is a curiosity, a propulsive system intended to utilise the reciprocal energy of pistons without its conversion to circular motion. The others are reports on steamships in the Hudson and Clyde.

The sixth group contains reports of a new class of warship, very much in its infancy: the submersible. Other papers on this subject appear in the appendix on gunnery and pyrotechnics.

Document List

Ship Design

Gabriel Snodgrass's Disquisitions on Ship-Building - 1799.[1] *II 585-591*

It is reasonable to suppose, that Providence in the formation of fast-swimming fish, has pointed out those principles which ship-builders should imitate as nearly as possible in the construction of their ships. Examine the fish which swim fastest; they will be found to have great length in proportion to their breadth, and very little depth, viz. the thickness from the upper part of the back to the under part of the belly; they also carry their breadth well forward, and diminish gradually towards the tail: whence it follows, that the column of water being displaced at once, it afterwards tends, when closing, to force them along.

2. For the same reason that a fast-swimming fish is long in proportion to its breadth, so should a ship be. But though nature in forming some fish to pass through the water quick, at the same time shaped others to avoid their pursuit, by enabling the short ones to turn round faster, and thereby escape the longer ones; so it is with ships. A ship very long, will not wear nor tack in the same space as a shorter ship of the same force; which cannot give any advantage to the latter one over the former, unless they sail equally well, which they cannot do if both are constructed on the best plans. A long ship will draw less water than a short one, which is a good property; and the resistance at the stem being less, she will therefore sail faster. Short fish have longer and larger fins in proportion to their length, and larger tails to skull with than long fish: therefore what has been said of short and long fish in this case is not quite applicable to ships; for a long, and therefore a fast-sailing ship, can always overtake a short one of the same force, and by superiority of sailing choose her station either to windward or to leeward.

3. Suppose the bow of a ship is in Fig. 1. A ship with such a bow will pitch, having nothing to support her; and being too sharp, after she rises to a sea, will again plunge deep.

Suppose the bow of a ship as in Fig. 2. Such a ship will not pitch, having a full bow to support her; for when she meets with a heavy sea, she will both rise and pitch easily. See also the bow, Fig. 8.

N.B. The greatest breadth at the knuckle timbers should be about four feet less than the extreme breadth; and as the quarters are the same breadth, the ship will be supported forward, and abaft, and of course be easy in a heavy sea.

5. If the stern or run of a ship is as in Fig. 3. such a ship, having no quarter to catch her, will dip her stern, when her bow rises to a sea, and will not be able to send in a gale of wind without a certainty of being pooped.

6. If the stern or run of a ship is as in Fig. 4 such a ship being too full abaft will not steer, as the column of water meets beyond the rudder.

7. The run of a ship should be neither too fine nor too full; but so that the column of water should exactly meet upon the stern-post; then the rudder will have its full power. The quarter should be very full above the water-line, to support the ship when rising forward to a sea, and also to enable her to send. See the run in Fig. 8.

N.B. the fashion pieces, or aftermost timbers on either side, should be at their greatest breadth asunder about six feet less than the extreme breadth and reach; the dead wood at a quarter of the draught of water abaft.

8. A ship with the bow Fig. 1 and a stern Fig. 3 will not pitch so much in carrying

---

1 These observations are by an officer in the Royal Navy, who has occasionally honoured us with his correspondence.

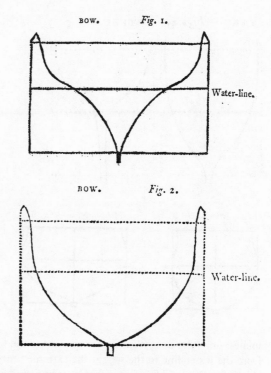

sail upon a wind, as a ship with the full bow as Fig. 2 and a stern Fig. 3 for at the water-line the breadth of the bow and quarter of the former ship is more equal than those of the latter: whereas the latter has a full bow (Fig. 2) will rise suddenly at the wave, and having nothing to support her abaft (Fig. 3) will dip her stern, and rise so high forward, that at the next pitch she will plunge deeper than if she had a sharp bow and struck through the wave at once. A ship of the former construction will be very wet in carrying sail, and a bad sea boat when lying-to: whereas the latter ship will lie to with safety, and will be more liable to ship a sea on the after-part of the quarter-deck than forward; and when carrying a press of sail upon a wind, will frequently be obliged to take in her mizen-topsail to prevent her pitching.

9. If the midship-frame of a ship is as in Fig. 6 which is quite a semicircle, a body of that form will roll continually and move like a pendulum.

10. If a midship frame of a ship is as in Fig. 6 which is a sharp bottom, such a ship will either draw too much water, or if otherwise will have no stowage, though but little rolling motion, and may sail well if a proper length and breadth.

11. If the midship-frame of a ship is as in Fig. 7 which is like a square box, such a ship will, no doubt, have the least rolling motion; but as she will never yield to the sea, every wave will make a breach over her.

12. The futtocks of a ship should therefore be straight; to obtain which, and stowage, the floor must be flat, with or without a rising is of no consequence; if with a rising, she will probably draw more water than without one.

13. As a general rule to go by in the midship frames of all ships, let their draught of water be what it will, take and draw a right-angled parallelogram similar to Fig. 8. - divide the floor into four equal parts: at the water-line set off on each side five or six

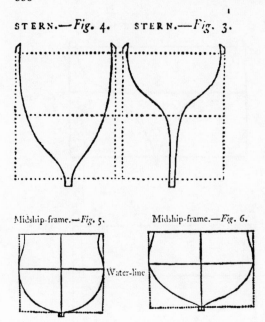

STERN.—*Fig.* 4.   STERN.—*Fig.* 3.

Midship-frame.—*Fig.* 5.   Midship-frame.—*Fig.* 6.

Water-line

inches; draw the lines from thence straight to the fourths of the floor; draw also lines from the water-line to the height the extreme breadth should be (suppose six feet in ships of the line and five feet in frigates): by rounding off these lines you will obtain the midship frame, and have a ship with a flat floor, a straight futtock, and the extreme breadth so placed, as to render her not only able to carry sail, but, if of the line, to fight her lower deck guns in a sea when other ships cannot venture to open their ports.

N.B. If the floor has a rising where it cuts the straight line at *a*, measure the distance from thence to the floor, and set off that distance one-third more or less outwards, to increase the breadth of the floor which rises to *b*.

14. If the extreme breadth lies at the water-line, or below it, in a ship, every inch she heels will expose a less half breadth on her inclined side to the surface of the water, and of course be crank, and come at once to her bearings. A ship whose lower-deck ports are low, but whose extreme breadth lies at the lower cill [sic] of the ports, will fight her guns better in a sea than a ship whose lower-deck ports are higher out of the water, but whose extreme breadth lies below the water-line.

15. To place the extreme breadth properly in all ships, it should lie six feet above the water line, in ships of the line, and five feet in frigates. The water is like so many perpendicular wires supporting a ship's body: the greater half breadth she exposes, the more of these points will bear to support her inclined side; so that every inch she heels, she become stiffer.

16. All ships should be built to sail upon an even keel, by which they will not be easily put out of trim: and as the keel will then be straight from the scarfing of the stem to the stern post, they will lie aground without straining, which in merchant ships is a good quality. A ship should carry her breadth well forward, and from her midships after diminish gradually: the several water-lines should be fair, and without hollows or concave lines, which latter, in the construction of a ship, impede her progress through the water. See Fig. 9.

Midship-frame.

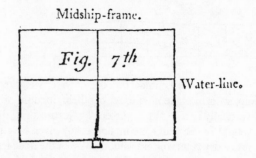

Water-line.

Fig. 8.
Midship-frame.
After-body.   Fore-body.

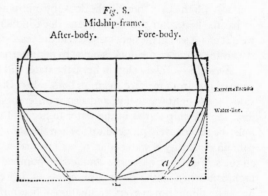

17. The stern-post of a ship should be perpendicular, and her stern should not overhang: the former gives the water a better opportunity of closing upon the rudder, and the latter contributes to ease her when dipping her stern.

18. The stem of a ship should rake a little: it gives an appearance of lightness, and does not injure her. Whether the hawse-pieces (viz. the timbers which rise to the stem from the knuckle timbers) are produced raking, or are built up bluff, like a Dutch fly-boat, is of no consequence in removing the column of water.

19. Shingle ballast is bad for two reasons: the first, because it creates damp vapour below; the second, because the weight being raised, the ship will be crank. If there was only iron ballast in a ship, skids might then be fixed fore and aft for the stowage of the ground tier. A ship would then carry sail better, and a perfect plan of the hold be delivered to the captain, when the ship was commissioned.

N.B. The French Ordinance de la Marine, for 1786, abolished the use of shingle ballast. The *Iphigene*, French frigate, had only iron ballast; and, from its being properly stowed, she was very easy in a sea when under her courses. Her extremities were not overloaded with cannon; for she carried only thirteen guns of a side, although she had room for fifteen. She was the best sea-boat, and fastest sailing ship, perhaps, ever built. Her length was something more than four times her extreme breadth, and she drew only fifteen, or fifteen and a half English feet water. To prove that length contributes to fast sailing, there was a smuggling lugger, at Boulogne-sur-Mer, manned with 36 men, all outlawed. They said, no vessel could overtake them. The length of the lugger was 64 feet upon deck; extreme breadth 11 feet, which lay at the gunwale; draught of water 6 feet; height of the gunwale above the water 3 feet.

20. To ascertain the exact tonnage of a ship or vessel, there are but three methods:

Fig. 9.

First, - As a cubical foot of salt water weights 72 lbs, let any common dock be filled up, so as to make it an exact parallelopinedon: let a scale of feet and inches be placed vertically in it. - When the dock gates are shut, the solid contents of the dock, and the weight of the water it contains at any given height, will be known. Let off that water into a dry reservoir or basin; then open the dock gates, and let water into the dock; after which, take a vessel in a light state into the dock; shut the dock gates after the water has run off with the tide; then fill the dock, by pumping the water into it from the reservoir or basin; the rise of the water in the dock higher than what it originally was, is the weight of a vessel in the light state. Load the vessel to her load water line. This additional rise of the water in the dock is equal to her internal capacity, which is her tonnage.

Secondly, - Take a ship in her light state, and let her load waterline be traced by a painted line from forward to aft on both sides. Bore trunnel-holes amidships on both sides, at the light water-line, and also at different distances above it, to the load water-line. As the ship settles in the water to her load water-line, let each of these trunnel holes be successively plugged up. When the ship floats at her load water-line, she will contain a quantity of water equal to her internal capacity, which is her tonnage: then let all the salt or fresh water she contains be pumped out into tubs, containing half a ton each; and when all the water is pumped out, her exact tonnage will be known, as also her best sailing trim in every graduation of her immersion, from her light water-line, to her load water-line.

N.B. As salt and fresh water differ in weight, the tubs must be proportioned accordingly.

Thirdly, - Take a quantity of iron ballast whose weight is known, and load the ship with it to her load water-line, which will give her internal capacity. That calculation is best which comes nearest to the tonnage given by these methods.

N.B. The above is intended as a general treatise on the property of ships; but should any person be desirous of obtaining accurate information respecting ship-building, I beg leave to refer them to the regular publications of the society for the encouragement of Naval Architecture.

On the Mode of Improving the Navy, 1801. *V 129-135*

In a letter from Gabriel Snodgrass, Esq. to the Right Hon. Henry Dundas, President of the Board of Commissioners for the Affairs of India, &c. &c. and to the Honourable the Chairman, the Deputy chairman, and court of Directors of the East India Company; with an Appendix

Gentlemen, I am sensibly flattered by your permission to dedicate to you the result of the experience which I have acquired in a series of years in the East India Company's service. It is a reward of which an honest man may be fairly proud - the approbation of his services by those who are the best able to appreciate their value.

While an attention to my duty produced improvements in the building and repairing of the Company's ships, I could not but feel an anxiety to extend those improvements to the Navy; in consequence, my strenuous endeavours have not been wanting to afford to my countrymen, in the fullest extent, what I conceived to be advantages material to Great Britain.

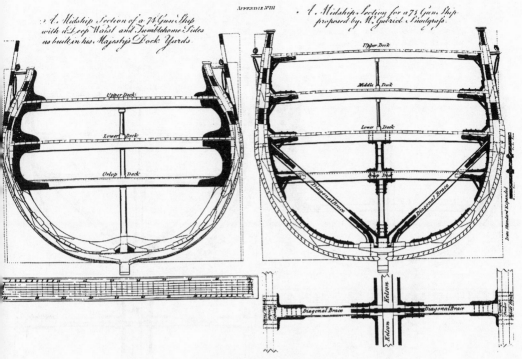

Snodgrass's Method of Strengthening a 74-Gun Ship. Plate 56

If the arguments I use in support of these opinions be too desultory, and if I express myself in a style not sufficiently polished, I am persuaded you will pardon these faults. I impute blame to no individual, I mean not to offend; if I speak truth you will approve it; - your approbation, and that of my country, is all I desire.

In the first place, I take the liberty of asserting (and from experience), that the East India Company's ships, as now constructed, are the first and safest ships in Europe. In support of the assertion which I have made in favour of the construction of those ships, I beg leave to submit in the Appendix (No. VII) a list of the number of ships built and repaired under my inspection, from the year 1757 to 1794, making in all 989, of which (as will appear by the said paper) there was only one, the *Earl of Chatham*, which was supposed to have foundered. If the improvements adopted in those ships were extended to the navy, much labour and expence would be saved to the nation.

Upon that idea the following remarks are founded; but, before I proceed to enumerate the particular circumstances which render the Company's ships superior to our ships of war, I must be permitted to remark, with deference to the opinions of the persons employed by government in the department of ship building, that radical errors appear to prevail respecting the article of timber.

In the first place, a much greater quantity of rough timber than can be necessary is kept in store; for I must contend that a stock sufficient for one year's consumption would equally serve the purposes to which it is at present applied in any of his Majesty's dock-yards.

No ship was ever yet built entirely with timber that had laid to season three years,

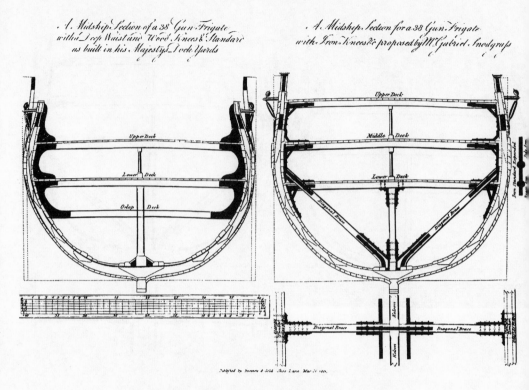

A Midship Section of a 38 Gun Frigate with a Deep Waist and Wood Knees & Standard as built in his Majesty's Dock Yards

A Midship Section for a 38 Gun Frigate with Iron Knees &c proposed by Mr Gabriel Snodgrass

Snodgrass's Method of Strengthening a 38-Gun Frigate. Plate 57

two years, or even one year; consequently, that part of the ship which was formed of the most unseasoned wood must be expected to decay first, and thus a progressive decay in the several parts of the ship, subjects her to the necessity of continual repairs, at an immense expence, and to the detriment of the service.

A second error is in the preparation of timber for service; upon this and upon the other point above mentioned, I cannot submit better information than what is contained in my answers to questions put to me by the Commissioners of the Land Revenue, in the year 1791 (Appendix No. II), which are published in their Eleventh Report to the House of Commons.

I there recommended that Government should always have twenty or thirty sail of line-of-battle ships constantly on the stocks, to be built by contract, and to stand to season under cover (as is described in my answer to the thirty-fifth question), by which means the ships would last from eighteen to twenty years, instead of only eleven years and three quarters, which is said by the Navy Board to be the average duration of ships of the present navy.

Indeed, I hope I shall be forgiven in requesting particular attention to those answers, as containing, in my humble opinion, suggestions which, if carried into execution, would be the means of reducing, not only the consumption of oak timber, but also the expence of building and repairing ships in the navy, by at least *one-half*. My opinions still continue the same as those which I then expressed.

No ship should ever have what is called a thorough repair, or *any timbers* shifted; instead of this, their bottoms and upper works should be doubled with three-inch oak plank, from keel to gunwale, and strengthened with iron knees, standards, and even with iron ryders, if necessary; all which might be done at a small expence; and ships so repaired would be stronger and safer, and be able to keep the seas longer, in the worst weather, than any new ships in his Majesty's navy.

This measure would be the means of saving great quantities of valuable straight and crooked (commonly called compass) oak timber, which otherwise must be expended by giving ships thorough repairs; and it should be more especially adopted with respect to such ships as have their top-sides of the absurd old fashion of *tumbling in* (Appendix No. III), than which nothing can possibly be more extravagant and ridiculous, as many of the timbers must be much weakened by being cut across the grain; and such ships as have had a second thorough repair, must also be further weakened, as the timbers are always considerably reduced in the moulding way on each repair, and those timbers are originally much too slight; on the contrary, great advantages would be derived from having little or no tumblehome to the sides, as it gives more room upon deck, a greater spread to the shrouds, additional security to the masts, makes the ship stiffer, a much better sea boat, and, in every respect, safer, stronger, and better.

As all ships of the navy are every way deficient of iron to strengthen and connect the sides and beams together, they should be built with diagonal braces (Appendix No. II), as described by me in the aforesaid eleventh report, and with the knees, standards, breast-hooks, and crutches of iron, it being obviously impossible, by any means, to make a ship equally strong with wooden knees, &c. The iron may be made to any size, strength, and length, to admit of as many additional bolts as many be judged necessary.

It is upwards of twenty-four years since I first introduced in the East India Company's shipping the mode of fastening on the outside and inside plank with bolts, and leaving the tree-nail holes open for air until the ships were nearly finished and ready for caulking, which has been, and is now universally acknowledged to be the best method of seasoning the timbers and plank of any yet adopted. But although this is a matter of so much importance to the preservation of the ships of the navy, it has not been practised in his Majesty's dockyards, nor have I ever heard of its being introduced into any contract for building ships of war in the merchants' yards.

It is more than seventeen years since I brought into use, for the East India ships, round headed rudders, requiring no rudder-coats. Experience taught me how dangerous the old fashioned rudder-coats were, particularly in small ships of the navy, many of which, I cannot doubt, were lost from the sea having carried away their rudder-coat.

The round-headed rudders are now universally acknowledged to be much superior, in every respect, to the square-headed rudders of the ships of the navy; and I am very anxious that these should be introduced into all ships to be built in the King's yards, and provided for in the contracts made, in future, for ships of war to be built in merchants' yards.

About twenty-seen years ago I also introduced four-inch bottoms to ships for the East India Company's service, instead of three-inch bottoms; and there are ships of less than six hundred tons burthen, built for that service, with four-inch bottoms, also with sheathing of three-fourths of an inch thick, and coppered as usual; whilst, on the contrary, there have been frigates of a thousand tons burthen, lately built for government in merchants' yards, with three inch bottoms, and a ship of eight hundred tons with a fir bottom only three inches thick; and there are ships of seventy-four guns, now building in those yards, of eighteen hundred tons burthen, with not more than four inch bottoms; which ships, I presume, are intended to go to sea, as usual, without any wood sheathing.

It appears to me that continuing the practice of *thin* bottoms tends to risk the loss of the ships and the lives of his Majesty's subjects, more especially if fir be taken instead of English, Quebec, or East country oak-plank, which may always be procured. In my opinion, no ships of four hundred tons and upwards should have less than a bottom of four-inch oak-plank; - all ships of the navy, of eight hundred tons and upwards, should have not less than five-inch plank; - line-of-battle ships should have bottoms at least six inches thick; - and all ships should have the addition of wood sheathing. The thickness of the inside plank of those ships may then generally be reduced in proportion.

It is many years since the keels of all the East India ships have been rabbitted in the middle, which is certainly safer and better than having the rabbit on the upper edge, as is the practice in the ships of his Majesty's navy at this time.

About twenty-six years since, I had the capstands to the ships in the Company's service fitted with an iron spindle, paul-head, and catch-pauls. This has ever since been allowed effectually to prevent the people from being thrown from the barts, which, is well-known, has frequently happened on board of his Majesty's ships, and whereby many lives have been lost, and great numbers crippled.

Every old capstand in the King's ships should be fitted with an iron spindle and catch-pauls, which may be done in a short time, and at a very moderate expence, compared with the great safety and other advantages that must attend this improvement.

I have made it a practice, for many years, to add iron knees under the beams to all old ships in the Company's service; and, of late years, to such ships as have made three voyages, I have frequently added an iron knee under every beam of the lower and middle decks, from the fore-mast to the mizen-mast, where there has not been a standard. If his Majesty's ship the *Centaur* (although French-built) and others that have foundered at sea, had been fitted in this manner, it would have prevented their sides from separating from the ends of their beams, and consequently might, in all possibility, have prevented those ships from foundering.

Indeed, I am persuaded that the loss of most of the ships of war and even merchant ships, that have foundered at sea, has been occasioned by their having been insufficient in point of strength.

After having stated, in my answers to the questions put to me by the Commissioners of the Land Revenue in the year 1791, every alteration I then thought necessary to be made in future, so as to prevent accidents of that kind, even in the worst weather, I cannot but sincerely regret that my remarks have not been attended to. I feel this the more when I consider the frequent losses of the King's ships, particularly the very recent catastrophe of his Majesty's ship *Leda*, when (as it is said) only seven of the whole crew were saved.

Out of the great number of ships that have been lost from getting on shore or striking on the rocks, there can be no doubt many of them might have been saved if their bottoms had been thicker when originally built, and the old ships doubled with three-inch oak plank when they required considerable repairs.

Whenever a ship is lost at sea, a strict inquiry ought always to be made of the survivors as to every particular, in order that the cause of such loss may be ascertained: - the result of such inquiry should be made as public as possible to the eye of observation.

The great number of King's ships, of all rates, which have foundered at sea, and the number of lives that have been lost in consequences, are striking proofs that those ships were not constructed, in all respects, as they might have been, so as to encounter the most severe storm. I am fully convinced that all ships may be so constructed, and I presume I have pointed out, in the different parts of this publication, effectual means for the purpose.

I sincerely hope that this will attract the attention of government, and also induce professional men to make such further observations on building, constructing and repairing ships for the navy of Great Britain, as may prevent the like dreadful consequences in future.

The principal causes of these misfortunes, in case of sudden violent storms, or the ships broaching to, appear to me as follows, *viz.*

In the first place, the deep waist in those ships, and more especially in the frigates and sloops of war, which occasions them to ship a great deal of water on the main-deck.

Secondly, the ballast, water, and every thing in the hold, shifting and falling to leeward, from want of shifting-boards and the pillars not being properly secured to prevent the same, whereby the ships are liable to become water-logged, and thus, before the hatches are sufficiently secured, they may fill and founder.

Captain Inglefield's narrative of the loss of the *Centaur* of seventy-four guns, will clearly evince that not only small ships, but all ships of war, however large, should have shifting-boards in the hold, and the pillars better secured; and as a farther security from the guns doing damage, in case of their breaking loose, I recommend substantial coamings to all the hatch-ways, at least two feet above the decks, also thick pieces of oak in mid-ships, between the hatch-ways, let down upon the beams, equally well secured and of the same height above the deck as the coamings, which must prevent the guns from going further to leeward.

The sterns of ships of war should have little or no rake, in order to give an opportunity of fighting a greater number of stern-chase guns, which cannot be done with safety where the sterns have a great overhanging, as is the case with the ships of his Majesty's navy. There should be strong dead-lights to their stern windows, and no quarter-galleries, which are not only unnecessary in those ships, as when they are close hauled, they very much impede their sailing, but are also dangerous (particularly in small ships) in case of the galleries being carried away; neither should there be any scuttles through the sides, or their [?] tillars under the gun-decks of any ships; there should be whole ports instead of half ports between decks, and no line of battle ships should work their cables on the lower deck.

I am confident if all ships had firm and flush upper decks, in place of deep waists (as I recommended in my answers in the year 1791, before mentioned) they would be far superior, not only as ships of war, but also in point of safety, as it would then be almost impossible (except through great neglect), for any ship to founder in deep water, even in the heaviest seas or the most severe storm. I feel myself so deeply interested in this subject, that I must take the liberty of referring to *Steel's* list of ships lost or foundered at sea,[2] and I am persuaded that I am rendering a service to the community by pointing out what I am certain would prevent those fatal consequences in future.

In addition to the above suggestions, which come more particularly within the professed object of this address, allow me, Honourable Sirs, to submit the following ideas to your consideration.

As it is apprehended there may be a want of oak timber in this country, I presume it is now time that Government should give orders to plant and enclose every part of the

2 Appendix No. I.

King's forests and waste lands with oaks, as I recommended in a report to an Open Committee of the House of Commons, printed in the year 1771.[3]

I would further recommend that, whenever a peace should take place, all those ships that were contracted for, or built for the East India Company's service, and purchased by government, should be returned to be employed in that service again, which would be the means of saving a great quantity of oak timber.

I am confident that the Surveyors of the navy may form such bodies for line of battle ships as would answer equally well for trade in times of peace, and such ships may be lent out to be employed in the East India Company's service as merchant ships. This measure would not only save an immense consumption of oak timber, give further time for improving the King's forests, and prevent the ships from rotting in the harbours, but would also save the public the usual expence of repairs, and they may be returned to government when required.

In my opinion, a great deal too much has been said in favour of French ships. I cannot myself see any thing worthy of being copied from them but their magnitude; they are, in other respects, much inferior to British ships of war, being slighter and weaker, in general draw more water, and they likewise commonly exceed the old ships of the present navy in the absurd tumble-home of their topsides. It must appear very extraordinary, that there are several line of battle ships and large frigates now building for government from draughts, copied from those ridiculous ships.

With respect to these humble ideas on the foregoing and other matters relating to ships of the navy, and of shipping in general, formed from long experience in that line, and which are more fully stated in my answers in the eleventh Report before mentioned, it does not become me to say why my plans were not thought worthy of adoption; but I owe to myself to explain to you, Gentlemen, upon whose good opinion I set so high a value, that I have left no proper means untried, from time to time, to impress on those who superintended the naval department of England, considerations which, as an Englishman, I thought it my duty to submit to them.

May I be permitted to add, that a principal inducement for troubling you with this address is that, under your auspices, the considerations contained in it may challenge a degree of attention, which, as the suggestions of an humble individual, they could not otherwise claim. I have the honour to be, very respectfully.

Gentlemen, Your most obedient and Faithful humble Servant,

GAB. SNODGRASS

East India House, the 9th November, 1796.

[Appendices etc. Vol. V 136-153; 227-233; 321-327.]

Particulars of the Weight of an Eighty Gun Ship - 1803. [X 113-114]

	pounds	tons & pounds	
The hull	3,568,726	1,593	406
The furniture	437,520	195	720
Guns and ammunition	521,427	232	1,747
Officers' stores	66,559	29	1,590
Provisions	1,792,870	800	870
Men and ballast	1,795,361	801	1,121
Sum.	8,182,463	3,652	1,983

3 Appendix No. III.

Weight of the Hull

Oak timber	3,200,802	1,428	2,082
Fir ditto	213,936	95	1,136
Elm ditto	27,040	12	160
Carved and lead work	4,651	2	171
Iron work	88,254	39	894
Pitch, tar, and paint	17,920	8	0
Cook-room	16,123	7	443
Sum.	3,568,726	1,593	406

Weight of the Furniture

Yards and masts	161,000	71	1,960
Anchors	39,996	17	1,916
Rigging	69,128	30	1,928
Sails	32,008	14	648
Cables	73,332	32	1,652
Blocks, pumps, boats	62,056	27	1,576
Sum.	437,520	195	720

Guns and Ammunition

Guns and Carriages	377,034	168	714
Powder and shot	116,320	51	2,080
Implements for powder	6,500	2	2,020
Ditto for crows and handspikes	21,573	9	1,413
Sum.	521,427	232	1,747

Officers' Stores

Carpenter's Stores	20,187	9	27
Boatswain's ditto	21,112	9	952
Gunner's ditto	8,964	4	4
Caulker's ditto	5,200	2	720
Surgeon and Chaplain's effects	11,096	4	2,136
Sum.	66,559	29	1,599

Provisions

Provisions for six months for 760 men with their equipage	858,970	383	1,050
Water, casks, and Captain's table	933,900	416	2,060
Sum.	1,792,870	800	870

Weight of the Men

Seven hundred men with their effects, including the Officers and their effects	316,961	141	1,121
Ballast	1,478,400	660	0
Sum.	1,795,361	801	1,121

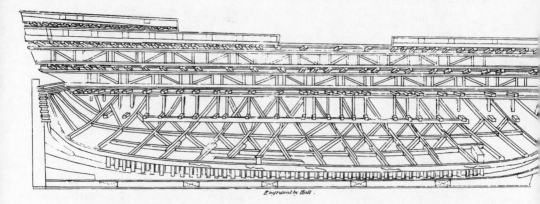

Engraved by Hall .

Perspective Section of a Third-Rate Ship of War, The *Tremendous*, re-built upon a novel construction. Engraved by Hall. [Plate 383]

The accompanying embellishment serves to illustrate the new system of architecture, on which a third-rate ship of war has been lately constructed internally, and represents what may be termed a perspective section of the ship. The beholder being supposed to stand about the middle of its length, with his eye nearly on a level with the orlop-deck.[4]

We are not in possession of the exact dimensions of this ship, which, we believe, was finished in 1810: but she may be supposed to have been rebuilt upon the model generally of her predecessor, which was built in 1784, and whose principal dimensions are understood to have been as follows: keel, 139 feet 6 inches; gun-deck, 170 feet 4 inches; breadth extreme, 47 feet 7 1/2 inches; depth of hold, 20 feet 4 inches; burthen, 1680 tons.

The following is a brief specification of this new construction:

In the hold, there is no plank or lining below the orlop-deck clamps; the perpendicular riders are also done away; the openings between the timbers, or ribs, are securely filled in and caulked within and without, to the height of the orlop clamps, or where the lining is omitted.[5] Diagonal riders are placed in the hold to the angle of 450, lying in opposite directions, in the fore to the aftermost part of the ship. Pieces of timber are placed in fore-and-aft directions, at the height of the floor and first futtock-heads, coming in contact against the sides of the said diagonal riders, to which they are secured. A piece of timber is also run in a diagonal direction in these compartments, thereby forming two triangles in each space. The whole of this is coaked, with circular coaks, to each other and to the frame or ribs of the ship; of course the bolts have no other office to perform, but that of keeping the materials to the timbers. The heads of the diagonal riders come in contact with an internal hoop, or shelf-piece, under the gun-deck beams, which forms the grand abutment, as well as a security to connect the beams to the sides, assisted by chocks and iron knees on a particular principle, upon which system all the decks are secured, the short plank between the ports (a certain quantity of which is placed in a diagonal direction) forming in the space between the ports two triangles. A great proportion of the lower and main deck is laid to the angle of 450 from the beams, and also the ledges of the decks; a proportion only of the plank lying in a fore-and-aft direction; *viz.* the sides and middle so secured that it forms abutments to the diagonal planks. The introduction of this principle has considerably reduced the price of timber, and also made use of that which was not applicable on the old

4 Certain improvements in this branch of hydraulic architecture are to be found detailed in Vol. 23 p. 112.
5 *N.C.* Vol. 3 pp. 62, 134.

principle of ship-building. Additional strength is given by the general combination of materials that compose this ship, probably with additional capacity for stowage as well as an opportunity to discover defects, and neat oeconomy in making them good; also a protection against worms externally, and rats internally, &c. The leading axioms of the project are, that strength is to be obtained rather by a judicious disposition of matter, than altogether by quantity; that partial strength produces partial weakness; and that no fabric is stronger than its weakest part. The triangle is the basis of this system, which is the only immovable figure known, to which form every part before described assimilates. By substituting the triangle for the rectangle (which latter figure the present mode of ship-building represents) the materials, *viz.* diagonal riders, trusses, decks, materials between the ports, &c are pressed upon as a pillar, or stretched as a rope by the varied action of pitching and rolling, sailing on a wind, &c. which is the strongest position fibrous solids can be acted upon. By the present practice they are acted upon in a transverse direction to a longitudinal position, which is the weakest, depending entirely upon the fastenings, which receive no contrary pressure; as is the case in the figure of a triangle, which cannot move but by forcing the matter it is composed of into a less space than it originally occupied, or in other words, the hypotenuse must have a tendency to insinuate itself into the space of one of the legs or sides of the triangle it forms a part of.

Royal William - 1813. [XXX 48]

The long service of the *Royal William*, protracted beyond those of any other ship ever built, are come to an end. She has been examined in Portsmouth Dock, when her timbers proved so generally defective, that she is ordered to be broken up. It is not ascertained when this memorable ship was first built. It is recorded of her, that she came into harbour on the 2d day of October, 1679, to be laid up in ordinary: she went out on the 16th of March, 1700: came in again on the 26th of July, 1702: was ordered on the 31st of July, 1714, to be taken to pieces, for the purpose of being re-built; and was undocked on the 3d of September, 1719. Particular orders have been given to report on the appearance of her timbers, when she is taken to pieces, to account, if possible, for her unusual duration; to observe if they have been charred or snail drawn (as, it is presumed, was the practice when she was built); and whether there appear to be any effects in them from any oxygenated matter on any other parts of her, from such a cause.

Manning of Ships of the Line - 1813
To the Editor of the Naval Chronicle, by 'A.B.', 5 August 1813. [XXX 140-141]

It appearing certain that the Americans are determined to try their strength with us in line-of-battle ships, which they are now building on a large construction, permit me, through the medium of your publication, to point out the inequality of manning in our line-of-battle ships, according to their size and tonnage:

Bellona, tons 1608, men 590; *Theseus*, tons 1680, men 590; *Sultan*, tons 1734, men 590; *Conqueror*, tons 1842, men 640; *Warspite*, tons, 1890, men 640; *Revenge*, tons 1929, men 640; *Ajax* (late), tons 1970, men 719; *Rochfort* [sic] (building), 2040, is to have 640.

By this list, you will perceive the inequality of the complement of our line-of-battle ships. The *Rochfort*, which is 200 tons larger than the *Conqueror*, is to have the same number of men; and the late *Ajax*, which was 70 tons smaller than the *Rochfort*, had 79 more men. The *Sultan* is nearly 130 tons larger than the *Bellona* - has only the same number of men.

A.B.

Ship Durability - 1813

To the Editor of the Naval Chronicle, by 'C.H.', Glasgow, 2 October, 1813.
XXX 407-408

[It has been reported in the daily papers, noted 'C.H.', that] Government has determined on building several immense frigates, the first of which is to be laid down in Plymouth yard, and to be called the *Java*: the length, breadth, and tonnage of these vessels is then reported, while the account is concluded by the following remarkable passage: "these frigates are *not* to be what is termed *serviceable* ships; they are to be built for the express purpose of running down the large American frigates," &c.: Is it really possible that the latter part of this sentence is correct? build unserviceable frigates! no, it cannot be; for by the term unserviceable is meant, I presume, that these frigates shall be made of such materials, as shall not be of long duration; pray, then, what are they built for; are the Americans to come out on purpose to fight these vessels? or is the puissant Commodore Rodgers, who flew from the *Alexandria*,[6] of little more than half his force, to embrace the first opportunity of coming out to engage an equal.

The truth is, the greatest attention must be paid to the building and equipment of these ships; for as the American frigates will be the principal object of their pursuit, and as these separate so much, it is impossible to say what weather our vessels may be exposed to: they must be equally fitted for pursuing the *President* to Greenland, or the *Constitution* to the Brazils, and be prepared for the gales which may occur between these regions.

Another occasion for not only the common but additional strength of these vessels is the weight of masts which these frigates, as I am informed, are to be equipped with, namely those of a seventy-four; this of itself, as I have stated, ought to be a sufficient reason for adding strength to these vessels; for every seaman knows how much, in a rolling sea, the heaviness of the masts increases the strain on the hull, and unless particular attention is paid to this the outfit of these vessels, we shall really find them to be immense, but unserviceable.

Lastly, let them be particularly strong, if we would nave them fight the American frigates: the manner in which our ships have been cut up in the various engagements with them, requires and demands this; and I think the commanders of our frigates should not be particular in having only common balls on board our ships; let similar pieces and bars of iron to those which Commodore Rodgers was seen to load his cannon with, when pursued by the *Alexandria*, let these be immediately adopted in our warfare with the Americans; the wounded on board our vessels demand reparation for their sufferings; and it cannot be unjust to use against an enemy the means by which he has succeeded in annoying us; and thus we shall have the hope of seeing the "proud old British Union" waving over the colours of the world as it was wont.

The Transit, Five-Masted Schooner

The Improvement of Rigging - 1800

Letter to the Editor by 'H'. II 422-424

I have lately seen the prospectus of an Improvement projected in Naval Architecture and Rigging, which ought to be noticed in your work.

6 An account of this was given by the captain of a whale-ship, who was at that time a prisoner on board the *President*.

There is a model,[7] now in London, made by the person who first suggested the idea, of rigging a vessel with five masts; for the service of either the Post-Office, or India-House, when expedition is particularly required. The inventor is Richard Hall Gower, Esq. who has been many years in the service of the Honourable East India Company. The object of the present Invention is to sail faster with a side wind, and closer to the wind, than vessels of the present construction can perform. The hull is calculated to admit her principal capacity to rest nearer the surface of the water. The sails are contrived to form a flatter surface, than sails at present do; and to make the fore-and-aft sails stand at the same angle with the wind, both below and aloft, which cannot be done in the present fore-and aft vessels. - For instance - to make the head of a Cutter's main-sail stand upon a wind, it is necessary to haul the boom in, almost fore-and aft; thus, in effect, by making the head of the sail serviceable, the foot is rendered almost useless. The sails too stand with that uniformity, and openness of situation, as not to take from each others power; which is repeatedly done in a ship by the lapping of stay-sail over stay-sail, and square-sail over square-sail; each destroying the effect of the other by back and eddy winds. - Again, the placing the sails upon a greater number of masts, not only admits the advantage of small and commodious fore-and-aft sails, which can be gybed with safety, and be managed by a few hands; but as it produces more weather leeches [ie. luffs], the united effort of the sails to accelerate the vessel, will be much augmented: for the weather leech of every sail is struck by the wind with more force than the lee leech; of course, if the same quantity of canvass be set obliquely to the wind, in detached pieces, their united efforts will be greater, than the same quantity of canvass in one piece, set to the same position. - Another advantage is easy and quick manoeuvering.

To *Stay* - merely put the helm down, and brace round the head yards at the proper time, as is now done in a ship, which is the whole duty to be performed, as the after sails of themselves will swing over to their proper angle, for the other tack. - To *Veer*, let fly the sheets of the three after masts; then proceed with the head sails, as we now do in a ship, gathering in the after sheets as the wind gets round upon the opposite quarter. Should it blow fresh, it will be proper in veering to brail up the three after top sails, and to take in the mizen and quarter courses. "*Laying to* is performed by bracing aback the head sails, and hauling in flat the after sheets; and at all times, the proper balance of helm may be produced by taking in one or other of the after sails."

A third advantage is the great safety, arising from the ease with which Sail may be reduced. "In a sudden Squall, the merely letting fly the mast sheets of the fore-and-aft sails, is an instant relief to all the after masts; the head sails only requiring particular labour, and attention. The topmasts, even at sea, are readily struck, without impediment to the working of the course sails; which sails, when the vessel is thus made snug, may be carried in very hard blowing weather, to the probable advantage of throwing her off a lee shore. As the masts do not depend upon each other, nor upon the bowsprit for their support, *one mast may fall, without endangering or destroying the effect of the rest.* The decks, apartments, &c. are calculated for a packet of 250 tons burthen, capable of facing all seas and weather with comfort to the crew. The fore cabin is for the people, which in the very worst of weathers, will have both air and light from the windows that open to the main deck: here they will be separated from the stores, and cargo, in a dry

7 It has lately been moved to Chichester: and the Inventor has met with so much encouragement, that he intends soon to construct a vessel on these principles.

airy cabin; which will preserve their health, and keep their conduct under the eye of the officer of the deck. The after cabin is appropriated to the captain, officers and passengers; and in very bad weather, when it may be necessary to put the dead lights into the stern windows, it will have both air and light from the main deck. - The capstern [sic] being forward admits of much snugness about the anchor gear, and much quicker heaving up than a windlass. In heavy heaving, it may be necessary to support the upper part of the capstern spindle, which is done by an *iron bar* from the *after bits to* the centre of the drum head."

A vessel contrived upon the plan of the model shewn in London, is not only calculated for the packet service, but, if pierced for guns, the Revenue service also; and, indeed, every employment requiring celerity of sailing. The Prospectus concludes as follows: "The author of the invention Mr. RICHARD HALL GOWER, has been long in the Naval service of the *Honourable the East India Company*. He has not solicited their employment for a considerable time, that he might have leisure to complete his model; and did his fortune permit him, with prudence to himself, to build a vessel on the plan proposed, he would cheerfully put it to the test of absolute experiment."

He hopes, however, to receive assistance from his country, in some form or other, either from the Government, the East India Company, a Society of gentlemen, or some patriotic individual; who may be willing to promote a scheme, seemingly fraught with benefit to Naval Architecture, and Rigging.

Trusting that you will consider the above as worthy of a place in the *Naval Chronicle*. I remain your Friend, -.

New Inventions - 1800. *III 412 & 505*

At Chichester, on the 10th [of May?], was launched the new vessel constructed by the ingenious Captain Gower, which is to carry five masts, and to exceed in celerity every vessel hitherto constructed. About eleven o'clock, A.M. a great concourse of spectators had collected at Itchenor, a small village on the Chichester River, where the vessel was built, and by twelve the opposite shores of Bosham-Hard and Chedham-Hard were completely lined. At a quarter past twelve, the signal being given, she descended gradually into the water in a majestic manner, amidst the shouts and well wishes of thousands. Among the company present were his Grace the Duke of Richmond, and a large party of his friends; General Lenox and Lady; several Captains and Officers of the Royal Navy from Portsmouth, &c &c The bottle was thrown by Captain Allen Charfield, with an ardour that bespoke his hearty good wishes for her success; and the exclamations of "Success to the *Transit*" resounded from all quarters. It is the intention of Captain Gower, the inventor, to have a trial of skill with one of our best sailing frigates, and immediately afterwards to proceed up the Thames.

In page 412, we gave an account of the launching of Captain Gower's newly constructed vessel, the *Transit*; we now inform our readers that a trial of her sailing has taken place. She sailed from the Motherbank on Thursday evening, the 19th inst. [June?] at six o'clock, with the wind at west, and arrived in the Downs at noon on the following day. At one on the same day she sailed for the River, turning up within Margate Sands through the Narrows, and over the Flats, with a double reef top-sail breeze at west, and arrived at Gravesend at midnight on the 21st; on the 22d in the morning, at eight o'clock, she again got under weigh, and turned up to Blackwall the same tide amidst the admiration and astonishment of the numerous beholders, who viewed the simplicity of her manoeuvres. It appears by the testimony of the Downs Pilot, Mr. William Norris, that she would have reached Gravesend on the second tide from the Downs, but for the darkness of the night.

The Transit - 1800. IV 50-52

This vessel, of which some account was given in the preceding volume, has been taken into Mr. Perry's dock, for the purpose of being coppered, and fitted for a foreign voyage. Her length by the keel is 97 feet; her extreme breadth at the gun-wale, which is the broadest part, is 22 feet; she is 11 feet deep in the hold, and is estimated at the burthen of 200 tons by the custom-house at Chichester, where she is registered. A more enlarged and particular account of this singular and highly patriotic exertion of the mind to effect an improvement in one of the most consequential sciences existing, will be given in our next. For the present suffice it to say, the following are the reasons given by the ingenious inventor in support of his new system.

The Objects of this Invention are numerous, and as follow:

First, Faster sailing with a side wind, and closer to the wind, than vessels of the present construction.
This, I think, will be allowed, upon a general view and examination of the vessel. The peculiar form of the hull admits her principal capacity to rest nearer the surface of the water, so that in her progress she may remove a volume of water more superficial than vessels of her tonnage of the present mould, inasmuch as that water nearer the surface is more readily removed than water deeper situated.

She possesses the property of being weatherly, from her length, depth of keel, and form of bow; and of great stability, even at a light draught of water, from the iron ballast being situated so much below her principal capacity, as, in effect, to produce the stiffness that would arise from a solid iron keel. This extraordinary stiffness is certainly objectionable in vessels as they are at present constructed; but that under consideration is exceedingly light rigged, and cannot roll with the violence of a stiff ship, from the nature of her form: of course, the masts will be infinitely less in danger of being carried away, notwithstanding the stiffness of the vessel.

[The description of sails and rigging given in the prospectus was abstracted in the previous number. Additional advantages of the design are that:]

Seventhly, The abridgement of chain wales for her rigging.
These can very well be dispensed with, on account of her tumbling out as she rises; which also gives her the advantage of coming alongside another vessel with safety.

Eighthly, The very great economy of every kind of store.
This circumstance arises from the equality maintained in masts, sails, and rigging, and from the sails being so contrived as to fill up the whole space between the masts, without that frequent over-lapping of canvass we meet with in a ship - one-third of the canvass will undoubtedly be saved.

Ninthly, The masts being equally spread throughout the vessel, will produce so even a strain when she labours, as not to wear and rack the hull partially.
This is not the case in cutters, brigs, or ships, particularly near the main-mast.

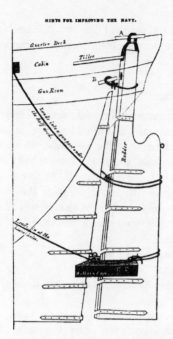

Newly Developed Naval Gear

An Emergency Rudder Mounting from Hints for Improving the Navy - 1802

To the Editor, Bath, October 20, 1802. ^{VIII 470-71}

Sir, It is possible the enclosed contrivance for securing a Rudder to steer by, after its having been beaten off, has not yet reached the public eye.

I stumbled on it this morning among some old ship papers, and thought (being unfortunately an *idler* on Terra Firma), an hour could not be passed better, than in copying and forwarding it for insertion in the *Naval Chronicle*, should you at any time find it not interfere with more useful nautical communication.

It was tried with good effect on board the *Hind*, commanded by the Honourable Captain Cochrane, in the North Sea, just before, or about the commencement of, the late war.

I am, Sir, Your humble Servant, A Sailor.

P.S. perhaps a *middle* hawser would add steadiness and security to the rudder.

A. The quarter-deck scuttled, with a bar across to hang the rudder.

B. Another bar with slings housed tight at the rudder-hole in the gun-room.

The upper hawser was fastened with a *clove-hitch* round the rudder, each end being brought into a port under the half-deck.

The lower hawser was *passed* through both bolts on the cap, and made fast on the opposite side.

[∞] Two bolts to secure the cap to the rudder.

The top-most part of the cap was cut to fit the rudder, and the *after* part *jawed* away, so as to work on the stern-post.

The helm could not be put hard over, but the *Hind* frigate *stayed*, and worked very well with it.

A New Marine Log - 1803. [X 292]

M. Leguin has invented a new log, by means of which the way made by a ship will be more easily and more accurately obtained than by the common long-line. The new log is furnished with wheel-work and an index:· the former is put in motion by the water, and the latter shews the way of the ship by the number of divisions it passes over in a given time. The public is already indebted to this gentleman for another mechanical instrument, invented in the year 1790, and approved by the board of Longitude at Amsterdam; by which the apparent distance of the centre of the moon from that of the sun, is reduced to the true distance, and consequently the calculations for obtaining the longitude of a place are simplified.

Improvement in Sails - 1805. [XIV 281-82]

A Mr. Malcolm Cowan has recently obtained a patent for sails for ships that may be reefed in a few minutes, in the most tempestuous weather, by very few seamen, &c.

The advantages proposed by this invention are as follow: To enable ships to reef their courses in a few minutes; 1st, on a lee shore, in stormy weather, when it may be necessary to reduce the sails, though at the same time it may be dangerous to take their effect off the ships by hauling them up to reef them on the yards; 2dly, when the ships' crews are reduced by sickness, by part of them being in prizes, or employed on shore, or weakened by labour or fatigue; 3dly, in gales of wind in frosty weather, when it is difficult to handle the sail; 4thly, in merchant ships with a few seamen, because the sails can be hauled up and set again in less time, as one part of the sail is taken off or set again at a time, and consequently requires less of the force of the wind.

We are also assured by the patentee, that when ships are obliged to carry a press of sail in squally weather, in chase, &c., the sails may be reefed and set again in a minute, without starting tack or sheet, or risk of splitting. If a sail should split in one part, it would be stopped by the reef-bands. When the sail is hauled up it will be almost furled to the yard, and bent to the cringles, on the rope of the reef-band. The weight of the reefs is removed from the yard to the foot of the sail, without increasing the strain on the yards. The sails being reduced at the foot instead of the head, will stand longer and better in a gale of wind, as the squarest part of the sail is taken off when reefed. These sails can be easily hauled up out of the fire of guns, &c., and the expense of them will be less; though they will last longer, from not being liable to split in hauling up or setting. Half-worn sails made in the usual form may be altered, and from the saving in the wear and tear will abundantly pay the expense.

The mode of working these sails is thus explained by the inventor:

When the courses are to be reefed, cast off the lower clews from the thimbles in the upper clews, haul up the slack sail by the buntlines, and haul tort [sic] the reef-line, one part at a time, from the middle of the sail towards the clews, and make it fast round the upper clews, so as to confine the lower clews.

To set the sail, reeve a few turns of the lashing for the clews, and haul them down, overhauling the reef-line and buntlines.

To reef the top-sails, send a man up to each lower yard arm, settle the haulyards, and haul the sail down by the reef-tackles, and pass the turns of the earrings through the thimbles in the earring cringles and on the foot-rope, and make them fast. Hoist the sail tort up, haul through the slack of the buntlines, and haul tort the reef-line on each side towards the clews, and make fast.

The top-gallant-sails are reefed in the same manner by earrings at the lower part, and a small gasket rove as a reef-line; or from the deck by the clewlines and a buntline.

The buntlines and reef-line will confine the slack-sail, when reefed, close up in the wake of the reef-band; and the buntlines will only require to be kept hand tort, as is usual, to prevent them from chafing the sail.

The *Minotaur*, of 74 guns, has reefed these courses in two minutes, in a gale of wind, without sending a man off the deck.

The patentee asserts, that sails made on this plan being adapted to square-rigged vessels of every description, may, in many situations, be the means of saving them from destruction, particularly in the winter season, when so many ships are unavoidably exposed in gales of wind to the danger of lee shores and narrow seas.

New-Invented Batteau - 1809. *XXI 457*

Lieutenant Browne, of the royal navy, lately crossed the Thames, and passed through one of the arches of Westminster Bridge, in the presence of some thousands of spectators, in a canvass batteau, invented by Colonel Browne, of St. Vincent's, for the use of the army, with thirty persons. This military batteau is made of prepared canvas, so as to be impervious to water. The batteau is seventeen feet long, five feet wide, and three feet deep, and when loaded with thirty persons only draws three inches water. It is capable of conveying 100 soldiers, with their arms, accoutrements, and baggage, across the widest river, provided they lie down, and 30 if sitting. This batteau weighs only 60 pounds, and can be fitted up or taken to pieces in three minutes, so that it forms an easy load for a soldier on a march. Two batteaus lashed together are capable of conveying the heaviest piece of ordnance, &c. and a number connected together form a bridge, for the passage of cavalry. This invention has been highly approved of by the Duke of York, Lords Moira, Mulgrave, Chatham, and Sir A. Wellesley. The Colonel intends fitting up one of his batteaus, to carry two six-pounders, one in the head, and the other in the stern.

Iron Knees - 1810. *XXIII 112*

A general failure of the required supply of wood knees, for ships in his Majesty's service, having rendered an effectual substitute a *desideratum* in naval architecture, Mr. Roberts, of the Navy Office, some time ago, happily succeeded in the invention of a method of securing the beams of ships to their sides, and of superseding the necessity of standards, top and breadth riders, and nearly of wood knees altogether. For this invention, he was presented by government with a pension of 800£ in consequence of a recommendation from the Lords of the Admiralty; and he has since been honoured with the silver medal of the Society of Arts.

The subjoined, is a list of such ships as have been built, and are building, for his Majesty's service, the beams of which are secured by iron knees, agreeably to Mr. Robert's plan:

Ships	Guns	Ships	Guns
Lively	33	*Aboukir*	74
Melampus	36	*Caledonia*	120
Jason	32	*Milford*	74
Hebe	32	*Cornelia*	32
Circe	32	*Nereus*	32
Pallas	32	*Bucephalus*	36

Alexandria	32	*Semiramis*	36
Thames	32	*Dolphin*	44
Resistance	38	*Ajax*	74
Spartan	38	*Conquestadore*	74
Undaunted	38	*Vigo*	74
Valiant	74	*America*	74
Elizabeth	74	*Berwick*	74
Cumberland	74	*Vengeur*	74
Venerable	74	*Scarborough*	74

Hollow Iron Masts - 1811. [XXV 221]

A Model of one for a first rate ship, on a scale of one-eighth of an inch to a foot, is now ready for inspection

This mast, the cylinder being half an inch thick, and the same height and diameter as a wood mast, will not be so heavy, will be considerably stronger, much more durable, less liable to be injured by shot, and can be easily repaired, even at sea. It will weigh only 12 tons, and at £45 per ton, will not cost more than £540 while its strength will be nearly fifty per cent. above that of a wooden mast, that weighs 23 tons, and costs nearly £1,200.

This mast is made to strike nearly as low as the deck, to ease the ship in a heavy sea - ships furnished with wooden masts are in such circumstances obliged to cut them away: ships furnished with iron masts will not, like others, be exposed to the risk of receiving damage from lightning. The iron mast being itself an excellent conductor, by using an iron bolt from the bottom of the mast, through the kelson and keel, the electric matter will be conducted through the bottom of the ship into the water, without injury to the ship.

Yards and bowsprits may also be made of wrought iron, at the same proportion of strength and expense as the mast, and chain shrouds and stays of iron, which may be used with those masts, will not cost half the expense of rope, while they will also prove ten times more durable. For many other purposes in shipping, wrought iron, employed as a substitute for the materials now in use, would have as great advantages as in the articles above-mentioned. Even the whole hull may be made of wrought iron.

Improvement in the Keeping of Water, in Ships - 1812. [XXVIII 102]

A sloop arrived lately at Portsmouth, with 52 cast-iron water-tanks which are to be fitted into H.M.S. *Minden*. They hold two tuns each; and the object is, to find a substitute for the present mode of keeping and preserving water on board ship, and in a more compact form.

Special Duty Vessels
Floating Mortar Battery - 1805. [XIII 193]

A floating mortar battery, for the bombardment of the enemy's ports, has been invented by Mr. Congreve, son of General Congreve, of the Artillery, which is proof both against shells and red hot balls. It is said to be so contrived, that though provided both with masts for any voyage, yet they can be securely disposed of in less than a quarter of an hour, so that the Battery then presents nothing but a mere *hull*, with sloping sides, upon the water, which is rowed by forty men under cover of the bombproofs, and may, by the peculiar construction of the masts and rigging, be brought under sail again as expeditiously as dismantled. The rudder and moorings are *entirely* under water, and protected by the bomb-proof, so that no disappointment as to them can possibly arise. The battery is armed with four large mortars for bombardment, and four 42-pounder carronades for self-defence, though from being covered with plates and bars of iron, she can neither be set fire to, nor be carried by boarding. Four such vessels, though they are not more than 250 tons burthen each, and draw less than 12 feet water, would throw upwards of 500 shells into any place in one tide, and with the greatest effect and precision; both because from their construction they have nothing to apprehend from approaching the enemy's batteries, and because from the peculiar contrivance of the mortar-beds, the elevation of the mortars is not affected by the rolling or pitching of the vessel. Several of our most eminent naval men have seen and approved of the contrivance, and it is said that ministers have attended to this gentleman's plans, and have it in contemplation to institute, with all expedition, vigorous and regular bombardments of such of the enemy's ports as contain any considerable accumulation of their flotilla.

Wrought Iron Caisson - 1811. ^{XXV 219-220}

Brief Description of a wrought Iron movable Caisson with a rudder, for docking a ship, while riding at her moorings, in any depth of water, leaving her keel dry in three hours, without removing her stores or masts. A model for docking a First Rate ship, on a scale of one eighth of an inch to a foot is now ready for inspection
This caisson or floating dock is made of wrought iron, half an inch thick, 220 feet long, 64 feet wide, and 30 feet deep, and will weigh about 400 tons, with a stanch six feet wide on the top, for the workmen to stand upon, and, also, to strengthen the caisson.

The weight of this caisson, when immersed in water, is nearly 350 tons, but, for reasons mentioned below, it is rendered nearly buoyant, being surrounded by an air receptacle capable of suspending the whole weight with great exactness, and which is riveted to it in such a manner as also to strengthen the caisson, and support the principal shores from the ship.

While light, this caisson will draw nine feet of water: when taken to the ship intended to be docked, the water is to be let into it at an opening or plug-hole in the bottom, and it is to be suffered to sink until the upper part is even with the surface of the water, the air tube still keeping it buoyant. A small quantity of air is then to be discharged, by opening a plug-hole in the air receptacle, until a quantity of water is let in just sufficient to sink the caisson below the ship's bottom. This being effected, the caisson (nearly buoyant) is then to be raised to the surface of the water, by ropes made fast from the caisson to each quarter of the ship. A pump, placed within the caisson, is then to be worked by a steam engine of 12 horse power, placed in a barge alongside, which will empty it in three hours, and reduce the draft eight feet of water; that is, from 26 to 18 feet; when she may be carried up into shoal water, *if required*, or alongside wharfs, or jetty heads of the dock-yards.

The ship's sides and bottom tending to fall outwards, by their own weight, and the sides and bottom of the caisson tending to be forced inwards, by the external pressure of the water, it is obvious, that by placing props, or shores between, both will be supported, while the ship will ride with all her stores on board, and masts standing, *nearly as easy* as when in water.

Should inconvenience be apprehended at any time from blowing weather, the caisson may be cast off and let fall to the bottom, where it cannot be injured, and whence it may be raised to the ship's bottom again at pleasure, with as little labour as weighing anchor.

The caisson will be 12 feet above water when there is a first rate ship in it; this is a sufficient height to prevent the sea breaking over.

By this plan a ship may have her bottom examined, and be out of dock again in six hours, without coming above the Nore, and without undergoing the tedious process of unshipping and reshipping her stores, waiting for spring tides, or fair wind, to enable her to reach or to return from the dock, which, on an average, now requires three months, accompanied with an expense of nearly £10,000 a month in wages, subsistence, &c. &c.

This plan may be practised in all countries, were there are no dry docks or flowing of tide.

Ships on many foreign stations when requiring to be docked are now obliged to be sent home, at a great expense of money and waste of time, others being sent to replace them. This may be avoided in future. Docks made in England may be sent out in pieces of five or six tons, with the necessary rivets and bolts, and ready to be put together where they may be wanted.

From estimation, we find, that a caisson capable of docking a first rate ship, will not cost above nineteen or twenty thousand pounds, (for merchantmen and smaller ships, the size and cost will be proportionably less) and, judging from the duration of wrought iron salt pans, will last 20 years without repair. When worn out, it will break up and sell for one third of its original cost.

By constructing this caisson, adapted to the local circumstances, ships of war and merchants' ships, with all their stores and cargoes on board, can be carried up rivers to wharfs and store-houses, where the depth of water is not above one half the ship's draft.

French Praam - 1812. *XXVI 384*

The following is a description of the praam, *la Ville de Lyons*, captured by the *Naiad* frigate, and now lying in the Thames:

She is ship-rigged, and of very light rigging, about 350 tons measurement, and has a square overhanging stern, one flush deck, and is bulwarked about five feet high; has a flat floor, about 11 feet depth of hold, and draws nine feet water; is a mere floating battery, and very leewardly, so as to be almost incapable of being worked at sea in a moderate gale; is about 110 feet long, by 26 feet beam, old, and rough in appearance, without any outside ornament, or interior accommodation; is armed with 12 guns, heavy French 24-pounders (nearly 30 English), each gun weighing about 50 cwt. In a seaman's eye she is, as a vessel, far from desirable, but as a battery, well manned and managed, would be a formidable enemy. Her lower masts are all wounded.

Torpedo Pilots - 1815. *XXXIII 25-26*

A British officer on the American station, in a letter to a friend, states as follows: - "American pilot vessels for towing torpedoes,[8] have been invented in New York, for the purpose of impelling through the water the infernal torpedoes intended to blow up the British line-of-battle ships. A winch inside this vessel turns two wheels on the outside, and which are placed on the larboard side. These wheels impel both the pilot vessel and

8 *Vide* Vol. XXX page 302; Vol. XXXI page 287.

The vignette head-piece (drawn by Pocock, and engraved by Berryman) represents the French prâme, *la Ville de Lyons*, which was taken, off Boulogne, by H.M.S. *Naiad*, Captain P. Carteret, on the 21st of September, 1811.

The stern of *la Ville de Lyons*, which is formed in a manner very similar to her bow, is presented to the spectator. Her gun deck is very roomy, from her breadth being continued very far forward. Her top-side is strait, but she has a fine water-line, and draws very little water. She has six ports on each side, with two stern, and two bow-chasers; in all, sixteen guns, 24-pounders, the shot weighing nearly 30 lbs. Her side ports are not opposite, as in other ships of war, but are placed alternately, so as to afford room for the guns to recoil, and be re-loaded, without occasioning any interruption or inconvenience to the men employed on the opposite side. Having neither quarter-deck nor forecastle, and consequently no gang-boards, or other cover than a netting, not very high above the gunwale, her deck is very much exposed to the carronades and small arms of a frigate's quarter-deck, &c. She is very roughly put together, and quite unfit for any but a temporary purpose, and near the shore.

Her three masts are nearly at an equal distance from each other; and are low and small for a vessel of her dimensions, but sufficient for impelling her swiftly, large, or before the wind; for which purpose, her shallow draught of water, and the form of her bottom, are adapted. She seems not, however, at all calculated to sail close-hauled. XXVII 1, 23-24

the torpedo attached to it, at the rate of four miles per hour. Within the vessel are 12 men. The bottom of it is not much unlike that of a boat, but its top is arched. The scantling are those of a ship of 100 tons: the planks are of inch and half stuff, and these being cased over with iron plates of half an inch thickness, are not to be injured by shot. On the top there is a scuttle for the crew to enter, and this opening is also the look-out where a sentinel is constantly placed. Two air holes forward and abaft, give sufficient air to the crew. The vessel draws six feet of water, but one foot only is to be seen above the water, and this being painted of a dingy white, is not perceivable. The torpedo is of course attached to the stern of this vessel, ropes leading to it from two ring bolts in the afterpart. The torpedo is filled with powder and combustible matter, and in its inside there is a gun-lock, to which is fastened a string, which leads to a scuttle of the pilot vessel. Having towed this infernal machine close to the vessel which it is intended to fire, this string is pulled the moment the torpedo touches her, and the pilot vessel altering her course, by means of a rudder attached to her, goes off in the general confusion."

Steamships
An Hydraulic Machine - 1799. [II 146]

Description of an Hydraulic Machine, invented by Monsieur Danzel, for making a Vessel or Boat advance in a Calm, or even against a Current
The mechanism of this hydraulic machine is extremely simple: it consists of a long pole, to the advanced extremity of which an apparatus, in the shape of a drawer, without back or front, is fixed in such a manner that, when impelled forwards, it folds itself back under the pole, and presents to *the water the thin cutting surface* of its three edges, viz. the bottom and two sides of the apparatus, shaped like a drawer. When the pole, after being pushed forwards from the vessel[,] is drawn back, the machine attached to it will assume a vertical position to the surface of the water; and by presenting its cavity, will press and resist the fluid infinitely more than a number of oars, while the re-action is less laborious.

We understand there is now on the river Thames a vessel having an apparatus constructed on principles somewhat similar to the above; and made to work in a calm or against a current by means of steam.

Livingston and Fulton's Steam Boat on the Hudson - 1808. [XIX 188-190]

The following extract of a letter, from a gentleman of South Carolina, dated September 8, 1807, gives a somewhat curious account of a newly-invented steam-boat:

"I have now the pleasure to state to you the particulars of a late excursion to Albany in the steam-boat, made and completed under the directions of the Honourable Robert R. Livingston, and Mr. Fulton, together with my remarks thereon. On the morning of the 19th of August, Edward P. Livingston, Esq., and myself were honoured with an invitation from the Chancellor [of?] and Mr. Fulton, to proceed with him to Albany, in trying the first experiment up the river Hudson, in the steam-boat. She was then lying off Claremont (the seat of the chancellor), where she had arrived in twenty-four hours from New York, being 110 miles. Precisely at thirteen minutes past nine o'clock, A.M. the engine was put in motion, when we made a-head against the ebb-tide and head wind, blowing a pleasant breeze. We continued our course for about eight miles, when we took the flood, the wind still a-head. We arrived at Albany about five o'clock, P.M. being a distance from Claremont of forty-five miles (as agreed upon by those best acquainted with the river), which was performed in eight hours, without any accident or interruption whatever. This decidedly gave the boat upwards of five miles an hour, the tide sometimes against us, neither the sails nor any other implement but the steam used. The next morning we left Albany with several passengers, on the return to New York, the tide in favour, but a head wind. We left Albany at twenty-five minutes past nine, A.M. and arrived at Claremont in nine hours precisely, which gave us five miles an hour. The current, on returning, was stronger than when going up. After landing us at Claremont, Mr. Fulton proceeded with the passengers to New York. The excursion to Albany was very pleasant, and represented a most interesting spectacle. As we passed the farms on the borders of the river, every eye was intent, and from village to village, the heights and conspicuous places were occupied by the sentinels of curiosity, not viewing a thing they could possibly anticipate any idea of, but conjecturing about the plausibility of the motion. As we passed and repassed the towns of Athens and Hudson, we were politely saluted by the inhabitants, and several vessels, and at Albany we were visited by his excellency the governor, and many citizens. Boats must be very cautious how they attempt to board her when under way, as several accidents had nearly happened when boarding her; to board a-head will endanger a boat being crushed by the wheels, and no boat can board a'stern. The difference between the wake of Neptune's chariot, and that of a common water carriage, is very materially open to observation; as when you approach the first you will be told by anticipation to pay respect to a lady in the chariot, as will be readily notified by the expansion of a wet fan, which forms the dimensions of her wake, but moving with great impetuosity from the warm repulsion. It is a curious fan; it only spreads by an aquatic latchet, being sprung by the kicking of the horses. I may now venture to multiply and give you the sum total. The boat is 146 feet in length, and 12 in width (merely an experimental thing); draws to the depth of her wheels two feet of water; 100 feet deck for exercise, free of rigging or any encumbrances. She is unquestionably the most pleasant boat I ever went in. In her the mind is free from suspense. Perpetual motion authorises you to calculate on a certain time to land: her works move with all the facility of a clock; and the noise, when on board, is not greater than that of a vessel sailing with a good breeze."

Steam Boats Clyde and Comet - 1814. ^{XXXI 365-366}

The extreme length of the *Clyde* steam-boat is 75 feet, its breadth 14, the height of the cabin is six feet six. She is built very flat, and draws from two feet nine to three feet water. The best or after cabin is twenty feet long, and is entered from the stern; between the after cabin and the engine there is a space allotted for goods, 15 feet long. The engine is a 12-horse power, and occupies 15 feet; the fore cabin is 16 feet long, and is entered from the side. The paddles, sixteen in number, form two wheels of nine feet diameter, and four feet broad, made of hammered iron; they dip into the water from one foot three inches to one foot six inches. Along the outer edge of these wheels a platform and rail are formed, quite round the vessel, projecting over the sides, and supported by timbers reaching down to the vessel's side. The *Clyde* runs at the rate of four or four and a half miles per hour, in calm weather; but against a considerable breeze only three miles. The steam boat can take in 250 passengers, and is wrought by five men. The engine consumes 12 cwt. of coals per day; and, if well constructed, will require very little repair for some years. The daily expense, while working, is nearly £40; the carpenter's work cost £500; the joiner's work £150 and the engine, with its apparatus, about £700. The funnel of the boiler is 25 feet high, and carries a square sail 22 feet broad.

The *Comet* steam-boat, after getting into the Frith [sic] of Forth, found her machinery of so little power in the rough water of the ocean, that the idea of proceeding to London was necessarily abandoned. She is now, therefore, with two others, plying constantly on the Clyde, between Glasgow and Greenock, for the conveyance of passengers and goods.

These several boats were fitted up with the greatest neatness, and with every accommodation, so as to render them attractive to travellers. They have already had a remarkable influence in reducing the prodigious number of post chases on this line of road; so much so, that the tolls have let this year for £1,400 per annum less than formerly; and four out of eight stage coaches are laid aside, in consequence of which, 60 horses less are employed on that road. The distance by water is 22 miles, and the boats generally make the voyage in four or five hours. They go and come every day, and sometimes in summer, when the weather is favourable, they have made three voyages a-day. The fare is 5s in the after cabin, and in the fore cabin 2s 6d. The expense by the mail and stage coaches is 10s or 12s. The noise and vibration of the machinery is, however, unpleasant, and to many people the smell of the steam is disagreeable. More boats of the same kind are building by Messrs Wood, calculated for towing lighters with goods between Glasgow and the sea ports.

Submersibles
New Invented Diving Machine - 1800. [IV 135]

An Experiment was lately tried at Rouen, upon a new invented Diving Machine, called *Bateau-Poisson*, or Fish-boat. This boat sunk of itself seven or eight times, and then rose of itself. The longest time it remained under water was eight minutes. The descent into the inside of this machine, is by an opening made in the form of a tunnel, which is about a demi-meter above the surface of the water. When those who conduct the experiment wished to descend altogether into the river, and disappear, they let down this opening, sunk entirely under the water, and lost all communication with the external air. The inventors of this ingenious machine are Americans, the principal of whom is called Fulton. Three of them went into the boat and remained during the experiment. The Prefect, and a vast concourse of spectators[,] were present.

American Diving Boat - 1802. [VII 270]

St. Aubin, a man of letters at Paris, and member of the Tribunate, gives the following account of the *bateau plongeur*, a diving-boat, lately discovered by Mr. Fulton, an American.

I have, says he, just been to inspect the plan and section of a *Nautilus*, or Diving boat, invented by Mr. Fulton, similar to that with which he lately made his curious and interesting experiments at Havre and Brest.

The Diving-boat, in the construction of which he is now employed, will be capacious enough to contain eight men, and provisions enough for twenty days, and will be of sufficient strength and power to enable him to plunge 100 feet under water, if necessary. He has contrived a reservoir for air, which will enable eight men to remain under water for eight hours. When the boat is above water, it has two sails, and looks just like a common boat. When she is to dive, the masts and sails are struck.

In making his experiments at Havre, Mr. Fulton not only remained a whole hour under water with three of his companions, but held his boat parallel to the horizon at any given depth. He proved the compass-points as correctly under water as on the surface; and that while under water, the boat made way to the rate of half a league an hour, by means contrived for that purpose.

It is not twenty years since all Europe was astonished at the first ascension of men in balloons; perhaps in a few years they will not be less surprised to see a flotilla of Diving-boats, which, on a given signal, shall, to avoid the pursuit of an enemy, plunge under water, and rise again several leagues from the place where they descended!

The invention of balloons has hitherto been of no advantage, because no means have been found to direct their course. But if such means could be discovered, what would become of camps, cannon, fortresses, and the whole art of war?

But if we have not succeeded in steering the balloon, and even were it impossible to attain that object, the case is different with the Diving-boat, which can be conducted under water in the same manner as upon the surface. It has the advantage of sailing like a common boat, and also of diving when it is pursued. With these qualities it is fit for carrying secret orders to succour a blockaded port, and to examine the force and position of an enemy in their own harbours. These are sure and evident benefits, which the Diving-boat at present promises. - But who can see all the circumstances of this discovery, or the improvements of which it is susceptible? Mr. Fulton has already added to his boat a machine, by means of which he blew up a large boat in the port of Brest; and if by future experiments, the same effect could be produced on frigates or ships of the line, what will become of maritime wars, and where will sailors be found to man ships of war, when it is a physical certainty, that they may every moment be blown into the air by means of a Diving-boat, against which no human foresight can guard them?

Submarine Explosion - 1807. ^{XVIII 381-82}

The notion of reducing the power of the English navy *under water* was first suggested by a Mr. Bushnell, of Connecticut, and was the subject of one of the papers of the Philosophical Society of America. As far as the vague description of the newspapers warrants, Mr. Fulton does not appear to have made any material improvement on the idea of Mr. Bushnell. The machine invented by the latter, consisted of a vessel capable of containing a single person, and furnished with such apparatus as would enable him to remain under water for the space of thirty minutes. It was moved by a single oar, and its course was directed by a rudder and a compass marked with phosphorus; to this vessel was attached a large powder magazine, capable of containing 150 lbs. of powder, with all the apparatus necessary for causing the explosion; the person contained in the vessel was likewise provided with instruments for attaching the magazine to the bottom of the ship. The time of the explosion might be regulated by an apparatus contained within the magazine, and constructed so as to run for any required length of time within certain limits; this apparatus communicated with a gun-lock, which gave fire to the magazine at the time proposed. By an additional apparatus, the vessel could be raised to the surface of the water, or lowered at pleasure.

Mr. Bushnell's experiments, however, never succeeded to his wishes; some mismanagement, some unforeseen accidents, always prevented their success - sometimes the operator, in boring the hole in the bottom of the ship destined for destruction, for the purpose of attacking the magazine, unluckily was stopped in his progress, by encountering a piece of iron in the hull of the vessel, and in removing to a more convenient place for his purpose, has absolutely been unable to discover the ship a second time, and has consequently been under the necessity of abandoning the attempt; at other times, the *unskilfulness* of the person employed has frustrated his endeavours, and frequently he has been disappointed in his prospects by the *motion* of the *tides* and *currents*.

Bushnell's last attempt was made in December 1777, on the Delaware, not far from Philadelphia, after the destruction of the Mud Island battery, by the British vessels. It failed, but he boasts that it occasioned such alarm as to be the means of bringing on the battle of the Hogs.

A Submarine Boat - 1814. [XXXI 287]

The singular vessel, in shape much resembling a porpoise, 27 feet in length, five in depth, and five broad, arched over, sharp at each end; her materials, principally consisting of wrought and cast iron, is in a state of considerable forwardness. The inventor of this extraordinary machine undertakes to sail her on the surface of the water as an ordinary boat; he can immediately strike her yards and masts, plunge her to any depth he pleases under water, and remain there 12 hours without any inconvenience or external communication, as occasion may require. To strike her yards and masts, and descend under water, is but the work of two or three minutes. He can row, and navigate her under water at the rate of four knots an hour; remain stationary at any particular depth, and descend or ascent at pleasure; this vessel is so strongly built and so well fortified as to defy the effect of a twelve-pounder at point-blank shot. It is supposed government designs this formidable invention to counteract the torpedo system of America: this proprietor can attach any quantity of gun-powder to any sunken body and explode the same at pleasure.

This volume is indexed in Volume V.